EXPOSITION OF GENESIS

By

H. C. LEUPOLD, D. D.

Professor of Old Testament Exegesis
in the
Capital University Seminary
Columbus, Ohio

VOLUME II

CHAPTERS 20-50

BAKER BOOK HOUSE
Grand Rapids, Michigan

Library of Congress Catalog Card Number: 55-11417

COPYRIGHT, 1942

THE WARTBURG PRESS

ISBN: 0-8010-5522-9

First Printing, January 1950
Second Printing, October 1953
Third Printing, December 1956
Fourth Printing, April 1959
Fifth Printing, September 1960
Sixth Printing, March 1964
Seventh Printing, January 1967
Eighth Printing, December 1968
Ninth Printing, March 1970
Tenth Printing, April 1971
Eleventh Printing, September 1972
Twelfth Printing, February 1974
Thirteenth Printing, April 1975
Fourteenth Printing, November 1976
Fifteenth Printing, February 1978
Sixteenth Printing, October 1978

PHOTOLITHOPRINTED BY CUSHING - MALLOY, INC.
ANN ARBOR, MICHIGAN, UNITED STATES OF AMERICA
1978

CHAPTER XX

10. Abraham and Sarah at Gerar

Abraham needs to be tried and purified still more before the promise can be realized. He is also to receive still further demonstrations of divine favor. However, the difficulty in which he finds himself is occasioned by Abraham himself. On the very eve of the fulfillment of the long-hoped-for promise, Abraham, largely through his own sins, imperils the precious hope. So once again, as so often in Genesis, the sovereign mercy of God is made to stand forth as supreme, that no flesh may glory before God.

It would be foolish to deny the similarity of this episode with those other episodes recorded in Gen. 12:10 ff. and 26:1 ff. It is equally foolish to claim the identity of the incidents on the ground that they merely represent three different forms of the original event, forms assumed while being transmitted by tradition. Critics seem to forget that life just happens to be so strange a thing that certain incidents may repeat themselves in the course of one life, or that the lives of children often constitute a strange parallel to those of their parents. Besides, there certainly are striking differences between this account and that of 12:10 ff. as well as striking points of similarity. Note the following six points of difference: two different places are involved, Egypt and Philistia; two different monarchs of quite different character; one, idolatrous, the other, one who fears the true God; different circumstances prevail, a famine on the one hand, nomadic migration on the other; different modes of revelation are employed — the one king surmises the truth, the other receives revelation in a dream; the patriarch's reaction to the accusation is quite different in the two instances involved — in the first, silence; then in the second instance, a free explanation before a king of sufficient spiritual discernment; lastly, the conclusions of the two episodes are radically different from one another — in the first instance, dismissal from the land; in the second, an invitation to stay in the land. We are compelled, therefore, to reverse the critical verdict: "it is impossible to doubt that the two are variants of the same tradition." We have here two distinct, though similar, events.

If we remember besides that about twenty years had elapsed between the two incidents (cf. 12:4 with 17:1), we can well understand how the memory of the first had paled upon the consciousness of the patriarch. Abraham should not have been so forgetful, but even the patriarchs were frail mortals and poor sinners. In any event, why should a nation perpetuate several forms of an incident that reflects no honor whatsoever upon its first father?

1. And Abraham journeyed from thence to the land of the South Country (Negeb) and dwelt between Kadesh and Shur; he also sojourned in Gerar.

We last met Abraham near Hebron, living amid the terebinths of Mamre (18:1). He "journeys" (literally: "pulls up") to go from thence toward the region called the Negeb, or the South Country; cf. 12:9. There his dwelling place — always shifting because he is a nomad — is in the broad stretch between Kadesh, i. e., Kadesh Barnea (see 14:7) and Shur (see on 16:7). From this region he penetrated northwest some forty or fifty miles till he finally also took up his residence in Gerar, the site now known as *Umm Jerar,* perhaps ten miles south of Gaza on

the Wadi Sheriah. Here criticism again seeks to discredit the account by seeking to identify the two
successive steps in the patriarch's journeyings, as
though the writer had said that Abraham went to
the region between Kadesh and Shur and *there* dwelt
in Gerar, though Gerar is not there. We have made
the successive steps involved more distinct by translating *wayyághor* not "and he sojourned" but "he
also sojourned." It is even possible that most of
Abraham's herds and flocks may have been scattered
over this region of the South Country while he was
taking up temporary residence (*gûr*) in Gerar. On
wayyághor cf. G. K. 72 t.

2. **And Abraham said of Sarah his wife, She
is my sister; and Abimelech, king of Gerar, sent and
took Sarah.**

The deception of 12:13 is renewed. It is as little
pardonable here as there. The expression *'amar 'el*
must here mean "to say of" someone (K. S. 327 g).
When Abimelech takes Sarah, that implies, not as
the phrase sometimes means, to take in marriage,
but only, to take into his harem. The silence of the
verse, in that it does not call the king of Gerar,
the king of the Philistines, cannot be pressed to
the point where it means that the writer holds that
he was not king of the Philistines, or even that the
Philistines were not yet in the land in those days.
Yet by this unfounded claim this passage (attributed to E) is made to clash with 26:1 (attributed
to J), and E is claimed to be the more accurate
and J is claimed to be in error. "Abimelech" means
"my father is king," or "Melech is father."

3. **But God came to Abimelech in a dream by
night and said to him: Behold, thou art going to
die, because of the woman whom thou hast taken;
for she is a man's wife.**

There must have been something about Abimelech that set him above the level of the idolatrous Canaanites dwelling in the land, for God deigns to reveal Himself to this man. As we proceed, we observe that Abimelech apparently feared God. Luther reckons him among the believers of his day. Yet Abimelech must have had but a limited knowledge of God, for He that appeared to him is here described only as the Deity, *'elohîm* not *Ha'elohîm*, "the true God." The mode of revelation employed is the "dream" (*chalôm*), a mode employed for those standing on a lower level of revelation. When critics claim all such passages dealing with dreams for E, like 28:12; 31:11, 24; 37:5, then Num. 12:6 must also be considered which belongs to J. Besides, 21:12, 14; 22:1 ff., and 46:2, all cited by Skinner, are only *assumed* to involve dreams. Consequently, such a claim has no solid foundation. The article with *layelah* is the categorical article.

The Deity informs the king that he has done a deed worthy of death: "thou art going to die," *meth*, the participle, must point to the future in this connection. This guilty deed of Abimelech is that he has taken a woman who already is a man's wife (*be'ulath ba'al* = "lorded over by a lord," i. e., "governed by a husband"). To take men's wives from them for one's self is a deed involving great guilt. This pronouncement of God's meets Abimelech on the level on which he stands. It expects of him to understand and to honor the sanctity of the marriage bond. It does not make an issue of another act of Abimelech's, where he adds eligible women to his harem, as though a king had the right to multiply wives to himself. Yet God's silence does not mean approval.

The difficulty arising in this connection as to the reason for Abimelech's taking Sarah is increased if one supposes that the king's reason was that he was infatuated with Sarah's beauty. For even when allowance is made for the greater length of the span of life of these days, yet Sarah, being ninety years old (17:17), would have been so far past middle-age as to have lost her charm. A kind of rejuvenation in connection with the impending birth of a son could have made no appreciable difference. Since the text ascribes no reason, we are just as much at liberty to choose the other alternative, namely that the king by marriage sought to create an alliance with this influential nomad and so increase his following. Critics, as usual, reject the second suggestion and adopt the first because of the difficulties which it creates, which seem to make this version of the story of 12:10 appear less credible.

4, 5. **But Abimelech had not approached her, and so he said: Lord, wilt thou slay even a righteous people? Did he not say unto me, She is my sister? And she, even she herself said to me, He is my brother. In the integrity of my heart and the innocency of my hands have I done this.**

The verb *qarabh* must here be a pluperfect "had approached" (K. S. 117). Abimelech has extenuating circumstances to point to and so prefixes this plea to his defense, "Wilt thou slay even a righteous people?" First of all, he seems to know that the Deity is not a tribal god but has power over all individuals and all nations alike. Secondly, he has full confidence in God's justice: God does not punish indiscriminately. When, however, the king speaks of the slaying of the "people," it must be because he recognizes that king and people here constitute a unity in that the people carried out the king's command willingly and so share in the guilt. Alarmed as he is, the king uses a hyperbole in speaking of those to be punished as "a people." He hardly means to refer to more than those who are directly involved in one way or another.

The meaning for *goy* adopted by some, namely "a person" or "one" cannot be substantiated. The question introduced by the interrogative *ha* here requires a negative answer (K. S. 353 f).

The tacit assumption of Abimelech, that it was, of course, perfectly proper for him to increase the number of women in his harem, or even, for that matter, to have a harem, again is not touched. It may well be that the king still lived in an age that was not yet ready to learn the truth in regard to this matter. At any event, only that part of the issue which directly concerned Abraham is taken in hand by God.

Both of the parties concerned had given Abimelech the assurance that Sarah was Abraham's sister. The answers quoted by Abimelech put the emphatic word first; he said: "My sister she"; she said: "My brother he." Under these circumstances Abimelech might well claim that the inner motive was unimpeachable ("integrity of heart") and the outward deed entirely proper ("innocency of hands"). In the latter expression the word for "hand," *kaph*, signifies "the palm of the hand," consequently, not even hidden uncleanness within the hand, — therefore complete innocency. Throughout the king gives the impression of being an entirely worthy and upright character, a man who truly feared God.

6, 7. And God said unto him in a dream: I too know that in the innocency of thy heart thou hast done this; and I prevented thee, even I, from sinning against Me; on that account I did not suffer thee to touch her. Now therefore restore the wife of the man, for he is a prophet, that he may intercede in thy behalf that thou mayest live. But if thou dost not restore her, know that thou shalt most assuredly die, as well as all that belong to thee.

Whatever the nature of a revelation by means of a dream may be, it surely allows for an interchange of thoughts — questions and answers, remarks and responses. He that replies is here called by a more specific name than that of v. 3: not *'Elohîm* but *Ha'elohîm* = "the true God." The advance in thought is, that the king first recognized the Deity, but the Deity is the only true God. Between these two designations stands Abimelech's address "Lord" *'adhonay* (v. 4). As such Abimelech had specifically acknowledged Him; that is what He was accounted by Abimelech to be — Lord of all. Such fine discrimination in the use of the divine names shows beyond a doubt that they are all used according to the specific meaning that underlies each.

Now it appears how the announcement of v. 3 was meant — "thou art going to die." God was not predicting an inexorable doom but was declaring what Abimelech in reality had merited and what would of necessity follow if Abimelech failed to give heed to the divine injunction. God recognizes the comparative innocence of the king. In fact, He Himself had so regulated the course of events that Abimelech had been prevented from approaching the mother of the promised seed: some sickness had incapacitated all of his household (v. 18). The sickness referred to was an event that was entirely providential for this very purpose.

These verses are supposed to exhibit "a vacillation." They are said to be "the first faint protest of the moral sense against the hereditary mechanical notion of guilt." Writers who say such things (like Skinner) first impute their misconceptions to the Biblical author and then they censure him. In the first place, no Scriptures, not even the earliest, teach a "mechanical notion of guilt." But there is hereditary sin, for which the sinners involved are also guilty. In the case before us the rule holds good: sin is sin and involves guilt, even when the perpetrator may have sinned in ignorance. Such ignorance does not constitute an extenuating circumstance. God acknowledges that here. Our story is not a protest against anything. It records facts in conformity with all the rest of revealed truth. On *chatô'*, infinitive construct, see G. K. 75 qq; on *neghoa'* G. K. 66 b.

7. The irregularity of which Abimelech is guilty must like all sins be adjusted at once, if such adjustment lies within the power of the one who has sinned. In this instance the offense is aggravated by the nature of the person against whom it is committed: Abraham is "a prophet," a *nabhî'*. This term is here to be taken in its usual and only meaning — *nabhî'* from the root found in the Arabic, *nába'a,* signifies "the speaker," in the active not the passive sense, i. e., not "the inspired one." Yet "speaker" in the eminent sense of speaking in behalf and in the name of the Deity is definitely the meaning implied (see K. W.). Though we observe no instances in Abraham's life, where he functions specifically as the organ of revelation, who delivers particular messages in the name of Yahweh, yet he had the truth in his possession and, no doubt, spoke it freely and so functioned as speaker in God's service. To press the meaning of the word down to the level where it means only a "man of God, whose person and property are inviolable" is a procedure warranted by no Scripture, and so merely an attempt to deflate terms.

Now the work of prophets has also in a special sense always been to intercede for others (cf. Deut. 9:20; I Sam. 7:5; 12:19, 23; Jer. 7;16). This function Abraham will in this instance employ in Abimelech's behalf, that he may live. Both clauses introduced by "and" are in this instance final: "and he shall intercede" = "that he may intercede"; "and live" (imperative) = "that you may live." Efficacious intercessory prayer was practiced from the earliest times. On the other hand, failure to adjust the wrong done will bring with it certain death both of the king and of all who belong to him. These latter persons are included, no doubt, because if the king persists in his wrong course, they that belong to him will have abetted and supported him in his position and so will be almost as guilty as he.

Surely, the word of the psalm in reference to this event covers the case, where God is represented as saying: "Touch not mine anointed ones, and do my prophets no harm" (Ps. 105:15). Charges of partiality on God's part are quite out of place. He who has mercy for all may surely exercise particular care over those who have served Him with unusual fidelity, especially if they be persons whom He is reserving for special purposes, like Sarah. That such protection is entirely unmerited goes without saying, for His saints too were fallible human beings, as our story demonstrates only too clearly. Since this is the correct Biblical approach to the problem, we must reject the attitude of Procksch, who tries to make an "adventure" out of this experience of Sarah and would have us believe that the purpose of the narrator is to show how high Sarah ranked in her day, namely, as a princess worthy to be taken into a royal harem; and so the whole episode is construed as a kind of glorification of Sarah.

8. **So Abimelech arose early in the morning and called all his servants and told all these things in their hearing; and the men were much frightened.**

Abimelech gives evidence of prompt obedience. It required a measure of humility to tell these things to his servants; but the servants had also been involved in the misdeed, even as they would have shared the punishment if the evil had not been adjusted. The

servants have their master's attitude of respect and
reverence for God, which here at the news of the
danger they had incurred made them to be much
afraid.

**9, 10. Then Abimelech called Abraham and
said unto him: What hast thou done to us? And
wherein have I sinned against thee that thou
shouldest bring a great sin upon me and upon my
kingdom? Thou hast done to me things that should
not be done. Abimelech also said to Abraham:
What didst thou meet with that led thee to do this
thing?**

When Abimelech called Abraham, that must
be understood in the sense that he had him summoned, even as v. 2 he did not go personally and
take Sarah. By this time, apparently, the situation
described v. 18 had developed fully, and everyone
may now after the lapse of several days have been
aware of grievous irregularities and of an unusual
affliction that had befallen the court and its retainers.
The blame for all this Abimelech lays at Abraham's
door: "What hast thou done to us?" Besides, the
king claims that the wrong was done quite unpro-
voked and that it amounted to this that Abraham
had made innocent persons, even the king practically
and his people, to do a great sin. The man who is
in a particular sense a friend of God must suffer
himself to be rebuked by one who actually stands far
below on the scale of spiritual opportunity and
advancement. Abraham must be told what should
not have been done. The imperfect *ye'asû,* "is done,"
readily passes into the meaning "should be done,"
on the supposition that men usually will be found
doing what they should (K. S. 181).

10. Apparently Abraham feels his guilt and says
nothing. So Abimelech proceeds to ask what it was
that led Abraham to do this thing. The expression

mah ra'itha, literally, "what didst thou see?" must
be meant in some such sense as, "what hast thou
encountered?" (B D B). Meek secures a vivid
translation but departs entirely from the basic idea
when he renders, "What possessed thee?"

**11-13. And Abraham said: (I did it) be-
cause I thought in no case is there any fear of God
in this place; so they will slay me for my wife's
sake. Also for a fact she is my sister, the daughter of my father, however, not the daughter of my
mother; and she became my wife. And so, when
God made me to wander from my father's house,
that I said to her: This is thy kindness that thou
show me: in every place to which we come, say of
me: He is my brother.**

Abraham's three excuses are listed in these
verses. Abraham lays no special emphasis upon them.
He attempts no exculpation. He simply seems to have
placed confidence in Abimelech and to have told him
exactly what motivated his course of procedure. In
the first place, he was afraid that the fear of God had
been lost here as practically everywhere else in
Canaan. With the respect for God gone, men would
hardly respect the rights of their fellow-men. Abraham mentions this first, for he gathered from the
king's words that Abimelech still stands in the fear of
God. So this part of the excuse practically amounts
to an apology. His words begin elliptically with *kî,*
which implies the suppression of some initial statement like: I did it, "because," etc.

12. The second excuse indicates that Abraham
was really not speaking a verbal untruth when he
declared Sarah to be his sister; she was his half-sister.
On the earlier levels of the development of the human
race such closer relationships of those married were
often necessary and so not abhorred as they came to
be later. The Mosaic law would not allow such con-

nections; see Lev. 18:9, 11; 20:17; Deut. 27:22. Whom Terah had first married or perhaps married after he had married Abraham's mother, we cannot determine. The particle *'akh*, "also," in connections such as these must mean "however."

13. The third excuse or explanation reveals a preconcerted arrangement agreed upon already when Abraham's wanderings first began: for all situations such as these this evasion was to be resorted to by both. This is not commendable, but it is the truth. These things had not been revealed to Pharaoh (12:18-20), no doubt because Abraham felt no kinship with Pharaoh, nor did he have the confidence toward Pharaoh that leads to such revelations.

The plural *hith'û* with the subject *'elohîm* is an entirely inoffensive Hebrew construction, where a plural of extent (cf. K. S. 259 c, d) is coupled with a plural verb or a plural adjective (cf. K. S. 260 b) without impairing the singular character of the object involved. Deut. 5:23 may also serve as a parallel, where the plural form of the adjective is coupled with a singular noun which is plural in form. The other explanation that Abraham is adapting himself to the polytheistic standpoint of the king would apparently involve on Abraham's part practically a denial of his own monotheistic standpoint. Note also the loose way in which *wayhî* attaches v. 13 to v. 12: "and it came to pass when God made me to wander," where *wayhî* functions in so secondary a fashion that we ventured to translate it merely: "and so when," etc. (cf. G. K. 111 g).

There is no complaint involved in Abraham's use of the verb He "caused me to wander." This is a mere statement of fact. He knew that his lot was to be that of a sojourner. He accepted that lot with open eyes. He is here merely referring to a situation that he himself accepts and which he will reveal to men of kindred mind.

14, 15. **And Abimelech took sheep and oxen and men servants and maid servants and gave them to Abraham; he also restored to him Sarah his wife. Abimelech also said: My country is at thy disposal; dwell, where it pleaseth thee.**

In addition to restoring Sarah, Abimelech gives tokens of goodwill in the form of generous presents of the type that a nomad could well use. Besides, he gives ample proof of a friendly disposition by inviting Abraham to settle down wherever he pleases. From passages like 26:18 we gather that Abraham stayed sufficiently long in the neighborhood to necessitate his digging wells. The offer was made in good faith and accepted in good faith. The expression "at thy disposal" reads in Hebrew "before thine eyes"; and the expression, "where it pleases thee" reads, "in that which is good in thine eyes."

16. **And unto Sarah he said: Behold, I have given a thousand shekels of silver to thy brother. This will be for thee a covering of the eyes in reference to all those who are with thee; and in all respects thou art justified.**

Abimelech is not said in v. 14 to have given Abraham any silver; but here he refers to his gift as something that has been made. Consequently, the thousand shekels of silver may be the value of the gift just confessed and not an additional gift. Considering that thirty pieces was the normal price of a slave, it would seem that he considered what he had bestowed in v. 14 a princely gift. Now in reference to Sarah this gift is to serve the purpose of a *kesûth,* "a covering of the eyes." Of the half dozen different interpretations offered for this expression the most fitting seems to be "the one that reckons

with the embarrassment that might be caused Sarah
when the news of what transpired becomes known
and those of her own household cast scornful and
embarrassing glances upon Sarah, because she did
what made her ridiculous. The effect of this generous
gift will be to give a token of the high esteem in
which Abimelech nevertheless holds this man and
wife. In view of this gift the patriarch's retinue
will feel the occasion for amused looks has fallen away,
and so the gift will serve as a very effectual veil
('covering of the eyes') might in warding off the
scoffing glance." The concluding statement confirms
this interpretation: "in all respects thou art justified."
The idea of covering the eyes of the household of
Sarah by covering the faces of all by veils seems less
appropriate than to have one woman shield her face
against curious glances by dropping her veil.

The supposition that the veil is to shield the
king against Sarah's angry or vengeful glances (Vilmar), is hardly suitable. References to a veil or
headdress of coins worn by married women and to
be secured by the use of this generous gift are still
less in place.

The last word *nokhā'chath* is best regarded as
Nifal participle feminine in pause; it gets its person from the preceding "thou" and "thine." Of
course, the common segolate participle feminine is
involved (K. S. 367 δ). Then the words immediately
preceding *we'eth kol* are an accusative of relation (K.
S. 288 k and 341 o) "in respect to all things" or
"in all respects." Luther's translation of the participle
can hardly be supported: *und das war ihre Strafe —*
"and that was her punishment" — for this was a gift
and not a punishment.

**17, 18. And Abraham interceded with God,
and God healed Abimelech and his wife and his
maids, so that they could bear children. For Yah-**

weh had completely closed up all the wombs of the house of Abimelech on account of Sarah, Abraham's wife.

Abraham does what God had ascribed to him as a prophetic function and privilege (v. 7), and as a result of his intercession the disability laid upon the king's entire household is healed. The very fact that this disability is described as something that was healed (*rapha'*) suggests that it should be classed as a sickness. This disability could hardly mean that pregnant mothers were prevented from bringing forth their offspring, as some interpret, but rather that conception, particularly the coitus, was rendered impossible. For so v. 18 is to be understood. This was Yahweh's mode of rendering the mother of the promised seed safe. Note the fine propriety of the use of the term "Yahweh" here: the faithful covenant God in mercy watches over the mother of the child of the covenant. Criticism resorts to the common expedient of calling v. 18 an addition from J, or a redactor's gloss, and tries to make v. 18 appear out of harmony with v. 17, where in reality it is the essential complement; for v. 17 requires an explanation.

HOMILETICAL SUGGESTIONS

If the customary theme is used for this chapter—the mercy of the Lord, a theme which has thus far appeared with many different variations, then certainly here an opportunity offers itself to show conclusively that mercy is not bestowed according to merit; for here is a case where the total absence of merit stands forth prominently. If the case in hand is to be approached from the moral angle, then it is seen to offer an illustration how even with God's best saints susceptibility to certain sins is not overcome by a single effort. These men of God, too, had their besetting sins and prevailing weaknesses. The repetition of the fall of Abraham under very similar circumstances, instead of constituting grounds for criticism should rather be regarded as a touch entirely true to life.

CHAPTER XXI

11. Birth of Isaac and Expulsion of Ishmael
(v. 1-21)

The long-deferred hope of the son of promise is finally fulfilled, but it is shortly followed by a grievous disappointment in another direction. This double experience demonstrates that, as God's dealings nurtured faith, so, on the other hand, less pleasant experiences kept the sojourner from feeling too much at home in a world that is not to be the final goal of our hopes.

1, 2. And Yahweh visited Sarah as He had said, and Yahweh dealt with her as He had spoken. So Sarah conceived and bore unto Abraham a son in his old age at the set time which Yahweh had designated.

With a solemn reiteration, indicative of the solemn joy occasioned by God's keeping of the long-deferred promise, the author records this event. It would hardly have been seemly merely to make a simple unemphatic statement of the fulfillment. Criticism fails to discern this and speaks of doublets within v. 1 and v. 6. The characteristic Hebrew idiom here employs the *paqadh*, "to attend to" or "to visit." God's drawing near to one, whether in mercy or in severity, is described by the term; and it always involves that some token of His attitude is distinctly in evidence after His visitation. A similar use in a good sense appears in 50:24, 25 and in Exod. 13:19. Here the verb practically implies that God comes and leaves the son. More appropriately, however, this act is attributed to "Yahweh," for the merciful God here kept His covenant promise. For emphasis, to recall forcibly that His Yahweh-character was involved, the subject "Yahweh" is repeated before "dealt." Meek's "dealt with" for "visited" is very flat and colorless.

2. What v. 1 reports in a general statement v. 2 reports in specific form: the aged woman actually "conceived"; she actually "bore a son" to her husband, Abraham had actually arrived at the time of "old age." "To old age" is here a temporal phrase (K. S. 286 c). The plural noun for "old age," *zeqûnîm*, a plural of condition, reflects the various conditions involved in that particular time of life. To convey the thought that everything was being done in strict conformity with the very specific promise, the statement is also added that this all transpired "at the set time which Yahweh had designated." The promise involved is found 17:16, 21.

3-5. And Abraham called the name of his son that was born unto him, whom Sarah bore to him, Isaac. And Abraham circumcised Isaac, his son, as as lad of eight days, just as the Lord commanded him. And Abraham himself was a man of a hundred years when his son Isaac was born unto him.

The Lord had appointed the name for this child, 17:17-19. There the joyous laughter of faith on Abraham's part was the direct cause for the choice of the name . At the same time, as far as Sarah was concerned, her laughter of unbelief (18:12) would be recalled to her by this name. For Isaac = *yitschaq* = "he laughs," Kal imperfect of *tsachaq*. At the same time the rejoicing in gratitude on Sarah's part (v. 6) brings in a new fulfillment of the possibilities latent in the name. The name even reflects, as Sarah there indicates, the holy joy of all who sympathize with Sarah's unexpected good fortune. The possibilities thus reflected by the name are manifold and even in the remarkable propriety of the name an additional indication of the control of divine providence over all that was connected with this young life. Note as parallel the case of Esau, whose name Edom = "red," because of 1) his appearance at birth (25:25) ; 2) because of the ominous red pottage (25:30) ; 3) because, as travellers have remarked, the soil and the mountains of Edom also have a peculiar reddish tinge in certain parts, as the paronomasia of Isa. 63:1 also indicates, from another point of view (cf. Rand and McNally's, *Bible Atlas,* p. 45). Criticism refuses to see such providential control of even the details of man's life and seeks devious rationalistic explanations for this simple fact. The unusual arrangement of v. 3 which holds the name Isaac in suspense till the close of the sentence yields a peculiar emphasis on this name. Apparently, the form *hannôl'ádh* (with short "a") is intended to be read as a participle and not as nifal perfect with the article (K. S. 52).

4. The commandment of circumcision laid down very precisely in 17:12 as a divine ordinance is fulfilled by Abraham to the letter. *Benô* is an accusative of condition (K. S. 332 k) "as a lad of," etc.

5. Though we are by no means ignorant of Abraham's age at the time of Isaac's birth (17:1), yet to avoid all misunderstanding and to recall how entirely God's mercy was operative in the birth of this son, specific mention is again made of Abraham's age. The word "Abraham," by standing first in the sentence, gains an emphasis by contrast, which we aimed to reproduce by "Abraham himself." The sign of the accusative stands with "Isaac" as a retained object after a passive verb.

6, 7. **And Sarah said: God hath prepared laughter for me; all that hear of it will laugh with**

me. She also said: Who ever said in reference to
Abraham, Sarah hath given suck to children; for I
have born a son unto him in his old age.

The word *tsechoq* may, of course, mean "laugh-
ing stock," as it undoubtedly does Ezek. 23:32. But
an experience such as Sarah's would not render her
ridiculous, least of all in the Orient. She herself
would have the reproach of a lifetime removed and
would consider this a piece of rare good fortune.
Therefore the word really stands first for emphasis:
"laughter hath God prepared for me." Likewise, all
who hear what befalls her will laugh, rejoicing with
her. The expression laugh "to me" (*lî*) is caught by
the German *zulachen*; the English "laugh *with* me"
is nearly correct. In faith Sarah attributes her good
fortune to a merciful act of "God." "Yahweh"
might properly have been used here from one point
of view; but that viewpoint was covered by v. 1.
Here the Creator's power in rejuvenating an aged
mother is best indicated by "Elohim."

7. The second *watto'mer*, opening this verse like
v. 6, is, of course, meant in the sense of "she also
said." The *modal* use of the perfect *millel*: "Who
would have said" (A. V.) is grammatically quite possible (cf. G. K. 106 p). However, the ordinary perfect yields equally good sense: "who (ever) said," and
is just as apt an expression of surprise at the unexpected good fortune of Sarah. Likewise, the next perfect *hênîqah* need not be taken as modal. There
would be a certain unnaturalness about reporting such
an event to the father, who would naturally know
of it before others could report it. Consequently, the
le before "Abraham" is not "to" but "in reference
to" (Strack). The ordinary joy of any mother here
gains added importance and a kind of sanctity because of the unusually momentous issues connected
with this child. For that reason these relatively less

important utterances are recorded one by one. When
God fulfills promises, his saints experience a rare joy.
The *le* before *zequnaw* is again temporal, as in v. 2.
Banîm is a generic plural like that used in I Sam.
17:43: "comest with staves," as Luther also already
pointed out (K. S. 264 c).

8. **And the child grew and was weaned, and
Abraham prepared a great feast on the day when
Isaac was weaned.**

At least something of the growth and development
of this child of old age would be recorded. In this
case there is nothing phenomenal for the present. The
weaning becomes the occasion for a "great feast."
We are made to feel that to Abraham everything connected with Isaac is important. It may well be that
such a custom prevailed more or less universally in
days of old. In Abraham's case, of course, such a
feast was an occasion for being joyful in the Lord.
Besides, a custom of the Orient needs to be remembered here: children were weaned as late as in their
third year (II Macc. 7:27, 28). *Higgamel* is an infinitive used as an equivalent of a relative clause
modifying "day." "Isaac" has the sign of the direct
object — a case of the retained object with a passive
verb.

Perhaps v. 9 does not directly attach to v. 8,
even though most commentators do connect the two.
Yet nothing actually indicates that what Ishmael does
is directly to be associated with the festivities of this
day. If the connection were as close as is usually
assumed, then Hengstenberg's remarks would be particularly apropos. For he claims: "Isaac, the object
of holy laughter, was made the butt of unholy wit
or profane sport. He (Ishmael) did not laugh
(*tsachaq*) but he made fun (*metsachcheq*). The
little helpless Isaac a father of nations! Unbelief,
envy, pride of carnal superiority, were the causes

of his conduct. Because he did not understand the sentiment, 'Is anything too wonderful for the Lord?' it seemed to him absurd to link so great a thing to one so small," (quoted by Keil). In any case, this explanation still covers the case. But v. 8 could as well close a paragraph covering v. 1-8 as begin a new paragraph v. 8-21 (A. R. V.).

In this connection Luther raises the question: "Why is it not reported that Abraham made a feast on the occasion of the more important event, the circumcision of Isaac?" In answer we suggest that silence does not argue for the absence of such a feast; for not everything could be reported in the Scriptures. The greater likelihood is that Abraham followed the custom prevalent in his time: at the time of weaning a feast would be prepared; for the event of circumcision no custom was as yet established.

9. **Now Sarah observed that the son of the Egyptian woman Hagar, whom she had born to Abraham, was (always) mocking.**

Everything in this verse hinges on the translation of *metsach(ch)eq,* which we have rendered, "was (always) mocking" — the "always" to cover the frequentative participle. They have only a show of reason who translate the word "playing," in that they claim that for the bad sense "mock," the *piel* of the verb, should be construed with a *be,* as in 39:14, 17. However, the following arguments support our contention: 1) the absolute use of the verb without *be* is here conditioned by the circumstances. The writer did not want to say that he mocked *Isaac,* because, apparently, Ishmael mocked the prospects of Isaac and his spiritual destiny, in fact, just adopted a mocking attitude over against *everything* involved in Isaac's future. 2) The *piel* stem is never used in a good and harmless sense, except when construed with *'eth* ("with"), 26:8. 3) To translate, as many

do, "he was *playing*" (Meek), certainly imputes to
Sarah the cheapest kind of jealousy, quite unworthy
of this woman of faith. 4) The παίζοντα of the Septuagint may also mean "give way to hilarity"
(Thayer), and when men give way to hilarity, they
seldom stay within the boundaries of the purely harmless. 5) But lastly, the interpretation of the New
Testament is overwhelmingly in favor of at least the
sense "mocked," for Gal. 4:29 says: "As he that was
born after the flesh persecuted (ἐδίωκεν) him that was
born after the spirit." This word of St. Paul's
can be based on no other passage than this. It interprets what Ishmael did to have been even more than
a mild mocking. It stamps this attitude, besides, as
descriptive of the constant attitude of the carnal-
minded over against the spiritually minded. One may
brush the New Testament inspired interpretation of
the event aside, as criticism does; but all who let the
chief norm of exegesis be, "Scripture must be interpreted by Scripture," find the case covered by Gal.
4:29.

Consequently, we are quite right in interpreting
Sarah's act ("Sarah observed," as we have rendered
wattére', literally, "and she saw") as one based on
sober observation and reflection. Sarah had actually
discerned the true nature of Ishmael sooner and more
correctly than Abraham. In harmony with this interpretation is also the designation of Ishmael, not by his
proper name but as "the son of the Egyptian woman
Hagar." The unsympathetic trait or racial antipathy
comes to the surface. Criticism here, too, fails to
penetrate so deeply into the choice of terms and errs
in concocting theories about the smelting together
of different source material, one of which sources
had lost the proper name of Hagar's son. In this
connection, fitting in very well with our interpretation, the frequentative participle indicates a thing

that Sarah had observed quite regularly in Ishmael's attitude toward Isaac — "always mocking." Besides, such a course of conduct indicated not only spiritual incapacity and inability to appreciate spiritual values but also a spirit entirely out of sympathy with the best treasures known to the household of Abraham, the hope of the coming Savior.

10. And she said to Abraham: Drive out this maid and her son, for the son of this maid shall not be heir with my son, with Isaac.

Because of the antipathy to spiritual treasures displayed by Ishmael, as indicated above, Sarah concludes that a radical cure of the evil should be taken in hand. The evil threatening is so grievous, and the damage it ultimately might do so alarming, that nothing short of expulsion of the Egyptian maid and her son can be deemed an adequate solution. True, Sarah refers only to the matter of sharing in the inheritance; but she evidently means this in the sense of sharing in the entire inheritance, which consists in spiritual as well as in physical assets. Else Gal. 4:30 would hardly have deemed her words worthy of quoting with approval. In conformity with this thought she designates Hagar as "this maid" and Ishmael merely as "her son," terms which indicate the lack of sympathetic understanding on the part of these two.

Of course, a superficial examination of the situation may lead to an interpretation which sees merely human rivalry involved and ascribes to Sarah a kind of vindictive cruelty. Such an approach makes it impossible to account satisfactorily for God's concurring in Sarah's verdict. A mediating position is not tenable, as when Delitzsch says that in this demand of Sarah's "justifiable disapproval is mingled with proud disdain."

11. And this demand was very displeasing to Abraham because of his son.

It must be observed that Abraham's disapproval is according to this statement based on his affection for his son, not on the higher considerations. The lad, whom Abraham had loved in a very special way as the child of his old age till Isaac came, was still very dear to him. Our interpretation, then, drives us to assume that Abraham's insight into the deeper issues of the case was in this instance blurred by the very strong affection he felt for Ishmael. The Hebrew idiom here says: "the thing was very bad in the eyes of Abraham." The masculine *yera'* is naturally to be taken as a neuter, "*it* was evil." On the form, Kal imperfect of *ra'a'*, cf. G. K. 67 p.

12, 13. And God said to Abraham: Let it not be displeasing to thee as far as the son and maid are concerned. In all that Sarah hath said to thee, give heed to her voice, for after Isaac shall thy descendants be called. But also, as far as the son of the maid is concerned, I will make of him a nation, for he is thy seed.

This divine communication is said to come from "God" not from Yahweh, for covenant issues in reference to Isaac are not touched upon so much as providential issues in reference to one who stood outside of Yahweh's covenant. Neither are we told in what manner the divine revelation came to Abraham. But as is always the case when God speaks to men they are definitely aware that it is He, and they know what He says. God reveals to Abraham that Sarah's demand is to be followed. Abraham's disapproval is to be dropped — "let it not be displeasing to thee." The entire demand of Sarah is to be carried out. Strack may claim that Sarah's *motive* is not sanctioned by God's word, but this claim merely grows out of the unwillingness to believe that Sarah was capable of having right motives in the matter. God's reason for sanctioning Sarah's demand is: "after Isaac shall

thy descendants (or seed) be called." The true descendants of Abraham — true as being of the same
mind and faith as Abraham — shall be found in the
line of Isaac. The truth of this statement is patent.
Ishmael's line quickly lost all spiritual kinship with
Abraham. All that Abraham regarded as of
highest moment, they cast off. Since, then, Ishmael
potentially is a foreign element among the offspring of
Abraham, he must be removed. That being God's reason for Ishmael's and Hagar's dismissal, why could
it not also have been Sarah's?

13. Reassurance in reference to the human
aspect of the case is offered to Abraham by a promise
which offers much more than that Ishmael should
not perish. For the promise looks into the distant
future and assures Abraham that for Abraham's sake
("for he is thy seed") God will make him to expand
into a nation. Consequently, Abraham need have
no misgivings as to whether the son will survive or
not. This gracious reassurance makes obedience easier
for Abraham.

Criticism, following its usual unsatisfactory
methods, here, at least in some explanations, tangles
up the situation badly in claiming that this portion
seems an insert from E in an attempt to secure a
motive for Ishmael's dismissal, but calls the attempt
"abortive" (Procksch), *was nicht allzu gut geglueckt
ist*. Such sallies at the reliability of the Word, though
poorly substantiated, are yet extremly harmful. The
initial *we* is adversative (K. S. 360 b).

14. **And Abraham arose early in the morning
and took bread and a water-skin, and gave them
to Hagar, put them on her shoulder, and (gave
her) the lad, and sent her away. And she went
forth and strayed about in the wilderness of Beersheba.**

Prompt obedience of faith on Abraham's part! Yet how hard it must have been for the natural feelings of the human heart! Luther, of all commentators, seems to display this aspect of the case best. The exiles are provided with provisions and water in the customary skin-bottle (*chémeth*) of the Orient. Men have asked, why did Abraham not provide better for Hagar and Ishmael and give money to them also? That may not have been recorded, being regarded as quite self-evident. The bread and the water are mentioned as the elements that must be noted to prepare for what follows. Surely, the concern that leads Abraham to supply these immediate necessities and even to lay them on Hagar's shoulder, will hardly have suffered him to omit further provisions for their welfare.

At this point, anxious to prove that the account, being a patchwork of unreconciled discrepancies, or else to set the author (E) at variance with the author assumed for 16:16 (J), modernists are wont to claim that the text plainly assumes that Ishmael is a mere toddling infant, who was also laid upon Hagar's shoulder to be borne by her. Some rearrange the text in the interest of their view, like Meek, who renders: "taking some bread and a skin of water, he gave them to Hagar, along with her son, and putting them on her shoulder," etc. The Hebrew order is as we have translated above. These words *may* be so construed as to make the words "and the lad" to be the object of "put." But they may with equal grammatical propriety be construed so that "and the lad" is the object of the preceding verb "gave"; so A. R. V.; A. V. ambiguous. An added consideration is the fact that women did not usually carry lads several years old on their "shoulder" but let them straddle the hip. Besides, the critics, who are practically unanimous on this point, would hardly believe that some author, perhaps the so-called E, would have himself believed that Ishmael and Isaac were both of the same age, or Ishmael perhaps even, as this view of the case might suggest, a bit younger than Isaac. Distorted tradition could hardly have grown blurred on so important a fact as the priority of the birth of Ishmael.

The mother goes forth; and whereas in the previous instance of her flight she had not lost her way, now, where both she *and her son* are involved, the tumult of emotion seems to have risen higher and caused her to miss the way, so that "she strayed about in the wilderness." This wilderness is here proleptically designated as that of Beersheba, although according to v. 31, apparently, this name was first bestowed upon the well and the region later.

Sam is an instance of asyndeton (for *"and* put") used epexegetically: "he gave" — (namely) "he put" (K. S. 370 m).

15, 16. And the water of the skin-bottle was spent, and she cast the lad under one of the bushes, and she went and seated herself opposite him making the distance about that of a bowshot, for she said: I cannot look upon the death of the lad. So she sat over against him and lifted up her voice and wept.

Having lost her way, she was inadequately supplied with water. One can imagine how carefully they portioned out the last swallows from the skin-bottle. Finally the lad, though (according to 16:16 combined with 21:8) easily seventeen years old, yet finds his unseasoned strength wavering before that of his mother — a situation not at all uncommon, for the lusty strength of youth often lacks seasoning and so falls short in point of endurance. For a time the mother supports the son, but her fast-failing strength cannot long bear to be doubly taxed. She finds one

of the bushes of the desert. Scant shade such as
may be offered is often sought out by those wandering in the desert when they need protection against
the sun's rays (cf. I Kings 19:4). The mother desires
to ease what appear to be the dying hours of the
lad's life. She drops him hastily in exhaustion, an act
for which the Hebrew uses the expressive *tashlekh*,
"she cast," or "threw" him. A parallel New Testament usage is found Matt. 15:30 ("they cast down
them i. e., the sick, at His feet"). Another parallel is
Gen. 24:64: "cast down" for "alighted quickly." In
view of all this it appears quite readily how poorly the
argument is grounded which insists that Ishmael is
regarded as a little child whom the mother has actually
been carrying. Here is another instance where with
almost complete unanimity the critics dismiss a substantial argument with a shrug, without actually
attempting to meet it squarely.

16. With fine skill the author delineates how
painfully the mother's love is torn by her son's distress. She must stay within sight. Yet she cannot
witness his slow death. At the distance of a bowshot (literally, "according to the shooters of the bow")
she hovers near. Her agonized cry rings out: "I cannot look upon the death of the lad." *'Al-'er'eh*,
literally, "let me not look," practically equals a potential, "I cannot look." There she sits and lifts up her
voice in lamentation.

The dative *lah* is a dative of interest, yet difficult to translate (K. S. 35). *Harcheq* is an absolute
infinitive used adverbially, something like "at a
distance" (cf. G. K. 113 h; K. S. 221 and 402 c).

17, 18. **And God heard the voice of the lad
and the Angel of God called unto Hagar from
heaven, saying to her: What aileth thee, Hagar?
Fear not, for God has hearkened unto the voice of
the lad where he is. Arise, raise up the lad and**

support him well, for I will make him a great nation.

All this gracious interest in the lost wayfarers is ascribed to *God* or to the Angel of God, because it still lies entirely in the field not covered by *Yahweh's* covenant. Nothing indicates that Hagar saw any manifestation of God. Yet there is likelihood that she saw the Angel of God, because He is the one through whom God specifically *manifests* Himself, the same one who in 16:7 under the name of Angel of Yahweh had previously appeared to Hagar. The difference in name does not bespeak a difference in person. Yet it should not be overlooked that the Angel of God in this case spoke unto her "from heaven." Since now such speaking may be regarded as a manifestation, we must at least admit that this may have been merely an audible manifestation and not a visible one. The thing that moved God to take pity was "the voice of the lad." Though it had not been said heretofore that the lad had cried out in distress, does that not go without saying? The Septuagint secures a mechanical harmony at this point by making v. 16 close with this idea — quite an unnecessary emendation.

By the question, "What aileth thee?" (literally: "What to thee?") the Angel recalls to Hagar that she had no cause for alarm, for she was forgetting what had been promised to her in 16:10 ff. She is bidden to drop her fears, for God, merciful and kind, had also heard the cry of the lad as he lay in his great distress. "Where he is" refers to the lad's pitiful condition and not to God in heaven (K. C.). For if the clause were to refer to God, it would hardly be immediately after the noun "lad" (*na'ar*).

18. In this case *qû'mî* must mean "arise" and not merely "come," for Hagar had actually seated herself (v. 16), and the remaining imperatives pre-

scribe the successive steps to be taken. The asyndeton "arise, raise" lends urgency to the command. The divine directions are so specific ("raise up the lad and support him well") because the distraught mother in the utter bewilderment of her agony needed clear directions how to proceed. The final statement ("I will make him a great nation") recalls the previous promise (16:10 ff.) and encourages the mother to build her faith on it. "Hold him in thy hand" (A. V.) is not in place, for the Hebrew says (literally): "Make strong thy hand on him."

19. **And God opened her eyes and she saw a well of water, and she went and filled the skin-bottle with water and gave the lad to drink.**

How much is actually implied in the statement, "God opened her eyes," is well covered by Whitelaw's comment: "Not necessarily by miraculous operation, perhaps simply by providentially guiding her search for water." Add to this the necessary observation that such wells in the wilderness were usually covered over to prevent excessive evaporation but were then usually marked by some sign to help travellers locate them, and the whole situation is quite readily understood. The mother fills the skin-bottle and from it administers reviving draughts to her son. With this colorful touch the incident as such closes. A brief statement follows (v. 20, 21) furnishing proof for the fulfillment of the promises God had made in reference to Ishmael.

20, 21. **And God was with the lad and he grew up, and lived in the wilderness and became an archer, a bowman. And he dwelt in the wilderness of Paran, and his mother got him a wife from the land of Egypt.**

"God was with the lad" implies that the promises made to Ishmael by God were being fulfilled: God's providence watched over him as he grew up. Luther extracts too much from the expression when he makes of Ishmael "a clever and learned preacher, who establishes a church among the heathen." There is likelihood that Ishmael, who (v. 17) had called upon God in prayer, and Hagar, who also had learned to believe in the true God while in Abraham's household, were both persons who stood in the faith all their days and, no doubt, sought to communicate this saving knowledge to their descendants. The disposition described in 16:10 displays itself in Ishmael's choice of a habitation — "in the wilderness." The distinguishing mark in the line of the young man's accomplishments was his skill in the use of the bow. Two terms cover this: the more general *robheh*, "shooter," the more specific *qashshath*, "a bowman." The second definitely limits the shooting or casting by describing the weapon involved. The German covers it well, *ein Schuetze, ein Bogenschuetze* (K. C.).

21. Whatever else we need to know is covered by the statement concerning the particular wilderness in which he moved about, viz., "the wilderness of Paran," the eastern part of the great wilderness *et-tih* on the Sinai peninsula, and by the statement concerning his marriage. His Egyptian mother procures for him an Egyptian wife. It this respect she does not display the wisdom used by Abraham in choosing, as he did, a god-fearing wife for his son.

Speculations about Hagar's ultimate return with Ishmael to Abraham's household shortly after this dismissal are poorly substantiated. The account as worded points to a permanent separation. In fact, there was need of having this group separated from Abraham's family—they were a group with a different spirit. Jewish attempts to identify Hagar with Ketura (25:1) are utterly without grounds.

12. Abraham's Covenant with Abimelech at Beersheba (v. 22-34)

This little incident shows forth clearly how influential and prominent a personage Abraham had become under Yahweh's blessing: neighboring kings were concerned about retaining his goodwill; he ranked on a par with the mighty men of his day. Besides, this groundwork of the story is essential to a proper understanding of Isaac's experiences with the Philistines. As usual, Abraham stands out as a man acting in harmony with his faith.

22, 23. It came to pass at that time that Abimelech and Phicol, the captain of his army, said to Abraham: God is with thee in all that thou doest. Now, therefore, swear unto me here by God that thou wilt not deal falsely with me or with my kith and kin; but according to the kindness that I have shown to thee, do thou deal with me and with the land in which thou sojournest.

The writer takes for granted that his readers know that Abimelech is, as v. 32 shows, king of the Philistines. Phicol accompanies him to show the importance of the occasion. "Phicol" may, if it be a Hebrew word, mean "mouth of all," and so the captain of the army may have occupied a post as representative of the people. God's favor to Abraham is so manifest that heathen men can recognize it. In a spirit that has much to commend it but may yet be largely the outgrowth of good governmental policy, Abimelech seeks to secure permanently the amicable relations now existing between his own people and Abraham's. The oath still has binding power and is highly respected. An oath-bound covenant with Abraham is what Abimelech desires: "swear thou wilt not deal falsely with me." The oath is to include furture generations, *nînî* and *nekhdî*, an alliterative pair of terms meaning literally, "my offspring and my descendant," and found always as a pair (Job 18:19; Isa. 14:22). We reproduced this combination less literally by a kindred phrase "kith and kin." Abimelech claims always to have shown "kindness" — *chésedh* (hardly "loyalty," K. W.) to Abraham and expects like treatment for himself and his land.

24-26. And Abraham said: I will swear. And Abraham reproved Abimelech because of the well of water which the servants of Abimelech had taken away by force. But Abimelech said: I knew not who had done this thing; and, furthermore, thou didst not tell me; and besides I had not heard of it before today.

Since, on the face of it the account seems to be inconsistent, men critically minded speak of unreconciled sources and pronounce verdicts such as, "This unreserved consent (cf. v. 24) is inconsistent with the expostulation of v. 26" (Skinner). However, the explanation of the difficulty lies so near the surface. When asked whether he is ready to make a covenant in the interest of an amicable relationship, he promptly assents. But if such a covenant is not to be deflected from its purpose and soon to become ineffective, obstacles that might arise later had better be removed at once. Such an obstacle is the taking away by force from Abraham of one of the wells which he had dug. However, had Abraham raised his objection first, before he expressed his assent, he would have created the impression he sought to avoid, namely that he seemed somewhat reluctant about taking steps to guarantee peace. Besides, there is no grammatical difficulty in the way of construing v. 25 thus. For the conjunction is not a *waw* conversive, necessitating the translation, "And as often as Abraham took Abimelech to task about the wells . . . Abimelech would answer" — a translation which throws the

Exposition of Genesis

whole account into confusion. Here is an instance where
the *waw* with a perfect merely expresses "a digression or an epexegesis," as K. S. (370 l) rightly contends and proves by many parallels; cf. 38:5, Num.
10:17 ff., etc. Meek and others, as a result of this
unnecessary translation, see themselves compelled to
reconstructions such as rearranging the sequence
of verses as follows to secure consecutive thought:
24, 27, 31, 25, 26, 28, 29 — an unnecessary juggling
with a good text.

26. But Abimelech has a strong defense whereby
he proves that he is being accused unjustly: "I knew
not who had done this thing." By this he means:
he neither knew who did it, nor that it had been
done. Neither had Abraham complained, nor had any
other person carried the knowledge of the irregularity
to him. This seemingly puts Abraham partly in the
wrong; he should have had confidence enough in Abimelech to complain before this day. In any case, it
becomes clear that the two men are both of such
a character that a covenant entered into by both will
be conscientiously kept.

Though no statement to this effect is inserted,
nevertheless it goes without saying that Abimelech
at once returned the well in question to Abraham.

27-30. **And Abraham took sheep and oxen and
gave them unto Abimelech; and they two made a
covenant. Abraham (namely) set seven ewe lambs
apart by themselves. And Abimelech said unto
Abraham: What mean these seven ewe lambs that
thou hast set by themselves? And he said: The
seven ewe lambs thou shalt take of my hand in order
that this may be a witness for me that I have digged
this well.**

The key to the understanding of what is narrated in these verses lies in the right understanding
of v. 27 b and its relation to v. 28. For v. 27 b

reports in advance the whole transaction, as does
Isa. 7:1 b. The details follow. We secure proper
coherence by introducing v. 28 by a "namely," as
we have done. The relation of the creatures mentioned in v. 27 ("sheep and oxen") to those mentioned
in v. 28 ("seven ewe lambs") then appears to be
this: the "sheep" of v. 27 include the "ewe lambs"
of v. 28. This difference in the use of these creatures,
apparently, must be established: those mentioned in
v. 27, apart from the ewe lambs, are to be used to
be slaughtered to establish the covenant; cf. 15:9-11
and our remarks on this passage. Then the ewe
lambs constitute a special friendly gift, not usually
made in connection with covenants; for Abimelech
asks (v. 29): "What mean these?" Abraham's explanation is that this gift shall serve as "witness"
(feminine, *'edhah*, German: *Zeugin*), that he has
digged the well. The *ki* (1) of v. 30 merely introduced the direct discourse, the *ki* explicative (K. S.
374 b).

**31. Hence the place was called Beersheba
(well of the seven), for there these two men took
an oath (beseventhed themselves).**

The play on words involved is not caught in English without some explanation like that of the paren-
theses employed above. For it so happens that the
root for "swearing" and the root for "seven" are
identical in Hebrew, *shabha'*, a fact nicely explained
by Luther, who says in this connection: *sie haben
beide geschworen, und, dass ich also rede, besiebent*
("beseventh"). What the deeper unity of these two
ideas is we are at present unable to discern. But
Be'er-shebha' does not mean "well of the oath," for
shebha' is never found in the sense of *shebhu'ah*
("oath"). Still the paronomasia appears in the original. The verb *qara'* is impersonal, which is conveniently rendered by a passive. So the famous well

got its name. K. W. translates *Sieben-brunnen;*
more acceptable than K. C., "Well of the oath." K. W.
also indicates that men have discovered five wells at
this point and indications of two others. This agrees
but poorly with the findings of other travellers who
were able to locate but one, or at most, two. Robinson
found but two, one twelve and a half feet in diameter,
a second five feet in diameter (Thomson, *The Land
and the Book,* p. 297).

32, 33. **So they made a covenant in Beersheba,
and Abimelech and Phicol, the captain of his army,
arose and returned to the land of the Philistines.
And Abraham planted a tamarisk tree in Beersheba,
and called there upon Yahweh, the Everlasting
God.**

The visitors return to their country, but Abraham
gives further acknowledgment of his indebtedness to
Yahweh for all the favors he enjoys. A memorial
tree, not a "grove" (A. V.), but rather a "tamarisk,"
as the Arabic parallel root suggests, a tree resembling
the cypress. Besides, Abraham acknowledged the
Lord in public worship; on *qara' beshem Yahweh*
see our remarks on 4:26. The new name by which
Yahweh is here designated, *'El 'ôlam,* "the Everlasting God," shows the new aspect of God's being
that had become apparent to Abraham as a result
of his recent experiences with God. It may be well
to compare that in 14:22 *'El 'Elyon* and in 17:1
'El Shadday had already appeared. The tamarisk
with its firm and durable wood was a fitting emblem
of the Everlasting God. Why some make a fetish
of this tree, or others say that the tree was only
"believed to have been planted by Abraham," is
beyond our power to explain.

34. **And Abraham sojourned in the land of
the Philistines many days.**

More and more Abraham sees, as Isaac also later did, that the southern extremity of the land is best suited to his sojournings. This verse does not clash with v. 32 where Abimelech, leaving Abraham, returns to "the land of the Philistines." For as Keil remarks, "the discrepancy is easily reconciled on the supposition that at that time the land of the Philistines had no fixed boundary, at all events, toward the desert."

HOMILETICAL SUGGESTIONS

Three sections make up this chapter. The first comprises the verses 1-7. It would seem proper to treat these verses under the subject "A Gracious Divine Visitation," building on the Biblical fact that the occurrences of our everyday life are more frequently than we admit instances of God's drawing near, that is of divine visitations. The next section v. 8-21 may well be approached from the angle suggested by Rom. 9:7. This would furnish a theme like "The Election of Grace," only, of course, with this caution, that the election involved is not an election to salvation but an election to prominence in the kingdom of God. The last portion v. 22-34 turns mostly about the idea of friendliness with the ungodly and may even be treated under that head. For Abraham is not unduly reluctant about being on terms of sincere friendship with those who know not the Lord, though, of course, such are not his intimate associates.

CHAPTER XXII

13. The Sacrifice of Isaac (22:1-19)

With this chapter we reach the climax of the faith life of Abraham — the supreme test and the supreme victory. This test of necessity had to come. The inner need of it becomes apparent when we weigh carefully how much love Abraham would naturally bestow upon his son Isaac. For Isaac was the son of his old age — long waited for and fervently welcomed. He was of a lovable, kindly disposition. He was the object of remarkable promises made by God. With him was linked up a fullness of promises tending to the salvation of mankind. But strong love on the part of man, even if such a love be good and natural, is apt in the course of time to crowd aside the higher love of God. Abraham was in extreme danger of coming by slow degrees and in a manner hardly observed by himself to the point where he would have loved his son more than his God. This problem must be faced and worked through. The love of God must consciously be set first. The love of his own son must consciously be relegated to its own proper place, not diminished but directed and purified.

This test, which makes Abraham face this issue and settle it, is here described as a "tempting." By this approach we see quite readily that the expression: "God tempted Abraham" is meant in a good sense and can, therefore, well be rendered by the expression which requires less explanation: "God put Abraham to the test." God brings Abraham into a position where he must face the issue and think it through.

God does not do this in order to bring him to fall, even though the possibility of a fall may not be excluded. Nor does the temptation aim to bring to light hidden sins, even though in this case the possibility of falling into a very grievous sin is discovered as lying very near. The temptation does not aim to uncover the evil in a saint of God but rather to make apparent what good God has wrought in this faithful believer.

Another question that had best be disposed of in advance is the one: "How could God demand a human sacrifice, when He is on principle unalterably opposed to such a practice?" The answer must be given as follows: What God actually wanted Abraham to give was the *spiritual* sacrifice of his son. Naturally, God is concerned about the giving up of the son, a thing which is done by the heart; for without that even a bloody sacrifice upon an altar is worthless. But then the problem arises, Why did God ask for the spiritual sacrifice in the form of a material sacrifice? Apparently, this question voices a common protest but is itself partly the outgrowth of a misunderstanding and is so worded as to mislead. God asked for one thing only: the spiritual surrender, the giving back to Him of this great gift which He had granted to Abraham. The terms employed by the Lord are taken from material sacrifices and, apparently, at this stage of the religious development of the race were the only terms available. God foresaw that a partial misunderstanding would result on Abraham's part. This misunderstanding was unavoidable, would not impair the trial that was being made, and could finally be corrected when it was about to lead to very grievous harm.

In the very nature of the case a very great perplexity must have arisen in Abraham's mind. The demand of God at this point seemed to be a flat contradiction of all the gracious promises ever given heretofore, and it may well have seemed to originate with none other than the devil himself. Yet herein the patriarch's faith proved itself a true faith, that he leaned in full trust upon his God that all must eventuate to the glory of God and to the eternal good of His children. So reason was taken captive under the rule of faith, and the test was successfully met.

There is no conflict between this interpretation of ours and the fact of the text where Abraham is bidden to go to the land of Moriah for the purpose of this sacrifice. For, in the first place, on the surface everything is transacted in terms of a material sacrifice. But, primarily, in the second place, even for thinking through and carrying out so fundamental a problem it is desirable to cut loose from customary settings and surroundings and there from the perspective that distance also lends to such matters to reach a satisfactory conclusion. If it still be protested that the expression "to bring or offer a burnt offering" is the regular expression for a bloody sacrifice upon a material altar, then it should also be borne in mind that such a sacrifice always demanded the spiritual sacrifice that it typified. Why, then, could not this essential thing stand in the forefront in this case?

1, 2. **And it came to pass after these things that God put Abraham to the test and said unto him: Abraham! and he said: Here am I! And He said: Take now thy son, thine only one, whom thou hast grown to love, even Isaac, and go for thyself to the land of Moriah, and offer him up there for a burnt-offering upon one of the mountains which I shall indicate to thee.**

The expression, "and it came to pass," is a loose mode of attaching what is to follow to the preceding event when no emphasis is to be placed upon the closer connection of time or events (G. K. 111 g). All preceding events ("after these things") practically lead up to the one now to be related. Other instances of God's putting to the test in mercy are found, e. g., Exod. 15:25; 20:20; 16:4; Deut. 8:2, 16; 13:3, 4. He that conducts the trial is "God," *Ha'elohîm*, not the Deity in general but the one true *personal* God. This work is very fittingly ascribed to Him, inasmuch as Abraham's *personal* relation to Him is under scrutiny. Besides, as Keil well points out, the trial originated with God not with the devil, not in Abraham's own thoughts as a result of his reflections upon the child sacrifices of the Canaanites or upon the question whether he loved the true God as much as they seemed to revere their idols in being ready to offer their own flesh and blood as sacrifices. We have no means of knowing exactly how this divine manifestation came to Abraham. Most likely it was in a vision by night. For dreams were employed in the case of those who stood farther removed from God. Besides, morning follows directly (v. 3). We are sure that this prophet of God (20:7) was able to discern clearly when he was receiving a divine communication and when not. Consequently, there is no doubt about the validity of the revelation. The double "Abraham" of the Septuagint is unnatural; the tenser emotion first comes v. 11.

2. The successive terms descriptive of the son who is to be sacrificed are employed, not to make the sacrifice harder but to recall to Abraham's mind how much he has "grown to love" him. For *'ahábhta*, the perfect, is a *perfectum resultativum*, describing that the father has grown to love the son and now stands deep in that love (K. S. 127). The successive terms are 1) "thy son," 2) "thine only one," 3) "whom thou hast grown to love," 4) his name "Isaac" the

epitome of the great joy that came with this son.
Taking his son, Abraham is to "go for himself." The
dative *lekha* here used, a dative of interest, rules out
the idea of others sharing in the test: Abraham
must fight this problem through alone. Luther and
others may not be far from the truth when they suggest that the patriarch told nothing of his purpose
to Sarah. The place to which Abraham is directed
to go is called by the general name "land of Moriah,"
which could better be rendered "region of Moriah"
(B D B) as the word *'érets* is also used in 19:28 and
Josh. 11:3, K. W. — *Gegend von Moriah.* No
doubt, the word "Moriah" is here used by anticipation,
i. e., proleptically, in view of the event here recorded,
which only afterwards gave the region this name.
Inclined to find fault without warrant, many commentators have all kinds of flaws to pick with this
expression. II Chron. 3:1 informs us that "Moriah"
was the name of the mountain or hill upon which
Solomon built the Temple. Why cannot a region get
its name from some prominent feature in it? God
Himself will have used some other designation of
the region, a designation which conveyed to Abraham
the very same thought that Moses conveyed to his
readers by this term. This unwarranted criticism
centers on the term "Moriah" (*Moriyyah*), claiming
for the most part a corrupt text or a misunderstanding
on the part of some inexpert writer or redactor — a
device frequently resorted to to remove some undesirable or inconvenient feature from the text. The term
may well mean "the place of the appearance of Yahweh" (*die Erscheinungsstaette Yahwehs* — K. W.),
the letter *'aleph*, which would mark the word as built
on the root *ra'ah*, having been assimilated, (as is
done not infrequently) for *mor'iyyah.* The prefix
mem often indicates place, the suffix *yah* is contracted for "of Yahweh." The numerous textual

changes suggested are quite unnecessary. ("Moreh"
[12:6]; or *mar'eh,* or *ha'emorî* = "of the Amorites,"
as if the Amorites had dwelt in any *one* place and
not scattered abroad in the land). The root of all
these objections is the fact that the critics find it
hard to believe that divine providence should have
marked the same spot twice by events far removed
from one another in point of time yet covered by
the same name. We, on our part, see an excellent
propriety about having the site of the Temple marked
doubly as "the place of the appearance of Yahweh"
in Abraham's time as well as from the time of the
erection of the Temple onward. Such instances of
divine providence prove truth to be stranger than
fiction.

The command, "offer him up there for a burnt-
offering," has been discussed in the introductory
remarks to the chapter. However, this must yet be
added, the "burnt-offering," (*'olah*), is the type of
sacrifice best suited for this purpose, because it typifies complete surrender to God. The term is derived
from the root *'alah,* signifying "to go up," i. e., in
the smoke of the sacrifice. Therefore, the son given
to Abraham is to be given back to Yahweh without
reservations of any sort.

That the sacrifice is to take place upon one of
the mountains which Yahweh would "indicate" (*'amar,*
"say," in the sense of "command," or "designate") to
him, is stated only here. There is no special statement showing that God later indicated which mountain
was to be used for this purpose. Nor is such a special
statement necessary at this point; in fact, it is lost
sight of under the strain of the stronger emotions that
prevail in the climax of the narrative.

Here we had best take note of the fact that no
mention whatsoever is made of Abraham's personal
reaction to this command from God. In purest epic

style the action alone is recorded not the emotions of the actors. Note now how entirely unfair is the criticism of those who continually aim to press down to the lowest possible level their estimate of patriarchal religion as well as of all Israelitish religion. Because Abraham expresses no revulsion at the thought of sacrificing his son, critics draw conclusions such as to phrase it very cautiously — "The writer does not say that Abraham took exception to this awful sacrifice" (Knobel quoted by Dillmann). Procksch is much bolder, speaking of "human sacrifice, the demand of which gives no offense to Abraham, and which therefore agrees with this earlier religious level." Now strict logic would demand that since nothing is said of the pain which tore the father's heart, therefore on this level of the development of the human race fathers felt no such tender emotions for their own flesh and blood. On this point, not governed by preconceived evolutionistic notions, the critics draw no such conclusions but are unanimous in speaking of the terrible struggle that arose in Abraham's heart. Such widely different conclusions, reached by the use of the argument from silence, are inconsistent. The second refutes the first.

So great a faith as Abraham's could not have allowed any room for such grievous misconceptions as the notion that human sacrifice should be offered by men. For the passages in the Pentateuch which forbid human sacrifices (cf. Lev. 18:21; 20:2 ff; Deut. 12:31; 18:10) either list such a practice among the vilest of deeds of which mankind is capable or else specifically stamp it as an "abomination" of the most degrading sort. Dods distorts the issue when he remarks: "Abraham was familiar with the idea that the most exalted form of religious worship was the sacrifice of the first-born"; or when he offers conclusions such as: "Abraham's conscience did not clash with

God's command." There is no instance whatever to show that in the earlier history of the people of God human sacrifice was ever resorted to. Jephthah's case (Judg. 11) does not belong here and positively does not involve the bloody sacrifice of his daughter. Very late in the degeneracy of the kingdom Ahaz first attempted this horrible practice (II Kings 16:3), a thing there mentioned as a foreign abomination. Hiel's story (I Kings 16:34) does not tell of human sacrifice but of sons lost by divine punishment.

3. And Abraham arose early the next morning, and girded his ass, and took his two servants with him, and Isaac, his son; and cut the wood for the burnt-offering, and arose and went to the place which God had indicated to him.

The article with "morning," being the article used for that which is self-evident (K. S. 299 a), is the equivalent of our "the *next* morning." Abraham's prompt and absolute obedience is here described. Here his faith looms up as positively heroic: God's behests are not to be questioned but executed. The various steps in the process are described from this point forward with a minuteness that makes the scene inexpressibly vivid. The ass is "girded" (*chabhash*) rather than saddled, for the beast must have been taken along to carry the rather sizeable load of wood sufficient to make a fire adequate for a burnt-offering. *Two* servants are taken to care for the beast and its burden as well as for the necessary supplies. They are "his two servants," i. e., those who specially wait upon their master, even as Balaam has two such (Num. 22:22) or Sarah had Hagar (16:3). The expression used would have been different if it was to have meant "two of his servants" (K. S. 304 a). No doubt, Abraham let the servants cut the requisite wood, though the common mode of expression is here used: "he cut" or "clave." Here

already every preparatory step taken by the father
was a painful one. The expression "he arose and
went" is the Hebrew idiom for our "he started out."

"The place which God had indicated to him," an
expression which bridges over from the initial command (v. 2) and implies that when Abraham arrived,
the very place of the sacrifice had been revealed to
him. This does not conflict with our claims immediately preceding v. 1.

Here we may add that Samaritan tradition claims
that Moriah is the region of Shechem. However,
the distance from *Be'er-shebha'* to Shechem is too
great for a three days' journey to allow time for a
sacrifice after arrival. Even Jerusalem is about fifty
miles distant; Shechem almost eighty. Forced
marches with alternate riding on the ass are out of
the question for an ass that bore the wood and for
an old man perhaps 120 years old.

**4, 5. On the third day Abraham lifted up his
eyes and saw the place in the distance. And Abraham said to his servants: Stay here with the ass.
I and the lad will go up yonder that we may worship,
and then we shall return to you.**

Maqôm here hardly means "sacred place," unless,
perhaps, by anticipatory use, for nothing indicates
that a sanctuary had been on the spot previously. The
account is in conformity with fact: the templehill did
not stand out so prominently as to be discernible at
a great distance. Therefore *merachôq* just means
"in the distance" in a moderate sense. Here the verb
with *waw conversive* follows a mere adverbial expression, which in sense, however, is the equivalent of an
adverbial clause (K. S. 366 l).

5. The two servants of Abraham could hardly
have understood what is to follow, so Abraham leaves
them far enough away as not to be able to witness
the impending sacrifice. The act about to follow is

rightly designated by Abraham as "worship" — the
imperfect used as a voluntative (G. K. 75 l). His
concluding remark is a statement of faith: "we shall
return." Heb. 11:19 interprets this remark: "account-
ing that God is able to raise up, even from the dead."
All God's promises received in the past gave him
warrant for reaching such a conclusion. To label
this word a "dissimulation" or "a somewhat confused
utterance" or a mere "hopeful wish," does not do
justice to its character. Knobel (quoted by Dillmann) goes to the limit of uncharitable exegesis
when he claims this is "an untrue statement like
12:30, and 20:12."

6. **And Abraham took the wood for the sacrifice and laid it upon Isaac, his son, and he took in
his hand the fire and the knife; and they two went
along together.**

The details still continue, in fact, they are multi-
plied, to let us feel how each successive step was an
added agony for the much tried father. In the
sturdy strength of youth Isaac is well able to bear
the load of wood up the hill. He may by this time
have arrived at the age of some eighteen to twenty
years. The aged Abraham, his strength cut by his
soul agony, could hardly have carried this burden.
With the resoluteness of faith he bears the two means
of destruction: a container, like a censer, filled with
live coals, and the fatal knife. The narrative gives
free play to our imagination as it pictures father
and son proceeding step for step up the hill. Isaac
cannot but sense that some unwonted burden depresses
his father past anything that the son had ever observed in the father before. This attitude on the
father's part causes some restraint between the two,
and a strange perplexity falls upon Isaac.

7, 8. **And Isaac said unto Abraham, his father:
My father! And he replied: What is it, my son?**

And he went on: Here are fire and faggots, but where is the lamb for the burnt-offering? And Abraham said: God will provide a lamb for Himself for a burnt-offering, my son. And they two went along together.

The splendid confidence existing between father and son cannot under these circumstances allow the father to divulge to the son the unspeakably heavy duty which seems imperative; nor does it prevent the son from asking about the seemingly very apparent omission — the sacrificial victim. The very address, "My father," must almost have been felt like a kind of knifethrust by the father. The reply, which literally runs: "Behold me, my son," or "Here am I," (A. V.), appears far too stilted by such a rendering, for it means no more than a kindly: "What is it?" as the Septuagint well renders τί ἐστιν, τέκνον, or the colloquial "Yes, my son" (Meek). The very thing that Abraham cannot utter is the matter about which Isaac asks: "Where is the lamb?" The question had to come even in the face of the unusual constraint that prevailed.

8. The father's love devises an answer which is a marvelous compound of considerate love and anticipative faith. He spares Isaac undue pain and leaves the issues entirely with God, where in his own heart he left them throughout the journey. In the light of what follows Abraham's answer is well-nigh prophetic: "God will provide." It marks the high point of the chapter, the one thing about God's dealings with His own that here receives emphatic statement. The verb used, *ra'ah*, usually means "see" — here "look out for," or "provide," or "choose," as in 41:33; Deut. 12:13; 33:21; I Sam. 16:1, 17. The iteration, "and they two went along together," here proves very effective (cf. v. 6). The *lô* "for him" = reflexive "for Himself" (G. K. 135 i; K. S. 27).

9. **And they came to the place which God had indicated to him, and there Abraham built the altar, and laid the wood in order, and bound Isaac, his son, and laid him on the altar upon the wood.**

With a straightforward simplicity the successive steps leading immediately toward the climax are recorded. The tension of the narrative grows. One feels how each successive step grew more difficult for the heavy-hearted father. One observes with wonder the strength of his faith which will not suffer him to waver.

We remarked above that nothing shows when God "indicated" to him that this was the particular "hill" chosen for the sacrifice. Abraham himself built "the altar" — the article signifies that the altar requisite for such a sacrifice is meant. The wood is arranged — *'arakh*, the regular word for setting the wood or the sacrifice in order upon the altar, yet it is not a highly technical term. So much for the impersonal elements utilized. Now, O marvel of marvels, he actually binds his own son! Isaac's submission to this act is best explained as an act of confidence in his father, a confidence built upon a complete understanding and a deep love which knew that the father could wish his son no harm. Therefore, even as it is not said that Abraham achieved the complete submission of faith, but the whole story is convincing evidence that he did; so in Isaac's case the same submission, only more passive in character, is also present. That Isaac suffered himself to be bound is an act of supreme faith in God and of full confidence in his father. Usually too little consideration is given to Isaac's heroism, which, if it were not for the more marvelous faith heroism of his father, could justly be classed as among the mightiest acts of faith.

**10-12. And Abraham reached forth his hand
and took the knife to slay his son, when the Angel
of Yahweh called to him from the heavens, saying:
Abraham, Abraham! And he said: Here am I.
And He said: Lay not thy hand upon the lad,
neither do anything to him; for now I know that
thou fearest God, seeing thou hast not withheld thy
son, thy only son, from Me.**

God knew that the hand that had the courage
to pick up the knife would not have hesitated to perform the sacrifice. He knew that in Abraham's heart
the necessary surrender had been made: Abraham
would suffer nothing to stand between him and his
God. God was Abraham's dearest treasure; God's
will, his chief concern. Though the external sacrifice
was not the object God sought, yet He allowed the
situation to develop to this point, to furnish full
evidence that the inner spiritual sacrifice was actually
achieved. In this connection it must be considered,
how often, especially in the matter of surrender or
self-surrender, a point which falls short of the total
surrender necessary, is often mistaken by a man for
complete surrender itself. In this case there were
to be no halfway measures.

11. He who speaks to Abraham is here designated
as "the Angel of Yahweh." As 16:7-11 and 21:17,
18 already indicated, this person is divine and specifically the one who later assumed the form of man.
In our passage His divine character is indicated by
the words that close v. 12: "thou hast not withheld
thy only son from Me." That one can be God and
yet so distinct from Him in one sense as to be
able to say, "I know that thou fearest God," is to be
explained on the ground of the distinction of divine
persons. In this case there is no need of His appearing on earth, because, as it seems, the emphasis in
His revelation lies upon the fact that God in high

heaven, the Supreme Ruler, who is justified in asking such a sacrifice as He did of Abraham, is satisfied with what Abraham has done. The double call, "Abraham, Abraham," gives proof of its urgency: Abraham is to be restrained on the spot. A remarkable indication of the fine spirit of complete submission to God's every call and purpose lies in Abraham's reply, "Here am I," still more concise in the original *hinnéni*, "Here I." Parallels to the double call in this verse are found in 46:2; Exod. 3:4; I Sam. 3:10; Acts 9:4.

12. In full conformity with His original purpose God restrains Abraham from carrying through the sacrifice. We may here yet take issue with an explanation that is a favorite with many, but, we hold, quite unsatisfactory. We refer to the explanation which represents God as merely pretending to be harsh in His demand and that for pedagogical reasons, but then after His purpose has been attained displaying His wonted loving-kindness. God cannot be guilty of pretense. He is not like parents who make themselves appear as though they cared little for their children but ultimately show their true attitude. Although this approach to the difficulty stands under the sanction of Luther's approval, we feel it to be strained and impossible.

Abraham is to do Isaac no harm whatsoever — (*me'ûmah*, "anything," has an old accusative ending *ah*, but is also used as a nominative). God Himself draws the conclusion as to what Abraham's act means: "I know that thou fearest God." The acme of true fear, i. e., reverence, of God consists in complete subjection to His sovereign will. Abraham's subjection was made without reservations. He had, indeed, feared God before; now he advances to the full measure of devotion, even as in the New Testament it is often said of believing disciples, "They believed

on Him" when a new level of faith was reached.
Here the mode of expression, besides, is quite
emphatic: "that a fearer of God thou," the normal
use of the participle for emphasis, *yere' 'elohîm* (K.
S. 241 i), and so the participle appears in the construct state. When God says, "Now I know"
(*yadháti*), that does not imply that at this earlier
stage of development, though God's omniscience was
granted, yet in cases where human freedom was involved, it was not always understood that God's knowing could cover them also (K. C.). Here *yadháti*
is used in the sense of "know by experience," and so
we have here not even an anthropomorphism.

It matters little how we construe the last clause
beginning with *welo'*. This may be regarded as a
causal clause introduced by *we* (G. K. 158 a), as
our rendering, following A. V., has done: "seeing
thou," etc., or else the copulative idea of *we* may
be retained, and the clause marks a climax or a
kind of result clause "and (therefore) thou hast not
withheld," etc. (K. C.).

13. **And Abraham looked up, and there was
a ram behind him, its horns caught in a bush; and
Abraham went and took the ram and sacrificed it
for a burnt-offering in place of his son.**

Providentially Abraham is led to look up at this
moment, and he discovers a ram, which because of
the intense preoccupation and mental struggle that
absorbed Abraham's being before, had not been
noticed. Perhaps, too, the beast had been quite
enfeebled by a long struggle and had held still till
now. Renewed efforts to liberate itself may just at
this moment have attracted Abraham's attention.
There is nothing so very marvelous about this as
in fairy tales where the necessary feature always pops
up (Procksch). Abraham's intense relief at being
prevented from sacrificing his son seeks expression

in a definite act of gratitude, which most logically
finds expression in a sacrifice. A devout mind cannot but regard the ram as providentially provided.
Words would not suffice to describe with what entirely
different emotions the ram is offered in place of the
"only son." It seems easiest to construe *ne'echāz*,
with long "ā," as a participle.

14. **And Abraham called the name of that
place Yahweh yir'eh; wherefore men say to this
day: In the mount of Yahweh provision is made.**

The fact that this verse says *"that* place" and
not *"this* place" indicates that after Abraham had
come away from the mountain and his thoughts on
this experience had crystallized he thus briefly caught
the meaning of it all in a kind of epitome: he had
said to Isaac as they went up the mountain side,
"Yahweh will provide"; Yahweh certainly had provided in a manner that most clearly displayed divine
providence. The event was so unusual, and the
character involved so prominent, and the formulation
of the importance of the whole experience so much
to the point that in Moses' day, as he wrote this
account, he had heard from trustworthy witnesses
that a kind of proverbial saying had perpetuated the
thought of this significant name in that part of the
country. Men were still wont to speak of that hill
as "the mount of Yahweh" and to recount the substance of the experience in the words: "In the hill
of Yahweh provision is made." This was as much
as to say: When men come to a particular test that
God imposes, God helps them in His gracious providence according to their needs. Of course, the divine
name "Yahweh" is here most appropriately used because God's covenant faithfulness is most emphatically
involved in the sparing of Isaac.

But the question remains: Is this translation
of *yera'eh* warranted? Does this mean: "provision

is made"? Shall we go back to the A. V., "it shall
be seen"? Shall we repoint the word to make a
Kal instead of a *Nifal?* Shall we attempt textual
changes? Nothing of the sort. We have a good
text. We have a sound tradition represented by the
vowel points. The only real difficulty is whether the
passive had not better be translated as a simple "it
shall be seen." In support of this contention it is
strongly claimed that the *Nifal* of the verb *ra'ah*
must mean "appear" (Keil). However, the whole
issue in this narrative has consistently turned on the
question, not whether Yahweh would "appear" but
whether He would "provide." If, then, in such a
connection the passive of *ra'ah* is used, it definitely
gains the meaning: "it is provided," or more idiomatically: "provision is made" (so also Meek). All
this is so simple and so natural that we must reject
as a weak evasion the verdict of Skinner: "The
words *behar Yahweh yera'eh* yield no sense appropriate to the context." Gunkel attempts an emendation claiming that the name of the sanctuary should
be *Yeru'el.* I believe that Luther's commentary gives
ground for interpreting his translation in the sense
we have given above, when he renders: *Auf dem
Berge da der Herr siehet,* i. e., *ersieht.* Cf. also
K. S. 160 b. Strack is guilty of the most incoherent
jump in thought when he claims that the phrase "to
this day" or "in this day" refers to the time of David
and to the event of the Angel's appearing at the
threshing floor of Araunah (II Sam. 24).

15-18. **And the Angel of Yahweh called to
Abraham a second time from heaven, and He said:
By myself have I sworn, oracle of Yahweh, because
thou hast done this thing, and hast not withheld
thy son, thine only son, I will most abundantly bless
thee, and most abundantly multiply thy seed as the
stars of the heavens and as the sand which is upon**

the seashore; and thy descendants shall possess
the gate of their enemies; and all the nations of
the earth shall bless themselves by thy descendants,
because thou didst hearken unto My voice.

At this point it is a good thing to remind oneself of Whitelaw's quotation from Oehler, that this
is a chapter "which is joined together like cast iron."
For since at this point the divine name *Ha'elohîm*
is abandoned and *Yahweh* appears, criticism must
attempt to make the different sources stand out prominently over against one another, and so the claim is
raised that the preceding section (from E) closed
definitely with v. 14 and had come to a natural close.
Then an effort is made to make the verses 15-18
appear as a manifestly later addition which is practically
foisted upon the preceding narrative. For this purpose the word *shenith* is even pressed as though it
could not have been used in the original account —
which is tantamount to saying: God cannot speak
a "second time" to a man in the course of one narrative. However, since covenant promises are being
made by a merciful God, God is naturally here
designated as appearing in His capacity as *Yahweh*.
Since in manifestations it is regularly "the Angel of
Yahweh" who functions, these words are appropriately
ascribed to Him. Besides, severe exception is taken
to the use of the phrase "oracle of Yahweh" (*ne'um
yahweh*) as though its use in a word from Yahweh
were entirely inadmissible. True, the phrase as such
appears only once more in the Pentateuch, viz. Num.
14:28. Yet in 18:14 God also refers to Himself in
the third person, and if in later prophetic usage the
expression *ne'um yahweh* comes to be very common,
it may well be that this usage builds upon our passage. As for the reasonableness of having a special
assurance together with reaffirmation of the former
promises given to Abraham in answer to his meeting

the supreme test, no one can deny that the occasion
practically calls for a divine utterance in a life where
every important juncture was marked by significant
utterances. Besides, it is quite appropriate that the
Lord's last word to Abraham should be an outstanding one embracing the substance of all those that had
preceded.

16. The outstanding feature about this word is
the new and entirely unique element of the divine
oath: God swore by Himself. No other instance of
God's oath by Himself appears in the Scriptures,
except when the oath is mentioned where God swears
that Israel because of its disobedience shall not enter
into the land of promise (Num. 14:28), or when it
is said that the Lord sware to give the Promised
Land to Israel. Yet it may be safely said, we believe,
that these latter oaths are implied in this first one.
Yet it remains as a remarkable fact that God, who is
truth, swore by Himself; not, however, as though it
were necessary but in order to give all possible
assurance to man. Here the oath of God in particular
stands in recognition of Abraham's supreme act of
obedience. God delights in rewarding faithful service:
Abraham did not withhold his best; God will bestow
His best.

We must note in this connection a correct observation that Luther makes. He points out that
the Scriptures speak of God's having sworn to *David*
that He would establish his seed forever (Ps. 89:3;
Ps. 132:11, etc). Yet we have no record of such
an oath in the Scriptures. Luther argues that since
the oath to Abraham involved the gift of the Messiah, if David is assured that the Messiah is to come
from his line, then the oath of Abraham transfers
itself to David. We believe this exposition to be
correct.

In the perfect *nishbá'ti* the action reaches over from the past to the present: in the past the decision was reached, now it is expressed. The *kî* following merely introduces direct discourse and is repeated at the beginning of v. 17.

17. The former blessings are repeated in most emphatic fashion, including everything promised since 12:1. The verbs, reinforced by the absolute infinitive in this case, are the equivalent of the verb idea plus a "most abundantly." Richest blessings, most remarkable increase are promised. To the blessing of the descendants like "the stars of heaven" (15:5) is added the new and more emphatic one of "the sand which is upon the seashore." The success of his descendants when they encounter enemies is indicated by the statement that they "shall possess the gate of their enemies." Since the gate was the keypoint in the question of control of a city, "to possess the gate" was the equivalent of gaining control of or capturing a city. This statement, however, does not guarantee that Israel shall conquer the world by aggression but merely shows what the outcome will be when Israel is assailed. Neither does the statement include spiritual conquest. That is covered by the next verse. Nor dare we forget that in reality this promise to Abraham's seed is conditioned by obedience. Only they who continue in the faith of Abraham and so are his true children may look to the possession of these things. Let it be observed that *weyirash* is not a converted perfect, as might have been expected, but an unconverted imperfect, a construction which makes the act stand out more distinctly over against the preceding (K. S. 370 s).

18. This verse does not contain the same promise that is found in 12:3, for *hithbarakhû* does not mean "be blessed." Yet for all that the thought of 12:3 is

implied, and the statement is without a doubt Messianic. *Hithbarakhû* is of the *Hithpael* stem, therefore reflexive: "they shall bless themselves." That means that when "all the nations of the earth" discern how great the blessing is that Israel enjoys, namely in the Messiah, then everyone "shall bless himself by thy descendants," i. e., he shall invoke upon himself the blessings that Abraham's children have in the Christ. That "all the nations of the earth" shall do this indicates the universal appeal that the Messiah has for all men and also indicates that He is to be a Messiah capable of bestowing blessings upon all. When the statement concludes with the words that God so richly blesses Abraham, "because thou didst hearken unto my voice," that does not mean that the blessing is an earned reward but rather a reward of grace.

19. **And Abraham returned to his servants and they arose and went together to Beersheba, and Abraham made his home in Beersheba.**

So the narrative concludes, telling how the group that had come from Beersheba returned thither and how Abraham "dwelt" there (A. V.), *yeshebh* being used, of course, in the sense of "made his home" there (Meek).

This remarkable event, historical and complete in itself in reference to Abraham, has prophetic import. Under God's providence this event becomes a type of the sacrifice on Calvary. The starting point for this consideration may well be the simple fact that God does not expect man to do for Him what He is not ready to do for man. Abraham and all men are expected to give up their dearest possession to God. God on His part gives up His dear Son. In Abraham's case the type is all the more to the point because Isaac is an only son, even as Christ is the Only Begotten. Nor is it merely a case of pious ingenuity when we

discover a parallel between these two. Rom. 8:32
sanctions this approach in a word that reads like an
allusion to this chapter: "He that spared not His own
Son but delivered Him up for us all . . . . ." A
proper exposition of this passage must, therefore,
point to this type that is involved as necessarily belonging to the exposition. In the homiletical use of the
passage at least two approaches are possible: either
one centers attention on Abraham and his faith life
and allows the type to be brought in incidentally, or
where one desires to use the text as a foundation for
the treatment of the subject of God's giving up of His
Son for us, the various typical elements of the text are
successively used, and everything centers about the
true sacrifice of Christ. Abraham and Isaac merely
appear incidentally by way of illustration.

14. **Nahor's Descendants (Rebekah) (22:20-24)**

20. **And it came to pass after these things that
someone reported to Abraham: Behold, Milcah,
too, has born children to Nahor, thy brother.**

The distance from Mesopotamia to southern
Palestine was so great that practically all contact between these two brothers, Abraham and Nahor, had
been lost. Now "someone reported" (*yuggadh* — "it
was told") to Abraham, perhaps, a chance traveler
in a caravan train. The individual in question was
fully informed and was able to give to Abraham the
exact names of the children. These names were faithfully noted and are here presented chiefly because in
the list of them Rebekah is to be found, concerning
whose identity we shall soon need information. The
"too" (*gam*) used with Milcah signifies that just as
Abraham's wife had born him legitimate offspring in
the son of promise, so Abraham's brother's wife had
also given him offspring.

21-24. **Uz, his first-born and Buz, his brother,
and Kemuel, the father of Aram; and Chesed, and**

Hazo, and Pildash, and Yidlaph, and Bethuel (and Bethuel begat Rebekah). These eight did Milcah bear to Nahor, Abraham's brother. And his concubine, whose name was Reumah, she also bare sons, Tebah, and Gaham, and Tahash, Maacah.

The remarkable coincidences that are here met with are that Nahor's case presents a strange parallel to that of Abraham as well as to that of Jacob. To Abraham's, in that Nahor has a wife and a concubine. To Jacob's, in that there are twelve sons. Critics, as we quite readily understand, see in this double coincidence proof of the legendary character of the account. Others again create artificial difficulty by claiming that at this time the third generation could not yet be reported in Nahor's line (Rebekah and Aram) when only the second is found in Abraham's. But it should not be forgotten that Isaac was born so very late as practically to place him parallel to the third generation.

Another difficulty is created by the assumption that since Jacob's twelve sons became the heads of twelve tribes, therefore these twelve sons of Nahor must be counted as tribes. The analogy is farfetched. The tribal theory in reference to these early ancestors has several fallacies. We must here even reckon with the possibility that perhaps not one of these twelve sons ever originated a tribe. So, of course, we cannot tell if, for example, the land of Uz, mentioned Job 1:1, is to be thought of as the land where the descendants of Uz, the son of Nahor, dwelt or not; or whether Elihu, the son of Barachel the Buzite, is a descendant of the Buz here mentioned or not. Even more problematic, then, becomes the question where these sons of Nahor lived.

Aram, the son of Kemuel, presents a problem in that 10:22 Aram is mentioned as one of the sons of Shem, and in that connection, without a doubt, as the founder of the tribe or people of the Aramaeans. However, the Aram in our chapter is hardly to be regarded as the founder of a nation; and if he were, then Keil's suggestion can relieve the difficulty. For a comparison of II Kings 8:29 with II Chron. 22:5 indicates that Arammim is another mode of writing Rammim. In case, then, that the Aram in question actually is the father of a tribe, he would be the father of the Rammim rather than of the Arammim. If he is an individual, Aram would be another form of the name Ram.

Homiletical Suggestions are embodied in the above comments.

CHAPTER XXIII

15. Death and Burial of Sarah (23:1-20)

After the climax of the preceding chapter the events of the life of Abraham taper off gradually toward the conclusion. A few matters that must yet be reported in order appropriately to close this significant life are presented.

The seemingly unimportant event of this chapter, an event that could have been reported far more briefly, is recorded at greater length because it is an act of faith, in fact, a rather outstanding act.

1, 2. And Sarah became 127 years old; that was the length of her life. And Sarah died in Kirjath-arba, (that is, Hebron) in the land of Canaan, and Abraham came to bewail Sarah and to weep for her.

We believe we have rendered quite idiomatically and correctly the first verse of this chapter, which, rendered more literally, would run as follows: "And was the life of Sarah 127 years, the years of the life of Sarah." It is true that the statement is somewhat detailed, but it represents a rather common mode of speech, about like the statement: she became so old, and that was all. Some try to doctor up the text, either by an addition or by an omission; but all such efforts grow out of an unwillingness to believe that men of old spoke and wrote much as we do.

It so happens that Sarah is the only woman whose age and death are reported in the Scriptures, as commentators have observed from days of old. This cannot be without design. She is the mother of

all believers, according to I Pet. 3:6, and so deserving
of some such distinction. *Chayyîm,* the customary
plural, expresses the multitude of aspects under which
life appears.

2. Sarah's death takes place at Kirjath-arba.
Though in 22:19 Abraham had taken up his residence
at Beersheba, yet since that time perhaps twenty years
had elapsed. For Sarah, being 127 years old at death,
lived 37 years after Isaac's birth (cf. 17:17 and 21:5).
If, then, Isaac had been nearly twenty years old at
the time of the sacrifice upon Mt. Moriah (cf. 22:6),
almost twenty years had passed since that time. During those years Abraham may have left Beersheba
repeatedly and come to Hebron, his earlier place of
residence (13:18; 14:13).

"Kirjath-arba" is identified by the more common
name "Hebron." The problem involved in the use of
these two names seems to be covered by the following
approach: according to Num. 13:22 the original name
of this ancient city appears to have been Hebron. At
the time Moses is writing, apparently, Arba, one of
the Enakim, had taken possession of the city and called
it "the city of Arba" (Kirjath-arba) ; cf. Jos. 14:15;
15:13; 21:11. According to these last mentioned passages the name Kirjath-arba was prevalent at the time
of the conquest under Joshua, but the propriety of
restoring the more ancient name, which apparently
had never been forgotten by Israel, seemed to appeal
to all. So also Moses here inserts the old familiar
name to identify the city by the name it had borne
in Abraham's time, "Hebron." Now Hebron, Hebrew:
chebhrôn, from *chabhar,* may mean: "city of treaty."
Since "Arba" was above shown to have been an Enak
prince, it is a proper name and cannot mean "four,"
as the Hebrew word otherwise could. The following
phrase "in the land of Canaan" is not superfluous;
for it recalls that in Canaan, the land of promise,

the mother of the children of Abraham died. (Cf. also
v. 19).

Whatever Abraham may have been doing at the
time of her death, he "came," when the news reached
him, "to bewail Sarah and to weep for her." Such
an expression as "he came" could hardly have been
used if he had been present at the time of her decease.
Not only was bewailing (*saphadh,* = "to beat one's
breast," "to lament") and weeping (*bakhah*) the
customary oriental mode of expressing grief, it was
also the natural expression of a deep and sincere sorrow on Abraham's part. True and loving husband
that he was, he felt his loss very keenly. Such
demonstrations of grief are as natural and as proper
to the Oriental as is our greater measure of restraint
to us. It was usually indulged in before the dead
body of the person who was being bewailed. "Bewail"
involves audible expression of one's grief.

**3, 4. And Abraham arose from beside his dead
and spoke to the children of Heth, saying: I am a
stranger and sojourner among you; give me a grave
for my own property among you and let me bury
my dead out of my sight.**

Much as he loved his good wife, the patriarch did
not sorrow above measure; also, because burial within
one day's time after death was the rule in this land,
he had to address himself to the task of securing a
grave. The "children of Heth" or the Hittites are
in possession of the city and its surrounding territory;
they must be consulted. In the Orient any transaction is preceded by an exchange of compliments. In
a measure this is the case in this instance, however,
apparently there is no idle courtesy or shallow, insincere flattery on the part of Abraham at all, and
on the part of the man Ephron very little, if at all.
The Hittites themselves speak as sincerely as Abraham does. Throughout the whole scene Abraham

demeans himself with fine tact and courtesy and the
utmost of sincerity but without obsequiousness.

4. Abraham begins by outlining briefly his position among his neighbors: he is "a stranger and
sojourner." The "stranger" (*ger*) is a foreigner
in a strange land possessing no property and having
no fixed habitation. The "sojourner," as we translate for want of a better term (*tôshabh,* from
yashabh, "to sit," almost = "squatter"), has a permanent dwelling but no property in the form of
land. Abraham can class himself as both of these,
for he sometimes settles down, sometimes wanders
about as a nomad. His reference to his status
recalls especially the fact that he does not as yet
possess any land in this country. He asks "for a
grave for his own property," literally: "possession
of a grave." The grave, of course, is a burial place
large enough to hold the remains of the family. He
desires to have this grave in the very midst of these
men ("among you"). There he hopes to bury his
dead (*meth,* common gender, since in the face of
death male or female is no issue). To bury *out of
sight* is simply a more expressive way of describing
burial. *'Eqberah* is a hortative imperfect.

The thought involved in this verse in the use of
the terms "stranger and sojourner" carries deeper
implications, as is shown by the interpretation given
by the author of Heb. 11:13-16. If these men, such
as Abraham and Jacob (47:9) spoke of their pil-
grim state on earth, even while thinking of the land
of promise, which did they regard as their true
home? The "better country, that is a heavenly"
(Heb. 11:16). This valid interpretation offered by
the New Testament shows us that it is not wise to
put too low an estimate upon the spiritual content
of the words of the men of God of the Old Covenant.

For the true faith which they possessed gave them deep insight and wisdom of utterance.

5, 6. And the children of Heth answered Abraham and said: Please listen to us, sir. Thou art a prince of God among us. Bury thy dead in the choicest of our sepulchres. Not a one of us would withhold his sepulchre from thee from burying thy dead.

A slight change of pointing is involved in our translation, without alteration of the text. The last word of v. 5 *lô*, "to him," seems to make good sense in the phrase, "saying to him." However, strange to say, the word "saying" (*le'mor*) is never followed by a *le*. Lev. 11:1 comes nearest to being a parallel but uses the preposition *'el*. By pointing *lô* as *lû* ("please") and joining it with the following verse we remove the difficulty. At the close of v. 14 the same situation is found.

One can hardly say that the Hittites appear reluctant to let Abraham acquire even this small bit of ground. They prove themselves very courteous and, it would seem, speak in all sincerity. For they give Abraham to understand that he needs to acquire no property, for they will all put their family sepulchres at his disposal, even "the choicest" of them. They explain why they are ready to grant so much by saying that Abraham has come to be ranked among them as "a prince of God." By this they mean that he is a "prince" (*nasî'*), a man of high station whom God has raised on high and upon whom tokens of divine favor have manifestly been bestowed, but who himself also stands in a relation of reverent obedience to God. Note how these heathen men use the word *'elohîm*, "God," not *Yahweh*. They know the divinity only in a general way. Besides, they could not use the expression *nesî' yahweh*, for that would mean "*the* prince of Yahweh" — which is not what they

mean to say.   Merely to class *nesî' 'elohîm* as a kind
of superlative (K. S. 309 l) is rather shallow.

Here we may also yet dispose of the problem
whether the Hittites could have dwelt as far south
as Hebron.   Some have claimed that the habitat of
this people must be sought from the Orontes east-
ward, but that it cannot have run as far as southern
Palestine.   K. C. quoting from Sayce shows why
such a claim as that of v. 3 and 5 is perfectly in place.
The three arguments advanced are 1) that also
Ezechiel traces the descent of Jerusalem from a
Hittite mother (16:3, 45) ; 2) the country of the
Hittites was promised to the descendants of Abra-
ham (15:19-21) ; 3) the testimony of the Tell-el-
Amarna letters agrees to this in that the sons of a
Hittite prince by name of Arzawia dwell to the south
of the land and take part in an expedition against
Jerusalem.

**7-9.   And Abraham arose and bowed to the
people of the land, to the children of Heth, and he
spoke with them saying: If it be agreeable to you
that my dead be buried out of my sight, then hear
me and intercede for me with Ephron, the son of
Zohar, that he give me the cave of Machpelah,
which belongs to him, which is at the end of his
field; for the full price let him give it to me in the
midst of you for a grave which is my own property.**

7.   Abraham is a man of fine courtesy, and so
he acknowledges the gracious compliment the Hittites
paid him by designating him as a prince of God and
by offering him the use of the finest of their sepulchres.
His acknowledgment consists of rising and bowing.
The regular inhabitants of the land are called "the
people of the land" — an expression which does not
bear the bad sense that it acquired later in Nehemiah's
time, when it applied to the heathen inhabitants
(*'am ha'arets*).   We do Abraham wrong if we let

either his actions or his words be thought of as insincere. His Canaanite contemporaries might use these same forms as idle gestures; not he, "the prince of God."

8. The Hebrew original has the expression "if it be with your souls," where "souls" may mean "inner purpose." This means, of course, "if it be agreeable to you." Abraham argues: if you are satisfied to let me use your sepulchres, you will not be averse to selling me a plot of ground as my own property. But in the Orient intermediaries are employed in all manner of business. So here the people assembled in the gate are to present Abraham's case to Ephron, whose the particular plot is that Abraham desires, and whom Abraham may not even have known personally. Now Machpelah, according to v. 17, also 49:30; 50:13, must have been a portion of ground upon which the cave Abraham desired, was located. The shorter expression, therefore, is "cave of Machpelah." Though *makhpelah* from *kaphal* may mean "double" (διπλοῦν) — Septuagint, yet here it cannot mean "the double cave" but the bipartite tract sought by Abraham comprising a portion of ground and a cave. This being "at the end of his field" will readily lend itself to purchase without necessitating the breaking up of Ephron's property.

9. Abraham wants no favors. He is ready to pay "the full price," Hebrew: "full silver" (*késeph male'*). Abraham desires to make the purchase one that is fully attested by the presence of an adequate number of witnesses, therefore "in the midst of you" let him give it. We have again rendered the expression "for the possession of a burial place" in better English as "a grave which is my own property." Note *wejitten* has no *waw conversive* and so makes the action stand out more distinctly (K. S. 364 l).

The *be* before *keseph* is *beth of price.* The mere
fact that an Assyrian expression like "full silver"
happens to have been discovered does not, however,
yet give warrant to draw far-reaching conclusions
from this correspondence as to the time of our incident, whether this Assyrian expression be found in
the time of later Assyrian kings or in the time of
Hammurabi. Such threads are too slender for hanging proofs on them.

**10, 11. Now Ephron was sitting in the midst
of the children of Heth; so Ephron the Hittite
answered Abraham in the hearing of the Hittites,
at least of all those who were wont to come to the
gate of his city, saying: No, my dear sir, do thou
listen to me. This field I give thee, and the cave
which is in it, that I give to thee in the eyes of
the children of my people; to thee do I give it to
bury thy dead.**

The Ephron that Abraham had referred to happens to be present in the city-gate where all such transactions were wont to be made and where the men
of the town continually congregate. Consequently,
there is no need of the functions of a mediator, and
so he speaks for himself. *Yoshebh,* the participle, does
not want to indicate that Ephron dwelt in this region
(A. V.), but since *yashabh* primarily means "to sit,"
that he was at that very moment sitting with the
townspeople there assembled (A. R. V.). This interpretation makes the statement fit so much the more
closely into the thought-connection, which goes on to
say that he replied to Abraham's proposal. That the
whole transaction was carried on "in the hearing of
the Hittites" marks it as an official piece of business,
fully attested and put on record. The phrase *lekhol*
serves as an apposition to the preceding genitive,
limiting it to those of the Hittites "who were wont
to come (*ba'ey,* participle expressing customary

action) to the gate of his city." Whoever happened to be present at a given time when a case like Abraham's was being disposed of, these persons constituted a kind of court and jury as well as witnesses. The translation "even of all that went in at the gate" (A. V.) does not fit in this case, though the verb *bô'* could mean "go in," because not all these could be present so that this case could have been transacted in their "hearing." Consequently, the *le* before *kol* gets a kind of restrictive sense — "at least." The expression *"his* city" in reference to Ephron does not give warrant to class him as the ruler of the city, for any man can call his home town *his* town. On *lekhol* see K. S. 280 e. The nounal force of the participle *ba'ey* definitely preponderates in this case, as the construct state also indicates (K. S. 241 d).

11. The initial *lo'* is used like our "No," and it is not to be altered to *lû,* which requires a different consonant. *'Adhonî* is respectful address like "sir" or "my dear sir." The perfect *nathátti,* called the "perfect of instant action" (Skinner), is used to express the certainty of an act in a treaty or agreement; the deed is to be regarded as good as done. Abraham should consider the field and the cave as already given to him. However, we are afraid, judging at least by what all Oriental travelers report under this head, that this remarkable liberality was an empty gesture. Orientals offer you as a gift whatever you admire; they do not expect that you will take it. Such an offer from God-fearing Abraham, however, would, no doubt, have been sincere. Even in case Abraham's sincerity had begotten a like sincerity in Ephron, it would, nevertheless, have been rather improper for Abraham to accept the generous offer, because in that case Abraham would really have been ready to receive from a heathen man what in reality he had already received from a higher hand,

though primarily for his descendants. To receive
from man what had been given by God would have
called in question whether God's gift was true and
valid.

**12, 13. And Abraham bowed before the peo-
ple of the land and said to Ephron in the hearing
of the people of the land: If thou wouldest only,
I pray thee, hear me. I am paying the price of
the field; accept it of me, and let me bury my dead
there.**

Many of these fine acts of courtesy ascribed to
Abraham were, no doubt, dictated by custom. So his
bowing before the people of the land was in acknowledgment of the fine offer Ephron, one of their
number, had made. Luther especially remarks what
fine manners also a good man of God may have and
recommends laying aside all boorish clumsiness.

13. At the beginning of this statement some
claim to have found an anacoluthon "expressing the
polite embarrassment of the speaker." We hardly
can accept the suggestion. The particle *'im* with
an imperfect gives an optative force (K. S. 355 x) ;
the *lû* increases the force of this optative; the *'akh*
equals "only." Abraham is not hemming and hawing
for very courtesy. Another perfect of instant action
follows: "I am giving or paying" — which translation seems to catch the force of this perfect better
than: "I will give" (A. V.). Abraham is more intent
upon concluding an honest purchase and burying his
dead honorably than upon anything else. So he
pleads to have the gift accepted that he may perform the burial.

**14, 15. And Ephron answered Abraham, say-
ing: If thou wouldest listen to me, O sir, a piece
of ground worth four hundred shekels of silver, what
is that between me and thee? Bury thy dead.**

As at the end of v. 5 we deemed it advisable to take the final word and point it to read *lû*, the optative particle, and read it with the following verb, so here.

15. With customary oriental politeness Ephron does not ask to be paid for his "piece of ground" (*'e'rets*); he merely suggests its probable worth but adds at the same time that such a sum is a mere trifle for men such as they are. It is true, 400 silver shekels, about $260, is not a big sum for a rich man. Nevertheless, if money had twenty times the present purchasing value in those days, as some claim, a sum of $5,000 for an acre or two is not a mere trifle. Apparently, Ephron is doing what Orientals regularly do: first they offer to give freely, not expecting their offer to be accepted; then they claim to fix a modest price, which is really quite exorbitant (cf. Delitzsch's examples), but which by common consent is really only to serve as a starting point for the bargaining proceedings that are to follow, and in which Orientals engage with the keenest delight.

16. **And Abraham hearkened unto Ephron, and Abraham weighed out to Ephron the money he had named in the hearing of the children of Heth, four hundred shekels of silver, current with the merchant.**

To us this looks like an instance where the nobler spirit of the God-fearing man stands out favorably by contrast with the conventional behavior of the heathen man. Abraham is above such a thing as haggling or driving a shrewd bargain over a burial lot: such bargaining is unworthy of a godly man at all times and is the outgrowth of an unseemly love of money. Under such circumstances Abraham would rather accept the offer, let Ephron take advantage of him and so demonstrate that he stands on higher ground than do his neighbors. To the astonishment

of all Abraham pays the full sum, pays it out by
weighing (*shaqal*), inasmuch as coined money was
not yet in circulation in those days. Besides, to
take advantage of the seller in no sense, Abraham
uses the higher standard "silver current with the
merchant," i. e., accepted on every hand as full value.
Socher is the itinerant merchant or peddler. '*Abher*
in reference to money means to be in current use.

**17, 18. So the field of Ephron which was in
Machpelah over against Mamre, the field and the
cave which was in it and all the trees that were
in the field within the entire confines of the field,
was assured to Abraham as his purchased property
in the sight of the children of Heth, that is, of all
those who were wont to come to the gate of his
city.**

So the transaction was concluded. This record
of it gives the details of the contract as they were
outlined at the time. Ancient contract tablets present
a close parallel to this case. Field, cave, trees are
all involved in the purchase. Apparently, everyone
present at the transaction knew exactly which field
was involved and what its boundaries were; and so
there was no need of a detailed description of the
boundaries. Incidentally, we are here informed also
what it was that prompted Abraham's desire for this
particular piece of ground: it lay "over against
Mamre," therefore directly within sight of Mamre
and contiguous to it. Abraham wanted a place of
burial as near as possible to his place of residence,
which since 14:13 apparently had always been the
terebinths of Mamre, when Abraham was dwelling
in the vicinity of Hebron. *Wayyáqom*, from *qûm*,
"stand," here bears the less usual meaning of "being
assured to" or of "passing into the possession of"
anyone; *auf das Konto jemandes eingetragen werden*
(K. W.).

18. The *le* before "Abraham" connects with the
first word of v. 17, making "to Abraham" a dative
of interest. The *bekhol* is of practically the same force
as the *lekhol* of v. 10 above, which see. The words following are identical with the words of v. 10. The
strong emphasis on the fact that this had been a
public sale closed according to the approved fashion
of that day, shows that the whole matter was one of
unusual importance in Abraham's eyes, both for himself and in reference to the future. For Abraham
in faith desired that his wife's and his own remains
might rest in the land that had been promised to him
and his descendants after him. He wanted his descendants to know that he had believed the divine
promise. The presence of his sepulchre among them
would in later years be mute but eloquent testimony
to them all that Abraham was sure of the validity
of God's promises. Consequently, the purpose of the
whole narrative is not to show that by this initial
purchase of one piece of ground Abraham secured a
kind of hold or perhaps an option on the whole, as
some contend. Abraham's title to the land rested
entirely on God's promise given in a clear word and
not on such devices as sale and purchase and legal
formality.

19, 20. **Thereafter then Abraham buried
Sarah, his wife, in the cave of the field of
Machpelah, over against Mamre, which is Hebron,
in the land of Canaan. And the field and the cave
which was in it were assured to Abraham as a
grave which was his own property bought of the
children of Heth.**

The burial is reported with a certain fulsomeness
of expression characteristic of the Scriptures in
recording notable events. The cave is mentioned, as
well as its location in the field of Machpelah, as well
as the fact that Machpelah faced Mamre. To this

is added the parenthetical statement that Mamre is Hebron and the reminder that this was "in the land of Canaan," a phrase which has the same force here as in v. 2. The statement that Mamre is Hebron appears to be made in the sense that Mamre is a part of Hebron.

20. At a time when the children of Israel were on their way to take possession of the land, Moses did well to remind them how in faith their forefather had secured at least "a grave which was his own property," and thus to arouse in them the desire to finish the work of taking into full possession what had so long ago been promised to them.

A few more problems need to be touched upon.

One is the critical problem. Practically unanimous is the verdict of criticism that the priestly writer (P) is the author of the chapter. We take up the question because we believe it furnishes a rather clear illustration of the shallowness of the critical method. Strack supports the contention of P's authorship by three arguments. The first is the use of the divine name "Elohim," supposed to be a mark of P (v. 6). But, as we showed above, if the sense of the divine names means anything, the term Elohim in the above connection was unavoidable to express the thought of the Hittites; and so the use of the word is not a stylistic criterion. Secondly, he claims the language is that of P. This argument builds on the claim which criticism believes so very well established: that the P sections all have a fullness of detail like legal documents and a certain repetitiousness. However, the same thing may be claimed for the following chapter (24) which is by common consent ascribed to J. Of course, chapter 24 has no legal terminology, because it does not report a legal transaction as does chapter 23. In the third place, Strack claims that later portions from

P refer back to this event repeatedly, and so it is supposed to be P's exclusive subject matter. The passages cited are 25:9 f; 49:29 ff; 50:13. Looking at these passages, we find that they appear to be ascribed to P (each being a brief section in the midst of material from a so-called different source) because originally chapter 23 dealing with the same event is ascribed to P. Consequently we have a perfect argument in a circle. Three passages are ascribed to P because they seem to build on a P passage, chapter 23. On the other hand, chapter 23 is from P because of these three passages. So weak and inconsequential is the textual critical argument.

Another problem is created by Acts 7:16, which ascribes Abraham's purchase of a tomb to a place at Shechem and names the seller as "the sons of Hamor in Shechem." This seeming confusion is not to be described as an error of Stephen's or Luke's, the writer of the Acts. Apparently, two separate events are under consideration. Abraham must have purchased two burial sites, one in Shechem, one in Hebron. Only the second purchase is mentioned in Genesis. The record of the first purchase, apparently, survived only in Jewish tradition. Another solution of the difficulty, though a less likely one, is that at an early date a copyist wrote "Abraham" for "Jacob" in Acts 7:16 and the error was not discovered until it had come into almost all manuscripts.

As to the identity of the cave of Machpelah the question seems far from settled. It is true that many agree that the present site of the mosque in Hebron, which is built over a cave into which a few Christians of more recent time have been permitted to look, is the very spot where the cave of Machpelah must have been situated. The name of this mosque is *Haram*, and it lies within the present city of Hebron. Others feel that the original Hebron must have lain a mile or so west from the present site, at a spot known as *er Rumeidy,* near which are several fine old tombs. Should excavators secure permission to explore both these sites thoroughly, the dispute might be settled.

As a matter of historical interest we record the fact that in Machpelah's cave Abraham himself was later buried (25:9), also Isaac (35:27, 29), also Rebekah and Lea (49:31), and lastly also Jacob (50:13). The Jewish interpretation which makes Kirjath-arba mean "city of four" in the sense that four patriarchs lie buried there — Adam, Abraham, Isaac, and Jacob — is, of course, pure guess as far as the burialplace of Adam is concerned.

HOMILETICAL SUGGESTIONS

It hardly seems feasible to break up this chapter into portions. Abraham's faith is again in evidence; and so we suggest some such subject as "A Testimony of Faith in the Face of a Loss by Death." This ought to prove a very practical text if treated from this point of view, for it gives occasion to emphasize that in the face of such losses faith should especially give testimony of its strength and its character.

CHAPTER XXIV

16. Isaac's Marriage (24:1-67)

A delightful chapter, charmingly written with much of detail, not because of its romantic character but because in it is recorded an act of faith which transfigures the ordinary experiences of life. The patriarch Abraham, believing the promises of Yahweh concerning the progeny to spring from his son, (namely a great nation and a great Redeemer), makes provision for the marriage of this son. This provision, however, is made in such a fashion that Abraham's full confidence in the validity of these promises is clearly displayed.

The marriage of Isaac can hardly be said to have come late in his life, though he was forty years of age at the time (25:20), inasmuch as the natural span of life at this time was about as long as it is now. The need of taking steps along this line had been suggested by Sarah's death and by the fact that Abraham, now 140 years old, felt the desirability of attending to this duty while he was still well and able to do so. The father's sole initiative in this direction and the entire passivity of Isaac on the occasion are to be accounted for by the fact that, first, it was primarily the function of parents to provide for the marriage of their children in those days; and, in the second place, Isaac was by character and disposition much inclined to be passive and unaggressive. Nothing points to the possibility that Abraham's death was imminent at the time he makes these arrangements. In fact, it would be a very queer style of writing which could overlook such a situation

if it had actually obtained, especially since v. 1 would
have presented a logical place for a statement conveying such a fact.

This simple narrative with its natural flow and
progression has fallen into the hands of a criticism
intent upon doing damage to the Scriptures wherever
it seems possible to do so and upon making a display of its ingenuity. Here criticism claims to be able
to detect two strands of narrative woven into one,
two strands which happen to diverge continually.
Apparently, he who wove the two together either did
not observe their divergence, or else put the two
together regardless of whether they harmonized or
not. The so-called divergences will be examined at
a few points to show the untenable nature of the
critical claims. Any unprejudiced person can readily
see that the so-called divergences are merely two sides
of one and the same story, supplementing without
contradiction. The critical efforts tend to read a
foregone conclusion into the evidence on the strength
of unproven and unconvincing evidence.

**1. Abraham was old and well stricken in age,
and Yahweh had blessed Abraham in all things.**

Abraham's being old is referred to in connection
with his choice of a wife for Isaac because his age
reminds him of the need of delaying in this important
matter no longer. The second statement "well stricken
in age" (Hebrew: "advanced in days," as in 18:11)
must in contrast to the first emphasize that the
infirmities of old age were coming to be more in
evidence. The reference to God's blessings which
Abraham had abundantly enjoyed in this connection
seems to indicate that there were no troubles so
engaging the thoughts of Abraham as to make him
forget this important duty. Besides, it indicates that
Abraham was financially well able to provide for his
son's marriage. But primarily, since it records the

fulfillment of 12:2, it seems to suggest that, since one part of this great promise (12:2, 3) had been fulfilled very manifestly, Abraham felt the necessity of making provision that no part of the things promised be delayed or interfered with, as it well might be if the son be not properly provided with a wife. "Yahweh" is referred to as the author of the blessing and throughout the chapter because the work of the gracious God of the covenant is primarily under consideration in this connection.

2-4. **And Abraham said unto his servant, the eldest of his house, who had control over all that Abraham had: Put, now, thy hand under my thigh, that I may cause thee to swear by Yahweh, the God of the heavens and the God of the earth, that thou wilt not take a wife for my son from the daughters of the Canaanites in the midst of whom I dwell, but that thou wilt go to my country and unto my relationship and take a wife for my son Isaac.**

It seems very strange that the account does not identify this servant. It may have been Eliezer of whom we last heard about sixty years ago (15:12). Still it seems a rather rare case that one servant should be in another man's employ for such a length of time. In fact, it would seem that Eliezer must have been in Abraham's employ more than twenty years to arrive at a position of such influence as he held according to 15:12. That would necessitate by the time of this chapter eighty consecutive years of service! "Eldest" (*zaqen*) often refers to rank rather than to age (cf. 50:7; Isa. 3:2; B D B says the term is used more than a hundred times as a technical term in reference to persons "having authority"). This individual had the complete management of Abraham's household in hand: *hammoshel* = "the one ruling" all Abraham had. In any case, he must have been a tried and true servant.

The gesture that is to accompany the oath under which this servant is put by Abraham is: "Put, now, thy hand under my thigh." The "now" (*na'*) gives a touch of mildness to the imperative. The "thigh" (*yarekh*) or "loins" is here indeed regarded as "the seat of the procreative powers" (B D B), and by metonomy it takes into consideration all the descendants of one. Note passages such as 46:26 ("all the souls that came out of his loins") ; Exod. 1:5; Judg. 8:30. Consequently, this form of oath has particular regard to the descendants and is taken in reference to them. But we cannot stop short with this correct statement. For when we consider how eagerly believers from the time of Adam looked forward to a Savior that was to be born, and also how Abraham (12:3) knew and believed that from his own line such a Savior was to follow, we cannot but accept the orthodox view held by churchfathers from days of old that this oath was administered in view of the Savior to come from Abraham's line. The whole course of procedure builds upon this prominent fact. This same form of oath is found besides only in 47:29. Consequently, we do not find here a remnant of some old custom now no longer understood, nor is this a remnant of some phallic cult, nor was this an oath by the *membrum virile,* for the hand was placed under the *thigh,* nor are the present-day analogies referred to by commentators as still obtaining among Arabs and Egyptians a good illustration or parallel. Here was a godly oath by a godly man taken and administered in the light of his greatest hope, the coming Savior. "Yahweh," as the covenant God, is most appropriately referred to as the one by whom the servant is to swear. The descriptive apposition "the God of the heavens and the God of the earth" reminds him that swears of Yahweh's omnipotence and omnipresence and so serves as an excellent indica-

tion of the exalted conception of God prevailing among
the patriarchs.

3. The *waw* introducing the first verb is final:
"that I may cause," as also in v. 14 and v. 51. The
thing so momentous as to require this solemn oath
is that the servant shall not "take a wife" for Isaac
"from the daughters of the Canaanites," among
whom Abraham was living. No doubt, material
advantage would have lain on the side of a marital
union with an influential Canaanite, to give Isaac
a foothold in the land, powerful connections and social
standing. Abraham's purpose, however, in abhorring
such a union will not only have been a desire to perpetuate pure Semitic stock, for the Canaanites were
Hamites. Such a purpose was incidentally involved,
for certain types of pure Semitic stock were, no
doubt, the depositories of a godly tradition. But the
patriarch's chief concern was to find a wife for Isaac
who with him knew and believed in Yahweh and
so would share with her husband a common faith
and so allow for the deepest of all harmonies in the
home, spiritual harmony. For again, only in a home
where true spiritual harmony prevailed would the
spiritual heritage of Abraham be jealously guarded
and faithfully transmitted to coming generations.
Besides, the Canaanite stock, which was already
deteriorating (9:25; 19:5, 32) and which was
destined to be destroyed ultimately by Abraham's
descendants, could hardly be found worthy for this
exalted purpose. Abraham, then, details this task
of finding the proper wife for his son to a servant
for two reasons. His own advanced age made such
a rigorous journey impracticable and, besides, all such
transactions in the Orient were arranged through
intermediaries (cf. 23:8).

4. The initial *kî* is adversative (K. S. 372 e;
B D B 474 a). Abraham regards the place of his

last residence, Mesopotamia, as his "country" (*'artsî*) ;
there is his "relationship." He is sure that some
suitable wife will there be avaiable if anywhere.

**5. And the servant said to him: Perhaps the
woman will not be willing to follow me into this land,
shall I then go so far as to bring thy son back to the
land from which thou camest?**

The servant sees the issues and difficulties clearly.
Not to be able to find a suitable person at all for
Isaac seems entirely out of the question. There is
likelihood that a woman will be available who meets
the spiritual qualifications. Socially Abraham's position makes his son a very suitable suitor. The very
real difficulty that may arise would be if the woman
were unwilling to break all ties of home and friendship, make a far journey and establish entirely new
connections. To find so courageous a woman would
indeed be rare. So in the other event what course
should be followed? Is the need so great in the case
of the woman's unwillingness as to allow the servant
to make the proposition that his master's son would
be ready to journey back to Abraham's early home?
The servant must be sure of his ground in advance.
The absolute infinitive added to the verb "bringing
back shall I bring back" is, we feel, covered quite
well by our free rendering above: "shall I go so far
as to bring back?" On the form of the interrogative
he see G. K. 100 n.

**6-8. And Abraham said to him: Take heed
not to bring my son back there again. Yahweh, the
God of the heavens, who took me from my father's
house and from the land of my relationship, and
who spoke to me and promised me under oath, To
thy seed will I give this land, He will send His Angel
before thy face and thou shalt get a wife for my
son there. But if the woman be not willing to
follow thee, then thou shalt be absolved of this my**

oath. Only, as far as my son is concerned, do not take him back there.

The servant's alternative is out of the question. Abraham strongly forbids it: "Take heed not to bring my son back there again." The Hebrew has, "take heed to thyself (*lekha*) lest thou bring" — *pen* with the imperfect, a negative final clause.

7. Abraham rightly concludes that Yahweh cannot desire a return to Mesopotamia, for He it was that brought Abraham forth. Besides, the land to be given to Isaac is the very land in which Abraham now lives. That land dare not now be forsaken. God spoke plainly to Abraham (12:7; 13:15) that this land should belong to his descendants. He even "promised under oath" (*nishba'* = merely "to swear") "to thy seed will I give this land" (15:17 f). He is the "God of the heavens" who has great resources at His command. "His Angel" has been wont to appear and succor God's own (16:7), and He is divine (see exposition of chapter 16). He will prosper the servant's journey, going before his face to remove difficulties. Since a wife is essential to the securing of descendants, Abraham is sure that Yahweh will provide.

8. To set his servant's mind at ease Abraham declares him absolved of this oath in case the woman be unwilling to accompany him. With solemn repetition Abraham forbids taking his son back to Mesopotamia. The *zo'th* after *shebhu'athî* has no article because of the suffix (G. K. 126 y; K. S. 334 y). "My oath" means not "the oath rendered to me" but "the oath administered by me" (K. S. 37); cf. also v. 3 and Josh. 2:17, 20. The initial *waw* naturally is adversative — "but."

9. **And the servant put his hand under the thigh of Abraham, his master, and he swore concerning this matter.**

After the issues are clear to both parties, the oath is given as it was demanded. The "master" relationship is emphasized on Abraham's part, because the servant recognized that this relation increased his obligation in the matter. This was not a case of friend pleasing friend but of servant obeying his master *'adhonaw* — a plural of respect — (*Herrschaftsplural*, G. K. 124 g i). The final *'al dabhar hazzeh* may also be rendered "on the basis of this thing" (B D B) or "thus" — *solches* — Luther.

10, 11. So the servant took ten of his master's camels and set out, and all sorts of his master's valuables were in his possession; and he arose and set out for Aram Naharaim, for the city of Nahor. And he made his camels kneel down outside the city by the well of water at evening time, at the time when the women came forth to draw water.

Ten camels are still regarded as a proper number for such a caravan (Thomson, *The Land and the Book,* p. 261 ff). Besides "the servant" (not "slave" — Meek) has "all sorts of (*kol* as in 2:9; 4:22; Lev. 19:23) valuables" — so Meek well translates *tûbh*. The camels bear him and his attendants as well as the necessary presents and will serve to convey the expected wife and her attendants as well. That the verb "set out," *wayyélekh*, should be repeated is quite natural and not an indication of two separate sources. The first "set out" reports in a summary way — so common in Hebrew, the second resumes after a few details have been inserted. Of the several Arams mentioned in the Scriptures this is the one "of the two rivers" (*naharayim*) which are not the Euphrates and the Tigris, for Aram did not extend to the Tigris, but the Euphrates and the Chaboras. Aram is a construct state in a proper name (K. S. 280 h). Nahor's city is Haran (27:43; 28:10).

11. The uneventful journey is skipped, and we are introduced in the colorful narrative to the scene witnessed upon the arrival at the outskirts of Haran. "Kneel" for camels is entirely proper, as it exactly describes how camels are brought down to rest. The customary well is located outside the city. *Sho'abhoth*, feminine participle, "drawers" of water, are the women whose regular duty it was to draw water, especially at evening. *'E'rebh* has no article, as is frequently the case in expressions more or less stereotyped (K. S. 294 f). *Tse'th*, infinitive from *yatsa'*, is the equivalent of a relative clause (K. S. 400 b).

12-14. And he said: O Yahweh, God of my master Abraham, let it befall before me this day and show kindness unto my master Abraham. See, I have taken my stand by the fountain of water, and the daughters of the men of the city are coming forth to draw water; so let it come to pass that the girl, to whom I shall say, Let down, I pray, thy pitcher that I may drink and she shall say, Drink, and I will water thy camels also, her thou hast adjudged for thy servant, for Isaac, and by this I shall discover that Thou hast showed kindness to my master.

This good servant has imbibed much of the spirit and the faith of his master Abraham. It is a problem sufficient to tax the finest ingenuity to the utmost without arriving at sure results. In a prayer of childlike faith the servant commits the issues to his Lord. The fact that he addresses Yahweh as the "God of my master" does not signify that Yahweh is not his own God but only Abraham's, but rather that he, the servant, first learned to know Him as the Yahweh who stood related to Abraham. Only a faith that knows God as Yahweh and trust like Abraham's would venture to submit such a prayer. Luther here

raises the question whether it be permissible to prescribe to the Lord what He is to do in answer to our
prayer and answers that this servant did not prescribe
to God what to do, but that the spirit of his whole
prayer is merely one of earnest desire: Oh, that it
would please thee, dear Lord, to let so and so happen!
Haqreh = "cause (it) to happen" — the indefinite
unexpressed subject "it" in this case being the finding
of the proper wife. Luther supplies as object "Thou"
or "Thyself" thus: "cause Thyself to meet me," *be-
gegne mir,* which is hardly admissible. A. V. renders
very acceptably: "send me good speed." His prayer
is quite unselfish, having regard only for his "master
Abraham," whom he apparently respects and loves
very much.

13. The servant outlines the situation, not as
though he would inform the good Lord but merely to
provide a basis upon which his prayer is to build up.
Nitstsabh is not so much "I am standing" as "I have
taken my stand" — a statement expressive of the purpose behind his being there. *Yotse'oth* indicates that
the daughters of the men of the city were already
"coming out," (cf. I Sam. 9:11).

14. After what preceded the *wehayah* will not
be: "and it shall come to pass," but rather optative:
"let it come to pass" (A. V.). The condition imposed
is unusually apt. Readiness to serve embodies a number of other virtues: cheerfulness, courtesy, unselfishness, readiness to work. The amount of service required in this case would demand the prerequisite of
good health and strength. For camels are notorious
for their capacity to absorb water. The servant's
stipulation was not for an ordinary favor easily bestowed. The girl measuring up to this requirement
would certainly be very distinctly marked from all
others by virtue of this accomplishment. Such a
prayer demands a very strong faith in the providence

of God, a certainty that the greater as well as the smaller happenings of life are very definitely controlled by the Lord's hand. The feminine suffix in *bah* covers the whole case as just outlined and serves as a neuter "by this" or "thereby" (Skinner). *Hokhachta* is really a bit stronger than "appoint" (A. V.) ; "adjudge" is better; Keil: "point out as right."

15, 16. And it came to pass before he had finished speaking, that, behold, there came forth Rebekah, who had been born to Bethuel, son of Milcah, wife of Nahor, the brother of Abraham, and her pitcher was on her shoulder, and the girl very beautiful in appearance, a virgin, and no man had known her, and she went down to the spring and filled her pitcher and came up again.

That the servant's prayer was not spoken audibly is so evident under the circumstances that the Greek translators made bold to add to the word "speaking" the phrase "in his mind." There is something startling about the promptness with which the answer to his prayer comes: before he is done praying Rebekah is on the scene. The Hebrew "behold" appropriately expresses this. The Hebrew *térem,* "not yet" or "before" usually stands with the imperfect; here we have a rare case with the perfect (K. S. 387 r; G. K. 152 r). Rebekah was identified already 22:23. Here, since emphasis lies upon the fact that one of the relationship of Abraham was required, this relationship is again traced down. Since Isaac is of the first generation from Abraham and Rebekah of the second generation from Abraham's brother, the relationship between Isaac and Rebekah is one that is termed second-cousinship. In anticipation of what she is about to do we are informed that "her pitcher was upon her shoulder." Even this touch of the narrative is claimed to be entirely accurate by some who have observed that around Mesopotamia pitchers are carried

on the shoulder, whereas in Egyt and elswhere they
are borne upon the head. In this verse *hinneh* with
the participle cannot refer, as so often, to the future
because of the connection.

16. In addition to meeting the qualifications of
the servant's prayer this girl has a few superadded
gifts which he had failed to include in his specifica-
tions. First, she is very beautiful. Secondly, she is
a "virgin," *bethûlah,* a term indicative of her age and
her station, not, however as the Talmud rightly observes (Delitzsch), in itself necessarily indicative of
virginal purity, for that is covered by the following
statement. The critical point of the narrative draws
near as the separate steps of her course are recalled
for us: she goes down, she fills her pitcher, she comes
up (for fountains or springs were usually approached
by a staircase). In eager anticipation the servant
has watched the girl.

**17-20. And the servant ran to meet her and
he said: Please, let me drink a bit of water from
thy pitcher. And she said: Drink, kind sir. And
she quickly lowered her pitcher upon her hand and
gave him a drink. And she finished letting him
drink and then said: Also for thy camels I will
draw water until they finish drinking. And she
quickly emptied her pitcher into the trough and
again ran to the well to draw water. So she drew
water for all his camels.**

In his eagerness to make the prescribed test to
which everything now points the servant "ran" to
meet her — a hyperbole, of course, implying no more
than his eagerness in approaching. His request is
quite courteous: the "please" and "a bit" stamp it as
entirely modest.

18. Her reply at first covers only the minor first
half of what the servant had stipulated. In fact, in
any case, it would have been unnatural for her to

offer to give his camels to drink also before he had
finished drinking. Nevertheless, the tension of the
narrative is increased by this delay. Rebekah's reply
also is courteous and modest, too, being couched in
few words. Travelers claim to have witnessed the
same procedure many a time, but none tell of the second
offer which Rebekah made. *Temah(h)er* is, as usual,
used practically as an adverb — "quickly" (cf. G. K.
120 d).

19. Koenig (K. C.) rightly contends for the
retaining of *tekhal* as an independent rather than a
subordinate clause, for it rightly stresses that Rebekah
patiently waited until the man had drunk his fill: "she
finished letting him drink." Then comes the statement
upon which everything hinged. Emphatically it places
the "camels" first in a very informal statement, just
as people are wont to speak in everyday life. With
impetuous goodness of heart she promises to give the
camels all they may require. Surely this is "hospitality
without grudging" — a fine and rare virtue.

20. The pitcher, which is still almost full, is
promptly emptied into the trough, and the girl with
a fine spirit of kindly service hastens to draw the rest
of the needed water. On the verb in apocopated form
watte'ar from *'arah* see G. K. 75 bb.

21-25. **But the man was gazing at her by himself, silently observing whether Yahweh had
prospered his enterprise or not. And it came to
pass, when the camels had finished drinking, that
the man took a golden ring a half shekel in weight
and two bracelets ten shekels of gold in weight for
her wrists, and gave them to her; and he said:
Whose daughter art thou, tell me, please? Is there
room for us to spend the night in thy father's house?
And she said to him: The daughter of Bethuel, the
son of Milcah, am I, whom she bore to Nahor. She**

further said to him: Besides we have both straw and fodder aplenty, also room to spend the night.

The fulfillment which the servant encounters seems in excess of what any man could have hoped for. He must note carefully whether there is any mistake; besides, he cannot yet be sure whether this girl will prove to be of Abraham's relationship. So for the present he was "gazing at her by himself" *mishta'eh, Hithpael* participle, durative, from the verb *sha'ah* a "by-form" of *sha'ah*. The time for speech has not yet come; so he is "silently observing," literally: "being silent to know whether." True faith uses caution to avoid the possibility of self-deception. The participle *mishta'eh* is in the construct state before a preposition. The interrogative before *hitsliach* has short "a" (G. K. 100 m).

22. A generous soul like this servant rewards unsought favors. The pregnant construction "he took upon" = "he took and put upon." Otherwise, as A. V. renders, he seems to take and dangle these presents before Rebekah without actually giving them to her. True, according to v. 47, the *nézem* was a nosering; cf. also Isa. 3:21; Ezek. 16:12; Prov. 11:22. But since this verse (22) omits mentioning that the servant put the nosering upon her nose, it seems to be the most likely explanation that he merely gave it to her. For a strange man after a few moments of acquaintance to venture to try such familiarity as affixing jewelry seems a bit out of place. Consequently we believe v. 47 to be a looser statement of the case: the servant ascribes to himself what really Rebekah carried out. However, for those days such jewels apparently were the most appropriate. Their weight indicates that they were gifts worthy of the master and of the occasion. The cue to the *béqa'* or "half shekel" is given Exod. 38:26.

23. Now the all-important and for this case crucial question: "Whose daughter art thou?" "Tell me, please," indicates the urgency felt by the faithful servant. However, not to give to the question too personal a note, in case the girl might yet after all prove to be unrelated to Abraham, he adds what for these circumstances is the most natural inquiry. "Is there room for us to spend the night in thy father's house?" *Beth* is an adverbial accusative = "*in* the house." (K. S. 330 k).

24. In speaking to a stranger it will hardly suffice to give a very brief identification. So Rebekah mentions her father, her father's mother and her grandfather. If the stranger had not heard of one, he might have heard of one of the others. The emotions of the servant would be difficult to describe as the hoped-for answer, which he might almost have deemed impossible, actually fell from the girl's lips.

25. Another *wattó'mer*, like the one beginning v. 24, is not merely "and she said" but "she further said." As the question was double, the answer was double. The answer, however, is broken up into two separate parts, perhaps because the questioner may for a moment have displayed an almost startled surprise at discovering the girl's identity, enough of a surprise for a moment to interrupt her answer. The final *lalûn* is an infinitive used as an attributive clause modifying "place" (*maqôm*), which we have rendered "room" in this connection and so retained the infinitive: "room to spend the night" for "place where we may spend the night." K. S. 400 c.

26, 27. Then the man bowed down and worshipped Yahweh, and said: Blessed be Yahweh, the God of my master Abraham, who hath not withdrawn his kindness and truth from my master; as for me, Yahweh has led me in the way to the house of my master's relatives.

True, the outcome of the enterprise as granted
to this man in answer to his prayer was as marvelous
a display of divine providence, perhaps, as ever a
mortal witnessed. Such mercy called for acknowledgment. But he that will make his acknowledgment as
freely and as openly as does this man is both a devout
and a courageous soul. It is true, Rebekah may have
been the only stranger present. But this confession
of the man together with the public praise he here
offers is in every sense most appropriate.

27. What a fine way of stating that the established
course, that God has without exception followed in
the treatment of Abraham, was always marked by
divine "kindness" (*chésedh*) and divine "truth" or
dependability (*'emeth*)! What happened here at the
well was merely one more token of God's consistent
mercies. Only a man in fullest spiritual sympathy
with the spiritual heritage of Abraham's household
could have stated the case so properly. Thinking of
himself (*'anokhî,* nominative absolute G. K. 143 b. c.)
and his part in the transaction, he says that it is
Yahweh who has directed his "way to the house of
his master's relatives." *'Achchim,* "brothers," is here
used in the common looser meaning of "relatives."
Therefore this last clause, with emphatic pronoun first,
really conveys the emphasis to the two pronominal
suffixes involved: "Right to the house of the relatives
of *my* master, Yahweh has led *me* this way" (as K. C.
well translates). The article before "way" has demonstrative force.

28-31. **And the girl ran and reported to her
mother's house what had happened. Now Rebekah
had a brother whose name was Laban, and Laban
ran out to the man to the well. Namely, as soon
as he saw the ring and the bracelets on his sister's
wrists, and as he heard the words of Rebekah his
sister, Thus the man said to me, he went to the**

man; and, lo, he was still standing by the camels by the side of the well. And he said: Come in, thou blessed of Yahweh, why shouldst thou stand outside, seeing that I have gotten ready the house and a place for the camels?

Naturally, such unusual experiences as Rebekah had had on this memorable evening had to be told at home, and the stranger's request had to be made known. What, however, had lent wings to the girl's return was the startling news, conveyed incidentally by the servant's prayer, that here was a delegate from Abraham, their own relative in Canaan. The daughter's course naturally tends to the mother when such startling news is to be communicated. Besides, the women had their separate compartments, as we gather also from 31:33f. — a separate tent. In any case, where bigamy was growing to be quite common, the bond uniting to the mother would be felt to be stronger than the bond uniting to the father; cf v. 50; chapter 34; II Sam. 13:22; Judg. 21:22; Lev. 19:3; 21:2. All these things do not, however, point to anything like the existence of a matriarchate.

29. Now the brother of Rebekah, Laban, figured prominently in the proceedings. Therefore the things he does are here reported, and in a preliminary way it is stated at once that "he ran out to the man to the well." This is a common characteristic of Hebrew narrative that it reports a certain result first, then the details that led up to this result, without a "namely" as we have done above. Now nothing in this account of Laban's doings reflects adversely upon his character. The greed of this man is displayed only in the later chapters. Yet in the light of what these chapters reveal we may well suppose that what the following verse tells is to be thought of in connection which his grasping disposition. But for the things reported in

following chapters one might almost suppose that Laban actually was a genial, generous host.

30. The gifts given to Rebekah were no trifles; they were enough to impress anyone who saw them. Whatever else might be in the offing, the man who dispensed such gifts was not to be ignored. Besides, apparently Laban understood also that this man represented his own relative, Abraham. After our explanation of v. 30 it will be seen that the verb "he went to the man" is not an indication of a duplicate expression derived from a different source after v. 29 had already said that "he ran out to the man." By way of making the account picturesque the writer tells us that the servant was "still standing" — we have inserted the "still" in order to express more distinctly the idea of the durative participle *'omedh*. The opening *wayhî* is the common mode of expressing a rather loose connection with the preceding (G. K. 111 g). The expression "he stood *by*" in Hebrew reads "he stood *over*," because the camels were crouched down (Strack).

31. Laban has gathered from Rebekah's words that Yahweh is still Abraham's and the servant's God. Laban himself may or may not still have believed in Yahweh. Later developments show that he very likely did not. Nevertheless, even from the polytheistic point of view it would be quite natural to acknowledge that the God whom one served had blessed him. Since "Yahweh" is a proper noun, its definiteness conveys itself to the preceding construct case; therefore "thou, the blessed one of Yahweh," a vocative with the article (K. S. 290 e). In this connection *Yahweh* is an active subject with a passive verb, *barûkh* (K. S. 336 n). It seems a bit more appropriate to translate the imperfect *ta'amodh* as a potential ("why should you stand") rather than as a present ("why standest

thou")? *Panah* ("turn") here means "to clear away," "to get ready." The invitation is put quite graciously and leaves nothing to be desired.

32, 33. So the man came to the house, and he unharnessed the camels and provided straw and fodder for the camels and water for the washing of his feet and of the feet of the men who were with him. And food was set before him that he might eat, but he said: I will not eat until I have delivered my message. And he said: Say on.

Everything proceeds as the customs of the time dictate. Chapter 18 already suggested that one of the courtesies of the times was to provide for a man's comfort as a guest and to serve him in every way also with food and drink before the business that may have brought the guest is looked into, and even then the initiative is taken by the guest. There is no need of altering the first verb to a Hifil: "he *brought* the man to the house" (*wayyabhe'*) merely because thereafter Laban is the subject. Subjects change very readily in Hebrew. *Yepattach* (subject: Laban) means only to "free" or "ungird" or "unharness" (Meek), not "unsaddle," because the saddle is not removed from camels when they are warm from driving. The beasts must adways be provided for before the men. Then the necessary footwashing (18:4) follows.

33. The *Keri* here seems preferable on the first verb, making it a *Hofal* passive: (literally) "and it was set before his face to eat." So urgent is the business in hand that in the servant's esteem the customary formalities are to be waived. He takes his commission so seriously that he cannot eat until he has delivered his message and ascertained whether the girl or young woman will actually follow him. The words "delivered my message" actually run thus: "spoken my words."

34-41. And he said: I am a servant of Abraham. And Yahweh blessed my master richly and he has become great; He has given him flocks and herds, and silver and gold, and maid servants, and camels and asses. And Sarah, my master's wife, bore a son to my master after she had grown old, and he has given to him all he has. And my master bound me by an oath: Thou shalt not take a wife for my son from the daughters of the Canaanites in whose land I am dwelling. But thou shalt go to my father's house and to my family to take a wife for my son. And I said to my master: Perhaps the woman will not follow. And he said to me: Yahweh before whose face I have walked will send His angel along with thee and He will prosper thy way and thou wilt get a wife for my son from my family and from my father's house. Then shalt thou be absolved of my oath, if thou come to my family and they do not give her to thee, then thou shalt be absolved of my oath.

Practically all this ground has already been covered by our exposition. Certain types of narrative, especially the epic, are wont to use far more frequent repetitions than do the Scriptures. A few things are new.

34. In a connection such as this *'ébhedh' Abhraham* must mean "*a* servant of Abraham" and not "*the* servant" — for Abraham had many servants (A. V. also inaccurate) ; cf. K. S. 362 g.

35, 36. For one who represents his master and his master's son in a marriage proposition it is essential that he make an accurate and complete statement of his master's standing and of his master's son's financial prospects. So a condensed account of Abraham's growth in wealth and cattle is given. But even in this matter the servant has caught his master's spirit and does not attribute the good fortune of his

master to anything other than to Yahweh's blessing.
The unusual story of Isaac's birth belongs into the
picture, else the hearers cannot know how the *son*
of one brother should be a candidate in marriage for
the *granddaughter* of another brother. Besides, the
incidental importance of Isaac's financial standing
receives just the proper amount of emphasis when it
is indicated that he is the sole heir to his father's
wealth. No unseemly importance is attached to this
fact to make it out a major motive to bring to the
favorable attention of Rebekah's family. *Ziquah* is
Kal infinitive (G. K. 45 d).

37. On v. 37 cf. v. 3 above. On v. 38 cf. v. 4.
On v. 39, v. 5. On v. 40 cf. v. 7.

41. After *yittênû* ("they will give") the object
"her" has to be supplied. Or the difficulty may be removed by translating: "if they refuse you" (Meek).
Instead of the word for "oath" used in v. 8 we here find
the synonym *'alah,* which originally means "curse."

42-48. **And I came this day unto the fountain and I said: Yahweh, God of my master Abraham, if thou art indeed prospering the way which
I am going, behold, I have taken my stand by the
fountain of water, and let it come to pass that the
girl that cometh forth to draw water, to whom I
shall say: Let me drink a bit of water, please, from
thy pitcher, and she shall say to me: Drink, and
I will draw water for thy camels also, she shall be
the woman whom Yahweh has adjudged for my
master's son. I had not yet finished speaking in
my heart, when, lo, Rebekah was coming forth, with
her pitcher upon her shoulder, and went down to
the spring to draw water, and I said to her: Please,
give me a drink, and she quickly let down her
pitcher from her shoulder and said: Drink, and
also thy camels I will give to drink. So I drank,
and she gave my camels to drink also. Then I**

asked her, saying: Whose daughter art thou? and
she said: The daughter of Bethuel, the son of
Nahor, whom Milcah bore to him. And I put the
ring upon her nose and the bracelets upon her
wrists; and I bowed down and worshipped Yahweh,
and I blessed Yahweh, the God of my master Abraham, who led me in the right way to take the
daughter of my master's brother for his son.

These verses run so close a parallel to v. 11-27
that there is no need of further comment. The more
important variations of expression have already been
discussed at one point or another. "Brother" in v. 48
is, of course, used as previously for relative. "Right
way" is perhaps better translated "sure way," B D B,
Weg der Zuverlaessigkeit (K. C.). V. 43 offers the
first instance of a transition from the participle to the
finite verb (K. C.).

49. And now if ye are showing kindness and
truth to my master, tell me, and if not, tell me, that
I may turn one way or another.

All the facts that bear upon the case have been
presented by Abraham's servant in a true, simple, and
straightforward fashion. Rebekah's family can come
to a decision. The hand of Yahweh must be as plain
to them as it was to the servant and, apparently, to
Rebekah. To grant the servant's request — which, by
the way, he does not even formulate but lets the facts
speak for themselves — is from one point of view
"kindness" (*chésedh*) which Abraham will appreciate,
and from another point of view "truth" (*'emeth*) or
"faithfulness," for where the hand of the Lord is
displayed by such clear tokens of divine providence,
man is true neither to God nor to himself if he does
not accept such guidance. The English idiom may
prefer the rendering: "deal kindly and truly" (A. V.).
Again, what A. V. has rendered, "that I may turn
to the right hand or to the left," appears in more

idiomatic present-day form when Meek translates: "that I may turn one way or another." This, then, does not mean: that I may seek a bride elsewhere.

50, 51. **Then Laban and Bethuel answered and said: That is the Lord's doing; we could not say anything at all. There is Rebekah; take her and go, and let her be the wife of thy master's son as Yahweh has indicated.**

Laban, the brother, as well as Bethuel, the father, are the two with whom according to custom the right of decision in such a case was lodged. Apparently, the full brother had as much of a voice in the matter as the father, for Laban is here mentioned first. The usual construction is found: verb singular at first: *wayya'an;* then plural: *wayyo'merû,* when the two subjects have appeared. Their answer is emphatic: "From Yahweh went forth the matter," which we would be inclined to express: "That is the Lord's doing"; Luther still better: *Das kommt vom Herrn.* The next clause is twisted quite out of shape when the Hebrew idiom, which A. V. retains: "We cannot speak unto thee bad or good," is taken to mean: "We dare not answer you adversely or favorably" (Meek and many others). For at once they answer favorably in the next words: "Take her and go." The difficulty is very readily solved when it is remembered that "good or bad" is one of the well-known cases where the two extremes are chosen to cover the entire area of the concepts involved. So here the statement comes to mean: "we could not say anything at all," in the sense: God has done the speaking; there is nothing more to be said (cf. K. S. 92 b for other such expressions). Procksch, after misconstruing, prefers to conclude that the text contradicts itself, merely to gain support for his idea of two parallel documents. He says: The first part of the verse "distinctly expresses approval, whereas 50 b leaves everything doubtful."

51. Whereas we say: "There is Rebekah," the
Hebrew idiom says: "Rebekah is before thee" (A. V.).
The family of the girl sees the leadings of providence
as manifestly as the servant. To them it is a case
where "Yahweh has indicated" (*dibber* = "he spoke")
what is to be done.

**52-54. And it came to pass that, when the
servant of Abraham heard their answer that he worshipped Yahweh bowing down to the earth. And
the servant brought forth articles of silver and
articles of gold and garments and gave them to
Rebekah and costly articles he gave to her brother
and her mother. Then they ate and drank, he and
the men that were with him, and stayed there overnight. In the morning they arose and he said: Let
me go back to my master.**

This is certainly an instance of fine piety and
bold confession on the servant's part, to acknowledge
Yahweh's hand in the matter by immediate worship
in deepest reverence as soon as he receives his verdict.
So Abraham would have done. To have servants such
as this reflects great credit on their masters.

53. A kind of dowry or wedding present was
regularly bestowed by a bridegroom when an agreement of marriage had been reached. Such a gift gave
proof of his financial competence. In this instance
there is first of all a gift to the bride, then a gift to
those who gave her in marriage. There is no purchase
involved here; merely a tangible way of bestowing
tokens and pledges of goodwill. We can hardly tell
now whether from this better custom there was derived
the inferior custom of the purchase of a wife or not.
Nothing in the Scriptures indicates that the Hebrews
were wont to purchase their wives. A dowry (*móhar*)
was regularly given. Since *kelî* has a wide variety
of meanings: "article, utensil, vessel," we had better
not here limit it to "jewels" (A. V.) or "vessels"

(A. V. m) but take the broader term "articles," which includes both and more besides. "Garments," too, are found in the Scriptures as commonly used for gifts. There is no reason for doubting that the gifts will have been of the richest sort to correspond to Abraham's financial standing. Like gifts in value, here called "costly articles," are given to the brother and the mother. *Mighdanoth,* also translated: "choice things," will hardly mean "spices" (Luther) here, although some such might have been included for the mother. The brother's right in the transaction is conceded by the gift; the father's gift may be thought of as included in the mother's. To this day a man visiting for a few days at a friend's house may express his gratitude by a gift to the wife of his friend.

54. Finally, when the business in hand was settled, food and drink claim their right. "Tarried all night" as a rendering of *lûn* is rather formal. We should say "they stayed overnight," hardly "retired for the night," because the verb covers more than the initial retiring. Knowing his master's anxiety to hear of the outcome of these betrothal proceedings, the servant is anxious to be on his way at once and asks for permission to return that very morning. *Shillach* means to "dismiss" or "let go"; "send me away" (A. V.) is too strong an expression. They who operate with the idea that the servant was executing a death-bed commission say that his anxiety to return was dictated by the hope of still finding his master alive. Why, then, does the narrative never say one word about Abraham's impending death?

55-58. **And her brother and mother said: Let the girl stay with us a few days or even ten; after that let her go. But he said to them: Do not delay me, since Yahweh has prospered my enterprise; dismiss me and let me go to my master. And they said: Let us call the girl and let us ask her**

decision. And they called Rebekah and said to her: Wilt thou go with this man? And she said: I will go.

Naturally such a proposal to leave that very day is all too sudden. Mother and brother wish to see a few days granted to grow accustomed to the thought of separation. To call this "reluctance to part with Rebekah an indication of refined feeling" is quite unnecessary. That injects the evolutionistic concept, making it appear that this group had barely risen above the level of selling off marriageable daughters like so much merchandise. Of course, the finer human emotions and attachment prevailed in a group that had departed but little (in some cases, perhaps, not at all) from the fear of Yahweh. Nothing is more natural than such reluctance, except on the part of the crudest savages. "A period of ten days," *'asôr*, is the most the family dares to suggest, not a "month" as the Samaritan Pentateuch reads.

56. The servant knows that protracted parting will make the parting harder. Besides, since Yahweh's hand in the matter was so clearly manifest, why delay in carrying out the will of Yahweh? This is his chief argument. He desires to leave at once, of course, with their permission ("dismiss me"). The *we* before *Yahweh* is causal: "since." K. S. should not oppose this construction.

57. Ordinarily, perhaps, the girls were not consulted as to their wishes. But it is equally possible that in better families, like that of Bethuel, there was no thought of arranging marriages obnoxious to the bride. In this case everything is so much out of the ordinary that the family feels that the daughter should be consulted. If Rebekah be willing to go at once, that should settle the case. In *niqra'* the final long syllable with *'aleph* takes the place of the usual *ah* hortative.

58. "Wilt thou go?" here must mean "go at once." So, apparently, Rebekah was not so far removed from the scene of the transactions as not to know what was being done. She understands that the question turns entirely on the matter of immediate departure and answers with a simple, resolute: "I will go." Courage, decision, and faith are reflected in her attitude. She is a wife who will amply supplement whatever deficiencies in the line of aggressiveness and activity her husband may have.

59, 60. **So they dismissed Rebekah, their sister, and her nurse and the servant of Abraham and his men. And they blessed Rebekah and said to her:**

Our sister, mayest thou grow to thousands of ten thousands
And may thy descendants possess the gates of their foes.

The case is settled; the caravan must be gotten ready. With Rebekah must go her nurse, both, no doubt, being much attached to one another. Of the nurse we shall hear again 35:8, in which passage we are also informed that her name was Deborah. *Meniqah* is *Hifil* participle from *yanaq*.

60. The blessing spoken by the relationship (they call her "sister") upon Rebekah is cast in a kind of poetic form with "parallelism of members." It may have been customary to bestow some such blessing upon brides. This blessing is recorded because it happened to meet with such literal fulfillment in the chosen family into which Rebekah was incorporated. Its substance is numerous offspring ("thousands of ten thousands") and victory in the conflict with foes ("possess gates of foes"), on "possess gates of enemies" cf. notes on 22:17. "Foes" literally: "haters" (*sone'im*). In *weyîrash* the usual converted Perfect is avoided, *we* being used with the imperfect to make

the act stand out as distinct from what preceded
(K. S. 370 s).

61. **And Rebekah and her maids started off
and rode on the camels and followed the man; and
the servant took Rebekah and went.**

Two groups are pictured as flowing together into
one: Rebekah and "her maids," who will naturally be
sent along with her, a lady of good rank and station —
they constitute the one group and mount "*the* camels,"
apparently those that the servant had brought along;
the other group is headed by the servant. Both points
of view here presented are very natural. On the one
hand, Rebekah and her maids may be said to "follow"
the servant, who actually has the leadership of the
group. On the other hand, the servant may very
appropriately be said to have taken (*yiqqach* = "he
took") Rebekah. Critics cannot see how natural all
this is and speak of the two sources (J and E) here
woven together. Nor can they conceive of one writer's
being able to set forth both points of view. In fact,
they see embodied in this harmonious statement a
double contradiction. Yet men can also quite readily
see that if v. 59 speaks of "the nurse" as nearest to
Rebekah, at that point the customary retinue of
"maids" may be taken for granted. Here where the
departure is graphically portrayed, the nurse may be
included in the whole retinue that Rebekah brings
along as "maids."

62, 63. **And Isaac was coming back from having gone to Beer-lahai-roi, for he dwelt in the land
of the Negeb (the South). And Isaac went forth
to meditate in the field at eventide, and he lifted
up his eyes and looked and, lo, camels were coming.**

The textual problem: the third word *mibbô'* is
said to be "impossible" in this connection: "he came
from coming." We still believe the construction makes

sense, as Delitzsch defends it. Merely to have said: "Isaac came from Beer-lahai-roi" would have created the impression that this was his residence at the time. Our construction says that he had just gone to this spot of the manifestation of the providence of God and was returning in order to be at home if the servant were to appear. Consequently, in this connection the first *ba'*, which we construe as a participle, must be "he was coming back" and the second after a *min* temporal must mean "after having gone." The explanatory clause, "for he dwelt in the Negeb," is essential that we may know that Isaac kept to the Negeb, or South Country. To change *mibbô'* to *mebô'* "entrance" (K. C.) does not seem to make good sense; what may the "entrance" to that spot have been? The change to *midhbar*, "wilderness," made by the Greek already, seems unnecessary.

Having just returned from this sacred spot, Isaac went forth "at eventide" (literally, "at the turning of evening") into the field "to meditate." *Sûach*, we feel, can so definitely be shown to mean "meditate" (A. V.) that the uncertainty of the Greek translators ought not disturb us. For the verb surely has that meaning in passages such as Ps. 77:13; 105:2; Ps. 119:15, 23 etc. Jerome also rendered *ad meditandum*. Though the verb may mean "to lament," yet it would hardly seem possible that about three years after his mother's death the man should still indulge in such an ample effusion of grief, even if he had been closely attached to his mother. On the "three years" cf. 21:5; 23:1; 25:20. If the Targum translates "to pray," that is simply a correct inference as to the type of meditation involved. Therefore Luther's *zu beten* is not to be condemned, though it is not literally exact. Changes of the text to *shût*, "walk about," and the like are not within the province of exact science. We feel the whole debate over the passage again grows out of an attempt to create the impression that the Hebrew text is a very unreliable article.

We gather now from this notice that this is a fine indication of the piety of the man Isaac. While his servant is absent on business vital to himself, Isaac at home stimulates devotion and engages in earnest prayer. Now we see why the servant's enterprise was so visibly prospered by the good Lord. While engaged in this pious exercise, Isaac lifts up his eyes and sees camels approaching without being able to discern at first whose they might be.

64-66. And Rebekah lifted up her eyes and saw Isaac, and she hurriedly dismounted from the camel. And she said to the servant: Who is that man walking in the field to meet us? And the servant said: It is my master. And she took her veil and covered herself. And the servant told Isaac all the things he had done.

They say that to this day when in the Near East a woman riding meets a man, courtesy demands that she dismount. Rebekah does the courteous thing. Although *naphal* means "to fall," we can readily see how a hurried dismounting can be described by that term; cf. II Kings 5:21; I Sam. 25:23. Luther's rendering: *sie fiel vom Kamel* presupposes that the reader will discern how it is meant. Rebekah seems to surmise that very likely her future husband would be the person most readily found abroad under these circumstances. Consequently her question. The infinitive "to meet" is not to be taken too literally; it usually means "coming toward us" or "over against us." It does not necessarily imply that Isaac had gone out to meet the approaching caravan. The *tsai'iph* is really much larger than a veil and is used to wrap around face and body. The covering in this instance is a sign of modesty and respect. Rebekah may be courageous, but she is not marked by an unseemly boldness. *Lazeh* ("this") is used besides only in 37:19.

66. The nature of things that had befallen the servant was such that Isaac needs must know them if he is to understand what manner of woman Rebekah is; why the servant returns so soon; and how remarkably Yahweh had heard the prayer of all concerned. The things require immediate telling. No doubt Rebekah stood by while they were being recounted, recognizing the need of an immediate report by the old servant.

67. **And Isaac brought her into his mother Sarah's tent and married Rebekah and she became his wife and he loved her; and Isaac was comforted after his mother's death.**

Isaac shows good courtesy in at once conducting his wife-to-be to a tent. He shows fine tact in taking her to a woman's tent. He honors his future wife by at once assigning to her the vacant tent of Sarah. Critics intent upon casting doubt upon the text assert that "a grammatical impossibility" (Procksch) confronts us here, a noun in the construct state with the article. Yet K. S. 303 a-g has collected a large number of parallel instances: Gen. 31:13; Exod. 9:18; Exod. 28:39 etc., etc. Still the phrase is cited in proof of the contention that two sources have been imperfectly welded together. "Married" is what is meant by the Hebrew expression: "he took her to wife." After Rebekah had become his wife, love grew up between them, for this may well be the case after marriage as well as before, especially where the union is sanctioned by heaven. In the course of time Isaac is completely comforted over the loss of his mother. Apparently he, the late-born son, and his mother had been close to one another. Still this does not support the textual changes of v. 63 nor the interpretation of the verb *sûach* as meaning "to mourn." For, we repeat, a three years' lamentation would be an indication of a morbid state of which we observe nothing in Isaac. The expression "after his mother" is condensed for "after his mother's death."

HOMILETICAL SUGGESTIONS

In this chapter everything centers about the subject "Marriage." It hardly seems feasible to use the chapter as a unit because of its length. The sections that do lend themselves to use are, first of all, v. 1-9, which gives an instance of the very practical and necessary truth that Godliness is the Chief Ingredient in a Proper Marriage. For certainly that is Abraham's major concern in the choice of his son's wife. The next section, v. 10-27, could be treated independently as an instance of Effectual Fervent Prayer; yet it would be essential even then to indicate that this prayer was made in anticipation of marriage and for the purpose of securing divine guidance in the choice involved. The next verses, v. 28-49, are practically a repetition of the substance of the chapter to this point and so are unsuitable for separate homiletical use. However, in order to maintain the high spiritual level of the chapter, the next portion, v. 50-60, should concern itself with a subject like Rebekah's Resolute Faith, for that is actually what the section aims to display. The last portion, v. 61-67, could be treated under the head of Proper Preparation for Marriage; for that is what is uppermost in Isaac's mind, and his conduct is exemplary under this head.

CHAPTER XXV

17. Abraham's Second Marriage and Death
(25:1-11)

In this portion Abraham's life record is brought to a close. To round out the story properly requires an account of his second marriage together with a list of his children by this marriage. For the promise 17:4 had given him the assurance that he was to be the "father of a multitude of nations." The facts recorded thus far hardly furnish the background for a "multitude of nations" to be descended from him. At the same time, if there be other descendants of Abraham, who, failing to hold fast the promise of a Savior to come, lapse into heathenish ways, it is important also to know of them that we might see that even Abraham's descendants are just another heathen group, if they fail to keep faith in God's promises. Yet, though Abraham's death is also reported in this connection, it is not to be forgotten that Abraham lived to the fifteenth year of the life of Jacob and Esau.

1. **And Abraham again took a wife, and her name was Keturah.**

We encounter the usual idiom: "he added and took" = "he again took" (G. K. 120 d). The wife's name is "Keturah," which K. W. interprets: *in Weih-rauchduft gehuellt* ("wrapped in clouds of incense smoke"). This wife is listed in v. 6 as having been only on the level of a "concubine," so also I Chron. 1:32. That raises the much discussed question whether Abraham had her as a concubine already during Sarah's lifetime. We may dismiss as utterly without foundation and most unlikely the Jewish notion that "Ketu-

(688)

rah" is merely another name for Hagar, who was later
taken back by Abraham. But whereas notable commentators are ready to concede that Keturah may have
been taken during Sarah's lifetime, yet that would
seem to conflict rather seriously with Abraham's pronounced monogamistic leanings; for he took Hagar
only as a last resort to realize God's promise. The
claim that in the event of his taking Keturah after
Sarah's death some of the six sons must have been
dismissed at the too early age of about twenty-five
years, should not be regarded too seriously. Though
ordinarily sons may have been married at the age of
forty and established for themselves, that is merely
a rather broad inference drawn from the exceptional
case of Isaac. Rom. 4:19 ("his own body now as good
as dead") is not to be taken too literally. Apparently,
the rejuvenation which the patriarch experienced,
enabling him to be father to Isaac, was of more than
merely the most transitory kind. Luther rightly
argues that Abraham saw that he was to beget more
children in order to fulfill the promise of 17:4 and so
in faith he proceeded to enter upon another marriage.
Consequently, no blame of any sort attaches to the
patriarch for this step: "he was not guilty of levity, nor
of intemperate lust," or of any other shortcoming in
this case. If he does not allow quite the same rank to
Keturah, it still is a regular marriage. But Abraham
must surely have felt that the rank of the mother of
the child of promise was to be regarded as higher than
that of any second wife. So even this distinction is
a necessary one. The coordinate clause "and her name
Keturah" is the equivalent of a relative clause "whose
name," etc. (K. S. 361 a, 369 m).

2-4. **And she bore to him Zimran and Jokshan
and Medan and Midian and Ishbak and Shuah. And
Jokshan begat Sheba and Dedan. And the sons of
Dedan were Asshurim and Letushim and Leummim.**

And the sons of Midian: Ephah and Epher and Hanoch and Abida and Eldaah. All these were the children of Keturah.

Parallel to this runs the passage I Chron. 1:32, 33. The following outline presents at a glance how far the descent is traced.

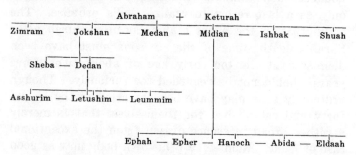

To argue at once, that because descendants of some sons are not indicated, the author's information was fragmentary, is less likely to cover the facts of the case than that some of these sons, like Zimran and Medan, simply were not founders of further tribes or nations. Jokshan, however, has through Dedan descendants who become the fathers of races through three generations. Brief as the table of Keturah's descendants is, it furnishes foundation for proof of the fact that a multitude of nations descended from Abraham. These, now, who are here listed are the fathers of Arab tribes who leave southern Palestine and migrate to the east, the southeast and the south. Apparently, in so doing they met with and absorbed, as Arab tradition also asserts, certain native Arab tribes. But, apparently, the element thus infused into the Arab tribes became the dominant factor and gave the name to the tribe.

Since very great uncertainty surrounds the identity of the individual groups or nations, we shall content ourselves with indicating briefly what seems the most reasonable identification we have been able to find.

"Zimran," perhaps identical with Zambran in western Arabia on the coast west of Mecca.

"Jokshan" apparently not yet identified satisfactorily.

"Medan," five days' journey south of Aila (Elath) which lies at the head of the Gulf of Akabah, located on the eastern shore of the Gulf.

"Midian" was a tribe which according to the Scriptures was scattered rather widely in northwestern Arabia, on the eastern portion of the peninsula of Sinai and even east of Palestine near Moab; cf. 36:35; 37:28; Exod. 3:11; 18:1; Num. 25:17; Jos. 13:21; Judg. 6:1 ff. So it need not surprise us that five subdivisions of this tribe should be mentioned (v. 4). "Ishbak" has not been identified. "Shuah" is somewhere in the Syro-Arabian desert mentioned as *Sûhu* by Assyrians and Babylonians.

3. "Sheba," cf. 10:7, belongs down into southwestern Arabia. "Dedan" apparently must be sought in the same region. Dedan's descendants are not reported under the name of individuals but, as the plural ending (*im*) indicates, as peoples. For "Asshurim" we could correctly say "the Assurites," etc., "the Letushites," "the Leummites." Though the term "Asshurim" might as such refer to the Assyrians, the greater likelihood is that a north-Arabian desert tribe is meant. Since Nabataean names of persons, or Sabaean like these last three have been found in inscriptions, we shall class these last three as north-Arabian.

4. lsa. 60:6 would merely indicate that "Ephah" may have been Midian's most distinguished son. "Epher" — not located. "Hanoch" reminds of *Hanâkia* three days' journey north of Medina. It has been pointed out that these three names Epha, Epher and Hanoch, are found also among the children of Israel and incidentally just among those tribes that lay

nearest to Midian — Judah, Manasseh, Reuben. "Abida" and "Eldaah" had best be classed merely as Arab tribes not identified.

There is no reason for adopting the common attitude of our day that these are fictitious ancestral names invented by these tribes at a later date. Though nations frequently invented such fictions, that fact does not stamp our account as fictitious.

5, 6. And Abraham gave all he had to Isaac. But to the sons of Abraham's concubines, Abraham gave gifts and sent them away from Isaac his son during his own lifetime, eastward to Kedem (East Country).

With wise forethought Abraham makes disposition of his property "during his lifetime" (on *'ôdhénû* see G. K. 100, o). The establishment as a whole goes to Isaac. The others are given adequate presents to enable each to make a proper beginning in life. This would involve about so much of cattle and goods as would constitute a reasonable nucleus to make possible a fair ranch. If all except Isaac are called "sons of Abraham's concubines," we have shown above in what sense this is meant in reference to Keturah. "Abraham's" is expressed by a clause, "which to Abraham," in order to avoid a succession of construct relationships (K. S. 282 e). In addition to giving gifts to the other children Abraham dismisses them so that the separation is made by his authority. They are said to have gone "eastward" (*qedhemah*) which is here used roughly to include north-eastward and south-eastward. Or else, if it were actually meant in the strict sense, then at first all did go eastward but in succeeding generations spread farther to the north and the south. All this involves the supposition that our attempted identification and location of the names v. 2-4 was at least relatively correct. The original expression used to indicate this direction taken by the descendants is:

he sent them away "eastward to the East-Country,"
which we have ventured to translate "eastward to
Kedem," because "Kedem" is at times used almost
like a proper noun. It also appears quite readily that
those who were sent away were not children of the
second and the third generation here listed but only
his actual sons. The historian (Moses) adds the later
names as a result of his knowledge of how the original
tribes divided or subdivided. After his original dismissal Ishmael may have returned home, at least
for a time.

**7-10. The whole length of Abraham's life was
one hundred and seventy-five years. And Abraham
expired and died at a good age, an old man and
having had his fill (of days), and he was gathered
to his people. And his sons, Isaac and Ishmael,
buried him in the cave of Machpelah, in the field
of Ephron, the son of Zohar, the Hittite, which was
over against Mamre, the field which Abraham
bought from the Hittites. There Abraham was
buried with Sarah, his wife.**

In concluding so memorable a life, whose details
have been given at such length, it is but natural that
the writer use a measure of fulness of expression.
Besides we are familiar since 5:5 with the fulsome
Hebrew expression: "the days of the years of the life
which he lived," which we have made free to translate:
"The whole length of the life." As is customary in
compound numerals, the item counted — here "years"
— is repeated in Hebrew (K. S. 314 e).

8. Here we still have the somewhat fuller style
of expression "he expired and died" (*gawa'* and *mûth*).
Of course, since all this more formal and elaborate
expression is ascribed to the mythical P, one need
not marvel to find the other uses of the phrase declared
to be marks of the style of P — "all P" says B D B —
although there are only two other passages where the

double expression occurs (25:17; 35:39). It must
appear at a glance that this is mere "reasoning in a
circle."

The first word (*gawa'*) pictures the act of drawing one's last breath; the second (*mûth*), the general
act of dying. By Abraham's time apparently the span
of life had been so much curtailed that 175 years
deserve to be described as a "good age." *Zaqen* is the
most common designation of an old man, but it involves
primarily the idea of dignity or rank growing out of
riper experience (see remarks on 24:2). The next
word *sabhé'a* we have rendered "having had his fill
(of days)" — in one word: "sated." This does not
mean "disgusted with life" or "tired of life," as some
are wont to construe Luther's rendering: *lebenssatt.*
The term has a good meaning; it implies that all wants
and all expectations have been satisfied. What 15:15
promised was fully realized.

The last expression used is particularly noteworthy: "he was gathered to his people." This cannot
mean: buried with his relatives or ancestors, for we
know that none of his kin except his wife lay buried
at Machpelah. Apparently, the expression is then
equivalent to the one used 15:15, "to go to one's
fathers." Those who have gone on before in death
are regarded as a people still existing. This is a
clear testimony to the belief in a life after death on
the part of the earliest patriarch. Though no specific
revelation on the subject seems to have been given
to these patriarchs, faith in the Almighty God drew
its own proper conclusions as to whether God would
ultimately let his children perish, and its conclusion
was correct: He cannot. This passage confirms that
conclusion. If Scripture is to be explained by Scripture, then Heb. 11:13-16 offers the fullest confirmation
of our interpretation. Therefore the prevalent exposi-
tions which aim to deny the possibility of faith in a

life after death on the part of the patriarchs will all
have to be discarded. They may assert: "The popular
conception of Sheol as a vast aggregate of graves in
the underworld enabled the language to be applied
to men who (like Abraham) were buried far from
their ancestors" (Skinner), but this "popular conception" is invented to cover a case like this. Such ra-
tionalizing explanations fail to do justice to the natural
meaning of words. Luther saw the implications of
these words very clearly: "If now there is another
'people' apart from those among whom we live, there
must be a resurrection from the dead." K. C. points
out that the passage cannot mean "to be laid in the
family sepulchre," because it is used in cases where
only one ancestor lay in the tomb (I Kings 11:43;
22:40) or none at all (Deut. 31:16; I Kings 2:10;
16:28; II Kings 21:18). Of course, when one's
"people" are thought of as having gone on before,
they are thought of as assembled in the Sheol, which
in this connection can mean only the "afterworld" or
the "hereafter." Nothing in this passage or in other
instances of the use of the expression (cf. 25:17;
35:29; 49:(29), 33; Num. 20:24; 27:13; 31:2; Deut.
32:50) indicates that the existence in the hereafter is
regarded as dull, shadowy or unreal. Since practically
in each case men of outstanding godliness are involved,
it would even seem strange if such were the ultimate
issue of a godly life. True, the New Testament fullness of revelation is not yet found in the Old. But the
common assertion that the Pentateuch knows nothing
of a life hereafter and of the resurrection from the
dead is merely a preconceived error. True, we shall
have to resort in part to reasoning like that employed
by Christ Matt. 22:31-33, but in reasoning thus we
follow a very reliable precedent.

9. Apparently there is no alienation between
Isaac and Ishmael at this time any more. Either the

death of Abraham had helped to bring the two sons
together, or else (K. C.) Isaac had succeeded in effect-
ing a reconciliation and an understanding (cf. 24:62)
before his marriage to Rebekah. In any case, both
are at one in arranging for the burial of their father.
There can be no doubt in their mind where the father
had wished to be buried (cf. ch. 23). Recalling all the
transactions that gave Abraham this burial plot at
Machpelah, the writer makes a rather detailed reference to the purchase of the cave and its location.

11. **And it came to pass after the death of
Abraham that God blessed Isaac his son, and Isaac
took up his dwelling at Beer-lahai-roi.**

We see that attention is about to center on a new
character in the narrative. This verse might be regarded as a kind of transitional paragraph. It is true
that after the general plan of Genesis the matters of
lesser importance must be disposed of first, and so
before the formal heading v. 19 there must be a brief
treatment of the descendants of Ishmael; but a few
verses (12-18) suffice for this purpose. Outstanding
about Isaac from the outset was the fact that God's
blessing was resting upon him. Everyone could discern that fact after brief observation. Besides, we
need to know that Isaac's more or less permanent
dwellingplace was the scene of the Angel's appearance
to Hagar, Beer-lahai-roi. This place apparently had a
strong attraction for Isaac (cf. 24:62). The blessings
received by Isaac are attributed to *Elohim* not to
Yahweh, because here only such blessings are thought
of as the Creator-God, Elohim, is wont to grant to
those who serve Him faithfully. Isaac also received
other blessings. These are not being reflected upon
for the present.

7.   **History (Toledoth) of Ishmael** (25:12-18)

With the distinctive heading employed ten times
in the book of Genesis this section is introduced and

clearly marked as a new section. As a section it may
be rather brief. But the alien elements, the portions
that have only incidental connection with the development of God's kingdom, these are always disposed of
quite briefly. The Bible retains the memory of such
groups but it allots to them their proper place. What
is not a part of the people of God, unfortunately, is
unimportant.

12-17. **This is the history of Ishmael, the son
of Abraham whom Hagar the Egyptian slavegirl
of Sarah bore to Abraham. These are the names
of the sons of Ishmael named according to their
generations: the first-born of Ishmael Nebaioth;
and Kedar and Abdeel and Mibsam, and Mishma
and Dumah and Massa; Hadad and Temah, Jetur,
Naphish and Kedemah. These, they are the sons
of Ishmael, and these are their names according
to their settlements and encampments, twelve
princes according to their nations. And this is the
length of Ishmael's life, a hundred and thirty-seven
years, and he expired and died and was gathered
unto his people.**

The more formal style and precise phraseology
are the chief reason for assigning this whole section
(v. 12-18) to the so-called P. But is not style bound
to assume some such form when a concise report is
being made? We still consider the man Moses capable
of varying his style according to the matter. When
condensed reports were to be offered, he lapsed into
this precise formal tone. On v. 12-18 compare I Chron.
1:28-31.

12. That Ishmael's story or "history" (see 2:4)
is given at all is really due to the fact that Ishmael is
"the son of Abraham." But when the added explanation
is given, "whom Hagar, the Egyptian slavegirl bore
to Abraham," the story of chapter 16 together with the
promises of 21:18 are called to mind. So we observe

that this account, brief as it is, aims to furnish proof
for the fulfillment of God's promises in reference to
this first-born son of Abraham. Ishmael did develop
into a "great nation."

13-15. As above v. 2-4 so here the identification
and the location of these twelve princes descended
from Ishmael offer difficulties. We shall briefly catalogue a few possibilities along this line. There is no
valid ground for departing from the plain meaning
of the text. These twelve were actually direct descendants of Ishmael, perhaps all twelve actual sons, for
the first is distinctly marked as "first-born." "Assumed
eponymous ancestors" is critical conjecture.

Apparently, generally speaking, the Ishmaelites
for the most part occupied a territory somewhat more
to the east and south of the Sons of Keturah. Skinner
assigns to them the region "intermediate between the
Arabian Cushites on the south; the Edomites, Moabites,
etc., on the west; and the Aramaeans on the north —
The Syro-Arabian desert north of Gebel Shammar"
(which lies almost in the center, or north-center of
Arabia).

"Nebaioth" are now usually identified with the
Nabayâti of the inscriptions of Asshurbanipal. Yet
K. W. still retains the old identification with the Naba-
taeans, who after the Exile made Petra in Edom their
stronghold and capital. Pliny also speaks of *Nabataei*
and *Cedrei* ("Kedar"). According to Isa. 60:7 they
were rich in flocks. North Arabia will, for the most
part, have been their home.

"Kedar" — cf. above. The cuneiform inscriptions
offer the parallel *Qidri*. These Ishmaelites were re-
nowned as archers (cf. Isa. 21:16 f.; Jer. 49:28 ff.).
Ps. 120:5 alludes to them as the remotest of strangers.

"Abdeel" sounds so much like the *Idibi'il* or
Idiba'il of the inscriptions of Tiglath-Pileser III that

we may regard this as a satisfactory identification. North-arabian.

"*Mibsam*" — unidentified.

14. "*Mishma*" — unidentified. "*Dumah*" lies in Northern Arabia also and may be identical with *Dumath al-Jandal*, seven days' journey southeast of Damascus. Of course, throughout this section, when we take the personal name and treat it as a place name, we imply that the original personal name came to be identified with a certain locality and so became a geographical term. The "Dumah" of Isa. 21:11 may be the same as this. "*Massa*" perhaps lay also in Northern Arabia. It may be identical with the *Masa* of the Assyrian inscriptions of Tiglath-Pileser.

15. "*Hadad*" — unidentified. "Tema" again seems to be four days' journey south of Dumah, now called *Taimâ'u*, or *Teyma*. About "*Jetur*" we know from I Chron. 1:31 that it was an Arab tribe with which Reuben engaged in conflict in the days of the conquest. Strabo speaks of Ἰτουραῖοί τε καὶ Ἄραβες. The New Testament "Ituraea" (Luke 3:1) seems to be derived from it. "*Naphish*" — unidentified. "*Kedemah*" — likewise.

16. Now appears our justification for the remark on v. 14 that personal names and place names are treated as identical because the place derived its name from the particular prince who settled there: "these are their names according to their settlements and encampments." It is somewhat difficult for us to see where the difference between "settlements" (*chaiserîm*) and "encampments" (*tîrôth*) lies. K. C. makes the former more protective — (*schirmendes Zeltlager*) and the latter distinctly made up of tents (*Zeltlager*). Skinner takes the former to mean "villages," the latter "a circular encampment of a nomadic tribe." But the main point at issue is that proof be furnished that the promise of 17:20 concerning the "twelve princes" was

fulfilled. The *beth sphaerae* or "beth of enumeration"
occurs in *"according to* their settlements" (K. S. 402s).

17. Ishmael, though according to 16:12 a somewhat wild and independent character, does not come
near Abraham's age, dying at the age of 137 years.
He, too, was gathered unto his people, whether these
now in Sheol were the lost or the saved. There is the
possibility that a man such as he, a man, who was
the object of a divine word of promise, (16:11, 12;
17:20) and who had grown up under the influence of
a godly man like Abraham, may have retained faith
in God all his days. The expression 16:12 ("wild ass")
implies no moral stigma.

18. **They had their dwelling place (in the region) from Havilah unto Shur, which lies east of
Egypt in the direction of Assyria. He settled to the
east of all his brethren.**

According to the prominent geographical terms
of that day a summary is given of the territory inhabited by Ishmael — *wayyishkenû* — "and they
dwelt" = "they had their dwelling place in the region,"
etc. In 10:7 we assigned to "Havilah" the sandy
regions east of Egypt. "Shur" lay somewhere nearer
the Egyptian border (cf. 16:7). The expression *'al-
peney* here appears to have the common (see B D B,
818 b) meaning "to the east of." "Assyria" (*'ashshûr*)
here would appear to be the well-known eastern country and not some scarcely known tribe of the immediate vicinity, for general directions are being given.
Naphal, "to fall," here means to "settle down," though
no parallels can be cited. To render "he died in the
presence of all his brethren" (A. V.) has no point.
Luther, who translates *er fiel* in his commentary, later
abandoned this rendering for "he opposed" — *er legte
sich wider alle seine Brueder.* But "he abode" (A. R.
V.) or "he settled" (above) is more in harmony with
the context.

8.   History of Isaac   (25:19-35:29)

Again a new "history," *toledoth,* (see 2:4). Though a more or less passive character, Isaac's life dominates the earlier stages of Jacob's life, so much so that though much more is told about Jacob up to 35:29, yet Isaac must have been the dominating influence of Jacob's life to that point.

1)   Birth and Early History of the Twin Brothers (25:19-34)

19, 20.   This is the history of Isaac, the son of Abraham.   Abraham begat Isaac.   And Isaac was forty years old when he married Rebekah, the daughter of Bethuel the Aramaean of Padan Aram, the sister of Laban, the Aramaean.

The opening statement cannot be translated "the following are the descendants" (Meek and others). See 2:4.   Since the new history is beginning, the relationships are recapitulated in a rather formal fashion. This accounts for having the author recall that Isaac was Abraham's son.   This is also done because immediately a strange parallel between the case of Abraham and that of Isaac is to be touched upon.

20.   The events of the preceding chapter are here summarized and the additional notice is given that Isaac was forty years old when he "married" (Hebrew: "took to wife") Rebekah. The patriarchs practiced fine self-restraint and were not unduly hasty about getting married.

21.   And Isaac interceded with Yahweh in behalf of his wife, for she was childless; and Yahweh granted his entreaty and Rebekah his wife conceived.

As Luther has pointed out, Isaac is the only patriarch till now whose intercession is recorded, and he accounts for the exception by the fact that this prayer was of unusual moment, being concerned with the promised Seed. The verb *'athar* means "to pray," the Arabic parallel signifying another form of devout exercise, "to sacrifice." The idea of particular urgency does not lie in the verb, as older commentators suggest. The preposition used with this verb *lenókhach* means "over against" in the sense that in thought his wife stood over against him as the object of his prayers. We should naturally translate "for" or "in behalf of." It is remarkable, indeed, that for a second time the wife of one who perpetuates the line of promise should be barren. However, it is to be made as apparent as possible that divine grace and not human endeavor or achievement is operative in these matters. For that reason, too, the faithful gracious God "Yahweh" is entreated, not Elohim. The same verb is used as before but now in the passive, in the sense of "He suffered Himself to be entreated" or He "granted his entreaty" — using an active construction. The *lô* with the passive expresses the agent (K. S. 102 a). It indicates a high value put upon motherhood and a proper estimate of the greatness of the gift of children when prayer to Yahweh is resorted to in order to obtain offspring. In this case, without a doubt, the thought of the Messiah to come was involved on Isaac's and on Rebekah's part. Conception or the absence of conception is more directly due to the omnipotent power of the Creator than men are wont to believe. Procksch presses the Arabic parallel beyond what Hebrew usage allows for when he makes the verb *'athar* signify "to sacrifice" and then construes *lenókhach* to mean that Rebekah was present before Isaac during the sacrifice.

22. **And the children jostled one another within her, and she said: If it be so, for what then am I (destined)? And she went to inquire of Yahweh.**

Rebekah was pregnant with twins without being aware of it. The children, as little able to agree now as later in life, "jostle one another" (Meek). *Yithrotsatsû*, Hithpael of the verb *ratsats*, "to crush," can hardly have so violent a meaning as "crush" or "thrust or strike" (B D B). Even "struggled" (A. V.) is a bit strong. Luther's *stiessen sich* = "jostled," as Meek renders it. The mother is alarmed, for she feels more than mere movements of the foetus. The unusual movements seem portents of unusual things. Yet she knows that pregnancy came as a gracious answer to prayer. "If (now) it be so" that these alarming movements within her accompany her pregnancy, then this must mean something for her too. She wonders what: "for what then am I (destined) ?" By supplying this "destined" (as K. C.) we give a simple, natural meaning to the question: "for what then I?" Of course, we then resolve *lammah* into its component parts — "for what" rather than to use the other common meaning "why" (A. V.). The divine answer given reveals to her to what she is destined: to bring forth two nations. This solution of this difficult passage should prove quite satisfactory, inasmuch as the other more acceptable of the many suggestions offered: "wherefore do I live?" (A. R. V.; Targum) has to supply the chief idea "live." Besides, it is hardly thinkable that movement of the foetus should at once cause Rebekah to despair of life.

We have no means of determining how and where Rebekah "inquired" (*darash* = "to seek or enquire") of Yahweh. Perhaps it was at some sanctuary where Abraham had been wont to worship. To speak of her as resorting to an "oracle" imports heathenish notions into the Hebrew text. Luther supposes that she will have consulted Shem. The answer may have come in a dream or vision (cf. 15:1).

23. **And Yahweh said unto her:**
Two nations are in thy womb,
Two peoples shall be separated from thy
bowels;
One people shall be stronger than the
other,
And the elder shall serve the younger.

A significant word revealing the destiny of nations. Since it has to do with the fulfillment of
covenant promises, it is ascribed to Yahweh. It is
somewhat mysterious as to import, but only until the
fulfillment becomes apparent. In reality each of the
four clauses is clear-cut in its meaning. We claim a
certain mysteriousness only in the sense that at first
hearing it seems somewhat difficult. But that characteristic is no doubt inherent in these words to
challenge further reflection. The first thought is:
Rebekah is to be a mother of twins who will be the
ancestors of two nations. She had through her husband
asked for a child; she now inquired as to what her
destiny in the matter of these children should be.
Rebekah finds that Yahweh is rich exceeding abundantly above what we ask and think. She sought to be
a mother of a child; she becomes a mother of two
nations.

The second part of the promise is pregnant in its
brevity: "two peoples shall be separated from thy
bowels" means, of course, that two children shall come
forth and shall develop into two distinct nations who
shall be separate from one another (K. S. 213 c).
Yipparedhû carries the emphasis in the sense that
these two nations shall have nothing in common. They
shall "separate" because they are so radically different
and shall remain apart for ever. To make "peoples"
by metonomy stand for "ancestors" (K. C.) is not
necessary.

The third advance in thought reveals that one of the two shall exceed the other in strength: one strong nation, one weaker nation.

Lastly, it appears that the reverse of what would have been anticipated will be the case: "the elder shall serve the younger." Now it is true, the Hebrew reads: "great shall serve small." But, since clearly the two sons are under discussion, it is not to be supposed that of two sons one will always be "great," consequently the matter of age only is here under consideration. Besides, *tsa'îr* usually means "young." Consequently, the only feasible translation will have to be: "the elder shall serve the younger." Ordinarily pre-eminence would seem to be associated with the first-born. Here we are clearly told that this rule is to be reversed.

The whole divine oracle is cast into poetic form. The clauses are parallel in structure 1 with 2 and 3 with 4. *Le'om* ("people") is a poetic word. The absence of the article is characteristic of poetic arrangement. Whether the substance of this utterance was originally cast into this very form or not is difficult to determine. The likelihood is that the word is recorded just as it was transmitted to Rebekah, form and substance dating from the Lord Himself.

Nor should it be overlooked that this significant word lays down more than a particular ruling applicable in this one instance. Paul's use of it (Rom. 9:12) indicates that at the same time the concluding statement ("the elder shall serve the younger") offers a general principle holding good for all times in the kingdom of God. For in this kingdom, first of all, every natural advantage of the carnal man is of no account in God's sight in the matter of salvation. The power and the claims of the natural man have to yield precedence to God's choice and election by grace. In the second place, a moral principle is also involved:

whatever excellence man may possess, it is all to be put to the service of the fellow-man, the strong serving the weak. This further application of the word does not, therefore, assign a double meaning to it. Rather, the general principle and its specific application blend into one in this instance.

Though we claim that the somewhat mysterious character of the word challenges deeper thought on the part of the recipients of it, we hold just as definitely to the contention that it was clearly understood by them from the very outset. God's primary purpose in giving revelation to men is that the revelation might *reveal*. Prayerful meditation upon this significant divine utterance established its meaning and its purpose very definitely for all involved. We even venture to say that this word became one of the guiding stars of this patriarchal family. Nor can there be any doubt that what Rebekah clearly understood will have been imparted without hesitation to Isaac. Such divine words in their very nature were intended to be common property of the family involved. Secretiveness about the matter will have been unthinkable. Consequently, as the two sons came to years of discretion, this word will have been communicated to them. This, of course, makes our problem all the more difficult when we come to explain how Isaac could afterward have attempted to ignore this word in the matter of blessing Esau. But we see absolutely no reason why Rebekah should have withheld this revelation from the rest of the family. Nor do we believe that so definite a word could have been misunderstood.

24-26. **When the time for her delivery came, behold, there were twins in her womb. And the first one came forth red, all over like a hairy garment, and they called his name Esau (Hairy). Next his brother came forth and his hand was holding Esau's heel; so his name was called Jacob**

(Heeler).   And Isaac was sixty years old when they were born.

What had been revealed previously by a word from Yahweh now becomes manifest in the hour of birth: there are "twins in her womb." The form *tômim* ("twins") is a shorter spelling for *te'omim.*

25.   The first-born is *'adhmonî* — "red" or "reddish-brown." Besides he is entirely covered with hair so as to resemble a "garment of hair" — *'addéreth se'ar.* In *se'ar* there seems to be involved an allusion to the land of Seir where Esau later took up his dwelling.   So also *'adhmonî* forms the basis for the name "Edom," for which more particular cause is found expressed in v. 30.   In any case, we have a record here of a child that seems unusually rough and rugged — a sturdy healthy child abounding in animal strength.   I fail to see in this a humorous allusion to Esau's appearance as being like that of a little hairy goat (Gunkel).   Such explanations aim to make the Scriptures ridiculous.   However, this very remarkable feature about the child's appearance is sufficient to give a name to the child.   "Esau" does mean "hairy," as the Arabic parallels indicate.   It may be objected that this matter of appearance is too trivial to account for the actual giving of a name.   But men familiar with the Orient find this to be a characteristic scene, quite likely to have occurred.

26.   The significant thing about the second twin is that "his hand was holding Esau's heel."   Now commentators have disputed much about the possibility of such a thing.   It is not, however, said that he already held the heel while both were in the mother's womb. For, in any case, who could have seen that the younger brother did thus? Here it is said that he did so as he came forth. Hos. 12:3 says: "In the womb he took his brother by the heel."   Both statements can be reconciled on the supposition that as the first was born

and before the umbilical cord was cut, the second reached forth his hand, perhaps while the first was still emerging, and laid hold on his brother's heel. Surely, that was very irregular, since an hour usually elapses between the birth of twins. But cases have been known, on the one hand, where the interval became as much as three days between the birth of twins. So, on the other hand, the case is thinkable where one twin follows immediately upon the heels (!) of the other. That case, again, is so significant that it may well furnish occasion for the giving of the name. For *ya'aqobh* is derived from the root *'aqebh* ("heel"). Consequently, though we translate the name "Heeler," we mean it in the sense of "Heel-gripper" (Meek), and that naturally leads to the other interpretation given to the name by Esau himself (27:36). Consequently there is no ground for claiming that this is a shortened form of "Jacob-el," just because this latter name appears as the name of a place in a list of Thotmes III and again as a personal name on a Babylonian contract tablet of Hammurabi's time. Such a claim grows out of the attempt to reduce things Israelitish to the Babylonian or the Egyptian level. Rather, here is a unique name of unique origin. From the concluding remark we learn that these parents had waited twenty years for children; cf. v. 20. No need of a textual change in the last clause, for *belédheth* can well refer to the father: "in (his) begetting them"; compare any lexicon on this use of the word — B D B says it occurs twenty-two times.

How inconclusive Scriptural evidence is for the critic appears from remarks such as: "The question whether Jacob was originally a tribe, a deity, or an individual man thus remains unsettled by etymology" (Skinner) — as though the remaining evidence aside from the etymological were weak.

27, 28. And the boys grew up, and Esau became a skillful hunter, a man living in the open country, but Jacob was a man of peaceful habits, as a tent dweller. And Isaac loved Esau, for game pleased him. But Rebekah loved Jacob.

The disparity between the two lads became increasingly apparent as they grew up. Esau develops into a "skillful hunter," literally: "knowing hunting." The parallel expression, "man of the field" (*'ish sadheh*) cannot mean that he followed agricultural pursuits (*ein Ackermann,* Luther), but rather the opposite: he was a man who disdained agriculture and was a "man of the open country," i. e., a man roving about everywhere. Examining this description a bit more closely, we notice that he turned his attention not to what would naturally have been his calling but that he loved excitement, activity, change and freedom. Consequently, he grew up to be an undisciplined character. Besides, as the fathers were wont to remark, the continual pursuit of a life of hunting makes characters harsh and cruel. The pursuit of it has no ennobling effects when it becomes an obsession. Apparently, the word *tam* in reference to Jacob aims to describe the very opposite traits. Though *tam* signifies "complete," "perfect," here it means: adequately filling the requirements of his calling, not roving about but "a man of peaceful habits," as we have rendered above. Luther's *fromm* may cover that, for it does not refer to a pious disposition only. "A plain man" (A. V.) is beside the point; "quiet" (A. R. V.) is better. So, too, "dwelling in tents" (A. V.) misses the point. Why mention at all where he dwelt? Traits are being discussed. *Yosebh 'ohalîm* means: as a man dwelling in tents is wont to be, here then: a typical nomad. That thought is to the point; for being destined to live a nomadic life, he gave himself to the pursuits typical to his class. He was intent upon filling well the place in life prepared for him.

28. Strange to say, Isaac loved Esau. The reason assigned is: "game pleased him" — literally, "(was) in his mouth," *bephîw*. It would hardly have gotten into his mouth if he did not like it; consequently our translation. Luther has about the same: *ass gern von seinem Weidwerk*. So A. V. is meant. This cannot be the only thing that bound these two characters closely together. In itself this fact suggests a character unduly given to the things that tickle the palate. But besides, the more passive Isaac finds himself attracted to the more active and bold Esau just because he himself lacks these qualities. Whereas Rebekah understands and loves the diligent and dutiful Jacob better. Rebekah had spiritual ambitions, in a good sense. They prompted her originally to cast in her lot with Isaac. Jacob had a kindred spirit. This kinship was the bond uniting the two. Luther's remarks cover the rest of the case: "Just as mothers are wont to love the sons who are of a more quiet and friendly disposition rather than those who are wild and bold, so fathers love those sons who are a bit more lively and bold." No inferior ground is adduced in referring to Rebekah's love for Jacob. Still, on the whole, a measure of partiality was involved on the part of both parents. We take this verse to imply a rebuke for both parties.

29, 30. **And Jacob boiled pottage and Esau came from the field faint with hunger, and Esau said to Jacob: Let me swallow, please, some of that red stuff there, for I am faint with hunger. (That is why he is called Edom — [Red]).**

A characteristic prosaic incident is here recorded, an incident fraught with far-reaching consequences, as certain almost trifling occurrences sometimes come to be of greatest moment. — The first expression used = Jacob "seethed a seething," *yázedh nazîdh*. The

expression is quite vague for the present. Later it
develops that the "seething" was lentils, a savory
dish. Esau returns from his customary pursuits out
in the open field. On this occasion he seems unusually
famished. *'Ayeph* actually means only "faint," or
"weary." In this case the faintness which results from
hunger; consequently: "faint with hunger." With the
ravenous appetite resulting from outdoor activity Esau
can hardly restrain himself. His words are expressive
of his uncontrolled hunger. He asks not merely with
a mild "feed me" (A. V.) or an equally mild "let me
taste" but *hal'îţenî*, "let me swallow," almost, "let me
gulp." Besides, his haste does not allow him even to
try to name the pottage under preparation; he just
designates it: "of the red, that red." Just as we should
say: "some of that red stuff there," (so also Meek).
Incidentally, this significant incident gave occasion
also for calling him "Edom" — for *'adhom* was "the
red." Now this second etymological explanation within the same chapter for the name Edom does not
conflict with the first (v. 25). It only shows that by
a peculiar guidance of Providence two events occurred
that gave rise to the name, or, better still, the original
name was doubly confirmed by this particular experience. By the way, the repetition of *'adhom* above
was not for emphasis (K. S. 309 m) but an indication
of impatience.

**31-33. And Jacob said: Sell me thy birth-
right first. And Esau said: Behold, I for my part
am going to meet death; of what use is the birthright to me? And Jacob said: Give me an oath
on this first, and he gave him an oath. So he sold
his birthright to Jacob.**

At this point the interpretations usually run afoul
of an old misconception: they assume that Jacob gives
evidence of crafty duplicity, that Jacob is all wrong
and Esau all right, although the account closes (34 b)

with a criticism of *Esau*. Behind this misunderstanding lies a second one, formulated best perhaps in the naive claim of Dods: "The character of Jacob is easily understood." Fact of the matter is, Jacob's character is one of the hardest to understand; it is complicated, it has many folds and convolutions. But in this particular incident the Scriptural point of view must be maintained: *Esau* was primarily to blame.

Another explanation must be inserted here. Jacob was really a spiritually minded man with appreciation of spiritual values and with distinct spiritual ambitions. Especially in the matter of carrying on the line of promise from which the Savior would come did Jacob have ambitions. The aspirations apparently, however, were begotten by the divine word of promise (v. 23). Yahweh had destined Jacob to pre-eminence. Jacob gladly accepted the choice and aspired to attain to the treasure promised. His eagerness was commendable. His choice of means in arriving at the desired end was not always above reproach. He felt he had to help the good Lord along occasionally. He was not fully confident of God's methods for arriving at the goal. He felt the need of occasionally inserting a bit of assistance of his own. Such an attitude was one of mistrust: confidence in human ingenuity rather than in divine dependability — in one word — unbelief. But his spiritual aggressiveness was by no means to be despised, nor was it wrong.

Approaching this incident with these facts in mind, we seem compelled to assume one thing in order to understand Jacob's request. It appears, namely, that the subject of the birthright (*bekhorah* = "first-bornness," "primogeniture," then the *right* of the first, i. e., "birthright.") had been under consideration between the brothers on a previous occasion. It would also seem that Esau had made some derogatory remark about its value, or had even spoken about his own readiness to part with the privilege. Otherwise we can hardly believe that Jacob would have made this special request without further motivation, or that Esau would have consented to the bargain without more ado. This, indeed, puts Jacob into a more favorable light, but so does our text (v. 34). Indeed, there is left on Jacob's part a measure of shrewd calculation in so timing his request that he catches Esau at a disadvantage, a form of cunning which we must condemn without reservation. Yet the act does not call for such strong criticism as: he was "ruthlessly taking advantage of his brother, watching and waiting till he was sure of his victim" (Dods).

Besides, to clarify issues we had better notice that the material advantages of the birthright were not under consideration by Jacob, whatever these advantages may at Jacob's time have been. According to the Mosaic law of a later date the right of the first-born involved a double portion of the father's inheritance (Deut. 21:17) and a kind of supremacy over one's brethren and his father's house (Gen. 27:29). But observe how obviously humble Jacob appears after his return from Mesopotamia, yielding the pre-eminence to Esau in all things. *Mikhrah* ("sell") is an emphatic imperative (G. K. 48 i). The expression *kayyôm*, literally: "as the day," "according to the day," comes to mean "at once," "first of all" (B D B) as in v. 33, I Sam. 2:16; I Kings 1:51.

32. Esau's answer seems a bit puzzling in its first part: "Behold, I for my part am going to meet death." Can he really mean: "I am at the point to die" (A. V.) from hunger? Shall we, then, subscribe to the interpretation of Dods: "Who does not feel contempt for the great strong man declaring he will die if he is required to wait five minutes till his own supper is prepared?" Esau is hardly such a big baby. Sturdy hunter that he was, he must have been some-

what inured to privations. Or does he then mean: "I
shall die sooner or later anyhow"? That's rather a
flat notion in this connection. So we conclude that
'anokhî hôlekh lamûth, with the emphatic pronoun
first, means: "I, for my part," in my dangerous
calling, "am going to meet death" rather soon anyhow;
so "of what use is the birthright to me?" This latter
statement now actually displays Esau's real sentiments: he has no appreciation of, or desire for, spiritual advantages or values. He despises the intangible
spiritual entity as altogether too nebulous. In this
sense he was a profane person (Heb. 12:16). His was
a coarse, entirely unspiritual nature. What if there
was a chosen line from which a Savior would ultimately spring? To be associated with that ideal prospect was not worth aspiring after, thought he.

33. Jacob is so eager to obtain this advantage
that he wants more than a hasty word, that might be
regretted on the morrow, to bind the bargain. To give
proof of his eagerness and to let Esau give proof of
his sincerity in the matter, Jacob asks: "Give me an
oath on this first." The solemnity of the added oath
does not deter Esau; he promptly gives the oath.

**34. Then Jacob gave Esau bread and pottage
of lentils, and he ate and drank and arose and went
his way. So Esau despised his birthright.**

Well-pleased with his bargain, Jacob gives
"bread," which is really presupposed for a meal, together with the pottage of *'adhashîm* ("lentils"). Well-
pleased with his bargain, Esau eats, drinks, rises and
goes away. There is something carnal about the attitude of Esau, so carnal as to rouse a feeling of contempt. The severe condemnation of this statement,
he "despised his birthright," as well as that of the
letter to the Hebrews (12:16): "a profane person"
(βέβηλος) puts the emphasis where it belongs. Now
we can understand why God had not chosen Esau to

carry on the line of the Messiah. Total spiritual incapacity was characteristic of this man. He could hardly serve as guardian of mankind's dearest hope. On *wayyesht* see G. K. 75 q o.

On the whole transaction Luther draws attention to a basic fact that should not be overlooked: this was not a valid purchase, because Jacob was attempting to purchase what was already his. With equal correctness it might be said that Esau was attempting to sell what was not his. Consequently, Bishop Hall's remark (Jamieson) was only partly true when he said: "There was never any meal, except the forbidden fruit, so dear bought as this broth of Jacob."

HOMILETICAL SUGGESTIONS

Most of the matter of this chapter is not directly adapted to homiletical use. For the list of Abraham's children by Keturah and the disposition made of his property are not readily adaptable to sermonic purposes. One would hardy care to use v. 5, 6 for the purpose of enforcing the desirability of making proper division of one's property. The theme is hardly big enough for a Gospel preacher, good as it may be on occasion to offer solid instruction on this head incidentally, where the subject that is being treated may allow for such instruction. Also the subject matter of v. 19-26 is not suitable for use in the pulpit for obvious reasons. If one needs would treat a subject like that of v. 23—"the elder shall serve the younger"—and the broad principle that is involved, it would be better to use Rom. 9:12 or as much of the chapter in Romans as is deemed suitable. The last part of the chapter v. 27-34 seems to us to come under a head such as Spiritual Aggressiveness, or even, The Right Goal but the Wrong Way. In any case, it should specially be borne in mind that the one censured by the text is Esau not Jacob.

CHAPTER XXVI

2) Various Scenes from Isaac's Life (chapter 26)

The incidents recorded in this chapter are the only ones in which Isaac figures as chief character. Immediately thereafter other persons stand out more prominently. This is in keeping with the character of Isaac. He is not the prominent, aggressive figure that Abraham is. Isaac, himself a great man in his own right, is quite overshadowed by the towering figure of Abraham. True, Isaac is a quiet and unassuming man, patient and submissive in his contact with others. But to infer from this that he is unworthy of the patriarchal position would be wrong. He is a man of strong faith. But it is not given to all men to occupy equally prominent positions in the kingdom of God. The distinct advance made in Abraham's day is carefully guarded by Isaac. Isaac lives in the fulness of truth revealed to Abraham. Spiritually he is a true son of his father. It has well been said that the experience of Moriah put its stamp upon Isaac and taught him that in patiently submitting to the Lord's will one shall see the Lord's salvation.

The pronounced parallel between events in Isaac's life and those of Abraham's can only disturb those who are too shortsighted to see that similar characters under similar circumstances in a given age are very likely to have similar experiences. A bit less of theorizing about such situations and a bit more of observation of real life will furnish a multitude of parallels equally startling.

a) Sojourn in Philistaea (v. 1-11)

1. **And there came a famine in the land, other than the first famine that was in the days of Abraham; and Isaac went to Abimelech, king of the Philistines, to Gerar.**

The writer, conscious of the similarity of Isaac's situation to that of Abraham's, is at pains to remind us that this could not be the famine of Abraham's time, and that we, therefore, have an entirely new case to deal with. In fact, a bit of computation reminds us that a full century had passed since that time. The second half of the verse is best construed as giving in characteristic Hebrew fashion the whole event in a summary fashion: Isaac went to Gerar. The details, beginning back in point of time before he actually started out, follow, beginning at verse 2. The Abimelech here mentioned can hardly be the Abimelech of chapter 20, who ruled Philistaea eighty years before. The common assumption that Abimelech was a standing designation of all Philistine kings, like Pharaoh for the Egyptian, finds definite support in the heading of Ps. 34, where Abimelech is used as a title for the man who I Sam. 21:10-15 appears as Achish. "Gerar" appears to be identical with *Umm-Jerar,* about ten miles south of Gaza.

2-5. **And Yahweh appeared to him and said: Do not go down to Egypt; dwell in the land I tell thee of; sojourn in this land and I will be with thee and I will bless thee. For to thee and to thy descendants do I give all these lands. And I will fulfill my oath which I swore to Abraham, thy father, and I will multiply thy descendants as the stars of the heavens, and I will give to thy descendants all these lands, and all the nations of the earth shall bless themselves in thy seed; because that Abraham hearkened to my voice and kept my charge, my commandments, my statutes, and my laws.**

The situation is sufficiently important to call for divine intervention. God appears to Isaac as well as to Abraham; but only twice to Isaac: here and v. 24. He appears in the capacity of "Yahweh," because His graciousness as the covenant God watching over the covenant people is displayed. According to our interpretation of v. 1 this word was spoken before Isaac set out from southern Palestine. Isaac may actually have contemplated a temporary sojourn in Egypt. This is denied him. Divine providence alone can determine whether what is permissible in one case is advisable in another. The statement, "dwell in the land I tell thee of," means, "in whatever land I may designate from time to time." There Isaac is to sojourn, and in every case he will be sure of the attendance of the divine presence as well as of the divine blessing. The blessings spoken upon Abraham are here being definitely renewed for Isaac in all their fulness with certain modifications of expression. The correspondence part for part with these earlier promises is too obvious to require to be pointed out: descendants, a land for these descendants, God's blessing upon them in that land. If incidentally the one land is now thought of in terms of the constituent parts: "all these lands," the difference in expression is merely nominal. *Ha'el*, the shortened form for *ha'elleh*, is one of the peculiarities of the Pentateuch. All such gifts as are here promised are based upon that basic oath spoken to Abraham (22:16 f.) which is important enough to be alluded to again.

4. The promise of numerous offspring is as much in place for Isaac as for Abraham, for in Isaac's case, too, the chosen family had not yet displayed numerical strength. The second half of the verse brings the distinctly Messianic element in the promise. For there is but one thing sufficiently important to challenge the strongest interest of "all the nations of

the earth" and that is the Messianic blessing. Here, however, a slightly different point of view obtains. In 12:3 the simple passive (*Nifal*) had been used, "be blessed." Here the reflexive (*Hithpael*) appears, "bless oneself." Naturally the latter is not radically different from the former, nor does it cancel the idea of the former. The passive speaks of objective blessings. The reflexive shows the subjective reaction: nations shall "bless themselves," i. e., wish themselves the blessings conferred through Abraham's seed, the Messiah in particular. Heretofore we have been translating *zéra'* ("seed") as collective: "descendants" (also v. 3), but here we definitely believe that the One great Descendant is primarily under consideration, "the Seed," the Christ. We also hold that in the light of 3:15 (see explanation there) men like Isaac will have interpreted this word as referring specifically to One — a fact denied almost universally in our day but yet true.

5. Though, indeed, this promise originally given to Abraham was a promise of pure grace, without any merit or worthiness on his part, yet God's mercy deigned to note with delight the one thing that Abraham did, which kept him from making himself unworthy of the divine promises: Abraham obeyed every divine injunction. Therefore, these manifold blessings, Isaac is told, come upon him for Abraham his father's sake, or rather, because of Abraham's faithful obedience. Remarkable is the scope of divine blessings that are mediated through faithful Abraham. In order to make prominent the thought that Abraham conscientiously did all that God asked, the various forms of divine commandments are enumerated; sometimes, of course, a divine word would fall under several of these categories. They are a "charge" or "observance" if they are to be observed (*mishméreth* from *shamar*, ("observe"). They are "commandments"

(*mitswôth*) when regarded from the angle of having been divinely *commanded*. They are "statutes" (*chuq-qôth*) when thought of as immutable, and "laws" (*torôth*) insofar as they involve divine instruction or teaching. Under these headings would come the "commandment" to leave home (ch. 12), the "statute" of circumcision, the instruction to sacrifice Isaac, or to do any other particular thing such as (15:8) to sacrifice, or (13:17, 18) to walk through the land, as well as all other individual acts as they are implied in his attitude toward Yahweh, his faithful God. By the use of these terms Moses, who purposes to use them all very frequently in his later books, indicates that "laws, commandments, charges, and statutes" are nothing new but were involved already in patriarchal religion. Criticism, of course, unable to appreciate such valuable and suggestive thoughts, or thinking Moses, at least, incapable of having them, here decrees that these words come from another source, for though J wrote the chapter, J, according to the lists they have compiled, does not have these words in his vocabulary, and so the device, so frequently resorted to, is employed here of claiming to discern traces of a late hand, a redactor.

6, 7. **And Isaac dwelt in Gerar; and when the men of the place asked him about his wife, he said: She is my sister, for he was afraid to say: She is my wife lest the men of the place slay me because of Rebekah, for she was beautiful to look at.**

Isaac, constituted much like his father, finding himself in a situation identical with the one in which his father has figured, does exactly as his father. The very strange thing about this action is that it is as wrong here as there, if not more wrong. For Isaac must have known how the matter turned out in the case of his father. But then, for that matter, sin is never logical.

Criticism, with almost complete unanimity (we know of only Koenig as an exception) calls this a later (Isaac) version of the original (Abraham) legend, or else calls chapter 26 the original and chapter 20 derivative. Yet the differences, aside from the very plain statements of the text to the same effect, point to two different situations: here a famine, there none; here Rebekah is not molested, there Abimelech took Sarah; here accidental discovery, there divine intervention; here no royal gift, there rich recompense. Of course, criticism usually points to 12:10 ff. as being merely another form of the same incident. Yet at least one aspect of the critical approach can be refuted completely on purely critical grounds. For, as K. C. observes, it is unthinkable that J, to whom chapter 12 as well as chapter 26 are attributed, should have preserved two versions of one and the same incident.

8-10. **And it came to pass after quite a number of days had passed, that Abimelech, king of the Philistines, looked out of his window, and, behold, Isaac was caressing Rebekah, his wife. And Abimelech summoned Isaac and said: Look here, she certainly is thy wife, and how is it that thou saidst: She is my sister? And Isaac said to him: (I did it) because I said: that I might not die on her account. And Abimelech said: What, now, hast thou done to us? Quite easily some of the people might have lain with thy wife, and so thou wouldest have brought guilt upon us.**

The situation comes to a climax after "quite a number of days had passed" (literally, "the days had grown long for him"), when Abimelech, looking out of a "window," (one of the small latticed openings looking beyond the confines of the court), happened to see Isaac, who dearly loved his wife (24:25), "caressing" her (*metsach* (*ch*) *eq* — "fondling," "sporting." A. V.), a course of procedure not followed with sisters. Though the term "sister" is sometimes used loosely, even the relative truth involved by such use would in Isaac's mouth have been employed in order to deceive, and would thus certainly have been an untruth.

9. The *wayyiqra'* can hardly here mean: "he called out to him" from the window (Procksch), by which boorish behavior on the king's part a lifelike touch is supposed to be secured. Rather, he formally "summoned" Isaac. The king's mode of stating the case implies suspicions that he has held right along: "Look (here), she certainly is thy wife," a shade of thought caught by Meek when he renders: "So she really is your wife." Taken to task for his lie, Isaac weakly admits that he had been afraid: men might have put him to death on her account. *'Amûth* ("die") is here really used in the sense of "lose my life." The *kî* is best explained as "because," and so it involves an ellipsis ("I did it").

10. Abimelech administers a well-deserved rebuke. The memory of what happened to his grandfather may perhaps have still been fresh at court. *Kim'at* could mean "almost," but that would imply what the text otherwise does not indicate, that some individual had been on the verge of approaching her. So "easily" (A. V.) is more in place. This Abimelech also has a measure of the fear of God still left in his heart, for he knows that adultery involves "guilt." However, obversely, by the argument from silence we dare not infer, as some do, that the king considered carnal intercourse with a maiden as entirely right. For it appears far more likely that a man who seeks to avoid guilt on the part of himself and his people will not have stood on so low a level morally, and will have referred to "guilt," *'asham,* in the sense of "great guilt." After *kim'at* the perfect always is used (K. S. 175). *Hebe'tha* with ē (G. K. 76 h).

Mah-zo'th could mean "what is this?" perhaps "why?" but most likely the demonstrative is used for a mild emphasis: "what, now?"

11. And Abimelech gave orders to all his people, saying: He that toucheth this man or his wife shall without fail be put to death.

The king is a man who desires to have righteousness strictly upheld among his people, so he gives orders to all his people, apparently by some public proclamation. Hebrew: "this man *and* his wife" means "this man *or* his wife" (K. S. 375 f). The same result is arrived at by construing the thought thus: "he that toucheth this man *and* he that toucheth his wife." In *mûth yûmath* the *Hofal* of the verb is strengthened by the *Kal* absolute infinitive, by which construction the verbal idea is made more positive not intensified; therefore: "shall be put to death without fail."

b)   His Prosperity (v.12-17)

12-14. And Isaac sowed in that land, and reaped that year a hundred fold; and so Yahweh blessed him. And the man prospered and kept right on and prospered until he was exceedingly prosperous. And his property consisted of flocks and herds and many servants; and the Philistines were envious of him.

If Abraham cultivated fields at all, he did not do sufficient of such work to make it important enough to record. Isaac ventured into agriculture to such an extent as to allow us to classify him as a kind of semi-nomad. Consequently, though following for the most part in Abraham's footsteps, Isaac must, nevertheless, be credited with a measure of initiative. He also dug new wells (v. 19 ff.). For "reaped" the Hebrew text has "found" (*matsa'*), involving the idea of coming into the field and discovering how rich the crop really

is. *She'arîm* means "measures," here most properly
a hundred measures = "a hundred fold." Such remarkable fertility was sometimes found in days of old
and is claimed for the Hauran, east of the Jordan, to
this day. Here, however, a rich harvest is a token of
divine favor. Therefore the "and he blessed" (*waybhárekh*) is meant in the sense "and *so* Yahweh
blessed" (K. S. 369 g). Though such a material blessing could most properly have been ascribed to *Elohim*,
here the ascribing of it to Yahweh involves that He
was blessing him because Isaac stood in covenant relation with Him.

13. In terms and construction reminiscent of
7:18, 19 the increase of Isaac's prosperity is here
described. *Gadhel*, "be great," can hardly here be
used of achievement or renown, and so we have rendered it "prospered." The Hebrew idiom for "he kept
growing richer and richer" is: "he went forward,
going on, and became prosperous." *Halokh*, absolute
infinitive (G. K. 113 u).

14. Since Abraham already was very rich (13:2;
14:23) and the bulk of his property had gone to Isaac,
such an increase as this in Isaac's wealth must have
brought his possessions up to a startling total. However, his wealth was that of the nomad only, "flocks,
herds, servants." The Hebrew designates the first
two as "possession of flock" and "possession of cattle."
Apparently, he had abstained from raising camels
and asses. However, a requisite number of servants
also belonged to his establishment — "many servants"
— *'abuddah*, abstract "service" (*Dienerschaft*) for
concrete "servants." A problem resulted from this
unusual prosperity: the Philistines grew envious. This
is here added to explain the clash with the Philistines
on the subject of wells, which is about to be touched
upon.

15-17. Now all the wells which the servants of his father had dug in the days of Abraham, his father, these the Philistines stopped and filled with dirt. And Abimelech said to Isaac: Go away from us, for thou art altogether too powerful for us. So Isaac went away and pitched tent in the valley of Gerar and settled down there.

Envy on the Philistines' part turns to spite. The wells so essential to the herds of nomads, wells that dated back to Abraham's time, and may for half a century or more have been recognized as the peculiar property of Abraham's family because he himself had had them dug, these the Philistines now begin to fill with dirt (*'aphar*) and so stop them up. Such a loss is very painful, for it shuts off the prime necessity of physical life. So the result of the envy of the Philistines is described. Criticism quite commonly insists that v. 15 is a later insertion. Critics would have preferred v. 16 as the continuation of v. 14. But what strange reasoning! Before the final result is related, we have the summons to depart. Why cannot another intermediate stage be recorded, namely, instead of 1) envy 2) summons, 1) envy, 2) spite 3) summons. In this latter case 2), 3) make a good sequence, for when the Philistines have done Isaac wrong, the king according to a common psychological procedure blames Isaac, asserting he has become too powerful. "Wells" — a nominative absolute (K. S. 341 c).

16. Numerically Isaac's household was so strong as to constitute a threat to the safety of the Philistines, had Isaac been minded to use his power selfishly. The king's summons is a combination of flattery ("thou art altogether too powerful for us") and of an ungracious attitude ("go away from us").

17. Isaac is a pacifist in the best sense of the word. Power is safe in his hands. He shows no in-

clination to abuse it. Secure in his strength but mindful primarily of his responsibilities to his God, he yields to pressure and moves farther up the valley, i. e., southeast from Gerar, and there pitches his tent with the intent of staying there permanently (he "settled down" — *yeshebh* = "sat down"). On *yichan* from *chanah* see G. K. 75 r.

c) Strife over Wells (v. 18-22)

18-20. **Then Isaac let the wells of water be reopened which had first been dug in the days of Abraham, his father, and which the Philistines had stopped after the death of Abraham, and he gave them the names which his father had already given them. Then Isaac's servants dug in the valley and found a well of running water. But the herdsmen of Gerar strove with Isaac's herdsmen, saying: Ours is this water. So he called the name of the well Esek (Contention), because they contended with him.**

It may seem like an account of prosy trifles to have such petty strife recorded in the Scriptures, but against the background of these trivialities the character of a man like Isaac is displayed to advantage. Trivialities serve to reveal true nobility of character when a man rises above them.

To understand the situation correctly (for criticism again believes v. 18 to be a later insertion) we must note that though Isaac had departed partly because of stopped-up wells (v. 15), yet Isaac's herds and flocks were spread over a great territory, and, apparently, very many wells had been stopped up all along the valley of Gerar. So abandoning those wells nearer Gerar, which had been one immediate source of contention, Isaac feels justified in reopening those wells at a distance from Gerar which Abraham had dug. The Hebrew construction: "and he returned and dug" = he "reopened." However, since the patriarch merely took steps to have this done, we may render: "he *let* the wells be reopened." The statement that they were wells that Abraham had first dug is not superfluous after v. 15 but clearly establishes Isaac's claims to these wells. To indicate, further, his right to these wells and to indicate his respect for what his father did, Isaac in every case revives the original names of these wells. On *shûbh* used adverbially for "again" see G. K. 120 d; K. S. 332 γ; 369 q. In *waysattemûm* ("and they stopped") the converted imperfect takes the place of the relative construction with *'asher,* which had preceded (K. S. 366 c).

19. This verse, of course, refers to additional digging operations carried on by Isaac's servants. Apparently, because of the rapid increase of Isaac's wealth there was need of additional wells. But the Philistines kept close watch. What could not be claimed by right of possession from Abraham's time was contested, especially in this case where "running water" (Hebrew idiom: "living water," *mayim chayyim*) was found.

20. The strife arises only among the herdsmen, the initiative, apparently, being taken by those of Gerar, who are mentioned first and whose assertive claim is mentioned: "Ours (emphatic) is this (demonstrative use of the article) water." No doubt, the distance from Gerar was sufficient to establish Isaac's claim to the well, otherwise this fair-minded man would never have sanctioned the digging. Isaac's policy is in keeping with the word, "Blessed are the meek." He leaves a memorial of the pettiness of the strife behind by calling the well *Esek* — "Contention" — the Quarrel Well. Perhaps a mild and tolerant humor lies in the name. Yet after all, what a fine testimonial to a great man's broad-mindedness and

readiness to sacrifice, lest the baser passions in men
be roused by quarreling.

**21, 22. Then they digged another well and
there was strife also over it. So he called its name
Sitnah (Hostility). So he moved away and dug
still another well, about which there was no strife.
So he called its name Rehoboth (Plenty of room),
saying: For now Yahweh has given us room and
we shall be fruitful in the land.**

A second attempt at a new well meets with the
same result. In this case the opposition seems to have
been even more spiteful, for the stronger name "Sitnah" (Hostility) is left behind for the well. But everyone must recognize that it is magnanimity and not
cowardice on Isaac's part when he yields, because
Isaac had ample manpower at his command.

22. Isaac goes as far as possible in the interest
of peace: he even "moved away." By this time his
generous example seems to have shamed the opposition. No doubt, too, the site of the latest well is still
farther removed from territory which Gerar may
rightfully claim. The resultant peace Isaac in true
gratitude ascribes to Yahweh, tokens of whose favor
he has been meeting with continually. The name
"Rehoboth" is to convey this reminder. *Rechobhôth*
means "wide places" and signifies in reference to the
well more than "room" (Meek), rather "plenty of
room." "Be fruitful" (*parah*) can hardly be referred
to good crops — *"we* shall be fruitful" — but rather
to numerical growth as in 1:28. Isaac is thinking
of v. 4.

d) The Appearance of Yahweh (v. 23-25)

**23-25. From there he went up to Beersheba,
and Yahweh appeared to him that night, saying:
I am the God of Abraham, thy father; be not afraid,**

for I am with thee, and will bless thee, and make
thy descendants numerous for the sake of Abraham,
my servant. And he built an altar there and called
upon the name of Yahweh and pitched his tent
there; and there Isaac's servants digged a well.

23.   Though Beersheba is said to lie lower than
Gerar, yet the general expression for approaching any
part of Palestine from the southwest is to "go up"
(*'alah*).

24.   "Yahweh" appears to Isaac, for covenant
issues are under consideration. Isaac has behaved in a
manner calling forth divine approval. Besides, Isaac's
faith needs to be strengthened in the matter of the
realization of the covenant promise. For one part of
this promise is: numerous descendants. Isaac has
been thinking along this line (see the close of v. 22).
He shall have to walk by faith very largely as did
Abraham. That this faith might be well established
he is informed that God will surely bring this promise
to pass. So we see that the situation is sufficiently
important to call for the appearance of Yahweh, the
second and last that is granted to Isaac. The substance
of Yahweh's promise is: Fear not as to the realization
of the promises given thee, for I am with thee, I the
God of Abraham, thy father, who never failed to
make good what I promised to him; I guarantee to
make thy descendants (Hebrew "seed") numerous,
for the sake of Abraham, my servant. It is here only
in Genesis that the title "my servant" is applied to
Abraham. By it another aspect of Abraham's relation
to the Lord is covered: he stood in God's service all
his days and faithfully did His will.

25.   A place marked by a divine appearance is a
sacred spot where Yahweh is to be worshipped in a
particular sense. So, following the good example of
his father, Isaac builds an altar, where, of course, he
offers sacrifice — a thing so obvious that it is not

even mentioned — and engages in public worship in
the course of which God's character and His works are
extolled, for this is involved in "calling upon the name
of Yahweh" (see notes on 4:26). Because of Yahweh's
manifestation such a spot becomes dear to Isaac, and
he pitches his tent there, and since a relatively permanent residence is involved, he has servants dig a
well here too. *Karah,* the verb for "dig" here used,
differs from *chaphar* used earlier in the chapter, in
that the former simply means "to dig," whereas the
latter involves the idea of "search." Both may imply
the successful completion of the digging operations.

e) Covenant with the Philistines (v. 26-33)

This passage presents a close parallel to 21:22 ff.
which covers a similar case in Abraham's day. But
why should the thought be so repulsive that in Isaac's
day the situations that had previously prevailed in
Abraham's time were duplicated? Have the critics
never noticed from their study of history how certain
problems and situations are perennial in certain
regions?

26, 27. **And Abimelech came to him from
Gerar together with Ahuzzath, his friend, and Phicol,
the captain of his army. And Isaac said unto them:
Why have ye come to me, seeing that ye on
your part hate me and have driven me away from
you?**

As "Abimelech" is the standing title of the Philistine kings (see on v. 1), so "Phicol" seems to have
been the standing title for the captain of the army.
The additional personage involved in this instance is
the king's friend "Ahuzzath" (on the Philistine ending
of the name cf. Goliath). The agreement to be entered
into is to be more than a private diplomatic arrangement. Isaac discerns the purpose of their coming

before they speak and points out a certain inconsistency
manifest in their attitude: first they drive him out,
then they follow after him to make a treaty of amity
and good will. Besides, his manner of stating the case
testifies to his innocence in the matter: "ye on your
part hate me." The emphatic personal pronoun (*'at-
tem*) indicates by an implied contrast that the ill will
is entirely on their side; he on his part never bore
them ill will, in fact, does not now. The Philistines had
deserved this rebuke. *Shillach* here is stronger than
"send away" (A. V.) ; they had actually "driven" him
away. In v. 29 the meaning "dismiss" is the one implied by the Philistines.

28, 29. **And they said: We plainly see that
Yahweh is with thee, so we said: Let, we pray,
an oath be between us — between us and you, and
let us make a covenant with thee, that thou wilt
do us no hurt, even as we have not touched thee,
and even as we have done only good to thee, and
have let thee go in peace — thee, now the blessed
of Yahweh.**

Through their whole speech this one idea shines
forth: we are impressed with Yahweh's blessings
which continually go with thee. The Philistines refer
to this at the beginning and at the close of their plea.
They do not think it safe to be on bad terms with
one who so manifestly stands in Yahweh's favor. That
the name "Yahweh" should be used by Philistines
need not surprise us. They naturally do not know
Him as the one who is what this name involves. They
simply take the heathen attitude: each nation serves
its own God; we have heard that Isaac serves Yahweh;
it must be Yahweh who has blessed His faithful follower. The "oath" (*'alah*) here is a "curse-oath," a
lower conception than is involved in *shebhû'ah*. Since,
indeed, the king and his captain may have been quite
innocent in the matter of the trouble over the wells,

they give the most favorable statement of their side
of the case and with a certain diplomatic glibness claim
for themselves that they always gave evidence of the
best of fair play. Isaac, the meek, will not broach a
fruitless argument on the subject and answers the
idle claim with a significant silence. The absolute infinitive (v. 28) *ra'ô* (G. K. 113 n) conveys some such
idea as "plainly." The jussive (*tehî*) is followed by
the cohortative *nikhrethah* (K. S. 364 g). *Ta'aseh* (v.
29) has *tsere* because it is not indicative (K. S. 183 c,
G. K. 75 hh).

**30, 31. And he made a feast for them and
they ate and drank. And they arose early in the
morning and gave the oath one to another, and
Isaac let them go, and they went from him in
peace.**

The customary thing in making covenants, apparently, was a covenant-feast in token of goodwill.
Isaac omits nothing that makes for a friendly relationship. The Philistines may be diplomats rather than
friends. The oaths are exchanged early the next
morning before departure. Here *shillach* is not meant
as "drove away" or "dismissed" — both of which
would conflict with Isaac's irenic treatment of his
potential allies; therefore, "let them go" (Meek). At
their departure the best of goodwill ("peace") prevails as a result of Isaac's discriminate handling of
the case. In the expression "one to another" *'ish*,
singular, does not strictly harmonize with the preceding plural verb but makes the two parties to the covenant individually more prominent (K. S. 348 w).

**32, 33. And it happened that day that
Isaac's servants came and told him concerning
the well that they had dug, and they said to him:
We have found water. And he called it Shibah
(oath); therefore the name of the city is Beersheba
unto this day.**

A coincidence, manifestly providential, marks that covenant day. After the departure of the noble guests Isaac's servants reported that the well on which they had been working had actually yielded water. Isaac regards this as a token of divine favor and gives a name to the well that is reminiscent of the oath of that date "Shibah." The difficulty about *shibh'ah* is that the word as such usually means "seven." Now it is true that there seems to be some deeper connection between the Hebrew roots "seven" and "swear." But here the matter is simplified if we give different vowel points to the consonants of the text, namely *shebhu'ah*, which is the regular word for "oath." Then all difficulty is removed. A slight difference, however, arises in connection with 21:31, where the meaning "well of seven" seems to prevail. But both points of view seem justified: there were originally "seven" wells; the place was the scene of an "oath." One account emphasizes the former; the other, the latter idea. For that matter, Isaac may well have remembered the name given to the place in Abraham's time and may have welcomed the opportunity for establishing that name. The expression "unto this day" simply carries us up to the writer's time and is, of course, very appropriate coming from the pen of Moses.

f) Esau's Hittite Wives (v. 34, 35)

34, 35. **When Esau was forty years old he married Judith, the daughter of Beeri, the Hittite, and Basemath, the daughter of Elon, the Hittite; and they were a grief of mind to Isaac and Rebekah.**

Esau's incapacity for spiritual values is further illustrated by this step. He is not concerned about conserving the spiritual heritage of the family. Wives, two of them, unfortunately, of the Hittite stock which gave evidence of Canaanite contamination, were married (Hebrew: "he took to wife"). *Yehûdhîth* is a

form that is quite possible without attempting to
derive it from Judah; it may come from the name of
the town *Jehûd* (Josh. 19:45) which lay in the confines
of the territory later inhabited by Dan.

35. "Grief of mind" (*morath rûach* = "bitterness of spirit") resulted from this marriage. The
corrupt heathenish way of these wives will have been
the source of this grief.

As to the location of the sites of Isaac's wells,
"Rehoboth" might well be *er-Rheibe,* some twenty
miles southwest of Beersheba. Robinson claimed to
have found a spot Wadi Shutain, or Schutnet, which
might be "Sitnah." Beersheba will, no doubt, be *Bir-
es-seba* in a wadi of the same name.

HOMILETICAL SUGGESTIONS

On v. 1-11 compare the remarks on chapter 12 that refer
to the similar event in the life of Abraham. For the remainder
of the chapter we see the several episodes as excellent illustra-
tions of certain Scriptures that furnish the dominant thought
for each episode. So v. 12-17 illustrates beautifully the truth:
"The blessing of the Lord, it maketh rich" (Prov. 10:22). The
section v. 18-25 furnishes a clear case of what is involved in the
word (Rom. 12:18) "as much as in you lieth, live peaceably with
all men." We prefer to include under this head v. 24, 25 because
they show the divine approval of the conduct of Isaac in this
instance. Then v. 26-33 may fall under the light of the word:
"When a man's ways please the Lord, He maketh even his
enemies to be at peace with him" (Prov. 16:7).

CHAPTER XXVII

3) Isaac Blesses Jacob (27:1-45)

This chapter offers one of the most singular instances of God's overruling providence controlling the affairs of sinful men and so disposing of them that the interests of God's kingdom be safeguarded. Usually the guilt of Jacob is overemphasized, and Esau is regarded as relatively or entirely the innocent party in the transaction. This traditional view requires modification and correction.

1-4. And it came to pass when Isaac was old and his eyes had grown dim so that he could not see, that he called Esau, his elder son, and said to him: My son; and he said to him: Here I am. And he said: See, now, I have become old and know not the day of my death. So now, take up thy weapons, thy quiver and thy bow, go out into the field and hunt some game for me, and prepare tasty things, as I love them, and bring them to me to eat, in order that my soul may bless thee before I die.

Luther's computations on the age of Isaac appear to be correct, when he sets his age at 137 years. For this figure compare the following passages: 47:9; 41:46; 31:38; 25:26. So it also appears that Jacob himself was about 77 years old. Ishmael, Isaac's half-brother, had lived to be only 137 years (25:17), having died fourteen years before this. It may have been this fact that led Isaac to surmise that his own end was near. Some particular sickness may besides have befallen him at this time. Yet it almost seems like a touch of helplessness, or at least a lack of aggressive-

ness, when he takes to bed more than forty years
before his death and actually makes preparations for
his end. In this account it is essential to the understanding of what follows to know that Isaac's eyes
had already grown so dim "that he could not see,"
mere'oth, involving a *min* with an infinitive, used as
an equivalent of a negative clause of result (G. K.
119 x; K. S. 406 n).

That the father actually calls *Esau* and makes
preparations to bestow the outstanding blessing upon
him, has always proved perplexing. This cannot have
been done because he had never heard the divine word
to Rebekah (25:23) ; for the relation between Isaac
and Rebekah was too intimate to allow for such a
supposition. Nor did Isaac fail to understand the
word aright: the word was too clear to allow for
misunderstanding. Nor could Isaac have forgotten
this notable word; it was too significant ever to forget
it. Nor was it rash and bold presumption on Isaac's
part or an attempt simply to fly in the face of God's
revealed will; it was not Isaac's nature to behave thus.
It seems psychologically most probable that Isaac
purposely forgot what God had determined; and at the
same time by clever little sophistries he led himself
to believe that if he bestowed the blessing on Esau,
the divine word uttered long before would not be
crossed. He that knows the duplicity and treachery
of the human heart will not find it difficult to understand how a man will circumvent a word of God, no
matter how clear it be, if his heart is really set on
what is at variance with that word.

2. Isaac gives his son to understand that the
matter to be attended to is suggested by the thought
that the father's days upon earth may be numbered.
If a particular sickness had befallen Isaac, it would
seem that that fact would have been mentioned. So
we seem to be left to the conclusion that the infirmity

of old age had seized upon the patriarch in a very
pronounced way.

3. In part Isaac's love for game prompts this
suggestion. Equally prominent is the fact that certain
important occasions call for a festive meal in order
to lend to them due solemnity and the spirit of festivity.
Telî (from *talah,* "to hang up") is the "quiver" and
arrows, not the "sword" (Targ.).

4. *Mat'ammîm,* from *ta'am,* "to taste," is any
thing that tastes good, "a delicacy," in the plural,
"tasty things," more than *ein Essen* (Luther). The
whole tenor of Isaac's words indicates that this preparation of "tasty things," chief among which was
the game taken by the hunter, was not a new thing.
Esau, knowing his father's love for game, had no
doubt shown this token of love many a time before
this and had noted what pleasure it afforded his father.
In this instance the momentous thing is that the father
purposes "to bless" his son. Esau well understood
what this involved. This was a custom, apparently
well established at this time, that godly men before
their end bestowed their parting blessing upon their
children. Such a blessing, had it been merely a pious
wish of a pious man, would have had its worth and
value. In it would have been concentrated the substance of all his prayers for his children. Any godly
son would already on this score alone have valued such
a blessing highly. However, the blessings of godly
men, especially of the patriarchs, had another valuable
element in them: they were prophetic in character.
Before his end many a patriarch was taught by God's
Spirit to speak words of great moment, that indicated
to a large extent the future destiny of the one blessed.
In other words, the elements of benediction and prediction blended in the final blessing. It appears from
the brief nature of Isaac's statement that this higher
character of the blessing was so well understood as to

require no explanation. From all this one sees that
the crude ideas of magic were far removed from these
blessings. The truth of our above claims is evinced
by the instances of such blessings recorded in Scriptures: 48:10 ff.; 50:24 f.; Deut. 33; Josh. 23; II Sam.
23:1 ff.; I Kings 2:1 ff.; II Kings 13:14 ff.

Perhaps it is true, as Keil claims, that Isaac
"wished to raise his spirits for imparting the blessing
by a dish of venison prepared according to his taste."
But more likely it is merely a case like so many others
in life, where a festive meal expresses the dignity and
importance of an occasion. We do not believe that it
was a sacrificial meal, as Luther and others surmise,
for as the later Mosaic Law did not allow for sacrifices
by the use of game, so the principle there involved will,
no doubt, have been understood at this earlier date
by the patriarchs. The expression "that my *soul* may
bless thee" does involve a bit more than the bare fact
that the word soul is used as a substitute for the personal pronoun. The expression actually indicates the
participation of one's inmost being in the activity
involved. But the soul does not "require strengthening
through meat and drink to be enabled to give a strong
blessing" (Procksch).

5-10. **But Rebekah on her part was listening
as Isaac spoke to Esau, his son. And Esau went into
the field to hunt game and to bring it. Now Rebekah
on her part spoke unto Jacob, her son, saying: Behold, I heard thy father speaking to Esau, thy
brother, and saying: Bring me game and prepare
for me tasty things, that I may eat and bless thee
before Yahweh before I die. Now, my son, give
heed to my voice exactly as I am now giving thee
orders. Go now to the flock and take from it for
me two good kids (of the goats) and I shall make
them up into tasty dishes for thy father as he loves**

**them.   Then thou shalt go to thy father and he shall
eat in order that he may bless thee before he die.**

The noun standing first becomes emphatic: "Rebekah on her part" — to mark a contrast with what
the others were doing.   The participle, durative,
(*shoma'ath*) indicates that she "was listening" all the
while that Isaac was speaking and so heard all.   Esau
at once gets under way into "the field" or open field,
not into the woods or the mountains.   Verse 5 a may
be regarded as a kind of parenthetical remark, for
attention has already begun to settle upon Rebekah.

6.   Here criticism gives an example of its strange
mode of procedure.   Procksch, yielding to the seeming
ingenuity of those who have separated the narrative
into portions from J and E, assigns v. 6-14 to E.   The
queer result of this comes to be the utterly unthinkable
situation freely admitted by Procksch, that then J's
account would have had no record of a conversation
between mother and son.   In other words, we are to
accept the possibility that J's account let Rebekah
act at once after hearing Isaac, and that Jacob was
automaton enough to carry out her wishes without a
question or an objection — an unthinkable situation!
The rest of the analysis of portions assigned to J and E
results in equally unbelievable absurdities if closely
examined — matters too trivial to discuss in detail.

Again the noun is placed first to show how
promptly "Rebekah on her part" acted.   "Her son"
(*benah*) here carries the particular connotation of:
the one whom *she* particularly loved.   The report of
what Isaac bade Esau do can be given very briefly,
because mother and son stand alike on the question
involved and thoroughly understand one another's
sentiments.

7.   This verse gives the kernel of the matter:
"that I may bless thee."   However, it contains an addi-

tion to the original in that it says: "before Yahweh."
One might dispose of the addition by saying that it
merely unfolds what Isaac naturally implied, namely
that he would give his blessing as before Yahweh, the
witness who would both enable him to give a true blessing and would also render the blessing efficacious.
But it is very doubtful if Isaac implied anything of
the sort, because with the sophistries he had employed
to persuade himself that he might with impunity bless
his favorite, he would hardly have God before his mind.
Apparently, by these words Rebekah reveals how *she*
regards the situation: this will be an act in which
covenant issues are involved, issues so momentous
that whether Isaac believes it or not, Yahweh will be
present to direct and control all, as He, Yahweh, does
always regulate all that bears upon the development
of the kingdom and the promises upon which the kingdom is built. Or as Hengstenberg (Whitelaw) puts
it: Rebekah regarded Isaac simply "as the instrument
of the living and personal God, who directed the affairs
of the chosen race." Of course, the phrase "before
Yahweh" does not have a purely local meaning, as
though a Yahweh image were present in the home.
It can be spiritual in its character as the "before me"
in 17:1 certainly is.

8. Rebekah's plan was apparently formulated
very quickly, for here it is complete in detail. She is
a woman of quick decision, as she was from the
moment of her first meeting with Abraham's servant
as well as on the occasion of her assent to the proposition to go back to Isaac at once. The Hebrew idiom
has: "listen to my voice" for our "listen to me."
Metsawweh points to the future, as the participle often
does: as I am now "going to give thee orders." We
have rendered *la'asher*, which literally = "according
as," by the more American: "exactly as."

9. The imperative "go" (*lekh*) is here made more urgent by *na'*. "The flock" is near at hand and time is precious. Esau may have good fortune in encountering game. The killing of the kids was a man's work. "Two kids" are chosen, because both together might make it possible to present on Isaac's platter bigger portions of meat such as might come from venison. "Kids of the goats" is an expression used in Hebrew to specify what with us is self-evident: kids are young goats. Rebekah must have had rare culinary gifts to presume to make a mess of kid's meat taste like game. Here the word "tasty dishes" is made to refer to the meat because the chief dish was without doubt to be the game.

10. Here the bold daring of Rebekah's plan stands forth in stark outlines: "thou shalt go in . . . that he may bless thee." One would hardly have thought such an undertaking possible. The strength of the plan lies in its daring.

11-13. And Jacob said unto Rebekah, his mother: Look here, Esau, my brother, is a hairy man, but I am a smooth-skinned man. Perhaps my father will feel of me, and I will count in his esteem as a mocker, and so I shall bring upon myself a curse instead of a blessing. But his mother said to him: Upon me let fall any curse intended for thee, my son. Only give heed to my voice, and go and get (them) for me.

Both seem agreed that since Yahweh has destined the pre-eminence to Jacob, the efforts they may make to secure what is rightfully Jacob's own are entirely in place. It must have been the case that there was a natural similarity between the voices of the twins. Anyone who has observed how pronounced such a similarity may be, will not think it strange that Jacob did not worry about this point. But another point of pronounced dissimilarity may be detected by the father.

The introductory *hen* is used like our "look here," not a formal "behold." Esau's hairiness was noted earlier (25:25). Jacob is *chalaq*, "smooth" or "smooth-skinned."

12. The possibility that Jacob suggests is by no means remote. The father may detect the difference in voice. Then after further test Jacob would surely be accounted "a mocker" (*metha'tea'*), one who was making sport of an old blind man, not a mocker in the sense of mocking at holy things; "deceiver" (A. V.) embodies an idea that does not really lie in the word. The upshot of that discovery would be a curse instead of a blessing. But the manner the father would in that case have employed to determine his son's identity would have been to "feel" of him, looking for the well-known characteristics of hairiness. *Yemush, shéni,* is to be derived from *mashash.*

Apparently, at this point Rebekah has not yet determined how to cope with this new difficulty; that problem seems to have been solved for her when she began the work of skinning the kids. For the present she is bold enough and so thoroughly convinced of the justice of the cause which she espouses as to be ready to assume any curse that may grow out of an eventual discovery. *Qillathekha,* "thy curse," involves a kind of eventual use of the possessive pronoun in the sense of "any curse intended for thee." Strack cites a parallel use in the expression "mine iniquity" Ps. 18:23, used in the sense of: "the iniquity into which I might have fallen." The boldness of Rebekah's reply appears reflected in its elliptical form: "Upon me thy curse." While she devises a solution of the difficulty, Jacob is to "give heed to her voice and go and get" for her. Her firm command gains in curtness when the verb "get" (*qach*) is used without an object. In English we have supplied a "them" (referring to the kids) in order to avoid unseemly harshness of expression.

**14-17.   And he went and got them and brought
them to his mother, and his mother made tasty things
as his father loved them.   And Rebekah took the
garments of Esau, her elder son, the choice ones,
which were with her in the house and she clad
Jacob, her younger son, in them.   And she put the
skins of the goats upon his hands and upon the
smooth part of the neck.   And she gave the tasty
things and the bread which she had made into the
hand of Jacob, her son.**

Jacob's chief difficulty was removed.   He had
been more afraid of detection than of duplicity.   His
mother, however, proved more resolute than he in
carrying through the plan.   Jacob provides the mate-
rials, Rebekah prepares them.   After more than ninety
years of married life she must have known pretty well
what "his father loved."

15.   Every eventuality has been considered: the
sense of sight is out of the question.   By the sense of
hearing Isaac may be brought to have misgivings.   The
sense of taste will be appealed to by cunningly devised
dishes.   The sense of smell will point definitely to Esau
if Jacob wears "the garments" of the elder, the
"choice" ones (*chamudhoth*, feminine to agree with
the feminine construction of the word *bégedh* which
is also found).   These are not by anything in the text
indicated to have been priestly garments, as the Jews
surmised.   They are simply the better ones that men,
especially men of means reserve for special occasions.
But these, too, had been worn by their owner roving
through the fields and woods and so had acquired an
attractive odor all their own, which the father may
have come to associate more and more with the
presence of Esau in the room, especially as the father's
eyes grew more and more dim.   Undue conclusions
should not be drawn from the fact that the mother
had these garments "with her in the house."   This

does not take us back in point of time to the days before
Esau had married but is quite adequately covered by
the assumption that Esau after his marriage still dwelt
in the same house with his parents. Criticism here
tries to prove the text guilty of incongruity. "House"
(*báyith*) points to the fact that a more substantial
dwelling may have been in use by the family just at
this time; yet, bearing in mind the avowed nomadic
character of life in patriarchal days, "house" may
simply be used in the sense of our "home," a use found
perhaps also in 33:17.

16. Now the difficulty arising from possible
detection by the father's sense of touch, Jacob's chief
difficulty (v. 11), is met. The skins, still very soft
and pliable and readily molded to any surface, and
besides of a much finer quality than the skins of young
goats as we know them, are applied to the hands and
the neck. *Yadh* will in this case cover more than the
mere "hand," for since garments were for the most
part sleeveless, the whole forearm might protrude
and is therefore enveloped in goatskin. All these
additional precautions might well have been disposed
of while the meat was roasting. No unseemly jokes
about the hairy Esau are attempted by this account,
rough like a goatskin (!).

17. The scene grows vividly dramatic as the
"tasty things" prepared are put into Jacob's hands
and he prepares to enter the father's room. "Bread"
is mentioned because the thin loaves were broken into
pieces, by the use of which meat and other viands
were conveniently taken in hand without soiling the
fingers, the thin bread being folded around the meat.

At this point criticism assumes too much by claiming that Gunkel has proved that the "garments" are
mentioned by J, the "goatskins" by E. Such contentions cannot be proved; they are subjective opinions
which are unconvincing but which seem to impress

the unlearned and the unwary because they are advanced by learned writers.

18-20.   And he came in to his father and he said: My father. And he said: Here am I. Who art thou, my son?   And Jacob said to his father: I am Esau, thy first-born. I have done as thou didst bid me.   Arise, now, take thy seat and eat, I pray, of my game in order that thy soul may bless me. And Isaac said to his son: How is it, then, that thou didst find so very quickly?   And he said: Yahweh, thy God, did bring it before me.

Perhaps a trace of suspicion may be detected in Isaac's first question: "Who art thou, my son?" He expects Esau; he seems to have heard Jacob's voice, though Jacob certainly will have been trying to imitate Esau's voice and mode of speech.

19. Jacob recognizes that hesitation or curt responses will arouse further suspicion and prove fatal to his enterprise, and so somewhat volubly he talks right on. He claims to be the first-born, to have carried out all instructions, and now he summons his father to "arise" from his bed and "take his seat" (*shebhah* — lengthened imperative — for *shebh* — "to sit down") and to eat. The double cohortative lends an urgency to his words, that make it appear that he is eager to receive the blessing. When Jacob calls the kid's meat "game," Whitelaw observes that this is the "third lie" in his words.

20. One surprising factor surely requires explanation: how did Esau find what he sought so very quickly? The boldness of Jacob's explanation certainly disposed of the question very effectively, but it is at the same time almost the most flagrant instance of abuse of the divine name recorded anywhere in the Scriptures. This is "lying and deceiving by God's name." By making the utterance doubly solemn, "Yahweh, thy God," the hypocritical pretense is made the more odious. Jacob's tricky device is decked out as an outstanding instance of divine providence: "Yahweh did bring it (*hiqrah* = cause to meet) before me." *Kî* merely introduces the direct discourse and is not to be translated.

21-23. And Isaac said to Jacob: Come near, please, and let me feel of thee, my son, whether thou indeed be Esau, my son, or not. And Jacob came near to Isaac, his father, and he felt of him and said: The voice is the voice of Jacob, but the hands are the hands of Esau. And he did not discover him, for his hands were like Esau, his brother's, hands, hairy — and so he blessed him.

But the father's doubt still persists. For the blind man the sense of touch must help to remedy the loss of sight. So Jacob is asked to step up that Isaac might feel of him. How correct had been Jacob's suspicion that he might be detected on this score. Luther, who entered quite successfully into the tenseness of this situation, said that had he been Jacob under scrutiny as here narrated, he would have dropped the dish and run away.

22. Though with trepidation, no doubt, Jacob steps up for closer examination. One sees the old father reach for his son with groping hand and feel of his hands and arms. Jacob will certainly have used all possible caution to prevent the father's hands from touching those parts where the kidskin was bound in place. The father's utterance reflects his perplexity: "The voice is the voice of Jacob," etc. The voice, by the way, is the only count on which misgivings arise.

23. Those who have not noticed the similarity of voice and manner of speech on the part of sons of one and the same family will think it strange that Isaac allowed the sense of touch and of smell to overrule the objections of the ear. But those who have

observed this similarity will not. Isaac may well have
recalled on how many occasions he had mistaken the
one for the other on the strength of this similarity in
speech. So "he did not discover him," — *nakhar,*
Hifil, implies "recognizing" or "discovering" on the
basis of a close scrutiny. The sum of Isaac's conclusion then is: "his hands were like Esau, his brother's
hands, hairy." That is to say: the voice has its variations and modulations, and so Esau may sometimes
sound like Jacob, but, surely, a man cannot change
his skin from rough to smooth or vice versa. When
now the conclusion of the verse says, "and so he blessed
him," this is simply one more of the many instances
where, according to the Hebrew style of narrative, the
result is reported first and the details are given afterwards. At this point Isaac's mind is practically made
up to proceed and to bless this one. For a moment the
critics, who claim to have at this point clear evidence
of the weaving together of two separate accounts,
seem to occupy a strong position when they claim that
according to E the blessing is bestowed at this point,
whereas according to J another question follows, then
the eating and the drinking, then the kiss, finally the
blessing. However, all these artificial constructions
discredit Scripture, in this case by letting the final
account as we have it contain a confused version of
events and so be unsatisfactory and devoid of even
the simple merit of clearness and correctness. Besides,
here again as practically always the critics diverge
quite radically from one another in their analysis of
the original sources. The account as it reads then
means: at this point Isaac addressed himself to the
task of blessing his son. But when v. 24 again records
a question of doubt from Isaac's lips, we are introduced
to a situation we can readily understand. In spite of
the resolution to go on with the blessing Isaac is

assailed by new misgivings. So, then, Isaac's *vacillation* is effectively brought to our notice by this style of the narrative.

24-27 a. And he said: Art thou really my son Esau? and he said: I am. And he said: Bring it near to me that I may eat of the game, my son, in order that my soul may bless thee. So he brought it to him and he ate, and he brought him wine and he drank. And Isaac, his father, said to him: Come here, now, and kiss me, my son. And he came near and kissed him, and he smelled the smell of his garments and he blessed him, saying:

We have just shown how the first question indicates new misgivings on Isaac's and a new lie on Jacob's part. But Jacob's answer is so positive, and, surely, Isaac was accustomed to truthfulness on the part of his sons. Jacob's persistence in his wrong course is to be accounted for, first, by the fact that he firmly believed in the justice of his cause, and then, secondly, by the fact that his mother so staunchly supported him in the enterprise. There may have been on the part of both of these an erroneous conception of the validity of a wrong blessing. For just as the curse causeless falls to the ground (Prov. 26:2), so the blessing granted in disobedience would have been futile.

25. The ending *ah* on the imperative and the imperfect make the hortative form help to express how Isaac is strengthening himself in his resolution to go through with the undertaking. When Isaac is said to have drunk wine at this point, the critics in a number of instances are greatly perturbed. They had not known that the patriarchs drank wine at this early date, consequently the text must be in error. Certainly a *non sequitur.*

26. The kiss appears here for the first time as the token of true love and deep affection. Isaac asks

for this token from his son. The treachery of the act
cannot be condoned on Jacob's part on any score: the
token of the true love is debased to a means of deception. The Old Testament parallel (II Sam. 20:9) as
well as that of the New Testament (Matt. 26:49 and
parallels) comes to one's mind involuntarily. The
emphatic imperatives with *ah* ("do come here and do
kiss me") show how strongly Isaac enters heart and
soul into his task. "My son" here implies: "my
favorite."

27 a.   Here Rebekah's clever foresight is further
vindicated as having coped with the situation. The
smell of Esau's garments recalls vividly to the father
the daily pursuits of his son and gives the immediate
ground for the blessing to be uttered. This smell
seems to have kindled Isaac's imagination.

> **27 b-29.   Behold, the smell of my son is as the
>   smell of a field which Yahweh has blessed,
> May the true God give thee of the dew of
>   heaven and of the fertile places of the
>   earth, and much of grain and wine.
> Let peoples serve thee, and nations bow down
>   to thee.
> Be master over thy brethren, and may thy
>   mother's son bow down to thee.
> Cursed be they that curse thee, and blessed be
>   they that bless thee.**

Isaac's blessing is poetic, being in an exalted
strain of noble feeling. On the formal side this poetic
character is marked by parallelism and the use of
poetic words like *re'eh* for *hinneh* and *hawah* for
hayah.

Starting with a reminiscence of the odoriferous
herbs whose smell clings to Esau's garments, Isaac
rightly interprets this smell as a token of things blessed
by Yahweh. The sweet smell of the fields is, in reality,

a reminder of the good Lord who displays His goodness
by many an attractive grace. Since, then, God's grace
is under consideration, He is rightly spoken of as
"Yahweh," at least at first. Besides, the use of this
name suggests that Isaac may originally have intended
to bestow upon Esau the full covenant blessing. But
the change to *ha'elohîm* (v. 28), "the true God," seems
to indicate that the patriarch's purpose wavered in the
midst of the blessing, and so he bestowed little more
than a material blessing. Of course, the expression
ha'elohîm would more naturally cover the case of blessings like dew and fertile soil. These two would result
in the total of good crops. For the heavy Palestinian
dews almost make up for the lack of rain during the
dry season. Such "dew of heaven" is heaven's gift;
whereas *shemannîm* are not merely "fat things" but
fat "fertile places." "Dew" and "fertile places" as
a cause should yield the result of "grain" and "new
wine," the essentials of food and of drink. So much
for the blessings relative to daily bread.

29. Now for the political blessings that involve
relations to others and the question of rule and superiority. "Peoples" and "nations" can hardly be distinguished as to their relative import. To have such
"serve" and "bow down" to one implies a position of
rule and authority, not the position of a servile nation.
In particular, the relation to the brother now comes
under consideration. When Isaac says: "be master
over thy brethren" he means to let Esau's descendants
dominate Jacob's; and so he was by these words trying
to annul and invalidate God's original verdict in
reference to the relationship of these children (25:23).
Certainly, then, from this point of view the word was
bold and presumptuous, even a defiance of the Almighty. "Brethren" and "sons," used in the plural,
do not involve an incongruity. The father is looking
forward to those who shall yet spring from both. In

reference to Jacob they will be "brethren" in so far as they are descended from Esau. In reference to Rebekah all Esau's descendants are "sons." The closing line is an echo of 12:3 a, not of 3 b. This is very significant. In 12:3 b is found the essence of the Messianic element in Abraham's blessing. This Isaac does not dare to bestow upon his favorite. That is too sacred an element to be tampered with. In 28:4 he finally bestows it upon Jacob intentionally. Still the blessing: "Cursed be they that curse thee, and blessed be they that bless thee" is a very substantial one. It fends off harm and bestows tokens of goodwill. The unusual sequence of plural and singular conveys a shade of meaning about as follows: "Thy cursers, may each one of them be cursed; thy blessers, may each one of them be blessed," (K. S. 348 t to ᵃ).

On the whole, who would not covet such a blessing? Bestowed by a godly father upon a godly and a deserving son in accordance with the will and purpose of God, it surely would constitute a precious heritage.

30, 31. And it came to pass when Isaac had finished blessing Jacob and Jacob had yet just about gone out from the presence of Isaac, his father, that Esau, his brother, came in from the field. And he too prepared some tasty things and came in to his father, and said to his father: May my father arise and may he eat of the game of his son in order that thy soul may bless me.

The *'akh* ("yet" or "only") marks how very nearly Jacob was detected. He had just about closed the door, divested himself of the borrowed garments and the kidskin disguise, when his brother appears on the scene.

31. Quite unsuspecting he prepares what he has caught and in due course of time steps into his father's presence, using practically the same words Jacob had used. For one thing, that shows at least how carefully

Jacob had planned his deception; he knew about what Esau would say when stepping into his father's presence. The jussives *yaqûm* and *yo'khal* are, it would seem, a bit more "deferential" ("may he rise and may he eat") than Jacob's imperative ("arise, take thy seat and eat"). But then Jacob acted under greater strain, which may, indeed, have been reflected in an attempt at bolder utterance. From all this no conclusion may legitimately be drawn as to which of the sons actually reverenced his father the more. In all likelihood it was Jacob.

32-35. And Isaac his father said unto him: Who art thou? And he said: I am thy son, thy first-born, Esau. And Isaac trembled most excessively and said: Who, then, is he who caught game, and brought it to me, and I ate of it all before thou camest in, and I have blessed him? Yea, blessed shall he be. When Esau heard the words of his father Isaac, he gave vent to an exceedingly loud and bitter outcry and said to his father: Bless me, me too, my father! And he said: Thy brother entered in treacherously and took thy blessing.

One can hear with what startled emphasis the cry breaks from Isaac's lips, *mî 'attah*, "who thou?" So, too, one can feel the surprise expressed in the tone of Esau's answer, as much as to say: "Why should you be surprised that I am come with my tasty things, seeing you made me prepare them for the blessing?"

33. What Esau witnessed immediately after he had given his answer was enough to startle any man. The Hebrew employs three devices to convey the desired emphasis, piling one upon the other: the cognate object, the modifying adjective, the adverbial phrase, "He trembled a trembling, a great, unto excess." Our rendering: "he trembled most excessively" is still too weak. What a pitiful sight to see the venerable patriarch under the stress of so violent an emotion.

It is almost unbelievable that one brother should thus have impersonated the other to secure the blessing designed for the other and that he should have done it so successfully. The pained perplexity stands out in the father's question: "Who, then, is he who caught game," etc.? But by the time the question has been formulated the problem has been solved. The vague "who is he?" has narrowed down to the one and only possibility that could be involved in this case. Isaac knows it was Jacob. Isaac sees how God's providence checked him in his unwise and wicked enterprise. From this point onward there is no longer any unclearness as to what God wanted in reference to the two sons. Therefore the brief but conclusive, "yea, blessed shall he be." But his trembling was caused by seeing the hand of God in what had transpired.

34. Esau's conduct in the case does not impress us favorably. His unmanly tears are quite unworthy of him. His "exceedingly loud and bitter outcry" is further evidence of lack of self-control. He who never aspired after higher things now wants this blessing as though his future hopes depended all and only on the paternal blessing. We cannot help but feel that a superstitious overvaluation of the blessing is involved. In fact, he now wants, as though it were his own, that which he had wilfully resigned under oath. The right to the blessing which Esau now desires was lost long ago. In fact, up to this point there was a double conspiracy afoot. Isaac and Esau, though not admitting that it was so, were conspiring to deflect to Esau a blessing both knew he had forfeited, in fact, was never destined to have. But at the same time Rebekah and Jacob were consciously conspiring to obtain what God had destined for Jacob and what Jacob had also secured from Esau. The pronoun in the nominative (*gam 'anî*) stands in apposition with the objective (G. K. 135 e).

35. The father refused to be moved. He admits Jacob's treachery (*mirmah*, primarily "deceit"), but he knows the case cannot be altered. Esau "found no place for repentance" (Heb. 12:17) in the sense of the more correct rendering: "he found no place for a change of mind (in his father)" (A. R. V.). Perhaps Isaac too now saw for the first time that in reality Esau did not stand on the level of the ideals of the patriarchs. Isaac's refusal to alter the blessing is not to be explained by calling upon the idea of something like a fetish character of the blessing. The true patriarchal religion was not encumbered by such trash. Nor are we to claim that the blessing "works in purely objective fashion and cannot be retracted, and so we have here a fate-tragedy of antiquity" (Procksch). The true patriarchal religion nowhere gives indications of a belief in fate.

36-38. And he said: Is he not rightly called Jacob, for he has twice overreached me: my birthright he took and, lo, now he has also gotten my blessing. And he said: Hast thou not laid a blessing aside for me? Isaac answered and said to Esau: Behold, I have made him thy master and all his brethren I have made his servants; with grain and wine have I supplied him, and as for thee, what shall I now do for thee, my son? And Esau said unto his father: Hast thou only one blessing, my father? Bless me, me too, my father! And he lifted up his voice and wept.

The thought expressed with so much bitterness by Esau becomes entirely clear when we remember that "Jacob" practically means "Overreacher" — he is rightly called "Overreacher" because he has twice "overreached" me. A strange but emphatic paronomasia is also involved in the second part of his bitter outbreak: first he took my *bekhorah* (birthright), now he takes my *berakhah* (blessing). Though there is

truth in what Esau says, he does not do well to play
the part of injured innocence. His birthright he sold
right cheerfully, and was far more at fault in the
selling of it than Jacob in the buying. The blessing,
on the other hand, had been destined for Jacob by God
long ago, and Esau knew it. The verb *'atsálta* very
distinctly means "lay aside" and so "reserve" (A. V.).

37. A blessing in the sense in which Esau wants
it cannot be bestowed, for that would require the
cancellation of the blessing just bestowed. Jacob's
blessing Isaac cannot revoke because he clearly sees
that God so disposed of events that Isaac finally did
what God had originally appointed. This startling
instance of God's overruling providence fills Isaac's
thoughts completely. He is not like a man who has
run out of ammunition and so has nothing more to
say. This is not the spirit of his answer but rather
the thought: we cannot alter Jacob's blessing for it
has God's sanction: "I have made him your master
and all his brethren I have made his servants."
Material wants have also been provided for. Really,
what is there left for Esau? *Daghan* and *tîrôsh* are
adverbial accusatives, *"with* grain and wine" (G. K.
117 ff).

38. Poor Esau's grief is pathetic, a startling case
of seeking a good thing too late. The blessing of the
father seems to be the one thing of the whole spiritual
heritage that has impressed Esau. Unfortunately, it
is not the chief thing.

39, 40. **And Isaac, his father, answered and
said unto him:**

> **Behold, away from the fertile places of the
> earth shall thy dwelling be
> And away from the dew of heaven from above.
> By the sword shalt thou live
> And thy brother thou shalt serve.**

**And it shall come to pass when thou shalt shake
    thyself
Thou shalt tear off the yoke from the neck.**

At this point prophetic utterance came upon Isaac
and he foretold what the distinctive lot and fortunes
of his son Esau would be. It is not said that he blessed
him, for this is not a blessing but a prophecy. Nor
could it rightly be called a curse. But the inferior
lot of Esau is made very apparent by this word. Misunderstanding has arisen from the fact that in point
of form both blessings use the preposition "from"
(*min*), especially in the two phrases "from the dew"
and "from the fertile places."   If the *min* of source
(B D B p. 579 b) be assumed for both cases (so Luther
and A. V.), then we are confronted by the impossible
situation that, whereas Isaac had insisted that Jacob's
blessing must stand, distinct from what Esau may
attain to, in the end Isaac reverses his decision and
gives Esau a blessing almost as good as Jacob's, and
so Esau would have lost little, only the pre-eminence.
Consequently, modern commentators, positive and
negative, are practically unanimous in construing the
preposition in the case that applies to Esau as a *"min
separative"* (B D B p. 578 a) : *"away from* the fertile
places . . . *away from* the dew." With this interpretation agrees the predominant impression conveyed
by the land of Edom.   In spite of fertile spots it is
mostly very bleak, rocky and barren, allowing scant
opportunities of cultivation, especially the western
part, of which travelers have claimed that they have
seen no region to equal it for barrenness.

40.   To "live by the sword" (this use of *'al* in
Deut. 8:3) implies violence and continual conflict. But
yet for all that he is to be in continual subjection to
his brother. Attempts at liberation from this yoke
shall be many.   In fact, whenever he "shall shake

himself," then will he succeed in "tearing off the yoke
from the neck," but he could not keep shaking himself
forever.   These words describe attempted freedom
rather than achieved freedom. So from David's time
onward Edom was kept subject to Israel. Though
rebelling frequently, they were always being sub-
jugated again, until finally John Hyrcanus (126 B. C.)
completely subdued them and compelled them to accept
circumcision.   The rather common interpretation of
this statement, that it implied that ultimately Edom
would "have dominion" (A. V., also Luther) is based
upon a misunderstanding of the verb *rûdh*.   In any
case, the rule of Herod the Edomite over Israel can
hardly be called the dominion of Edom, the nation,
over Israel, for Edom had ceased to be a nation by
this time, and, in any case, Herod's rule did not involve
Edom's rule. Herod ruled alone as an individual. However, the meaning of *rûdh*, "to shake," or "to shake thyself," or, as Keil puts it, "to shake, namely the yoke,"
is pretty well established. So this becomes the one
part of Isaac's word in which some success is promised
to Esau. His people shall at least occasionally be rid
of Israel's yoke. In so far, then, this statement involved an interruption in Jacob's blessing. For Jacob's
wrong in deceiving his father the blessing bestowed
was to be curtailed in part.

After all this examination of what Isaac did the
verdict of Heb. 11:20 may still seem a bit strange:
"By faith Isaac blessed Jacob and Esau, even concerning things to come."   But this word will be felt
to be entirely true if we but bear in mind that the
erring saint had been corrected by God in the midst
of his attempt to transfer the blessing. He had
accepted the correction and repented, and so in the
end what he did was an act of faith after all. Both
words told "concerning things to come" and were
spoken in faith and in the strength of God's Spirit.

The ethics of the case should be scrutinized a bit more closely. That Jacob was in part at fault has not been denied. That Esau was far more at fault has been pointed out. This contrast is usually overlooked. Jacob is criticized quite roundly, and the greater sinner, Esau, is pitied and represented as quite within his rights. That the whole is a most regrettable domestic tangle cannot be denied, and, as is usually the case in such tangles, every member involved bore his share of the guilt. But if it be overlooked that Jacob's aspirations were high and good and in every sense commendable and besides based on a sure promise of God, a distorted view of the case must result.

They that insist on distorting the incident claim that the account practically indicates that Jacob was rewarded with a blessing for his treachery. The following facts should be held over against such a claim to show how just retribution is visited upon Jacob for his treachery: 1. Rebekah and Jacob apparently never saw one another again after the separation that grew out of this deceit — an experience painful for both; 2. Jacob, deceiver of his father, was more cruelly deceived by his own sons in the case of the sale of Joseph and the torn coat of many colors; 3. from having been a man of means and influence Jacob is demoted to a position of hard rigorous service for twenty years.

41. **And Esau harbored enmity against Jacob because of the blessing wherewith his father had blessed him, and Esau said in his heart: The days of mourning for my father are not far off; then will I kill my brother Jacob.**

Good-natured, easy-going Esau is changed in his attitude toward Jacob. Bitter enmity takes up residence in his heart. All his thinking still seems to center about the lost blessing. This confirms our inter-

pretation of v. 39, 40, because if Esau had construed these words as a substantial blessing, he could
hardly have cherished animosity. But one thing restrains Esau: he does not want to cause his aged
father further grief. He does, however, believe that
his father will not live long. This is the meaning
of the word: "the days of mourning for my father
are not far off." He expects to wait till his father
is dead; then will he kill Jacob. Esau does not
mean: I will kill my brother, and in that sense
days when my father must mourn are coming upon
him. But it is strange that he who so readily parted
with the birthright now so firmly resolves to commit murder, even fratricide. *'Ebhel 'abhî* is "mourning for my father" not "of my father" — therefore
objective genitive like Amos 8:10; Jer. 6:26. The
expression "said in his heart" means "to himself"
or "in his own circle," because v. 42 Rebekah hears
the report of it.

**42-45. And the words of Esau, her elder son,
were told to Rebekah, and she sent and called Jacob,
her younger son, and said unto him: See, Esau, thy
brother, is about to take vengeance upon thee by
killing thee. Now, my son, give heed to my instruction: up, flee thou to Laban, my brother, to Haran,
and live with him for a while until the fury of thy
brother turn away, until thy brother's anger turn
away from thee and he forget that which thou hast
done to him. Then will I send and get thee from
thence. Why should I be bereft of both of you in
one day?**

Esau's intention somehow comes to the ear of
one who is friendly disposed toward Rebekah, perhaps
one of the feminine members of the establishment.
With her customary alacrity of decision Rebekah acts
and calls Jacob in order to dismiss him at once. The
participle *mithnach(ch)em* from *nacham*, "to com-

fort," could be rendered "comforteth himself" (A. V.)
or "eases himself" (B D B) but very likely the comfort that one of Esau's mind administers to himself
is vengeance. The participle then expresses the durative "is planning vengeance" or "is about to take
vengeance." Then the infinitive must be rendered
"by killing thee" — a kind of gerundive use.

43. Rebekah's attempt to make her warnings
emphatic show how sure she is of the need of immediate action: "now, my son, give heed to my instruction." Flight to Laban to Haran offers sure asylum.

44. Her desires color her thoughts. She hopes
it may be only "for awhile," *yamîm 'achadhîm* — "a
few days." Men of Esau's disposition often let their
native good-naturedness dissipate their "fury" (*cha-
mah* — from *yacham* = "burning" "hot anger").

45. The repetition of the thought — "until thy
brother's anger turn away from thee" — shows how
eagerly her thoughts hope that this may come to pass.
This parting must have been hard for both. So
Rebekah tries to make herself believe that it will be
but for a short time and Esau will "forget that which
thou hast done to him." Her thoughts run to what
she regards as perhaps an early prospect: "I will
send and get thee from thence." When Rebekah
expresses the thought of the possibility of being "bereft of both her sons in one day," she means "at one
time." Of course, she refers to the possibility of
Esau's slaying Jacob. Then at once someone would
take it upon himself to play the part of the "avenger
of blood" and so slay Esau, perhaps very shortly
thereafter.

4) Jacob's Dismissal from Home and His First Vision (27:46-28:22)

The Jewish custom of choosing a more or less
weighty utterance to be the initial word of a new chapter led to the addition of v. 46 to chapter 27, in order

that 28:1 might make a seemly beginning. Yet, without a doubt, v. 46 has to do with the matter of Jacob's dismissal from home. K. C. penetrates a bit more deeply into the essence of the situation when he gives as a title for this section, "The Beginning of the Exile and of the Training (*Erziehung*) of Jacob." But the second half of this title is defective, for Jacob's "training" did not begin at this point, though at this point it becomes more intensive.

For once let an analysis of the critical contentions be made on the section 27:46-28:9, which is with great unanimity ascribed to P.

The argument seems quite imposing when we are told that the following terms, which are said to be characteristic of P, are found in the passage: *'el Shadday* ("God Almighty") v. 3, *'elohîm* ("God") v. 4; *ha'arammî* ("the Aramaean, or the Syrian") v. 5; *paddan 'aram* v. 2, 5, 6, 7; *'érets meghurîm* ("land of sojournings") v. 4; *benôth kena'an* ("daughters of Canaan") v. 1, 6, 8; *qehal 'ammîm* ("company of peoples") v. 3. But note how very flimsy all this becomes on closer investigation.

Take *'el Shadday*. This term does occur besides in 17:1; 35:11; 48:3; Exod. 6:3. But in 17:1 "God Almighty" appears to Abraham and assures him of His strength to carry out His promise. This is not a stylistic peculiarity; this is a designation *God* employed to describe Himself. Similar is the situation in 35:11 where Jacob is addressed, where God's comfort will mean so much more to Jacob if it is couched in terms long familiar from Abraham's time. Why then in 48:3, where Jacob blesses Joseph's sons, should he not use the very terms God used for Him? And most particularly Exod. 3, where God reappears after a long interval to Moses, why should He not employ names familiar from patriarchal times to describe Himself? This use of a specific divine name here is not a peculiarity of style on the part of one author. This name most appropriately grows out of a given situation. It is used also Gen. 43:14, which some critics assign to a priestly redactor and not to P. There, surely, is little convincing proof in the use of this term.

On the use of *'Elohîm* (v. 4) little can here be said; we shall dwell on the propriety of the term later in this connection.

The word *ha'arammî* ("the Syrian") v. 5 is supposed to belong to the vocabulary of P. It appears twice in 25:20. But why not in a formal beginning of a new section as 25:19 ff. use fuller titles, "Bethuel, the Syrian," "Laban, the Syrian"? Aside from our passage, 28:5, appear the two instances of its use 31:20 and 24, which, however, Strack ascribes to E. Surely, nothing like proof for a peculiarity of style has been offered.

Paddan 'aram is next. True, it appears in 48:7; 25:20; 28:2, 5-7; 31:18; 33:18; 35:9, 26; 46:15. This point is supposed to build up on the divergent use found in J, who in 24:10 used for Syria the name *Aram Naharaim*. Note the invalidity of trying to prove J's style by a *single* instance. We know too little about the use of these names to build arguments on them. But the inconclusive methods employed to make the argument appear impressive come to light when we notice that in 31:18 and 33:18 critics label just this *one* verse in a supposedly different source as belonging to P merely on the strength of the appearance in it of the word "Paddan Aram." After it is first consigned to a supposed P, it is quoted as a P passage to prove that P uses the word — a perfect argument in a circle. The same use is made of 25:20, where v. 19 and 20 are alone ascribed to P. Since now the likelihood is that "Paddan Aram" was the usual designation of the country, what else could

P say? This is not a peculiarity of style on his part.

Now *'érets meghurîm,* used 17:8; 28:4; 36:7; 37:1. First of all, the nature of God's remarks requires that it be emphasized both in the case of Abraham (17:8) and of Jacob (28:4) that for the present they are dwelling in a "land of sojournings." Two passages of such a character do not suffice as evidence to build up a peculiarity of style. Critics admit that they are not sure to which source 36:7 is to be ascribed. But on the strength of the first two passages cited above they claim 37:1 for P, ascribing, however, only v. 1 and 2 to P. If this is to be called "proof," we do not know what the word "proof" means.

The case of the critics keeps growing flimsier. The use of the term *benôth kena'an* ("daughters of Canaan") borders on unmeaning proof. In the passage we are studying the expression occurs three times, in v. 1, 6, 8. Of these three v. 6 quotes v. 1 and v. 8 is a direct reference to the two preceding. Then, as far as peculiarities of style are concerned, there is really only *one* passage before us in chapter 28. Now the only other instance of the use of the expression is 36:2, whose authorship is doubtful (Strack). What now? On the strength of *one* passage, then, this expression is said to be a part of the vocabulary of P. Could any procedure be more unscientific?

The case of *qehal 'ammîm* is about as flimsy. The only instances of its use are 28:3 and 48:4. Can that suffice as an argument for assigning both passages to P, or even for claiming the expression as peculiarly P's? So shallow are the critical contentions.

46. And Rebekah said to Isaac: I am disgusted with life because of the daughters of Heth. If Jacob is going to take a wife of the daughters

of Heth like these, of the daughters of the land, what's the use of living?

First of all this verse throws a side light on 26:34, indicating how great the bitterness of heart caused to Esau's parents by the unbelieving, ungodly Hittite wives really was. *Qâtstî* = "I abhor," "I am disgusted with." However, Rebekah's complaint is preparatory to having Jacob sent away before Esau does him harm. What Rebekah says is true: her vexation over these daughters-in-law is excessive, but Rebekah uses this situation as an indirect argument to move Isaac to send Jacob to Mesopotamia. Should Esau, then, hear what Isaac had done, respect for his father would certainly check him from laying hands upon his brother, who would merely have done what his father had bidden him do. The verse thus furnishes a good illustration of the methods employed, perhaps more or less commonly, on Rebekah's part in dealing with Isaac. Sending Jacob to Mesopotamia to get a wife was a splendid idea. Inducing Isaac to take steps in that direction by her complaints about Esau's wives was not the most frank procedure in achieving her purpose, but it secured the desired result.

HOMILETICAL SUGGESTIONS

This chapter, at least the major part of it, is so much a unit (v. 1-40) that it would not do to take portions of it; for these would be but fragment texts. Yet, without a doubt, forty verses are too long a text. Too many elements in it cannot receive adequate treatment. Yet, if one should determine to use it, he should primarily emphasize the inadequacy of a faith that builds on human ingenuity. It would still seem that the text as a whole is sufficiently well known through Sunday school instruction so as not to require specific homiletic treatment. The remaining portion of the chapter, v. 41-45, furnishes an illustration of the bitter fruit of duplicity. Yet, if it were desired as a text, it might justly be questioned whether it does not rather tend toward a so-called morality-sermon rather than to broader and bigger themes of the Scriptures.

CHAPTER XXVIII

1, 2. And Isaac called Jacob and blessed him; and he laid commandment upon him and said to him: Not shalt thou take a wife from the daughters of Canaan. Up, go to Paddan-aram, to the home of Bethuel, thy mother's father, and take a wife to thyself from the daughters of Laban, thy mother's brother.

We cannot help but feel that, had Rebekah told Isaac of Esau's murderous plans, Isaac would, or at least could, have taken a hand in restraining Esau. For reasons best known to herself Rebekah does nothing of the sort. Her words of 27:46 have the desired result. She had agreed (27:13) that any eventual curse resulting in the case of miscarriage of her plans might light upon her. For the same reason she feels the responsibility for keeping Jacob safe from Esau's wrath. Jacob is called, though, indeed, Isaac should have taken care of the matter of Jacob's marriage without solicitation by his wife. The expression "and blessed him" is here used in the summary way common in Hebrew narrative, giving the entire story beforehand, then following with the details: cf. 21:27; 24:29 b; 27:33 b. Why a separate act of blessing really is yet necessary after the formal blessing of the preceding chapter, will appear when we examine v. 4. Of the words that Isaac speaks, v. 1 b and v. 2 may be regarded as a preliminary condition that ought to be met by the recipient of the weighty blessing of v. 3 and 4. However, the matter of avoiding one kind of wife and choosing another is not merely suggested as helpful counsel. The full patriarchal authority is employed: "and he laid commandment upon him." On this question Isaac felt as Abraham had. There is even the possibility that Isaac may have learned of the part Rebekah played in the preceding chapter. Yet he felt that a woman of Rebekah's type, in spite of what minor failings she may have displayed here or there, was infinitely superior by reason of her faith.

2. Isaac does not delegate some old reliable servant to go to secure a wife for Jacob, as had been done in his own case, possibly because he recognized Jacob's capacity to handle the situation himself. The two imperatives, "up" (*qûm*) and "go" (*lekh*), impart an urgent tone to the command. Here is a commandment that is to be carried out now, not a suggestion to be acted upon ultimately. "Paddan-aram" may signify "field of Aram" as many, on the strength of Hos. 12:12, conjecture. The only ones Isaac knows of that have spiritual ideals sufficiently akin to those of the chosen race are the relatives in Mesopotamia. He may have felt that there would be opportunity for Jacob to secure a wife from this group because they on their part might till now have been reluctant too about marrying off their daughters to men given to idolatry. Here was not, as some suppose, merely a case of trivial conceit where men were intent upon preserving the strain of blood pure.

3, 4. And may El Shaddai (God Almighty) bless thee and make thee fruitful and multiply thee and mayest thou become a company of peoples; and may He give to thee the blessing of Abraham, to thee and to thy descendants with thee, that thou mayest possess the land of thy sojourning, which God gave to Abraham.

In giving "the blessing of Abraham" how natural to revert to the language the Almighty Himself had used on that occasion; note the resemblance with 17:1, 2. In point of fact, how appropriate is here the name

"God Almighty." Blessings certainly depend upon
the Almighty's power to render them effectual. How
much in place is the wish, "make thee fruitful and
multiply thee," now at a time when the father of
the chosen group is still but *one*. So Isaac would
naturally speak. How trivial to say: so P naturally
writes. The idea "company of peoples (*qehal
'ammîm*) in a connection where strength of numbers
alone is under consideration could hardly involve the
Messianic thought of the spiritual subjugation of
many nations. The Messianic thought finds expression
in v. 4. Nor is this a blessing that went wide of the
mark, failing of fulfillment. Apparently, the separate
tribes that came from Jacob are to be understood here,
each being viewed poetically as the equivalent of a
"people" (*'am*). This involves a figure of speech but
does not yet, as K. W. contends, establish the meaning
of "tribe" for *'am*. Consequently, we do not here find
an expansion of the blessing of Abraham.

4. In fact, the identity of this blessing with the
one given to Abraham is established by the words,
"may He give thee the blessing of Abraham." By
these words Isaac conveys the most important part of
the patriarchal blessing, the part relative to the Messiah, which he had not quite ventured to bestow previously when he still thought that he was dealing with
Esau. Sobered by the failure of his attempt and
made wiser, he freely gives what he fully understands to have been divinely destined for Jacob. "The
blessing of Abraham" is fully as much as was promised
to him but no more. Since previously (27:27-29)
Isaac also had not ventured to bestow the land of
promise on the one who presumably was Esau, now
he unmistakably bestows it on Jacob, that which is
now a "land of sojourning" where the patriarchs have
as yet no permanent possession except a burial place.
Lerishtekha, "for thy possessing," has a *subject*

suffix (G. K. 69 m). God "gave" this land to Abraham, of course, only by promise but none the less actually.

5. So Isaac sent Jacob away; and he went to Paddan-Aram to Laban, the son of Bethuel the Aramaean (Syrian), the brother of Rebekah, the mother of Jacob and Esau.

In rather a formal fashion the author reports how Jacob obeyed the paternal injunction. The formality consists in repeating the name of the place to which, as well as that of the person to whom he went. The identity of this person is also established in a formal manner — his nationality and his relation to Jacob's mother also being appended. This formality is the Hebrew way of emphasizing the importance of an event. For, certainly, very much hinged on this momentous journey, and very important issues depended on it.

6-9. When Esau saw that Isaac had blessed Jacob and had sent him away to Paddan-Aram to get a wife there for himself, and that as he blessed him he also commanded him, saying: Not shall thou take a wife from the daughters of Canaan; and that Jacob hearkened unto his father and unto his mother and went to Paddan-Aram; and when Esau further saw that the daughters of Canaan pleased not Isaac, his father, then Esau went to Ishmael and took to wife Mahalath, the daughter of Ishmael the son of Abraham, and the sister of Nebaioth in addition to the wives that he had.

Hardly with a touch of irony and yet as an indication of Esau's obtuseness in the more spiritual issues, the author now reports how Esau felt impelled to take a non-Canaanite wife. Esau observes, first of all, that Jacob is sent away for a wife. Besides, Esau either himself hears or hears by report that in the blessing spoken at the dismissal (observe

how the infinitive construction goes over into the finite
verb, K. S. 413 a-e) Isaac even commanded Jacob not
to take a Canaanite wife. Then Esau observes — for
apparently v. 7 is still object of the *wayyar'* of v. 6
— that Jacob obeys this command emanating from
father and mother.

8. The initial *wayyar'* of v. 6 is resumed —
"and when Esau further saw." Apparently, at this
late date Esau first discovers, or at least begins to
reckon with the fact, that the heathen Canaanite
wives pleased not Isaac. What a dullness of spiritual
perception! Growing up in a household where it
was well known why Abraham had taken pains to
secure a non-Canaanite wife for Isaac, Esau never
seems to have understood why this was done. The
entire spiritual heritage and all spiritual traditions
had not as yet begun to mean anything to Esau.
These few verses help us to understand very clearly
why God could not use Esau in the building of the
kingdom. Besides, it is quite significantly reported
that Esau noted only that these Canaanitish wives did
not please his father. Apparently, he never troubled
to discover his mother's reaction — and she was vexed
most. The expression "pleased not" gives a milder
touch to the Hebrew, which originally said: "were
evil (*ra'ôth*) in the eyes of."

9. Even in his attempt to go right Esau still
goes at least half wrong, for he takes a wife from
stock which has already been cast off by God, from
Ishmael's family, who may, indeed, yet have preserved some of the good traditions of the house of
Abraham. Procksch has an idle and erroneous speculation when he remarks in this connection: "It is
here indicated that the blessing had to come upon
Jacob and not upon Esau because it is tied up with
the purity of the blood." Spiritual issues not blood
issues govern the case. Esau could not have visited

Ishmael in person, for, as we showed at the beginning of the preceding chapter, Ishmael had died about thirteen years before this time. The preposition *'al* here bears the less common meaning of "in addition to," as in 31:50 (B D B, 755 a). It must further be observed that Esau's attempted remedy of the evil is no remedy. He allows the evil to continue and merely adds something that may be half right. The existing wrong is not broken with, and so the moral indecision of the man is made very apparent.

10, 11. And Jacob went forth from Beersheba and came to Haran. And he lighted upon a certain place and spent the night there, for the sun had gone down, and he took one of the stones of the place and laid it as his head place and he lay down in that place.

A characteristic Hebrew way of summarizing the whole story before the details are given: he "went forth from Beersheba and came to Haran," cf. "and he blessed" (v. 1). Was Jacob a fugitive? In a mild sense, Yes. But they let their imagination play too freely, who make him run forth in haste from home in continual fear of being overtaken and let him cover the entire distance from Beersheba to Bethel — about 70 miles as the crow flies over mountain roads — in one day. Esau had threatened to kill his brother only after the death of Isaac. It may have been about the third day when Jacob arrived at this spot after traveling leisurely, for he had a long journey before him.

11. "Lighted upon" (*pagha'*) is to be taken much in the sense of "he chanced upon." However, we avoided the latter rendering because the Scriptures know of no "chance." The verb implies that there was no design or purpose behind Jacob's coming here. However, is *maqôm*, "place," here meant, as often in the Scriptures, as "the cult-place" belonging to

a certain town? We doubt it very much. Such a "cult-place" would hardly have been a seemly place for Yahweh to reveal Himself; for perhaps without exception these places were set apart for the idols of the land. Yahweh has nothing in common with the idols. Such a spot would be an abomination to Yahweh. The article *bammaqôm* — "upon the place" — does not overthrow our contention, for as Skinner admits, "the rendering 'a certain place' would be grammatically correct (G. K. 126 r)." Meek renders the phrase in the same way. The article simply marks it as the place which was afterward to become famous. Jacob spends the night just there because that was all that was left for him, for "the sun had gone down" and the night had fallen swiftly, as oriental nights do. The hardy shepherd is not disturbed by the experience, for shepherds often spend the night thus and are observed to this day sleeping with a stone for a pillow. Here *mera'ashtaw* does not actually mean "pillow" but "head place" — a proper distinction, for pillows are soft, "head places" not necessarily so.

They who must find rational explanations for everything here conjecture about some stony ascent which Jacob saw in the rapidly descending dusk and which then afterward in the dream took the form of a ladder (even Edersheim). Dreams, especially those sent by the Almighty, require no such substructure.

Not quite so harmless is the contention of those who import liberally of their own thoughts into the text and then secure a sequence about as follows: The stone used by Jacob is one of the pillars or sacred stones of the "cult-place," (a pure invention). Jacob unwittingly takes it in the semi-darkness and prepares it for a headrest. The charmed stone then superinduces a dream. On awakening, Jacob is afraid,

because he realizes he has rashly used a sacred stone
and quickly makes a vow to fend off possible evil consequences and to appease the angered Deity. Such
interpretations transport the occurrence into the realm
of superstition, magic, fetish and animistic conceptions, debasing everything and especially the
patriarch's conception of things.

**12, 13 a. And he dreamed and, behold, there
was a ladder set upon the earth and its top touched
the heavens; and, behold, the angels of God were
going up and down on it; and, behold, Yahweh stood
above it.**

This is the first theophany that Jacob experiences of a total of seven according to the following
count: the second, 31:3, cf. 11-13; the third, 32:1, 2;
the fourth, 32:24-30; the fifth, 35:1; the sixth, 35:9-
13; the seventh, 46:1-4. Men may differ in their mode
of counting but not to any very great extent. Dreams
are a legitimate mode of divine revelation. On this
instance the ladder is the most notable external
feature of the dream. The word *sullam,* used only
here, is well established in its meaning "ladder." If
it reaches from earth to heaven, that does not necessitate anything grotesque; dreams seem to make the
strangest things appear perfectly natural. Nor could
a ladder sufficiently broad to allow angels to ascend
and descend constitute an incongruity in a dream.
The surprise occasioned by the character of the dream
is reflected by the threefold *hinneh* — "behold": behold a ladder, angels, and Yahweh. The last prepositional phrase, *'alaw,* could mean that Yahweh was
standing "over him," but grammatically simpler and
fitting better into the picture is the old "above it"
(R. V., also Luther). Such a clear-cut dream must
embody a deeper symbolism. Why a ladder? Why
the angels? Why the Lord above it? Answer: In
order to convey by a visible sign what the words

themselves also convey as Yahweh speaks. The ladder symbolizes the uninterrupted communion between heaven and earth, mediated through God's holy angels and instituted for the care and the needs of God's children on earth. The angels bear man's needs before God and God's help to man. For this reason Jesus could, alluding specifically to this passage (John 1:51), claim that the truth involved was most significantly displayed in His own life, for in Him the divine and the human met in perfect union. So Jacob becomes a type of the Christ, though, indeed, an imperfect one. The many other interpretations that have been attempted must be rejected: the ladder does not symbolize the church, or faith; nor "the heavenly source and goal of the revealed religion of Abraham and Israel" (K. C.) ; nor "the mystery of the incarnation" (Luther), at least not so immediately as Luther construes it.

13 b-15. And He said: I am Yahweh, the God of Abraham, thy father, and the God of Isaac — the land upon which thou liest, to thee will I give it and to thy descendants. And thy descendants shall be as the dust of the earth, and thou shalt spread abroad to the west and to the east and to the north and to the south. And in thee shall be blessed all the families of the earth and in thy seed. And, behold, I am with thee and will keep thee withersoever thou goest; and I will bring thee back to this land, for I will not forsake thee, until I have done what I have told thee.

Is the Lord blessing a cheat and prospering one who secured a blessing by craft? By no means. Our interpretation of the preceding chapter confirms itself at this point. Jacob is being strengthened in the faith and supported by liberal promises, because he was penitent over his sin and stood greatly in need of the assurance of divine grace. Besides, Jacob was deeply grieved at being called upon to sever the ties that bound him to house and home, and he was apprehensive of the future as well. The Lord meets him in his need and grants him the support of His grace.

After identifying Himself as Yahweh, the God of Abraham and Isaac, and so tying up this present revelation with those that preceded, Yahweh, the merciful covenant God, proceeds to confirm to Jacob "the blessing of Abraham," which Isaac had bestowed upon him just at his departure. The first element of the promise bestowed by the Lord is the possession of the land ("the land upon which thou liest") on which he now lay practically an exile. *Ha'árets* is a nominative absolute (K.S. 341 c).

14. The second portion of the blessing that is specially confirmed to him is that of numerous descendants like "the dust of the earth" (13:16 cf. 22:17). For "spread out" the Hebrew uses *parats*, "to break through," in the sense of bursting all restraining bonds. Emphasis is added to the thought by letting the expansion extend to all points of the compass.

15. Lastly, protection during the time of his absence from home is promised to Jacob, protection due to nothing less than God's personal presence — "I am with thee and will keep thee." "Whithersoever thou goest" implies that Jacob's wanderings will be extensive. The protection promised involves being brought back to this very land of promise, and it is further confirmed by the added assurance not to be forsaken until all that is promised has been attained. *'Asîthî*, a perfect, practically = a future perfect — "until I shall have done" (G. K. 1060). "To this land," *'adhamah* = to "this piece of ground," for Jacob is to experience the providence of God in being brought back even to this very region and this very spot.

16. **And Jacob awoke from his sleep and said: Surely, Yahweh is in this place and I knew it not.**

This verse and the next record Jacob's immediate reaction to the dream, spoken while the effect of the dream was still strongest upon him. This word indicates what had been uppermost in his mind. Jacob had felt himself severed from the gracious presence and the manifestation of Yahweh, which he knew centered in his father's house. Jacob understood full well the omnipresence of God, but he knew, too, that it had not pleased God to manifest and reveal Himself everywhere as Yahweh. Now the patriarch receives specific assurance that God in His character as Yahweh was content to be with Jacob and keep and bless him for the covenant's sake. That Yahweh was going to do this much for him, that is what Jacob had not known. To understand the word rightly note that Jacob could not have said — for it would have involved an untruth —: "Surely, *God* is in this place and I knew it not." Of course he knew that. Any true believer's knowledge of God involves such elementary things as knowledge of His not being confined to one place. Such crude conceptions the patriarchs never had. To suppose that the account is trying to picture Jacob as on a lower level than Abraham in spiritual discernment is misunderstanding.

17. **And he was afraid and said: How awe-inspiring is this place! This is none other than the house of God and this is the gate of heaven.**

Since Jacob, a sinful man, had come near to God, this nearness caused fear. Any other reaction would have been improper. The Hebrew *nôra'*, "awe-inspiring," is the passive participle of *yare'*, "to be afraid." The translation could cover this by the rendering: "he was awed, saying: 'How awesome,' etc." Since here is a place where God meets man, Jacob gives expression to this thought thus: "This is none other that God's house," for to him this was at the same time as kindly an experience in spite of his fear as though he had been allowed to enter God's dwelling-place and meet Him. But to be at such a place was practically equivalent to having found a gate leading to heaven. At such places where God had once revealed Himself men with good reason felt that they would be sure to be able to meet God again. Yet on the other hand, besides construing "gate of heaven" as gate leading to heaven, it is equally proper to construe it as gate leading from heaven, through which, when it so pleases God, He steps forth into contact with men. The divine name *'Elohîm* appears here because Jacob wishes to express the simple thought: Contact with the Deity is possible here. Yet previously (v. 16) he had recognized that Yahweh in His mercy granted this revelation.

Criticism makes another of its unproven claims, when, largely because of the divine name Yahweh, the verses 13-16 are described as a Yahwistic insertion in an Elohistic narrative: "v. 17 follows v. 12 without sensible breach of continuity." Now, without a doubt, the climax of the whole divine revelation was the word spoken v. 13-16; that is the golden jewel of the chapter. Yet so discerning a writer as the supposed E had lost the best part, which then had to be supplied from J. This creates a problem that criticism will never explain and which overthrows its contention.

Witness also the following exposition, the most fantastic of all: the entire experience is supposed to convey the thought that from this gate to heaven access to the heavenly sanctuary is gained, as it were by the ladder — "when to this (to the idea of a sacred stone or sanctuary at Bethel) was added the idea of God's dwelling in heaven, the earthly sanctuary became as it were the entrance to the heavenly temple, with which it communicated by means of a ladder" (Skinner).

Luther's rendering, "here is none other, etc." for "this is none other, etc.," is also entirely permissible; for the demonstrative *zeh* is used as the adverb "here" (cf. Ges. Buhl, and K. S. 43).

18. **And Jacob arose early in the morning and took the stone which he set as his head place and set it up as a pillar and poured oil upon the top of it.**

The words spoken in v. 16 and 17 were uttered during the night immediately after the dream. Whether Jacob again fell asleep or not is not told. In any case, he arose early in the morning and took the stone used for a head place and set it up in a manner calculated to make it stand out and so to mark the precise spot where the dream-vision had occurred. The stone must have had enough size so that when it was set up it might be classed as "a pillar" (*matstsebhah*). Since the pillar marked a holy experience, it was in this instance consecrated by the pouring out of oil upon it (cf. Exod. 40:9-11). It has been claimed that travelers would in olden times regularly carry a horn of oil with them so that the oil might be used for purposes of anointing and for food. In addition to the consecration expressed by the anointing there is the possibility that the oil also gave expression to the idea of sacrifice and was offered as sacrifice, for in 35:14 in consecrating the Bethel altar Jacob poured a drink offering and oil upon tne altar. In any case, we need not wonder that Abraham and Isaac had not set up memorial stones heretofore; they had no direct occasion to do so as Jacob here had. Good parallels are seen in 31:45; Josh. 4; 24:26 f; I Sam. 7:12. So natural is it to do a thing of this sort that anyone of us might in our day do a similar thing with the utmost of propriety. Later, when the Canaanite shrines for idolatrous worship had these "pillars" regularly set up ˙round about the "holy place" (*maqôm*), as excavations still amply prove, and Israel stood in danger of copying heathen abominations, the Lord saw fit to forbid the use of such *matstsebhoth* and bade Israel to destroy them — Exod. 23:24; 34:13; Lev. 26:1; Deut. 12:3; 16:22. The idea of a fetish stone simply does not enter into this case. Efforts to inject it by claims very boldly stated are quite futile; as when it is said: *matstsebhah* — "originally a fetish, the supposed abode of a spirit or deity — a belief of which there are clear traces in this passage." Koenig has successfully refuted such claims by pointing out that Jacob says: "How awe-inspiring is this *place*" — not "this *stone*."

It is much to be deplored that on this point another attempt to cheapen the holy record is made by identifying Jacob's anointing of the stone with the so-called Baetylian stone worship. That such a practice as stone worship existed rather widely in days of old is, of course, true. That such anointed stones were called in Greek βαίτυλοι is also known. But this accidental point of coincidence proves nothing about Jacob's experience as belonging into this class. It might possibly be admitted that a distorted record of the Bethel experience began to circulate among the Gentiles and gave rise to stone worship. But even that assumption has great difficulties. For, in the first place, the name βαιθήλ ("Bethel") does not occur in this chapter of the Septuagint, being rendered "house of God," and if it did appear, as Keil points out, it would be quite inexplicable how the ϑ was changed to the τ in βαίτυλοι. Besides, it is claimed that Baetylian worship in days of old centered around meteoric stones, which were thought to have been dropped down from high heaven by the gods. In

any case, if a superstitious practice existed among
the heathen, must everything similar at once be put
into the same class?　Then with equal propriety
sacred memorials that we might set up in our day
would also have to be classed as Baetylian worship,
especially if the practice of anointing stones should
be revived.

19. **And he called the name of that place
Bethel, whereas the name of the city had formerly
been Luz.**

Beth-'el means "house of God."　The substance
of the thought of v. 17 is incorporated in this name.
Jacob may have meant the name for this particular
spot only.　The city that already may have stood
there then, or perhaps was first built there or near
there later, presently came to bear that name.　Originally it was called Luz, remarks the well-informed
author, who had used the name Bethel already in
12:8 by anticipation.　Josh. 16:2 does not conflict with
our passage, for there, according to v. 1, "Bethel"
must mean "mountains of Bethel."

20-22. **And Jacob vowed a vow, saying:　If
God will be with me and will keep me in this way
which I am going, and will give me bread to eat
and clothes to wear, and I shall return in peace to
my father's house, and Yahweh will be God to me —
then this stone, which I have set up as pillar, shall be
a house of God and of all that Thou givest to me, I
will surely give a tithe to Thee.**

Jacob's gratitude for the much needed comfort
and encouragement finds expression in an appropriate
vow, of which v. 20, 21 forms the protasis and v. 22
the apodosis.　True, the greater promises concerning
the possession of the land and of being a blessing to
all the families of the earth are not mentioned.　That
does not say that Jacob does not understand them

and is not grateful for them. They, in the nature
of the case, are seen to lie in the distant future. For
the other tangible blessings which the next years are
to bring Jacob vows to give tangible tokens of gratitude. For the greater blessings, what shall or can
he return to the Lord? Nothing except praise and
thanks, because these blessings are unspeakably
great. In enumerating protection, food, clothing and
safe return Jacob is not displaying a mind ignorant
of higher values but merely unfolding the potentialities
of God's promise (v. 15), "I will keep thee and bring
thee again," etc. When he says: "If Yahweh will
be God to me," he is paraphrasing the promise (v.
15): "I am with thee." Consequently, in all this
Jacob is not betraying a cheap, mercenary spirit, bargaining with God for food and drink and saying:
"If I get these, then Yahweh shall be my God."
That would be about the cheapest case of arrogant
bargaining with God recorded anywhere. In fact, it
is difficult even with the very best construction that
it is possible to put upon the words to draw the
clause *wehayah yahweh lî le'lohim* into the apodosis:
"then shall the Lord be my God" (A. V. and Luther).
The Lord was his God. Jacob was not an unconverted
man still debating whether or not to be on the Lord's
side and here making an advantageous bargain out
of the case. They who postpone his conversion to a
time twenty years later at the river Jabbok completely misunderstand Jacob. Not only does the construction of the Hebrew allow for our interpretation,
it even suggests it. The "if" clauses of the protasis
all run along after the same pattern as converted perfects = future: "if He will," etc., including: "if
Yahweh will be, or prove Himself, God to me." Then
to make the beginning of the apodosis prominent comes
a new construction: noun first, then adjective clause,
then verb.

22. By "house of God" (*beth-'el*) Jacob does not mean a temple but a sacred spot, a sanctuary, which he purposes to establish and to perpetuate. How Jacob carried out the vow is reported in 35:1-7: he built an altar to Yahweh on the spot. Nothing is reported about his giving of the tithe, perhaps because that is presupposed as the condition upon which the maintenance of the sanctuary depended. The silence of the Scriptures on this latter point by no means indicates that it was neglected. Incidentally, this constitutes the second Scriptural reference to the voluntary tithe (cf. 14:20).

HOMILETICAL SUGGESTIONS

If the first five verses of this chapter are to be used as a text, the last verse of the preceding chapter should be prefaced to them. Though a similar text is found in the beginning of chapter 12 and repeatedly thereafter, this text should be evaluated according to its connection and should be used to show that the Messianic hope was clearly understood and realized to be the crowning glory of God's revelation to Abraham. The next portion, v. 6-9, is not to be recommended for use, for its subject is too largely negative: the folly of an unspiritual man. The last section, v. 10-22, is unusually fruitful. The most natural approach is to regard it as an excellent demonstration of God's providential care for His erring children. It sets forth a broader comprehension of what God's omnipresence means to His children. Since John 1:51 is an evident allusion to this experience of Jacob, it would be very much in order to approach the text from the angle that suggests that Christ is the perfect embodiment of continual communion with the Father in heaven.

CHAPTER XXIX

5. Jacob's Double Marriage (29:1-30)

In this chapter the major emphasis lies on God's gracious providence: in the preceding chapter Yahweh had promised to manifest His grace to Jacob; here definite tokens of that grace are received. Jacob finds those of his mother's family without difficulty; he meets with a pleasant reception; his years of work are rendered delightful; he secures a wife from the relationship of his mother; children come from this union. In the second place, of course, there are also indications of just retribution when the deceiver is also deceived.

Writers of our day are inclined to stress particularly the romantic phases of the chapter. These phases are, incidentally, an added ornament; but to regard the whole narrative from this point of view makes the incidental paramount. It is not to be denied that the Scriptures also glorify true and honorable love but always without growing sentimental about it. Those who are without spiritual discernment may consider the matter of this chapter as being altogether off the spiritual plane and dropping to the level of the almost trivial. However, in the ordinary events of everyday life true faith finds its right sphere of activity, and the trivial things of one's daily task become great and important if in them a man expresses his faith, as Jacob does. It is especially Luther's exposition that knows how to set forth this important angle of the case.

On the matter of the critical analysis of the chapter we need say little. The majority of the critics seem to agree that v. 1 comes from E, v. 2-14 from J, v. 15-30 from E; perhaps v. 24 and 29 from P. In this case J never bridged over the gap from Bethel to Haran, an absurdity, which Procksch in the interest of defending the critical analysis expressly defends. Aside from this it need only be remarked that criticism is entirely committed to the proposition that as soon as both sides of a case are presented this fact is a trace of dual authorship. J and E for all their commendable qualities never have quite risen to that fine level of discernment which sees two or more sides in a proposition. Then, too, though the so-called critical analysis of the chapter is admittedly difficult, nevertheless all critics cheerfully and almost positively make it and quite staunchly defend their findings.

1. **And Jacob got under way and went to the land of the children of the East.**

"He lifted up his feet," says the more colorful Hebrew expression for "got under way." Naturally the expression "land of the children of the East" is a bit vague, but the use of it in the Scriptures always seems to take the land west of the Euphrates into consideration. To try to extend the term to include Mesopotamia and so Haran is quite unwarranted. But this does not now point to different sources with different or conflicting viewpoints. The whole matter is as simple as daylight. Between Mesopotamia, Jacob's goal, and Palestine lay "the land of the children of the East." Consequently, Jacob strikes out for it next in order to traverse it and so to arrive at Mesopotamia. The uneventful journey as such is passed by.

2, 3. **And he looked about and, lo, there was a well in the open field, and, lo, three flocks of sheep were there lying beside it, for from this well men were wont to water the flocks, and the customary**

**great stone lay on the mouth of the well; and thither
all the flocks were wont to gather, and then they
would roll away the stone from the mouth of the
well and would water the sheep.   Then they would
replace the stone on the mouth of the well.**

The unusual thing, marked as unusual by a
double *hinneh* ("behold," or "lo"), was that Jacob
encountered at once the very well where the sheep
of his kinsfolk were regularly watered.   In "the open
field (*sadheh*) three flocks of sheep" would be quite
conspicuous and stand out distinctly the one from
the other.   The Hebrew says they lay '*al* ("above")
rather than "beside" the well, for it regards the fact
that the water always lies on a lower level.   The
imperfect *yashqû* marks the habitual thing in this
instance, "men were wont to water" (K. S. 157; G. K.
107 e).   The third person plural indicates the indefinite subject "men."   The article *ha'ébhen* indicates
the customary thing: "the customary great stone,"
which always covered the opening of these wells.
Travelers like Robinson and Thomson testify to the
prevalence of this type of well down to the present.
Usually these wells do not contain "living water" but
stored-up water.   First the opening is covered by a
large flat stone with a smaller opening in the center,
which in turn is covered by a smaller stone.   The
"large stone" prevented theft by individuals.

3.   The converted perfects are brought into align-
ment with the *yashqû* of the preceding verse and are
so made to express the rest of the habitual acts:
flocks would gather, men would roll away the stone,
and water sheep and replace the stone.   In order not
to conflict with v. 10 we do best to regard the waiting until all the flocks were assembled partly as a
matter of necessity partly a matter of common consent.   For if a girl like Rachel tends her father's flock,
like Jethro's daughters near Mt. Sinai (Exod. 2:16)

at a later date, then others of the shepherds may well
have been young men, in fact, quite young men, who
would require their united strength, or at least that
of some two or three of the lads, to remove the stone.
Now apparently, in order to be the first to water their
flocks, shepherds would frequently come in rather early
in the afternoon and there lie awaiting their turn,
when they might yet have been out in pasture. It is
this part of the procedure that somewhat perplexes
Jacob (v. 7), that grazing time should thus be lost.

4-6. **And Jacob said: My brethren, whence
are ye? And they said: We are from Haran. And
he said to them: Do ye know Laban, the son of
Nahor? And they said: Yes. And he said to
them: Is all well with him? And they said: He
is well, and, see, Rachel, his daughter, is coming with
the sheep.**

The conversation that follows is the most natural
and true to life imaginable. The shepherds are not
a taciturn lot, but Jacob, being about seventy-seven,
was much older than they, and so the younger men
wait till they are spoken to. With good tact, Jacob
addresses them "brethren" — the wider use of the
word *'ach*, as members of the same people; for
Jacob's ancestors came out of their midst. Apparently,
too, both yet spoke the same language. The first thing
for Jacob to determine is where he is. The well in
the open field is not a town; but if Jacob learns where
the shepherds come from, he will know which is the
nearest town. Imagine the glad surprise of Jacob
when they answer: "We are from Haran." Without betraying too much of his identity to total strangers Jacob can learn what he needs to know if they
should happen to know Laban, whom he here calls,
"the son of Nahor" rather then Bethuel's son, naming
the grandfather, as, no doubt, the more illustrious
ancestor; cf. II Kings 9:20 with v. 14; also Ezra

5:1 with Zech. 1:1 for similar cases. The "a" of the
interrogative particle lengthened before *Schwa*.

6.   Next Jacob must know whether after all these
newsless years Laban, his mother's brother, still fares
well: *hashalôm lô* = "Is there peace to him?"
"Peace" in connections such as these refers to a
state of well-being in which nothing essential is
lacking.   This question meets with an affirmative
response.   Besides, even then the shepherds were
anticipating the arrival of Laban's daughter, Rachel.
Perhaps the *hinneh* ("see") points to her as she becomes visible at some distance.   *Ba'ah,* with the
accent on the last syllable, is the feminine form of the
durative participle — "is coming."

Though "Rachel" signifies "ewe" and "Leah"
"wild cow," that fact in itself does not support the
groundless contention that the early stages of the
patriarchal religion included totemism.   For nowhere
do these or other names of wild beasts or tame appear
as totems, nor are there indications anywhere of
totemism in the legitimate religion of Israel.

7, 8.   **And he said: Lo, the day is far from
spent; it is not yet time for gathering the cattle.
Water the sheep and go and pasture them.   But
they said: We cannot, until all herds are gathered
together.   Then they roll the stone from the mouth
of the well, and then we water the sheep.**

At that time there were still hours left for pastur-
ing.   The efficient shepherd Jacob is pained to see
good time wasted thus.   That is not what he would
have done.   So he urges them to do the necessary
watering and then again lead the flock out to pasture.
Besides, it is very manifest that by this maneuver
Jacob is trying to remove the onlookers from the scene
against the time when Rachel arrives.   "The day is
big" is the Hebrew expression for our: "the day is
far from spent."

8. Now it appears that they are agreed to wait till all are assembled before the stone is removed. Compare also our remarks on v. 3. In this instance the assembled shepherds are just as loath to miss the meeting between this stranger and Rachel as Jacob is anxious to remove them from the scene. We take the expression "we cannot" as involving moral inability (they have agreed to act in unison) as well as physical.

9, 10. While he was still speaking with them, Rachel arrived with her father's flock; for she was a shepherdess. And it came to pass when Jacob saw Rachel, the daughter of his mother's brother, Laban, and the sheep of his mother's brother, Laban, that Jacob drew near and rolled away the stone from the mouth of the well and watered the sheep of his mother's brother, Laban.

'ôdhénû = "still he" (G. K. 100 o), with the participle here goes to make up an adverbial clause of time. Here the form *bá'ah* (accent on the first syllable) is the perfect "she arrived." It may not have been customary in all lands also not among the Israelites to have girls tend flocks. Consequently, the explanation: "for she was a shepherdess" is necessary.

10. It is really a very characteristic trait observed by the author at this point that Jacob took separate note first of Rachel, then of Laban's flock. Nor should the second observation surprise us in one who had been a shepherd all his days. Nor need we wonder at the threefold repetition of the phrase "of his mother's brother, Laban." What else would a man like Jacob, loving his mother with particular affection, do under such circumstances than keep saying to himself: "This is the daughter of my mother's brother, Laban, whom she has mentioned so often; these are his sheep"? But what of the fact that he

rolls away singlehanded a stone which required the united efforts of the rest? That is to be explained partly by the fact that he was naturally very strong, then partly by a mixture of two facts: his joy at finding his kinfolks and his joy at finding such a pretty cousin stirs him greatly and makes him strong. It may be that we here have a Biblical instance of love at first sight, although even that had more fitly find mention in connection with the next verse. But to talk only of that love and to make Jacob act like a young fellow who tries to impress his ladylove by feats of strength is just a bit shallow by way of interpretation. Life here, as usual, was rather a complex of various motives that surged strongly in Jacob's heart. The text by its threefold repetition of the phrase "of his mother's brother, Laban" shows on what his thoughts dwelt at the moment. It has remained for Gunkel and men of his type to ascribe to the narrative the attempt to make out Jacob to be a man of Herculean strength, a gigantic fellow — fabulous elements in the story. Such conclusions in reference to Jacob are, to say the least, most fantastic and farfetched. *Wayyághel* is Kal — G. K. 67 p.

11, 12. **And Jacob kissed Rachel and lifted up his voice and wept. And Jacob told Rachel that he was her father's kinsman and that he was a son of Rebekah. And she ran and told her father.**

The other shepherds now fade out of the picture. Whether they still were present when Jacob kissed Rachel is not told, though it seems quite likely. Such matters are so entirely secondary to the author's purpose that they may well be ignored. Allowing for the fact that in those days, among a different people, a kiss of cousins was a proper greeting, there is little doubt that Rachel was taken quite unawares and may well have been astonished, for as yet she knew

nothing of this strong shepherd's identity. The more
natural procedure would have been to explain first
who he was, then to give the kiss of greeting. The
reverse of the procedure indicates how his glad
emotions ran away with him. No man will determine
how much of this emotion was plain joy at seeing a
cousin and how much incipient love for pretty Rachel,
and Jacob himself, perhaps, at the moment would have
been least able to make an accurate analysis of
what his heart actually felt at the occasion. We
can hardly go wrong in claiming to detect a trace
of love at first sight.

The strength of Jacob's emotion is attested to
by the fact that after having bestowed the kiss "he
lifted up his voice and wept" — not a dishonorable
or unmanly thing for the Oriental then or now, for
he is a man inclined to make a greater display of
his emotions. At the same time, what he does betrays, on the one hand, how keenly the loss of the
association with the loved ones at home was missed
by this quasi-fugitive, and, on the other hand, how
deeply the new joy of the promise of attachment of
his kinfolk touched him. When the identity of Jacob
is revealed to Rachel, she makes haste to impart the
welcome news to her father, not like Rebekah to her
mother. In fact, Rebekah's mother is not even mentioned in these narratives and may already have
been dead. *'Ach*, "brother," here appears in the
broader use as "kinsman," it could also be rendered
"nephew."

13, 14. **And it came to pass when Laban heard
the report about Jacob, his sister's son, he ran out
to meet him, and embraced him and kissed him repeatedly and brought him to his house. Then he
reported to Laban all these matters. And Laban
said to him: Thou certainly art of my own flesh
and blood. And he lived with him a month's time.**

The Hebrew uses the expression: "he heard the
hearing," which means: "he heard the report."   "The
report of Jacob" must be "report about Jacob" —
objective genitive. The strength of Laban's interest
in a nephew, whom he had never seen and who brings,
in fact, the only direct news that has come from his
sister, who left almost a hundred years previously,
is attested to by the fact that he on his part "ran
out to meet him."   We need not impute only base
motives and emotions to Laban, though many of the
things he did must call forth our sharpest disapproval.
Without a doubt, the man was glad to meet his nephew
and "embraced him" in all sincerity and "kissed him
repeatedly" with true affection.   Yet the *Piel* stem
yenashsheq does not mean just "give a kiss" as does
the *kal wayyishshaq* (v. 11).   Perhaps the overplus
of affection displayed carries with it a trace of in-
sincerity, for the truest affection does not make a
display of itself.   When Jacob has been escorted
courteously to his uncle's house, it behooves him to
give an account of himself.   So "he reported to Laban
all these matters."   How much is to be included in
haddebharîm ha'elleh ("all these things") ?   Without
a doubt, the most recent occurrences concerning the
meeting with the shepherds and Rachel.   But will
not his unattended coming, so different from that of
Abraham's servant who led Rebekah back, have called
for an explanation?   Not to explain this difference
would have raised justifiable questions and even doubts
in the minds of his kinsmen.   Consequently, if Jacob
came as a godly man and one repentant of his recent
deceit, as we have every reason to believe that he
was, then he could not do otherwise than relate the
direct and the more remote reasons of his coming.
Consequently, "these matters" will have included an
honest report concerning the things of chapters 27

and 28. Otherwise Jacob would have been sailing under false colors.

14. Jacob's report at least conveyed, first of all, to Laban full proof of Jacob's identity: this man was truly his kinsman, a blood relative, or, as the Hebrew says: "my bone and my flesh," for which we have substituted the more common English expression "my own flesh and blood." A total stranger had, of course, to furnish unequivocal proof of his identity. Laban is so thoroughly convinced by Jacob's account of himself that he prefaces his acknowledgment with a "certainly" (*'akh*). Nothing definite is agreed on for the present, except that Jacob should "live" (*yeshebh*) there. So "a month's time" elapses. The Hebrew expression has been variously rendered. *Chódhesh yamîm*, "a month of days," employs the term "days" in the common meaning of "time," consequently, the almost colloquial English expression "a month's time" is very satisfactory. "The space of a month" (A. V.) is very good, also Luther: *ein Monat lang*. Attempted improvements are wrong, such as "a full month" or "about a month."

15-17. **Then Laban said to Jacob: Shouldest thou serve me for nothing, just because thou art my kinsman? Tell me what shall be thy wages? Now Laban had two daughters; the name of the elder was Leah and the name of the younger Rachel; and Leah's eyes were weak, but Rachel was of beautiful form and beautiful looks.**

By this time Laban has discerned that in Jacob he would have a very competent shepherd. No doubt, Jacob began to serve in this capacity at once. His faithfulness and his industry were immediately apparent. A measure of selfishness enters into Laban's proposal without a doubt. But most likely it is a compound of honest and selfish motives. The good features in it are that he wishes to bind a relative to himself, especially as this relative is unusually competent. Besides, he wants to arrive at a definite understanding as soon as possible in order to obviate future misunderstandings. Furthermore, it behooves him as the elder to steer toward a definite agreement. Each of these good motives had an admixture of selfishness, for Laban was basically a selfish and a tricky man. No doubt, he was planning to gain this competent young man as a son-in-law. Laban must have anticipated the proposal that was actually made. Perhaps Laban had noticed that Jacob had fallen violently in love, and now Laban hoped that if he let Jacob set the terms, Jacob's newborn love would incline to make a generous proposal.

The basic statement is correct in every way: "Shouldest thou serve me for nothing, just because thou art my kinsman?" The second is not generous. For though in a sense Jacob was for the moment impecunious, yet Laban had clearly discerned that he was prospective heir to a very great fortune. Even if Jacob failed to tender the customary *móhar*, or dowry, that lack was more than compensated for by his potential wealth. The formality of the case could well have been met by a nominal service of one year.

16. Here criticism makes a very positive assertion: v. 16 as it stands could not have been written thus by the same author who had written v. 6; and so the critics claim to have firm ground for assigning v. 16-30 to E. We claim — since here only an unproved and unprovable claim has been advanced — on the contrary: Without a doubt the author of v. 6 could have written v. 16 just as he did and be perfectly consistent; there is not the slightest difficulty in the way of this assumption.

17. "Leah" (meaning "wild cow"), though the
elder, has "weak (*rakh*) eyes." This, according to
the oriental standard, did not imply defective vision
but merely the absence of that clear-cut brilliance
and lustre that the Orientals love. "Tender" (A. V.)
is in a sense even more correct than "weak." By
contrast Rachel's eyes are not specifically referred
to but seem, indeed, to have been dark and lustrous.
But a "beautiful form and beautiful looks" are attributed to her. Add to these her natural assets the
dramatic meeting at the well and it becomes very
clear why Leah did not even enter into consideration
for Jacob. Yet by v. 16, 17 we are prepared fully to
understand the later complications that arise.

18. **And Jacob loved Rachel, and so he said:
I will serve thee seven years for Rachel, thy younger
daughter.**

True love between man and woman is here approved by the Scriptures. In the month's time spent
with his relatives Jacob had come to know very definitely what his heart felt. Everything indicates that
his was a very true and lasting devotion. A man
deeply in love makes the terms that follow — seven
year's service — and certainly does not look primarily
to his own advantage.

19, 20. **And Laban said: It is better that I
should give her to thee than that I should give her
to another man. Stay with me. And Jacob served
for Rachel seven years and they seemed to him like
just so many days for the love he had to her.**

To this day Orientals and specially Syrians and
Arabs much prefer to marry their daughters to those
in their own relationship. Higher motives will have
entered into the case on Laban's part. Jacob's worth
of character and his true religiousness may have
made a strong appeal to a man who had himself
departed from this higher standard — a silent tribute

often paid by the less godly to the more godly. The
comparative with *min* — "good from" — is used here
(G. K. 133 a). Laban's ready assent leads us to think
that he had anticipated some such proposal and found
Jacob's terms so very generous that he closed with
them at once.

All they who attempt to reduce the transaction
here described to the level of a purchase are injecting
foreign elements into the text. At no time in Israel's
history were wives purchased. The customary *móhar*,
or dowry-money, was regarded as proof of financial
competence on the bridegroom's part.

20. Without sentimentality or cheap emotional-
ism the author describes very beautifully and most
effectively the strength of Jacob's love. Years seemed
like mere days "for the love he had to her." *Yomîm
'achadhîm* is strictly "a few days." We have rendered it more colloquially, "just so many days."
'Ahabhathô, "his loving," is an infinitive used as
a feminine noun with a suffix. *Wayyihyû* is masculine
though it really has *shanîm*, a feminine noun, as its
subject. But this strange anomaly grows out of the
tendency almost always to begin sentences with the
masculine (G. K. 145 p), especially in the plural.

21. **And Jacob said to Laban: Give me my
wife, for my time is up that I go in unto her.**

Laban should have taken the initiative at the end
of the seven years. Selfishness lets him wait. Jacob
must remind him. For "go in unto" we should say
"marry." *We'abhô'ah* is a final clause (G. K. 165 a).
Jacob's somewhat curt demand indicates that he has
come to know his father-in-law's character pretty well
by this time.

22-24. **And Laban gathered together all the
men of the place and made a feast. And it came
to pass in the evening that he took Leah, his daughter, and brought her in to him and he went in unto**

her. **Also Laban gave Zilpah his maid to Leah, his daughter, as her own maid.**

Now the crafty and cunning dealings of Laban come to light. First of all, though, indeed, custom demands that "all the men of the place" be invited to the marriage banquet, yet that arrangement will serve Laban's purpose well. When the prank played on Jacob becomes known to all, it will not be easy for Jacob to cast off Leah, and so Laban will have disposed advantageously of a daughter whom perhaps none would have desired. The expression "all the men of the place" may involve a natural hyperbole, unless Haran had still been but a tiny place, which is not very likely.

23. This was about one of the meanest pranks ever played on a man. It almost seems as though this boldly conceived plan could not have succeeded. But if one considers that Jacob had absolutely no reasons for suspicion; that his wife was brought in under the cover of darkness; that she was, no doubt, veiled (24:65); that two sisters, utterly unlike only as to facial appearance, may yet have had a pronounced physical resemblance otherwise as to size and stature; that the conversations of the bridal night may have been entirely whispered; that reticence on the bride's part would hardly seem unnatural under the circumstances; that intimate association, commonly found in modern courtships before marriage, were unthought of in days of old; and that Jacob may well be thought of as under the spell of a strong infatuation, which may have led him to overlook what at other times might have aroused suspicion — we say, if one considers all these circumstances, it becomes clear that it may all have happened just as it is here told.

24. Here is a convenient place to insert the comment that Laban gave his daughter a handmaid to be specifically her own. We shall need to know this fact

later. We combine the *lah* with the final *shiphchah* to make "as her own maid." It is true, Laban did not deal with his daughters as generously as Bethuel had dealt with Rebekah. For Rebekah according to 24:59 received a "nurse," but according to 24:61 there were "damsels" in the train. Laban's greed and parsimoniousness comes to light more and more. "Zilpah" perhaps means "nearness," "intimacy."

Leah's part in the plot requires explanation. She cannot be absolved from guilt even on the score that it behooved her according to the conceptions of those days to submit to parental authority. She knew that Jacob was to be deceived. Common decency and uprightness would have demanded that she apprise Jacob of the fact at the risk of severe parental displeasure. A moral issue was involved. Apparently, though, indeed, far less guilty than her father, Leah was guilty in so far as she was not entirely averse to the whole scheme. She may have loved Jacob secretly. She may have considered this her one chance to get a husband. She may have thought this an unsought, and therefore justifiable, opportunity to steal a march on her sister. Even absolving her from all improper motives, we cannot entirely condone her action on the ground of the need of absolute obedience to her father as the times demanded it.

25-27. **And it came to pass in the morning that, lo, it was Leah. And he said to Laban: What is this that thou hast done to me? Was it not for Rachel that I worked for thee, and why didst thou trick me? And Laban said: Not is it customarily done so in our community, to give the younger before the elder. Finish the week with this one, and also the other shall be given to thee in return for the service which thou shalt do with me for yet another seven years.**

After the bridal night comes the rude shock of the discovery that it is Leah. Jacob recognizes that the fault lies preponderantly at the father's door. So Jacob at once takes his father-in-law to task. First he addresses to him the justly outraged question: "What is this that thou hast done?" This question implies that Laban has made a sport of all the finer and truer aspirations of men, has toyed with loyalty, truth and pure love. Next Jacob casts the terms of the original contract into Laban's teeth and adds to them the question: "Why didst thou trick me?" Surely, Jacob had been remiss in nothing. He had served with the truest fidelity. He had taken advantage of his father-in-law in nothing. Yet Jacob's words are comparatively few, his self-justification quite brief. For one who has been so grievously wronged he submits rather tamely after all, at least after the first outbreak. One cannot help but feel that the memory of the treachery he practiced on his brother and his father was being refreshed strongly and sealed his lips from making further accusations. The justice of God's retributions seems to have overwhelmed Jacob and made him very docile on this occasion. Now Jacob felt what it meant to have a piece of deceit practiced on one in reference to things that are especially prized.

26. Everyone recognizes at a glance that if this really was the ironclad rule in this "community" (*maqôm* = literally, "place") that the elder be given in marriage before the younger, then the time for saying so would have been at the time the agreement was originally made. The imperfect *ye'aseh* here expresses customary action; therefore we rendered: "not is it customarily done so."

27) Observing his son-in-law's unexpected meekness and realizing the difficult position into which he has put Jacob — Jacob would be the laughingstock

in any case, and Leah doubly so if Jacob simply cast her off — Laban makes a new set of terms, which have regard exclusively to Laban's advantage. He suggests seven years' service for her for whom Jacob has just rendered the stipulated seven years. For downright, galling meanness these terms could hardly be surpassed. For despicability Laban takes the prize in the Old Testament. "The week" mentioned is the bridal week, which the Syrians still term the "king's week," the time during which bridegroom and bride are respectively addressed as king and queen. What a tumult of disappointment and vexation for Jacob during this festive week! The brazen impudence which prompts Laban to add the terms for receiving Rachel as being "for the service (*beth* of price) which thou shalt do with me for yet another seven years," almost passes belief. We believe *nittenah* fits better into the connection if it be construed as *Niphal* perfect with waw conversive, rather than as a *Kal* imperfect, first person plural; for "*we* shall give" is quite out of place in a case where only Laban had done the giving.

Fully to understand the entire situation it becomes necessary to answer the question: "Were Jacob and Leah guilty of adultery, or would their union have to be classed as adulterous if Jacob had refused further to consort with her?" Luther was right when he said, No. Their union was not marriage at first, because there was no free consent between these two. It was not adultery, for Jacob consorted with one whom he certainly did not desire. Consequently, Jacob could on ethical grounds have rejected Leah and would still have been guiltless.

28-30. **And Jacob did so and finished the week with this one, and then he gave to him Rachel, his daughter, for wife. And Laban gave to Rachel, his daughter, Bilhah, his handmaid, to be her hand-**

maid.   And he went in also unto Rachel, and he
loved Rachel more than Leah.   And he worked for
him still another seven years.

Summarizing our previous contention, we believe
that Jacob, smitten with a sense of guilt because of
his own deception practiced on father and brother
and also having consideration for the sorry plight
into which Leah would fall if he were to reject her,
consented to "finish the week," that is pose as and
actually be her husband.   Then, not waiting till the
second period of seven years' service was terminated,
Laban at once gave Rachel to Jacob.   Very likely,
Laban sensed that Jacob would be adamant in insist-
ing on his right, at least on this one point, and so
Laban conceded what could not be avoided.

29. Here, as in v. 24, appears to be the most
convenient place for inserting this notice essential
for the understanding of the next chapter.   No matter
where these notices about the maids are inserted, they
are always bound to make the impression as being
additional bits of information, which is exactly what
they are and are intended to be.   But that furnishes
no ground for the critical contention that other
sources are involved.   As long as writing is done, supplementary bits of information have to be added at
certain points by all authors, and yet this fact does
not point to other sources.   "Bilhah" may mean "terror" or, perhaps, "terror is God."

30. The marriage with Rachel is also consum-
mated.   Here the very natural fact is recorded that
Jacob loved Rachel more than Leah.   This by a very
natural interpretation involves that a measure of love
also grew up for Leah.   Here, then, we have the
strange case of a man who is a bigamist, primarily
by accident, certainly not by choice.   Still we must
claim in the interest of the true conception of a truly
monogamous marriage that Jacob would have done

right only if he had refused Leah and married Rachel and so loved one wife only. His own earlier sin made him timid and prevented his carrying out this only correct solution of the difficulty. We are also here informed that Jacob was as good as his word: he had agreed to work "still another seven years" and so he lived up to his agreement. The second *gam* must be a copyist's error. Perhaps the copyist's eye ran into the wrong line, and so the *gam* should have stood before *'eth-Rachel* v. 28 (K. C.). In any case, neither of the two very ancient witnesses, the Septuagint and the Vulgate, have it. It certainly does not make sense.

6. Jacob's Children and His Increasing Wealth
(29:31-30:43)

The last five verses of chapter 29 plainly belong to the subject matter of chapter 30. Now the account centers on the fulfillment of Yahweh's promise to be with Jacob and to bless him. But incidentally parallel with this most delightful fact runs the observation that the house of the bigamist is a house divided against itself and the fruitful source of much mischief and the effectual disruption of all true discipline. Though the statement is not explicitly made that bigamy is bound to be a grievous evil, the chapter as such by its objective record conveys the truth of this statement.

31, 32. **And Yahweh saw that Leah was slighted, so He opened her womb, but Rachel remained barren. And Leah conceived and bore a son, and she called his name Reuben ("behold, a son"), for she said: . . . . because Yahweh hath looked upon my affliction; for now will my husband love me.**

For a third time in the line of Abraham barrenness occurs, but parallel with it runs fruitfulness

on the part of the less beloved wife. For *senûah*,
literally "hated," in connections such as this (cf.
Deut. 21:15) means only "less beloved" or "slighted"
(Meek). Yahweh, who has regard to his promise
to Abraham as well as to the affliction of Leah, grants
to the less beloved wife a son. "Rachel remains
barren" in order that husband and wife may learn
the more to trust in God's mercy. It seems that
Jacob's love for Rachel savored too much of infatu-
tion growing out of purely physical attraction. Higher
motives should animate those to whom God's rich
promises are entrusted.

32. On the etymology of the proper names of
this and of the next chapter it has been remarked:
"The popular etymologies attached to the names are
here extremely forced and sometimes unintelligible"
(Skinner). Such a statement is the result of the
critic's confusion. He acts on the assumption that
these etymologies are to be scholarly efforts based
on a careful analysis of Hebrew roots according to
the Hebrew lexicon. Whereas, in reality, these are
not etymologies at all but expressions wrought into
the form of proper names, expressing the sentiments
or the hopes associated with the birth of these sons.
So someone or even the mother may have remarked
at the birth of the first-born, "Look, a son," *Re'û - bhen.*
Result, the proper name "Reuben." What is there
"forced" or "unintelligible" about such a name? The
added explanation as to what further thoughts Leah
associated with this name "Reuben" do, indeed, not
grow out of the words, "look, a son," but they lay
bare the inmost thoughts of her heart. Leah knows
God as "Yahweh," an index of fine spiritual understanding and faith, and ascribes to him her fertility.
She sees that Yahweh delights in being compassionate
toward them that have "affliction," and hers was a
state of affliction; and she anticipates that her hus-

band will love her more. *Kî* involves an ellipsis: (I
have named him so) "because."

**33. And she conceived again and bore a son
and she said, ... because Yahweh hath heard
that I am hated, and so He hath given me this one
too. And she called his name Simeon (Hearing).**

Yahweh "heard" (*shama'*), so she calls him
"hearing" (*shim'ôn*). So in Hebrew the idea becomes more readily apparent. Leah implies that she
had asked for this child in prayer. Again she ascribes
the son to the graciousness of "Yahweh." She must
have been a woman of faith.

If after the simple and convincing explanation
given, "Simeon" is by some deduced from the Arabic
root — which signifies a beast which is a cross between a wolf and a hyena, we can but marvel and
let such an explanation pass as an instance of critical
arbitrariness.

**34. And she conceived again and bore a son,
and said: Now this time my husband will grow
attached to me, for I have borne him three sons.
Therefore his name was called Levi (Attachment).**

Here the play on words centers upon the root
lawah which in the passive signifies "grow attached
to." How poor Leah must have thirsted for the love
that was denied her. Leah now stands on pretty
firm ground: any man would be grateful for three
healthy sons; especially are men in the Orient minded
thus. On *happa'am* see 2:23.

**35. And she again conceived and bore a son
and said: This time I praise Yahweh. Therefore
she called his name Judah (Praised). Then she
ceased bearing children.**

Apparently her hopes are by this time realized;
she is no longer disregarded or loved but little. But
in a sense of true devoutness she lets all praise be

given to Yahweh and here contents herself with pure praise. Without knowing Hebrew one can hardly see the connection between the name and the words spoken. "I praise" = *'ôdheh*, a *Hifil*, active form. The passive, third person, is *yûdheh* = "he will be praised." This form distends itself into *Yehudhah*, a form still having the same meaning.

HOMILETICAL SUGGESTIONS

We cannot persuade ourselves that this chapter furnishes material for homiletical use. The portion, v. 1-20, could be used; but. for that matter, chapter 24 has already furnished more suitable texts on the same subject. Besides, the instruction of the Sunday school will always keep the subject matter of this chapter fresh in the memory of men. Certainly, v. 21-35 is not well adapted for use in the pulpit, important as the issues involved may otherwise be in sketching the development of Jacob's character, the just retribution of God, and the essentials of the beginnings of the history of the fathers of the twelve tribes.

CHAPTER XXX

6. Jacob's Children and His Increasing Wealth (Continued) (30:1-43)

1, 2. When Rachel saw that she was not bearing Jacob children, Rachel became jealous of her sister and said to Jacob: Give me children, or else I die. And Jacob's anger against Rachel was kindled and he said: Do I stand in God's place, who hath withheld from thee the fruit of the womb?

The sequence of time is not necessarily being followed very strictly throughout this account. For, surely, it would seem quite unreasonable to suppose that Rachel never experienced a trace of envy until Leah had borne four sons. The likelihood is that already when Leah's first, or at least her second, son had been born, Rachel's jealousy put in its appearance. So the closing verses of the preceding chapter apparently grouped together the first four births for convenience' sake. Nowhere does the author claim to follow a strict sequence in his narrative. Yet, on the other hand, lumping together a series of kindred happenings is always permissible and in this case particularly expedient.

Rachel, the well-beloved, finds her secure position less satisfactory than it once was. Desire for offspring is a healthy and a natural desire. In childbearing woman fulfills her destiny. But Rachel's jealousy is not excusable and her impatience far from harmless, for both in the last analysis question the wisdom of God. Her impatient demand is positively sinful, though it very accurately reflects her spiritual state.

In the chosen race God was making it very apparent
that human ambitions and human devices were not
going to carry on the line of promise and furnish the
desired offspring. Strong, indeed, must have been
Rachel's jealousy and impatience to dictate so unreasonable a demand and to back it up with the contention
that she would die unless her wish were granted.
The participle *methah,* as is frequently the case, points
to a future event: "I shall soon die," *moritura ego*
(K. S. 237 d). In the phrase *methah 'anokhî,* the
threatening *methah* is in the emphatic position (K. S.
239 g).

2. Jacob's anger is justifiable, for his wife has
given vent to a foolish and a sinful utterance. She
certainly has every reason to know better than to
speak thus. Therefore Jacob very properly reminds
her that conception and the bearing of offspring lie
in the will and the power of God alone, who is here
designated as *'elohîm,* because to *'elohîm* creative
works are to be attributed. The rhetorical positive
question, "Do I stand in God's place?" is the equivalent
of a direct negative claim (K. S. 352 a) : I am not in
God's place. *Tachath* in the sense of "in the place of"
appears also in 2:21; and 22:13. It is by no means a
superstitious notion on Jacob's part when he ascribes
fruitfulness or its absence to divine will and control.
Here is simply another instance of the deeper insight
characteristic of the patriarchal religion. "Fruit of
the womb" for children is a characteristic, as well as
expressive, Hebrew idiom.

The expedient adopted in v. 3 indicates that Keil
is right in charging Jacob with lacking capacity to
comfort his wife, inasmuch as he at the time, apparently, was not sufficiently strong in faith to bring
the problem before God in prayer together with his
wife. Isaac's example (25:21) should have taught
him what was to be done in such a case, and, surely,

Jacob had learned from his mother about that incident. Again, the miscarriage of Abraham's plan when Sarah substituted Hagar should have taught Jacob the inadequacy of the plan that was being devised. Jacob still appears as a man who has quite a bit to learn.

3, 4. And she said: There is my handmaid Bilhah; go in unto her, that she may bear children upon my knees, that so I too may build up a family through her. So she gave him Bilhah, her handmaid, to wife, and Jacob went in unto her.

The expression found in Hebrew, "Behold, my handmaid," is like our: "There is my handmaid." This demonstrates the variety of translations that must be made of the interjection *hinneh*. "Go in" is the usual euphemism for sexual intercourse. If Bilhah is to "bear children upon the knees" of Rachel, that is simply another way of saying that Rachel will take the children her maid bears and set them upon her own knees and treat them as her own. It may also be that setting the children upon the knee was a formal mode of the adoption of such children. The handmaid's wishes were not consulted in the matter. She was originally bestowed upon her mistress at the time of the marriage of the mistress, partly in view of the possibility of the barrenness of her mistress, that then the mistress might give the handmaid to her husband. So did Sarah, and so Rachel, and so Leah. The expression "build up a family through her" is borrowed from Meek's admirable translation of the statement which in the original merely says: "that I may be built of her." This possibility of translation grows out of the fact that the word for "house," or "family" in Hebrew has the root *banah*, "to build." In *mimménnah* the agent is introduced by *min* (K. S. 107).

4. It is no credit to either Jacob or Rachel that this device is resorted to. God's institution of the order of marriage is ignored. The lesson taught to

Abraham is not heeded. Human expedients are trusted in rather than God's blessing.

5, 6. **And Bilhah conceived and bore Jacob a son. And Rachel said: God has vindicated me and has hearkened also to my voice, and has given to me a son. Wherefore she called his name Dan (Vindication).**

As far as securing its immediate object is concerned, this new union was indeed successful — a son is born. Some faith must be ascribed to Rachel. She too, in spite of what she said in a rash utterance in v. 1, recognizes that children are the gift of God. This foster child may be looked upon as a means whereby God has vindicated her. Though *dîn* does primarily mean "judge" (A. V.), in a case such as the one before us the judging is meant in the sense not of pronouncing sentence but of securing one's rights for him, *jemanden sein Recht finden lassen* (K. W.). In other words, Rachel was relatively justified in expecting that she as really the one destined to be Jacob's wife would be privileged to bear her husband children. She believes that God, in giving success to the substitute expedient adopted, has vindicated her right publicly. By her explanation she indicates that both she and her sister had with chaste desire made this a matter of prayer. Now she says: "God has hearkened also to *my* voice," i. e. as well as to Leah's. She does not rise to the level of Leah's earlier utterance, who (29:32) ascribes her offspring to the faithful God, *Yahweh*. Rachel thinks of God only as the Creator and Source of life, *Elohim*. The higher covenant issues involved do not seem as yet to be discerned by her. In the Hebrew the relation of *dan* ("vindicator" or "vindication") to *dîn*, "vindicate," is quite apparent. To extract from v. 6 the meaning: "God brought judgment upon me, but now has heeded," etc., is made impossible by the name *dan* ("judge") which would in that case commemorate not the deliverance but the preceding disfavor.

7, 8. And Bilhah, Rachel's handmaid, conceived and bore a second son to Jacob. And Rachel said: Wrestlings with God have I wrestled together with my sister and I have prevailed, and she called his name Naphtali (Wrestling).

Though it goes without saying that Bilhah is "Rachel's handmaid," yet the appositional statement is inserted to indicate that she bore a son only in her capacity as a maid. He did not count as her own, nor was the disposal of his lot in her hands. Where the previous verses indicated how strenuous contentions with her sister were, this verse (v. 8) makes is still more apparent. On the one hand, though, indeed, it merely looks like rivalry between two sisters, there is a higher element involved on the part of both: they strive with one another in rivalry and with God in prayer. This is what Rachel means by her remark, "wrestlings with God have I wrestled together with my sister." In the expression *naphtûley 'elohîm* the construct relationship represents a prepositional relationship which immediately afterward in the case of the sister is expressed by the preposition *'im*. To regard the use of the divine name in this connection as merely a device for expressing a kind of superlative, as does K. S. (309 l), is the shallow approach of rationalism. That such a construction may replace the prepositional construction is apparent from K. S. 336 d. "Wrestlings with God," however, in the last analysis are wrestlings for God's mercy. We may wonder that one and the same situation may present such a tangle of jealousy and faith; but the soul's workings are often just such a tangled thing. The name given to the son, "Naphtali" ("Wrestling"), preserves the foster mother's sentiment for later consideration. They who find fault with some of

these names as not being strictly etymological forget
what popular etymologies are in the habit of doing:
they work very freely with words.

A peculiar side light falls on the critical method
at this point. The critical verdict is that in JE the
names are usually bestowed by the mother. The
verdict of history is: when the mother has particular
reason for doing so, *she* gives names to her children.
Circumstances, not authors, explain this fact.

The untenable exegesis of rationalism furnishes
one of its best contributions on this verse, when Meek
renders: "It was a clever trick that I played my sister,
and I succeeded too." There was at least a measure
of reason behind translations which rendered: "It was
a veritable God's bout," in the sense of a superhuman
struggle. But "clever trick" can never be deduced
from *naphtulim* by any legitimate device, to say nothing of the questionable attitude of such a statement
as a whole.

**9-11. When Leah saw that she had ceased
from bearing children, she took Zilpah, her handmaid, and gave her to Jacob for wife. And Zilpah,
Leah's handmaid, bore Jacob a son. And Leah
said: Good Luck! and she called his name Gad
(Luck).**

Leah might have continued without resorting to
the devise employed by her sister to secure children
had it not been for the fact that she herself ceased
bearing children. When this, however, happened she
followed in her sister's footsteps and gave Zilpah to
Jacob for wife. When v. 10 repeats that it was Zilpah,
"Leah's handmaid," who did the bearing, this again
emphasizes, as did v. 7, that only in this capacity does
her childbearing come into consideration.

11. The significant name given to the son in this
case is *gadh*, "luck" or "fortune" — based on the foster
mother's exclamation on the occasion of his birth, when

she said *begadh,* "with luck" or "in luck" — an ellipsis
for, "we acted with" or "we are in luck." To us it
seems that "good luck," as an exclamation, well covers
the case. It is true that this necessitates adopting the
textual reading followed by the Greek translators and
by Jerome. But still this reading seems simpler than
bagadh, which the marginal reading (*keri*) alters to
ba'gadh = "fortune has come." An exclamation is
more natural here than the formal statement.

Since Leah nowhere else gives indications of polytheistic leanings, and since Jacob surely would have
tolerated no names for his children that were allusions
to Aramaean or other divinities, we believe that the
interpretation which draws upon the fact that there
was a god of luck, Gad, has absolutely nothing to do
with our case. Besides, how unnatural to call a child by
the very name of the god of luck! Interpretations that
claim this to be the source and the import of the name
are attempts to degrade and to make light of the
patriarchal religion.

12, 13. **And Zilpah, Leah's handmaid, bore
Jacob a second son and Leah said: Good fortune,
for daughters shall call me fortunate — and she
called his name Asher (Fortune).**

Zilpah has the same measure of success: she too
has two sons. Leah's sentiments on the occasion are
so much the same as in the previous instance that the
name of Asher is practically only a synonym of Gad,
as is also indicated by dictionaries. K. W. gives
Glueck as the meaning for both. Only, of course, the
motivation of the name must needs be a bit different.
Here it is derived from the fact that Leah exclaims:
"Daughters shall call me fortunate" — the verb being
'asher in the *piel* stem, *'ishsherûnî.* Leah alludes to
the well-known custom that in lands where many sons
are deemed the finest gift a wife can bestow upon her
husband, daughters will naturally extol a mother of

whom such praise can be spoken. To be consistent,
Procksch invents the idea that "Asher" must be the
name of a Canaanite-Aramaean divinity, masculine to
the feminine "Asherah."

14, 15. **And Reuben went out in the days of
the wheat harvest and found mandrakes in the field
and brought them to Leah, his mother. And Rachel
said unto Leah: Please, give me some of the mandrakes of thy son. And she said to her: Is it not
enough that thou hast taken my husband away from
me, that thou wouldest take my son's mandrakes
also? And Rachel said: Therefore he shall lie
with thee tonight for thy son's mandrakes.**

Rivalry and jealousy in the bigamist's household
continue even though the two wives are sisters, or
perhaps all the more on that account. One object of
the narrative, without a doubt, is thus to portray the
evils of bigamy in a drastic fashion. The major purpose, of course, is to show how the fathers of the
twelve tribes came into being. For though on the
human level petty jealousies and the natural longing
for offspring are the things that are chiefly in evidence,
on the divine level the forebears of the chosen race
are being called into being, and the basis is being laid
for the rapid increasing of the seed of Abraham.

By this time Reuben may have been a lad of
about four years, just old enough to toddle out into
the field after the reapers. Childlike, he gathers what
especially attracts the eye, the yellow berries of the
mandrake about of the size of a nutmeg. The Hebrew
knows them as *dûda'îm,* which according to its root
signifies "love-apples." The ancients and, perhaps,
the early Hebrews, too, regarded this fruit as an
aphrodisiac and as promoting fertility. Had that
thought not been involved here, this innocent episode
could hardly have given rise to such a clash between
the sisters. Reuben, as little children will, presents

the mandrakes to his mother. Rachel, present at the time and much concerned as usual about her sterility, thinks to resort to this traditional means of relieving the disability and asks for "some of the mandrakes" (*min* = "some of") of Reuben. She had hardly thought that this harmless request would provoke such an outbreak on her sister's part. For Leah bitterly upbraids her with not being content to have withdrawn her husband from her, but, she petulantly adds, Rachel even wants to get the mandrakes of her son Reuben. Apparently, her hope that her husband would love her after she had born several sons (see 29:32) had not been fully realized. Childless Rachel still had the major part of his affection. Quite unjustly Leah charges Rachel with alienation of affection where such affection had perhaps never really existed. Leah still was being treated with more or less tolerance. So Leah certainly begrudges her sister the mandrakes, lest they prove effective and so give her sister a still more decided advantage. Yet the English idiom, "is it not enough," etc.? is not quite the same as the Hebrew which says: "is it a little thing that," etc.? We follow Luther for an easier idiom.

Rachel desires to preserve peace in the household and so concedes to yield the husband to her sister for the night in return for the mandrakes which she nevertheless purposes to eat. The frank narrative of the Scriptures on this point makes us blush with shame at the indelicate bargaining of the sisters — one of the fruits of a bigamous connection.

The efforts of critics to make the text appear at variance with itself here draw attention to the fact that nomads are said to be harvesting grain ("wheat harvest"). However, the contention is obviously unwarranted. It is not said that the nomads did the harvesting; and, surely, no one would deny the possibility of their using the expression "wheat harvest"

to mark a definite season of the year even if they
themselves did no harvesting. In any case, it may be
only the author's remark, used to fix a particular season
when, as his readers knew, mandrakes usually ripened.
Or may not the lad have followed along in the fields
of some neighbors, farmers, and gathered his mandrakes? Where several possibilities suggest an easy
explanation, critics select the one best suited to their
constructions and treat it as the only one: "the agricultural background shows that the episode is out of
place in its present nomadic setting" (Skinner). Without good reason K. C. makes *lakhen* concessive —
"nevertheless." Besides, on occasion the patriarchs
sowed and reaped (26:12), perhaps also in Mesopotamia.

16. **And Jacob came from the field toward
evening and Leah went forth to meet him, and she
said: To me shalt thou come in, for I have indeed
hired thee for my son's mandrakes. So he lay with
her that night.**

Jacob's lot cannot have been a very happy one.
To an extent he was shuttled back and forth between
two wives and even their handmaids. Almost a certain
shamelessness has taken possession of Jacob's wives
in their intense rivalry. Leah almost triumphantly
claims him as a result of her bargain, as he comes in
from the field. The *Beth* in *bedhûdha'ey* is the *Beth
of price.*

17, 18. **And God hearkened unto Leah, and she
conceived and bare Jacob a fifth son. And Leah
said: God hath given me my reward, because I
gave my handmaid to my husband. And she called
his name Issachar (Reward).**

For all the jealous and indelicate bickering on
Leah's part there must, nevertheless, have been also
a measure of faith, for she had called upon God in
her distress, and her cry cannot have been without

faith, for "God hearkened unto Leah, and she conceived," etc.

Yet the jealous struggles that went on day by day had dragged Leah down to a lower level than the one she had first occupied when she had attributed her offspring to "Yahweh," the God of covenant grace (29:32). Now she merely regards him as *'Elohim,* the God of power over his creatures. She actually believes that when she so humbled herself as to grant her handmaid to her husband for offspring's sake, God recognized her sincerity and is now rewarding her for it. Truth and error blend in that opinion. God may, indeed, have recognized her humble unselfishness. But God does not sanction bigamous proceedings, much as a certain age may condone them. The name "Issachar" embodies Leah's idea; for the simplest analysis of the form is still the one which sees the name as a compound of *yesh* and *sakhar* = "there is reward." This explanation would account for the otiose "s" or "sh," consistently found in the writing of the *Hebrew* name; as a *Keri perpetuum.* A parallel to this name is found in Jer. 31:16.

19, 20. And Leah conceived again and bore a sixth son to Jacob. And Leah said: God has bestowed an excellent gift on me; now my husband will dwell with me, for I have borne him six sons. And she called his name Zebulon (Dwelling).

The second period of fertility into which Leah enters results in two more sons. Her statement resulting in the naming of the child offers a kind of a pun. For the first word: "God has bestowed an excellent gift on me" operates with the verb *zabhadh,* "to present"; with the cognate object it literally means "present a present." Now as the result of the *zabhadh* Leah expects her husband will *zabhal* ("dwell") with her. This derivation makes the double propriety of the name Zebulon very apparent.

21. **Afterward she bore a daughter and called her name Dinah.**

This statement is inserted at this point because it prepares most appropriately for the events of chapter 34.   We know from 37:35 and 46:7, 15 b that Jacob had other daughters.   There was no occasion for making reference to them at this point.   In fact, Dinah may actually have been born shortly after the sixth son.   The name Dinah is about the same in meaning as Dan and could mean "Vindication."

22-24. **And God remembered Rachel and God hearkened unto her and opened her womb.   And she conceived and bore a son and she said: God has taken away my reproach.   And she called his name Joseph (May he add) saying: May Yahweh add for me another son.**

Criticism offers some strange reasoning on the verb "remembered."   Only P is supposed to use it.   So entirely mechanical is a man's style supposed to be that so common an idiom is supposed to be P's exclusive property.   Critics actually believe J could not have said: "God remembered."   Such remembering, *zakhar*, in cases such as these involved "granting requests" (B D B).

By this statement ("God remembered") the author indicates that Rachel's conception was not due to the mandrakes but to the omnipotent power of God, who is the Author of all life.   In any case, the story has advanced several years beyond the point where the mandrakes were eaten.   Yet Procksch claims without sufficient evidence that the birth of Joseph must originally have stood in connection with the mandrake episode.

23. Quite humbly Rachel, who early in her marriage may have been a more or less haughty and self-sufficient personage, now gives God the glory and rejoices that He "has taken away" her "reproach."

Sterility brought reproach, as though God had deemed a wife unworthy of children. Rachel still stands on the lower level of faith when she makes this remark, for she thinks only of the sovereign power of God. Yet her experience of divine help raises her faith to the higher level where she asks for grace from the faithful covenant God Yahweh: "May Yahweh add for me another son."

24. A double thought plays into the name Joseph: it incorporates both of Rachel's remarks. For *yoseph* may count as an imperfect of *'asaph*, "to take away." Or it may also count more definitely as imperfect (*Hifil*) of the verb *yasaph* "to add." We must admit this to be very ingenious. But why deny to a mother a happy ingenuity on the occasion of her greatest joy? Why try to inject the thought of a confusion of two sources?

25, 26. **And it came to pass that when Rachel had borne Joseph, that Jacob said to Laban: Let me go that I may depart to my place and to my country. Give me my wives and my children for which I have served thee and let me go; for thou knowest what service I have rendered unto thee.**

From what is here said it appears that Joseph must have been born at the end of the fourteen years of service. However, it must also be remarked here that apparently there is no attempt made to report the birth of Jacob's sons in a strictly consecutive fashion. If that were the case, seven years would never have sufficed for eleven children. Apparently, the children born of one mother are listed in a group in order to dispose of all of them at once, except in the case of Leah where about a year may have elapsed between the birth of the fourth and the fifth son. Whitelaw summarizes the possible sequence as concisely as it may be put when he says: "The six sons of Leah may have been born in the seven years, allowing one year's complete cessation from pregnancy, viz. the fifth; Bilhah's in the third and fourth years; Zilpah's in the beginning of the sixth and seventh; and Rachel's toward the end of the seventh, leaving Dinah to be born later." So by this time Jacob's family was almost complete as to numbers, and he might well think of looking to the establishment of an independent home. The birth of Joseph had rounded out the one gap which had been felt till now.

"Let me go" is a bit stronger in the original and could be rendered, "send me away" or "dismiss me." "My place and my country" are mentioned side by side in the sense where we sometimes refer first to a more definite then to a more general object; therefore we could render: "that I may go to my place, and in general to my country." For even after Jacob comes to his native country he will not confine himself strictly to his "place," for he is a nomad and must wander about.

26. Since Jacob had pledged himself to seven years of additional service for the possession of Rachel, he could not strictly call his whole family his own until the second seven years were fulfilled. He now wants Laban to acknowledge the fulfillment of his contract by giving him his wives and his children that he might depart. In a sense all had been Laban's or at least under Laban's acknowledged jurisdiction. Laban is asked to admit that this is cancelled. Jacob's experience with Laban has not been such as to make Jacob desirous of staying with him any longer. Jacob realizes that the service he has rendered during all these years was in an eminent sense marked by faithfulness, so he remarks, "thou knowest what service I have rendered to thee." Jacob implies that what he has done will bear closest scrutiny and must be acknowledged to be a faithful performance of his own part of the agreement. There is no obsequiousness

about Jacob's attitude, no diffidence. He knows his
father-in-law must be dealt with firmly. On the other
hand, he also knows how to treat him with becoming
respect.

**27, 28. And Laban said unto him: If I have
found favor in thy sight — I have consulted the
omens and find that Yahweh hath blessed me for
thy sake. Besides he said: Fix the wages I am
to pay thee, and I will pay them.**

Laban is quite deferential to this son-in-law whom
he respects for his character and his success. He
begins with the somewhat elaborate oriental courtesy:
"If I have found favor in thy sight" — an ellipsis.
Perhaps it involves a courteous protest like, "please
don't talk about leaving," or else the conclusion might
run, "tarry" (A. V.). In any case, the superstitious
old fellow had surmised right along that Yahweh was
granting blessings to Jacob's endeavor. Now recently
he had "consulted the omens" (*ni(ch)cháshtî*), and
they had pointed to the same conclusion. What heathen
device Laban had resorted to in consulting the omens
cannot be determined. But the act as such does reveal
a departure from the true service of God and practically stamps him as an idolater. His reference to God
as Yahweh is merely a case of accomodating himself
to Jacob's mode of speech. Laban did not know Him
as such or believe in Him. Any man with even a
measure of insight could have determined without
augury what Laban claimed had been revealed to him
by augury. Jacob's faithful service of Yahweh was
not kept hidden by him.

28. Laban is ready to go almost any limit to
retain a man whose services have been so advantageous to himself. Laban is an eminently selfish man.
He makes Jacob a proposition which at once substan-
tially alters Jacob's status. From the position of a
bound servant he is raised to that of a partner who

may freely dictate his own terms. Now, indeed, such
an offer is not to be despised, for it puts Jacob in a
position where he can build up a small fortune of his
own and so removes him from the necessity of returning home practically a penniless adventurer, though
a man with a good-sized family.

**29, 30. And he said to him. Thou thyself
knowest what service I have rendered thee and how
thy cattle fared under my care; for it was but a
little that thou didst own before I came, but it expanded tremendously and Yahweh let blessings follow wherever I went. And now when am I to provide for my own house also?**

Apparently, before Jacob began to take steps to
leave Laban had never admitted that he owed his
newly won prosperity to Jacob. Since he admits at
least so much, Jacob improves the situation by driving
home that point and emphasizing it. Again he tells
Laban that he is very well aware of the type of service
his son-in-law has been rendering: this is the emphasis
conveyed by the statement "thou thyself knowest."
Jacob adds as a particular illustration how well Laban's
cattle have fared. For in the case of nomads practically their entire wealth consisted in cattle. The
phrase *'ittî* must mean "under my care," or literally
"with me." Apparently, Laban had had but indifferent
success before. Jacob frankly tells Laban that Laban
had "but a little" before his coming, *lephanay* (literally: "before my face or presence"). A change must
have been apparent at once upon Jacob's arrival, for
from that time onward Laban's wealth "expanded
tremendously" (*larobh* = "unto a multitude"). But
it would ill behoove this true follower of Yahweh's to
ascribe such wealth to himself. Here is his opportunity
roundly to confess his faith in Yahweh's blessing, and
he does it in no uncertain terms: "Yahweh let blessings follow wherever I went." This last statement

really reads: "Yahweh blessed me upon the foot."
Now *leraghlî*, "to my foot," usually means "after me,"
as I Sam. 25:42 and Hab. 3:5 show. From this it follows, if blessing go after him, blessings attend wherever he goes. Where such is the case, a very high
measure of blessings is certainly being bestowed. The
rest of Jacob's argument now runs modestly as follows:
I have done all in my power to provide for you and
have done my work very successfully; "when am I
to provide for my own house also?" The fairness of
the demand can hardly be questioned.

**31-33. And he said: What shall I give thee?
And Jacob said: Thou shalt not give me anything.
Yet I will again pasture thy flocks, yea, and guard
them, if thou wilt do for me this thing: I shall
pass through thy entire flock today removing from
it every sheep that is speckled and spotted and every
one of the lambs that is black, and the spotted and
speckled among the goats; that shall be my pay.
Then my righteousness shall answer for me on any
future day, if thou shalt come upon my hire before
thee; everything that is not speckled or spotted
among the goats or black among the lambs, it shall
count with me as a thing stolen.**

By his question, "What shall I give thee?" Laban
admits that Jacob is quite justified in asking for a
substantial flock for himself and appears quite ready
to give it on the spot. Jacob knows the niggardly
disposition of his father-in-law and that he will rue
very shortly having parted with any of his goods. So
Jacob says: "Thou shalt not give me anything"
(*me'û'mah*, second last syllable accented because the
ultima is an old case ending, S. G. 90 f). Yet Jacob
will do the work of a shepherd (*'er'eh* — "I will pasture") "yea, also guard them," i. e. use the best of
caution in all his work on one condition which he is
about to state, v. 32, 33. The plan suggested puts the

possibility of acquiring wealth entirely in the providence of God. Jacob does not know whether it will
please God to have him acquire wealth. Now to understand what follows it must be borne in mind that sheep
are normally white in the Orient (cf. Ps. 147:16; Song
4:2; 6:6; Dan. 7:9); goats are normally black or
brown-black (Song 4:1 b). The exceptions to this
rule are not numerous. Yet Jacob will take only the
exceptions. If he is to acquire wealth according to
God's will, the Almighty Disposer of events must
grant it. This was a fine act of faith on Jacob's part.
He cast himself wholly upon God's mercy.

32. Jacob proposes to go through all the flocks in
person and separate that very day every one of the
abnormally colored sheep or goats, i. e. the *naqôdh*,
covered with smaller spots, or "speckled," and the *talû'*,
marked by larger spots, or "spotted." Though he says,
"that shall be my pay," yet this remark must be held
against his initial statement: "Thou shalt not give me
anything" (v. 31). Jacob is not now changing his
mind. He merely means all *future* speckled or spotted
lambs and goats shall be my pay. He actually asks
for nothing at the outset. *Haser* is an absolute infinite
used as an accusative of relation expressing mode
(G. K. 113 h, K. S. 402 b).

33. Jacob expects that from time to time suspicious Laban will come, bent on investigating. Jacob
expects to have a very clear case in such an event;
for either flocks consist of such as are normally colored,
or they do not. One glance will always suffice to tell
whether Jacob is dealing fairly or not; in other words,
"my righteousness shall answer for me on any future
day." If anything appears in Jacob's flocks "not
speckled or spotted," that is to be dealt with as "a
thing stolen," that is to say, Laban may promptly
remove it and claim it for his own. The issue will be
very clear-cut. Deceit will be out of the question.

With good reason, at least from this point of view, Jacob chose such a basis of division.

Jacob cannot be charged with tempting God in this case and, as it were, seeking to induce God to work a miracle for him. For when Jacob was still at Bethel, God had promised to care for him; and since his arrival in Canaan Jacob had had ample tokens of divine favor. He may, therefore, well commit the issues entirely to God. We repeat, Jacob's proposition to Laban was a fine act of faith.

34. And Laban said: Right; let it be as you say.

Laban is only too ready to close with an offer such as Jacob's. *Hen,* "behold," expresses a kind of eagerness, like our exclamation of assent "right." The Hebrew wish is really a bit more formal than our translation indicates, for it says: "would that it might become according to thy word."

35, 36. And on that day he removed the striped and spotted he-goats and all speckled and spotted she-goats and all that had white on them, and all the black among the sheep and put them in the care of his sons. And he put a distance of a three days' journey between himself and Jacob; but Jacob tended the rest of Laban's flock.

Verse 35 can mean only this, that Laban himself did the separating of the ones that were to be kept apart from the rest, yet v. 32 Jacob had stipulated that he himself would take care of that work. Laban's interference indicates his mistrust of Jacob, not a warranted mistrust but the mistrust of a man who is himself not to be trusted. Whatever promptings of generosity Laban may have felt at the time when he stood in danger of losing the valuable services of Jacob, these promptings are all dissipated as soon as he sees that the son-in-law will continue in his service. Two other indications of mistrust on Laban's part are that he puts the abnormally colored under the care of his sons, lest Jacob tamper with them and perhaps use them for breeding purposes, where, of course, the chance of abnormal offspring would be proportionately greater. The original agreement had no such proviso in it: Jacob had always been treated as perfectly competent and dependable for the care of any part of the flock. But Laban's conduct and attitude become downright insulting when he gives a third indication of mistrust in putting "a distance (Hebrew "way") of a three days' journey between himself and Jacob." Had Jacob not displayed a fine tolerance at this point, he might well have been tempted to sever connections with Laban on the spot in spite of any agreement that might have just been made.

It is true, the enumeration in v. 35 is not complete, but everyone understands that the ones not mentioned are to be supplied in thought. A number of new terms appears here, apparently the ones that were used at this point by the contracting parties to define more closely the terms previously used. So "striped" (*'aqud-dîm*) appears for the first time, for, indeed, the "striped" are neither "speckled" nor exactly "spotted," and yet Jacob must have had them in mind originally. So, too, the "she-goats" are separately mentioned, though there could have been no thought of exempting them. Likewise, "all that had white on them" must have been included in any reasonable definition of what was to be included in this group. *Hannôtharoth*, plural, agrees *ad sensum* with the collective singular *tso'n* (K. S. 334 i).

37-39. **And Jacob took fresh rods of poplar, almond, and plane trees, and peeled white stripes on them, laying bare the white part of the rods; and he laid these rods which he had peeled in front of the sheep in the gutters of the watering troughs to which the sheep came to drink. And they were**

in heat when they came to drink. So the cattle bred before the rods and the cattle bare striped, speckled and spotted.

The bargain relative to Jacob's wages, as it was originally made, was actually an act of faith on Jacob's part. But when Laban's several acts of mistrust came to light, it seems Jacob was somewhat shaken from his resolution to make an issue of faith of the whole matter; and so on his part he resorted to tricky devices in order to be assured of success. Mistrust lies behind Jacob's devices.

If now biologists raise the issue that prenatal influence cannot determine the color of sheep or of goats, as far as we can discern, they must add the qualifying statement: "as far as their observation goes." Here seem to lie certain problems with which they have not sufficiently grappled. Though, indeed, there may be curious superstitions on the part of people in reference to some of these matters, yet as the Biblical record here runs, its meaning without a doubt is that Jacob's crafty device helped determine the color of the lambs and the goats. The observations of the ancients, backed by the experience of many moderns, seems to confirm the practicability of the device here described.

Quite another question is the one of the ethics of Jacob's act. Here it must be conceded that when Jacob originally made his bargain, he certainly meant that the varicolored sheep and goats were to be his, but only those that would be born under perfectly normal circumstances. If Laban's acts led him to feel that certain schemes are thereby justified, Jacob is in the wrong in thinking so. True, the text says nothing of the sort, but then the issue is sufficiently clear without a statement of the text, and 31:9 does not conflict with our claim, as we shall presently show. Certain extenuating circumstances, however, certainly appear in this case, which, if they do not justify Jacob, at least lessen his guilt.

Jacob's device, then, as here described is to lay peeled rods of trees that peel more readily than others and show a particularly white surface after peeling — the white "poplar" as the name *libhneh* ("white") indicates, the *lûz*, or "almond" and the *'ermôn*, or "plane tree," whose bark naturally peels off in large slabs — to lay these in the troughs where the sheep drink during the breeding season. Breeding took place with these speckled or spotted objects before the eyes of the she-goats and the lambs. Now, especially the lamb is said to be susceptible to the things seen at the time of copulation or during the period of gestation by way of having the effects of such sight passed on to the offspring. And yet, certainly, another influence must be allowed at this point. Surely, man cannot so definitely control nature. Biologists admit the possibility of prenatal influences that they have not yet fully discerned. One such influence in this case was the overruling providence of God which in an unequal contest between two men gave the advantage to the one who was relatively innocent. In v. 37 *machsoph* is a verbal noun, like an absolute infinitive (G. K. 117 r). Again, *pitstsel petsalôth* gives an instance of a cognate object. In v. 38 the collective singular *tso'n* has a plural verb. In v. 39 *yechemû* ("they bred") is masculine but is quite naturally replaced by a feminine *teladhnah* ("they bore") with again the collective *tso'n* a subject for both.

40. And the lambs Jacob set apart and set the faces of the flock toward the striped and all the black in Laban's flock and he made separate herds for himself and did not put them together with Laban's flock.

Here many insist that the thought of the verse is an impossibility. How, they ask, could the cattle under

Jacob's care see Laban's flock, a three days' journey distant? Without a doubt, the author is not guilty of any such absurdities. For the understanding of the verse it must be remembered that Jacob had Laban's flock — the white sheep and the black goats — that is, the normal color. Laban had Jacob's flock — all the abnormally colored. The preceding verse had mentioned "the striped, speckled, and "spotted" that were born. These v. 40 groups together under the term "lambs." These were to go under Laban's care according to contract, so they are called "Laban's flock" by anticipation. These "lambs" are not at once taken over by Laban, but, no doubt, the shepherds would wait until they were weaned and had gotten old enough to be moved some distance away. But as long as Jacob had them under his own care he made a separate unit of them as much as possible and would so pasture all of Laban's sheep that were under his care that he "set the faces of the flock toward the striped and the black" in the expectation that this sight, an unusual one, would impress itself on the white flock in advance and so prepare the influence that would be intensified later by the peeled rods. With this interpretation the second half of the verse agrees, except that "Laban's flock" is now used to refer not to the flock Laban tended but to the flock which he owned but which Jacob tended. Everyone understands how the expression "Laban's flock" would continually be used in two senses as long as the arrangement they had agreed upon remained in force.

41, 42. **And it came to pass whenever the sturdier cattle were breeding, Jacob would place his rods before the eyes of the cattle in the drinking troughs in order that they might have breeding heat among the rods. But when the flocks showed feebleness, he did not lay out (his rods). As a result,**

the more feeble were Laban's, and the sturdier, Jacob's.

In v. 41 the converted perfects equal the frequentative imperfects, even as the imperfect of v. 42 *yasîm* is frequentative (K. S. 401 p, 367 e, G. K. 112 ee). Since the flocks bore twice a year, apparently Jacob's experience had taught him that those born in the fall were the "studier" or hardier. He so adjusted his device that it would react upon these and omitted to use it "when the flocks showed feebleness" (B D B). But for v. 42 one might argue that he, indeed, employed the device, but the text as such says nothing of its effectiveness. It must be conceded that v. 42 states that his device proved effective; but again we add: only in the providence of God.

43. And the man became exceedingly rich and had large flocks and handmaidens and servants and camels and asses.

The Hebrew says: "the man burst out exceedingly exceedingly." Our translation catches the import of the statement, though in a less colorful fashion. To take care of the ever increasing flocks a multitude of servants became necessary, and camels and asses as well, for keeping in touch with the various movements of the flock and for moving from place to place with the nomadic establishment. God had fulfilled His promise of 28:15 beyond what Jacob could ever have anticipated. Observe *rabbôth*, plural adjective with *tso'n*, singular collective (K. S. 346 d).

HOMILETICAL SUGGESTIONS

Important as the revelation of this chapter may be from several points of view, again it does not happen to be suited for use in the pulpit. For without a doubt, no man would care to lay bare the rivalries between Rachel and Leah as recorded v. 1-24. Still less adapted to sermonic use is v. 37-43. That would leave v. 25-36, which again would fall under the same general heading as 26:12-17: "The blessing of the Lord, it maketh rich."

CHAPTER XXXI

7. Jacob's Flight from Laban; their Treaty
(31:1-54)

It may seem very strange to regard the preceding chapter and the present one as still belonging to the "story of Isaac," as the heading 25:19 suggests. But though Jacob is the active figure, Isaac still dominates this portion of the history of the chosen people: v. 18 Jacob is going back to Isaac under whom he belongs; v. 53 Jacob swears by Isaac's God or "fear." Jacob's "story" begins 37:2. These headings ("history," or "story" = *toledôth,* see 2:4) are aptly chosen.

The chapter before us may be divided into three parts: a) the flight of Jacob, v. 1-21; b) the interference of Laban, v. 22-42; c) the treaty, v. 43-54.

a) The Flight of Jacob (v. 1-21)

1, 2. And he heard the words of Laban's sons, who said: Jacob hath taken all that belonged to our father; and from that which was our father's hath he achieved all this abundance. And Jacob observed Laban's face, and it certainly was no longer as it had formerly been.

Jacob thrived far more abundantly than Laban. Apparently, Laban himself was doing far better than when Jacob first arrived. But Laban's sons have too much of the niggardly spirit of their father. When they observe that Jacob is growing wealthy, they vent their displeasure in grumbling remarks, which, perhaps, are not heard by Jacob directly but are reported by others. Jealousy leads the sons of Laban to overstate the case, almost absurdly: "he hath taken all

(828)

that belonged to our father," as though Laban had
been impoverished, and as though Jacob had been
guilty of some form of theft. Another statement of
theirs ran thus: "from that which was our father's
hath he achieved all this abundance." Here *kabhodh*
is better taken as "abundance" (B D B) or *Masse*
(K. W.) rather than wealth, for the heads of cattle,
numerous as they were, are under consideration.

In addition, though Laban is more adroit and
refrains from saying what might be used against him,
yet he has dark looks for Jacob in place of the hypocritical smiles that once wreathed his face. We render
kithmol shilshom, "formerly," though literally it
means: "yesterday (and) the third day." By
synecdoche the special is used for the general (K.
W.) and so the expression is little different from our
"formerly." We take the liberty of rendering *hinneh*,
("behold,") "certainly," which points out as definitely
as "behold." The expression *me'asher* must mean
"from *that* which" (G. K. 138 e). *Peney* is not
"attitude."

3. **And Yahweh said to Jacob: Return to the
land of thy fathers and to thy relationship, and I
will be with thee.**

Many times before this Jacob may have desired
to return, especially since living together with Laban
was becoming increasingly difficult. We have every
reason to believe that, godly man that he was, Jacob
had been submitting his difficulty to his God in
prayer. Since he had been living under God's direct
guidance ever since the time of the Bethel vision,
Jacob would not presume to return unless God so
directed. The substance of the Bethel promise (28:
15) is here renewed. God indicates that now Jacob
may feel free to return. Most appropriately He is
here designated as *Yahweh,* the faithful Lord, who
had kept all promises made to Jacob. After all the

promises made to Abraham, Jacob well understood the necessity of returning to "the land" of his fathers.

4-6. So Jacob sent and called Rachel and Leah out into the field to his flock, and he said to them: I have been observing your father's face, for it is no longer toward me as it formerly was; but the God of my father hath been with me. And you for your part know that I served your father to the best of my ability.

The wives are to be apprised of Jacob's purpose to flee. The fact that Jacob sends for them to come "out into the field" — *hassadheh* used adverbially (K. S. 330 c) — gives the first indication that Jacob is determined to flee secretly. This plan is not to be commended. If the separation from Laban was permissible and right, and God has even sanctioned it, then it should have been carried out openly as the honorable thing that it actually was. Fear of the consequences should have been dismissed, since divine approval was assured. Here, too, Jacob is seen putting undue confidence in purely human devices.

Rachel is mentioned first because she still ranked pre-eminent in Jacob's esteem. The wives are not only to be informed; their active co-operation is to be enlisted. It would seem as though Jacob had never fully spoken his mind to his wives on this subject. The patriarchal manner of life seems to have made such a step as Jacob here contemplated appear too much like rebellion to allow him even to discuss it with his wives prior to this time. Emancipation desires were not the order of the day then as now.

5. "I have been observing" (*ro'eh*, participle and first by way of emphasis) indicates that Jacob wishes to assure his wives that this is not an impression based on a glimpse or two of Laban's face. Laban's ill will has now already become a fixed attitude. The expression relative to the change in Laban's face

involves in this case active and harmful enmity, because Jacob hastens to point out by way of contrast (*we* adversative) that God had definitely taken Jacob's part to guard him against the harm which Laban's attitude presaged or even may already have attempted. The expression, "God of my father," does not mean that He is not Jacob's God, but rather that He is giving proof of the faithfulness which the fathers experienced. *Elohim* is here used because Jacob is thinking of the power which the Creator displayed in overruling the things that Laban did to overreach his son-in-law.

6. Jacob, however, knows himself to have been quite undeserving of such treatment as he has been receiving at Laban's hands, and he knows how thoroughly his wives understand the justice of his cause: they have seen day for day how faithfully their husband was serving their father. Therefore *'atténah,* first by way of emphasis — "you for your part" or "you, at least."

7-9. **But your father has deceived me and changed my wages ten times; but God did not allow him to do me harm. If he said thus: The speckled ones shall be your wage, then the entire flock bore speckled ones. But if he said: The striped ones shall be your wage, then the entire flock bore striped ones. So God has taken away your father's herd and given it to me.**

Now we learn, what had not yet been revealed in chapter 30, that Laban had repeatedly altered and realtered the original agreement in an effort to fleece Jacob. Whereas at first it was merely stipulated that all that was unusual in color should be Jacob's (30:32), Laban had changed these terms so that only one particular class of the off-color sheep or goats should be Jacob's, such as *only* "the speckled" (*nequddim*), i. e., those with smaller spots, or *only* "the striped ones"

('*aquddim*), always hoping that surely the man Jacob
could not continue to be so particularly favored. The
statement "ten times" here stands as a round number
signifying as much as: just as often as he could.
Apparently, Jacob, secure in the confidence of divine
favor, had acceded to each new request, exorbitant
though it was. Jacob throughout ascribes his success
to "God," *Elohim* who as Creator can well control
His creation. Under these circumstances Dillmann
should not have described Jacob as God's "favorite"
(*Schuetzling*). For Laban was actually "deceiving"
(*hethel* — Hifil from *talal*) Jacob, for the original
agreement, which was to have covered all relations
between the two, was always being invalidated by
Laban. Besides, without a doubt, Laban was trying
every possible demand or combination of demands of
which he was capable. Of course, in these later
instances Jacob could not longer resort to devices
mentioned in the previous chapter, for no device
could be calculated to produce such nice differentia-
tions in coloring as the new contracts made necessary.
So, without a doubt, Jacob himself was led to ascribe
all success he had to God's providence. On the other
hand, it must have been very strange that Laban
could not sense divine interference. *Hethel* used
with *be* implies a despising of the object (K. S.
212 f). *Hecheliph* is really iterative: "he has kept
on changing" (K. S. 367 h).

9. The absolute statement of this verse is certainly to be taken as being only relatively correct:
surely, Laban had not lost everything, nor had Jacob
come into possession of all. But God certainly had
taken away from the one and given to the other. The
verb "take away" (*natsal* in the Hifil) bears an unusual shade of meaning here. It usually means "to
deliver" and here practically implies that for a flock

to come out from under the hand of Laban was the
equivalent of a deliverance. In v. 8 the *yihyeh* is
singular, being influenced by the predicate noun
rather than by the subject (K. S. 350 a). In v. 9
the suffix on *'abhikhem* is masculine representing
the infrequent feminine (G. K. 135 o; K. S. 9).

10-13. **And it happened at the time when the
flock was hot in breeding that I lifted up my eyes
and saw things in a dream, and, lo, rams that were
leaping upon the goats were striped and speckled
and spotted. And the angel of God said unto me
in a dream, Jacob; and I said: Here I am. And
he said unto me. Lift up now thine eyes and see:
all the rams that are leaping upon the goats are
striped, speckled and spotted, for I have taken note
of all that Laban hath done to thee. I am the God
of Bethel where thou didst anoint a pillar and didst
vow a vow unto me. Up now, go forth from this
land and return to the land of thy birth.**

We must first dispose of the problem whether
God actually inspired this dream and actually spoke
in the dream to Jacob, or whether the dream was conjured up by Jacob's excited imagination or subcon-
scious mind which had been busied rather intensively
with the problem the dream reflects. Keil and Strack
and others, without offering proof, assume the latter.
They do not attribute deception to Jacob; they allow
that he may have had such a dream but simply state,
e. g., "it is certain that God did not shown Jacob the
rams in a dream" (Strack). However, such a dream
of a man of God, if it were a subjective delusion and
yet reported in the Scriptures, would be quite without analogy. In fact, in all other cases such men
were sure that a divine revelation had come to them,
and Jacob is no less sure than they. As for the question whether God will stoop to reveal such trivial, if

not even unseemly, matters as the details of breeding, it must be remembered that such matters could hardly be offensive and trivial to a shepherd like Jacob. It is an injustice to the man Jacob to assume that he reported as a divine revelation a dream whose origin may have seemed doubtful to him and used the dream to influence his wives and to justify himself.

This dream, then, is not for the purpose of suggesting to Jacob what lambs and what kids he is to select the next time he bargains with Laban, for, as we just learned, *Laban* was the one who kept altering the terms of the agreement. This dream is rather a revelation given to Jacob at a particular breeding time to make him aware of the fact that even this matter was being regulated entirely by God's providence, and that Jacob could put full confidence in God to guard his best interests. Surely, what Jacob saw in the dream (v. 10) was not necessarily what was happening in reality. Yet even here we must concede that God might so have regulated the matter that only "the striped, speckled and spotted" rams did the breeding. However, according to a well-known biological law that would not guarantee offspring only of the color of the rams. Therefore this part of the dream may have been suggestive, indicating to Jacob that God had the issues fully under control.

Berudhim ("spotted") seems to involve bigger spots than *nequddim* ("speckled") which seems to involve a being mottled. Therefore K. W., *grossfleckig* for the former.

11. The one who addresses Jacob is "the angel of God." Yet in v. 13 this person identifies himself with God and so cannot have been a created angel but must have been divine. Here 16:7-11 as well as 22:11, 15 should again be compared, together with the comments there made. The fact that previously

He was called "angel of Yahweh" but here "angel of God" makes no appreciable difference.

12. The Angel of God specially draws Jacob's attention to what he sees. Jacob is not to regard the thing seen as trivial but as indicative of the fact that God had "taken note of all that Laban had done" to him and was, of course, Himself taking measures to safeguard Jacob in what seemed like an unequal contest.

13. Very definitely God identifies Himself to Jacob as the one who formerly had appeared at Bethel and to whom Jacob had anointed a pillar (*matstsebha*) and vowed a vow. This is another way of saying that what He had promised then to do for Jacob is now actually being done. For assuredly, but for divine interference Jacob would have suffered irreparable loss. Strangely, *ha'el,* though construct state, has the article. Yet this is not so difficult if it be noted that the generic noun *'el,* as it passes over into use as a proper noun, retains the article, so that the whole combination *ha'el* becomes the proper noun (cf. K. S. 295 i; 303 a; G. K. 127 f).

This dream, of course, did not need to be repeated every year when a new situation arose, for *mutatis mutandis* it indicated what God was doing. Very likely, what v. 3 reports in summary is given in fuller detail in v. 10-13. There is no need of assuming a series of dreams, as does Lange.

V. 13 b = v. 3. It is the climax of this dream revelation. The time for departure is at hand. This land of adoption must be forsaken. The land of birth is to be sought. Such a declaration as Jacob here reports must have deeply influenced Jacob's wives. It would not seem as though this divine vision had ever been told to them before. Jacob knew that sacred spiritual experiences were not to be discussed too freely. Perhaps, too, his wives were not yet spi-

ritually ready for this information. Coming to them
at this juncture, it may have been overwhelming in its
impression.

**14-16. And Rachel and Leah answered and
said to him: Have we still any share or inheritance
in our father's house? Have we not been accounted
as foreigners by him? for he hath sold us and hath
entirely used up the money that should have been
ours. For all riches which God hath taken away
from our father really belong to us and to our children. And now as for all that God bade thee,
do it.**

The two wives are of one mind and agree entirely
with their husband. The construction indicates that
Rachel took the lead and spoke first — *watta'an,*
singular, though a double subject follows; yet that
alone is a common enough construction and used as
an alternate for the plural verb (cf. K. S. 349 u).
Yet Rachel is placed first, indicating that the initiation
lay with her. The wives recognize that they no longer
share the interests and the objectives of their paternal
home. B D B under *cheleq* suggests quite aptly that
the idea "obligation to the paternal home" is involved.
Anteil (K. W.) could cover the case. Then, coming
to more material concerns, their "inheritance" apparently need not be hoped for.

15. In fact, the father has treated his own
children not as though they were his own flesh and
blood but as though they were of as little concern to
him as *nokhriyyoth,* "foreigners," i. e., those of an
unsympathetic foreign group. "Strangers" (A. V.)
is not quite exact. Proof of this unpaternal attitude
lies, first, in the manner in which he disposed of his
daughters: it was a case of sale (*makhar* = "he
sold"), and their mode of referring to it indicates
that the daughters knew a better mode of giving in
marriage to have been the custom even in their day.

Seven (or fourteen) years of service constituted the price paid. But besides, whereas a less greedy father would have used the gift from his prospective son-in-law to provide a dowry for his daughters, Laban "entirely used it up" (Hebrew, "eaten up" — *'akhal* with absolute infinite = "entirely") most likely by investing it directly in his flocks and herds so that it was completely absorbed. Consequently, *kaspénu* = not "our money" but "the money that should have been ours," or perhaps, "the money he acquired through us" (K. C.). Yet our translation lies closer to the facts under discussion.

16. From one point of view the wives are correct when they assert that all the present wealth of their father belongs to them and to their children, because he apparently had not been wealthy before Jacob came who by his assiduous and skillful management increased his father-in-law's "riches" enormously. By all canons of right Jacob's family ought to have been adjudged as deserving of a good share of these riches. But the wives saw that their father was not minded to give them or their husband anything at all. Apparently, the long pent-up grievances find expression in these words. Ultimately, then, the wives arrive at the conclusion that the best thing Jacob can do is to obey God's command and depart. Their mode of arriving at this conclusion is not the most desirable: they finally conclude to consent to what God commands because their best material interests are not being served by the present arrangement. Jacob, no doubt, approached the problem on the higher plane: he was obeying the God of his fathers, who had made promises to Jacob previously and was now fulfilling these promises. So in Jacob's case we have fidelity to God; in the case of his wives a greater measure of interest in material advantage. For that reason, too, Jacob's wives refer to Him only

as *Elohim.* There is no special reason for regarding
the introductory *ki* as "so that," since the customary
"for" is quite adequate, tying back, however, to the
idea of considering his daughters as "foreigners."

**17, 18. So Jacob proceeded to set his children
and his wives upon camels, and he drove away all
his cattle and all his substance which he had
acquired, the cattle constituting his property which
he had acquired in Paddan Aram, in order to go to
Isaac, his father, to the land of Canaan.**

The Hebrew "rose up" (A. V.) *wayyaqom,* is
often used in the looser sense of addressing oneself
to a task; therefore: "he proceeded" (Meek). With
skillful and picturesque detail the father is shown
getting his family under way for the flight, "he set
them upon camels." The original has even a bit more
of color — *nasa'* = "he lifted up."

18. "He drove away" indicates not a leisurely
departure but all possible haste, though, of course,
flocks had to be driven carefully lest they suffer from
overexertion and perish. In addition to the cattle
there were other possessions of Jacob that he had
acquired in Paddan-Aram or Mesopotamia. For
Jacob had not been, and was not intending to be after
his return, a nomad. By a repetition of *miqneh,*
"cattle," this part of his possessions is reverted to
as "constituting" the major part of "his property,"
qinyano, as K. W. well translates: *der Viehbesitz,
der sein Vermoegen bildete.* The statement is rounded
out by a double statement of the objective of his
journey: on the one hand, he was going back "to
Isaac, his father," under whose authority he felt he
still belonged, and "to the land of Canaan," which
according to divine decree was ultimately destined
to be the possession of his posterity. Such precise
formal statements including all the major facts are
wont to be made by Moses when he records a par-

ticularly momentous act. The very circumstantiality
of its form makes one feel its importance — a device,
by the way, quite naturally employed for similar
purposes to this day. Critics miss all these finer
points of style, for the supposed authors that the
critics imagine have wrought out parts of Genesis
(E, J, P, D) are poor fellows with one-track minds,
not one of whom has the least adaptability of style,
but all of whom write in a stiff, stilted fashion after
one pattern only. Critics ascribe most of v. 18 to P.

19-21. **But Laban had gone to shear his sheep;
and Rachel stole the teraphim which belonged to her
father. And Jacob tricked Laban, the Aramaean,
by not telling him that he was fleeing. So he and all
that were his fled. He proceeded, namely, and
crossed the River and set his face in the direction
of Mount Gilead.**

As it just happened, the rather important task
of sheepshearing was just engrossing Laban's attention. Among the ancients, at least of a later date,
the event was quite a festivity (cf. 38:12; I Sam.
25; II Sam. 13:23). Since Laban was at some distance from Jacob's flocks (30:36), and since all hands
were kept quite busy for a few days, no time could
have been more opportune. Because the father was
away from home, Rachel had a chance to carry out
a special project of her own: she stole her father's
household gods, the *teraphim*. The plural may be
a plural of excellence patterned after *Elohim*, and
so only one image may have been involved. Whether
these were larger, almost man-sized as I Sam. 19:13,
16 seems to suggest, or actually were only the small
figurines that excavations in Palestine now yield matters little; both types may have prevailed. Apparently, judging by the parallel Hebrew root, they were
regarded as promoting domestic prosperity, and so
were a kind of gods of the hearth, *Penates*. Appa-

rently, according to Zech. 10:2, they were also used for purposes of divination. It seems hardly fair to assume that the Israelites carelessly carried these household divinities over from the time of these early Mesopotamian contacts and continued to use them almost uninterruptedly. When Michal happens to have such a figure handy (I Sam. 19), that is not as yet proof that from Rachel's day to Michal's Israel had quite carelessly tolerated them. We should rather say that whenever Israel lapsed into idolatry, especially in Canaan, then the backsliders would also adapt themselves to the teraphim cult. Hos. 3:4 by no means lists them as legitimate objects of worship.

But of some moment is the question: "Why did Rachel steal this teraphim?" To be rejected are such conjectures as merely to play her father a prank; or to take them for their intrinsic worth, supposing that they were gold or silver figurines; or to employ a drastic or almost fanatical mode of seeking to break her father's idolatry — views current among Jewish commentators and early church fathers and to some extent to this day. More nearly correct might seem to be the opinion which suggests that she aimed to deprive her father of the blessings which might have been conferred by them. Most reasonable of all, though it does not exclude the last mentioned view, is the supposition that Rachel took them along for her own use, being herself somewhat given to superstitious or idolatrous practices. For though 30:23, 24 suggest a measure of faith and of knowledge of the true God, even as Jehovah, yet it would seem that as a true daughter of her father she had been addicted to his religion and now had a kind of divided allegiance, trusting in Jehovah and not wanting to be deprived of the good luck teraphim might confer. In any case, since she took what did not belong to her, she is guilty of theft — "she stole."

20.   Jacob, skilled in the use of devices to further his own interest, spread the veil of secrecy over what he did: "he stole the heart of Laban."   But since the heart is the center of mental activity, this idiom signifies to "trick" or "deceive" (B D B), not yet, however, "outwit" (Meek).   Laban is here called "the Aramaean" (*ha'arami*), which could also be translated "the Syrian" (A. V.).   The reason for this apposition is puzzling.   It hardly grows out of the Hebrew national consciousness which here proudly asserts itself.   Perhaps the opinion advanced by Clericus still deserves most consideration.   He believes Laban's nationality is mentioned because the Syrians were known from of old as the trickiest people; here one of this people in a kind of just retribution meets one trickier than himself.   Yet this is not written to glorify trickery.   The participle *bore(a)ch* expresses the idea that Jacob concealed that he was "making preparations for flight" (K. C.).

21.   Here is a typical example of Hebrew narrative.   First the summary statement: "Jacob fled"; then the details: "he proceeded (*wayyaqom*) and crossed (*wayya'abhor*) the River and set his face," etc. (*wayyásem*).   We have sought to express this relation by inserting a "namely" after the summary statement.   The necessity of our interpretation becomes apparent also from the peculiar sequence, if all verbs are supposed to be strictly consecutive: he fled, he proceeded, he crossed, he set his face.   Plainly, the last three give the details of "he fled."   The article before *nahar* ("river") is the article of distinction, and so *hannahar* is the Euphrates.   The point of crossing seems to have been the ancient ford at Thapsachus.   Naturally, from this point the next objective had to be the mountain of Gilead or "Mount Gilead."

b)   The Interference of Laban (v. 22-42)

22-24.   And it was told Laban on the third day that Jacob had fled.   So he took his kinsmen with him and pursued after him a seven days' journey and he overtook him in Mount Gilead.   And God came unto Laban, the Aramaean, in a dream by night and said to him: Take care not to say anything to Jacob.

According to 30:36 a three days' journey was set between Jacob and Laban.   Though this may not have been permanent or even the constant distance between the two flocks, in this case it at least took three days till the message came to Laban.

23.   Laban takes with him his *'achchim*, literally: "brethren," here most likely "kinsmen."   Jacob, encumbered with his herds, loses his three days' advantage by the time seven days of pursuit are ended. There can be no question in Laban's mind whither Jacob is going.   Besides, such a group as Jacob's train made must have left a broad trail in their going. Consequently, somewhere in Mount Gilead he practically comes up with his son-in-law and goes into camp, knowing that escape is out of the question for Jacob.

The distance covered by Jacob creates a problem. Some have computed that the distance involved is about 350 miles as the crow flies.   This need not necessarily be assumed.   We have accurate maps that represent it to be no more than about 275 miles to the fringes of Mount Gilead.   Besides, in shifting his grazing ground Jacob may have so arranged things before he took his flight in hand as to gravitate some three days' journey to the south of Haran — certainly not an impossibility.   If only fifteen miles constituted an average day's journey, the total distance would be cut down to almost 230 miles.   Now, cer-

tainly, Jacob will have pressed on faster than the
average day's journey, perhaps even at the cost of
the loss of a bit of cattle.   The cooler part of the
day and portions of the night may have been utilized
in order to spare the cattle.   Then, too, the boundaries
of Gilead may originally have extended nearer to
Damascus.   Skinner's criticism that "the distance is
much too great to be traversed in that time" is quite
out of place.   K. C. shows that "Gilead" is used for
the country east of Jordan in general.

24.   Apparently, during that last night God
appears to Laban in a dream.   Is he again called
"the Aramaean" in reference to his ingrained trickery,
which would have sought to inveigle Jacob into some
agreement disadvantageous to himself?   It almost
seems so.   The dream, employed especially for men
on the lower spiritual level, is the medium of approach
to Laban.   God's injunction laid upon Laban is, "Take
care (*hishshamer* — nifal, here more reflexive, like
'watch yourself') not to say anything to Jacob."   The
unusual Hebrew idiom has it: "not to speak from
good to bad."   This is an expression designed to
cover the entire scope of a concept, like "from the
least to the greatest," or "root and branch."   See
K. S. 92 b.   Here "from good to bad" means "anything."   Yet the statement involves an ellipsis.   Laban
is not forbidden even to speak with Jacob but to say
anything to influence Jacob to return, or to say anything by way of bitter reproach.   Luther stresses the
latter by rendering: "speak only in a kindly fashion"
— *nicht anders redest denn freundlich*.   The A. V.
rendering "either good or bad" is literal but bears a
connotation different from the Hebrew.

25-29.   **And Laban came up with Jacob.   Now
Jacob had pitched his tent on the mountain, and
Laban on his part pitched in Mount Gilead together
with his kinsmen.   Then Laban said to Jacob: Why**

didst thou undertake to deceive me and drive off
my daughters as though they had been captured
by the sword? Why didst thou flee secretly and
deceive me and not inform me? I should have sent
thee on thy way with joyful festivities and songs,
with timbrel and harp. But thou didst not suffer
me to kiss my grandchildren and my daughters.
Now that was foolishly done. It lies within the
power of my hand to do thee harm. But the God
of thy fathers spoke to me last night and said,
Take heed not to say anything to Jacob.

Above, v. 23 merely reported that Laban had
virtually caught up with Jacob. Now v. 25 describes
their actual meeting on the next morning: "Laban
came up with Jacob." We learn besides that Jacob
had actually pitched tent at this point, a thing that
had often not been done as his caravan and drove
progressed day for day. That Mount Gilead is
meant by "on the mountain" is entirely clear from
v. 23. In the case of Laban the specific statement
that it was "Mount Gilead" where tents were pitched
makes it entirely plain that both had pitched on
the same mountain though over against one another.
The critical correction, which tries to put Jacob on
Mount Mizpah, grows out of the desire to prove that
two threads of narrative intertwine. Critics are continually, though often unwittingly, "doctoring up" the
evidence.

26. Blustering and simulating righteous indignation, Laban demands to know why he was deceived
thus: "what hast thou done and thou didst deceive
me" = "why didst thou undertake to deceive me?"
He tries to present Jacob's course in the most un-
favorable light possible: "why drive off my daughters
as though they had been captured with the sword?"
Laban is as much aware of the extent of his exaggera-

tion as are all others who hear him. At the same
time he himself knows best why Jacob fled secretly
and without announcement. *Shebhuyoth* is plural
feminine of the Kal passive participle. *Chérebh,*
"by the sword," substitutes the genitive for the active
agent with the passive (K. S. 336 n).

27. The Hebrew idiom reverses the sequence in
"flee secretly" by the construction: "make secret the
fleeing," or "hide to flee." Says the smooth hypocrite: "I should have set thee on thy way with joyful festivities (Hebrew: "joy") and songs, with
timbrel (*toph,* a kind of tambourine) and harp"
(*kinnor,* perhaps originally an instrument more like
a violin). All this he would never have done. Jacob
interposes no defense for the present, knowing how
empty the boast is. Then Laban plays the part of
the outraged parent and grandparent. He was not
able to kiss his *banim,* i. e., "sons," here grandchildren,
and "daughters." For the present his bombastic
harangue reaches a temporary stop in the summary
statement: "now that was foolishly done."

29. Well remembering God's warning and not
for a moment daring to carry out his threat, Laban
nevertheless claims that he could do Jacob harm. He
mentions no wrong that Jacob did. He merely boasts.
But the overwhelming impression of God's warning
here compels him to admit all that God had said and
so explains why he utters all his threats as vain
words — a queer conclusion for one who thus far tried
to play the part of a man grievously wronged.
"Power" = *'el,* a form which has a full parallel in
another *'el* from the same root, (*'alah,* "to be strong")
and meaning God. It is useless to try to contend
for the fact that *'el* must always mean "God"; for
in Deut. 28:32; Micah 2:1; Prov. 3:27; Neh. 5:5
such certainly cannot be the case.

Laban throughout this section is a good illustration of the man who has fallen away from the true God, still knows of Him, feels impelled to heed His Word, but otherwise has put God on the same level with heathen deities, and lives a life such as a renegade might live.

30-32. So now thou hast indeed gone, for thou didst long very much after thy father's house. Why didst thou steal my gods? Jacob answered and said to Laban: Because I was afraid — because I said — that thou wouldest take thy daughters from me by force. With whomsoever thy gods be found, that one shall not live. In the presence of our kinsmen make a search for thyself what of thine I have and take it for thyself. For Jacob knew nothing of the fact that Rachel had stolen them.

The familiar versions (not so, however, the Septuagint) have made a subordination of clauses in this verse that is not so desirable and that erases the peculiar flavor of the thought. We should not read: "*though* thou wouldest needs be gone." But rather by way of summary: "thou hast indeed gone (verb plus infinitive absolute), for thou didst long very much after thy father's house" (again verb plus infinitive absolute). Now very abruptly in order to catch Jacob unawares: "Why didst thou steal my gods?"

31. Now Jacob gives an answer but not at once to the last question, because the reason for his secret flight has been demanded. Apparently he has resolved to use no subtleties. The truth of the matter actually is that he was "afraid." He even anticipated that Laban might use his power as patriarch of his tribe and take from Jacob by force the wives whom he had grown to love. Resuming the construction already once employed, Jacob begins: "Because

I was afraid — because I said — that," etc. Apparently, Jacob is conveying the thought: I was afraid
and had also said I was afraid. The deeper reason
for departure, God's command, Jacob does not mention, apparently for the reason that Laban would
not have believed that God appeared to Jacob. But
all this Jacob disposes of quite briefly because he
feels Laban was only blustering and certainly cared
little about an explanation. Laban knew better than
anyone else why Jacob had fled. But since Jacob's
cause was just and since he had just been charged
with theft, Jacob feels the necessity of answering the
last question or charge. He is so sure that no one
would have been guilty of such a deed that he boldly
asserts that the thief shall die, should he be found.
Such a punishment for such a crime may have been
suggested by the prevalent attitude of the times reflected in the Code of Hammurabi — a few centuries
old by this time — that they who stole the property
of a god (or temple) should die. Yet, though in himself entirely certain of his ground, Jacob ought never
to have made such an assertion. Seemingly Jacob
feels this, for as he invites a search, he merely asks
Laban to take whatever he thinks Jacob or his retinue have taken wrongfully; he does not again
threaten the death of the idol thief. That nothing
be covered up Jacob asks that the search be made
"in the presence of our kinsmen" — (*'a(ch)chim* =
"brothers"). Finally the necessary explanation that
Jacob had never for a moment thought Rachel capable
of such a deed.

The suffix on the last verb ("stolen *them*") suggests that at least a couple of teraphim may have
been involved. In 35:16, 18 Rachel's death is reported as occurring rather a short time after this
event. It is hardly correct to call this death an event
that was fulfilled as a result of Jacob's prediction, as

the rabbis believed. We rather hold that Rachel's death so soon after this word was a merely accidental coincidence.

33-35. So Laban went into Jacob's tent and into Leah's (also into the tent of the two handmaidens) and found nothing; and he came forth from Leah's tent and went into the tent of Rachel. But Rachel had taken the teraphim and put them into the camel's litter and sat upon them. And Laban felt all over the tent and found nothing. And she said: Let it not vex my lord that I cannot rise up before thee; for the manner of women is upon me. So he searched and did not find the teraphim.

The search begins. First Jacob's tent is combed through — the piel of *chaphas* v. 35, being an intensive, suggests the thoroughness of the search. Next comes Leah's tent. The two handmaidens are inserted parenthetically for completeness' sake. Separate tents for the husband and the wives and the handmaidens apparently were the rule in those days. Disregarding the parenthesis, the writer goes on, working up to the climax of the search: he (Laban) came out of Leah's tent and entered Rachel's. Rachel is a match for her father in craftiness. She has taken the teraphim and put them into "the camel's litter," a capacious saddle with wicker basket attachments on either side. Some describe it as a palanquin. Apparently it was so constructed that even when it was removed from the camel it offered a convenient seat for travelers. Laban feels over everything in the tent. The litter is all that remains. Had Rachel raised her protestation or excuse before this time she would have roused suspicion. By waiting till the last critical moment she diverts attention from the fact that she may be sitting upon the teraphim. For who would care to trouble a menstruating woman suffering pain? Besides, it may actually have been true what she was asserting. Nothing appears here of the taboo that some tribes and some races associated with women in this condition, taboos which temporarily rendered such women untouchable. So Jacob appeared justified, for a painstaking search revealed no theft. We may well wonder what he would have done if Rachel's theft had come to light.

36, 37. **So Jacob grew angry and stern with Laban; and Jacob answered and said to Laban: What am I guilty of? wherein have I sinned? that thou didst hotly pursue after me. For thou hast felt over all my goods. What hast thou found of all thy household goods? Set it here before my and thy kinsmen, and let them give the verdict over both of us.**

The long pent-up emotions of years find expression in this eloquent defense of Jacob's. He is justifiably angry, he "strives" (*ribh*), i. e., settles the matter of controversy between them in a heated expostulation. First he protests his innocence, and apparently on good grounds: he has neither guilt nor sin in this case. Least of all has anything called for such a pursuit as this which might justly have been inaugurated against an evildoer (*dalaq* = "to pursue hotly"). There was a high measure of indignity about Laban's treatment of Jacob throughout, also in the matter of feeling over all his goods. Jacob waxes bold and challenges Laban to set forth before all their kinsmen whatever of his own he may have found. The kinsmen can serve as arbiters or judges to render a public verdict, which must be all the more fair because it will be a jury composed of adherents of both parties. This challenge must have embarrassed even thick-skinned old Laban. Now for the rest of Jacob's self-defense.

38-42. **Look here, for twenty years I have been with thee. Thy ewes and thy she-goats have not** miscarried; the rams of thy flock I have not eaten. If anything would be torn, I did not bring it to thee; it was I who used to make good. Thou didst hold me responsible for that which was stolen by day as well as for that which was stolen by night. I was a man whom heat consumed by day and frost by night; and sleep would flee from my eyes. Look here now, for twenty years I have been doing service in thy house, fourteen years for thy daughters and six years in connection with thy cattle, and thou hast altered my pay ten times. If the God of my father, the God of Abraham and He whom Isaac reverenced, had not been for me, surely now thou wouldst have let me go empty-handed. But my misery and the toil of my hands, God saw it and reproved thee last night.

"These twenty years" (A. R. V.) or "this twenty years" (A. V.) would require a different Hebrew construction, aside from the bad grammar of A. V. The initial *zeh* is an expression of impatience, which we have tried to cover by "look here." First, then, Jacob reminds Laban how during the past twenty years no losses were suffered by miscarriage — a matter largely attributable to the careful oversight of the shepherd at the time of the birth of lambs and of goats. Even the occasional ram that custom allowed to the shepherd Jacob did not take for fear of being criticized later.

39. Sellin reminds us that a custom of the East provided that as long as a shepherd could lay before the owner the torn beast, the shepherd was not held chargeable, inasmuch as the torn beast counted as evidence that the shepherd had boldly driven off the predatory beast. Jacob was accorded no such consideration. He was held accountable. The *'achaténnah* is durative — "I used to make good." "Thou didst hold me responsible" in the Hebrew idiom reads

thus: "thou didst seek it at my hand." The passive
participle construct has an archaic case ending to
mark it as used as a noun rather than as a verb
genubhti (K. S. 241 a; 272 a; G. K. 90 l); genitive
construction for the adverbial (K. S. 336 q).

40. The broken construction of the sentence
bears testimony to its strength of feeling — "I was
one — by day heat consumed me," etc. The more
intense the heat by day in the near tropical regions,
the more acute the cold. Out in the open Jacob's
shepherd duties exposed him aplenty to both. Short
rations of sleep were almost the rule besides.

41. The same expression of impatience as in
v. 38 only here intensified by a kind of ethical dative
(*zeh — li*) "look here now." *Be* used before daughters
is a kind of genitive of price; not so before "cattle,"
because his service was not being regarded as work
by which he should acquire cattle. The cattle were
rather acquired incidentally. In return for this rather
generous period of service Jacob had been rewarded
by tricky salary alterations.

42. Finally Jacob traces down the true source
of his own prosperity and cheerfully confesses to his
unbelieving father-in-law that God was the one to
whom alone he owed all blessings. In calling God
"the God of my father" Jacob is reminding Laban
that while he (Jacob) has remained true to the
ancestral religion of truth, Laban has departed from
it. So for special emphasis Jacob also designates Him
as the God of Abraham as well as the one "whom
Isaac reverenced" (literally, "the fear of Isaac"). In
true faith Jacob confesses God to be the Disposer of
the affairs of men and the Judge of evildoers. At
the same time Jacob charges Laban with having been
ready, but for God's intervention, to send his son-in-
law away empty-handed (*reqam*). So little does Jacob
give credence to the above protestations of love and

concern (v. 26-28). Jacob boldly closes with the
assertion that God had finally taken a hand in the
matter and reproved Laban.

c) The Treaty (v. 43-54)

**43, 44. And Laban answered and said to
Jacob: The daughters are my daughters and the
children are my children and the cattle is my cattle
and all that thou seest belongs to me; and, as for
my daughters, what can I do to them this day or to
their children which they have borne? And now
come let us make a covenant, I and thou, and let it
be for a witness between me and thee.**

Laban skillfully avoids the issue, which centers
on the question whether Jacob has ever treated him
unfairly, and substitutes another, namely, whether
there is any likelihood of his avenging himself on
Jacob and his family. In a rather grandiose fashion
he claims that all that Jacob has — household and
cattle — is his own. The only use he makes of this
strong claim is that, naturally, these being his own
family, he would not harm them. It hardly seems
that he has been "cut to the quick" by the justice of
Jacob's defense. He is merely bluffing through a contention in which he was being worsted. But being
a suspicious character, he fears that Jacob might even-
tually do what he apparently would have done under
like circumstances, namely, after arriving home and
having grown strong, he may come with an armed
band to avenge all the wrongs of the past. To forestall this he suggests a "covenant." This covenant
might serve to deter Jacob, of whose justice and
fairness he is convinced, and who, Laban trusts, will
keep a covenant inviolate.

**45-47. And Jacob took a stone and raised it
up as a pillar. And Jacob said to his kinsmen:
Gather stones. And they gathered stones and made**

a heap and they ate there upon the heap; and Laban called it Jegar-sahadhutha, but Jacob called it Galed.

Because Laban suggested the making of the covenant it would seem that he should have made the witnessing pillar and heap. So sure of this are some critics that they call the word "Jacob" at the beginning of v. 45 a mistake. Historical evidence must be judged according to its face value not by subjective expectations. The objective facts indicate Jacob's personal readiness to preserve peace and harmony, showing that he even took the initiative in sealing a treaty that he might well have resented. Jacob himself raises a memorial stone or "pillar," a *matstsebha,* meaning, "a thing raised up," as in 28:18.

46. Jacob goes a step farther: he summons his kinsmen to make the memorial more substantial by gathering stones. These were, perhaps, heaped around the one stone which stood up pillar-like. Such a heap is called *gal.* Here apparently the *gal* served as a kind of table upon which the covenant feast was eaten. For to the full sealing of a covenant belonged a solemn covenant feast.

Very strangely the critics, who are intent upon proving that two documents giving two recensions of the event are woven together, here hit upon the pillar, or monolith, and the heap or cairn, and claim these two as one of the things that prove their point. Instead of pointing to a double recension or to two authors this merely points to the fact that Jacob was ready to go the limit to keep peace and harmony, as he always had been doing. The critics' argument is a *non sequitur.* All the rest of their so-called proof is of the same sort and too flimsy to refute.

47. Here Moses inserts a notice to the effect that Laban and Jacob each gave a name to the cairn, and

each man in his native tongue, that of Laban being Aramaic and that of Jacob Hebrew. Nothing indicates that this is a later insertion. Why might not Moses consider it a matter worthy of record that in Mesopotamia Aramaic prevailed; whereas in Canaan Hebrew, perhaps the ancient Canaanite language, was spoken? The exactness of his observation is established by this definite bit of historical information. The two names are not absolutely identical, as is usually claimed, though the difference is slight. *Jegar-sahadhutha* means "heap of testimony," *gal'ed* means "heap of witness" or witnessing heap. For "testimony" is an abstract noun, "witness" is a personal noun or name of a person.

We observe, therefore, that at the beginning of their history the nation Israel came of a stock that spoke Aramaic but abandoned the Aramaic for the Hebrew. After the Captivity the nation, strange to say, veered from Hebrew back to Aramaic.

48-53. **And Laban said: This heap is a witness between me and thee this day. That is why he called its name Galed, and also Mizpah (Watch); for he said: May Yahweh watch between me and thee when one of us cannot see the other. If thou shouldst treat my daughters harshly, or if thou shouldest take other wives in addition to my daughters, with no man to check up on us, may God see it, as witness between me and thee. Laban also said to Jacob: See, this heap and this watch-station (Mizpah) which I have planted between me and thee — a witness is this heap and a witness is this pillar, that I will not go past this heap against thee, and that thou wilt not go past this heap against me, neither past this pillar to do any harm. The God of Abraham and the God of Nahor they shall judge between us — the gods of their fathers. And Jacob swore by the Fear of his father Isaac.**

Here the critics hold that the redactor, who wove
the threads of E and J together, made a sorry job
of his task. They are very confident that since the
cairn of stones is called a "heap" and a "pillar" this
difference in terminology quite fully substantiates that
E and J here each used his own term. But when a
third term *mizpah,* "watch," or "watch-station," enters
upon the scene, describing the same cairn, then they
decree that a textual or copyist's error alone can
account for the third term and proceed to alter the
text to conform to their previous conclusion — — very
unscientific! But the true cue to the whole section
is completely missed. And why, by the way, cannot
one and the same writer have ingenuity enough to
discern that one thing may be regarded from two,
yea, even from three, points of view?

The whole matter involved in what seems a rather
diffuse and verbose passage is very simple: Moses
describes Laban as using so many and so varied terms
because he actually used so many terms. Not to be
trusted himself, not being a man of his word, Laban
uses many words to cover up his untrustworthiness.
Besides, as Luther already discerned, the undependable
man is trying to make the dependable one appear as
undependable by using many turns and expressions
and so creating the impression that Jacob is a slip-
pery character who has to be bound fast by a whole
series of stipulations. At the same time Laban seeks
by hard and sharp terms actually to terrify Jacob,
the godly man, as though he were ungodly and needed
to be threatened. We shall try to trace out briefly
how this crafty fellow goes about his unholy work.

There is craft even in the opening remark, "this
heap is a witness between me and thee this day."
Laban was not the one who made "the heap." That
was Jacob's idea. Now Laban appropriates what
Jacob made, as though the idea had been his (Laban's)

own, originated for the purpose of binding a crafty opponent. That was the spirit in which Laban had given the name "Galed." Of course, there cannot be an inaccuracy here in the statement, as the literalist critics claim, saying: the writer makes Laban speak Hebrew instead of Aramaic. Any man not absorbed in finding fault, recognizes that the writer is going back quite naturally to the use of the Hebrew equivalent of "Jegar-sahadhutha."

49. In his craft Laban invents another idea that may be attached to the cairn: it may serve as a *mizpah*, "a watch" or "watch-station" or "sentry," standing aloft between these two when they cannot keep watch upon one another. Here again, of course, the idea implied is that Jacob is the one who bears watching. For that reason Laban employs the name of the true God "Yahweh." Whoever may be Laban's god, Laban does not require watching; but may Jacob's God watch over Jacob and keep him from harming Laban. "When one cannot see the other" really reads in the original "when we are hidden (not 'absent' A. V.) one from another." But the Hebrew plainly involves, as our translation indicates, when one cannot keep an eye on the other. It is unfortunate that this unkind word, full of suspicion, should in our day so often be used as a benediction at parting. This almost amounts to a wicked perversion of Scripture.

50. To cast a further shadow upon Jacob's character Laban conjures up what was in reality a highly improbable situation. Suppose Jacob should treat Laban's daughters harshly (*'anah* = "afflict, oppress"), or should take other wives in addition to the ones he had. But Jacob had never given the least indication of being inclined to treat his wives harshly. Gentleness and goodness are characteristics of Jacob. Besides, as the account reads, Jacob had more wives

already than he had ever desired. He apparently
recognized the evils of bigamy sufficiently in his own
home. Both these cases mentioned by Laban as possible are in themselves harsh and unjust slanders. The
statement, "there being no man with us," does not
refer to the present (Luther) but to a future eventuality and should therefore be taken in the sense,
"with no man to check up on us." Very solemnly
God is adjured to act as a witness in such a case, and,
of course, to act as avenger. For all the solemnity
of the adjuration there is nothing good about this
word. It is an effort to slander a good man and do
it with the sanctions of apparent piety — in other
words, it is wicked hypocrisy.

51. Very solemnly Laban begins again, saying
nothing new, but desirous of creating the impression
that this dangerous character Jacob must be tied as
firmly as possible. Only now he lays emphasis on
the possibility of Jacob's coming back on a punitive
expedition. It is true that Laban's bad conscience
may actually have induced him to reckon with such
a possibility. But in any case he merely suspects
Jacob of being capable of such a deed because he himself would no doubt have avenged himself thus. In
this case (v. 51, 52) Laban refers to the cairn only
as "heap" and as "pillar" (*matstsebha*), the latter
expression involving the idea of a *sacred* pillar.
Laban safeguards himself by all possible sanctions
and calls upon Jacob's religious scruples. Incidentally,
so as not to make the aspersions too direct and so
defeat his own purpose, Laban also pledges himself
not to "go past this heap" against Jacob "to do any
harm" (Hebrew: "for evil").

53. In conclusion Laban offers his most solemn
adjuration, stronger than v. 50 b; for God is called
upon not only to "witness" but to "judge." Besides,
he is called by the solemn title "God of Abraham."

In fact, another god is invoked, "the god of Nahor."
If v. 29 and v. 42 are compared, it seems most likely
that two different deities are under consideration:
the true God; and Nahor's, that is also Laban's idol.
The plural of the verb "judge" (*yishpetu*) therefore
points to two different gods. So the polytheist Laban
speaks. The more gods to help bind the pact, the
better it is sealed, thinks Laban. Without directly
correcting Laban or his statement of the case, Jacob
swears by the true God under the same name as
that used v. 42, the Fear (i. e., object of fear, or
reverence) of his father Isaac. Had the renegade
Laban perhaps meant to identify his own god with
the true God of Abraham? And is Jacob's statement
of His name an attempt to ward off such an identification? This is not impossible.

54. **And Jacob offered a sacrifice upon the
mountain and called upon his kinsmen to eat bread.
So they ate bread and spent the night upon the
mountain.**

We view Jacob's sacrifice as one of thanksgiving
that this last serious danger that threatened from
Laban is removed. We cannot conceive of Jacob as
joining with the idolater Laban in worship and sacrifice. Consequently, we hesitate to identify the "eating
of bread" with the partaking of the sacrificial feast,
unless the "kinsmen" here are to be regarded only
as the men on Jacob's side, as *'a(ch)chim* is used
throughout the chapter. In that event the kinsmen
are to be thought of as having the same mind as
Jacob on questions of religious practices. But the
summons to eat bread might also signalize that the
transactions between Jacob and Laban are concluded. The events of the meeting between Jacob and
Laban may well have consumed an entire day, and so
the night has to be spent in the same place.

We cannot drop the chapter without indicating

to what unwarranted extremes critical analysis has gone. Procksch assigns to J verses 1, 3, 20-23, 26, 27 b, 31, 36 a α, 38, 39, 40, 42 a, 10, 12, 45, 49, 50, 51 b, 53 b, 54. The rest, with the exception of a part of v. 18, is ascribed to E. The tortuous reasoning by which this separation is supported is one feature against the analysis. The manifest desire to see two threads in a narrative marked by singleness of purpose constitutes a second count on which we reject the whole approach. Add to this Koenig's verdict, "the attempt to separate the successive strata rests very often on indecisive criteria."

We have nothing certain as to the location of the heap called "Galed" or "Mizpah" in Mount Gilead. "Mizpah" itself is a rather general term: there were many points of eminence in the land which could serve as "watch-stations." We personally do not believe that the Mizpah located in Jebel Ajlun is far enough to the north. We can only be sure of this that according to chapter 32 it must have lain to the north of the River Jabbok.

HOMILETICAL SUGGESTIONS

One may well question whether this chapter offers suitable matter for preaching. Certain negative matters loom up rather prominently—Laban's treachery and duplicity; Rachel's theft, involving incipient idolatry at least on her father's part; Rachel's lie. Though such material could be used for illustrative purposes in sermons, yet it is not of a character to furnish a text or a theme. In the section v. 1-16, v. 12 is an essential part, yet offensive for public use. Again the portion v. 22-32 consists mostly of the protestations of a hypocrite. Even if one should think v. 36-42 suitable in a sense as the defense of a faithful workman, surely the evangelical pulpit needs more comprehensive themes. The concluding section v. 43 ff. reports for the most part how a suspicious and utterly untrustworthy fellow seeks to safeguard himself by binding others through solemn contracts and covenants. All this should be taught with necessary omissions to the youth of the church, and such use will always have its value.

CHAPTER XXXII

8) Preparations for Meeting Esau (31:55-32:32)

This caption may at first glance seem somewhat inapt for the chapter, but further reflection will indicate that in v. 1-3 (Hebrew) God is preparing Jacob to meet Esau. Then Jacob's preparations by the sending of messengers, by the division of his caravan train, and by prayer are recorded. Jacob's further preparations by the conciliatory gift which is tendered Esau are next related (v. 13-21). The rest of the chapter describes his spiritual preparation in which God again takes a hand and in which indeed broader issues are involved than mere preparations to encounter Esau, though the latter still stand in the forefront.

31:55-32:2. And Laban arose early in the morning and kissed his grandchildren and his daughters and blessed them. Thereupon Laban went and returned to his place; whereas Jacob continued along his route. And angels of God met him; and Jacob said, when he saw them: This is God's host. And he called the name of that place Mahanaim (double host or camp).

We group these three verses together as the Hebrew text does (32:1-3), apparently because the first events of the day after the treaty are here recorded, though certainly the first verse could serve as a conclusion of the matters recorded in chapter 31 (So A. V. and Luther). As 31:28 reported, Laban's ground for complaint was that he had not been allowed to take affectionate leave of his kin, young and old. For all his faults toward Jacob, Laban may not have been deficient in love for Jacob's family. The grand-

father kisses the grandchildren first. Following patriarchal custom, Laban bestows a blessing. Then he
returns to his place. Jacob, however, goes on along
the route that he had been following (literally, "according to his way"). The accusative *'ethhem* has a
masculine suffix for the feminine (K. S. 13).

He may now be considered as crossing the borders
of the land of promise, when suddenly he beholds
"angels of God": they "met him." This does not
necessarily imply that they came toward him but
simply that they encountered him. They may for the
brief time that they were seen have been accompany-
ing Jacob's train. They may merely have been discovered as present. In any case, it is quite appropriate
that here at the borders of the land of promise they
put in their appearance. Their object was, without
a doubt, to afford Jacob reassurance at a time when
he was about to need it sorely. For scarcely had he
gotten rid of the danger that threatened from Laban,
when a new danger and a grievous one had to be
reckoned with — Esau's attitude. As angels had re-
assured Jacob at Bethel (ch. 28), so here; but now
especially because Jacob was following a course prescribed by God.

2. Luther delights in pointing out in this connection how a certain exultation of faith was roused
in Jacob by the sight of the angels, and so, to mark
the place of this experience, Jacob designates it by
the name "Mahanaim." The singular may mean
"camp" or by metonomy "host." Here, since *macha-
náyim* is a dual, the name must signify a "double
camp or host," depending on whether the Lord's
army was seen encamped or moving along. The latter
seems more likely since (v. 1) they "met him." The
most likely meaning intended by "double host" would
then be to designate the angels' host as well as Jacob's.
Jacob would no longer feel unprotected. Though
Mahanaim is repeatedly mentioned in the Scriptures,

we cannot be sure of its exact location. It must have lain somewhere east of Jordan near the confluence of the Jordan and the Jabbok. The present site *Machneh* often mentioned in this connection seems too far to the north.

But how did Jacob "see" this host? Nothing suggests a dream of the night. Whether the inner eye beheld it or the physical eye may be almost impossible to determine. Jacob, as spiritually the most mature, seems to have been the only one to see the angels.

3-5. **And Jacob sent messengers on in advance to Esau, his brother, to the land of Seir, the region of Edom. And he gave them orders saying: Thus shall ye say to my master, to Esau: Thus saith thy servant Jacob: I was staying with Laban and was detained till now. And I have ox and ass and flock and servant and handmaid, and I am sending to inform my master that I may meet with his favor.**

Jacob's first object in dealing with Esau is to conciliate him. Rebekah has not sent for Jacob, as she was to do when Esau's wrath relented. Jacob has no indication that Esau's intentions are kindly. A delegation, acknowledging Esau as one entitled to receive reports about one who is about to enter the land — such a delegation may produce goodwill on the part of the man thus honored. So Jacob sends messengers "in advance," i. e. *lephanaw* — "before his face." The region where Jacob anticipated that Esau could be met is "the land of Seir" south of the Dead Sea. "*Seir*" means "shaggy," i. e. "wooded." The apposition adds to the name one more readily understood, "the region of Edom."

4.   Jacob prescribes the exact message that is to be delivered. With good diplomacy Esau is to be addressed as the "master." Jacob describes himself as the "servant" of Esau. Nor is this diplomacy insincere. Jacob, well aware of his pre-eminence as

rooted in God's blessing, is ready to concede to Esau
every outward advantage and honor. He makes no
secret where he has been; he was with Laban. He
indicates further that his stay was temporary, for
garti from *gûr* signifies "to stay as a stranger," "to
sojourn," and therefore implies: temporarily. But
'echar (contracted from *'e'echar*, G. K. 68 f) adds "I
was detained" (K. C., *musste bis jetzt zurueckbleiben*),
suggesting that his stay had become more protracted
than he had at first intended that it should be.

5. Nor should Esau get the impression that an
impecunious beggar dependant on Esau's charity is
coming back as a suppliant. So the messengers enu-
merate all that Jacob brings with him. Yet here again
a modest statement of the case is made so as not to
arouse Esau's jealousy. The enumeration of Jacob's
possessions is made in collective singulars: "ox, ass,"
etc., as our translation indicates. Yet it should be
noted that similar enumerations in the Scriptures are
regularly found in the singular. The concluding statement of the report sounds like a humble request for
permission to enter the land — "I am sending to inform
my master that I may meet with his favor." In
wa'eshlekhah the converted imperfect has the added
syllable *ah*, (*yaqtul gravatum*) rather common for
such a form in some books (see G. K. 49 e; K. S. 200).

Here again, in the interest of tracing down sources
more or less out of harmony with one another, critics
assert that these verses (v. 3-5) assume Isaac's death
and Esau's occupation of the land which he in reality
only took in hand somewhat later, according to 36:6,
which is ascribed to P. Isaac, with his non-aggressive
temperament, may have allowed the far more active
Esau to take the disposition of matters in hand. So
Jacob may well have been justified in dealing with
Esau as "master." This is all quite plausible even if
Isaac had not died. Furthermore, in speaking of "the
land of Seir, the region of Edom" Jacob may only imply

that Esau had begun to take possession of the land
which was afterward to become his and of whose
definite and final occupation 36:6 speaks. In any case,
"master," used in reference to Esau, only describes
Jacob's conception of their new relation. Jacob did
not need to enter into negotiations with Isaac, his
father, in approaching the land. His welcome was
assured at his father's hand. But the previous misunderstanding called for an adjustment with Esau.
At the same time our explanation accounts for Esau's
400 men: they are an army that he has gathered while
engaged upon his task of subduing Seir, the old domain
of the Horites. Skinner's further objection: "how he
was ready to strike so far north of his territory is a
difficulty," is thus also disposed of.

6. **And the messengers returned to Jacob saying: We came to thy brother, to Esau, and he is
already coming to meet thee, and there are four hundred men with him.**

What is recorded in v. 4-14 apparently takes place
within one day. The messengers are anticipating a
journey of several days to the land of Edom and meet
Esau the selfsame day. News is known to travel with
incredible swiftness in these lands, as travelers have
reported in many instances. So Esau has been apprised of Jacob's return and is already on the way
several days. He receives Jacob's messengers. He
sends no reply. He seems desirous of informing himself in person exactly as to how things stand. His
intentions were, without a doubt, none too clearly
defined in his own mind. He must first see for himself just what Jacob intends to do and what his personal
attitude is. For the present Esau's following may
serve to impress Jacob, and should it have seemed
desirable, Esau may actually not have been averse to
employing his martial escort to harm Jacob. Esau

seems to have been about as uncertain in his own mind
as to his plans and purposes as Jacob was in reference
to these same plans and purposes. The very uncertainty
of the report of Jacob's messengers makes it all the
more alarming.

7, 8. **And Jacob was very much afraid and
distressed, and he divided the people that were with
him and the flocks and the herds and the camels into
two camps; and he said: If Esau come against the
one camp and smite it, then the remaining camp may
have a chance to escape.**

The courage engendered by the vision of angels
is dissipated. The exaltation of faith gives way to
the agony of despair as soon as the stern reality of
Esau's coming with 400 men is encountered. No one
knew better than Jacob how deeply Esau's grudge
had taken root. The failure of Esau to give an answer
to Jacob's messengers seemed ominous. Jacob's fear is
very great; he finds himself "distressed" (*yétser* —
from *tsarrar*, "to be tightly pressed"). A quick precautionary measure is taken — his entire train is
divided into two sections. We have translated *machaneh* "camp" to remind of the similarity of the "camps"
or "hosts" of v. 2. "Sections" would have been a better
rendering. Half the men and half the beasts go into
each section.

8. The explanation that he gives while making
the division is that if Esau should attack and smite
the one section, "then the remaining camp (section)
shall be for escape," plainly meaning "may have a
chance to escape." The *we* before *hayah* introduces
the apodosis. This seems to have been a stratagem
resorted to with caravans in the East from days of old.
Procksch charges Jacob with smooth trickery (*Schlau-
kopf*) on account of this stratagem, whereas Jacob
is employing nothing other than justifiable prudence.

Nor can the same writer prove "camels" to be a gloss
merely by the absence of the sign of the accusative. No
writer is perfectly consistent in such matters.

**9-12. And Jacob said: O God of my father
Abraham and God of my father Isaac, O Yahweh,
Thou who didst say unto me, Return to thy land and
to thy relation and I will do thee good, I am unworthy of all the acts of kindness and of all the faithfulness which thou hast bestowed upon thy servant;
for with only my staff I crossed this Jordan, and
now I have become two companies. Deliver me
from the hand of my brother, from the hand of Esau,
for I am afraid of him, lest he come and smite me —
both mothers and children. Yet thou didst say unto
me, I will do only good to thee, and make thy seed
as the sand of the sea which is too plentiful to
count.**

Now Jacob betakes himself to prayer. He should
not be sharply criticized for taking precautionary
measures first and praying afterward. Many a man
in the face of extreme danger has lost his sense of
proportion. Besides, there are emergencies that call
for action first and prayer afterward. "God of my
father" does not imply: not my God, but does ask: As
Thou wast faithful to them be faithful to me. "Yahweh" specifically implies the idea of God faithful in
performing His merciful promises. The special promise under consideration is the command to return to
his own land with the prospect of receiving good at
God's hand. Jacob can therefore plead that he was
not following his own devices but God's orders. It is
almost unbelievable that Tuch should have been scan-
dalized because Jacob reminds God of His promises.
But is not that the approach of all true prayer,
taking one's stand firmly on divine promises? Equally
deplorable is Procksch's estimate who terms the whole
prayer "a specific creation of J." Was ever a prayer

truer to life? There are few prayers from which we can learn more. It loses all its worth if it is to be regarded as a clever fiction which a fictitious J put upon Jacob's lips.

10. "I am unworthy" is *qatónti* — "I am little." The perfect implies: I always have been too little and still am (K. S. 127) — too little, of course, to deserve them, not to repay them. *Chasadhim,* "mercies," or "kindnesses," means acts of kindness, freely bestowed. *'E'meth* is "truth" in the sense of "faithfulness." The measure of these gracious gifts at God's hands is best illustrated by the contrast between what Jacob was when he first crossed the Jordan and what he now has upon his return to Jordan. The *be* before *maqlî* is the *be* of accompaniment. The adjective idea in *qatonti* used with *min* results in a comparative (K. S. 308 b). "With my staff" means, as Luther translates, "with only this *staff.*"

It is hard to understand how men can claim that "the element of confession is significantly absent" in Jacob's prayer. True, a specific confession of sin is not made in these words. But what does, "I am unworthy," imply? Why is he unworthy? There is only one thing that renders us unworthy of God's mercies and that is our sin. Must this simple piece of insight be denied Jacob? It is so elementary in itself as to be among the rudiments of spiritual insight. Let men also remember that lengthy confessions of sin may be made where there is no sense of repentance whatsoever. And again, men may be most sincerely penitent and yet may say little about their sin. If ever a prayer implied a deep sense of guilt it is Jacob's. Behind the critics' claim that "confession is absent" from this prayer lies the purpose to thrust an evolutionistic development into religious experiences, a development which is "significantly absent." It was not first "in later supplications" that this element became "so prominent." It was just that in this earlier age the experience of sin and guilt particularly impressed God's saints as rendering them unworthy of God's mercies (cf. also 18:27 in Abraham's case). *Maqqel* is the shepherd's or the wanderer's staff. A rare specimen of misinterpretation is that of A. Jeremias who refers to a traditional belief that three stars of the constellation Orion are still regarded as Jacob's staff — a very questionable tradition — and so give evidence that a mythological motive — some astral myth — underlies this story. Are such farfetched vagaries deserving of refutation?

11. From profession of unworthiness or confession the prayer turns to petition: "Deliver me" (*hatstasiléni*, from *nasal*). "From the hand" may be construed to mean "from the power," for in reality Jacob is at Esau's mercy. The eagerness of the petition is reflected in such a repetition as "from the hand of my brother" followed by "from the hand of Esau." The critic rejects the one or the other for metrical (!) reasons, in spite of the fact that it is even very dubious whether there is any poetical meter in these parts of Genesis. Jacob admits freely to God that he is afraid that Esau may "come and smite" him. Naturally, Jacob will not suffer alone. The attack will center on him, but should it come, mothers and children will suffer as well. Jacob says literally: "mother upon children," apparently using a proverbial expression, *'em*, singular, because usually there is one "mother," and *'al banim*, "upon children," because in case of attack the mother would bend over her children in an effort to shield them with her own body. The whole expression is one of those, like "root and branch," which covers the entire range of a concept (cf. 31:24), as K. S. defines, 92; and so this means: "me and all mine."

12. The only ground upon which godly men can take their stand in times of distress is God's Word. It alone is sure, as Luther so beautifully argues in connection with this passage. Jacob remembers exactly

what form God's promise took: "doing good I will do
thee good," meaning either: "I will surely do thee
good," or "I will do thee only good." Then, too, God
had said (22:17) to Abraham that his seed was to be
"as the sand of the sea, which is too plentiful to count."
But when Jacob had become the bearer of the Messianic promise (28:13, 14), all the things spoken to
Abraham in that connection became applicable to
Jacob as well. Jacob has a correct estimate of the
situation from this point of view. Naturally there is
a certain boldness about holding God's promises before
Him and taking one's stand on the ground of them;
but such an attitude distinctly belongs to faith. Imperfects like *yissapher* convey a modality of thought like
"it *cannot* be counted." (K. S. 186 b.)

13-16. **And he spent that night there; and he
took of that which came to his hand a present for
Esau, his brother: two hundred she-goats and
twenty he-goats, two hundred ewes and twenty rams,
thirty milch camels and their colts, forty cows and
ten bulls, twenty she-asses and ten foals; and
entrusted them to the care of his servants, each
herd for itself, and he said to his servants: Pass
along ahead of me, and leave intervals between the
herds.**

The night is spent at that place, which later is
found to be at the ford of the river Jabbok (v. 22).
Though the major work is accomplished, for Jacob
committed all the issues into God's hands in the prayer
recorded above, yet prudence and foresight are to find
their place in the course followed by Jacob. Prayer
does not necessarily result in inaction. Luther states
the case quite strongly when he says, "men should
not tempt God but should employ every device and
means that is available." The device Jacob employed
was to send a substantial gift on before to his brother
Esau as a token of good will. A check-up will reveal

that the total count of the beasts sent is 580, not an inconsiderable number. Jacob must have been enormously wealthy to be able to afford such a present. Certainly it was good psychology on Jacob's part to prepare so substantial a gift. Goats and sheep predominated among the possessions of Jacob. Cows and asses have not been mentioned heretofore, but that need not surprise us, for they were proportionately few in number. But, surely, asses and camels were essential for the oversight of so large a semi-nomadic establishment. Besides, camels' milk was a regular article of diet. Each type of stock constituted a separate "herd" or drove. The ratio of male and female is that which is usually maintained by those who breed stock, according to the old rule cited by the Latin writer Varro.

In v. 13 the expression "that which came to his hand" means, whatever he was able to assemble as it came along. It does not mean, of what he owned, because such a statement is quite unmotivated; what else could he give? It does not imply that he made a careful selection: Vulgate: *separavit*. We must remember that it was night and that the gift had to be gotten ready in great haste, for Esau was near. Besides, the separate droves had to be arranged. All Jacob could do was to assemble quickly whatever he could lay hands on. In v. 15 *gemalîm*, though masculine in form, is construed as a feminine as the *Hifil* participle *meniqôth* indicates. In *benehem* the masculine suffix is used for the less common feminine, as in 31:9. In v. 16 the repetition *'edher 'edher* gives a distributive sense, "by droves" or "each herd for itself" (G. K. 123 d; K. S. 85).

The shrewd forethought displayed by Jacob is most clearly revealed by his arrangement of the gifts. First comes a drove of 220, then an interval; then another drove of 220, again an interval; now a drove of sixty, then a drove of fifty, and the last of thirty.

The effect is cumulative. Yet Jacob, the giver, the brother who left twenty years before had not appeared, for all these "passed along ahead" (*'abhar*) of Jacob.

17-21. And he gave orders to the first one saying: If Esau, my brother, meet thee and ask thee: To whom dost thou belong, and whither art thou going, and whose are these animals before thee? then thou shalt say: They belong to thy serv- ant, to Jacob, and are a present sent to my master, to Esau, and, see, he himself is coming along after us. And he gave the same orders to the second fellow, and to the third, and to all that followed their herds, telling them: Speak exactly these words to Esau when ye meet him, and ye shall say: And see, thy servant Jacob is right behind us. For, he thought, I will conciliate him by the gift that goes on before me; afterwards I can see by his face whether he will receive me kindly. So the present passed on ahead of him, and he spent that night in the encampment.

Jacob does not depend on the ingenuity of the shepherds to whom he entrusts the separate droves. Their message is given to them practically *verbatim*: they are to make sure that they ascribe all these herds to Jacob but describe Jacob as Esau's "servant" (*'ébhedh*, a strong term implying even "bond-servant" but here definitely describing Esau as his superior). At the same time Esau is to be addressed as Jacob's "master." Jacob is actually ready to accord to Esau any external advantage of position and any honor that he may desire, if only peace and concord be preserved. Then they are to inform Esau that all this is a gift from Jacob. The words to be used are repeated for each shepherd separately. *Ri'shon* is here used for the more common *'echchadh.*

19. Note that the shepherds are described as "following" their herds. In the Orient the shepherd

usually goes before his herd. In this case perhaps the
herd was to impress its ultimate recipient before the
shepherd could deliver his message. *Kaddabhar hazzeh,*
"according to this word," is like our "exactly these
words " *Bemotsa'akhem* is the infinitive of *matsa'*.

20. Each man is to conclude his message: "And,
see, thy servant Jacob is right behind us." *'Amar*
here very likely means "thought" rather than "said."
Jacob's purpose is to "conciliate" his brother. The
Hebrew idiom for this idea is rather unusual; it says:
"I will cover his face." The gift "covers" and, as it
were, prevents the wronged person from seeing the
wrong that has been done him. As a result he becomes
"conciliated" or reconciled. This procedure by no
means involves anything unworthy or improper. The
gift is not a bribe but a token of goodwill. When Jacob
then finally comes up himself, he will be able to read
from Esau's countenance whether a kindly reception
awaits him. However, perhaps after all the current
translation should be preferred to ours for the second
half of this verse. As A. V. has it: "afterward I will
see his face; peradventure he will accept me." For
"accept me" the original has the idiom "receive
my face."

21. "The present passed on ahead of him";
otherwise it would have failed entirely of its effect.
It must meet Esau part by part on the following
morning, and Jacob himself must be the climax of the
procession. So Jacob stays behind in the encampment,
at least it is his purpose at first just to spend the night
where he is. As the next verse indicates, this purpose
is somewhat modified. In a sense, however, Jacob
stays with the camp through the night.

Now follows the story of the mysterious prayer-
struggle that marked this night as well as the climax
of Jacob's spiritual development. To a degree, at least,
this experience is for Jacob what the offering of Isaac

on Moriah was to Abraham. Here Jacob is brought
to the point where human devices and carnal ingenuity
are no longer equal to the need that has arisen. His
own cleverness on which he has so largely leaned in
the past proves inadequate. Jacob has only the Lord
left in this extremity and learns in faith, though it
costs him a hard struggle, to cast himself wholly and
resolutely upon God's mercy alone. But to do so involves an agony of prayer that leaves its mark upon
the man.

22-24. **And he arose in the course of that
night and took his two wives and his two handmaids
and his eleven sons and crossed the ford of the Jabbok. He took them, namely, and brought them
over the brook and brought over all that he had.
And Jacob was left alone, and a man wrestled with
him until dawn arose.**

Danger threatens. At first it seems very surprising that Jacob should lead his entire train directly
into the face of danger. Some see behind this act a
return of the spirit of courage and resolution on
Jacob's part. They describe him as the same old,
confident, resourceful Jacob that he always was, trusting even now that in some way or other his ingenuity
will not fail him in these emergencies as he clashes
with his more slow-witted brother. But nothing really
indicates that the great fear that in part prompted
the above prayer (v. 8-11) has subsided. That fear
was very real, and nothing had happened to allay it.
Yes, a certain measure of boldness is displayed in the
course followed by Jacob. He had not cast off utterly
his confidence in the word of the Lord, which had bid
him to be on his way. Furthermore, he saw that to
retreat and to flee would invite attack. So the only
course left was to proceed confidently and so to create
the impression of courage and confidence. However,
it would hardly have been wise to allow himself to be

caught in the midst of the somewhat disorderly business of fording the stream. The need of having this
work of crossing out of the way occurs to Jacob as
soon as the gift has been dispatched. He promptly
arises and takes steps to have the business of fording
disposed of at once. The Jabbok is the *Wady-ez-Zerka,*
as almost all commentators agree — *ez-Zerka* signifying "the blue" i. e. the clear mountain stream. "Jabbok"
means "Wrestler," reminding of Jacob's experience.
Jacob is still on the north side of the Jabbok. Now
when Jacob remains behind after the others have
crossed, that could hardly be called exposing them to
undue danger inasmuch as the Jabbok is perhaps
thirty feet wide and at most about hip-deep. Jacob
could cross over and be on the other side in a minute's
time. The wives, handmaids, and sons are brought
over first. Only the sons are mentioned, as the one
daughter Dinah was not as important for later history
as the sons were. The seeming repetitions are to be
accounted for by the style of Hebrew narrative which
first gives a summary statement that gives the final
result ("he crossed," v. 22) then follows with details
which in this case continue until v. 32 where the final
crossing occurs. The expression "that night" somewhat irregularly omits the article before the demonstrative.

23. In addition to his family there was all the
cattle as well as all other possessions that had to be
brought across ("all that he had"). Though fording
may present difficulties, especially by night, there are
several attendant circumstances that may well have
aided Jacob on this occasion. There may have been
moonlight. The water may not have been at its
greatest depth. Again, in those days when bridges
were unknown Jacob's men may have negotiated many
a fording and have known how to go about it.

24. The natural thing for the master of the entire
establishment to do is to stay behind to check whether

all have really crossed or whether some stragglers of
this great host still need directions. In the solitude
of the night as Jacob is "left alone," his thoughts
naturally turn to prayer again, for he is a godly man.
However, here the unusual statement of the case
describes his prayer thus: "a man wrestled with him
until dawn arose." Rightly Luther says: "Every man
holds that this text is one of the most obscure in the
Old Testament." There is no commentator who can
so expound this experience as to clear up perfectly
every difficulty involved. This much, however, is relatively clear: Jacob was praying; the terms used to
describe the prayer make us aware of the fact that
the prayer described involved a struggle of the entire
man, body and soul; the struggle was not imaginary;
Jacob must have sensed from the outset that his opponent was none other than God; this conviction
became fully established before his opponent finally
departed. The verb *'abhaq* is correctly translated
"wrestled," as just about all translators agree. It
matters little whether it be derived from the noun
'abhaq, which means "dust" and so the verb is construed to mean "roll in the dust," or "to become
dusty" or "to raise the dust"; or whether the root
chabhaq is compared, which means "to clasp," as
wrestlers do.

The Biblical commentary on the passage is Hos.
12:4: "Yea, he had power over the angel, and prevailed; he wept and made supplication unto Him."
The antagonist is here described as an "angel." But
since the theophanies of the Old Testament regularly
involve the Angel of the Lord, we need not be surprised
that He who usually assumed angelic guise here assumes, as later in the Incarnation, human form.
Again, by way of commentary, "wrestling" is defined
as "he wept and made supplication unto Him." That
certainly is a description of agonizing prayer. However, when v. 3 of Hos. 12 is compared, we learn that

this struggle in Jacob's manhood was the culmination of the tendency displayed before birth, when by seizing his brother's heel he displayed how eager he was to obtain the spiritual blessings God was ready to bestow. This experience and this trend in Jacob's character is held up before his descendants of a later day that they may seek to emulate it.

We mention certain modern interpretations of this experience of Jacob's as instances of how far explanations may veer from the truth and become entirely misleading. It has been described as a "nightmare" (Roscher). Some have thought that Jacob engaged in conflict with the tutelary deity of the stream which Jacob was endeavoring to cross (Frazer), and so this might be regarded as a symbolical portrayal of the difficulties of the crossing. But the stream has already been crossed by this time. One interpreter considers the wrestling as a symbol of "the victory of the invading Israelites over the inhabitants of North Gilead," (Steuernagel), but that is a misconstruction of history: the conquest began much later. Some call the experience a dream; others an allegory. The most common device of our day is to regard it as a legend, "originating," as some say, "on a low level of religion." All such approaches are a slap in the face for the inspired word of Hosea who treats it as a historical event recording the highest development of Jacob's faith-life. For there can be no doubt about it that the motivating power behind Jacob's struggle is faith and the desire to receive God's justifying grace; and the means employed is earnest prayer. Why it pleased the Lord to appear in human guise to elicit the most earnest endeavors on Jacob's part, that we cannot answer.

25-28. **When he saw that he could not prevail against him, he touched the hollow of his thigh, and the hollow of Jacob's thigh was dislocated in his**

wrestling with him. And he said: Let me go for
dawn is arising. But he said: I will not let thee
go except thou bless me. And He said to him:
What is thy name? And he said: Jacob. And he
said: Not Jacob shall thy name be called from now
on, but Israel, for thou hast striven with God and
men and hast prevailed.

There is nothing ambiguous about the subject of
the verbs found in v. 25, as critics would have us
believe. God saw that he could not prevail against this
adversary. This statement does not impugn God's
omnipotence, but it does effectively portray the power
of prayer. God does allow the prayer of men to be
mighty in His sight. At the same time there is a
certain measure of truth to the idea that God is the
opponent of believing men as they pray. God is not
pretending. But God must oppose because the sinful
will of those that pray often is not yet reduced to full
accord with the divine will. As the will of man learns
ever more perfectly to submit to God's will, God can
no longer "prevail" against such a one. Yet in this
case the struggle for submission involved so much for
Jacob that he actually needed a memento of his victory
as a warning against relapse. The memento consisted
in a physical disability which marked the physical
being of him who had so long put undue confidence in
carnal devices. He is to be reminded that in his own
person there had hitherto been a seriously crippled
state which had much impeded his progress. God
secures this disabling of Jacob by a mere touch. The
words used do not suggest that something in the nature
of a wrestler's trick was used. "The hollow of the
thigh" seems to have been the ball-and-socket joint.
This joint "was dislocated," *teqa'* from *yaqa'* meaning
"to fall or slip out." We are not informed whether
this infirmity was permanent or only for a few days
or weeks. Speculation on this point is quite futile.

26. The struggle continued through the night to the early hours of the morning. Some admire "the powerful imagination" of the author who here creates a story of "a silent wrestling in a pitch-black night." This is however no creative genius; the author merely writes a historically accurate account. As dawn rises, the divine Opponent asks that He be let go. There is a simple and a sound Biblical reason for this. Exod. 33:20 teaches us that man shall not "see God and live." The frailty of sinful man could not have endured the sight of this Pre-incarnate One. Not for His own sake but for Jacob's He asks that Jacob let him go. Just a little too prosy in the explanation which says: since daytime is the season for a man's labors and duties this Divine One was asking Jacob to let Him go and be about his daily duties. Entirely off-key is the explanation which parallels this noble account with fairy tales, which insist that fairies and all spirits of the night must return to their confinement at dawn of day. He who has so little spiritual discernment as to be unable to recognize this fact cannot be convinced even by sound argument. But Jacob has recognized the divine character of his opponent and has persistently sought a blessing. He will not yield except he receive this blessing. All true faith, having taken its stand on God's promises, must have something of this persistence. How and when Jacob became aware of the character of the "Man" with whom he wrestled, we are quite unable to say. Jacob must from the outset have been most distinctly aware that this was not a struggle merely between man and man in physical opposition.

27. This question is addressed to Jacob not for information's sake but to center Jacob's attention upon what was about to come and upon the thought which his name connoted. "Jacob," "the supplanter" (27:36), was to recall how heretofore he had primarily

displayed the characteristics of one who would in emergencies resort to stealth and stratagem.

28. Speaking as one who possesses authority, He says: "Not Jacob" (the negative immediately before the word affected) shall thy name be called from now on but Israel." He adds a reason: "Thou hast striven with God and men and hast prevailed." *Sarah* means "to strive" or "fight" — *'el* is "God." *Yisra'el,* according to this explanation, is "The fighter with God," i. e. the one who fought with God, of course, in a good and honorable sense. "Persist" (B D B) for *sarah* is hardly a strong enough term to cover the experience of this night, which had previously been described as a "wrestling." Buhl and K. W. both offer the meaning "to fight," *kaempfen.* This meaning fits better with the second object, "men," as well. Apparently Jacob encountered much opposition on the part of men, as his clashes with Esau and Laban illustrate. But there, too, Jacob had fought through his contests until he had prevailed. In maturity (Hos. 12:4) this would seem to be the characteristic that best described the man. It is true, in Genesis the name "Israel" is not used from this time on to the exclusion of all others. Apparently, then, since it represents a personal achievement rather than a divine destiny, as by way of contrast "Abraham" does, it is used interchangeably with Jacob, according as the older or the newer type of character predominates. In this respect the use of the name Peter in the Gospels is a close parallel. With the explanation of the text as the final verdict as to the meaning of the name, we hold the case of the meaning of the name to be closed. Attempts to make it mean *'ish rachel,* "the husband of Rachel" (Steuernagel) are untenable, as well as grammatical impossibilities. So, too, are the efforts to get nearer the original meaning of the word by comparing Egyptian or Assyrian transliterations; for transliterations are often surprisingly far removed from the original.

29-31. **And Jacob asked and said: Reveal thy name, I pray? And He said: Why then dost thou ask for My name? And He blessed him there. And Jacob called the name of the place Peniel (The Face of God). For I have seen God face to face and my soul is preserved. And the sun rose upon him as he passed by Penuel, and he was limping because of his thigh.**

The partly unsolved problem for Jacob is the identity of the Wrestler who opposed him. Though relatively sure, as his request for a blessing indicates, he wants full confirmation. The thing that suggested to him to ask at this time was the fact that he had just been asked his own name. But the question: "Reveal thy name, I pray?" implies, according to the Hebrew idiom, that the name is the index of the character or personality. We should have said: "Reveal thy identity." The reply is in part the same as that of the Angel who was asked the same question by Manoah (Judg. 13:18), only here the continuation of the answer is omitted — "seeing it is wonderful." Several reasons for the somewhat evasive reply may be discerned. The one that presents itself first is that the question in reply practically means: "Why ask to know My identity, seeing you already know it?" Add to this the fact that, as Luther indicates, the failure to reply leaves the name as well as the whole experience shrouded in mystery, and mysteries invite further reflection. In spiritual experiences there is and must be the challenge of the mysterious. A spiritual experience so lucid that a man sees through and is able to analyze every part of it must be rather shallow. And lastly, the blessing about to be imparted is a further revelation of His name and being, that carries Jacob as far as he needs to be brought. "Asked" and "said" are also in Hebrew two verbs coinciding in one act and expressed by *waw conversives* (K. S. 369 o). *Zeh* is not a demonstrative but an emphatic particle.

The blessing spoken of is an added blessing. For the entire experience may also well be regarded as a blessing. The substance of this added blessing we do not know. Luther's supposition is as much to the point as any when he remarks that it may have been the great patriarchal blessing concerning the coming Messiah through whom as Jacob's "seed" all the families of the earth were to be blessed.

On the question of learning the name, they who put Scripture record and legend on the same level can rise no higher than the supposition that he who has gotten possession of the name of a deity (the name-taboo, as it were) has control of that deity. This, they say, was Jacob's purpose in asking for the name. Do such shallow misinterpretations deserve serious refutation?

30. Divine manifestations deserve to be commemorated in every possible way. Jacob marks this one for himself and for his descendants by giving a distinctive name to the place where it occurred. Though "Peniel" like "Mahanaim" has not been definitely located, it may be a still used ford of the Jabbok near Jordan and is mentioned Judg. 8 and I Kings 12:25. This name should not be said to be "derived from an incidental feature of the experience." That would be the equivalent of saying: Jacob was unhappy in his choice of a name for this memorable spot. Of course, his experience was a purifying one that was to break self-trust and cast him wholly upon God's mercy. But this experience centered in a personal encounter with God, a direct meeting of God, a seeing of Him, though not with the eye of the body. Does not the whole experience, then, sum itself up as a seeing of God and living to tell of it, though sinful nature should perish at so holy a contact? The name touches upon the essence of Jacob's experience. For *Peni'el* means "face of God." The explanation really says more than "my

life, or soul, was *spared.*" For *natsal* means "delivered" or "preserved." God did more than let no harm come nigh Jacob; He again restored him, who otherwise would surely have perished. Luther gathers up this idea in "recovered" (*genesen*). *Panim* has no article, being a customary phrase (K. S. 294 f).

With an adequate and a historically accurate account of the origin of the name "Peniel" before us, we may well wonder at those who under such circumstances go far afield and try to account for its origin by comparing the Phoenician promontory of which Strabo speaks, which was called θεοῦ πρόσωπον ("face of God"). Those who have lost their respect for God's Word no longer hear what it says and make fools of themselves in their wisdom by inventing fanciful explanations for that which has been supplied with an authentic explanation.

31. The details of the memorable event stayed with Jacob. He distinctly recalled when in later years he told of this experience how as "he passed by Penuel, the sun rose upon him," (*Penu'el* has an old case ending *û* for the construct in place of the other old case ending *î* in *Peni'el*). However, the propriety of this symbolic sunrise is what chiefly prompts this statement: a new day of light and of hope was dawning for Jacob after the night of gloom and despair. Analogous by way of contrast is the remark made in connection with Judas Iscariot's departure on the night of betrayal, where after he went out the evangelist remarks: "and it was night" (John 13:30). What men observed as they saw him approaching was that "he was limping because of his thigh" (*tsoléa'*, durative participle, yet saying nothing as to whether the infirmity continued long thereafter). The expression *'al yerekho* may mean "upon his thigh" (A. V.) or perhaps a little more exactly "because of his thigh" (Meek).

32. **Therefore the children of Israel are not in the habit of eating even to this day the sinew of**

**the hip muscle which is upon the socket joint of
the hip, because that He touched the socket joint of
Jacob's hip on the sinew of the hip muscle.**

God did not demand this ritual observance in the
Mosaic law, but the descendants of Israel of their own
accord instituted the practice because they recognized
how extremely important this experience of Jacob was
for him and for themselves. Some interpret this *gidh
hannasheh* to be the sciatic nerve. Delitzsch tells us
that Jewish practice defines it as the inner vein on the
hindquarter together with the outer vein plus the
ramifications of both. The imperfect *yo'khelu* expresses what is habitual: "are not in the habit of
eating."

Generally speaking, critics assign the most of
v. 10-13 to J, and v. 14 b-22 to E; 23 ff. is hard to
analyze. Procksch, as usual, makes a very intricate
analysis on very flimsy grounds. We do wonder that
v. 30 (English) Jacob says: "I have seen *God*," *'Elohim*, where surely it was Yahweh. But his choice of
the divine name is motivated by the idea of the contrast between a creature encountering the Creator-
God, i. e. *'Elohim*.

HOMILETICAL SUGGESTIONS

The central portion of this chapter, v. 13-21, is, indeed, an
example of fine prudence, but there are not many that would
feel inclined to use it as a text. However, the initial section,
v. 3-12, or also v. 1-12, is rather suggestive from several points
of view. One angle of approach would be to consider primarily
the latter part of the section and treat of Pleading God's Promises. Looking at the central part of the section, suggests The
Extreme Danger of a Saint of God. Looking at v. 1-2, one might
incline to set down as a theme God's Rich Assurances, or The
Strong Protection of God's Holy Angels. Of necessity, the
entirely different types of approach would lead to a very different type of treatment of the various elements in the text.
The portion v. 22-32 would be treated adequately under a theme

such as The Crowning Victory of Jacob's Faith-Life. If Jacob himself sums up his experience in the designation that he coins for the place—"Peniel"—no one could question the propriety of this name as a theme. For that matter, the new name given to Jacob—"Israel"—is the embodiment of the whole experience and therefore most suitable as a theme. In the case of these last two proper names, nothing would be more essential by way of introduction then an immediate simple definition of the words.

CHAPTER XXXIII

9. Reconciliation with Esau; Settlement in Canaan (33:1-20)

The chapter as a whole furnishes an outstanding example as to how God turns the hearts of men "withersoever he will" (Prov. 21:1). A delightful reconciliation takes place between brothers long estranged, but this reconciliation comes from God as an answer to earnest prayer.

1-3. And Jacob raised his eyes, and looked, and there was Esau coming, and with him were four hundred men. So he divided the children among Leah and Rachel and the two handmaidens. And he put the handmaidens and their children first, Leah and her children next, and Rachel and Joseph last. But he himself went on ahead of them, and bowed low seven times until he had come close to Esau.

The preparations recorded in the previous chapter are apparently just completed, and at daybreak Jacob had just crossed the stream when he looked ahead "and there was Esau coming." One glance suffices to show that the men in attendance are the four hundred that had been reported. One last precautionary measure can yet be taken. To put himself first in the way of danger, if there really be any, induces Jacob to come to the forefront and to arrange his wives and his children in climactic order so that the most beautiful and best beloved come last and so may be spared if none else will. Each mother stands with her own children and Rachel last with Joseph, who, as some seem to compute with a fair measure

of accuracy, was now a lad of perhaps six years.
Ri'shonah is an adverb. *'Acharonim* as an adjective
agrees with its nearest noun.

3. *'Abhar* does not here mean "cross over," for
the stream had been crossed, but "went on ahead."
"He bows," *'artsah,* i. e., "to the earth," but we have
not translated the phrase thus because there is another
expression which signifies the deepest bow in which
the face actually touches the earth. "Low" seems
strong enough here. Jacob bowed, advanced a few
steps, and bowed again, until seven obeisances were
made. Such tokens of respect to the number of seven
were the customary homage tendered to kings according to the el-Amarna tablets. Jacob indicates only
his deep respect and courtesy toward his brother.
Jacob's deceit in the matter of the blessing had made
an unceremonious fraternal greeting impossible. Yet
Jacob does not indicate Esau to be ruler over him,
but he does strongly indicate his willingness to show
Esau all due respect and consideration. We have no
reason for questioning the sincerity of Jacob's courteous approach. The spirit of cunning which had often
dominated Jacob in the past had been put aside in
the experience of the previous night. *Gishto* is infinitive of *naghash* (G. K. 66 b). The words from the
el-Amarna tablets referred to above run thus: "At
the feet of the king, my lord, seven times and seven
times do I fall." The expression is found on these
tablets more than fifty times.

4-7. **And Esau ran to meet him and embraced
him and fell on his neck and kissed him, and they
wept. And he lifted up his eyes and saw the women
and the children, and said: What relation are they
to thee? And he said: The children whom God
hath graciously bestowed upon thy servant. And
the handmaidens approached — they and their children — and bowed. Leah also drew near and her**

**children and bowed; and then Joseph and Rachel
drew near and bowed.**

The much dreaded encounter resolves itself into
as friendly a meeting as Jacob could ever have
wished. Esau was impulsive. All rancor and bitterness are forgotten at the sight of his only brother. If
Esau had himself not been clear in his own mind
at first as to the attitude he would take, now all
thoughts of vengeance evaporate. That was God's
doing. Esau makes the first move: he "runs" and
"embraces" Jacob and "falls upon his neck" and
"kisses" him. These many verbs are by no means
indications of the smelting together of two original
accounts but a historically correct record of what
actually transpired in the excess of strong feeling at
the moment of meeting. We can hardly determine
now what prompted the Masoretes to put the "extraordinary points" over the verb "kissed." Later rab-
binical commentators believed the word was a mistake
for "bit." But the sincerity of Esau's approach need
not be doubted; nothing casts suspicion on his attitude. He is frank and straightforward. The word
tsawwa'raw should, apparently, have the ending *ro*
rather than *raw*, being a word that may be regarded
as a singular (*ro*) or as a plural.

5. Esau's eyes fall upon the women and the
children immediately before him — the handmaidens
and their offspring. He may well inquire as to whose
they all are, for when Jacob had left home he was
still unmarried. Esau asks: "What relation are these
to thee?" literally: "What these to thee?" Oriental
custom does not suggest that a man take much interest in another man's wife; so Jacob replies only
in reference to the children, that they have been
"graciously bestowed" upon him by God. *Chanan,*
written with double *n* because active (G. K. 67 a).
"God" is referred to as *'Elohim,* it seems, because

Jacob desires to avoid reference to *Yahweh*, whose blessing he secured at his brother's expense.

6, 7. Then the handmaidens and their children approach, bowing respectfully as Jacob had done. Then comes Leah and her children; lastly, Joseph and Rachel. How it happened that Joseph came before his mother we do not know. *Niggash* is the *Nifal* of *naghash*, used for the *Kal* (G. K. 78).

8-11. **And he said: What about all this host that I met? And he said: To find favor in the sight of my lord. And Esau said: I have much, my brother; keep what thou hast. And Jacob said: Please, no. If only I might find favor in thy sight and thou wouldest accept my gift at my hands! For on that account have I beheld thy face, as one sees the face of God; and thou hast graciously received me. Accept, I pray, my gift of welcome which I have offered thee, for God hath dealt graciously with me, and also because I have everything. So he urged him, and he accepted.**

Some commentators confuse the whole story at this point by claiming that the "host" referred to is one-half of Jacob's train. This they claim, because "host" (*machaneh*) in 32:8, 9 is used in reference to one-half of Jacob's goods but nowhere in reference to Jacobs "present" to Esau. But is not the case as simple as it can be? Is not the present so substantial as to be naturally described as a "host"? Making "host" here refer to half of Jacob's train lets the story lose sight of Jacob's "present" entirely; and, besides, it makes Jacob lie smoothly to the effect that he had intended to give one half of his goods to Esau. This type of exegesis presses words at the expense of common sense, no matter how inadequate the account as such becomes. K. C. perhaps did well to ignore the whole issue as too trivial to mention. Esau's question really has a *lekha* ("to thee") in it;

"What to thee is all this host?" We felt that our form of the question might come fairly close to the original: "What about all this host that I met?" But it was Jacob's present, had not Jacob's servants told Esau what Jacob intended by it? Naturally; but Esau, by ignoring what they have said, implies that he could not be the recipient of so great a gift. But Jacob plainly states his purpose: "to find favor in the sight of my lord."

9. Esau could hardly receive so generous a gift without protestations of his unwillingness to do so, if his meeting with his brother just before had actually been a meeting in brotherly love. He seems to have been quite rich himself. He does not say: "I have enough" (A. V. and Luther), but: "I have much" (*rabh*). He actually does not want anything from Jacob.

10. Jacob pleads urgently. His offer was sincere. Esau's acceptance would be the surest token of his having been reconciled to his brother. If the customs of the Orient of our day are an index of the attitude of bygone days, then the acceptance of the gift of the person seeking reconciliation would have been the surest proof that all was well. The two perfects after *'im matsathi* and *laqachti* are the expression of a wish, although the wish takes the form of conditional sentences (K. S. 355 w) : "if I might find favor . . . . if thou wouldest accept." The expression "for on that account" (*ki 'al - ken*) — namely, that thou mightest accept my gift — introduces again in a loose popular style a result just mentioned. The statement: "I beheld thy face as one sees the face of God," is not fulsome flattery meant as if Jacob had been as glad to see Esau as one would be to see the Lord Himself. Such excessive compliments would be obnoxious. Strong but sincere courtesy rules all these utterances. What Jacob means is that in the

friendliness beaming from Esau's face he saw a reflection of divine favor, because he knew that it
was God Himself who had changed Esau's heart to
make it friendly. Passages like I Sam. 29:9 and
II Sam. 14:17 are analogous. Skinner runs to extremes when he makes the expression mean, "with
the feelings of joy and reverence with which one
engages in the worship of God." Since the expression
is plainly figurative, Procksch introduces too literal
a thought when he draws a parallel between the relief
experienced at the danger of death which Esau's
presence threatened, even as God's countenance would
normally be death to the beholder; but from the one
a man is delivered with the same feelings as from
the other. K. C. overstates the case when he calls
Esau's countenance as "worshipful and comforting"
as would be the Lord's. "Thou hast graciously received
me" is *tirtseni* from *ratsah*, "to accept favorably."
The infinitive *re'oth* has no subject expressed — which
allows for the indefinite subject "one"; yet "I" might
well be supplied from the context.

11. The urgency of Jacob's plea that his gift be
accepted is further reflected by the enclitic *na'* after
"accept." *Berakhah*, "blessing," also means "gift,"
but in this case a "gift of welcome" (K. W.). Two
further reasons for the acceptance of this gift are
added: the first, "God hath dealt graciously with
me," therefore a generous gift will not impoverish;
and the second is like unto the first, "I have everything." It has often been remarked that Jacob, sure
of having the Lord on his side, can boldly claim that
he has everything. Esau, not resting his confidence
in the Lord, can only say, "I have much" (v. 9). Esau
recognized the propriety of the motive behind Jacob's
gift and saw that acceptance of it would be the
strongest proof of thorough reconciliation, so "he accepted" when thus "urged."

12-16. **And he said: Let us depart and be
on our way, and I shall go along parallel with thee.
But he said: My lord knoweth that the children
are of tender age, and that flocks and herds that
are giving suck are upon my hands. If they be overdriven but one day, they will die — all the flock.
Let my lord, I pray, pass on ahead of thy servant,
and I shall drive along at my leisure at a gait suited
to the cattle before me and at a gait suited to the
children, until I come to my lord to Seir. And
Esau said: Then let me leave with thee as guard
some of the men I have with me. And he said:
Why then? Only let me find favor in my master's
sight. So Esau returned that day on his way to Seir.**

Esau anticipates that Jacob will at once proceed
at least down to Hebron. As an expression of his
friendly disposition he suggests that both companies
advance together, his four hundred men moving along
parallel with Jacob's flocks — "parallel with," *lenegh-
dekha* = "as over against thee" not "before thee"
(A. V.). Meek says: "alongside." Jacob suggests
that this be not done, not because he mistrusts Esau's
sincerity or expects the brotherly goodwill to be of
short duration, but exactly for the reason that he
assigns, which reason, therefore, is not a pretext. The
cattle have actually been driven to the limt in Jacob's
escape from Laban, and caution must be used lest
they be overdriven. On the other hand, the slow
progress of Jacob's cattle would have proved irk-
some to Esau's unencumbered soldiery. Nor were
Jacob's children equal to a strenuous journey, for
Reuben, the eldest, could not have been more than
twelve years old. Many of the cattle were with
young, *'aloth* = "giving suck"; *'alay* = "upon me" or,
as we should say, "upon my hands." *Debhaqum* =
"they overdrive them," indefinite subject, conveniently
rendered as a passive.

Jacob seems to have had another reason for refusing Esau's company and protection, though out
of delicacy he does not tell it before his brother:
Jacob like Abraham (14:23) was conscious that he
owed his entire wealth and success to God's blessing
and, therefore, he felt the necessity of maintaining
his independence, lest it might seem as though others
had contributed to his wealth. The masculine suffix
on *debhaqum* refers to the feminine *'aloth* — an irregularity (K. S. 15).

14. Jacob suggests that each proceed at the
pace best suited to his condition, Esau "passing on
ahead." Throughout these discussions Jacob main-
tains the respectful address that he had used upon the
first approach — "my lord" — "thy servant." *'At* is
really "gentleness"; but "to my gentleness" = "at
my leisure." So *réghel*, "foot," here means "gait."
Mela'khah, "work," means "the product of one's work,"
here Jacob's "cattle." The statement that so by easy
stages Jacob would finally come to the point where
he could come to Esau "to Seir" is not pretense. This
evidently was Jacob's sincere purpose. Though it may
have been delayed, why should we doubt that Jacob
did visit his brother, perhaps even repeatedly? The
Scriptures cannot report every major and every minor
incident.

15. Esau at least would leave a guard with Jacob.
For the reason assigned above under v. 12 Jacob
feels that this kind offer cannot be accepted. *Yat-
sagh, Hifil,* means "to set up"; here it must mean
"leave a guard." Jacob sincerely means: your goodwill is quite sufficient for me. Jacob really dominates
the entire interview, and Esau goes on his way. *Lammah zeh,* "why then," can, of course, also be construed: "what needeth it?" (A. V.). The imperfect
following is optative. *Min-ha'am,* "from the people,"

presupposes some such indefinite pronoun as "a few of the people" (K. S. 81).

16. This verse does not say that Esau was also permanently established in Seir. He may have been busied about the task of subduing the land. But he may also still have had a part of his establishment somewhere in the vicinity of Hebron or Beersheba. Without a doubt, he recognized that his ultimate domain had to be Seir.

As to the question of Esau's spiritual status we can hardly agree with Luther, who with great charity assumes that Esau was by this time a man who had come to the faith and was ultimately saved. Of course, the personal salvation of Esau need not be ruled out. But one thing surely stands in the way of regarding Esau as a man who has come to the true faith. Had his faith accepted what the Lord had ordained, he would have held to Jacob as the possessor of the divine promise. His failure to do this seems to indicate that the true spiritual values were not grasped nor understood by him. This prevents his being classed as a man of faith, though in the end the spiritual truth communicated by Isaac may have turned his heart to the Lord.

17. **Jacob started out for Succoth and built himself a house, and for the cattle he made booths (succoth); therefore the name of the place was called Succoth.**

Succoth is now usually identified with *Tell Deir-'Alla,* a short distance east of the Jordan and north of the Jabbok, i. e., near the point of confluence of the two rivers. To reach this place Jacob naturally had to ford the Jabbok again. The fact that he built "a house" indicates a residence of several years, as does the fact that, according to chapter 34, when Dinah comes to Shechem she is already quite mature.

After Esau's departure Jacob may have become aware of the fact that the cattle required more extensive care. This may have necessitated the postponement of his journey to Seir. Thereafter other circumstances may have made a continued stay at Succoth desirable. The name "Succoth" (feminine plural of *sukkah,* "booth") was derived from the peculiar type of hut or booth, built for the shelter of cattle. These booths are described by travelers as something still occupied by the Bedouin of the Jordan valley, and as being "rude huts of reeds, sometimes covered with long grass, and sometimes with a piece of tent" (Whitelaw).

18-20. And Jacob arrived safe and sound at the city of Shechem, which is in the land of Canaan, upon his return from Paddan-Aram, and he encamped in front of the city. And he acquired the portion of the field where he pitched his tent from the hand of the sons of Hamor, the father of Shechem, for a hundred kesitas. There he erected an altar and called it: El-Elohe-Israel (i. e. A Mighty God is the God of Israel).

How long the interval was between v. 17 and v. 18 we are unable to determine; cf. on v. 17. But in reality the land of Canaan was not reached till the Jordan was crossed. But a special significance attaches to the entrance into the land proper, for 28:15 had specially promised this to Jacob. So the fulfillment of this promise is being recorded when it is said that "he arrived safe and sound" and that the city of Shechem to which he came was "in the land of Canaan." *Shalem* is hardly a proper name (A. V. and Luther) but means "safe and sound" (*unversehrt*). The remark that this was the case "upon his return (literally: 'in his coming') from Paddan-Aram" helps to remind us that the fulfillment of the above promise was involved. He encamps "in

front of (literally, '*eth peney,* 'by the face') the city,"
an expression which here definitely means "to the
east of."

19. As a testimony to the fact that he expects
permanent possession of all the land, because it had
been promised to him, he purchases the portion where
he encamped from the sons of one Hamor, who by
way of anticipation of the events of the next chapter,
is described as the father of Shechem. It would
hardly seem as though the name Shechem already belonged to the city at that time. The following events
may have attached the name to the city in years to
come. So the writer uses this name proleptically. We
do not know the value of a "kesita" (*qesitah*). K. C.
is a bit too positive when he simply asserts that it
was "of the value of ten shekels." This is the only
place where the coin is mentioned. This parcel of
ground was remembered by Jacob's descendants.
There Joseph's bones were buried (Josh. 24:32).

20. After the example of Abraham (12:8) as
he entered the land Jacob also builds an altar unto
the Lord. The name of the altar embodies the sum
of Jacob's spiritual experience, which he sought to
transfer to coming generations. So he gives the altar
a name which is in itself a statement to the effect
that "the God of Israel" is an '*el,* i. e., "a Strong One,"
i. e., "a mighty God." Jacob is remembering God's
promise, and God has in an outstanding way proved
Himself a God well able to keep His promises. The
common name for God, '*el,* covers this thought. By
the use of his own new name, "Israel," Jacob indicates
that the restored, new man within him was the one
that understood this newly acquired truth concerning
God. We believe those to be in the wrong who assume
that while Jacob was in Paddan-Aram he lapsed into
the idolatrous ways of men like Laban and so practically forsook the God of his fathers. Nothing points

in that direction. The meagre evidence available rather points to a fidelity on Jacob's part, which, though it was not of the strong ethical fibre as was that of Abraham, yet kept him from apostasy. Since it stood in need also of some measure of purification, God took Jacob in hand, especially at Peniel, and raised his faith-life to a higher level.

HOMILETICAL SUGGESTIONS

If the account of v. 1-17 is used as text, the treatment of it must center around the thought of the reconciliation of the two brothers. Some very practical thoughts are offered by this text. In the first place, the emphasis is very clearly on the fact that a true change of heart in the relation of man to man must originate with the good Lord, who can change even the most stubborn of hearts and make them to be inclined to peace and amity. In the second place, this is a Scripture that offers a significant silence: the two brothers do not discuss either at length or in brief the issues that had set them at variance with one another. There are persons who believe that the all-essential thing is *discussions*. However, there may be a perfect and a satisfactory harmony between men who had failed to agree, and the basis of such harmony may be the tacit agreement to let bygones be bygones. The last part of the chapter, v. 18-20, could be used to furnish a theme that embodies the idea of Jacob's Manly Confession.

CHAPTER XXXIV

10. **The Outrage on Dinah Avenged by
her Brothers** (chapter 34)

It would really be better to begin this chapter
with v. 18 of the preceding chapter, telling of Jacob's
arrival at Shechem. For, apparently, the things recorded in it followed immediately or almost so upon
the arrival.

It must also be determined how much time has
elapsed since Jacob's return to Canaan. If Joseph,
according to 37:2, was seventeen years old at the time
there described, which again was shortly after the
events of chapter 34, and Joseph was only about six
years old at the time of Jacob's arrival in Canaan,
it would be safe to assume that the events of our
chapter transpired about ten years after the return
to Canaan. Dinah must have been at least fourteen
years old; fifteen is not impossible.

1-3. **And Dinah, the daughter that Leah had
borne to Jacob, went out to see the women of the
country; and Shechem, the son of Hamor, the Hivite,
a prince of the country, saw her, and took her, and
lay with her and ravished her. And he was much
attached to Dinah, the daughter of Jacob, and he
loved the girl, and comforted the girl's heart.**

For the better understanding of what follows it
is well to know that Dinah was "the daughter that Leah
had borne to Jacob." It would hardly seem that her
act of going out would be referred to as "going out to
see the women of the country," if Dinah had been wont
to go out thus many times before. It is useless to
speculate whether mere idle curiosity prompted her,

(897)

or whether she went without consulting her parents,
or whether she even went forth contrary to their
wishes. We are unable to determine to what extent
she was at fault, if at all. In any case, it seems she
should have known that Egyptians and Canaanites
(12:15; 20:2; 26:7) regarded unmarried women
abroad in the land as legitimate prey and should not
have gone about unattended. Shechem happens to
find her. The fact that he is the son of Hamor, a
Hivite prince, seems to make him feel that he especially
has privileges in reference to unattended girls. We are
not told whether she was pleased with and encouraged
his first approaches. At least, the young prince was
bent upon seduction. This his object was accomplished,
whether she resisted or not. If 48:22 informs us that
the inhabitants of Sechem were Amorites, the apparent
contradiction seems to be solved by the fact that the
general name for the Canaanite tribes was Amorites.

3. At least, wrong as his deed was, Shechem
"loved" Dinah; we read "he was much attached" to
her, an expression rendered in Hebrew: "his soul
clung to her." After her seduction he sought "to comfort the girl's heart" — an expression for which the
original has: "he spoke upon the heart of the girl."
For "girl" the common gender form *na'ar* is regularly
used in the Pentateuch, always pointed *na'arah* by the
Masoretes (G. K. 17 c), a word supposedly belonging
to J, as though only he could write about "girls."
Shechem, therefore, was not like cruel Amnon (II Sam.
13). This occurrence serves to illustrate the low
standard of morals prevalent among the Canaanites.
Any unattended female could be raped, and in the
transactions that ensue neither father nor son feel the
need of apologizing for or excusing what had been
committed. But Shechem in his "comforting" no doubt
promised marriage to Dinah and otherwise sought to
relieve her fears.

4-6. **And Shechem spoke unto Hamor, his father, saying: Get me this damsel for wife.** And **Jacob on his part heard that he had defiled Dinah, his daughter, but as far as his sons were concerned, they were with his cattle out in the field. So Jacob kept still till they came. And Hamor, the father of Shechem, went forth to Jacob to consult with him.**

Shechem is so much in earnest about actually having Dinah to wife that he at once goes to his father and asks him to take the steps necessary to secure her. For as the story of Samson (Judg. 14:2) also indicates, the ones who arranged for marriages were the parents. The brevity of Shechem's demand — "Get me this damsel for wife" — indicates the young man's urgency.

5. The arrangement of verses would seem to indicate that before Hamor came to Jacob news of the misfortune of Dinah had already reached Jacob's ears. Since both "Jacob" and "his sons" stand first in their respective clauses for emphasis, the peculiar emphasis that these clauses gain runs thus: *Jacob* heard, but his *sons* were in the field. This definitely implies that in the matter of the disposal of a daughter or of safeguarding her rights the brothers, if of age, acted jointly with the father. The father could according to the custom of those days do nothing without the consent of the full brothers of the girl. Naturally, so large an establishment as Jacob had would keep the individual members of the family pretty well scattered till perhaps toward evening. Despite his great grief Jacob "kept still" — the perfect with *waw* conversive makes a durative imperfect (K. S. 367 i). Everyone can understand how the father's heart must have been lacerated by this tragic news. Dinah could not have been the one who informed her father, because she was kept in Shechem's house (v. 26). The critics call *timme'*, "defile," a ritual term and therefore assert

that a later Levitical hand inserted it. B D B proves
that the term is used in an "ethical and religious"
sense as well as being a ritual term. So the critical
objection falls away.

6. Hamor "went forth" because Jacob dwelt
outside of the city as a newcomer.

**7. And the sons of Jacob on their part came
in from the field, when they heard of the matter,
and the men were pained and very angry that folly
had been committed against Israel by lying with
Jacob's daughter — which thing ought not to be
done.**

Bad news spreads quickly, especially if it be as
disastrous as that which we have here. As soon as
the sons of Jacob receive the report, they come in from
the field. Again the subject stands first, because, as
in v. 5, their share in the following transactions is
specially under consideration. Critics, failing to appreciate this feature of these two verses, call both v. 5
and v. 7 poor Hebrew — a patent self-condemnation
of scholars proud in their own conceit. The worst
offender is Procksch.

The first step on the part of the brothers naturally is to hear the entire story. Their first reaction
is pain or grief (*yith'atsebu,* "they were hurt"). The
second is anger *yichar lahem me'odh,* "it burned for
them exceedingly." Both these reactions are seen to
be more than the ordinary carnal reactions of brothers
when the explanatory clause is heeded which we find
attached immediately: "that (or "for") folly had been
committed against Israel." The sons of Jacob appreciate the honorable destiny which was laid before
all descendants of Jacob when God Himself bestowed
the honorable epithet of "Israel" on their father. They
knew that the tribe was destined to become a great
people. God's promises were preserved among them.
Two explanations are here possible, which really differ

but little in the final analysis. Either Jacob's sons
consider their tribe already the Israel out of which
the nation Israel is soon to develop and then they
mean: "folly has been committed *in* Israel." Or else
they think of the sacred dignity vested by God in their
father Israel and mean: "folly has been committed
against Israel" — for *be* may mean "against." The
infinitive *lishkabh* ("to lie") is here used in a modal
sense, called by some a gerundive sense; "by lying with
Jacob's daughter" (K. S. 402 z). The last clause may
be rendered as above: *wekhen lo' ye'aseh* = "which
thing ought not to be done." K. C. arrives at nearly
the same result by assuming a transition from indirect
to direct discourse with the omission of the verb "and
they said"; then we render after the verb of saying:
"So ought not to be done." The obligation ("ought")
is covered by the imperfect (G. K. 107 w).

So far Jacob's sons are to be commended. Canaanite moral indifference and lascivity would have
found what Shechem had done quite natural and certainly not reprehensible. Jacob's sons live on the
level of true faith, at least in part, and as a result
have clear ethical concepts. Yet, as the sequel shows,
a measure of the carnal enters in and blurs their spiritual vision. Usually they are condemned too harshly
as being utterly devoid of a sense of higher values.
This verse in its use of the name "Israel" compels us
to allow a measure of spiritual understanding on their
part. They err largely in their choice of means for
solving the difficulty involved.

8-12. **And Hamor spoke with them saying:
As for Shechem, my son, he is dearly attached to
your daughter. Do give her to him for wife. Intermarry with us: your daughters ye may give us;
and our daughters ye may take for yourselves. Then
ye may live with us, for the land lies open before
you. Dwell in it, travel back and forth in it,**

establish yourselves in it. And Shechem said to her father and her brethren: Let me find favor in your sight; I will give whatsoever you say. Make the demand for dowry and gift heavy. I will pay it, no matter what you say. Only give me the girl for wife.

Though (v. 6) Hamor had set out to speak with Jacob, in the meantime Jacob's sons have come home, and so Hamor speaks "with them," here really including the sons and the father. But the Canaanite laxity of morals is apparent in both the father's and the son's words: neither admits that a wrong has been done. They are ready, however, to make an adjustment just as it might have been made for any regular marriage. What has occurred does not constitute an irregularity. They feel that Jacob's clan should feel honored at the proposal of a matrimonial alliance with their own princely line. Or at least they anticipate that a financial adjustment may smooth out all misunderstanding. Neither of the two modes of settlement dare be agreeable to Jacob's sons if they purpose to remain true to their spiritual heritage.

Hamor apparently first comes up alone and speaks first. His proposal is that Jacob consent to have Dinah be Shechem's wife because "he is dearly attached" (Hebrew, "his soul clings") to the girl. He calls her by a kind of zeugma *"your* daughter," though she is but Jacob's daughter; however, all have the disposal of her in hand. This step Hamor visualizes as the inauguration of the general practice of intermarriage. *Chathan* in the *Hithpael* actually means "make oneself a daughter's husband" (B D B). "Intermarry" is a loose equivalent about as inaccurate as the German *verschwaegern.* Naturally, where two tribes freely intermarry they will "live with" one another. This again was quite feasible because larger stretches of unclaimed country still lay available here and there

in those days: "the land lies open before you." Then
Hamor tries to paint an attractive picture of the advantages accruing to Israel from such an alliance:
they "may dwell' in the land, "travel back and forth
in it" (*sachar*, however, implies traveling mostly for
the purpose of trading) and they "may establish
themselves in it," departing from their more nomadic
way of life and adopting agricultural habits. In v. 8
"Shechem" stands first — nominative absolute — his
attitude is primarily under consideration.

11. In the meantime Shechem has come up also
and makes a different set of proposals in pressing his
suit. Being younger, he courteously asks "to find
favor in their sight" and then talks in terms of a
financial settlement. He surely displays willingness
as far as meeting the customary conditions is concerned. Let them set the terms as high as they will,
he is ready to meet them. Infatuation speaks in the
young man. He will give "dowry" (*móhar*, here, no
doubt, actually the purchase price paid to parents for
their daughter, though Israelites never bought wives)
and "gift" (*mattan*, the wedding gift presented to
the bride).

13-17. **And the sons of Jacob answered
Shechem and Hamor, his father, with guile, and
they spoke because he had defiled Dinah, their
sister. And they said to them: It is impossible
for us to do this thing, namely to give our sister to
an uncircumcised man; for that were a disgrace for
us. Only on this condition will we accede to your
request, if you will be as we are, and have all males
among you circumcised. Then will we give our
daughters to you, and shall take your daughters
unto ourselves, and we will dwell with you and we
two shall become one people. And if you will not
listen to us and be circumcised, then will we take
our daughter and go our way.**

Though right in refusing the proposition of the Hivites — for had Israel accepted, his descendants would have disappeared among the more numerous Canaanites and their spiritual heritage would have been sacrificed — yet Jacob's sons sin grievously in the manner of their refusal. "They answered with guile" — *mirmah* = "deception." The next verb may be taken to mean, "they spoke treacherously," because *dabhar* according to the Arabic *dábara* originally meant "be behind" and so, perhaps, "speak behind one's back," though no other instance of such use can be cited. We offer another simpler solution: they might have kept a grudging silence, but "they *spoke,* because he had defiled Dinah." In other words, all the while they were speaking this outrage kept running through their mind, and so all their speaking had to do with avenging this outrage. Whichever explanation be accepted, there is no need for textual alterations.

14. Rightly they insist that they cannot mingle in marriage with the uncircumcised — but, of course, mere carnal circumcision cannot make any nation worthy to share with them in their rare heritage. So Jacob's sons are guilty of treating the sign of the covenant lightly and of dishonoring it.

15. This verse contains rather a sweeping demand, but behind the demand must lie the fact that many nations and tribes practiced circumcision. *Ne'oth* ("be agreeable" or "accede") is derived from the unused *Kal 'oth.* *Zo'th* — feminine — represents the neuter and signifies, "on this condition."

16. The *waw* conversive (*we*) in *wenathannu* introduces the apodosis in this instance; for that reason we have rendered it "then."

17. The condition imposed by Jacob's sons is made rather strong, because if this condition is not met without exception by all inhabitants of their city, the stratagem of Jacob's sons would fail.

We may well ask, Where was Jacob when his sons made these conditions that he certainly would in no case have sanctioned? Above, v. 13, these terms and conditions are attributed to "the sons of Jacob" exclusively. There is the possibility that after the transactions were under way Jacob retired in the great grief of his heart and trusted that his sons would well be able to handle the case. It is quite certain that they kept their father in the dark both in regard to their original demand as well as in regard to their further purpose.

18, 19. Their proposition appealed to Hamor and to Shechem, the son of Hamor. The young man did not hesitate to do this thing, because he delighted in Jacob's daughter, and he especially was honored by all who were of his father's house.

The original says, "their words were good in the eyes of Hamor," etc. We should say, "their proposition appealed to Hamor," etc. The son is agreeable because he above all things wants the girl. The father is agreeable for his son's sake and also because the demand was quite in keeping with customs prevalent at the time. Hamor will have regarded their demand as the outgrowth of a tribal practice or taboo which they felt they dared not violate.

19. The son's attitude is explained at once; but "he did not hesitate" does not mean that he submitted to circumcision on the spot but that he was the first one to submit to the operation after the townsfolk had been found agreeable. Further, by way of anticipation of the agreement of his kinsfolk to the plan, it is explained that he happened to be "honored by all who were of his father's house." This implies that another young man less respected than Shechem might not have been heeded by the villagers in the proposition on which his marriage hinged.

20-23. And Hamor and Shechem, his son, came to the gate of their city and they spoke to the men of the city saying: As far as these men are concerned, they live harmonious with us and they will dwell in the land, and they will travel back and forth in it; and as far as the land is concerned, it is spacious enough on either side before them. Their daughters we will take to ourselves for wives, and our daughters will we give to them. Only on this condition will the men accede to our request to dwell with us and become one people if every male among us be circumcised, even as they are circumcised. Their cattle and their possessions and all their beasts of burden, shall they not be ours? Only let us accede to their request and they will stay with us.

The gate of the city is the natural place for all transactions of a public or even of a private character. The substance of their speech is given in one unified whole, the various arguments with which father and son plied their friends being smelted together. It is an artful speech. With clever rhetoric the acquisitiveness of the Hivites is appealed to. Things that had never been mentioned to Jacob's sons are introduced. They are really inferences that may well be drawn, results that must follow if intermarriage on a general scale is introduced. These additional things are that the Hivites will come into possession of the Israelite "cattle" — *miqneh* — about the same as "stock" (Meek), of their "possessions" and of their "beasts of burden" — that must be the meaning of *behemah* here. One other thing not mentioned to Jacob's sons and yet on the whole an inevitable consequence was: both would "become one people." The Hivites apparently predominated in numbers, and so there was no danger that they would become submerged in the process; so to them it may be mentioned. Note how at

the beginning of the speech nouns are placed first in
the sentences pointing to the various issues involved:
as for these "men" — as far as "the land" is concerned;
also in v. 23 as far as their "cattle" "possessions," and
"beasts" are concerned. This is a touch true to life.
The last *yeshebhu* of v. 23 seems to mean "stay" rather
than "dwell." In v. 21 the dual *yadháyim*, "on both
hands," means "on either side." In v. 22 the infinitive
běhimmol, "in being circumcised," is the equivalent
of a conditional clause (K. S. 404 a).

**24. And they hearkened to Hamor and unto
Shechem, his son, all who went out of the gate of
his city; and all the males, all who went out of the
gate of his city, were circumcised.**

The entire male population is referred to as adopting the proposed plan. In apposition with "males"
twice stands the phrase "all who went out of the gate
of his (i. e. 'his own') city." The participle *yotse'ey*
implies the habitual: they were wont to go out. This
phrase, however, refers to the city gate as the customary council chamber or courthouse; they that go
out are the ones that are entitled to sit there. The
reason why the expression is used twice is to emphasize
that this was a valid decision properly arrived at by
those competent to make it. *Yotse'ey* is a participle
construed primarily as a noun (K. S. 241 d).

**25, 26. And it came to pass on the third day
when they were suffering pain, that the two sons
of Jacob, Simeon and Levi, full brothers of Dinah,
each took his sword and came upon the unsuspecting city and slew all males. Hamor and Shechem,
his son, they slew with the edge of the sword, and
took Dinah from the house of Shechem and went
forth.**

Wounds come to a kind of crisis on the third day.
In this instance it was known to be the third day
when a man was incapacitated in a very special sense:

ko'abhim, they "were suffering pain." Simeon and Levi deem it to be a matter involving their honor in a very special sense, because they were *'achchim,* "full brothers." But so were Reuben and Judah as well as two more. Reuben with a sense of the responsibility of the first-born refrained at least from active participation. Judah, a man of nobler cast, also lent no active assistance when this first step of the plan was carried out. Yet neither of these two seems to have offered active opposition. But then there is the possibility that Simeon and Levi finally decided to carry out their nefarious purpose without informing the rest who seemed more than reluctant. Without a doubt, the murderers took their servants, for even two very courageous men could hardly venture to attack a city. At the time both could not have been above twenty or twenty-two years old. *Betach,* according to its position, as practically all now recognize, belongs to "city" and means "unsuspecting" *sorglos* (K. W.), being an adverbial accusative and the equivalent of a condensed clause, "as it lay there unsuspecting" (G. K. 118 q; K. S. 402 k). The men especially involved in this slaughter are specifically mentioned by name, "Hamor and Shechem, his son." Dinah, their sister, who must have been kept by Shechem in his house till now, was taken, and so they "went forth," i. e. from the wretched city.

One shudders to think of the bloody cruelty that animated these two brothers in their carnal pride. Not a word can be said to excuse these murderers. The account, as Moses offers it, is strictly objective neither commending nor condemning; he trusts his readers to posses sufficient ethical discernment to know how to judge the deed. Those who class these accounts as being largely legendary may well pause at this chapter. For no nation was wont to develop legends about events that reflected dishonor upon their nation, here in particular upon the tribal father of the priests — Levi.

Lephi chérebh, "according to the mouth of the sword," means: as the sword is wont to devour, or "according to the usage of war" or "without quarter" (Skinner).

27-29. And the sons of Jacob came upon the slain and plundered the city that had defiled their sister. Their flocks and their herds and their asses they took, both what was in the city and what was in the field. And they captured all their wealth, and all their little ones and their wives, and they plundered even everything that was in the houses.

"Sons of Jacob" here refers to all of them. Strangely, they who seemed to have scruples or fears about taking part in the slaughter have no compunctions of conscience about taking a hand in plundering the city. This act of theirs again does them little credit. The thing that rankled in the bosom of all was that this was "the city that had defiled their sister." They are, indeed, largely correct in imputing to the city a share in the wrong done; for the city condoned the wrong and had not the slightest intentions of taking steps to right it. But only the most excessive cruelty can demand such a wholesale retribution for a personal wrong.

28. The cattle is mentioned first in the plunder, no doubt, because the wealth of the Shechemites consisted primarily in cattle. "Flocks" and "herds" and "asses" are listed because these were constituent parts of cattle or stock.

29. Then to show how thoroughly Jacob's sons were in the heat of their vengeance the author reports that also "all their wealth and all their little ones and their wives" were captured, the latter, no doubt, being kept as slaves. Then to produce the im-

pression that the sacking of the city was done with
utmost thoroughness the writer adds: "and they
plundered even everything that was in the houses."
By translating thus we remove the necessity of textual
changes which the critics regard as necessary. We
hold our translation to be quite defensible.

**30, 31. And Jacob said unto Simeon and unto
Levi: Ye have brought trouble upon me by causing
me to become odious to the inhabitants of the
land, the Canaanites and Perizzites, whereas I have
but a small following. Now they will gather together against me and smite me and I shall be
destroyed, I and my family. And they said: Should
our sister be treated like a harlot?**

It is almost unbelievable that Jacob should be
reproached by commentators at this point for what
he is supposed to have failed to say, namely for not
rebuking Simeon and Levi for "their treachery and
cruelty." Yet such a man as Jacob could not have
failed to be in perfect accord with us in our estimate
of this bloody deed of his sons, for Jacob was a truly
spiritual man, especially in these his later years. Nor
was the moral issue involved in the least difficult to
discern. The chief reason for the writer's not mentioning Jacob's judgment on the moral issue is that this
issue is too obvious. Furthermore, that judgment is
really included in the statement, "ye have brought
trouble upon me." Then, lastly, the author is really
leading up to another matter that specially calls for
discussion. Since, namely, the entire Pentateuch aims
to set forth how God's gracious care led on the undeserving people of His choice from grace to grace, the
author is preparing to show another instance of such
doing and prepares for it by mentioning how greatly
troubled Jacob was by this deed. For 'akhar, which
means "disturb," "destroy," here means "bring into
trouble." In what sense he means this in particular

is at once explained, "by causing me to become odious (literally: 'to stink') to the inhabitants of the land." That surely implies that the deed done was both obnoxious and dangerous. In comparison with the inhabitants of the land Jacob had "but a small following," or, says the Hebrew, "men of numbers," i. e., men easily numbered. Had God not intervened, the outcome would inevitably have been as Jacob describes it: they would have gathered together and smitten and destroyed him and his family. Though without a doubt the deed of Jacob's sons gave evidence of great courage, it certainly also entailed even greater rashness. The thoughtlessness of young men who rush headlong into ill-considered projects was abundantly displayed by this massacre.

31. Simeon and Levi are still a bit impatient of rebuke. What they say is true enough: their sister should not be treated like a harlot (*ye'aseh* — an imperfect expressing a potential "should," *durfte* — K. S. 181). But Delitzsch very properly adds: "Simeon and Levi have the last word, but the very last of all comes from Jacob on his deathbed" (49:5-7), where Jacob's verdict is clearly recorded for all times: "Cursed be their anger."

We are greatly amazed in reflecting upon the event as a whole that descendants of the worthy patriarch Abraham should almost immediately after his time already have sunk to the level upon which Jacob's sons stand in this chapter. A partial explanation is to be sought in the crafty cunning of their father which in the sons degenerated to the extremes here witnessed. A further bit of explanation is to be sought in their environment: hardly anywhere except in their own home did they see any manifestations of a godly life. Then, in the third place, we must attribute a good measure of the guilt of an improper bringing-up of these young men to the irregularities of a home where bigamy ruled. All true spirit of discipline was cancelled by the presence of two wives and two handmaidens in the home — practically four wives.

Lastly, the chapter as a whole furnishes a clear example as to how much the critics are divided against themselves in spite of their strong protestations of unanimity. Skinner claims that two recensions are interwoven here, but he says they are not J and E; rather he introduces two new sources, I and II, but admits that their accounts may have been revamped by J^x and E^x. A few stand as he does, but Procksch claims to find the usual strands of J and E tradition. Koenig contents himself with the modest assumption that a story of J has been filled out a bit. But the critics as a whole for the most part wrest the simple harmonious account, trying to make themselves and others believe that two tales have been woven into one.

HOMILETICAL SUGGESTIONS

We may well wonder if any man who had proper discernment ever drew a text from this chapter. As a rule, the Sunday school scholars do not even hear of this event in the life of Jacob. Men who followed the mechanical procedure in the work of preaching, which consisted in treating in strictly consecutive order the chapters of a Biblical book that they had selected for such treatment, of necessity had to use this chapter also. As a whole it is an invaluable sidelight on the lives of the patriarchs. It is rightly evaluated by the more mature mind and could be treated to advantage before a men's Bible class. But we cannot venture to offer homiletical suggestions for its treatment.

CHAPTER XXXV

11. The Last Events of Isaac's History (35:1-29)

If we are to follow the outline offered by the author himself, we must have some such title as the above. For the "history" (*toledôth*) of Isaac closes with this chapter; he has, unaggressive person that he was, still dominated Jacob's action up to this point. Jacob becomes an independent factor after his father's death, and his own "history" begins with 37:2.

1. And God said to Jacob: Arise, go up to Bethel and tarry there, and make there an altar unto God who appeared to thee at the time of the flight from before Esau, thy brother.

Since the divine name *'Elohim* or *'El* dominates this chapter, it appears plainly that the writer regards the various acts and words of God here recorded as displaying the activity of the *Creator-God* in His authority as He deals with His creature *man*. In this capacity *Elohim* authoritatively bids Jacob fulfill his vow; the altar is to be erected to Elohim (v. 3), who showed forth His power in protecting Jacob. The God who controls the nations lets a terror fall upon the inhabitants of the land lest they harm Israel (v. 5). It is *Elohim*, who appears to Jacob, blesses him, changes his name, and bestows upon him the blessing of Abraham; for *Elohim* alone possesses authority to do these things. Without a doubt, some of these acts, like the last, do also show forth the *Yahweh* character of God; but we sincerely believe the *Elohim* character predominates.

We have no way of knowing in what manner God spoke to Jacob. If this appearance is analogous to that of v. 9-13, it would seem that He appeared under some visible guise, because (v. 13) He "went up from him." But more puzzling is the question why Jacob should have deferred fulfilling the vow of 28:22 and should have to be bidden by God to do according to it. The readiest explanation is that Jacob had kept putting it off until a more convenient season. The level of faith arrived at at the close of chapter 32 had not been maintained. God Himself prevents further sinful delay by allowing Jacob no choice in the matter. That God demands the building of an altar where Jacob had vowed to build a "house" shows how Jacob had meant his vow: he had intended to establish a sanctuary, whose most prominent feature in days of old could be nothing other than an altar. He should "tarry" (*shebh*, imperative from *yashabh*; here not in the sense of "dwell" but "tarry") just long enough to carry out the injunction laid upon him. Jacob was not to "go up to Bethel to live" (Meek). This rendering creates an unnecessary conflict with what Jacob actually does.

2-4. And Jacob said to his household and to all who were with him: Discard the foreign gods which are in your midst, and purify yourselves and change your garments. And let us set out and go up to Bethel; and there I shall make an altar unto El (God) who answered me at the time of my distress and was with me on the way that I went. And they turned over to Jacob all the foreign gods in their possession and the rings that were in their ears, and Jacob buried them under the terebinth near Shechem.

Such a command as Jacob has just received requires more, as Jacob clearly sees, than a mere literal keeping. A general repentance and reconsecration of all that are with him should accompany the outward act. Certain of the more recent happenings had taught him the need of such a purging of his house-

hold. His sons had given evidence of a very carnal
and cruel disposition. His daughter may at least have
displayed undue levity. The grave danger growing
out of the present situation had contributed to stir
his conscience. But most important of all, there had
been a most pernicious and dangerous practice subtly
at work poisoning the fountainhead of all true religion
— idols were worshipped. Most of this evil must have
kept under cover. It now appears that Rachel's purpose in stealing her father's teraphim (31:19) may
well have been at least occasionally to engage in
the worship of them. Then it is highly probable that
the servants acquired in Mesopotamia may in many
cases have still been idolaters. The sacking of Shechem may have brought additional "foreign gods"
into the possessions of the plunderers, and the mere
having of them will have constituted a grave danger
for the possessors. Without a doubt, Jacob will as
a faithful patriarch have instructed his entire household to serve Yahweh, the only true God, and, as
Luther frequently reminds, will have been a faithful
preacher in his own household. But now the drastic
action that might well have been taken long before
marks a courageous and thoroughgoing attempt to
root out the evil. Patriarchal authority certainly
made Jacob's course possible and effective. *Hasiru*
means more than our "put away" — that might imply
"storing away"; the verb is rather an emphatic "discard." The command, "purify yourselves," may include ceremonial washing, as in Exod. 19:14, but
its essence would be: purge your hearts and lives
of this noxious influence. Again as at Mt. Sinai the
changing of garments was to do honor to the occasion
and further symbolize the putting off of the old and
the putting on of the new. For "foreign gods" the
Hebrew uses the noun in place of the adjective —
"the gods of the foreigner."

3. With the preparations demanded in v. 2, which may well be regarded as a repentance of heart, the people as a whole are ready to "set out" (literally: "rise up," *qum*) and "go up" ('*alah*, for Bethel lies 1,000 feet higher). In recounting by way of thankful confession what God did for him Jacob remembers what strength God displayed in guarding him against all harm and therefore designates Him as '*El*, the "Strong One." Jacob's confession includes the statement that '*El* answered him "in the day" (*beyom*) or "at the time of my distress." The following words are a definite allusion to 28:15; for this was just what God had promised at Bethel, to be with him on the way that he went. Since, without a doubt, Jacob had frequently told the story of God's promise, this word will have been recognized by those that heard him as an acknowledgment of God's faithfulness.

4. When "they gave" (*nathan*) to Jacob the objects he had asked them to discard, it was with the purpose that he might dispose of them as he pleased; therefore we translate *nathan* they "turned over" to Jacob. Apparently they entered wholeheartedly upon the plan, for they gave "*all* the foreign gods in their possession," as well as earrings, which must have served as amulets and tokens of some idolatrous practices. Jacob buries all they give him "under the terebinth near Shechem." Such a terebinth ('*elah*) was mentioned as having been at Shechem in Abraham's day (12:6), although there we read, "the terebinth of Moreh," which, as we remarked on this passage, hardly bears any idolatrous connotation. Since it may, nevertheless, be the prominent terebinth under which Abraham had stopped and at which the Lord had appeared to him, the article may here recall that event; and the sacred

memories associated with it may well accord with the memorable event of our chapter, and so the tree becomes a memorial tree of the notable religious events. Reluctant to accept Scriptural suggestions and seemingly anxious to obscure a simple text, one critic remarks: "The burial of idolatrous emblems under this sacred tree has some traditional meaning which we cannot now explain." The claims to the effect that some Canaanite cult was associated with this tree rest upon a weak foundation. The dative is here expressed by the preposition *'el*, (K. S. p. 263, 1). In Joshua 24:26 Shechem becomes the scene of an event much like that of Jacob's days.

5-7. **Then they departed; but there was a terror of God upon the cities round about them, so that they did not pursue the sons of Jacob. And Jacob came to Luz, which is in the land of Canaan — that is to say, Bethel — he and all the people that were with him. And he built there an altar and called the place El-Bethel (God of Bethel), for there God had been revealed to him in his flight from Esau.**

God gives plain tokens of his favor and approval of the step just taken by Jacob in purging out idolatry by putting restraint upon all Canaanite projects of revenge for the Shechemites. Certainly, here again God's favor far exceeded the deserts of the chosen group, but on the other hand Jacob's reformation had prepared his family for holier living. The "terror of God" was a supernatural terror — "of God" being either a descriptive genitive or a genitive of source. Apparently, the neighboring cities had intended a murderous pursuit, and in point of numbers they certainly had the advantage. But God had purposes for the future in reference to Abraham's seed and so spared them. "Terror," *chittah*, a feminine noun, has a masculine verb because of the tendency to let sentences begin with masculine verbs (K. S. 345 a). Cf. also II Chron. 20:29.

6. We are reminded of 28:19 where already Jacob had altered "Luz" to "Bethel." The mention of Bethel is a definite allusion to the former experience at this site. So, too, the mention of the coming of Jacob "and all the people that were with him" aims to show how marvelously God had fulfilled His promise to bring Jacob back unharmed. The critics do not believe the Elohist, so called, capable of making any such point, so they ascribe at least 6 a to P. Naturally, such points are too important for the writer, Moses, to overlook.

7. Then the altar is built, no doubt, more than the simplest kind of a place of sacrifice. If in making his vow (28:22) Jacob had spoken of a "house of God," we are justified in thinking here of a permanent sanctuary, such as the needs of that day would require, the task of building which may have required weeks. Yet everything centered about the *mizbéach,* "the place of slaughtering" or the "altar." Here now, without a doubt, *maqom* must mean "holy place" or "sanctuary." This holy "place" therefore receives the name *'El-Bethel,* "the Strong God of Bethel." Those translators who failed to recognize that the holy place was meant (e. g. Septuagint) altered the name to a mere "Bethel." The propriety of the name Jacob chose is readily apparent: "The Strong One" who had so often delivered him as He had promised at "Bethel" is the one whose altar Jacob has built. The experiences of twenty years are perpetuated pointedly in this name. To make the reason for the erecting of the altar clear beyond all doubt the reason of v. 1 is again repeated here: "God had been revealed to him in his flight from Esau." The verb *nighlû* is plural with *ha'elohim,* a plural of

potentiality, a harmless construction explained above
on 20:13; which see. Such expressions never contain
reminiscences of a former polytheistic standpoint.
Here in particular all such possible allusions are
ruled out by *'Elohim* with the article *ha*, a combination always of the strictest monotheistic import, for
it means: "the true God."

8. **And Deborah, Rebekah's nurse, died and
was buried below Bethel beneath the oak; so it
came to be called the Oak of Weeping.**

Of Deborah we read in 24:59 without being apprised of her name. It will forever remain a puzzle
how she came to be with Jacob at Bethel. The
simplest surmise is that after Rebekah's death she
may have chosen to attach herself to Jacob, because
she had loved and tended him in infancy and in
youth. Even on Jacob's part there may have been
an attachment for one, who in our day might be
referred to as an old "mammy." Deborah must have
been very old at this time. Since Jacob may have
been nearly 110 years old at this time and was born
rather late in his mother's life, an age of 170 years
for Deborah is not unlikely. But Isaac lived to be
180 years old (v. 28). But these unexplained and
unusual features constitute no reason for questioning
the historicity of this event. The confusion of our
event and the person of Deborah (Judg. 4:5) does
not lie in these passages but in the minds of the critics.
The Deborah of a later date "judged" and dwelt "under
a palmtree between Ramah and Bethel." Our Deborah
"died" and was buried "under an oak below Bethel."
More important to observe is the fact that the Scripture regards the death and the burial of this menial
worthy of notice; and that fact would lead us to infer,
as Luther does, that "she was a wise and godly matron,
who had served and advised Jacob, had supervised
the domestics of the household and had often coun-

selled and comforted Jacob in dangers and difficulties." So the "Oak of Weeping" became a monument to a godly servant whose loss was deeply mourned by all.

9-12. And God appeared to Jacob again as he came from Paddan-Aram and blessed him; and God said unto him: Thy name is Jacob; thy name shall no longer be called Jacob, but Israel shall be thy name. So He called his name Israel. And God said to him: I am God Almighty; be fruitful and multiply; a nation and a group of peoples shall come from thee, and kings shall come forth from thy loins. And the land which I gave to Abraham and to Isaac, I now give to thee; also to thy seed after thee will I give the land.

Apparently the author's point of view is that Jacob is to be regarded as still on his way home from Paddan-Aram. Only in v. 27 does Jacob actually return home to his father Isaac. But since Jacob has returned again to Bethel, at least the significant point of departure had again been reached. To confirm and ratify the promises made at the time when God first appeared to him at this place, God deems it good and necessary for Jacob that He appear to him again. With this appearance is coupled a ratification of the change of name which was first determined 32:28. Since the whole of God's dealings with Jacob in this manifestation may be designated as the imparting of a divine blessing — even the change of name may be regarded from this point of view — it is here said and He "blessed him."

10. It must remain a divine prerogative to determine when men need manifestations such as these. So, then, it must have appeared necessary and good in the eyes of the Lord first of all to confirm the change of name and so to reimpress the obligation involved in the new name. If, then, this episode is closed with

the assertion: "so He called his name Israel," this is
no denial of 32:28 but a reaffirmation of it. But
criticism will persist in thinking this account in conflict with the earlier experience. But why should
God not repeat what He wishes to emphasize
strongly?

11, 12. These verses are a reaffirmation of the
promise formerly given at Bethel 28:13-15. In the
earlier passage Jacob is assured that his seed shall
be as the dust of the earth, and that he shall spread
abroad to all quarters of the land. Here the blessing
of fruitfulness and of multiplying covers the same
ground, except that here in addition it is specified
that "a nation and a group of peoples shall come"
from him, as well as kings. In both words possession of the land is assured to Jacob and his seed.
There God designates Himself as the faithful Yahweh;
here, as *'El Shadday*, i. e., God Almighty. Strangely,
the earlier passage 28:14 b offers the Messianic
thought ("in thy seed shall all the families of the
earth be blessed"), which is not restated in the
passage before us. May this be due to the fact that
this most prominent part of the blessing had been
laid hold upon by the faith of Jacob so decisively
and retained so firmly that it required no repetition?
It seems so. We know no more appropriate explanation.

13-15. **And God went up from him in the
place where He had spoken with him. And Jacob
erected a pillar in the place where God spoke with
him, a pillar of stone, and poured a libation on it
and also poured oil upon it. And Jacob called the
name of the place where God had spoken with him
Bethel.**

The unusual expression "went up from him in
the place where He had spoken with him" implies
that as God had spoken to Jacob from a position

above Jacob so from this point His visible ascent
occurred in a plainly visible fashion. For *me'alaw*
means "from above him" and marks the starting point
of His departure. It is hardly to be expected that the
stone erected in 28:18 in commemoration of the previous event will still have been standing after a lapse
of thirty years, during which time Jacob had had no
occasion to visit the spot. The *matstsebha* is in this
instance again a sacred memorial pillar; and since
wooden pillars may occasionally have been used, this
one is specified to have been "of stone." The libation
is poured out (*nasakh nésekh* = "pouring out a
pouring," i. e., a drink-offering or libation) as a
quantity of wine that here constitutes an independent
offering but later was always used in conjunction
with other offerings. The oil is the oil of consecration. On drink-offerings see Deut. 32:38; Exod.
29:40; 30:9. Though this constitutes a repetition
of what transpired 28:18, it, like the appearance of
God, is a second and a distinct act: God appeared
twice; Jacob anointed a stone twice. But no one who
reads the account fairly would claim to find evidence
here of the fact that "these monuments were doubtless
originally objects of worship," or that the "libation
was in the first instance an offering to the dead."
Such interpretations impute to the patriarch superstitions of which not one trace appears in the text.
Such "debunking" of the patriarchs and their religion
deserves the sharpest rebuke. Note the omission of
the dagesh forte in *yitsoq* (G. K. 71).

15. If it seem strange that the name of the
place should a second time (cf. 28:19) be called
"Bethel," i. e. "house of God," let a distinct difference
be noted. Then there was but one person; now there
is a multitude. Then the one expressed his godly
sentiments in a memorial; now a whole tribal group
shares in the experience, even if, perhaps, Jacob alone

witnessed the divine manifestation. This time the word "Bethel" expresses what all feel or are to feel.

16-18. And they departed from Bethel, and when they were still some distance from Ephrath, Rachel brought forth a child and had great difficulties in the birth. And it came to pass when her labor was extremely hard that the midwife said to her: Do not be afraid, for this one too shall be a son for you. **And it came to pass as her soul departed — for she was dying — that she called his name Ben-oni** (Son of my sorrow), **but his father called him Benjamin** (Son of the right hand).

Jacob is on the way to his father at Hebron. Rachel's travail comes upon her "when they were still some distance from Ephrath." Now *'ephrath* means "fruitful region" and must have been a certain fruitful area within which Bethlehem was the most prominent town. In Jacob's day the limits of that area may have been more distinctly marked so that, as they were approaching it, their location would be marked in reference to the proximity of Ephrath. Unfortunately, no light has as yet been thrown upon the expression *kibrath*. Luther says *ein Feldwegs*. Does he mean a distance like the length of an ordinary field? A. V. imagines the distance to have been greater, saying: "still some distance" — so above. The Syriac Peshito seems to go too far when it calls the distance "a parasang," i. e. about six miles. The expression must mean a familiar distance and hardly seems to imply a great distance. The birth is first recorded in a summary way: *watteledh,* "and she brought forth a child." In characteristic Hebrew manner the details follow: she "had great difficulties (literally: "she had a hard time of it" or "she was hard beset") in the birth." *Lidhtah* — infinitive from *yaladh*.

17. The *Hifil* stem of the verb *qashah* here differs little in meaning from the *Piel* of v. 16; if anything, it may be a bit stronger: "her labor was extremely hard" vs. "she had great difficulties." The "midwife" was none other than some older woman experienced in helping at birth. She comforts Rachel when she discerns that this child too is to be a son, as she had prayed 30:24 that he might be.

18. Rachel's birth struggle terminated fatally. Since *néphesh* means both "soul" and "life," we may translate either: "as her *soul*," or "as her *life* went forth or departed." There is a very tragic note in this that her dying word is an expression of the anguish of her soul as she gives the name to her son — *Ben-oni,* i. e. "son of my sorrow." It would, indeed, have been almost morbid to allow a son to bear such a name through life. So the father promptly alters the name to at least a similar one: *Benjamin.* Though literally translated: "son of the right hand," this name may signify "a child of good fortune" because the right side was commonly regarded as the stronger and more honorable and so came to symbolize good fortune. *Glueckskind* has aptly been suggested as a rendering. From Jacob's point of view this is the son that rounds out the number of his children to a perfect twelve, and so his birth is a token of good fortune. It hardly seems likely that this son's birth is contrasted with that of the other sons in that he was born after Jacob became free, whereas the other eleven are the sons begotten in the state of relative bondage.

19-21. **So Rachel died, and she was buried on the way to Ephrath, that is Bethlehem. And Jacob set up a pillar at her grave. This is the pillar of the grave of Rachel until this day. But Israel moved on and pitched his tent beyond Migdal-eder.**

After Rachel's death the sad duty of love, burial,
devolved upon Jacob. The writer gives us the location
of this grave very definitely for a reason which will
soon become apparent. He says it was "on the way
to Ephrath." This does not necessarily involve that
the burial took place at the very spot where she died.
Yet it cannot have been far from there, because in
v. 16 they were "still some distance from Ephrath."
Nor are they now there. Ephrath is identified, for
strictly speaking it is more in the nature of a common noun ("fruitful region") than a proper noun,
or according to its meaning there may have been
several such Ephraths in the land. The closer identification says: "that is Bethlehem." Since Bethlehem
is a town in a region Ephrath — so also in Micah 5:2
— this identification must be meant in the sense that
Bethlehem was the best known or most important
town in this tract. Another possibility is this: "way"
may be supplied before the second noun, thus: "on
the way to Ephrath, that is the way to Bethlehem."
Then the region would be mentioned first; thereafter
the specific spot in the region. Such a construction
has nothing harsh or unnatural about it. Usually
critics call the parenthetical identification — "that is
Bethlehem" — a blunder on the writer's part. They
say that the writer did not know that the region
and the town were not identical. Strange ignorance
on his part! But with our second explanation another difficulty vanishes: Jacob in coming from Bethel
and approaching Ephrath may have been just past
the site of Jerusalem when Rachel died. Near there
he buried her. But now the two passages that are
usually said to conflict with this point of view lose
their point, viz., I Sam. 10:2 and Jer. 31:15. The
first places Rachel's sepulchre in the border of Benjamin. But the border between Benjamin and Judah
ran diagonally through Jerusalem. All we, then,

need to assume is that Jacob had not yet passed Jerusalem when Rachel died.

The second passage (Jer. 31:15) represents the mother of Benjamin weeping over her slain children at Ramah. Now Ramah lay about five miles north of Jerusalem. However, though Rachel is represented as rising from her tomb and lamenting over her slain descendants that does not say that her sepulchre has to be at the same spot where she weeps. The only discrepancy would then be the traditional site of Rachel's tomb, the *Kubbet Rachel* about two miles north of Bethlehem.

Somehow the peculiar interest attaching to the tomb of Rachel in Moses' day lay in the fact that the pillar, which Jacob set up as a memorial at Rachel's tomb, was still to be seen after a lapse of four hundred years. How it came that this pillar was not dislodged by the Canaanites or did not fall of itself we may not be able to determine. Sometimes burial sites enjoy even the respect of strangers. Neither have we any means of determining how Moses came into possession of this interesting fact. But all this casts no shadow of doubt upon its correctness. Moses, however, inserted such notices to arouse interest in the land of promise on the part of the people whom it was his business to lead there.

21. He that departs from the scene of his sorsow is designated as "Israel," as it would seem to indicate that he bore his grief as his better, newer nature helped him to do, and so "moved on" a chastened but a more seasoned saint of God. But for the present he did not move far. For "Migdal-Eder," meaning "the tower of the flocks," i. e. a lookout tower for shepherds, was, according to Micah 4:8, (rightly interpreted), on the southeast hill of Jerusalem on old territory of the tribe of Benjamin (Josh. 18:28; Judg. 1:21).

22 a. **And it happened while Israel dwelt in that land that Reuben went and lay with Bilhah, his father's concubine. And Israel heard of it.**

A sad testimony to the demoralization of Jacob's sons! Jacob is here called Israel to remind us that in doing this vile deed Reuben dishonored Israel, the eminent hero of faith. Vile, incestuous lust here has its sway among men who should have been worthy to bear the honorable title sons of Israel. Though Bilhah was heretofore described only as Rachel's "handmaid," she is now after Rachel's death described in her relationship to Jacob against whom the wrong is done and is designated as Jacob's "concubine." Critics cannot see such simple proprieties and promptly seize upon such points as proofs of a supposedly different style of different authors. Need we be told the self-evident thing that Jacob disapproved and was deeply grieved and shamed? We are merely informed that he became aware of what has happened: he "heard of it." This prepares us for 49:4 where his disapproval finds lasting expression for all future time. Criticism's verdict again cannot satisfy: it calls this statement "probably a temporal clause of which the apodosis has been intentionally omitted." The infinitive *bishkon* = a temporal clause (G. K. 45 g).

22 b-27. **Now Jacob had twelve sons: the sons of Leah — the first-born of Jacob, Reuben, and Simeon, and Levi and Judah and Issachar and Zebulon; the sons of Rachel — Joseph and Benjamin; the sons of Bilhah, the handmaid of Rachel — Dan and Naphtali; the sons of Zilpah, the handmaid of Leah — Gad and Asher. These are the sons of Jacob which were born to him in Paddan-Aram. And Jacob came to Isaac, his father, to Mamre, to Kirjath-Arba — that is Hebron — where Abraham and Isaac had sojourned.**

Summaries or recapitulations serve a good purpose in narratives. Here it can be seen to be very appropriate to have those twelve who are Jacob's sons listed together, first, to reimpress their names on the mind and to show what potentialities for development into a numerous people lay in Jacob's descendants at this point already. Critics, of course, call this one of the characteristics of P, to write such summaries and discourse on their supposed findings but fail to see how naturally any writer, or writers, summarize at important junctures of their narratives, as here where Jacob presents himself to his father Isaac.

These sons are listed according to their mothers rather than according to age because those of one mother would naturally find themselves drawn closer together. Then, again, it is but natural that the sons of the wives be listed first, then those of the hand-maidens. But among the wives, though Rachel was the favorite, Leah had borne many sons long before Rachel began; consequently her children are listed first. These twelve are all said to have been born in Paddan-Aram, though everyone knows that Benjamin was born in Canaan. *Yulladh* as a singular with a plural subject ("these" being the antecedent) is to be accounted for by the fact that after they have been summarized, they appear to the writer as one group. The passive of this verb is a convenient mode of avoiding the mention of numerous subjects (K. S. 108).

27. Comparing with 18:1, we notice that Mamre will most likely be a briefer designation for "the terebinths of Mamre." The well-informed writer lists both names of the ancient town, giving "Hebron" parenthetically as the better known name for "Kirjath-Arba," i. e., "the city of Arba." To mention that Abraham and Isaac "had sojourned" there does not

serve the purpose of imparting new facts but suggests what it was that drew Jacob to Hebron: the place was redolent with the memories of his godly forefathers.

The break in v. 22 indicates, as it were, the beginning of a new paragraph. The double accent on *yisra'el* suggests the two possible modes of reading: *athnach* for private reading, making a pause according to the sense, the *metheg* for public or liturgical reading to indicate direct continuation, slurring over the vile deed.

28, 29. And the length of Isaac's life was one hundred and eighty years. And Isaac expired and died and was gathered unto his people, an old man and sated with days; and Esau and Jacob his sons buried him.

From this time onward Jacob enters into the full patriarchal heritage, having at last attained to a spiritual maturity which is analogous to that of the patriarch. Coincident with this is Isaac's receding into the background. Consequently Isaac's death is now reported, though it did not take place for another twelve or thirteen years. For shortly after this, when Joseph was sold into Egypt, he was seventeen years old. When he stood before Pharaoh he was thirty (41:46). Seven years later when Joseph was thirty-seven, Jacob came to Egypt at the age of 130 (47:9). Consequently Jacob must have been ninety-three at Joseph's birth and at the time of our chapter 93 + 15, i. e. about 108 years. But Isaac was sixty years old when Jacob was born; 108 + 60 = 168 = Isaac's age when Jacob returned home. But in closing the life of Isaac it is proper to mention his death, though in reality this did not occur for another twelve years. Strange to say, Isaac lived to witness Jacob's grief over Joseph.

29. *Gawa'*, "he expired," describes the process; *muth*, "he died," marks the conclusion of the process. That he "was gathered unto his people" certainly implies more than being laid in the common ancestral grave or even than passing out of this life. They to whom he goes are a "people" whom he joins. How strong and clear the hope of eternal life was in those days we cannot now tell, but this word bears testimony to such a faith. With the progressive weakening of the human race Isaac at 180 years was counted as an old man. How much of life God had let him taste is indicated by the statement that "he was sated (*sebha'* = 'full') with days." He had seen as many as his soul might desire. It is a pleasant fact to note that at the death of their father the once estranged brothers are still united.

On the sources of this chapter the critics, though far from being of one mind, claim to have discerned a pattern about as follows: E wrote 1-8, 16-20. To J must be ascribed 21, 22 a. This leaves for P 9-15, 22 b-29 (K. C.). Aside from the fundamentally wrong presuppositions about discernable sources we have pointed to several additional weaknesses of this construction. To one not blinded by the glamor of pseudo-criticism and its claims the manifest unity of the chapter and its natural sequence of parts will be sufficient proofs of its original unity.

Other untenable claims by more extreme critics are these: v. 22 describes an old marriage custom of the Reubenites; v. 18 the birth of Benjamin in Canaan is supposed to indicate that the tribe was formed after the conquest of Canaan. Attempts to discover astral myths relative to sun and moon reflected in the appearing of the brighter Jacob (sun) after the dimmer Isaac (moon) are extravagant impossibilities.

HOMILETICAL SUGGESTIONS

The first episode (v. 1-8) suggests some such subject as Spiritual Housecleaning, or since Jacob is performing his vow, why not use the approach suggested by the psalm: Perform Thy Vows unto the Most High? A very practical treatment of that theme is suggested by these verses. Since v. 9-15 is in a double sense a repetition of matters found previously in Genesis, why not make that a prominent feature of the treatment of the section and speak of the Repetition of Spiritual Experiences?

CHAPTER XXXVI

9. The History of Esau (Chapter 36)

On the heading ("history" for *toledôth*) see remarks on 2:4. Quite in harmony with his previous procedure the author, having concluded the "History of Isaac" and being about to take in hand the "History of Jacob," disposes first of the less relevant "History of Esau." For, at least briefly, the marvels of divine grace in reference to Esau are worthy to be recounted. In 27:39, 40 a blessing had been pronounced upon Esau, a blessing which was not meaningless. It is worth tracing down how it pleased the Almighty to bless Esau and to make him to become a nation. This skeleton history of Esau serves this purpose and at the same time bears testimony to a breadth of interest on Moses' part that was indeed worthy of emulation. For though Esau had, indeed, begun to display its inveterate animosity quite fully at Moses' time, Moses believed that it behooved Israel to have a generous interest in this brother-race. The information conveyed by the chapter is so obviously correct that it has been remarked that "the chapter evidently embodies authentic information regarding the history and ethnology of Edom" (Skinner).

A word on the meaning of the proper names of the chapter may serve a purpose. As usual the meaning of many of these names is far from certain, as, for example, Whitelaw's comments amply indicate. The meaning of some, which are reasonably sure, shows how in many cases they reflect the natural surroundings of the people. *'Ahah* (v. 2) may mean

"ornament" or "morning." *'Elon* (v. 2) may mean
"a region of deer" or *wildreiche Gegend. Zibe'on*
signifies "hyena." *Basemath* (v. 3) means "perfume."
'Eliphaz seems to mean "pure gold." *Re'u'el* (v. 4)
is "friend of God," though this very likely is to be
taken in an idolatrous sense. *Je'ush* (v. 5) may mean
"helper (is God)." *Nahath* (v. 13) means "rest,"
Zerah = "rising" or "east"; Dishon (v. 21) =
"gazelle"; *Alvan* (v. 23) = "wicked"; *Shepho* =
"bald"; *'Ajah* (v. 24) = "hawk"; *'Eshban* (v. 26) =
"restorer"; *Ithran* = "advantage"; *Cheran* = "tur-
tle"; *'Akan* (v. 27) = "swift"; *'Aran* (v. 28) =
"mountain goat"; *Jobab* (v. 33) = "jubilation";
Bozrah = "fold"; *'Achbor* = "mouse," etc. We have
listed these to give a representative selection and
to show how groundless the assumption is that we
find in these names traces of a totemistic religion,
especially on the part of the old Horites. For as
Procksch rightly remarks, first of all we know nothing about the religion of the Horites; and, secondly,
the giving of names of beasts and birds may be occasioned by many other motives: some names may be
"satire" (*Spitznamen*), some a "boast" (*Prahl-
namen*), some merely "figurative," as found among
all nations; cf. even our "Leo" and "Agnes."

We now offer an outline of the chapter to demonstrate at once that it aims to do much more than
merely to sketch a brief list of descendants. For
from the outline it will immediately become apparent
that we are apprised also of the non-Edomitish
elements that were incorporated into the race and
of the "chiefs" and "kings" that were men of prominence among this people. The outline of the contents of the chapter runs thus: 1) Esau's wives and
children and their settlement in Seir (v. 1-8);
2) Esau's descendants (v. 9-14); 3) the Edomitish
chiefs (v. 15-19); 4) the Horite chiefs (v. 20-30);

5) the Edomitish kings (v. 31-39) ; 6) the Edomitish chiefs — after another classification (v. 40-43).

Strangely, I Chron. 1 :35-54 gives lists parallel to these.

1) Esau's Wives and Children and their Settlement in Seir (v. 1-8)

The following outline shows the relation of names:

a) Adah   b) Oholibamah   c) Basemath
   | ┌───────┼────────┐ |
Eliphaz   Jeush   Jalam   Korah   Reuel

Our chief difficulty arises from a comparison of the names of Esau's wives as they previously appeared. In 26:34 the Canaanite wives bore the names, "Judith, the daughter of Beeri the Hittite," and "Basemath, the daughter of Elon the Hittite," whereas in 28:9 the Ishmaelite wife was described as "Mahalath, the daughter of Ishmael." Apparently, then, Judith must be identified with Oholibamah, Basemath with Adah — for both are followed by the name of the same father "Elon" — and Mahalath must be the Basemath of our list, because in each case follows the father's name, "Ishmael." The reason for identifying Judith with Oholibamah may be made somewhat more convincing by noting that Oholibamah is described (v. 2) as "the daughter of Anah." Now Anah, according to v. 24, discovered "hot springs"; but *be'er* is the Hebrew word for spring. However, in the former list he is described as *Beeri* — "springman." Such changes of names need surprise no one, for Orientals commonly go under several names, especially the women, who frequently receive a new name at marriage. Men should, therefore, not speak here of a "contradiction as to Esau's wives" and call this "a crucial difficulty."

1-5. **And this is the history of Esau — that is Edom. Esau married women who were Canaanites: Adah, the daughter of Elon, the Hittite, and Oholibamah, the daughter of Anah, the granddaughter of Zibeon, the Hivite; and besides, Basemath, Ishmael's daughter, the sister of Nebaioth. And Adah bare Eliphaz to Esau; and Basemath bare Reuel; and Oholibamah bare Jeush and Jalam and Korah. These are the sons of Esau which were born to him in the land of Canaan.**

The parenthetical, "that is Edom," recalls very briefly 25:30. The Hebrew expression for "married" is here again the common idiom, he "took" wives. This sense plainly obtains here; the author is not writing the "took" that is resumed in v. 6, for that would make an exceedingly clumsy construction. Since the Anah of v. 2 no doubt is a man (cf. v. 25), the word *bath* ("daughter") following it cannot refer to him but must be used in the looser sense of "granddaughter" and naturally refers to Oholibamah. This same Anah appears here as a "Hivite" but in 26:34 as a "Hittite." The difficulty resolves itself quite readily when we observe that "Hittite" is simply a more general designation of Canaanites, which use of the term is found in Josh. 1:4; I Kings 10:29; II Kings 7:6. For the Hittites were a very prominent group among the inhabitants of the land and so came to stand for all of them. If in v. 20, however, Anah appears as a Horite, a term meaning "cave dweller," why should not one, originally a Hivite, also be able to dwell in a cave and so merit the additional cognomen "Horite"?

A summary expression like "these are the sons of Esau which were born to him in the land of Canaan" is not a mark of any particular author's style (such as P) but a necessary summary, lest we overlook that these five were distinct from all other descendants also in this that they were born in Canaan.

6-8. And Esau took his wives and his sons and his daughters and all individuals of his household and his flocks and all his cattle and all his possessions which he had acquired in the land of Canaan, and went to a land where he was far away from Jacob, his brother. For their property was too great to allow for them to dwell together, nor was the land where they sojourned able to support them in view of their flocks. So Esau dwelt in Mount Seir — Esau is Edom.

We are brought to the time where Esau sees the necessity of leaving the land of Canaan, which has definitely been assigned to his brother Jacob. It will be difficult to determine whether he took this step before Jacob's return from Mesopotamia or some time thereafter. For there is the possibility that Esau's and Jacob's flocks could not subsist together even when the flocks which were potentially Jacob's were still in reality under Isaac's care. The more likely construction to put upon the case would be that Jacob with his large flocks and herds, freshly returned from Mesopotamia, made the problem a critical one. But Esau on his part was by this time resigned to his lot that he yield the preference to his brother to whom the better blessing had been given, and when a clash like that which threatened between Abraham's and Lot's herdsmen seemed imminent, Esau showed prudence in promptly yielding. The *naphshoth betho*, "souls of his house," here are the "members" or "individuals of his household." The word *'érets*, "land," must be construed as being closely connected with the word immediately following *mippenê*, "from the face of," and so the words signify "a land far away from," or "where he was far away from" — to use a freer rendering. To concede that some word like "Seir" had fallen away after *'êrets* is therefore unnecessary.

7. Apparently Esau, too, under the blessing of Almighty God, had grown enormously wealthy. Besides, these patriarchs were at a very special disadvantage for the present: Canaan was "the land where they sojourned," literally: "the land of their sojournings." Therefore they were only journeying about, utilizing unclaimed pasturage, and yet, no doubt, wealthier than the actual inhabitants of the land. The resulting jealousy of the native inhabitants will have made their position still more difficult. The negative clause of purpose that some languages might use is covered by the infinitive with *min — mishshébheth* — "from dwelling" = "to allow them to dwell" (K. S. 406 h). The expression "from the face of their flocks" means, of course, "in view of their flocks."

8. "So Esau dwelt in Mount Seir" means that he chose this land south of the Dead Sea for his permanent home. "Seir" — or "Mount Seir," since it is such mountainous terrain — is the original designation of the land. Exactly how this occupation proceeded we do not know. Perhaps several modes of procedure blended into one another. As we suggested in the preceding chapter, a process of conquest may have been involved. As the material of this chapter suggests, intermarriage with native Seirites or Horites figured quite largely in the process. Sometimes intermarriage may have preceded, sometimes it may have followed upon certain stages of the conquest, until the aboriginal inhabitants are eliminated and the Edomite stock has become the dominant factor.

2) Esau's Sons (v. 9-14)

9-14. **This is the history of Esau, the father of the Edomites, in Mount Seir. These are the names of the sons of Esau: Eliphaz, the son of**

Adah, the wife of Esau — Reuel, the son of Basemath, the wife Esau. And the sons of Eliphaz were
Teman, Omar, Zepho, and Gatam and Kenaz. And
Timnah was a concubine of Eliphaz, Esau's son,
and she bore to Eliphaz, Amalek. These are the
sons of Adah, the wife of Esau. And these are
the sons of Reuel: Nahath and Zerah, Shammah
and Mizzah. These were the sons of Basemath,
the wife of Esau. And the following were the sons
of Oholibamah, the daughter of Anah, the granddaughter of Zibeon, Esau's wife: she bore to Esau
Jeush and Jalam and Korah.

Verse 1 began as does v. 9, the difference being
that from v. 9 onward we have "the history of
Esau . . . . *in Mount Seir.*" What preceded was
his history in the land of Canaan. Where in v. 1-8
we had only the names of those who in the strictest
sense were "sons of Esau," here the same expression
is used in the looser sense and takes in the grandsons,
at least those of Eliphaz and Reuel and incidentally
also Amalek. The grandsons of Oholibamah are not
listed. Regard 12 a as parenthetical and the summary statement, "these are the sons of Adah," fits
perfectly into the picture. The following diagram
makes the entire section clear at a glance:

	Esau			
of Timnah and Eliphaz	Reuel	Jeush	Jalam	Korah
(Amalek) 1. Teman	1. Nahath			
2. Omar	2. Zerah			
3. Zepho	3. Shammah			
4. Gatam	4. Mizzah			
5. Kenaz				

Trying to force history into certain patterns
according to which its author was supposed to have
written it, Gunkel claims that the author devises
twelve patriarchs for Esau as well as for Jacob —

an attempt on Gunkel's part indirectly to prove how history is manufactured by Biblical writers according to preconceived notions. But he obtains the twelve by the omission of Amalek, whom Moses definitely includes in the list.

If we note Amalek as belonging among the Edomites (v. 12), we can understand how, being the son of a concubine, he may have been discriminated against and how that may have resulted in his separation from his brethren. For according to Exod. 17:8 and Num. 13:29; 14:25 the Amalekites must have held territory much farther to the west. According to Judg. 5:14 and 12:15 they must once have occupied territory much farther to the north. Gen. 14:7 points to the fact that Amalekites had once dwelt much farther eastward, although in this passage the term refers to territory which later was occupied by Amalekites. All of this cannot seem strange if it be borne in mind that all these tribes may have been more or less nomadic in their day.

How Strack can claim that the Kenizzites of 15:19 may have sprung from the Kenaz of v. 11 is difficult to see in view of the fact that these Kenizzites have a land called after their name already in Abraham's day, five generations before Kenaz was born.

In v. 9 we have an instance where the name of an individual doubtless is used as a tribal name, for Esau is called *'abi 'Edom*, "the father of Edom," in the sense of "father of the Edomites." Though such a use of proper names indubitably occurs, this use is not to be as freely assumed as is done in critical works.

3) The Edomitish Chiefs (v. 15-19)

15-19. **These are the chiefs of the descendants of Esau: the sons of Eliphaz, the first-born of Esau: chief Teman, chief Omar, chief Zepho, chief Kenaz,**

chief Korah, chief Gatam, chief Amalek. These
are the chiefs of Eliphaz in the land of Edom.
These are descendants of Adah. And these are
the sons of Reuel, the son of Esau: chief Nahath,
chief Zerah, chief Shammah, chief Mizzah. These
are the chiefs of Reuel in the land of Edom. These
are descendants of Basemath, the wife of Esau.
And these are the sons of Oholibamah, the wife of
Esau: chief Jeush, chief Jalam, chief Korah. These
are descendants of Esau and these are their chiefs —
that is Edom's.

A diagram of the chiefs yields the following
result:

Sons of Eliphaz	Sons of Reuel	Sons of Oholibamah
Chief Teman	Chief Nahath	Chief Jeush
Chief Omar	Chief Zerah	Chief Jalam
Chief Zepho	Chief Shammah	Chief Korah
Chief Kenaz	Chief Mizzah	
Chief Korah		
Chief Gatam		
Chief Amalek		

Comparing this diagram with that covering v.
9-14, we note that all the descendants of Esau on the
former list rose to the rank of "chiefs." We need
not find it strange that Amalek should be listed
among the chiefs who trace their ancestry to Eliphaz,
though he was born of a concubine. But the fifth
name "Korah," identical with the last son of Oholibamah as far as name is concerned, does surprise us.
It is idle to try to settle speculations such as: did
he come into this list by some matrimonial alliance,
or is he merely another person of the same name?
No one knows. Elaborate conjectures leave us just
as much in the dark.

But this is the significant thing about this list:
it shows how at a comparatively early date Esau's

descendants advance to positions of prominence and honor. For *'alluph,* "chief," may well mean "chiliarch," "ruler over a thousand," for *'alluph* is from the root *'éleph,* which means a "thousand." Now, though the idea of "thousand" is not to be pressed, in any case a rather outstanding dignity was involved in the case of those who bore the name; they were men who ruled a "thousand," or "a thousand families." In these lists the mothers are always prominently mentioned, the reason for this most likely being the fact that Edomites attached importance to the line of maternal descent, and yet this fact could hardly point to a matriarchate.

4) The Horite Chiefs (v. 20-30)

20-30. **The following are the sons of Seir, the Horite, the inhabitants of the land: Lotan and Shobal and Zibeon and Anah; and Dishon and Ezer and Dishan. These are the chiefs of the Horites, the sons of Seir, in the land of Edom. And the children of Lotan were Hori and Hemam; and the sister of Lotan was Timna. And these are the children of Shobal: Alvan and Manahath and Ebal, Shepho and Onam. And these are the children of Zibeon: both Ajah and Anah. It was this Anah who found the hot springs in the wilderness, as he fed the asses of Zibeon, his father. And these are the children of Anah: Dishon and Oholibamah, the daughter of Anah. And these are the children of Dishan: Hemdan and Eshban, and Ithran and Cheran. And these are the children of Ezer: Bilhan, and Zaavan, and Akan. These are the children of Dishan: Uz and Aran. The following are the chiefs of the Horites: chief Lotan, chief Shobal, chief Zibeon, chief Anah, chief Dishon,**

chief Ezer, chief Dishan. These are the chiefs of the Horites in the land of Seir, chief by chief.

The object of this section is to show the ones who comprised the descendants of Seir, that other major group which entered into the making of the Edomites; and at the same time to show how these Seirites were of ancient and honorable stock, for they, too, numbered many "chiefs" in their race. Though "Seir" usually designates the *land* of the Edomites, extending south from the lower end of the Dead Sea to the Elanitic Gulf, here, without a doubt, it signifies a person, the ancestor of the Horites ("cave dwellers"), who occupied the land before the children of Esau overcame them (cf. Deut. 2:12, 22). *Chori* from *chor,* "cave," is very properly construed to mean "cave dwellers."

A diagram of the "Horite chiefs" together with their descendants will show at a glance what the list of v. 20-30 offers:

Seir						
Lotan (Sister-Timna)	Shobal	Zibeon	Anah	Dishon	Ezer	Dishan
1. Hor	1. Alvan	1. Aiath	1. Dishon	1. Hemdan	1. Bilhan	1. Uz
2. Heman	2. Manahath	2. Anah	2. Oholibamah	2. Eshban	2. Zaavan	2. Aran
	3. Ebal			3. Ithran	3. Akan	
	4. Shepho			4. Cheran		
	5. Onam					

Chiefs of the Horites

1. Lotan   5. Dishon
2. Shobal   6. Ezer
3. Zibeon   7. Dishan
4. Anah

It appears at a glance that every son of Seir became a chief. There are no others who succeeded in rising to the level of this honor as was the case in the list of the Edomitish chiefs. From this list we also discover that the Anah, who was the father of Oholibamah, was a son of Seir.

Trying to identify these names with certain others mentioned in the Scriptures, which are either similar or identical, is seldom safe. So to seek to connect "Lotan" (v. 20) with Lot, Abraham's nephew, is utterly impossible (though Procksch does it), for one was descended from Seir, the other from Haran (11:31). "Bilhan" (v. 27) can for the same reason not be identified with Bilhah, Rachel's handmaid.

In v. 25 *beney,* "sons," is used where of the two descendants one is a son and another a daughter. The same usage appears in 46:23; Num. 26:8.

In v. 24 Anah is said to have discovered *yemim.* The Jews had lost the meaning of the word and so invented the conjecture that it meant "mules" (A. V. and Luther), an idea that may be traced to Jewish antipathy for the Edmonites, whom they by this fiction describe as men tampering with the original purpose of the Creator. The Vulgate already had the correct meaning of the word, which, as K. W. demonstrates, is not farfetched or doubtful. Hot springs, it is claimed, are still found at the point where the ancient pilgrimage route from Damascus crosses the Wadi Hesa, about ten miles southeast of the Dead Sea, and so in Edomite territory.

The linguist will be interested in an observation by Skinner to the effect that "the endings — *an* and — *on* in this list point to a primitive *nunation,* as contrasted with sporadic cases of *mimation* in the Edomite names" (cf. Gatam, Jalam).

The man "Uz" (v. 28) may have given name to the land of Uz from which Job came (Job 1:1). Who knows?

The different form of the names in a few instances in the list of I Chron. 1: 38-42 may be accounted for on the score that some of these names quite naturally had variant forms.

Nothing is said concerning the Edomitish or the Horite "chiefs" to indicate that they ruled successively. Rather, if one notes that they were all children or grandchildren of the same generation, the conclusion becomes inevitable, as Luther already pointed out, that these "chiefs" held office simultaneously. In other words, Edom was not governed by a long *succession* of "chiefs" before a long succession of "kings" came to power.

5)　The Edomitish Kings (v. 31-39)

31-39. The following are the kings who ruled over the land of Edom before the ruling of a king for the children of Israel. Now there ruled over Edom Bela, the son of Beor, and the name of his city was Dinhabah. And Bela died and Jobab ruled in his stead, the son of Zerah of Bozrah. And Jobab died and there ruled in his stead Husham of the land of the Temanites. And Husham died and there ruled in his stead Hadad, the son of Bedad, the man who smote Midian in the field of Moab, and the name of his city was Avith. And Hadad died, and there ruled in his stead Samlah from Masrekah. And Samlah died, and there ruled in his stead Shaul from Rehoboth-hannahar. And Shaul died, and there ruled in his stead Baal-Hanan, the son of Achbor. And Baal-Hanan, the son of Achbor, died and there ruled in his stead Hadar, and the name of his city was Pau, and his wife's name was Mehetabel, the daughter of Matred, the granddaughter of Mezahab.

Verse 31 is to this day listed by the critics as belonging definitely to the *post-Mosaica*, i. e. statements written later than the time of Moses. Some merely make their assertion to this effect without troubling to offer proof. So sure are they of being right. K. C. offers labored proof, but what he offers is ineffectual. For what an unbiased exegete must admit is that the statement is a very natural one for a man like Moses to make if he knew definitely that also the descendants of Israel were destined to have kings in the course of time. To one who remembers besides that Jacob (Israel) and Esau were brothers such a comparison very naturally suggests itself. Now Moses had previously indicated that kings would come of Israel's line (35:11; cf. 17:4 ff.). In fact, a common meaning for the verb *malakh* is not only "be king" or "rule," but to "become king." Note how naturally our interpretation fits into the picture when we render: "the following are the kings who ruled over the land of Edom before a king (cf. G. K. 129 c) of the children of Israel became king." All claims, therefore, that this list of Edomitish kings must have been made in Saul's or David's time or even Solomon's are poorly substantiated. In fact, our contention gains added support from the fact that the death of the last king is not mentioned. This could easily be accounted for by the fact that Moses, who was well informed on the subject he treated, mentions the last king as contemporary with the time of his writing. For himself Moses does not know how many additional kings Esau will have or how long it will be before Israel has kings. But it certainly is very proper in a chapter where the rapid development of the Edomites is sketched to show how in the matter of instituting the royal office they outran Israel by many years.

If now kings began to rule about the third generation after Esau, that is about a generation after the "chiefs" began to rule or about 1850 B. C., and Moses wrote about 1450, that would seem to allow 400 years for the eight kings of this list. But that offers no grave difficulty. The kingdom may have been established a century later than we suggest. This idea gains support from the fact that "chiefs" and "kings" ruled simultaneously in Edom, as a comparison of Exod. 15:15 with Num. 20:14 ff shows. Besides, in those days, at least in the earlier of these four centuries men lived longer. Besides, interregna may have occurred between the kings of this list. For it should also be noted that the line of succession in Edom was not hereditary. Not one of these eight kings succeeded his father. Note what things the following list reveals:

Kings of Edom

1. Bela — son of Beor — his city Dinhabah.
2. Jobab — son of Zera — of Bozra.
3. Husham — of the land of the Temanites.
4. Hadad — son of Bedad — his city Avith.
5. Samlah — from Masrekah.
6. Shaul — from Rehoboth-hannahar.
7. Baal-Hanan — son of Achbor.
8. Hadar — — — — — — — — his city Pau.

Three of these kings had each "his city," which must mean, his royal city where he established himself as king. Either the other five had no city, or else after one had become king, he continued to use the royal city of his predecessor until his successor in turn shifted to another capital city. The list most clearly shows that not one of the kings was descended from another.

"Hadar" (v. 39) is called "Hadad" in I Chron. 1:50. That, however, by no means identifies him with the Hadad who was Solomon's adversary, I Kings 11:14. In fact, this last named Hadad was not a king but only a man "of the king's seed."

In v. 37 the town "Rehoboth" is followed by the word *hannahar*, i. e. "of the river." This expression (noun plus the article) almost invariably refers to the Euphrates, unless the connection points to another stream. K. C. therefore places Rehoboth on the

Euphrates. Foreign conquerors have sometimes established themselves in a land even if they came from afar. Yet it cannot be denied that in a connection such as this *nahar* might refer to almost any stream.

Attempts have been made to identify *béla'*, the son of *be'or* (v. 32), with *bil'am*, the son of *be'or* (Num. 22:5). Though the names are strikingly similar, the identity is far from likely. Nor is the *Jobab* (v. 33) to be regarded as the same person as Job, whose Hebrew name is *'iyyobh*. Even Michaelis already declared this latter view an *insignis error*.

6) The Edomitish Chiefs — a geographical classification (v. 40-43)

We already had one list of Edomitish chiefs in v. 15-19. Only a few of the names of that list recur in v. 40-43. The cue to the difference between these two lists therefore seems to be found in v. 40 in the statement: "These are the names of the chiefs of Esau by clans according to their places of residence (*limqomotham*)." Dillmann, therefore, seems to be entirely correct in calling the first list of chiefs "historic-genealogic" and our list "geographic-statistic." Then *Elah* (v. 41) may be identical with *Elath* (Deut. 2:8) on the Elanitic Gulf. Then, of course, all the proper names are place names not personal names, as the following translation shows:

40-43. The following are the names of the chiefs of Esau by clans according to their place of residence, name by name: the chief of Timna, the chief of Alvah, the chief of Jetheth, the chief of Oholibamah, the chief of Elah, the chief of Pinon, the chief of Kenaz, the chief of Teman, the chief of Mibzar, the chief of Magdiel, the chief of Iram. These are the chiefs of Edom according to their

habitations in the land of their possession. This is Esau, the father of the Edomites.

It can hardly be doubted that the last word *'edhom* must be translated "Edomites" and not "Edom."

A brief explanation as to the so-called sources of this chapter as the critics see them. The following outline will show quite clearly what a problem the critics have on their hands and how little harmonious "the assured results" of criticism are. Skinner's position is covered by the statement that the chapter contains "partly P," for he recognizes the problematic nature of many of the conclusions. Strack says: P: 6-8, 40-43; JE: v. 31-39. Procksch: P. 9, 6, 7, 40, 41; J: 8, 10-14; 20-28; 31-39. Koenig: P: 7, 9, 31; J: 8, 10-30.

Source analysis here too is "groping blindly."

CHAPTER XXXVII

10. History of Jacob (chapters 37-50)

This portion of the book of Genesis is, without doubt, the most interesting and dramatic of the entire book. The author's skill as a narrator is throughout displayed to excellent advantage. A part of the interest of the narrative lies in the greater wealth of detail. If the author employed available sources, as it seems most likely that he did, his source material, apparently, was more copious the farther he advanced in these early histories. But on the other hand, it seems equally true that the nearer he gets to the events of his own day, the more would his readers desire full information. Moses is now writing history that involves the fathers of the twelve tribes. There is much in this history that the tribes themselves should be acquainted with for their comfort and their admonition.

But when we say that the dramatic element begins to predominate more in the narrative, we do not imply that the author injected it. Truth still is stranger than fiction. It was not the author's skill that rendered these tales dramatic. These things actually transpired as they were narrated. The drama involved is practically nothing other than the unusual display of divine providence, which shines forth more brilliantly here than perhaps anywhere else in sacred history. Step for step God's providence watched over the chosen race as it was about to go into the depths of national enslavement. One element of encouragement for these trying days was to be the remembrance of the signal tokens of divine grace experienced shortly before.

One very noticeable feature of this "history (*tole-dôth*) of Jacob" is the predominance of Joseph practically throughout the entire section. Yet for all that, though he is the mainspring of the movement of the history, Jacob is still the dominant character. We remind of this, for though Joseph is prominent, he is not to be estimated too highly. God never appeared to him as he did to his father Jacob, or to Isaac and to Abraham. Joseph dare not be ranked higher on the level of faith than his forefathers. It is a case of misplaced emphasis to say that "the hero himself is idealized as no other patriarchal personality is . . . (Joseph) is the ideal son, the ideal brother, the ideal servant, the ideal administrator." In contact with non-Israelites Joseph surely achieved remarkable prominence, but for the inner, spiritual history of the kingdom of God he does not come up to the level of his fathers.

There is another feature of his life which is rather striking and demands closer attention. In a more distinct way than in the lives of his fathers Joseph stands out as a type of Christ. Abraham exemplifies the Father's love who gave up His only-begotten Son. Isaac passively typifies the Son who suffers Himself to be offered up. But in Joseph's case a wealth of suggestive parallels come to the surface upon closer study. Though these parallels are not stamped as typical by the New Testament, there can hardly be any doubt as to their validity. For as Joseph is a righteous man and in this capacity is strongly antagonized and made to suffer for righteousness' sake but finally triumphs over all iniquity, so the truly Righteous One, the Savior of men, experiences the same things in an intensified degree.

Lange lists the details of this type in a very excellent summary. He mentions as prefiguring what transpired in the life of the great Antitype, Jesus Christ, the following: "the envy and hatred of the brethren against Joseph and the fact that he is sold; the realization of Joseph's prophetic dreams by the very fact that his brethren seek to prevent his exaltation by destroying him; the fact that the malicious plot of the brethren results in the salvation of many, however, in a very particular sense for the brethren and for Jacob's house; the judgment of the Spirit upon the treachery of the brethren and the victory of forgiving love; Judah's surety for Benjamin and his rivalry with Joseph in the spirit of self-sacrifice; the revival of Jacob in his joy over the fact that the son long deemed dead was alive and eminently successful."

This angle of the case is beautifully supplemented by Pascal (*Pensées,* quoted by Delitzsch): "Jesus Christ is prefigured by Joseph: the beloved of his father, sent by the father to his brethren, the innocent one sold by his brethren for twenty pieces of silver and so made their lord, their savior and the savior of strangers and the savior of the world; all of which would not have happened if they had not had the purpose to destroy him, if they had not sold and rejected him. In prison Joseph the innocent one between two malefactors — Jesus on the cross between two evildoers: Joseph predicts good fortune to the one and death to the other, though both appear alike — Jesus saves the one and leaves the other in his just condemnation, though both stood charged with the same crime. Joseph begs of the one who is to be delivered to remember him when he is restored to honor, and he whom Jesus saves asks to be remembered when He comes in His kingdom." The ways of divine providence could hardly be stranger, and God's guiding hand in history is marvelously displayed to the eyes of faith.

1. And Jacob dwelt in the land of the sojournings of his father, in the land of Canaan.

This verse is plainly a transition verse and at the same time it constitutes a contrast to the preceding chapter. In every preceding instance the words *'elleh toledoth,* which open v. 2, have stood at the head of each of the preceding nine major divisions of Genesis. Consequently, v. 1 cannot be brought in as an introductory verse to this *toledôth* or "history." It does, however, remind us that as Esau (chapter 36) settled in the land of Seir, so Jacob after the separation of the brethren continued in the ancestral territory, a sojourner, where his father had sojourned. Nothing was more natural than that he, who continued the line of promise according to God's choice, should also settle in the land of promise. By this word, furthermore, it is indicated that Jacob had actually left the land east of the Jordan, where he had first stayed after his return from Mesopotamia, and had come to the land west of Jordan, which alone ranks as the land of Isaac's sojourning — and for that matter to the southern part of this land, where Isaac had been found, namely the vicinity of Hebron, Beersheba and the region toward the west, bordering on the Philistine land. Isaac, though his death was reported proleptically 35:29, continued to live for perhaps another twelve years and so shared in Jacob's grief over Joseph. But at this point Jacob supersedes Isaac and begins to carry on the history of the chosen race.

1) Joseph sold into Egypt (37:2-36)

2. This is the history of Jacob. Joseph at the age of seventeen years was doing a shepherd's work among the flocks together with his brethren, and

in fact he was a servant together with the sons of
Bilhah and the sons of Zilpah, the wives of his
father; and he brought the report about them,
which was evil, to their father.

Strictly speaking, the caption, "History of
Jacob," that is set down as a heading for the chapter,
should appear after v. 1 with the subhead that we have
set above v. 2. In any case, it is the author's own
title and so at the same time an indication of the
beginning of the last subdivision (compare remarks
on 2:4). Consequently, to label this section, "The
Story of Joseph," (Meek) indicates complete disregard
of the authors's mode of treatment of this section
and labels his point of view as trivial or unimportant.
One reason why critics so consistently ignore Moses'
own divisions of the book seems to be, because to let
the author's plan or outline emerge clearly would
display what they deny — the manifest unity of the
entire book.

True, from our point of view, it may seem strange
to begin Jacob's history with details about Joseph's
experiences. But does not the father's life express
itself in his sons? First we are told Joseph's age
at the time under consideration: he was seventeen
years old. Next we are informed as to his occupation:
"he was doing a shepherd's work" — *ro'eh,* literally:
"he was shepherding." He was not with the cattle
but "among the flocks," *tso'n — Kleinvieh.* In this
work he stood on the same level as his brothers who
shared the work with him. The next "and" (*we*),
as is frequently the case, offers more specific details,
as we should say, "and in fact" (*und zwar*). He had
not yet advanced to the point of being a master shepherd; he was merely "a servant" (*na'ar* commonly
bears this meaning — see B D B, p. 655, 2 a). The
following phrase "with the sons," etc., would seem to
indicate that these brothers of his perhaps were also

still learning how to be competent shepherds. "The sons of Bilhah and the sons of Zilpah" are his companions because in point of age they stand nearest to Joseph, hardly because of Joseph's humility in associating with those who were less proud than the sons of the regular wife, Leah. For sons of concubines ranked but slightly inferior in social standing. Joseph was associated with just these brethren more by virtue of his father's choice than by his own. Bilhah's sons were Dan and Naphtali (30:5-7); Zilpah's, Gad and Asher (30:9-13).

"The report about them" (*dibbatham* — with object suffix as a kind of objective genitive — "their report" — from a root analogous to the Arabic signifying "to flow along slowly," "to glide along") Joseph brought to his father. Not his own observations so much as what others said. No doubt Joseph recognized on the strength of what he saw that this report was the truth. In any case, the report was "evil." Joseph's motive in conveying this report seems to have been good. He was the one son who had spiritual kinship with his father. He had nobler ideals than did his brothers. He felt that it behooved Jacob to know these reports. But Joseph hardly did wisely in telling what his brothers were said to do. It seems quite likely that a trace of spiritual pride tainted what may otherwise have been prompted by a good motive. For a youth to know himself better than his brothers and not to feel a measure of self-exaltation is hardly thinkable.

3, 4. **Now Israel had come to love Joseph most of all his sons, because he was the son of his old age and he made him a long-sleeved cloak. But his brethren observed that their father loved him more than all his brethren and they hated him and were not able to speak peacefully with him.**

The perfect *'ahabh* must express something that has come to a conclusion; consequently, "he had come to love" as a result of contact over many years — rather than just simply he loved. "Israel" stands first for emphasis to indicate how he stood related to the brothers between whom a tension was growing. The primary reason assigned for Jacob's preference of Joseph is "he was the son of his old age" (*zequnîm*, plural of condition, to mark the various aspects involved in such a situation). It is commonly to be observed that children of old age enjoy preference and are pets. Here other factors contributed to make this preference more pronounced. The whole narrative indicates that not one of the sons came as near to the father's spiritual stature as Joseph did. The outward distinction which the father bestows upon this son is "a long-sleeved cloak," *kethóneth passim*. The *kethóneth* is the undergarment or tunic, which usually was sleeveless — a thing of about knee-length. But *passim* means "ankles" or "wrists." Consequently, this tunic was sleeved and extended to the ankles. It was not, therefore, a garment adapted to work but suitable to distinguish a superior, or an overseer. By this very garment the father expressed his thought that this son should have pre-eminence over the rest. For Reuben had sacrificed his claim by incest. Simeon and Levi were poor candidates for leaders because of their headstrong cruelty. Besides, the converted *we'asah* means rather "he used to make" — when one such cloak was worn out the father furnished another. Such distinction by the father was hardly wise. Luther's translation *bunter Rock* (like the A. V.'s "a coat of many colors") was a shrewd guess on the translator's part who confessed: "I confess freely that I do not know what the term means." But he surmised that the father wished to designate the son as a ruler and used *bunter Rock* because the garments of the ruling classes were more brilliant in color in his day.

4. This ill-advised distinction bestowed upon this young brother moved the others to actual hatred. They would hardly ask the question, Does he deserve this preference? but would be stirred by the petty jealousies characteristic of those of one family. Besides, Joseph's dreams created additional antipathy. This verse describes the situation after it had developed to the point where they were no longer "able to speak peaceably with him." In *dabberô* the direct pronominal object had taken the place of a dative object, like our "bespeak him" in place of "speak to him" (K. S. 22). In *leshalom le* is dative of norm (K. S. 332 q): "according to peace." This translation is to be preferred to the one which renders "greet him," because the latter calls for the verb *sha'al* rather than for *dabhar*.

5-8. **And Joseph dreamed a dream and told it to his brethren with the result that they hated him still more. For he said to them: Do hear this dream that I dreamed. Look, we were binding sheaves in the midst of the field, and, look, my sheaf rose up, and even remained standing, and, look, your sheaves gathered around it and made obeisance to my sheaf. And his brothers said to him: Dost thou really expect to be king over us? or dost thou at least expect to rule over us? And they hated him still more for his dreams and for his words.**

The narrative shows how the hatred already engendered was fanned to a brighter flame by successive events. Joseph's dream need not be regarded as divinely inspired. Nothing shows that it originated in any other way than do other dreams. It may have in part grown out of the ambitious thoughts of

the young shepherd. It certainly was divinely controlled so as to express what afterward actually
transpired. It need not be thought of as involving
a reference to Joseph's work as grain regulator. For
binding sheaves is work that stands far removed
from grain conservation. Besides, it is not a prophetic
dream such as prophets have. The Lord was not
informing Joseph concerning things that would come
to pass, yet God so controlled the dream that later
it was seen to be in conformity with fact.

The expression, "they hated him still more," involves the familiar Hebrew idiom: "they added still
to hate him" — the chief verb in Hebrew being actually
rendered as an adverb in English. An instance of
hasty inference and unwarranted critical alteration
of the text appears in the striking out of 5 b after
the example of the Septuagint. It is claimed by
Procksch to be premature because "he has not as
yet said a thing." But does not 5 a ("he told it")
cover in a summary form what Joseph said; and
cannot the result of such telling be reported before
the dream is told?

6. "And he said" (*wayyo'mer*) must mean "for
he said" or "namely he said," for the details of the
dream mentioned in v. 5 are to be given. The opening statement shows the eager interest or the enthusiasm the dream had roused in the lad's heart, who
well saw what the dream implied. In his enthusiasm
Joseph begins: "Do hear (*shim'ûna'* — literally:
'hear, pray') this dream that I dreamed."

7. Three times *hinneh*, "behold," occurs in the
sentence. We have rendered it "look." The word
betokens not so much surprise as eager interest.
Joseph none too wisely grows quite enthusiastic over
the prospect of rising above his brethren. The dream
involves a situation common enough in the family life
of those days. In harvest time all able-bodied men

were in the field. Though partly nomadic in its habits, Jacob's family was also partly agricultural, as was Isaac's (cf. 26:12). But, for that matter, such groups are found in Palestine to this day, partly nomadic and partly agricultural in their pursuits. Criticism here, as usually, misconstrues the statements in favor of two different viewpoints originating from two distinct sources.

Now what happened in the dream was simply this: the sheaves that had been tied lay about in the field as usual. Perhaps all brothers had started binding simultaneously. Each had just tied a sheaf when Joseph's rose up and also "remained standing" (*nitsabh* — Nifal from *yatsabh*). Then the sheaves of the others gathered around this one and "made obeisance" — a verb used of any token of respect to a superior.

8. The meaning of the dream was so very transparent that the brothers catch its import at once. The construction which reinforces the verb with the absolute infinitive (*malokh timlokh* and *mashol timshol*) in this case is expressive of their indignation. Literally they say: "Being king wilt thou be king?" and "ruling wilt thou rule?" We feel that the translation: "Dost thou really expect to be king over us? or dost thou at least expect to rule over us?" just about reproduces these sentiments of theirs. The "at least" that we have inserted in the second member of the question grows out of the fact that from "being king" to "ruling" the idea is stepped down very noticeably.

In v. 7 the *hinneh* with the perfect *qamah* merely makes the statement vivid (K. S. 131). *Hinneh* with the imperfect *tesubbénah* makes a historical present, marking the act as not brought to a conclusion (K. S. 158).

Though Joseph has had only one dream according to this report up to this time, yet (v. 8, conclusion) they hated him "for his dreams" (plural). This construction apparently involves a kind of generalization: because he was dealing in such things as dreams (K. S. 264 c).

9-11. **And he again dreamed a dream and told it to his brethren, and he said: Look, I have again dreamed a dream; and, look, the sun and the moon and eleven stars were making obeisance to me. And he told it to his father as well as to his brethren. And his father sharply rebuked him and said to him: What dream is this that thou hast had? Shall we indeed come — I and thy mother and thy brethren — to make obeisance to the earth before thee? And his brothers were envious of him, but his father bore the thing in mind.**

The Hebrew uses an expression which we would deem redundant when it says: "he again dreamed another dream." To us this would seem to indicate a third dream. The Hebrew regards it as a strong expression that the dream was actually another one. Caution and discretion should have taught Joseph to keep silence about this dream in the presence of his brethren, for he must have noticed how the former dream had displeased them. This indiscretion gives us cause to think that a secret pride possessed Joseph. The double *hinneh* ("look") used in the telling of it shows how the thought suggested by the dream personally pleased Joseph. The dream as such is typically a dream: impossible things are happening. How else but in a dream could luminaries make obeisance? The participle *mishtachawîm* is durative — "they were making obeisance," that is, they were doing it repeatedly.

10. Since this verse translated literally begins: "and he told it is his father and his brethren," the

second "and" before brethren must be a *waw adaequa-tionis* (K. S. 375 i) meaning "as well as," because we have already been told v. 9 that he told it to his brethren. This way of stating the case implies that the previous dream had not been told his father. We then get the impression that the impression created by the second dream emboldened Joseph to venture to tell what in the first instance he had dreaded might incur the father's displeasure. The father could well sense that a secret pride and self-satisfaction prompted the telling and administered a deserved rebuke. *Ga'ar* means *anschreien*, "to scream at," and so, at least, he "sharply rebuked him." The father sees what the dream signifies. The numbers coincide so perfectly with Jacob's family. Therefore He interprets the luminaries to mean, "I and thy mother and thy brethren." The question quite naturally arises: how can the mother, though dead, make obeisance? The simplest answer is that though she was dead she lived in the memory of this son and the father. Besides, who would expect historical accuracy from a dream? Stranger incidents than this have figured in dreams. It is, therefore, unnecessary to say that "mother" must here refer to Leah, who had mothered Joseph since Rachel's death; or to one of the handmaids; or by synecdoche to Jacob and his family in whom Rachel lived.

11. To the hatred of v. 8 jealousy or envy is now added. For this dream went beyond the former one. Previously Joseph's supremacy over his brethren was indicated. Now it is the supremacy over the entire family that is suggested. But Jacob, like Mary (Luke 2:19), bore the thing in mind. Strange things seemed to be foreshadowed by these remarkable dreams. In a measure they coincided with Jacob's own purposes, which he had intimated by the special cloak he had been providing for his favorite son. On

the whole the folly of parental partiality is only too effectively portrayed.

The notion, advanced so positively by Jeremias and accepted as quite likely by such as Skinner, that the eleven stars are a mythical designation of the signs of the zodiac is really too untenable to be regarded seriously. The signs of the zodiac are twelve. Eleven is not twelve. Very fanciful, too, are the explanations why one of the twelve is suppressed. Then, too, the signs of the zodiac are groups of stars, constellations. Our chapter speaks of single stars. The astral myth theory of patriarchal history is a subjective claim.

12-14. **And his brethren went to shepherd the flock of their father in Shechem. And Israel said to Joseph: Do not thy brethren shepherd the flock in Shechem? Come, let me send thee to them. And he said to him: Here am I. And he said to him: Go now, look to the welfare of thy brethren and to the welfare of the flock, and report back to me. So he sent him forth from the valley of Hebron, and he went to Shechem.**

It does seem a bit strange that Joseph's brethren should venture back to Shechem again after the events of chapter 34. Perhaps the fear of God (35:5) was still upon the place. Equally plausible is the explanation that these were bold men who sometimes courted danger. Or did these men wish to use the portion of ground their father owned there? (John 4:5). The points set in the Hebrew text over *'eth*, the sign of the accusative, show that the Masoretes had misgivings about retaining the word. Yet we cannot see why.

13. Israel himself is not entirely at ease about the venture. The question asked of Joseph is a characteristic Hebrew way of making a positive assertion: he *knows* they are "shepherding" (*ro'im*, plural

participle from *ro'eh*) the flock there. He desires to
send Joseph because he knows he can depend on him
for reliable information. Yet Jacob seems strangely
ignorant of the attitude of the other brothers to
Joseph. Joseph himself seems hardly to have
suspected that their enmity was strong. He presents
himself as ready to carry out his father's wishes:
"Here am I."

14. Joseph gets his orders. "Go now, look" is
called "a conventional asyndeton" (K. S. 357 i). We
have rendered *shalom*, usually rendered "peace," as
welfare, because the broad use of the term here applies
also to the flock. The rest of Joseph's orders are to
"report back" to the father — the Hebrew idiom:
"bring me word again." So Joseph leaves the pleasant
valley in Hebron and unsuspectingly goes to Shechem.

15-17. **And a man found him, and, lo, he was
straying about in the field; and the man asked him,
saying: What art thou seeking? And he answered:
It is my brethren that I am seeking. Tell me, pray,
where they are shepherding. And the man said:
They moved from here, for I heard them saying:
Let us go to Dothan. And Joseph went after his
brethren, and found them in Dothan.**

The distance from Hebron to Shechem is more
than fifty miles as the crow flies. The trip must
have taken Joseph more than a day. The "lo" here
indicates what is in the nature of a surprise both to
Joseph as well as to the reader. Here was an outcome with which Joseph had not reckoned. It is quite
understandable that a stranger, seeing Joseph "straying about" (*tho'eh* — durative participle), should
have seen at a glance that the man was looking for
someone. Consequently he asks: "What art thou
seeking?" *Mah*, "what," rather than *mi*, "whom,"
introduces the question, the stranger assuming that

perhaps cattle had been lost. *Hinneh tho'eh* without a *hu'* is unusual; see G. K. 116 s.

16. The word order in Joseph's answer puts the object emphatically first, an arrangement possible in English by the use of some construction like: "It is my brethren that I am seeking," again the durative participle, *mebhaqqesh.* Apparently the conversation that took place is being recorded in a much condensed form. The stranger has some knowledge of Joseph's identity, and in those days Jacob's sons may have been known far and wide. Consequently Joseph's question is in place: "Where are they shepherding?" *Ra'ah* implies watching over a flock and frequently stands without an object.

17. This stranger had overheard the brothers, while they were still in Shechem, saying that they were making Dothan their next objective. We shall never be able to say how many other persons Joseph may have asked before he met this stranger. Now Dothan lay perhaps twenty-four miles farther north. So Joseph sets out and actually finds them in Dothan. Two forms of the name of this town appear here, one with a dual-like ending *dotháyin,* the other *dothan* is contracted from this.

18-20. **And they saw him at a distance, and before he came near to them they knavishly planned against him to put him to death. They said, namely, one to another: Look, here comes this dreamer. And now, come, let us slay him and cast him into one of the cisterns, and we shall say: A wild beast hath devoured him. Then we shall see what will come of his dreams.**

This may be as good a place as any to take issue with the perplexing question how sons of Jacob and direct descendants of Abraham could ever have become so debased as a group as to stoop to the iniquities about to be retailed. We see two factors loom up

prominently by way of explanation. The one, these
fruits are largely the outgrowth of a bigamous
home; a home lacking inner harmony and true discipline, as must needs be the case where there are
more wives than one, produces misbegotten children.
The other factor is this: depending on a godly ancestry,
these men neglected to watch and pray, each man for
himself, and so they fell prey to the clever devices of
the wicked one.

Joseph is spied at a distance. His gait, his figure,
his special cloak — all these identify him. The distance separating the brothers from paternal influence
seems to remove all restraint that they might otherwise have felt. Their whole scheme is described in
advance in the summary statement, "they knavishly
planned against him." Their devices were certainly
in the class of the most dastardly of crimes. The
details are given in v. 19 where the initial *wayyo'merû*, literally, "and they said," must mean "namely
they said," for their knavish plans are to be revealed
in their genesis. One speaks to the other (Hebrew:
"a man to his brother," K. S. 348 w). The group
hums with schemes. First comes the mocking greeting of recognition: "Look, here comes this dreamer."
Ba'al ha(ch)chalomoth is literally: "master of
dreams," not in the sense of "you master-dreamer"
(Skinner). For *ba'al* is just about the most general
"noun of relation" known. Anyone who is characterized by specializing in some one thing may be
said to be a *ba'al* of that thing. So here it means:
this fellow who has been having so many dreams —
certainly a coarse mocking description.

20. Their plan takes shape with singular rapid-
ity: to slay — to cast the body into a pit — to cover
up the deed with a ready lie. The sequence of persons is not entirely congruent at this point: "come"
(*lekhu, second* person imperative) "and let us slay

him" (*wenaharghehu, first* person plural hortative) ;
cf. K. S. 344 g. But every language has just about
the same combination without feeling any irregularity
to be involved. The *bor* into which they purpose
to cast Joseph's body is just one of the many artificial
cisterns for the collecting of rain water, found here
and there in the fields. Apparently, at this season
they were dry, as often happened toward the close of
the dry season.

When men like Gunkel see a certain motif come to
the forefront here — the motif of trying to invalidate
an oracle that has been spoken but failing, as often
happens in Grimm's *Fairy Tales* — we refuse to take
such trifling seriously. He that cannot see that this
story moves on a much higher plane would be impervi-
ous to refutation.

V. 18, *betérem* is regularly construed with the
imperfect (G. K. 107 c). On the suffix of *'akhalathu*
see G. K. 59 g.

**21-24. And Reuben heard it and delivered
him from their hands. He said namely: Let us
not take his life. Furthermore Reuben said to them:
Let us not shed blood. Cast him into this pit which
is in the wilderness, but a hand — do not raise it
against him — in order to deliver him from their
hand and send him back to his father. And so it
happened when Joseph came to his brethren, they
stripped Joseph of his coat (the long-sleeved coat
that he wore), and they took him and cast him into
the pit. But the pit was empty. There was no water
in it.**

Reuben has had no hand in formulating the plans
for evil, which had developed so rapidly among the
brethren. He had not opposed at once, possibly because he felt his loss of prestige due to his sin of
incest. Now he bethinks himself of his moral responsibility as the first-born. Murder would very likely

have been committed by the brothers in the revenge-
ful frame of mind that was upon them. Consequently,
in the summary report, which in true Hebrew style
covers the entire episode in a brief statement, the
statement: he "delivered him from their hands" is
entirely correct. The translation attempted by quite
a few — like Meek's: "he *tried* to save him" — cannot be extracted from the verb. But the following
verb "and he said," *wayyo'mer*, is one of the many
cases where "and" means "namely" — "he said
namely." So, apparently, with a measure of diffidence
as to how his interference may be treated he first
ventures a brief objection: "Let us not take his
life." The Hebrew idiom is quite unusual: "Let us
not smite him as to the soul or life," *néphesh*, an
accusative of specification. *Nakkennû* is Hifil imperfect from *nakkah*, with suffix attached by a *nun
epenthetic.*

22) After this first brief venture Reuben speaks
again. This explains why the double "and he said"
is not clumsy composition; but the second is meant
as: "furthermore he said." (K. S. 368 c.) Reuben
makes his plea more strongly. First he states what
their slaying would amount to — it would be a
"shedding of blood" — a thing that should be repulsive
to any man. Then he proposed an alternative, making
his suggestion more definite by pointing to a cistern
near at hand. The fact that this pit is "in the wilderness" (*bammidhbar*) suggests that the deed will not
readily be discovered and so can be perpetrated with
impunity. The reason for our unusual translation
of the next clause — "but a hand — do not raise it
against him" — is to recapture the particular emphasis
of the original order of words, which, of course, suggests very strongly that not even a hand should be
raised against the brother (K. S. 339 m). Reuben's
words are immediately followed by a purpose clause,

showing what good object he had in mind by his
suggestion, namely to deliver Joseph and to send him
home. This purpose clause is directly introduced by
lema'an — "in order that" (K. S. 407 e), to make it
stand out more prominently as what it is, for *lema'an*
is the most emphatic introduction to purpose clauses.
The good objective of Reuben is in part cancelled
by the fact that he sought to meet evil with cunning
craft. This craft failed of its purpose. More resolute
opposition to the evil plans of the brothers should have
been interposed.

23. This part of the drama was being enacted
while Joseph was still approaching his brothers. Now
we see how Joseph fares at his brothers' hands. If
the account intends to be complete as to details, the
brothers proceed step for step with a grim, spiteful
silence. They strip Joseph of his coat — *pashat* with
a double object, G. K. 117 cc — the coat that had become to them an object of special aversion. Then
they seize him and cast him into the pit with a sort
of grim ferocity — and perhaps without explanation.
Fortunately the pit was "empty." Now since this is
a relative term and may involve that no water stood
in the cistern but perhaps deep mire, the additional
asyndetic clause — "there was no water in it" — seems
to point to a cistern completely dry at the bottom.
The asyndetic clause here represents a subordinate
relative clause — "in which there was no water"
(K. S. 361 e).

25. **Then they sat down to eat, and lifted up
their eyes, and there they saw a caravan of Ishmaelites coming from Gilead; and their camels bore
tragacanth gum, balsam and myrrh, and they were
going to bring it down to Egypt.**

Bread was a part of every meal. Consequently
the expression "to eat bread" came to mean "to eat
a meal," or, as we have translated, "to eat." Apparent-

ly, the disposition that they had just made of their
brother did not deeply affect these men: their appe-
tites were unimpaired. When we note Joseph's treatment of Simeon (42:24), we may well conclude that
he had been a ringleader in the whole affair; and
what a hardened fellow he was we saw already 34:25.
A road passes a short distance to the north of Dothan,
another more prominent highway goes a bit farther
to the east coming from across the Jordan, passing
Beisan or Bethshean and continuing down through the
center of the land to Hebron and from there deflecting
southwestward to Egypt. To see a "caravan"
(*'orechath* — feminine participle from *'arach* — feminine to denote the collective, K. S. 255 d) coming
along this road must have been a rather common
occurrence. Gilead, a country noted for gums and
balsams ("Is there no balm in Gilead?" — Jer. 8:22)
was the country from which they had come. Their
wares were primarily "tragacanth gum" (*nekko'th*),
a substance exuding from a bush two or three feet
high; "balsam" (*tsori*), another gum secured by making incisions in the bark of the mastic tree; and
"myrrh" (*lot*), also called "laudanum," "an aromatic
gum exuded by the the leaves of the cistus-rose." All
these articles will have been particularly sought by
the Egyptians for embalming as well as for medicinal
purposes.

And now the "Ishmaelites" mentioned in this
verse. The close connection of v. 25-28 makes it
imperative to consider them as identical with those
of v. 27 and v. 28. But these, in turn, must be identified with the Midianites of v. 28 — mentioned again
v. 36. It would not make sense to say in one breath:
"Let us sell him to the Ishmaelites," and then in the
same breath without explanation show how he was
sold to Midianites, who, by the way, again appear
as Ishmaelites before the end of the verse. Inci-

dentally, in v. 36 a modification of the name Midianites
occurs; they are called "Medanites." Nor is the difficulty grave. First of all, Ishmaelites and Midianites
have one ancestor, Abraham (16:15; 25:2). In Judg.
8:24 Midianites are called Ishmaelites. Both groups
may have been in this caravan. The Ishmaelites may
have been the dominant faction, the Midianites the
more numerous. In such a case both designations
would be suitable. Instead of striving to reconcile
a surface discrepancy critics press the different names
in the interest of proving that the material of the
chapter came from two different sources. Procksch
is the most extreme, inserting after v. 24, "then the
brethren went out to the pasture." With the brethren
off the scene, he lets the Midianites come along v. 28,
draw out Joseph and sell him to the Ishmaelites.
Skinner says, that is what v. 28 really means but
"the composite narrative requires us to assume that
the brethren are the subject of 'they drew and lifted
up Joseph' against the natural construction of the
sentence." Koenig goes to extremes and interprets:
"And they (the *Midianites*) drew and lifted Joseph
out of the cistern, and they (the *brothers*) sold Joseph
to the Ishmaelites." In support of this contention he
points to 40:15 where Joseph emphatically protests
that he "was stolen away out of the land of the
Hebrews." But would you expect Joseph actually
to reveal what his brethren had done to him? That
passage would hardly cover the case of the Midianites
who are supposed to have drawn him from a well.
For to draw an abandoned wretch from a pit and to
sell him is hardly theft.

26-28. **And Judah said to his brethren:
What advantage is there if we slay our brother
and cover up his blood? Come, let us sell him to
the Ishmaelites; but let not our hand be upon him,
for our brother is of our own flesh. And his brethren**

listened to him. Then they passed by — Midianite men, traders — so they drew Joseph up and brought him forth out of the cistern, and they sold Joseph to the Ishmaelites for twenty pieces of silver. But they brought Joseph to Egypt.

Now another brother espouses Joseph's cause, the brother who ultimately displays the finest traits — Judah. His appeal does not express his purpose to the full but merely addresses itself to utilitarian considerations. His main object is manifestly to prevent murder. To tell the truth, nothing is gained by slaying the brother and covering up his blood — therefore *mahb - bétsa'* — "what profit" — *mah* the interrogative pronoun being used as an adjective (K. S. 68, 69). He mentions covering up the blood, because since Cain's time shed blood is regarded as crying out to heaven. Covering it up would seem to prevent disclosure. Yet there is a heartlessness about Judah's proposition which is but little short of the attitude of the others. For selling into slavery is certainly exposure to a hard lot. But then, perhaps, Judah clearly discerned that nothing short of such harsh treatment would satisfy the brothers' vengefulness. In the end, to Judah belongs the credit for having averted murder. He further reinforces his plea by the consideration that in case they slew Joseph their hand would be upon their own brother — a cruelty like Cain's — for their brother is after all of their "own flesh." We say our "own flesh and blood." All the while Judah is thinking in reference to the approaching caravan, to which the general designation for all such bands is applied — "Ishmaelites." Judah's plea is successful: "his brethren listened to him."

28. Instead of confusion we have here the finest of order. Since the previous words of Judah were spoken with one eye on the Ishmaelites, the next

verb *wayya'abheru* — "and they passed by" — can
refer only to these men. Closer inspection reveals
their more exact identity, which the writer inserts
parenthetically, "Midianite men, traders." Since these
were the ones to whom they had agreed to sell Joseph,
naturally *Joseph's brothers* now "drew Joseph up and
brought him forth out of the cistern." They also are
the ones who "sold Joseph to the Ishmaelites." This
all makes sense so readily and so consistently that
it certainly does not redound to the credit of the
astuteness of the critics that they have made such a
mess of the passage, charging it with the clumsiest
of contradictions. The "twenty pieces of silver" would
hardly be coins. In fact, the word omitted in
the original — "for twenty of silver" — is *shéqel*,
which root means "to weigh." Consequently this represents the *weight* of silver paid; for coined money
was not yet in circulation at this early date. Moses
later fixed this amount as the value of a boy between
five and twenty years (Lev. 27:5). So this price
fits well for Joseph who was seventeen. The average
price of a slave of full physical maturity was thirty
shekels (Exod. 31:32). For the present a brief statement covers the ultimate destination to which Joseph
was brought: it was Egypt. If the road we described
before was followed, Joseph may have passed quite
near to his father's house at Hebron. But of all this
we know nothing.

29, 30. **And Reuben returned to the cistern
and, lo, Joseph was not in the cistern; and he
rent his garments. And he returned to his brethren
and said: The lad has disappeared; and as for me,
whither shall I go?**

The statement that Reuben "returned" (*way-
yáshobh*) is sufficient indication that Reuben was
absent at the time of the sale. Perhaps he had inten-
tionaly gone away to allay suspicion as to his further

purposes. It is just as likely that the other brothers purposely disposed of Joseph during the absence of the first-born, lest he again interfere. We can well imagine Reuben's consternation as he comes to the pit by himself with none of the others near and finds it empty. His grief expresses itself in the conventional fashion by the rending of the garment, seizing the inner garment, the tunic, at the neck and rending downwards a few inches. Thoroughly alarmed, he returns to the brethren with the cry, "the lad has disappeared," literally *'eynennu,* i. e., "is not." Their lack of surprise will soon have made him aware of the fact that they themselves had disposed of him. His further cry, "as for me, whither shall I go?" shows his complete bewilderment. Shall he attempt a rescue? Shall he hasten home? Shall he call a rescue party? To translate: "And I, how can I go home" (Meek) is too specific a limitation.

31-34. And they took Joseph's cloak, and killed a goat and dipped the cloak in the blood. And they sent the long-sleeved cloak and had it brought to their father, and said: This we found; examine it whether it be thy son's cloak or not? And he examined it and said: It is my son's cloak. Some wild beast hath devoured him; Joseph has certainly been torn in pieces. And Jacob rent his robe and put sackcloth upon his loins and demeaned himself as a mourner for his son many days.

The brothers are resourceful. They seem to be planning at the same time to take revenge on their father for having preferred Joseph. Their resourcefulness lets the cloak be profusely stained with goat's blood. Their revenge thus prepares a cruel shock for the father. Had the father controlled his grief he might have found it suspicious that the cloak was not torn but only stained with blood. We translate *wayyabhi'u* "they had it brought" — the third per-

son plural may express an indefinite subject, rendered
by a passive; for they certainly "sent" the cloak and
did not bring it themselves. The message accompany-
ing the cloak has a certain blunt brutality about it.
They did not try to soften the blow.

33. Everything works out according to schedule:
the father examines the cloak, arrives at the desired
conclusion. In fact, he expresses his conviction more
drastically than his sons, because of his greater grief:
"Joseph has certainly been torn to pieces." *Taroph*
— pual — is reinforced by a kal infinitive *taraph*
(K. S. 215 d; G. K. 113 w). The sackcloth Jacob
puts upon his loins was a very coarse garment — if
it deserved to be called a garment, being in the nature
of old gunny sacks — usually worn over the inner
tunic. Jacob's greater grief displays itself more
fully: *Yith'abbel*, a hithpael, should be rendered as a
reflexive: "demeaned himself as a mourner."

35, 36. **And all his sons and all his daughters
rose up to comfort him, and he refused to let himself be comforted, and said: No, for I shall go down
in grief to my son to Sheol. So his father bewailed him. But the Midianites sold him in Egypt
to Potiphar, a eunuch of Pharaoh's, captain of the
bodyguard.**

The cruel device of the brothers succeeded too
well. Jacob's grief proved excessive; he was simply
inconsolable. Alarmed and prompted by a feeling
of guilt, the sons without exception sought to administer comfort. How hard it must have been for
them and how hypocritical it must have sounded to
them! His daughters joined them in these efforts —
"daughters" including daughters-in-law and daughters
born later than Dinah. But the grief was too deep;
they had not realized how deep the love was. Jacob
anticipates to die of his grief and so to go to where
his son has gone, to the afterworld, i. e. "to Sheol,"

where all go after death. It is visualized as being
below, as higher things are visualized as being above.
Yet this does not warrant attributing to the Hebrews
the conception that Sheol actually "lay beneath the
surface of the earth," even though the verb *yaradh*
("go down") is used in reference to it. Still less
tenable is the view that the conception of Sheol is
derived from Babylonian sources. Israel and Babylonians both drew upon a fund of original tradition,
which Israel retained uncontaminated.

36. For preliminary information we are apprised
of the name and the official position of Joseph's
master. "Potiphar" is traced (K. W.) to the Egyptian word signifying "he whom Ra (the sun god)
gave," a typically Egyptian proper name. Though
married, he is a *saris*, i. e. a eunuch. Besides, he is
"captain of the bodyguard," *sar hattabachim*. i. e.
"captain of the slaughterers."

On the chapter as a whole criticism claims that
it offers some of the plainest proof of duality of
sources, mostly J and E, with a slight admixture of
P. The following supposed doublets are stressed:
two dreams, or two occasions for the hatred of the
brothers: the cloak and the dreams; the efforts at
liberation by Reuben vs. those of Judah; Ishmaelites
vs. Midianites, etc. Procksch, as usual, has two
separate stories to which he gives two different titles,
viz. a) the Sale of Joseph; b) the Treachery. In some
instances radical changes of the text are made in
order to secure the needed evidence. We believe our
interpretation has shown the futility of these misconstructions. Life is manysided. When the writer
shows this manysidedness, he simply proves himself
to be a shrewd observer. The fictitious writers of
criticism, E, J, and P, are never able to see or to
record more than one side of an event — an unheard-
of narrowness!

To conceive of the narrative as a Hebrew version of the Tammuz legend is simply a farfetched vagary.

HOMILETICAL SUGGESTIONS

There are, no doubt, many points of view from which the preacher may approach this chapter. Lest it be overlooked, we should like to suggest first that method of treatment that lays emphasis on the providential factors—Divine Providence in the Early Years of Joseph's Life. One must at the outset limit himself to the matter found in the chapter, because so many indications of providence occur throughout the rest of Joseph's life. In this chapter the following providential features stand out: the father's godly influence; the warning example of the wicked life of the brothers; the strong encouragement of the double dream; the sparing of Joseph's life when his brothers had determined his death; the selling into Egypt, the land of destiny for Joseph and for Israel. An entirely different approach to this chapter, or more specifically to the part v. 1-28, would be the evaluation of Joseph as a Type of Christ. We have indicated above the major items involved. Again only those features could be treated which the text offers. Though v. 1-28 be utilized, v. 36 ought to be added, because it gives occasion to introduce the thought: "Out of Egypt have I called my Son."

CHAPTER XXXVIII

2. The Danger that threatened Jacob's Sons
(Chapter 38)

He that has made up his mind that since Joseph's story was treated in the last chapter, chapter 38 must needs continue the story, will find this chapter out of place. The heading 37:2 showed that *"Jacob's History"* is being considered. Our portion under consideration shows a very definite angle of Jacob's History. Jacob's family was a minority group. For the present, no matter how strongly Jacob's sons may have believed in the divine destiny of their family, they were running grave danger of being submerged by the Canaanite element, making matrimonial alliances with them, adopting Canaanite ideals of life, and so being ultimately absorbed by this dominant element. For it is to be observed repeatedly that, though the Canaanites were already far inferior to Israel morally, they were very amiable and ready to establish closer contacts with the descendants of Abraham. Realizing this, we can the more readily see why a sojourn in a land like Egypt was a necessity from the Lord's point of view. For the Egyptians of old were noted for their aversion to strangers, especially to shepherds (46:34).

We are struck at the same time by the rhetorical skill of the author who makes this chapter serve the purpose of letting us feel the lapse of time after the sale of Joseph.

The events recorded in the chapter show a decline to a low moral plane. Things positively offensive to good taste are here recorded. But every attentive reader will have to admit that the manner of relating these events is calculated to produce a deeper abhorrence of sin. It is just as true to state that a remarkable impartiality pervades the entire account. Israel's past was not glorified at the expense of truth. Add to this what Luther emphasized, that these records that show the grievous faults of God's weak saints and the forgiveness they received are of great comfort to all poor sinners of our time.

1-5. **And it came to pass at that time that Judah went down away from his brethren and pitched his tent near a man of Adullam, whose name was Hirah. And there Judah saw the daughter of a Canaanite man whose name was Shua, and he married her and went in unto her. And she conceived and bare a son and he called his name Er. Again she conceived and bore a son and she called his name Onan. Even once more she bore a son and she called his name Shelah. It happened at Chezib that she bore him.**

Is there a strict sequence of time between chapters 37 and 38? It seems so. "At that time" would mean: just after Joseph had been sold into Egypt. We need not assume that only the climax of the event recorded in this chapter took place after the sale of Joseph (Strack, and many from Augustine down; also Luther). For about twenty-two years intervene between the sale of Joseph and the settlement in Egypt (13 years till Joseph's promotion + 7 years of plenty + 2 years of famine). Judah has time to marry, to have a son whom in his seventeenth year he gives in marriage; to have a second son whom in *his* eighteenth year he gives to the same wife; and two years remain for the rest of the events of this chapter. Then the items involved fit closely together: Judah departs from his brethren in vexation over their treatment of their brother Joseph and over their hypocrisy in the

sight of their father. At least some such reason for
his going "away from his brethren" (*me'eth 'echaw*)
is possible. His next step was *wayyet 'adh 'ish* — *yet*
shortened imperfect from *natah*, "to stretch" or
"bend." This verb is to be considered as used absolutely, omitting the common object "tent," and so
meaning "he pitched" (his tent), or else in the sense
of "bend," i. e. "turned aside to a man of Adullam."
K. W. suggests both possibilities; commentaries waver;
the result is about the same in either case. Judah does
approach more closely to a Canaanite man, who appears to have been friendly and welcomed the approach.
"Adullam" lay in the western part of the later territory
of the tribe of Judah, very likely in the foothills, the
Shephelah. In place of a relative clause a co-ordinated
clause is preferred: "his name Hirah" for "whose
name Hirah" (K. S. 361 a).

2. A further contact with Canaanites follows.
A man by the name of Shua (a name meaning perhaps
"opulence") has a daughter, whom Judah takes to
wife. Whether resentment against his brethren had
anything to do with this, or whether easygoing friendship with Canaanites lay at the bottom of it all, is
hard to say. Three sons are born of this union. To
the first the father gives the name; to the second and
the third, the mother. As Whitelaw points out, the
giving of the name by the father is supposed to be an
idiosyncrasy of the Elohist; yet this chapter is un-
hesitatingly assigned to J. "Er," from *'ûr*, may mean
"watcher" or in a theophoric sense: "God is watcher."
Onan may mean "strength." Then by contrast *Shelah*
may mean "weak," "drooping," if the lad was less
robust than his brothers. Or the name may also mean
"rest." At least the birthplace of the latter is definitely
recorded as "Chezib," a town near Adullam. This is
mentioned for the definite information of the descend-

ants of Shelah of the tribe of Judah (Num. 26:20),
that they might know their birthplace or ancestral city.
Since "Chezib," or Achzib, could mean "town of lies"
or "Lieham" (K. C., *Lugheim*), the insertion of its
name as suggestive of Judah's deception in the matter
of giving Shelah to Tamar is possible, yet hardly seems
likely. The allusion would be too subtle. Skinner,
intent upon discrediting a good text, labels the *wehayah* of the last clause as "impossible." The clause
being a digression has no *waw* conversive, simply *waw*
conjunctive (K. S. 370 l).

6-10. **And Judah procured a wife for Er, his
first-born, and her name was Tamar. And Er,
Judah's first-born, was wicked in the estimation
of Yahweh, so Yahweh let him die. Then Judah
said to Onan, go in unto thy brother's wife and
marry her as brother-in-law, and raise up offspring
to thy brother. But Onan knew that the offspring
would not be his own, so it happened that each time
he went in unto his brother's wife he took preventive
measures so as not to give offspring to his brother.
And that which he did was evil in the estimation of
Yahweh, and He let him die also.**

Whereas Judah had gone out to select as a wife
whom he pleased, apparently he acted without consulting his father. Yet Judah selected his son's wife.
Our reckoning above displayed that the son must have
been comparatively young at the time. Did the father
perhaps by an early marriage seek to steer his son
clear of Canaanite vices in matters sexual? It would
almost seem so. Er's wife's name was "Tamar," a
word meaning "palm tree." They that think the Scriptures to be on the same level with folklore generally
here attempt to establish a parallel between this story
and the Tammuz myth or with the Babylonian Ishtar
myth — the "goddess who slays her lovers" — but the

evidence advanced by way of support of their contention is quite inconclusive.

7. But "Er was wicked in the estimation of the Lord." Specific mention is made of this wickedness. It is the direct cause for the death of Er. The modifying phrase is appended: "in the estimation (Hebrew: 'in the eyes') of the Lord." From this last phrase alone we should conclude that the wickedness involved called forth the heaviest divine disapproval. We conclude that it may well have been some sexual perversity, for it is mentioned in connection with Er's marriage. This man was therefore guilty, in a special sense, and "so Yahweh let him die." We find in this fact a direct indication of the truth, "the soul that sinneth, it shall die," — an echo that rings through the entire Old Testament (cf. Gen. 2:17; Ps. 90:7 ff.; Prov. 10:27).

8. The custom of levirate marriage seems to have prevailed quite universally at the time, as it is known to have been customary among many nations ancient and modern. Judah does not appear as an innovator in this instance. Levirate marriage implied that if a man had died without leaving a son, the next brother of the deceased, if unmarried, would take the widow to wife with the understanding that the first son born would carry on the line of the deceased, but all other children would be accounted his own. The Mosaic code refers to the custom Deut. 25:5 ff. and made what had previously been a custom among such as the Israelites a divine ordinance. See a further reference in Matt. 22:24. The root *yabam* means "brother-in-law." The *Piel* of the derivative verb could then be translated "marry her as brother-in-law," the ultimate purpose of course being "to raise up offspring" (Hebrew: "seed") to the brother.

9. Onan knew of this provision and intentionally prevented its realization. Selfishness may have

prompted him; he did not care to preserve his brother's family. Greed may have been a concurrent motive; he desired to prevent the division of the patrimony into smaller units. But in addition to these two faults there was palpably involved the sin of a complete perversion of the purpose of marriage, that divine institution. What he did is described as "taking preventive measures." The original says: "he destroyed (i. e. the semen) to the ground." From him the extreme sexual perversion called onanism has its name. The case is revolting enough. But plain speech in this case serves as a healthy warning. Yahweh let him die even as his brother. On *wayyéra'* see G. K. 67 p; on *wayyámeth*, G. K. 72 f.

11. **And Judah said to Tamar, his daughter-in-law: Stay a widow in thy father's house until Shelah, my son, grow up. For he said: Lest he die too like his brethren. So Tamar went and stayed in her father's house.**

A peculiar situation obtains here: it rests with Judah, the father-in-law, how Tamar is to be disposed of in marriage; Tamar's temporary home, however, until such disposition is made is her father's house. Social customs prevalent at the time were the norm governing such cases. But Judah is using deceit in counselling Tamar to wait (*Shebhi* — imperative from *yashabh*, "to sit or dwell" — here "stay"), nor does he directly promise to give her to his son. His unexpressed thought, "lest he die too like his brethren," shows his attitude. He believed Tamar was a woman who brought bad luck. Yet, as we have just been informed, the reason for the death of the first two sons lay in their own sinfulness. Somehow the father failed to see this and instead became obsessed with a kind of superstitious notion, worthy rather of a heathen Canaanite than of a member of the chosen family. *Beth* is accusative of place where (G. K. 118 g).

12-14. And quite a number of days passed, and the daughter of Shua, Judah's wife, died. Then when Judah had recovered from his grief, he went up to his sheepshearers, he and Hirah his friend, the Adullamite, to Timnah. And it was reported to Tamar: Look, thy father-in-law hath gone up to Timnah to shear sheep. So she laid aside the garments of a widow, and covered herself with a veil, and completely disguised herself and sat down at the entrance to Enayim, which is on the way to Timnah; for she saw that Shelah had grown up, and she was not being given to him as wife.

The Hebrew says, "and the days grew many." We should say, "quite a number of days passed." That does not mean "years," at least not many years. But for a woman destined to be married to the next son it may have seemed like quite a while. Judah's wife dies in the meantime. When he has "recovered from his grief" (*wayyinnachem* really means "was comforted") it happens to be the time for sheepshearing, a season of general festivity and hilarity. Since they are his own sheep that are to be sheared, he goes to the scene of their shearing to Timnah. This cannot be the Timnah down in the plain, mentioned Josh. 15:10; 19:43, but must be another that lay in the mountains, mentioned Josh. 15:57, as "went up" shows (Keil). Hirah, Judah's Canaanite friend (v. 1), goes with him.

The report of what Judah is doing comes to Tamar's ears. The course that she adopts as a result perplexes us a bit. She makes calculations that seem to have but one chance in a hundred of being realized, but just that one chance is sufficient. It seems she is determined to secure offspring if she can, and if her father-in-law has thwarted her, she purposes to thwart him. Mere lust cannot be laid to her charge. On the other hand, her course is far from innocent. It almost

seems as if she had calculated on two things, namely
that the sheepshearing festivities would lead to con-
viviality and more generous drinking of wine (cf.
I Sam. 25:36), and, then, one is almost inclined to
believe that she had heard of other escapades of Judah.
Or, at least, she calculated that the widower would at
such a time be peculiarly susceptible. In any case,
she puts on the disguise that makes her appear as a
harlot — "a veil," (Hebrew: "the veil," the article of
the customary thing for such a case, K. S. 299 b), "and
completely disguised herself" (Hebrew: "wrapped herself up"). Then she sat down by the wayside, as such
did who plied this iniquitous trade. She chose "the
entrance" (*péthach*, not *sha'ar*, "gate") of Enayim,
called also Enam (Josh. 15:34), "which is on the
way to Timnah." Here her grievance is recorded:
Shelah had grown to be as old as his brothers had
been when she was given to them in marriage, and
Judah was doing nothing to keep his implied promise.
Without a doubt, had any stranger or any other man
than Judah approached her, she would have refused
them.

**15-19. And Judah saw her and took her for
a harlot, for she had her face covered. And he
turned to her by the wayside and said: Look here,
I want to go in to thee, for he did not know that
she was his daughter-in-law. And she said: What
wilt thou give me for coming in to me? And he
said: I on my part will send thee a kid from the
flock. And she said: If thou wilt give a pledge
until thou send it. And he said: What is the
pledge that I should give to thee? And she said:
Thy seal, thy cord, and thy staff which is in thy
hand. So he gave these to her and went in unto
her; and she conceived of him. And she arose and
went away and put aside her veil, and clothed herself with her widow's garments.**

What Tamar had designed actually came to pass. Judah does not appear to very good advantage in this account. He seems to know altogether too well how to carry on a transaction of this sort. Since the veil merely seems to be the customary device to give herself the appearance of coyness, such as persons of this sort may use, it effectually serves the purposes of disguising Tamar. When, besides, it is indicated that Judah did not know that she was his daughter-in-law, we see that Judah surely would not have consciously made himself guilty of incest. *'El dérekh* rather means "by the wayside" (K. C.) than "to the way." Some compensation should fall to the harlot's lot. She bargains as others might in such a case. The customary fee seems to have been a kid (Judg. 15:1). They that suggest that in classical antiquity the goat was sacred to the goddess of love may have the correct explanation. For Canaanite standards prevail throughout this vile episode. Tamar's answer, "if thou wilt give a pledge until thou send it," is an unfinished statement, an aposiopesis, the omitted conclusion being, "I shall be satisfied." *'Erabhon,* traced to a Phoenician source meaning "pledge," went over into the Greek as ἀρραβών.

18. Shrewdly Tamar asks for what she can use as evidence of a conclusive sort, should circumstances make it necessary: seal, cord, and staff. The "seal" (*chotham*) may have been a ring or even a cylinder seal, such as the Babylonians commonly used. This was always carried around upon his person by the well-to-do man, suspended by the "cord" (*pethil*) ; cf. Song 8:6. The "staff" may have been like those which, according to Herodotus, the Babylonians carried, having at its head a specially carved figure of "an apple, or a rose, or a lily, or an eagle, or any such thing, for no man may carry a staff without a device,"

(Herodotus 1:195, cited by Delitzsch). *Wattáhar* anticipates the result far in advance of the sequence of the narrative (K. S. 369 c). Having achieved her purpose, Tamar lays aside her disguise and arrays herself in the garments of widowhood, which custom demanded.

20-23. And Judah sent the kid by the hand of his friend, the Adullamite, in order to recover the pledge from the woman's hand; and he could not find her. So he asked the men of her place, saying: Where is the sacred prostitute, the one that sat in Enayim by the wayside? And they said: There was no sacred prostitute here. So he returned to Judah and said to him: I could not find her. Furthermore, the men of the place said there was no sacred prostitute there. Then Judah said: Let her keep them for herself, lest we bring disgrace on ourselves. In any case, I sent this kid, and thou wast not able to find her.

This is the conclusion of the very regrettable tale. Judah sends his pledge. A certain shame may have led him to choose a less sensitive Canaanite to pay his whorish debts. The Adullamite seems to regard such service as a true token of friendship. It follows that very shortly after Judah's falling into her snare, she was no longer to be seen at that place, nor did she appear as a whore. Compelled to ask for her whereabouts, even the Adullamite tries to give the case a better color by asking for the *qedheshah,* "the sacred prostitute." A *qedheshah* considered her debasing of herself a votive offering brought to the goddess of love, whether this was merely an occasional act or whether she was a professional (cf. Hos. 4:14 and Deut. 23:18). So depraved were also the Canaanite morals. But even such a one the men of the place had not seen. Tamar had apparently waited at Enayim so short a time as

to be noticed by no one. Hirah reports his failure to
Judah. Judah sees the advisability of letting the matter ride and making no further inquiry, for, surely,
by extensive inquiries Judah would have advertised
his deed. So Judah, content to have done what lay
in his power to redeem his pledge, says, "let her keep
them for herself."

**24-26. It came to pass after about three
months that is was reported to Judah: Tamar, thy
daughter-in-law, has played the harlot; and, mark,
she is also pregnant as a result of her harlotry. And
Judah said: Bring her forth that she may be
burned. When she was brought forth, she sent to
her father-in-law and said: By the man to whom
these things belong have I become pregnant. She
further said: Look closely now, to whom do these
things belong — this seal, these cords, this staff?
And Judah looked closely and said: She is more
in the right than I, for I did not give her to Shelah,
my son. And he never again had intercourse with
her.**

Judah is the head of the family and responsible
for all that transpires in it. So even his former
daughter-in-law, or, as she may also be called, his
potential daughter-in-law comes under his jurisdiction.
When her condition becomes apparent, it is reported
to him as a grave moral offense. We consider
kemishlosh as compounded of the inseparable prefix
ke + *min* + *shelosh* — no *dagesh forte* in the *sh*,
because the consonant is supported only by a *Schwa*.

Judah's verdict may only have been the traditional
one for delinquents who were virtually betrothed. It
hardly seems right to assume that Judah designed an
especially rigorous punishment for her. At this point
already Judah's conscience may have stirred: this
would hardly have befallen Tamar had he given her
to Shelah for wife. But, then, very likely he will have

regarded this outcome as a convenient release from
the necessity of ever giving her to his youngest son.
The Mosaic law fixed the penalty of burning only for
the case of a priest's daughter who had become guilty
of harlotry (cf. Deut. 22:20-24 with Lev. 21:9). The
usual mode of execution for other cases was stoning.
Here then Judah orders, "bring her forth," i. e. out
of the house where she naturally would be found. The
word "bring forth" has a forensic flavor. The next
clause, *wethissareph*, "and she shall be burned," is
final: "that she may be burned." The *le* before
zenunim is a *le* of relation (K. S. 105) — "she is
pregnant relative to her harlotries," in which plural
lies an exaggeration.

25. Tamar is completely prepared for this outcome. She has reason to believe that for all his delin-
quencies Judah will give her fair play. So she takes
Judah's three articles of pledge and sends them to
him with the statement that she will not conceal the
paternity of the expected child: the owner of these
articles is the father. She invites Judah by messenger
to look closely whose they be. For "cord," *pethil*,
Tamar uses the plural *pethilim*, perhaps because of the
several strands twisted together to make the stronger
cord. Meek translates "seal," *chothémeth*, as "signet
ring." Should the *chothémeth* actually have been a
seal cylinder, this rendering would not fit. This verse
begins with a participle and continues with *waw* conversive with the finite verb (K. S. 412 n).

26. Judah is taken under circumstances that
make evasion impossible. Most likely he would not
have attempted evasion anyhow. The mysterious
qedheshah of three months ago suddenly stands revealed
very clearly. Judah is not ignorant of Tamar's guilt
in the case, but his own is double: refusal of Shelah
and illicit whoredom. He makes a manly confession.
To word this confession: "she hath been more right-

eous than I" (A. V.) sounds too much as though two
relatively righteous persons are being compared.
Therefore we prefer a rendering like Meek's, "she is
more in the right than I." Judah seems to see that
the guilt involved is not hers, especially since he himself did her the wrong of refusing the son promised
as a husband. After such incestuous connection it was
right neither for Judah nor for his son to have her.
A notice covering this case closes this part of the
episode. We cannot support the statement that claims:
(the author) "presents Judah's behavior in as favorable
a light as possible, suggesting extenuating circumstances for what could not be altogether excused; and
regards that of Tamar as a glory to her tribe." Many
of us from the days of our earliest youth in reading
this account have had the impression which later years
has but deepened that Judah and Tamar are both
represented as guilty of a grievous, yea, even a shock-
ing, moral lapse. The extenuating circumstances ap-
plying to the cases of both are also truthfully recorded
by the sacred writer.

K. S. has an unusual translation for *tsadheqah
min*: *sie hat ein Uebergewicht von Momenten der
Normalitaet*. However, since *tsedhaqah*, the root involved, means "normalcy," this seemingly cumber-
some translation is really quite accurate (K. S. 308 b).
The expression *ki-'al-ken* is not to be rendered "for
on that account," as many still claim. For, as K. W.
has demonstrated, a kind of popular pleonasm is involved — *'al ken* is really only an amplied *ki* or "for."

27-30. **And it came to pass at the time of birth,
lo, there were twins in her womb. And it happened in birth that one put out a hand and the
midwife took it and tied a scarlet thread on his
hand, saying: This one came out first. Then it
happened that he drew back his hand, and lo, his
brother came out. And she said: How you have**

forged your way through! And they called his name Perez (forging through). And afterwards his brother came out, upon whose hand was the scarlet thread. And they called his name Zerach.

This conclusion of the chapter records what would be of interest to the descendants of Judah, the birth of Tamar's twin sons. In v. 28 *wayyitten yadh* is an instance of an indefinite subject: *"one* put out a hand" (G. K. 144 a). Apparently, the midwife's only reason for using a scarlet thread to mark this one was because it happened to be conveniently at hand and certainly could serve as an identification tag. It naturally would be anticipated that he would be born first. Such, however, was not the case. Of course, to have a hand emerge is an indication that delivery is not about to be perfectly normal. When his brother preceded him who first put out the hand, he was greeted by the midwife with the remark: "How you have forged your way through" — an expression of wonder, for which the Hebrew idiom says: "How hast thou breached a breach (*parátsta pérets*) for thyself" — a cognate object, not as A. V. has: "How hast thou broken forth? this breach be upon thee," a rendering which like Luther's (*solchen Riss getan*) involves the idea of causing a serious rent or rupture. The rendering used above is copied from Meek. Again the two verbs (v. 29 and 30) *wayyiqra'* ("and he called") involve the indefinite subject and may be rendered "and they called." "Perez" means "forging through" rather than "breach." What "Zerah" means we do not know; it hardly means "scarlet."

Criticism regards the chapter as a whole "a pure specimen of Yahwistic narration." Phrases that have been discovered as common to the sections ascribed to J and also exclusively used by him are cited as proof for this claim: "evil in the sight of" (v. 7, 10), "come now" (v. 16), "for therefore" (v. 26), "Yahweh"

(v. 7, 10). This exclusive use is purely accidental, however, even as it is unreasonable to suppose that such common stock terms should be stylistic peculiarities. "Yahweh" is used in v. 7 and 10 because God is thought of as the covenant God of Abraham, who watches over the moral integrity of His chosen people.

HOMILETICAL SUGGESTIONS

Entirely unsuited to homiletical use, much as the devout Bible student may glean from the chapter.

CHAPTER XXXIX

3. Joseph's Imprisonment because of his Steadfastness (39:1-23)

Several purposes are served by this chapter, which manifestly directs the current of the narrative into the channel of the experience of Joseph.

First of all, we cannot help but notice that in a twofold way the things narrated serve to prepare Joseph for the portion he is to fill later in life. In Potiphar's household he becomes familiar with Egyptian life in general and with the elements of successful business administration. In the humiliation of the prison, however, Joseph is seasoned so that he is later able to endure being placed in an exalted position without danger of falling into conceit.

Besides, Joseph's character is purged from dross by the trying experiences of these years. He personally stood in need of a measure of purging, for he, too, had an admixture of pride in his disposition. After being himself purged Joseph is an instrument qualified to work in the direction of purging the character of his brothers. Joseph unrefined would hardly have been suited for his task.

At the same time the chapter stands in strong contrast with the preceding one. Judah has been contaminated by the laxity of morals characteristic of the Canaanites. Joseph, who has grown up under the same circumstances, has preserved the ideal of the godly patriarchs. The one falls, the other stands. At the same time the victory of true virtue is so represented as to be a lesson and an encouragement for all that are of a godly mind.

Besides, the impressions of the thirty-seventh chapter are confirmed relative to the innocent sufferings of righteous men. They that walk uprightly are not to expect the reward of their righteousness as a necessary and an immediate result. Their lot may at least for a time be entirely out of harmony with their deserts. This valuable lesson, amply confirmed by the experiences of many, is taught very plainly by the early experiences of Joseph.

1-4. And as for Joseph he was brought down to Egypt, and Potiphar, a eunuch of Pharaoh's, captain of the bodyguard, an Egyptian man, bought him from the Ishmaelites who had brought him down there. And Yahweh was with Joseph, so that he became a successful man, and he stayed in the house of his master, the Egyptian. And his master noticed that Yahweh was with him and that Yahweh made everything that he did prosper under his hands. So Joseph found favor in his sight and became his personal attendant. Besides he appointed him over his house and gave all his possessions into his hands.

The current of the narrative turns back to Joseph. This fact is indicated by the prominent position of the noun *yoseph* before the verb, a construction somewhat like our, "as for Joseph, he," etc. The repetition of the words, "Potiphar, a eunuch of Pharaoh's, captain of the bodyguard" from 37:36 ties the thread of the narrative back to the previous mention of Joseph and leads us to reflect more on this important personage who figures prominently in the following narrative. It seems very strange that a eunuch should be married, as we learn of Potiphar in this chapter. Two possibilities confront us, and the choice between them is difficult. It actually happened in days of old that eunuchs had wives. On the other hand, the term "eunuch" (*saris*) very likely lost its

original meaning and came to signify: prominent
court officials. The name "Pharaoh" has been traced
down by Egyptiologists to mean "great house" and
is used by metonomy for him who has his seat in the
great house or royal palace (K. W.).

It is just another of the guesses of criticism when
these repeated words are said to be a redactional insertion into the J document. In like manner, criticism
claims that the apposition, "an Egyptian man," originally standing in J, makes J refer to this character
as a nameless person. The case is much simpler than
that. Men who were not Egyptians must also have
been employed in state offices in those days. In this
instance the fact that Potiphar was of Egyptian
blood is brought to our attention. If all this happened in the era of the Hyksos domination, the phrase
in question is all the more readily understandable.
The closing words, that it was Potiphar who "bought
him from the Ishmaelites who had brought him down
there," complete the tie-up with the last mention of
Joseph. Having heard this, we are ready to resume
the narrative.

2. It pleased Yahweh to lend His kind help
to Joseph from the very outset. Joseph's sufferings
were not unknown to Him, and His first token of
favor consisted in letting Joseph experience His help.
This act is rightly ascribed to "Yahweh," because it
was the covenant God who for the sake of the promises
made to the fathers and for the sake of the future
destiny of this chosen race helped Joseph. Yahweh's
favor appeared in this that Joseph "became a successful man." Whatever he took in hand thrived. Besides, to understand what developed later we are told
that "he stayed" (literally: "was") in the house of
his master, the Egyptian, not in the servants' quarters.
Potiphar desired to have this helpful man near at

hand and showed his appreciation for services rendered by housing him well.

3. In fact, that Joseph's success was traceable to more than human ingenuity was apparent even to the Egytian, who in truly heathen fashion ascribed it to Him whom Joseph openly acknowledged to be his God and the source of his blessings — Yahweh. Joseph, for one, certainly recognized the universal power of Yahweh and never for a moment thought of Him only as a tribal god. The Egytian, by his admissions, must himself have recognized something of this. *Matsliach* here has a meaning different from that found in the preceding verse: there it meant "prosperous," here, "making to prosper." The participle *'oseh*, which we rendered "all that he did," should actually be rendered "was doing," and so it creates the impression that the projects of the past as well as those which were even then passing through Joseph's hands, all gave evidence of being successful.

4. As the account progresses, we are made to feel the successive and, no doubt, gradual stages by which Joseph moved forward in the process of time: God with him; God prospering him; Joseph living in the Egyptian's house; the Egyptian taking note of Yahweh's blessing; his taking note of the fact that every project of Joseph's thrived; the resultant increase of favor that Joseph enjoys, and so forth. This "favor" (*chen*) would seem to imply a personal attachment which the Egyptian formed for him as a result of which he "became his personal attendant." For *yeshareth* (G. K. 64 g) means "to wait on." Hitherto the service had been more impersonal; now Joseph must personally attend to his master's wants. We can understand all this. The indolence of Orientals readily allows them to turn responsibility and duties over to competent hands. So finally

"he appointed him (*hiphqidh*) over his house and gave all his possessions (literally: 'all that was to him') into his hands." In the expression "all that was to him" the relative "that" is implied in a certain conciseness of the original (K. S. 337 v; G. K. 130 d). Joseph could hardly have risen higher. We gather besides from the emphasis laid upon his advancement as being a very significant one, that the estate of Potiphar must have been considerable. This would follow already from Potiphar's official station as "chief of the bodyguard."

5, 6. And so it happened that from the time he appointed him over his house and over all that he possessed that Yahweh blessed the house of the Egyptian for Joseph's sake, and Yahweh's blessing was upon all he possessed in the household and in the fields. So he left all he had in Joseph's hand, and, having him, he had no concern for anything, except the bread which he on his part used to eat. Besides, Joseph was of beautiful form and of beautiful appearance.

Still another step in the progression recorded concerning Joseph's advancement is to be noted: from the time of Joseph's advancement to the point of being in complete charge Yahweh's blessing began to rest on the Egyptian, apparently in noticeable measure. But it was all for Joseph's sake and could be discerned indoors and out-of-doors. God was encouraging Joseph and displaying His sovereign power and goodwill in the eyes of the Egyptians. Yet, strictly speaking, all this was done for the chosen race out of pure mercy, and so it is rightly and consistently ascribed to "Yahweh."

6. So all things were thriving better than they ever had when Potiphar himself supervised more closely. Why should he not leave everything in Joseph's hand? The exception mentioned really is no exception. For we cannot follow those who think that Potiphar supervised only his food that it might conform to the Egyptian rules of cleanliness. For if Joseph was so trustworthy in all things else, why should he have been untrustworthy in the dietetic regulations that Egyptian ceremonies demanded? The having "no concern for anything (*lo' yadha'* here means 'have no concern') except the bread which he on his part used to eat" does not mean that he personally supervised the food he ate and its preparation. It does mean he only interested himself in his meals and that only because his appetite drove him to do so.

These preparatory statements need to be supplemented by the fact, recorded very briefly at this point, that Joseph was beautiful as to form and appearance — well-built and good-looking, as we should say. Of only two other men is it said in the Scriptures that they were beautiful — David and Absalom. The Hebrew idiom says "beautiful in form" and "beautiful of appearance," using the construct relationship (K. S. 336 h). We believe that *'itto,* "with him" used here is taken in the sense of "having him" (Meek).

7-10. **And it came to pass after these matters that his master's wife began to observe Joseph, and she said: Lie with me. But he refused and said to his master's wife: See, my master, having me, does not concern himself what is in the house, and all that is in the house he has given into my hand. He is not greater in this house than I; nor has he withheld anything from me except thee, inasmuch as thou art his wife. How then can I do this great evil and sin against God? And it came to pass as she spoke to Joseph day by day, he would not listen to her to lie at her side, or even to be with her.**

Previously Potiphar's wife had not noticed Joseph. As he was advanced in her husband's favor he came to wear garments in keeping with his station, garments which set off the beauty of his person to advantage. So she "began to observe Joseph." The Hebrew says: "she lifted up her eyes to Joseph." For the present this only means "observe," not yet, "take a fancy to." But her observation rapidly ripens into desire. Shamelessly she proposes at once "lie with me" — a euphemism for intercourse. Keil and others have pointed out that Egyptian women were noted for their lascivious and unfaithful ways. *Shikhbah* is a stronger form of the imperative from *yashabh* (G. K. 48 i).

8. Joseph's answer was unmistakable: "he refused." He makes his refusal the stronger by a statement calculated to give pause to his master's wife. There are three major considerations that he presses upon her notice: 1) the unlimited confidence that his master has bestowed upon him — he concerns himself about nothing; has put everything into Joseph's hands; he is not greater in his own house than Joseph. The baseness of betraying so complete a trust is what Joseph stresses first. The greater the confidence given, the baser the betrayal of it. 2) Joseph emphasizes that the woman is withheld from him, for she is Potiphar's wife. She herself may esteem this position rather lightly. It still involves obligations. 3) Such a deed would be a "great evil" and a "sin against God." Joseph realizes what the woman may not perceive, that sins against man are sins against God. For Joseph it would have been a sin against Yahweh, who had prospered him. Over against the woman, whose spiritual insight is very limited, he merely calls it a sin against the Higher Being, *Elohim.*

10. The shameless hussy was not in the least impressed by any of the higher considerations that Joseph had sought to drive into her conscience. "Day by day" (Hebrew: *yom yom*) she approached him. She was as persistent in her solicitations as he in his steadfastness: "he would not (Hebrew: 'did not') listen to her to lie at her side." In fact, he took double precautions: he took care not even "to be with her." The infinitive construction (*kedhab-berah*) goes over into the finite verb construction (*shama'*), cf. G. K. 114 r.

11-15. And it came to pass, as was customary, that he came into the house to attend to his work, and there was no man of the men of the household there in the house. And she laid hold of his coat and said: Lie with me. And he left his coat in her hand and fled, going out-of-doors. And it came to pass when she saw that he had left his garment in her hand and had fled out-of-doors, that she called the men of the household and said to them: Look, he brought us a Hebrew man to make sport of us; he came in to me to lie with me, and I raised a loud outcry; and it came to pass when I lifted up my voice and cried out, that he left his coat by my side and fled, going out-of-doors.

In spite of his careful avoidance of the woman Joseph could not keep out of the house entirely. The difficult expression *kehayyom hazzeh*, "as this day," seems to be elliptical and perhaps not as "elusive" as Skinner would have us believe. For K. W. has aptly suggested that it may mean "as was customary," filling in the ellipsis: "as this day (shows)." This at least makes very fitting sense. Joseph is intent upon some necessary work. The woman either has arranged that no man be in the house or has carefully waited till such a coincidence occurred. This time her insistence passes beyond mere words: she actually lays hold

of his coat (*béghedh* — "garment") and repeats her
shameless invitation. Joseph must have realized
that the situation called for immediate and drastic
action and let her have the coat and fled, not merely
into the next room but "out-of-doors" (*chûtzah* — "to
the street").

13. This was definitely a case of spurned love
but different from all previous instances, for Joseph
had left his coat behind and had fled out-of-doors.
Now either servants might come and see the coat
and raise incriminating questions, or they might also
have witnessed the hasty exit of Joseph. In either
case Potiphar's wife would stand under strong suspicion. To divert suspicion to Joseph she hastily goes
on the offensive by raising an outcry, summoning the
men of the household and making the protestation
of an outraged innocence. When her passion put her
in danger, its unholy flame burns against Joseph without any consideration of what might befall him. In
this respect she presents an analogy to Amnon (II Sam.
13:15-19). By raising an outcry she puts herself
in the class of those who are mentioned Deut. 22:24
and have a claim upon innocence by virtue of their
outcry. The charge that Joseph at least acted indis-
cretely in leaving his coat behind overlooks the fact
that an emergency had actually arisen, calling for
immediate and determined action. The critics here,
as usual, construct artificial distinctions: they assign
v. 8 and 9 (so Procksch and others) to E, where
Joseph reasons with the woman. Then our verses
(11-15) are said to be J's account, said to be more
effective than E's, for J lets Joseph flee in speech-
less fear. But the critics frequently are more intent
upon separating sources or making sources than upon
valid exegesis.

14. Potiphar's wife seems to refer to him a bit
disparagingly when, without mentioning his name,

she lets him be the nameless "he" — "*he* brought us a Hebrew man." This latter designation of Joseph as "a Hebrew man" (*'ish 'ibhri*) is the term used for all the descendants of Eber (11:16). "Hebrews," as a term, therefore, included a much broader scope than the later term "Israelites." Only after Jacob's family became a more prominent group, did the later term come into vogue. The term *'ibhrim* ("Hebrews") may, therefore, correspond to the *Habiri* of the Tell-el-Amarna tablets, although the incursions coming from the south at that time may have nothing to do with Israelites. Jacob's sons preferred to refer to themselves as Hebrews in speaking to men of another nationality (40:15). It is not reported that the men of Potiphar's household made any response when his wife explained to them how she came into possession of Joseph's coat. They may not have been unduly impressed by her protestations of innocence.

16-18. **And she laid the coat beside her until her lord came home, and she spoke to him after these very words, saying: The Hebrew slave whom thou didst bring to us came in to me to make sport of me. And it happened when I lifted up my voice and made an outcry, he left his coat beside me and fled out-of-doors.**

There is a cleverness about this woman's presentation of the case. The garment by her side looks like a substantial bit of evidence, which she in her indignation has laid aside as positive proof. The verb "to make sport of" (*tsa(ch)cheq*) is also euphemistic here (v. 17) as above in v. 14 and implies attempted rape. Above (v. 14) the woman includes as potential objects of rape all the other female members of the household. The preposition *be* with which this verb is construed involves the idea of disparagement of the object involved (K. S. 212 f). *Wattánach* is Hifil of *nûach* (G. K. 72 ee).

19, 20. **And it came to pass when his master heard his wife's words which she spoke, saying: So and so thy slave did to me, that his anger flared up; and Joseph's master took him and threw him into prison, the place where the king's prisoners lay bound. So he lay there in the prison.**

It is significant that we do not read that the master's anger flared against Joseph. Perhaps it was caused chiefly by the vexation created by the whole bothersome incident. Since he could not disprove his wife's statements — it would hardly have done to take a foreign slave's word against his wife's — all that remained was to do the conventional thing and to punish Joseph and incidentally to get rid of a most efficient business manager. This interpretation of the master's anger is confirmed by the further consideration that the customary punishment for adultery was extreme. To be cast into a prison was a relatively light penalty. In view of the things that are yet to develop the writer tells us that the prison was the one used for the king's prisoners. Joseph, the chief servant of the captain of the bodyguard, was as important a man as the king's prisoners. We are not able to say whether the king's prisoners had better treatment than the ordinary run of prisoners or whether such confinement was unusually rigorous. "So he lay there in prison" implies that this new situation in Joseph's life did not soon undergo a change. *'Adhoney* as a plural expresses quality rather than number (K. S. 304 d). The word for prison *beth hassóhar*, "the house of enclosure," is different from the other Hebrew expressions for the same thing found Exod. 12:29; Isa. 42:7; Judg. 16:21. *Meqom* is unusual, being construct state, though instead of having a noun attached to it, we have a complete relative clause (K. S. 337 z; G.K. 130 c). The marginal reading *'asirey* appears to be the more correct, being a regular noun, whereas the following *'asurim* is a participle. K. S. says: this means, the *captivi* of the king were *capti* there (235 d).

21-23. And Yahweh was with Joseph and made him the object of goodwill and gave him favor in the sight of the overseer of the prison. And the overseer of the prison put all those that were lodged in the prison into Joseph's care, and everything that men were doing there, he was responsible for it. The overseer of the prison himself gave no attention to anything that he had turned over to him, inasmuch as Yahweh was with him, and whatsoever he would undertake, Yahweh would make it succeed.

Grievous as Joseph's disappointment was at this second serious setback, Yahweh did not let him go on long without tokens of divine favor. These were the more necessary, humanly speaking, because in this instance Joseph's calamity was certainly not caused by his own sin, as it was in part at least in the first instance. Here a man was very definitely suffering for righteousness' sake. But the gracious God who had covenanted to be with his chosen ones — *Yahweh* — "was with Joseph." This involves that the comforts of being conscious of God's presence and favor were experienced by Joseph from the outset. This hardly allows us to think of Joseph as being tried severely in his faith and as utterly downcast in spirit. The first tokens of such divine presence were that Yahweh "made him the object of goodwill." So the *Hebrew* phrase is meant: "he turned to him goodwill" (*chésedh*), of course, the goodwill of others. In particular "He gave him favor in the sight of the overseer, (*sar* = 'captain') of the prison." God, who turns the hearts of men as the water brooks, was actively interposing in Joseph's behalf. *Chinno* has a suffix used as an

objective genitive: "his favor" = favor toward him
(K. S. 37).

22. It was not long, apparently, before the overseer of the prison reposed as complete confidence in
Joseph as Potiphar formerly had. He must look after
the prisoners and their welfare. His administrative
ability is recognized, and Joseph puts it to use with
the same faithfulness as when he was outside of the
prison. He is made responsible for all things done
in prison; literally the statement runs: "everything
that they were doing (indefinite subject for the participle, K. S. 324 n) there, he was the one doing it."
Nor was Joseph proving unworthy of such trust. All
things that he undertook were proving successful.
But all this was not due to Joseph's ingenuity, though
that may have been great enough, but to Yahweh's
blessing: "Yahweh would make it succeed" — Yahweh
matslíach, "was causing it to thrive."

Criticism stands divided on the question of sources.
Some say that aside from "a sprinkling of E in
variants . . . . . the whole passage is from J."
Wellhausen assigned v. 6-19 to E. Procksch gives E
v. 6-10. And they are both reputable critics.

Most reprehensible of all is the treatment of this
historical narrative as though it were a document of
fiction with different trends woven in according to
the author's fancy. A similar Egyptian tale has been
discovered on the papyrus of Orbiney — the tale of
the two brothers, of whom the one is solicited by
his brother's wife but refuses to do such wrong to
his brother. Men without due respect for God's Word
in some cases assume that because of this similarity
the writer of the Genesis account must have woven
the Egyptian tale with modifications into his Joseph
tale. Such assumptions are groundless. To approach
Biblical accounts as though they were borrowed and
unreliable, indicates strong prejudices against them.

For a thorough refutation of all attacks upon the historical reliability of these chapters we refer the careful student to Koenig's *Commentary,* where in the section immediately preceding our chapter he thoroughly disposes of these ill-founded attacks.

HOMILETICAL SUGGESTIONS

Since the element of providence stands out so distinctly in Joseph's life, it would be well to follow through from this point of view and so to treat this chapter as a unit from the point of view of the *Mysterious* Providence of God. Equally proper would be that type of approach which emphasizes that here the Scriptures offer an excellent example of Suffering for Righteousness' sake. This particular approach, however, may be put under the caption: "Whom the Lord loveth, He chasteneth."

CHAPTER XL

4. Interpretation of the Prisoners' Dreams by Joseph (40:1-23)

The things that transpire in this chapter are in preparation for Joseph's deliverance. He was not forgotten and forsaken as he may at times have deemed himself to be. The experiences of this chapter lead directly to Joseph's advancement.

1-4. And it came to pass after these things that the butler of the king of Egypt and the baker offended their master, the king of Egypt. And Pharaoh was angry at his two eunuchs, at the chief of the butlers and at the chief of the bakers, and put them under guard in the house of the chief of the bodyguard, the prison, the place where Joseph was bound. And the chief of the bodyguard entrusted Joseph with them and he waited on them; and they were under guard for quite a while.

The chapter connects very directly with what was last narrated. After Joseph had advanced to the position of trust and responsibility where all things were directly under his responsibility, the two high officers of the court incurred the royal displeasure. When it is said that they "offended" their lord, the verb used, *hate'u* implies actual guilt on the part of each, for literally it means, "they sinned." This verb does not connect with the introductory verb "it came to pass" by the customary "and" (*waw*). For parallel instances see K. S. 370 b. The offending officials, who according to v. 2 are the chief of their class in each case, are here merely designated as "the butler" and "the baker." But already the article is practically equivalent to "the chief of." Where critics regard this difference as indicative of two different authors, they are arguing on the assumption that an author would not care to alter expressions for variety's sake.

2. These two officials are designated as "eunuchs" *sārisaw*, with long "a" — so-called *qamets impurum*. We have no means of determining whether in this case the men actually were eunuchs, or whether the term had come to signify merely a royal officer. In any case, we know both from secular parallels as well as from Scriptures (Neh. 1:11 — Nehemiah; and II Kings 18:17 — Rabshakeh, which Aramaic name means "chief of the cupbearers") that at least the butler's office was one of the most influential, and presumably the baker's also. *Mashqeh* is strictly a participle and means "giving to drink," so "cup-bearer." Since such persons had to be trusty individuals not involved in the frequent court intrigues, it is not to be wondered at that other responsibilities were laid upon them and that they constituted a group with a chief (*sar*) over them. Since v. 1 said "they sinned," v. 2 very likely speaks of a justifiable anger on Pharaoh's part. To impute their imprisonment to some drunken whim is quite unwarranted. Again, the Jewish supposition that these officials had shared in a plot to poison their lord is too harsh. Such a deed would have called for more than temporary imprisonment.

3. Here it appears for the first time that the superintendent of the prison must have been Potiphar, "the captain of the bodyguard," and that "the prison" (*beth hassohar* as in 39:20) was in some way connected with Potiphar's palace. So we see that the "keeper of the prison" (39:21) was this same Potiphar. These prisoners of high station apparently received better treatment than the common run of prisoners. Of them it is said: they were "put under guard" — not just cast into prison — "guard," *mish-*

mar from *shamar*, "to guard." By a dispensation of divine providence these two prisoners come to the very prison which is "the place where Joseph was bound." *Meqom* is construct state before a relative clause. Some light is thrown on the expression "bound" in reference to Joseph if we compare Ps. 105:18. Apparently, Joseph lay bound for a time when he first came to this prison. Afterward the expression is used as a loose synonym for "confined."

4. Prisoners of such high rank are deserving of special attention. The captain of the bodyguard may have reckoned from the very outset with the possibility of the restoration of these important prisoners. For their sake as well as for his own "he entrusted Joseph with them." *Paqadh* here really means he "appointed" or "assigned" Joseph to be with them. Besides, Joseph "waited on them" — *shareth* for higher forms of service, not like *'abhadh,* which covers the menial tasks of a slave. Though *yamim* means only "days," here it may well signify "for quite a while," for in some cases the expression even means "years." (G. K. 139 h).

5-8. **And both of them dreamed a dream, each man his own dream in one night, each man a dream with its own particular meaning, the butler and the baker of the king of Egypt, who were lying bound in the prison house. As Joseph came to them in the morning he noticed that they were out of humor. So he asked these eunuchs of Pharaoh which were with him in ward in his master's house: Why are your faces so gloomy today? And they said to him: A dream we have dreamed, and as for an interpreter — we cannot get one. And Joseph said to them: Interpretations are God's matter. Pray tell me about it.**

To tell the truth, it is rather unusual that dreams should be so numerous at this point of the Genesis

narrative after the many earlier instances we have
encountered; cf. 20:3; 21:12; 28:12; 31:11, 24;
37:5 ff. But to tell about dreams is not a peculiarity
of style of one man, as E. Why should J and P
not be ready to record a dream if they know of one?
The simple solution of the artificial problem created
by criticism is just this: Moses wrote of dreams
as they had bearing upon his subject and, therefore,
as they actually occurred. It pleased God in His
providence to let dreams play a more important role
in the history of His people at this time. Persons
who stand on a lower spiritual level are the ones to
whom revelation comes through dreams.

Yet there is a difference between dreams and
dreams. Vilmar has this to say: "The dreams of
this and the following chapter are not to be put on a
par with the dreams of Abraham and Jacob, in which
the Lord appeared to them. They are phenomena of
the natural *psyche*, the *nephesh chayyah*, but yet not
entirely natural. In a secondary sense they appear
as manifestations of God. For God's revelation has
a great variety of stages (Heb. 1:1). They may,
therefore, be conceived of about as follows: God
arouses the natural soul to be able to discern things,
which according to God's purpose are about to
transpire."

5. The first statement stresses the fact that these
dreams have something in common: they both come
on the same night; they both have a meaning. But
it stresses also that both have a very distinct difference — "each man a dream with its own particular
meaning." The Hebrew way of putting this is: "each
man according to the interpretation of his dream."
But *pithron*, "interpretation," must mean "significance." So we believe our rendering covers the
thought in idiomatic English. Stating this now, the
story indicates that God so adapted these dreams as

to give them this difference. It was not a matter
of accident or something that developed in the sequel,
namely that these dreams are actually indicative of
the things to come. God or the devil may influence
dreams, as may also a poor digestion; but in this
case it was God. It is not a meaningless repetition
here to recount that the ones who dreamed were "the
butler and the baker of the king of Egypt, who were
lying bound in the prison house." This is repeated
to show us that divine providence was reckoning with
these details when it roused these dreams in the souls
of these men.

6. Joseph takes note that the men are out of
sorts or "out of humor." *Zo'aphim* refers to any state
of perturbation, whether more or less severe. We
hold that the term is stronger than "sad" yet not
quite "excited" (*erregt*) K. C. For Joseph to notice
this at once indicates his kindness in attending upon
the men who have been allotted to him.

7. He asks these men "with him" (*'itto*), that
is "under his care": "Why are your faces so gloomy
(*ra'im* — 'evil') today?" The mode of putting the
question betokens kindliness, interest, respect. He
asks as one who may be told and will be of whatever service he can. The whole expression "with
him in ward in his master's house" recalls that his
position really demanded of him to take note even
of such a thing as their moods and feelings. They
had been "entrusted" to Joseph (v. 4), and Joseph
took all such commissions very seriously. Therein
lay a large measure of the secret of his success. Had
Joseph not inquired of them why they were so gloomy,
the entire chain of events that followed might have
been rendered impossible.

8. Their answer indicates what was uppermost
in their thoughts. The Hebrew sentence order in the
first two clauses throws the emphatic word forward,

thus: "A dream we have dreamed, and an interpreter — none" (cf. K. S. 339 h). *'Eyn* before *'otho*
is still construct state (G. K. 152 o). The manner of
statement of these high officials indicates that on
general principles they believed in dreams and would,
had they been at liberty, at once have resorted to
some acknowledged interpreter. Being under restraint
in this latter respect makes them "out of humor" and
"gloomy." Joseph's reply is a revelation of Joseph's
principles and convictions. The claim, "interpretations are God's matter," would strike a responsive
chord in the Egyptians' heart, though they would take
it in the sense of some particular god who dominated
such activity. Joseph meant: Only the one true God
can interpret what he has sent. In the Hebrew the
affirmation is made strong by putting the obvious
truth in the form of a question which expects an
affirmative answer: "Is it not that to God (belong)
interpretations?" Joseph well knows, that even
though a dream may reveal something, yet no man
can detect what it is unless God grant him insight
(cf. Dan. 2:11, 28, 47). Yet he asks, somewhat eagerly: "Pray tell me about it," literally: "tell, pray,
to me." More than interest or curiosity lies behind
this request. Appearing in the connection in which
it does, it strongly suggests that Joseph surmised
that under the circumstances God would grant the
favor of interpretation to him, and he asks with this
in mind.

9-11. **And the chief of the butlers told his
dream to Joseph and said to him: In my dream,
see, a vine was before me; and on the vine were
three tendrils; and as soon as it sprouted, blossoms
had come upon it and its clusters had ripened out
grapes. And Pharaoh's cup was in my hand, and
I took the grapes and pressed them out into**

Pharaoh's cup and gave the cup into Pharaoh's hand.

The butler speaks first. This may have been due to the fact that he had no misgivings about his dream, much as it may have puzzled him. His account is very clear as it would be if the dream left a definite impression. But still it is a dream. If certain elements of the impossible are encountered, that will not surprise us: that is a usual feature in dreams. First, there was a vine standing directly before him. Three "tendrils," or "branches" (A. V.) are on this vine. This feature of the dream impressed the butler as an outstanding one. The season for sprouting is upon it, and the very process of sprouting takes place with visible progress before his very eyes. The quick succession of the ensuing steps in the process is indicated by unconnected perfects after *khephoráchath* — "as it was sprouting" (*'alethah* = "there had come up"; *hibhshilû* = "they had ripened out" — K. S. 119). Blossoms develop into grapes, which appear in complete clusters, which in turn are ripe almost on the spot. At this point the butler finds Pharaoh's cup, no doubt a beautiful example of the goldsmith's art, ready in his hand. While the grapes still hang on the vine, he takes them and presses them out into Pharaoh's cup and then proceeds to hand the cup to Pharaoh, the final assumption being that with all these accelerated processes involved, by the time the cup was in Pharaoh's hand its contents was the customary wine. The whole makes up a dream just as fantastic as those which every man has dreamed many a time.

Certainly, the deduction that the kings of ancient Egypt drank only fresh grape juice is exceedingly farfetched. Archaeological conclusions are not based on dreams as source material. The claim of some

that Moses slipped up on a matter of archaeological
accuracy has since been dropped. The monuments of
earlier days show various drinking utensils, men
treading the wine press, men drinking wine to excess,
even drunken women (Delitzsch). The Scriptural
references, therefore, referring to Egyptian vine culture are very much in place (Ps. 78:47; 105:33; Num.
20:5). Hengstenberg has given the subject thoroughgoing treatment in *Die Buecher Moses und Aegypten*,
in the first chapter.

**12, 13. And Joseph said to him: This is the
interpretation of it: the three tendrils stand for
three days; yet three days and Pharaoh will lift
up thy head and restore thee to thy position; and
thou wilt hand Pharaoh's cup to him, according to
thy manner when formerly thou wast his butler.**

Luther suggests that at this point, immediately
upon hearing the butler's dream, Joseph sought pri-
vacy and approached his God in prayer, as Christians
are wont to do in all things in their daily life. We
cannot think of Joseph as forgetting or overlooking
prayer after what he had just said to the butler. God
grants Joseph to discern the interpretation of the
dream with perfect clearness. Therefore we see no
wavering or uncertainty on Joseph's part. He seizes
upon the essential features of the dream that are now,
after the interpretation of the dream, seen to stand
out all the more clearly: three tendrils, the days;
in three days restoration to former position and duties.
Whatever parallel from heathen antiquity may be
cited for tendrils signifying days, all such bear at best
only an accidental similarity and never could have in
any case made an authoritative interpretation possible.
The expression, "lift up thy head," is idiomatic and
takes its meaning from its connection. Here it must
refer to putting an end to the butler's gloom, when

he had hung his head. A parallel thought is found
4:6, 7. A parallel case II Kings 25:27.

14, 15. **Only thou wilt remember me by thyself when it goeth well with thee, and do thou, I
pray, show kindness to me and do thou bring me to
Pharaoh's remembrance and do thou bring me forth
from this house. For I was of a truth stolen from
the land of the Hebrews; and here too I have
done nothing that they should have put me into the
dungeon.**

Usually the translations give a different turn to
the first words of v. 14 than the original allows for:
they make the perfect a precative — an impossibility
— "but think on me" (A. V.). *Ki'im* = "only." The
perfect of *zekhartáni* is, indeed, used in a futuristic
sense: "thou wilt remember." The thought then is:
everything will again be with you as it formerly was,
except that from time to time "thou wilt remember
me by thyself." This will happen when he is alone
by himself and his thoughts revert to these unpleasant
prison years. Then, when it "goes well" with him,
the contrast may serve as a reminder, and the butler
will be in a position to "show kindness" to Joseph and
to bring his case to Pharaoh's attention. The perfects
(*'asíthi* and *hizkartáni*) are converted and so become
hortative or precative futures.

15. If a prisoner lays claims to liberation, he
must offer some explanation for his right to be
liberated. Joseph covers both the more remote past
as well as the more recent. He came to Egypt, he
says, having been "stolen from the land of the
Hebrews." That should appeal to the butler: Joseph
has done no wrong; wrong was done to him. That
accounts for his presence as a Hebrew in the land
of Egypt. The rest of his claim is that here in Egypt
he has "done nothing that they should have put"
him "into the dungeon" (here *bor*, i. e. "pit"). The

whole explanation bears the stamp of verity. It is not too brief or so vague as to lead to the supposition that something is being suppressed. It is not so lengthy as fictitious explanations are liable to become in an effort to achieve plausibility. It bears all the earmarks of truth. "Land of the Hebrews" — a fitting expression, not an anachronism, for "Hebrews were all the inhabitants of Palestine of whatever race, who spoke the Phoenician — Canaanite — Hebrew tongue" (Bailey and Kent, *History of the Hebrew Commonwealth*, p. 414).

The critics stress the verb "stolen" at this point setting it over against "sold" (37:28). This is supposed to be a very strong proof for the different tales of J and E. Procksch says: "One ought to see into the fact that stealing and selling are two different things." However, the case is quite simple. If a great injustice is done to me by selling me into slavery, I am justified in calling that: stealing me, for that is what it amounts to. One ought to be able to see into that fact also. The only possibility the critics would allow for is that Joseph tells exactly what transpired. Of course, the critics cannot tell what transpired. For them there are two unreconciled and unreconcilable accounts in this story — J's and E's. But apart from that, they fail to see Joseph's charity, which refuses to incriminate his own brothers, guilty as they are. He merely says in a general way that a great injustice was done him. He may in view of the underhanded way in which the transaction was carried through by his brothers well say that he was stolen.

16, 17. When the chief of the bakers saw that he had interpreted something promising, he said to Joseph: I too had a dream, and in my dream there were three baskets of white baked goods upon my head; and in the top basket there was

some of every sort of Pharaoh's food — handiwork of the baker — and birds were eating them out of the basket upon my head.

From one point of view the chief of the bakers could hardly be blamed for expecting a favorable interpretation of his own dream, for there surely was at least something of a striking similarity between his dream and that of the butler. Both had the man who dreamed busied with the things relating to his former office. Both had the element of three prominently figuring in them. Now the butler had heard "something promising" (Hebrew: *tobh* — "good"). The baker tries *his* luck, *'ani* emphatic. He tells of the three baskets — no doubt one on top of the other — with *chori* in them. This is best taken as coming from the root *chur*, meaning "white" — here "white baked goods" — not "open-work." The top basket had a variety of "some of every sort of Pharaoh's food — handiwork of the baker." From this top basket birds did eat. Now all this had nothing unusual about it, as was the case in the butler's dream. For baskets were commonly carried on their head by men, though not exclusively by them, as Herodotus claimed. And birds are liable to be especially bold in a land where, as was the case in days of old, no beast or bird was molested. But one thing the baker failed to notice, which is really one of the outstanding things of the dream and which was really ominous: he was unable to drive the birds off; they ate unmolested.

18, 19. **And Joseph answered and said: This is its interpretation: Three baskets stand for three days; yet three days and Pharaoh will lift up thy head from off thee, and hang thee on a tree, and birds shall devour thy flesh from off thee.**

God enables Joseph to discern the distinctive feature of this dream and to interpret very definitely

and correctly. Three days are signified by the three
baskets. But now a very radical difference: "lifting
up the head" (*nasa' ro'sh*) must have an entirely different meaning because it is followed by "from thee."
That must mean decapitation, a common form of
capital punishment in Egypt. This is to be followed
by hanging on a "tree" or "wood," *'ets,* a less common mode of punishment. Then will the birds of prey
be able to eat his flesh from off him. Whether this
interpretation, which reads rather like a sentence
than like an interpretation, was offered with all possible sympathy, or spoken bluntly and harshly we
cannot know. If the baker had been a wicked fellow,
the latter is the more likely. But judging by Joseph's
kindliness, we are rather inclined to favor the view
which holds that he broke the unwelcome news as
kindly as he knew how. The writer says nothing on
this score so as not to detract from major issues.

**20-23. And it came to pass on the third day,
Pharaoh's birthday, that he made a banquet for his
courtiers, and he lifted up the head of the chief of
the butlers and the head of the chief of the bakers
amongst his courtiers; namely, he restored the chief
of the butlers to his butlership, so that he again
placed the cup in Pharaoh's hand; but the chief of
the bakers he hanged, as Joseph had interpreted for
them. But the chief of the butlers did not remember
Joseph; he forgot him.**

As usual, an important step in the narrative is
introduced by *wayhi,* "and it came to pass." The
significant "third day" happened to be "Pharaoh's
birthday," *yom hullédheth,* the latter form being
infinitive Hophal (G. K. 69 w) and is used as an attribute: "day of his being born" (K. S. 227 b), the sign
of the direct object being retained before the noun
Pharaoh though construed with a passive verb (K.
S. 109). Royal birthdays were celebrated by "ban-

quets" (*mishteh* — a "drinking") and by amnesties, if the king was so minded. Both are common features of antiquity for royal birthdays at least for the Ptolemaic period according to the Rosetta stone. The ones invited are the "courtiers," strictly *'abhadhaw,* "his servants." The play of words on "lifted up the head" is maintained, and the difference in the use of the phrase is at once adjusted. The one is restored to his "butlership," *mashqeh,* literally "drink," but by metonomy here the office. The fuller description of his reinstatement shows him again placing the cup in Pharaoh's hand. The other courtier is hanged. Joseph's interpretation of the dreams stands justified. Only the immediate sequel is disappointing: the butler did not "remember," he "forgot." This cannot have been an accidental forgetting. The thought of his promise must have kept recurring, but it was put off either for a more convenient season or because the butler just was not a man of his word. This surely was a culpable forgetting.

Nothing indicates that Joseph's fate came as a punishment for his having presumed to interpret these dreams. We find no trace of presumption in what Joseph did. Joseph just was not yet fully tested in God's crucible. For the great elevation impending a very thoroughgoing preparation was essential.

A sample of critical analysis of the chapter may be appended more as an illustration of presumption than as proof of scholarship. Procksch arrives at the following conclusions, accepted with many differences of opinion by critics as a whole; he ascribes to J 1, 3 a, 5 (5 b), 6, 14 b, 15 b; and to E: 2, 3, 4, 5 a, 7:9, 10-12, 14 a, 15 a, 16-23. Consequently, E gets the lion's share. We have showed the idle grounds for this division in some major cases in our exposition.

HOMILETICAL SUGGESTIONS

Several Scripture passages could be used as the key for the approach to this chapter. If one prefers to develope more fully the mysterious providence of God, then one would operate with the Scripture truth embodied in the words of the hymn,

"God moves in a mysterious way
His wonders to perform."

Very similar would be the approach that builds on the word, "We walk by faith, not by sight." But Joseph at the same time fulfills the requirement that his Lord makes of him by proving himself one who "is faithful in that which is least" by humbling himself to perform lowly service for those committed to his care. It might also be quite proper to approach the chapter from the angle of Warranted and Unwarranted Use of Dreams.

CHAPTER XLI

5. Joseph's Exaltation (41:1-57)

For the third time dreams figure prominently in the history of Joseph. Yet really none of these dreams, except perhaps the first set, were primarily for Joseph. Joseph's connection with them was primarily that of interpreter, after his own first set of dreams had been interpreted by his own father. Since then it was chiefly for the sake of others that these dreams were granted. There may be truth in Dod's suggestion: "If these men were to receive any knowledge beyond what their own unaided efforts could attain, they must be taught in a language they understood." Men like Jacob and Joseph could receive revelation perhaps by a word or in a vision, but not Pharaoh and his courtiers.

1-4. **And it happened at the expiration of two years that Pharaoh was dreaming, and, lo, he was standing by the side of the Nile; and, lo, from the Nile there were coming up seven beautiful fat cows, and they grazed among the reeds. And, lo, seven other cows were coming up after them from the Nile, ugly and skinny, and took their place by the side of the first cows by the bank of the Nile. And the ugly looking and skinny cows ate up the seven beautiful fat cows. Then Pharaoh awoke.**

Two full years elapse before the case of Joseph comes to Pharaoh's attention. *Shenātháyim* alone means "two years." The added expression *yāmîm,* "days," on the one hand, seems to indicate that it was "two whole years" (Meek); but on the other, it almost seems as if the expression recalls how Joseph was by this time eagerly counting the days. The two nouns are not in construct relationship but purely appositional, as is often the case with terms of weight and measure (K. S. 333 e).

Pharaoh "was dreaming" (*cholem*) ; the participle implies that after idle dreaming had been going on for a time, the dream suddenly took very tangible shape. What he became definitely aware of is drawn to our attention by a *hinneh*, "*lo.*" He himself was standing by the Nile. The Hebrew says *'al* ("over") because the bank is always higher than the stream. *Ye'or*, a form in which, apparently, an Egyptian and an Assyrian root blend, standing in reference to Egyptian surroundings, always refers to "the River" of Egypt, i. e. the Nile. A participle like *cholem* may be used in place of a finite verb in the past tense also (K. S. 238 b).

2. Again the participle lets the scene progressively re-enact itself — *'oloth* — "they were coming up." Apparently, these cows left nothing to be desired: they were "beautiful" and "fat" — the Hebrew expressively says "fat of flesh." The "reeds" in which they graze are *'achû*, a distinctly Egyptian word. The scene could hardly be more characteristically Egyptian. In "beautiful of appearance" — "appearance" (*mar'eh*) is an accusative of specification.

3. The second seven cows are in every way the opposite of the first: "ugly and skinny" — *daqqôth basar*, "beaten, or thin of flesh." *Watha'amódhnah* = "and they stood" — we render they "took their place." Apparently, the two groups of seven each first appear side by side for a while in order to make the contrast between them forcibly apparent. But as to their origin in the dream it is noteworthy that both groups come from the same river.

4. Cow eating up cow is the strange thing that now follows; and yet in a dream such an occurrence is entirely of the type that might be expected. Still that part of the dream was so utterly strange as to startle Pharaoh into a waking state.

5-8. And he fell asleep and dreamed a second time: and, lo, there were seven ears of grain coming up on one stalk, plump and nice; and, lo, seven ears, thin and blasted by the east wind, were sprouting up after them; and the seven thin ears swallowed up the seven plump and full ears. And Pharaoh awoke, and, lo, it was a dream. And it came to pass in the morning that his mind was wrought up and he sent and summoned all the magicians of Egypt and all her sages, and Pharaoh told them his dream. But there was no man who could furnish an interpretation for Pharaoh.

The second dream is as distinctly Egyptian as the first, at least, objects familiar to the Egyptian are involved. Egypt was known as the granary of the ancient world. Seven ears on a stalk were not at all uncommon. These seen in the dream were so "plump" (literally: "fat") that it was a pleasure to behold them: they were "nice" (literally "good," *tobh*).

6. The seven lean ears have the same word applied to them that was used in reference to the cows, *daqqoth*, "thin." In addition, as they were developing in their wretched state, apparently the withering "east wind," *qadhim* — for Egypt more usually a southeast wind — had blasted what little remained. This wretched wind, called to this day *chamsin*, utterly wilts all green things upon which it blows. Since these last seven ears are not said to have come upon a single stalk, the implication is that each grew on its own stalk. In *shedhuphoth qadhim*, "blasted of the east wind," a genitive construction replaces the construction which offers an

active subject (K. S. 336 n). On this "east wind" see Hos. 13:15; Jer. 18:17; cf. also Jonah 4:8.

7. The lean "swallow up" the plump. We interpret that to mean more than that in their weedlike growth they crowded out and smothered the plump, as Strack suggests. The "thin" were too "blasted" for that. Grotesque as dreams are, this one actually showed the one group swallowing up the other, an act in itself as unnatural as that cows should turn carnivorous. The uniqueness of the scene again startles the king awake. The remark, "lo, it was a dream," leads us to conclude that, as often happens, the dream had been so realistic that for a time the king had almost believed that it was an actual occurrence, even though his reason was protesting at its impossibility.

8. The resultant impression is so strong that even on the next morning Pharaoh's mind (Hebrew: "spirit") was still "wrought up." Unable to decipher his dreams, he calls upon the *chartumîm*, the men versed in deciphering hieroglyphics, wherefore the Septuagint describes them as ἱερογραμματεῖς, "men versed in the sacred writings." No doubt they also cultivated arts such as astrology. The root as such means one who wields a writing instrument, *Griffel-fuehrer* (K. W.). "Magician" seems to cover the case most nearly. To these are added the sages (*chakhāmîm*, "wise men"). They hear the double dream and find themselves unable to interpret it: *'en pother'otham* = "there was not an interpreter of them." The suffix on "his dream" is singular, treating both dreams as one.

We must admire the honesty of these men. To offer some makeshift interpretation would seemingly have been so easy. Perhaps they were entirely conscientious: their science offered them no clue; they admitted it. Yet the whole thing seemed so very obvious, as has often been pointed out. The part that the Nile plays in at least the first dream is too evident to demand explanation. Let Dods tell the rest of the story: "The cow also was reverenced as the symbol of the earth's productive power. If then . . . . God wished to show to Pharaoh that seven years of plenty were approaching, this announcement could hardly have been made plainer in the language of dreams than by showing to Pharaoh seven well-favored kine coming up out of the bountiful river to feed on the meadow made richly green by its water." Apparently, the hand of God was upon the interpreters, making their own devices of no effect, in order that the revelation might come by His own chosen instrument.

9-13. **And the chief of the butlers spoke to Pharaoh saying: My sins do I for one call to mind this day. Pharaoh was angry at his servants and put me under guard in the house of the chief of the bodyguard, both me and the chief of the bakers. And we dreamed a dream in one night, both I and he, each man dreaming according to the particular interpretation of his own dream. And there, with us, was a Hebrew lad, a servant of the captain of the bodyguard; and we told him, and he furnished us with an interpretation of our dreams; he interpreted for each man as his dream demanded. And it came to pass that everything turned out as he interpreted for us: me he restored to my position, and him he let be hanged.**

The chief of the butlers could hardly have forgotten Joseph under these circumstances. The sequence of thought in what he says regarding Pharaoh's anger leads us to believe that his word "my sins" (*chatā'ay*), A. V., "my faults," is only a reference to his own misdeeds over against the king and does not mean that he remembers how shabbily he treated Joseph in not pleading his cause. To him Joseph is the Hebrew prison-slave; he himself, however, is the noble courtier. Then follows his story how Joseph had furnished an entirely reliable interpretation to clear up the butler's great perplexity, and how the interpretation furnished to the baker had also proved correct. The details are explained in the preceding chapter.

In v. 11, in *nachalmah* the ending *ah* with waw conversive is quite the exception (G. K. 49 e and K. S. 200). In v. 12 *'ébhedh lesar* = "a servant of the captain," because the intention is to leave the first noun indefinite, therefore *le* in the construct relationship (K. S. 280 l). "To each one," *'îsh,* furnishes an instance of a *casus pendens,* the noun standing as an absolute rather than as a dative as the construction demands (G. K. 139 c). "Me he restored" = of course, "I was restored," etc.

14-16. And Pharaoh sent and let Joseph be summoned and brought in haste from the prison; and he let himself be shaved and provided with a change of garments, and he came to Pharaoh. And Pharaoh said to Joseph: I have dreamed a dream and no man can interpret it. Now I for my part have heard about thee that for thee to hear a dream is to interpret it. But Joseph answered Pharaoh: Not at all! God will give Pharaoh a favorable answer.

Pharaoh's need is urgent: it matters little who will furnish the interpretation. The utmost of meticulous cleanliness was essential for those who were to be presented to the Pharaoh. Consequently also the shaved head as well as the shaved body would present rather a delay in this instance. Besides, adequate raiment had to be provided for such a presentation. Several of the verbs used refer to what was ordered to be done rather than to what the subject executed in person. *Wayyiqra'*, "and he called" = "he let Joseph be summoned," and in reference to Joseph *waygalach*, "and he shaved" = "he let himself be shaved," and the next verb: "he let himself be provided with a change of raiment." For this impecunious prisoner would hardly have had the proper shaving utensils or a change of raiment.

15. Very concisely Pharaoh formulates the problem which led to this unceremonious summons of Joseph. Equally concise is Pharaoh's statement concerning the report he has heard about Joseph. To lend the needed dignity to his urgent presentation of the case, Pharaoh refers to his royal person with emphasis: "I for my part have heard," *'anî shamá'ti*. What he has heard is really: "thou hearest a dream to interpret it." That must mean: "for thee to hear a dream is to interpret it." That clearly claims unfailing ability to cope with all dreams. "The Hebrew subordinates the emphatic clause where we would subordinate the condition" (Skinner).

16. Joseph's reply is usually given too much emphasis in its first part; *bil'adhay* is not: "it is not in me" (A. V.), nor really quite as we have rendered, "not at all" (B D B), nor yet as Luther rendered: *das stehet bei mir nicht.* For the word means: "quite apart from me." Certainly Joseph is disclaiming unfailing ability to interpret. We believe that, roughly paraphrased, the remark means: "leave me aside for the present," and it is followed at once by a statement that lodges all power and all honor with God — here *'elohim*, for Pharaoh had no acquaintance with *Yahweh*. Yet the implication of the brief but courteous reply is that God will use Joseph as the medium for his revelation. We may well be astounded at the downright honesty which refuses to profit even in an emergency by a slight distortion of the truth. As far as Joseph was con-

cerned, absolute truthfulness in guarding God's honor
was far more important than personal advantage.
After twelve years and more of injustice Joseph's
first consideration is not deliverance but to take care
that his relation to his God be entirely upright. In
the original "a favorable answer" is an "answer of
peace," or more literally: "God will answer the peace
of Pharaoh," i. e., that which will be conducive to
Pharaoh's well-being. Note also the tactful courtesy
of Joseph's reply: he does not by unwarranted claims
take advantage of a situation that might make him
appear a great expert and all the court magicians poor
bunglers — an attitude that would have antagonized
these courtiers.

17-24. **And Pharaoh spake unto Joseph: In
my dream, lo, I was standing on the bank of the
Nile; and, lo, from the Nile there were coming up
seven cows, fat and beautiful, and they grazed
among the reeds. And, lo, seven other cows were
coming up after them, thin, very ugly and poor looking — I never saw such poor specimens in all the
land of Egypt — and the skinny, ugly cows ate up
the first seven fat cows; and they went down into
the midst of them and it was not to be noticed that
they had gone down into the midst of them; and
they looked just as bad as they had before. Then
I awoke. And I noticed in my dream, and, lo, seven
ears of grain were coming up on one stalk, plump
and good; and, lo, seven ears of grain, hard and
dry, and blasted by the east wind, were sprouting
up after them. And the thin ears swallowed up
the good ears. Now I have spoken to the magicians,
and there is not a man that can enlighten me.**

Pharaoh is so vitally interested in what seems a
matter of great importance to him, that he retells his
dreams himself. Everything is as true to life as it
can be. You would expect the major terms used to

be the same as those found in the first account. You
would expect some points to be stressed a bit more:
the account has not been rehearsed so frequently as
to become utterly stereotyped. On the face of it,
it would appear ridiculous to attribute an account
that varied slightly from the first account to a different source, as ridiculous, we say, as it would be
unnatural to have both accounts entirely the same.
First the poor cows are merely "ugly and skinny";
now they are "thin, very ugly and poor looking." Besides, further reflection on the whole dream has now
led him to remark: "I never saw such poor specimens in all the land of Egypt." In the first recital
the latter seven merely ate the former seven. Now
he recalls "that they went down into the midst of
them and it was not to be noticed that they had gone
down into the midst of them; and they looked just
as bad as they had before." But who would venture
to put the second recital at variance with the first?
Even Skinner says: "The slight differences in
phraseology are due to the literary instinct for
variety." Though we believe our explanation to be
far more natural, we are surprised that the tendency
to set source, so called, at variance with source does
not control all critics here.

Similar minor differences appear in reference to
the second recital of the second dream. After it has
been given, the king, impatient for a solution, summarizes very briefly, concluding: "there is not a man
that can enlighten me" — Hebrew: "there is not a
one telling (*maggidh*) me."

In v. 21 *qirbénnah* really has a plural suffix (G.
K. 91 f) and *mar'êhen*, all appearances to the contrary, a singular one (G. K. 99 ss). In v. 22 *Wa'ē're'*
is rather an unusuel form for the first person (G.
K. 75 o p). In v. 23 the masculine suffix on *'ach(ch)a-*

rêhem, being the one more frequently used, has displaced the feminine (G. K. 135 o).

25-32. Then Joseph said to Pharaoh: Pharaoh's dream is but one; God has made known to Pharaoh that which He is about to do: The seven good cows stand for seven years, and the seven good ears stand for seven years — the dream has one meaning. The seven skinny and ugly cows coming up after them, they also stand for seven years; and the seven ears, empty and blasted by the east wind, mean: there will be seven years of famine. This then is the thing that I told Pharaoh: God has showed Pharaoh what He is about to do. See, seven years are about to come — great plenty throughout all the land of Egypt. After these shall arise seven years of famine, and all the plenty in the land of Egypt shall be forgotten, and the famine shall consume the land. And it shall not be known that there was plenty, because of the ensuing famine. For it shall be extremely grievous. As far as the fact is concerned that the dream came twice to Pharaoh, this signifies that the matter is fully determined by God, and that God will carry it out promptly.

With deft skill and with the sure touch of one who knows, Joseph interprets as God reveals it to him. Though nothing is said under this head, it seems too obvious for words specifically to recount how one, who had ascribed all ability to God, first made his earnest silent prayer to God for help. Then comes the swift unravelling of the tangled skein. First: the two dreams have the same interpretation; there is really only one dream. Secondly: God is revealing to Pharaoh what He is about to do (*'oseh* is future, G. K. 116 d).

26. "The seven good cows stand for seven years" — the adjective *tobhoth* has the article, because the

numeral "seven" made the preceding noun definite
(K. S. 334 v) — "and the seven good ears stand for
seven years." This clinches the point that the dual
dream has a unit meaning. This was the one difficulty — seven cows = seven years — which had bar-
ricaded the approach to the whole interpretation.
With this key item clear, everything literally falls
into its proper place. The seven skinny cows must
be years, too, and bad ones — that is to say "seven
years of famine." At once all difficulties are removed,
and the interpretation may proceed to clinch all vital
points. Once again Joseph repeats the fundamental
point of view which should govern the entire approach:
"God has showed Pharaoh what He is about to do."
Hû' haddabhar reaches back to 25 b, which is almost
entirely identical with 28 b. Joseph's life and his
thinking are theocentric. These dreams are centered
in God's merciful kindness; Pharaoh should gratefully
record that fact.

29. The inference to be drawn from the above
premises is that a first heptad of years is coming —
"great plenty throughout all the land of Egypt" —
"plenty" stands in apposition to the "seven years."
Related to one another, the seven famine years shall
make the years of plenty "to be forgotten" — they
"shall consume the land" — "it shall not be known
that there was plenty" ("known" in the sense of
"realized"). Since a needed warning is involved,
Joseph summarizes in respect to the famine: "it shall
be extremely grievous."

32. Now the last essential fact: the repetition
of the dream points to the fact that the events revealed will come to pass at once. "The matter is fully
determined by God." It is not contingent upon the
possible outcome of other matters that are still pending. Besides, "God will carry it out promptly"
(Hebrew: "God is making haste in reference to the

doing"). The opening clause of this verse in literal translation runs thus: "and upon ('al) double occurrence (hishshanôth) of the dream to Pharaoh" (is built the fact that) "the matter is fully determined" (K. S. 403 f).

One is amazed how this man Joseph, inspired by God, cuts through the Gordian knot. Every Egyptian magician must have been convinced of the correctness of the interpretation and have marvelled that so obvious a solution did not occur to him. Here the contrast between the certainty of divinely given truth and the unreliability of human thoughts is demonstrated with unusual clearness.

33-36. And now let Pharaoh pick a man who is shrewd and wise and set him over the land of Egypt. Let Pharaoh act and appoint administrators over the land and let him take a fifth part of the produce of the land of Egypt during the seven years of plenty. And let them gather all the food of these seven good years that are about to come, and let them heap up the grain under Pharaoh's hand for food in the cities and let them guard it there. And this food shall be for a deposit for the land during the seven years of famine which shall be in the land of Egypt. Then the land will not be ruined by the famine.

The Spirit of God did more than merely enable Joseph to interpret the king's dreams; he enabled him to furnish a comprehensive plan to meet this unusual emergency. This plan is as masterful as was the interpretation that preceded. First, a chief administrator is needed. He must have two qualifications: he must be "shrewd and wise." "Shrewd" — nabhôn, from the root bîn = "to have insight." He must, therefore, be a man who has keen insight into the situation and its needs. But the capacity for acting constructively in a way to meet these needs is covered by *chakham,* "wise," which always implies constructive capacity.

34. Joseph's energetic counsel tended toward instantaneous action. So sure was he of the correctness of the interpretation and of the need of action. Therefore *ya'aseh,* optative — let Pharaoh "act." Even as there was need of centralized authority to meet the emergency (v. 33), so there was need of sub-"administrators" (*peqidîm* — "appointees") over portions of the land, whose business would primarily be to *chimmesh,* "fifth," the land, i. e., "take a fifth part of the produce." "A fifth part" would, indeed, be a double tithe, but in years of plenty that would hardly count as a hardship. Had this surplus not been gathered, it might largely have been wasted by careless management. A further likelihood is that Pharaoh will have secured this surplus by purchase not by merely impounding it. The low prices of bumper crop years will have made greater purchases possible. In no event need the charge of harshness be laid against Joseph's plan as outlined. The jussive *ya'aseh* is without the usual apocopation *ya'as.*

35. The grain thus gathered is usually called *'okhel,* "food," for from that point of view it is usually considered. Once in this verse *bar,* "grain," is used. "Food" may, of course, include everything that could have been preserved. In the last analysis Pharaoh is to have complete control as the words "under Pharaoh's hand" (i. e., by his authority) indicate. Observe how well co-ordinated this plan is and yet how simple in all its parts. The "cities" are indicated as the logical center for storage of the grain. Besides, provision is to be made properly to "guard" (*shamar*) this food after it has been laid up. So, then, when the inevitable famine comes, the land will not "be ruined" (*tikkareth* = "cut off" — A. V. "perish").

We feel rather keenly that Joseph never for a moment thought of himself as a possible candidate for head administrator. Verse 16 shows how little Joseph thought of turning the situation to his own advantage. How utterly unreasonable for one who had never held an office of state, who, besides, was a foreigner and still almost smelled of the prison whence he had been brought — for such a one to anticipate immediate advancement to a position second only to that of Pharaoh! The last few years had stifled all ambitions to hold a prominent position. Joseph would have considered himself fortunate indeed merely to be set at liberty.

37-41. And the proposition appealed to Pharaoh and to all his courtiers, and Pharaoh said to his courtiers: Shall we find a man with the Spirit of God like this man? Then Pharaoh said to Joseph: Seeing that God has revealed all this to thee, there is no man as shrewd and wise as thou art. Thou shalt be over my house, and all my people shall be entirely obedient to thee. Only in the matter of the throne shall I be greater than thou art. Besides, Pharaoh said to Joseph: See, I have set thee over the entire land of Egypt.

37. Joseph's lucid plan meets with immediate approval by Pharaoh and his courtiers. Its merits kept suggesting themselves so forcibly upon this group, which a moment before was so entirely at a loss, that the next suggestion of Pharaoh also meets with the full approval of all. The thought that stands out in reference to Joseph is that he has "God's Spirit" (*ru'ach 'elohîm*). The Egyptians still had so much spiritual discernment as to be able to see that a supernatural element had been involved in this interpretation. Pharaoh senses that this same element as a divine equipment will be essential to carry out

a plan of such magnitude as the one Joseph just outlined. *Nimtsa'* is not potential, "can" or "could we find" but a plain future: "shall we find" (K. S. 187). Apparently, there was a measure of the knowledge and fear of God still left to the Egyptians at this point in history.

39. Pharaoh reasons quite cogently: the God who revealed the dream and this excellent plan to you would very likely equip you to carry it out rather than any other man. He observes in Joseph both shrewdness and wisdom. Joseph's prompt response arouses a kindred prompt resolution in Pharaoh. Using his power as supreme ruler, he appoints Joseph over his "house" first of all. When we consider the importance of the major-domus of the Merovingians or of the officials of Israel's court bearing practically the same name (cf. I Kings 4:6; 16:9; Isa. 22:15), we see that the position was easily as influential as that of a secretary of state. Joseph's position in reference to the people is also defined at once: "all my people shall be entirely obedient to thee," Hebrew: " they shall hang upon thy mouth" (*nashaq* = "cling to," "attach oneself to" — and so "be entirely obedient" *vollkommen gehorchen* — K. W.). Apparently, the verb is not as doubtful as some claim, and the rendering of the Septuagint gives a good lead — ὑπακούσεται. Still Pharaoh will be the supreme ruler; yet he graciously states the case as much in Joseph's favor as possible: "only in the matter of the throne (*hakkisse'* — accussative of specification) shall I be greater than thou art." The additional statement rounds out the broad scope of Joseph's authority in reference to the land as a whole: "I have set thee over the entire land of Egypt."

Only a man like Joseph, schooled by adversity and sorrow, could meet a sudden elevation like this with-

out pride and self-exaltation. His rigorous training
enabled him to encounter success without succumbing
to its blandishments.

**42-45. And Pharaoh removed the signet ring
from his finger and put it upon Joseph's finger and
clad him in linen robes and put a golden chain
around his neck, and had him ride in his second
chariot, and men cried out before him: Bow the
knee. So he was set over the entire land of Egypt.
And Pharaoh said to Joseph: I am Pharaoh; but
without thy permission not a man shall move hand
or foot in all the land of Egypt. And Pharaoh
gave Joseph the name Zaphenath-paneah, and gave
him a wife Asenath, the daughter of Potiphera,
priest of On. And Joseph went forth throughout
the land of Egypt.**

Everthing has a strictly Egyptian coloring:
"signet ring," "linen robes," "golden chain," "chariot."
The students of Egyptiology are wont to point out these
details. The "signet ring" (*taba'ath* from *taba'*, "to
sink down," viz., into the clay upon which the signature
is affixed) gives its possessor authority to sign documents with the equivalent of royal authority. Robes
of "linen" (*shesh* = byssus, the chararacteristic fine
linen of the Egyptians) were considered the most
elegant. The "golden chain" seems to have been a
rather general symbol of authority — especially in
the XVIII and XIX dynasty (Procksch). The "second
chariot" must have been a vehicle sufficiently splendid
to be recognized as second only to Pharaoh's. So all
the outward trappings of authority are provided by
Pharaoh himself. The last step taken serves to introduce Joseph formally to the people at large. The
word cried out before Joseph's chariot was *'abhrekh*.
This word has caused much difficulty. Perhaps it was
intended to remind the Hebrew of the root *barakh*, "to
bow the knee," and it may have ranked as a kind

of *Aphel* form. Popular etymology may have put some such meanings upon it. This view is reflected in our versions. Luther, however, attempts an unetymological interpretation, guessing at the second half of the word after he removes '*abh* which may mean "father" — *dies ist des Landes Vater.* B D B lists no less than seven attempted explanations. K. W. offers *pass auf*, "look out" — which seems rather inadequate. "Bow the knee" seems to fit the needs of the case most aptly. *Nathôn*, absolute infinitive, continues the sequence after the finite verb (G. K. 113 z).

44. The king's word, "I am Pharaoh," is best understood if one recalls the exalted reverence that was shown to such rulers in days of old. Meek seeks to express the thought by rendering: "Although I continue as Pharaoh, yet, etc." The king is telling Joseph that there can be no thought of his ranking as high as does the king, but he tells it very considerately; he practically appoints Joseph dictator: "without thy permission (Hebrew: apart from thee) not a man shall move hand or foot in all the land of Egypt" — an effective hyperbole.

45. Now Joseph has everything except the requisite social standing. This is provided by egyptianizing his name and giving him an Egyptian wife of priestly extraction. "Zaphenath-paneah" may mean "abundance of life" (K. W.), although the consonants are usually construed to mean, "the god speaks and he lives" (B D B and K. W.) — not in a monotheistic sense. "Asenath" appears to mean "the one belonging to Neith" (a goddess of the Egyptians). "Potiphera" is said to mean: "he whom Ra (the sun god) gave." The city "On" was the well-known center of worship of the sun god, Ra. Of course, the Potiphar of chapter 39 is quite distinct from this Potiphera. In any case, much as the Egyptians may have felt

an aversion to foreigners, yet to be introduced to one under such auspicious circumstances, to one who besides has contracted so favorable a matrimonial alliance, ought to cancel all prejudice. Students of Egyptian history tell us besides of certain periods where even the reserved and superior Egyptians were possessed of a strange mania for foreign innovations and customs. The last statement is quite in place: "Joseph went forth throughout the land of Egypt" on an initial tour of inspection. Only by securing adequate firsthand information would Joseph be able to estimate rightly the problems involved in his gigantic task. Alterations of the text like: "His fame spread throughout the land of Egypt" (Meek) are without warrant.

46-49. Joseph was a man of thirty years when he entered the service of Pharaoh, king of Egypt. So Joseph went out from Pharaoh's presence and traversed the whole land of Egypt. During the seven years of plenty the land produced bumper crops. And he gathered all the food of the seven years which came in the land of Egypt, and put this food into cities, and he put into each city the food from the fields round about. And Joseph heaped up grain like the sand of the sea, exceedingly much, until men left off counting; they could not keep count of it.

At such an important juncture in Joseph's life the reader naturally grows desirous of knowing just how old this food administrator was, and the writer meets this legitimate desire by telling him. Critics do not concede such flexibility of style and ascribe all such data to the fictitious P. However, if the picture is to be complete and the measure of favor that God grants is to be rightly evaluated, we practically need to know that these high honors and responsibilities were laid upon one so young — thirty years old.

The expression "stand before the face of," '*amadh liphney,* means to "serve one" or here "enter the service," not merely "to stand before," which here at least would be an empty designation. Nor does the next verse merely duplicate 45 b. The verb is different, '*abhar,* "traverse," and the territory covered is greater, "all the land of Egypt." So after Joseph's first trips of exploration and investigation there followed extensive journeys leaving no part of the land untouched.

47. What Joseph so confidently foretold actually happened: the land produced *liqmatsîm,* "with full hands," i. e., "bumper crops." The very practical plan was followed of gathering the abundance found round about the individual cities into these cities. The amount laid up in reserve must have seemed needlessly abundant. Ultimately those entrusted with keeping the records lost count of what reserves they actually had. Perhaps arithmetic had not advanced sufficiently to deal with such enormous totals.

50-52. **And two sons were born to Joseph before the year of famine came, sons whom Asenath, the daughter of Potiphera, priest of On, bore to him. And Joseph called the name of the first-born Manasseh, for God has caused me to forget all about my toil and my father's house. And the name of the second he called Ephraim, for God has made me fruitful in the land of my misery.**

The birth of Joseph's sons is set down as a matter of record as to how and when these two fathers of future tribes came into being, and also to give an indication how Joseph, the man of faith, viewed these tokens of divine favor. The name of the mother is again recorded so that we may take note how in an age of grievous irregularities Joseph remained faithful to the patriarchal standards of monogamous marriage, from which ideal only Abraham and Jacob had departed, and that under very unusual circumstances. *Menasseh*, as a verbal form, means "making to forget," as the explanatory word following also indicates (*nashshânî*, an unusual Piel form for *nishshânî*, G. K. 52 m). Though the statement is absolute: "Cod caused me to forget all about my toil and my father's house," there can be no doubt about it that Joseph means: the sting is gone out of the remembrance. "God" (*'Elohîm*) is said to have wrought this, for it is *'Elohîm* who is the mighty Ruler of the world and who disposes of the things in it according to His pleasure. *'Ephraim* means "double fruit" (K. W.). God had made his life "fruitful," i. e., exceedingly successful in a land where he had previously seen only "misery."

53-57. **And there came to an end the seven years of plenty which had been in the land of Egypt; and the seven years of famine began to come, just as Joseph had said, and there was a famine in all lands, but in all the land of Egypt there was bread. And when all the land of Egypt suffered hunger, the people cried out unto Pharaoh for bread, and Pharaoh said to all Egypt: Go to Joseph; all that he saith to you, do it. And the famine spread over the whole face of the land. So Joseph threw open all that was in it and started to sell grain to the Egyptians; and yet the famine was severe in the land of Egypt. And the whole earth came to Egypt to Joseph to buy grain, because the famine was so strong over the whole earth.**

Joseph's prediction was not only relatively true: things developed "just as he had said." The king and the nation must have relied implicitly on this infallible guide in these days. But the famine was of broader scope than merely to involve Egypt: "there was famine in all lands." Divine providence made these two famines to be coincident, the one in Egypt,

due to the failure of the annual inundation of the
Nile, the one thoughout Syria, due to lack of rain, no
doubt. For though here we read "in all lands" and
in v. 57 "over the whole earth," we hardly believe that
this is to be regarded literally. An intentional
hyperbole is used. The lands beyond Syria and the
Mediterranean litoral are hardly under consideration,
because distance forbade attempts to get grain from
Egypt on the part of those living in Mesopotamia and
beyond. Yet, on the other hand, we do not deny the
possibility of a world-wide famine at this time.

By way of explanation let this be said. The Nile
owes its regular overflow partly to the torrential rains
in Abyssinia, partly to the steady volume of water
maintained by the White Nile, which carries off the
melted snows from the high peaks of Central Africa.
Occasionally, however, the channel of the White Nile
grows choked with a sedge called *sud*. This takes
place in the marsh lands of the Sudan. As a result
the waters of the Nile lose themselves in these
marshes till the river has cleared a new channel. This
is usually regarded as the correct explanation for the
failure of the inundations of the Nile, which, by the
way, are not so very uncommon. Whitelaw records
a similar case; he says: " . . . . the most complete
parallel to Joseph's famine was that which occurred
in A. D. 1064-1071, in the reign of Fatimee Khaleefeh,
Eh Mustansir-b-rllâh, when the people ate corpses and
animals that died of themselves."

55. When the famine begins to be acute, the people naturally appeal to Pharaoh first. His confidence
in Joseph is so complete that he directs the people to
him and enjoins complete conformity to whatever plan
Joseph puts into operation. Either Pharaoh was weak
and recognized that Joseph had greater administrative
capacities than he himself did; or else Pharaoh was
discreet in recognizing superior capacity coupled with

a rare measure of providential guidance. Joseph, however, waited until the famine had spread "over the whole face of the land." Even the ample stores which he had gathered needed husbanding. When the need became imperative, "Joseph threw open (*yiphtach* = "open") all that was in it." *Bahem,* "in them," correctly refers to the plural "faces of" (*peney*) of the preceding clause. English demands the translation "in it." The text is not confused; neither is there "a slight discrepancy" between v. 54 and v. 55 (no lack of bread vs. they are famishing). The solution is immediately apparent: Joseph was controlling the surplus very strictly; consequently people had to suffer a bit of hunger so as not ultimately to die of hunger. For though the sale of grain had started, "yet the famine was severe in the land of Egypt."

57. Now the narrative definitely prepares the way for the following chapter, for when Jacob's sons come to Egypt for grain, they are merely one of many groups coming on the same mission.

It seems difficult to determine whether the famine of Joseph's day is mentioned in the monuments. Kyle, *The Deciding Voice of the Monuments,* p. 225 f., claims to have found the evidence. K. C. questions the validity of Kyle's conclusions.

The analysis of this chapter according to so-called sources offers no new problem and nothing substantial or constructive.

HOMILETICAL SUGGESTIONS

The chief difficulty confronting the preacher on a chapter such as this is its bulk. Clearly it would be improper to take anything less than what ends with v. 45 and still have a complete unit. Yet forty-five verses certainly comprise more of a text than any man could treat adequately. Yet since the facts of the story are well known on every hand and since the section beginning at v. 25 gives an adequate summary of the double dream, it would seem entirely satisfactory to take v. 25-45 as one piece and treat it under some such head as "The Exaltation of Joseph." Exaltation was the thing for which Joseph had been in process of preparation for the past twenty years. Yet two extremes should be avoided in the use of this text. Steer safely between the extravagant opinion which guarantees similar deliverance to all who are brought low, and, on the other hand, the attitude of unbelief which despondently says: I am brought so low that even God cannot raise me up. In the practical application God's power to do as much for any man, as He did for Joseph, should be stressed. Then v. 46-57 presents a good basis for treating the subject "Successfully Encountering Prosperity." For to cope with prosperity may be more difficult than to cope with poverty. Joseph (v. 51 and 52) recognized the mighty hand of God as being the only power that sustained him.

CHAPTER XLII

6. The First Journey of Joseph's Brethren to Egypt without Benjamin
(42:1-38)

First of all, at this point the Joseph story requires further development. The next logical step in this development is the contact between the exalted slave brother and the needy brethren who appear before him as humble and suspected petitioners. A broader point of view needs to be regarded here. Left to themselves, the sons of Jacob, yielding to the effect of sin, would have drifted apart and have lost all true unity as a family group. Joseph by his discriminating direction cancels the effects of incipient sin and leads the brothers to oneness of heart and purpose. In so doing, he prepares them so that they are found ready to go down into Egypt and there as *one group* to uphold the best traditions of their family. But for this reconstructed unity Jacob's family would have disintegrated in Egypt, would have lost its racial identity, and would have been absorbed by the Egyptians.

1-4. Now when Jacob saw that there was grain in Egypt, Jacob said to his sons: Why do ye look at one another? He further said: See, I have heard that there is grain in Egypt. Go down there and buy some for us there, that we may live and not die. So the brethren of Joseph went down — ten men — to buy grain in Egypt. But Benjamin, the brother of Joseph, Jacob did not send with his brethren, For, he said, lest harm befall him.

The scene seems to be laid in the time when news first reached Canaan that grain was being sold in

Egypt. The father and the sons apparently have not discussed this piece of news before. Besides, the entire family had arrived at the point where something had to be done about the famine. The father has noted the look of perplexity in his sons' faces. Each has been looking at the other (*ra'ah* in the *hithpael* = "to look questioningly one at the other") waiting for the other to suggest the next move. It seems rather an exaggeration to think that all regarded Egypt with a certain apprehension as the land to which Joseph had been sold and to which none now cared to go for that very reason. The general perplexity at facing this strange issue was all that their faces reflected. Occasional thoughts of the possible fate of Joseph will also have arisen in their minds.

2. *Wayyo'mer* must here mean: "he further said." Father Jacob is a man of decision of character. He knows how to act in different situations and holds his position as head of so large a household firmly in hand. Since men had begun to go down to Egypt to buy grain, that was the best course to follow. He commands his sons to take this trip and to make the necessary purchases. It really was already an issue of life and death, for he says, "that we may live and not die." *Shébher,* "grain," derives its meaning from the root *shabhar,* "to break," either as that which is broken or threshed, or as that which breaks out or sprouts. We may think it strange that Jacob did not venture to go to Egypt in time of famine as Abraham had (12:10). But in the first place, in Egypt itself the famine was strong; and then, the household of Jacob together with servants and cattle constituted so immense a group as to render such a journey in a measure impracticable.

3. The Hebrew word order might be rendered by our colloquial idiom: "the brethren of Joseph went down *ten men strong,*" for *'asarah,* "ten," is

in apposition to the subject, or it may be regarded as a predicate noun. It is a bit unusual to have the numeral appear without the article after a definite noun (K. S. 334 u). Here "grain" = *bar*, which according to its root means "clean," i. e., the clean grain after the chaff has been removed.

4. Benjamin is not allowed to go along with his brothers. Jacob does not necessarily harbor even a dim suspicion of what the other ten might do to his present favorite, Benjamin. He merely guards Benjamin with an apprehensiveness that has grown out of his loss of Joseph. Luther rightly indicates that such an attitude on Jacob's part is due to a lack of sufficient faith. But such weaknesses are everyday occurrences even in the lives of God's saints.

5, 6. **And the sons of Israel came to buy grain together with others that came; for the famine was in the land of Canaan. Now Joseph, he was the governor over the land, and he it was that sold grain to all the people of the land. Now the brethren of Joseph came and did obeisance before him with their faces to the ground.**

We are made aware of the fact that many were bound for Egypt on the same mission as Jacob's sons when we are told that these ten came "together with others that came." The Hebrew expression has it: "in the midst of the coming ones." There must have been a steady stream of purchasers coming from Canaan. For, as we are again reminded, "the famine was in the land of Canaan."

6. We are now told how Joseph's work at this time resulted in his coming into contact with his brethren. He acted in a double capacity, as the double *hu'* indicates (K. S. 340 e). He was both "governor" (*shallit* — or "vizier" or even "sultan"), in fact, "*the* governor," and also the one who "sold grain to all the people of the land." He personally managed the

sale of grain in every detail with such care that he
could well be said to have done all the selling himself. *Mashbir* = "causing to sell," a participle serving as the predicate (K. S. 409 a). Yet all this may
be construed to mean that he superintended all selling
and was at hand particularly to give personal attention to all extraordinary cases, especially those that
had to do with the sale of grain to foreigners. It
does not seem farfetched to us to suppose that Joseph
planned to be at hand when grain was disposed of
to men from Canaan in expectation of actually
encountering his brethren. So it actually came to
pass of a day that Joseph's brethren "came and did
obeisance before him with their faces to the ground."
"Did obeisance" is the same verb as that found 37:7.
"With their faces to the ground" is a modal accusative
(K. S. 402 h). Some trace Σάλατις, the name of the
first Hyksos king, (Josephus, *Cont. Ap.**) to *shallit*.
The connection is doubtful.

7-9. **And Joseph saw his brethren and
recognized them, but he acted as a stranger
toward them and spoke harshly with them, and said
to them: Where do you come from? And they
said: From the land of Canaan to buy food. Now
Joseph recognized his brethren, but they on their
part did not recognize him. And Joseph remembered the dreams which he had dreamed in reference to them, and he said to them: Spies ye are;
to see the nakedness of the land have ye come.**

So it was providentially ordered that Joseph was
actually present when his brethren stepped in. The
scene which he had actually visualized many times
before was now transpiring. Their could be little
difficulty about "recognizing" them. They were full

---

*Whiston's translation of the *Works of Flavius Josephus* —
(Hartford, 1916) p. 888.

grown men when Joseph had seen them last. In the years between twenty-five and fifty very radical changes in appearance seldom occur. They appeared in their native garb besides. Then there were just ten of them. By a strange play on words in the use of a different stem the Hebrew secures the meaning, "he acted as a stranger toward them" for "he recognized." So K. W., whereas B D B assumes two distinct roots. "He spoke harshly" in Hebrew = "he spoke hard things," *qashoth* — the feminine for the neuter (G. K. 122 q; K. S. 245 d). This harshness is not the outgrowth of a natural and almost justifiable anger. Nor do we "ascribe to Joseph an almost supernatural and superhuman sanctity" (Lange) if we assume that Joseph had his feelings and his purpose under full control from the very moment of meeting. For though vindictive anger would have been natural enough from one point of view, it is just as clear on the other hand that natural emotions of this sort had been purged out of Joseph by the fire of prison tribulation. Furthermore, now for a period of about fifteen years Joseph had enjoyed a position of unusual eminence at Pharaoh's court, a position to which he could hardly have advanced but for his brothers' treachery. Consequently, the perspective of divine providence will surely have helped Joseph long before this time to adjust himself in reference to his brethren and to map out a general plan of action. First and foremost in this plan will have been the purpose to redeem his brethren from their evil ways if they still stood in need of redemption, as was most likely the case. To forestall all possibility of recognition Joseph uses a harsh mode of address. The ancients had noted that the Egyptians were inclined to view all foreigners with suspicion. All who entered at the northeastern boundary were regarded as potential enemies. The first question grates harshly upon

their ears: "Where do you come from?" They
attempt to disarm suspicion by giving more information than was asked: they state what their homeland
is as well as what their purpose is: "From the land
of Canaan to buy food." Surely, theirs was a harmless purpose. Dozens of such purchasers were appearing daily.

8. Here another point is definitely settled. The
verse might well have been rendered: *"Though* Joseph
recognized his brethren, they on their part did not
recognize him." His side of the matter was discussed
above. Their side is this: Joseph may have altered
somewhat in appearance since the immaturity of his
seventeenth year. High position held for some time
puts a decided stamp upon a man's personality. Also
it would never have occurred to the brethren to look
for Joseph as the incumbent of such a position. Add
to that the disguise effected by the distinctive Egyptian
garb, which surely bore a stamp all its own. Then
consider the constrast between the bearded Israelite
and the clean-shaven Egyptian. Top all this off with
the harsh official tone of the foreign language and the
disguise is perfect.

9. The statement that "Joseph remembered the
dreams which he had dreamed in reference to them"
(*lahem* — dative of reference) indicates that as they
lay before him with their faces to the ground the
memory of his dreams came strongly upon him. The
guiding hand of Providence will have been very manifest to him at that remembrance. His seeming harshness therefore flows out of his higher purpose when
he says: "Spies ye are." Apparently, espionage of
nation upon nation was not so uncommon in those
early days, when the Asiatics and the Egyptians
already clashed rather frequently. "The nakedness
of the land" would be the *bare* or exposed places,
as our own idiom and that of many other languages

also represent the case. Furthermore, a very definite
suspicion had to seize upon Joseph from the very
moment he saw but *ten* brethren. Where was the
eleventh? It was easy enough to understand why the
father should have sent a big delegation of men —
they were to bring back as ample a store as possible.
Ten men could surely secure more than one or two.
But if ten, where was the eleventh? Benjamin might
have become the father's favorite after Joseph's dis-
appearance. Men who had not stopped short at what
was practically murder in the first instance might have
been less reluctant about disposing of the second
favorite. Besides, as Luther develops at length,
Joseph's dealings with his brethren were analogous
to those of God when he deals with sinners who are
to be led to repentance. Dods offers the key to the
situation in the words: "Joseph was, of course, well
aware that in the analysis of character the most potent
elements are only brought into clear view, when the
test of severe trouble is applied, and when men are
thrown out of all conventional modes of thinking and
speaking."

10-13. **But they said to him: No, my lord;
but thy servants have come to buy food. We all,
we are sons of one man; we are honest men; thy
servants have never been spies. But he said to
them: No; but the nakedness of the land, that
is what you have come to see. But they said: Thy
servants are twelve in number; we are brothers,
the sons of one man in the land of Canaan; and,
see, the youngest is with his father this day, and the
other is no more.**

All Jacob's sons can do is faithfully to reiterate
their story. One claim of theirs carries particular
weight — "we are sons of one man." There may have
been even a measure of physical resemblance to make
this claim more apparent. But if they had been sent

out as spies, no father would have sent practically
all his sons on so dangerous a mission. Or, to restate
the case, it was utterly improbable that ten brothers
should be traveling about as a group in order to spy
upon a foreign nation. Had Joseph not determined
to use the harshness commonly found in foreign officials who claim to have just grounds of suspicion, he
would have been compelled to admit the force of their
argument. Instead, he stubbornly holds to his original
contention: "the nakedness of the land, that is what
you have come to see" (so the Hebrew word order).
Now the brothers grow a bit more explicit. The circumstances demand a greater measure of detail. It
is rather an unsympathetic treatment of the case to
attribute this increase of detail to "the social clumsiness of the little fellow" (Procksch) who hopes to disarm suspicion by garrulous honesty. This is nothing
more than a natural attempt of honest men to tell
the whole truth and so to extricate themselves from
a difficult position. They reveal that there are really
twelve sons. The statement claiming that they are
"brothers, the sons of one man" implies that not all
have the same mother. Canaan is their fatherland,
though they will hardly have worn the distinctive
Canaanite dress. They also reveal the wherabouts of
the youngest (the adjective with the article = superlative, K. S. 309 b) — "with his father," and on the
question of "the other" their statement suddenly drifts
into a strange vagueness: "is no more." No doubt,
they actually believed that since nothing had been
heard of him these twenty years he must have perished.
Yet to Joseph this last statement reveals nothing about
their attitude of heart. True, here is not the place for
the confession of their great wrong. But the words
are quite unequivocal. But with men, who once revealed such readiness to resort to desperately cruel
means, it would have been wrong quickly to make a

few charitable assumptions. Perhaps even "the youngest is with his father this day" might not have been as harmless a statement as it seemed on the surface. Joseph did not dare take anything for granted. For the present the brothers must have a dose of their own medicine. As they once had refused to listen to a brother's plea, so now their pleas must be rudely rejected. The independent *lo'* (v. 10) = "No" (K. S. 352 f). Strack remarks that the briefer form for "we," *nachnû* (v. 11), occurs in but five more instances.

14-17. And Joseph said to them: It is just as I have been saying to you — Ye are spies. By this shall ye be put to the test, as surely as Pharaoh lives: You shall surely not go out from here except your youngest brother come here. Send one of your number and let him bring your brother, but as for you, ye shall be bound; and so your words shall be put to the test, whether ye are speaking the truth. If not, as surely as Pharaoh lives, ye are spies. So he confined them in prison three days.

Joseph's attitude has been well described by Skinner as "well-feigned official obstinacy." He keeps repeating after the manner of officers who put a man through the third degree, "ye are spies." First he makes the exorbitant demand that all except one must remain bound in Egypt until this one has gone home and brought the youngest along — a very unreasonable request. What would hinder this obstinate man from seizing the youngest brother also and thus hold all bound? Consequently, in any case, their hopes of freedom were slim. Yet it is quite true that the return of the messenger with the younger brother would constitute a fair test of the veracity of their claims. But even so, this unreasonable official might refuse to see the case from this angle.

The question is here raised whether Joseph did wrong in using the oath, "as surely as Pharaoh lives." Calvin cannot condone the oath. Luther finds nothing wrong about it. Apparently, a similar oath was in use in Israel at a later date, an oath by the life of the king, used in addressing the king: I Sam. 17:55; II Sam. 11:11. Heb. 6:16 countenances swearing "by the greater." Without a doubt, Joseph calculated to give his words as distinctive an Egyptian cast as possible. But as for himself, he will in the oath have remembered the Almighty and thus, though mentioning a ruler whom God acknowledged, he thought of the God that avenges false oaths. Joseph, however, does not swear that he will detain his brothers, as Luther construes the case; but that the brothers shall be put to the test. His second claim is hypothetically true: if a younger brother cannot be produced, then under the circumstances they would be spies. We are unable to depart in v. 16 from the original Jewish division of the verse and to take the "or not," *we'im lo'*, as belonging to the preceding clause. That would make Joseph use an insincere or idle oath: "as surely as Pharaoh lives, ye are spies," when he well knew they were not spies. The Jewish punctuation and our translation (also Luther, A. V., and A. R. V.) make the statement hypothetical and the oath permissible.

There was a very appropriate strategy as well as psychology about this imprisonment. The strategy involved what Dods has stated thus: "So new an experience to these free dwellers in tents as imprisonment under grim Egyptian guards worked wonders in them." The psychological reaction was bound to be a comparison between what their imprisoned brother must have suffered and what they are suffering now. The more or less dormant conscience was bound to awaken at this point. On *chey phar'oh* (v.

15) see G. K. 93 aa. The interrogative has *pathach* (v. 16) before a laryngeal (G. K. 100 m).

18-20. **And Joseph said to them on the third day: Do this and live — for I am a man wont to fear the Deity — if ye are honest men, one of your brothers may remain bound in your prison, but ye may go and carry home grain to meet the need of your households. But you must bring your youngest brother to me. So shall your words be proved reliable and ye shall not die. And they did so.**

Joseph cannot persuade himself to make his father's household suffer in working out this plan of the regeneration of his brethren. Three days are deemed sufficient to start their conscience working. At the same time Joseph needed at least so much time to think through his own course of procedure. In making his modified proposal to them — one stays; the rest go home — he represents himself as "a man wont to fear (present participle *yare'*) the Deity." Joseph naturally uses *'elohim* at this point, which, coming from the mouth of a man seemingly a Gentile, can mean no more than "Deity." In days of old it was already recognized that a proper relation to God brought about considerate treatment of men. The original fear of God, more or less a tradition among the nations of earliest antiquity, had not yet entirely died out in these days.

The injunction laid upon the brethren is made sufficiently serious by the reminder: if your youngest brother is brought, "ye shall not die." Their life is practically to be regarded as hanging in the balance. The summary statement "and they did so," includes what is developed in the verses following to v. 26. The expression *ra'abhon battêkhem* — literally: "the hunger of your homes," signifies: that which can remove the hunger from your homes, or "to meet the need of your households." See K. S. 336 e.

21-24. **And they said one to another: Verily, we are guilty in reference to our brother, because we saw the distress of his soul when he pleaded with us, and we would not listen. Therefore has this distress now come upon us. And Reuben answered them and said: Did I not say to you, Don't sin against the lad, and ye would not listen. And as far as his blood is concerned, behold, it is being required. And they knew not that Joseph heard, for there was an interpreter between them. And Joseph turned away from them and wept. Then he returned to them and spoke with them, and took one of their number, Simeon, and had him bound in their sight.**

Whatever they may have said in prison, now at least they speak in terms of their guilt in the matter of Joseph. Their conscience has awakened mightily during these three days. They feel that a just retribution has come upon them, and are apparently all of one mind in regard to the matter. They admit guilt, the "only acknowledgment of sin in the book of Genesis" (Inglis, quoted by Whitelaw). They find it to be just compensation — "because we saw the *distress* of his soul . . . and would not listen. Therefore has this *distress* now come upon us." Reuben comes to the forefront with a dire, "I told you so" — he gets some satisfaction from the fact that he had warned them, though he now makes his warning stronger than it then was (37:22). Now he rubs it in on himself as well as upon them that "his blood is being required" — *nidhrash* = "sought out." We should say: Satisfaction for his blood is being demanded. Nothing was farther from their thoughts in their self-accusations and recriminations than the thought that Joseph might understand. For Joseph had wisely throughout these proceedings availed himself of an interpreter, *melîts* — from *lûts* or *lîts*, "to mock," for speaking a strange language sounded like mockery. When Joseph "turned away" this seems to signify that he momentarily left the room, for later "he returned." Simeon is singled out to be held bound. It might have been Reuben, the first-born, but he had half acquitted himself by preventing more serious steps. Simeon seemed to stand in need of a special measure of corrective treatment. He was among the most cruel of the brethren; cf. 34:25; 49:5-7. To make the matter a bit more impressive Joseph lets Simeon be bound "in their sight."

25. And Joseph gave orders and they filled the receptacles with grain and they restored each man's money to his sack and gave them provisions for their journey. Thus was done for them.

At this point Joseph does what he normally longed to do for his family; he gave them ample stores of grain, restored their money, and furnished provisions for the journey. As far as his brothers were concerned, he well knew that this kindness would only cause consternation and perplexity, but that, he recognized, was good for them. *Yemal'û* has no dagesh forte in the "l"; cf. G. K. 20 m. *Bar* is accusative of material with verbs of filling and the like (G. K. 117 z). *Ya'as* is impersonal, therefore to be rendered as a passive (K. S. 324 d; G. K. 144 h).

26-28. Then they loaded their asses with their grain and departed. And a certain one opened his sack to give fodder to his ass at the lodgingplace, and he saw his money and, lo, it was in the mouth of his sack. And he said to his brother: My money has been restored to me, and, see, it is also in my sack! And their heart failed them, and in fear they turned one to another, saying: What is this that God has done to us?

The Egyptians give them the desired grain; the sons of Jacob must load it on their own beasts. At once they "departed," only too glad to get away so cheaply. How many days' journeys they had gone when the next episode occurred we are not told. Since they had "provisions for their journey," this would seem to imply also provender for their beasts. Consequently it may have been near the end of the return journey that some one of their number found it necessary to supplement what fodder he had been provided with in "the lodgingplace," i. e., the caravansary used for such journeys, an empty shelter by the roadside built to accomodate caravans. The article is used with *malôn,* signifying the particular one where all this happened. This individual to his great surprise "saw his money," for it was not buried deep in the grain but laid on top so as to be discovered at once. Therefore the remark, "and, lo, it was in the mouth of the sack," is not "unnatural" because "self-evident" as K. C. strangely claims, at least for v. 28. For the same reason that appears for making the first statement in v. 27 applies also for v. 28 where the one tells his brother exactly where he found it. Here practically all critical commentators agree that the text must be charged with being guilty of an omission. For after v. 28 a they assume that what happened was that all opened their sacks and discovered their money. So the critics feel the scare they received is better motivated. How unnecessary an assumption! Let them visualize what happened. Apparently, they think that each brother had only one sack, and that all sacks were opened at the end of the first day. Both of these are very improbable assumptions. If such a journey was to be of any consequence, each man would secure quite a number of sacks. Just by chance one man opened a sack before he came home, and it happened to be the sack containing the money. The others would not have thought of the possibility of having the money restored to each

of them, not in the wildest flight of their fancy. But
with consciences so badly alarmed as theirs were, and
nerves as jittery, even one such sack seemed to spell
calamity. Mindful of God's just punishment, they feel
that somehow God had a hand in what was befall-
ing them. This was not superstition. The training
of their youth received at the hand of a godly father
was reasserting itself. "In fear they turned to one
another" reads in Hebrew: "they trembled a man
toward his brother" — a pregnant construction with
'el (K. S. 213 a). "Their heart failed them," according to the Hebrew idiom = "their heart went out."
Here especially critical ingenuity displays itself: it
finds it unthinkable that either E or J could be so
clever as to use both "sack" and "bag," i. e., *'amta'-
chath* and *saq*; and they invent the opening of all
bags at the lodgingplace in order to make J's account
differ materially from E's, who has the rest open
their bags after they arrive home. All unwarranted
devices that are unworthy of the scholars that make
them.

29-34. **And they came to Jacob, their father,
to the land of Canaan and they told him all that
had befallen them, saying: The man, the lord of
the land, spoke harshly to us, and treated us as
if we were spying upon the land. But we said to
him: We are honest men; we have never been
spies. Twelve in number we are, brothers, sons of
our father, the one is no more, and the youngest is
this day with his father in the land of Canaan. And
the man, the lord of the land, said to us: By this
I shall know whether ye are honest — leave one
of your brothers with me and take what meets the
need of your households and go; and ye shall bring
your youngest brother to me; so shall I know that
ye are not spies but are honest men; so shall I**

**give your brother back to you, and ye may go about
in the land.**

This report covers what the preceding verses
record. Joseph is designated as "the lord (*'adhoney*
— plural of potentiality) of the land." It is rather
significant that they omit to tell their father of the
disgrace of spending three days in prison. Neither
do they inform him that Simeon was left behind bound.
That, of course, he discovered for himself.

**35-38. And it came to pass when they emptied
their sacks that, behold, each man had the bundle
of his money in his sack; and when they saw the
bundles of their money, they as well as their father
grew afraid. And Jacob, their father, said to them:
Me have ye made childless — Joseph is no more;
Simeon is no more; and ye would take Benjamin
also? on me are all these things fallen. And Reuben
said to his father: You may slay my two sons if
I do not bring him back to you. Entrust him to
my care, and I will return him to you. But he said:
My son shall not go down with you; for his brother
is dead and he alone is left. Should a mishap befall him on the way which you go, ye shall bring
down my gray hair with sorrow to the afterworld.**

The first report of his sons was borne with relative equanimity by old father Jacob. But now an
added disturbance arises, which, because it seems so
utterly inexplicable, seems all the more dire a threat.
All the brethren discover their "bundles of money"
(*tseroroth kaspêhem* — a kind of double plural:
"bundles of money" — K. S. 267 b) in their sacks.
This puts them all on the defensive and requires an
explanation they cannot furnish and lays every man
of them open to serious charges. Now even the
father's sober courage fails him. He sees all his sons

in danger. He foresees the direst outcome. Though it is unreasonable grief and fear that speak, yet the father hits closer to the truth than he guessed when he charges his sons with being the ones who were making him childless. How the sons must have winced at the charge, wondering how much their father actually guessed! How their already sensitive conscience must have smarted still more! Jacob anticipates losing at least three sons: Joseph, Simeon, Benjamin.

37. Now Reuben seeks to make good at least his share of the original wrong by a rather extravagant offer, which has been described as bearing the marks rather "or a crude heroism than of any common sense" (Lange). Luther charges Reuben with speaking without rhyme or reason: *Also hat Ruben allen Verstand und gemeinen Witz oder Vernunft verloren.* *Tamîth* is permissive rather than imperative: "you may stay." But why should the murder of grandchildren compensate for the loss of a son? For the present the father's refusal is categorical (v. 38): "My son shall not go down with you." Here it appears how deeply and how long he had grieved over the loss of Joseph. The sons of the favorite wife had been unusually dear to Jacob. After a life that had been marked by many severe buffetings of adversity Jacob feels he simply could not endure another major blow. This would bring his "gray hair" (*sebhah* — by metonomy = him as an aged man) with sorrow to the afterworld, i. e., to Sheol. Now *She'ol* in earlier Hebrew literature is the common place of abode for *all* the departed and is, therefore, as vague as "afterworld" or "grave." It asserts nothing about the state of the departed who have gone there. Much later it becomes the term that describes the abode of the wicked. Much has been imputed to the term without good grounds. It involves no thought such as Procksch

injects into it when he says: "He that departs to the realm of the dead full of grief rests there in eternal shadowy grief," and cites as proof Job 14:22. What Job said in his most grievous temptation does not reflect the normal belief of the saints of old. Job spoke while under the shadow of doubt, and his word hardly counts as a dogmatic proof passage, *a sedes doctrinae.* Jacob, therefore expresses only this thought: My last days, should Benjamin die, will be steeped in great grief under the load of which I shall die — not a very cheerful prospect.

HOMILETICAL SUGGESTIONS

Though the entire chapter makes a long text, its interest is sustained and so will carry the preacher past that difficulty. Two approaches strike us as feasible. Either, one may think in terms of the brothers who thought they had executed the perfect crime. From this angle the word is fulfilled which says: "Be sure your sin will find you out" (Num. 32:23). Or else, one may think in terms of Joseph and his magnanimous conduct toward his brethren. Then the treatment will yield some such approach as that suggested by the word: "Recompense to no man evil for evil" (Rom. 12:17).

CHAPTER XLIII

7. The Second Journey to Egypt with Benjamin (43:1-34)

The work of God upon the hearts of Joseph's brethren is only begun. Joseph himself is the instrument of God and knows himself to be at work in such a capacity. So far the brothers are ready to use self-accusations; they admit that a just retribution befalls the sinner. They have not, however, consciously broken with their sin, nor has it actually been overcome. They have not yet become regenerate men. The last steps in this work of restoration come in this and in the following chapters.

1-5. But as far as the famine was concerned, it was severe in the land. And it came to pass when they had entirely eaten up the grain which they brought from Egypt, that their father said to them: Buy a bit of food for us again. But Judah said to him: The man strictly admonished us, saying, Ye shall not appear before me except your brother be with you. So if thou art sending our brother along with us, we shall go down and buy food for thee. But if thou art not sending him, we shall not go down. For the man said to us, Ye shall not appear before me except your brother be with you.

By putting the noun *hara'abh* first, the author turns attention back to the famine. Its effects were beginning to be felt heavily; *kabhedh* is a very emphatic "be heavy" or "severe." "When they had entirely eaten up" is our way of rendering the Hebrew idiom: "when they had finished to eat," where *killû* is the chief verb and *'ekhol* an infinitive, yet the chief verb

is best rendered by the adverb "entirely." The same
construction appears in "buy again," where "again"
is practically the chief verb "return" (G. K. 102 g;
K. S. 361 m). We have no means of knowing how
long it took till their grain was "entirely eaten up."
A few months would seem to be the limit even with
the utmost of stinting. The father's request speaks
of "a bit (*me'at*) of food," because Egypt was selling
only in very limited quantities, and, besides, in any
case, no matter what amount was secured, it was
only "a bit" in comparison with the enormity of the
need.

3. Judah functions as spokesman. That others
may have contributed their bit to the discussion is
not excluded. Several substantial reasons may be
advanced why Judah stands in the forefront. The
negative aspect of the case is this: Reuben had forfeited his pre-eminence by incest (35:22) ; Simeon was
incarcerated; Levi had displayed cruel bloodthirst-
iness (34:25). On the positive side several factors
put Judah in the forefront. He was relatively innocent of disposing of Joseph (37:26). Besides, he
seems to have grown in solidity of character since
his sin of incest, unwittingly committed (ch. 38).
For that matter, he seems to have had the makings
of a really strong and resolute character, ready to
act in an emergency, more than did the others. But
for all his firmness in dealing with the present situation he displays proper respect for his aged father
throughout. For even the summons, "Buy a bit of
food for us," contains an evasion. The father was
reluctant to face the issue (42:34, 38). He knew
that Benjamin had to go along. Yet he had vowed
that Benjamin must stay home. Now he tries to send
the rest without the youngest — a natural evasion,
such as we poor humans often resort to when an unpleasant situation is encountered. Judah had rightly

gathered from the tenor of Joseph's demand that he was not to be trifled with. He expressed this, "admonishing he admonished us" or "strictly admonished," the usual construction of reinforcing the verbal idea by the infinitive absolute *ha'edh he'idh*, literally "testifying he testified," from *'ûdh*. The stern Joseph is evasively referred to as "the man." "Ye shall not appear before me" runs thus in Hebrew: "Ye shall not see my face." The ultimatum has to be reckoned with: "If thou art sending our brother along (*meshalléach* — Piel), we shall go down; if not, we shall not go down." This makes the situation hard for the father, but no harder than it actually is. Judah is actually helping Jacob to make an inevitable decision.

6-10. **And Israel said: Why have ye dealt so ill with me as to tell the man that you had another brother? And they said: The man closely questioned us about our family, saying: Is your father still alive? Have you a brother? and so we told him the facts of the case. Could we know in any way that he would say: Bring your brother down? But Judah in particular said to Israel, his father: Let the lad go along with me, and let us be up and going, that we may keep alive and not die, both we, and thou, and our familes. I personally will go bond for him. Demand him at my hand. If I do not bring him back to thee and set him before thy face, I shall count as guilty before thee forever. For if we had not procrastinated so long, surely by this time we could have returned at least twice.**

The name Israel appears here for the first time since chapter 37. Critics claims that as an index of different sources, attributing the name to J. However, this results in a very arbitrary division, especially in chapter 45. The simplest explanation of the use of the two names Jacob and Israel seems to be: where Jacob is used the man is represented as characterized more by his older nature which overlooked his theocratic destiny; and when Israel is used the man is represented as actually acting in the consciousness of his higher calling. For "Jacob" this surely holds good in 43:29-38. The true "Israel" speaks in 43:1-13; also in 45:28. But before the news of Joseph revived him 45:25-27 he thought in terms of "Jacob." The complaint: "Why have ye dealt so ill with me as to tell the man?" is a bit fretful. Israel seems to feel that the family was unduly endangered by incautious remarks. In *lehaggidh* the *le* of relation or sphere (K. S. 402 z) is used.

7. Now several brothers take part in the conversation — *wayyo'merû*, "and *they* said." A comparison with 42:13 would suggest that they had volunteered the information given about their family. However, 44:19 confirms the correctness of this seventh verse. Consequently 42:13 is more in the nature of an inexact account such as all men frequently give before the issues are clearly defined. For, without a doubt, much more was said in the course of the conversation than the few words recorded, which in a summary way indicate the major points touched upon. What we have rendered very loosely, "the facts of the case," reads in Hebrew: "according to the measure (literally, mouth) of these things." Again the absolute infinitive figures in, "Could we know in any way?" for the Hebrew has: "knowing could we know?" — *nedha'* — from *yadha'* — being an imperfect used potentially: not "will we know?" but "could we know?" (K. S. 187; G. K. 107 t). "Questioned us closely" also involves an absolute infinitive.

8. We translate *wayyo'mer jehûdhah*, "Judah *in particular* said," because this verse stands in contrast with the preceding where they *all* spoke.

It is good to observe that here the Kal imperative is used (emphatic form) *shilchah*; above in v. 5 the Piel appeared, *meshalléach*. The Kal is the weaker stem and does not imply so much a sending away as a letting go: "Let the lad go along with me" — and so the statement leaves more room for the idea of a return (K. C.). Sturdy resolution speaks forth in the words, "let us be up and going" — literally: "let us arise and let us go." The reference to possible death is not ill-timed, for death by starvation must have claimed many victims in those days. We feel that "we, and those, and our families" really constitutes a climactic statement, especially since the *tappénû* is not "our families" but really "our little ones." But no doubt, since children constituted the major part of the families, the term is used by synecdoche for the whole group.

9. The initial *'anokhî* bears the emphasis, "I personally." In the strongest possible terms Judah pledges himself to do everything humanly possible to guarantee a safe return of the young man. For though in v. 8 he is called *na'ar*, "youth" or "lad," he must have been easily twenty-one years of age. But the other brothers are so much older that he seems young by contrast. The verb *'arabh* means to "go surety" or "bond" or "to pledge oneself." Again *chata'nî* is rather, "I shall count as guilty," than, "I shall sin." Judah's proposition is not so extravagant as Reuben's was 42:37, and so is calculated to awaken more confidence. Judah closes his strong plea with the practical observation: But for this unnecessary delay the trip could have been made twice over by this time. Delay increases the suffering and mends nothing.

11-14. **And Israel, their father, said to them: If that be the case, then do this: take of the choice fruits of the land in your receptacles and take a present down for the man, a little balm, and a** little honey, gum, laudanum, pistachio nuts and almonds; and take some more money along, and also the money that was restored in the opening of your sacks, take it back with you; perhaps there was some mistake. Then take your brother, start out and return to the man. And may God Almighty grant you to find favor before the man and restore to you your other brother and Benjamin. But as for me, as I was childless, so have I become childless again.

Throughout this entire discussion are heard frequent references to "the man" — the ominous individual whose name they scarcely dare mention. Judah has summarized the issues very correctly. By so doing he has helped Israel to see the whole situation in the proper light, so that he finally says: *'im ken,* i. e., "if so," namely: "if that be the case." The unavoidable must be met. But a bit of careful foresight is still in place. He who once sought to placate Esau's wrath by a gift (32:13 ff) now orders a gift prepared for "the man." At best the gift must have been meagre, "a little balm, a little honey." Yet when grains do not grow, a few other delicacies may still subsist meagrely. These are described as "the choice fruits of the land," *zimrath ha'arets,* a term that has been much discussed. For the word *zimrah* may mean "music" or "praise" and so the thing praised or "choice fruits." The majority of scholars seem to interpret the term thus, as did in a way the old Greek translators, who used καρποί, "fruits." It seems as though some of the gifts sent were not indigenous to Egypt, like pistachio nuts and almonds. Consequently some conclude that "honey" must refer not to bee honey, which is found in Egypt but to grape honey, boiled down from fresh grapejuice to the consistency of syrup, a product of which Delitzsch reported that 300 camels' burden of it still was being exported annually to Egypt from Hebron in his day. "Balm," "gum" and "laudanum" were discussed 37:25. Besides, they were to take "more money" along. *Késeph mishneh* may mean "double money." But since the original money is mentioned besides, it seems to mean only "other money" (so K. W., *sub mishneh*). We simply say "more money." The manner of referring to "the money that was restored" indicates that it has been kept intact in its original bundles, a kind of unlucky coin which no one cared to use. The simplest explanation to be devised for the present is: "perhaps there was some mistake."

13. The word order puts "brother" first with an emphasis of about this sort: "And as far as your brother is concerned, take him." Seeing clearly that Benjamin must go, Jacob reaches a quick decision and settles the case that was so long pending. Of course, *qumû* means "arise," but usually its implication is to address one's self to a task. We therefore translate: "Start out."

14. "God Almighty" (*'el shadday*), Who was the covenant God of Abraham, is besought to afford the protection that human agencies cannot give. Note the faith of the man Jacob. He certainly tried to exhaust every human expedient before he exposed Benjamin to the dangers of the journey. Then he committed the issues into God's hand. Nor has he a limited and an unworthy conception of God. The term employed suggests the unlimited power of God. Nor is his God a local, tribal deity; He has power to control the hearts of men anywhere, and if it so please the Almighty, He will make the hearts of the unfriendly to be favorably disposed to God's people and will induce them to cancel their harsh deeds. Jacob's words at this point are not a timid wish but a powerful benediction spoken in faith. The adjective "other" after "brother" is without the article after a definite noun — a construction

often used with numerals after a definite noun (K. S. 334 w).

Israel's benediction and the spirit in which it was spoken indicate the character of the words that follow. They are not a weak complaint but a word of grief spoken in the spirit of faith. The King James Version makes it too much a word of resignation: "If I be bereaved of my children, I am bereaved." Besides, "be bereaved" would require an imperfect rather than the perfect *shakhólti*. Luther's translation makes it too much a word of bitter complaint: *Ich aber muss sein wie einer, der seiner Kinder gar beraubet ist*: "I must be as one who is spoiled of all his children." This rendering, too, clashes with the perfect. As a matter of fact, the perfect suggests: "As I was childless, so have I become childless again" — the second perfect *shakhálti* being a perfect of result, *perfectum resultativum* (K. S. 127 a). The thought is: not so many years ago I was a childless man, now I have practically again become such a one. The extreme hyperbole of grief expresses thus the thought: I am rapidly losing my children one after another. Extreme as the utterance is, being coupled with faith, it means: if it so please God, so let it be. Similar thoughts are similarly expressed in Esther 4:16 and II Kings 7:4.

15-17. And the men took such a gift, and twice as much money did they take along with them, and Benjamin. Then they started out and went down to Egypt and stood in Joseph's presence. And Joseph saw Benjamin with them and he said to the man who was over his house: Bring the men down to the house, slay a beast and prepare it; for the men are to eat with me at noon. And the man did as Joseph had said, and the man brought these men to Joseph's house.

The narrative moves along in the stately lapidary style of the Scriptures. Three things are taken along:

"this gift" (*hamminchah hazzo'th*) or as we should
say: "such a gift." Then "twice as much money" —
literally: "the double in respect to money" (*késeph*
being an accusative of specification). The verb "take"
is repeated for this second object to make this item
stand out prominently. Thirdly, since the father's
permission had been secured, they took Benjamin. We
see the apprehensive group get under way and "go
down" to the lower lying country of Egypt. And there
we meet them in the presence of the man who had
engaged their waking thoughts for the past months.
Apprehensiveness is written in every man's face.

16. A multitude of issues are settled for Joseph
the moment he sees Benjamin. The brothers have not
ventured to do anything to his younger brother like
what they did to him. Besides, all that the brothers
had said on this matter bore the stamp of veracity.
The time for Joseph to rejoice, at least over this fact,
is at hand. Without a moment's hesitation and glad
beyond measure to see his only maternal brother in the
flesh, Joseph gives orders "to the man who was over
his house." i. e., his stewart, to "bring these men down
to the house, slay a beast and prepare it." Joseph's
explanation is: "The men are to eat with me at
noon." A great man such as Joseph is does not stand
under obligation to his subordinates to account for the
seemingly unusual things that he does. For one in
Joseph's exalted position to select a group of foreigners
for such an honor for no apparent reason must have
seemed passing strange. The respect Joseph enjoyed
is displayed most significantly in his servant's attitude:
He "did as Joseph had said," and "the man brought
these men (both nouns repeated, instead of pronouns,
used to make the contrast the stronger: Joseph's
steward was a man of influential position) to Joseph's
house."

Here the question is usually discussed about
Joseph's eating meat, though he lived like a typical
Egyptian. The assumption usually is that since so
many animals were sacred in Egypt, the natives ate
no meat. It is known from Herodotus that Egyptians
so abhorred things foreign, that priests, at least, ate
and drank nothing that was imported, nor would they
use utensils for eating that had been used by Greeks.
Wilkinson, quoted by Whitelaw, informs us that "beef
and goose constituted the principal part of the animal
food throughout Egypt"; also that the monuments
indicate that "a considerable quantity of meat was
served up at those repasts to which strangers were
invited." So we need not fear that any inaccuracy
lurks in the command to "slay a beast." "Noon"
(*tsohoráyim*) is a dual because it marks the point
where the day divides itself into two halves, the noon
really extending into both.

18-22. **And the men were afraid because they
were brought to Joseph's house and they said: It
is because of the matter of the money that came
back to our sacks the first time that we are being
brought, that one may roll himself upon us and
cast himself upon us and take us for slaves and
our asses. And they approached the man who was
over Joseph's house and they spoke with him at
the door of the house, saying: Oh please, dear
sir, we merely came down the first time to purchase
grain. And it happened when we came to the lodgingplace and opened our sacks, that, lo, each man's
money was found in the mouth of his sack, our
money in full weight; and we brought it back with
us. And other money have we brought down with
us to buy food. We do not know who placed our
money in our sacks.**

It has been rightly remarked that Joseph first
confused his brethren by his severity, then by his

gracious invitation (Procksch). Who could interpret
such a complete reversal of attitude? Naturally the
men construe the invitation to be something in the
nature of a judicial summons and tie it up in their
thoughts with the returned money. As vaguely as
possible they speak of it as the money "that came back
to our sacks." For *shabh,* the participle, is to be construed actively, "came back," not "was returned" (A.
V., also K. S. 97). This vague expression, without
necessarily involving superstitious notions, indicates
their perplexity; they feel there is something mysterious about it all — but also something ominous.
This will furnish occasion for "one (Joseph is implied)
to roll himself upon" them and "to cast himself upon"
them, expressions indicative of their apprehension of
being overwhelmed by a calamity which is in the last
analysis "that man." Since a provision of the Mosaic
law (Exod. 22:3) provides that thieves be sold as
bondmen, it is quite likely that such a provision prevailed at an earlier date; and this led the brothers to
conclude that they would be impounded as "slaves,"
and also their "asses," they add with a mournful pes-
simism that visualizes the worst.

19. Before they ever get into the house, which
appears to them as a trap, they approach the steward
"at the door (adverbial accusative — *péthach hab-
báyith*) of the house." They plead their case very
humbly: "oh please, dear sir" — *'adhonî* — "my lord"
in the sense of our "dear sir." "Coming down we
came down," *yarodh yarádhnû,* here gives a meaning like "we merely came down" or "indeed we came
down." Here they condense the narrative without
anything remotely like falsification, for when they
claim that they opened their sacks at the lodgingplace, they mean only that their sacks were not opened
until they were too far removed from Egypt to return
and to restore the money. "Sacks" is a categorical

plural. It is to be observed in their report of things, whether made at home or before Egyptians, that these men are always strictly honest, a thing that certainly turned out very decidedly in their favor. "Our money in full weight" is really our money "according to its weight" (*bemishqalô*). This suggests that in these early days before the coinage of money "silver" (*késeph* — usually translated "money" because silver was the metal most used for such purposes) was weighed and apparently circulated as small bits, rings, bars and the like. The brothers express their readiness to restore this mysterious money as well as to pay for what they purpose to buy afresh, and they rightly say they cannot tell "who placed the money" in their sacks. Joseph's steward, no doubt informed as to that part of the situation, could check on the correctness of this last statement. *Wanniphtechah* (v. 21) is one of those rarer forms where an imperfect with *waw* conversive has an "*ah* hortative" (*yaktul gravatum*, K. S. 200), which ending has completely lost its force.

23-25. **And he said: Be at ease; do not be afraid; your and your father's God has given you a treasure in your sacks; your money came into my hands. Then he brought Simeon out to them. And the man brought these men into Joseph's house; and he gave them water to wash their feet; and he gave them fodder for their asses. And they prepared the gift against Joseph's coming at noon; for they had heard that they were to have their meal there.**

The double mention of the steward's bringing these men to Joseph's house found in 17 b and 24 a is not an indication of how two literary sources merged, as even Koenig unnecessarily concedes. A fine point of realism is lost by such an interpretation. It is far more to the point to construe the statement of v. 17 as marking the beginning of the steward's work along this line: he begins to escort the strangers towards his master's house. But they make a definite halt at the door, and only after their problem has been adjusted can the steward lead the men indoors: "he brought these men in." Such obvious and natural interpretations escape the critics because of their confusing source analysis.

"Be at ease" (the Hebrew, "Peace be with you") is a good rendering of Meek's. It shows that this expression sometimes has no deeper implications. Here it might actually be rendered: "Everything is all right." The steward has perhaps copied the more godly forms of speech of his master, or else he has caught his master's piety when he ascribes the return of the money to God. The Hebrew expression does not allow for a polytheistic interpretation of the expression "your God and the God of your father" (A. V.). Therefore we have translated, "your and your father's God." The Hebrew does not like to extend the construct relationship over a succession of nouns as K. S. 276 a explains; but rather prefers to repeat the first noun, viz., "the God of you and the God of your father." The steward calls the money a "treasure," i. e., "a buried thing." This answer or reassurance is given to the brothers outside the door. Further to increase their confidence Simeon is restored to them. Then they are led indoors and treated as honored guests, being provided with water for the washing of their feet. In fact, even their asses are provided with fodder. Then they make ready their gift, which their father had suggested, "against Joseph's coming at noon." For by this time it has come to their ears that they were "to have their meal there" — Hebrew idiom: "eat bread there." It seems the Egyptian custom was to have the more substantial meal at noon; the Hebrew custom, at evening.

26-31. **Then Joseph came home, and they
presented to him the gift which was in their
hand, bringing it into the house, and they bowed
down before him to the ground.** And he inquired
after their well-being, and he said: Is your father
well? the old man of whom ye told me; is he yet
alive? And they said: Thy servant, our father,
is well; he is yet alive. And they did obeisance
and bowed down. And he raised his eyes and saw
Benjamin, his brother, the son of his mother, and
he said: Is this your youngest brother of whom ye
told me? And he said: God be gracious to thee,
my son. And Joseph hurriedly sought a place to
weep, for his feelings were stirred at the sight of
his brother; and he went into an inner room and
wept there. Then he washed his face and came
back and kept himself under control, and said:
Serve the meal.

Joseph, the busy food administrator, cannot be
home before noon. When he arrives, they present their
gift first. Nothing is said as to how Joseph received
it. Apparently, Joseph knew that he had to take care
to keep himself well in hand. To take too much note
even of so small a thing as this gift might have caused
him to lose his cool reserve. The expression in reference to the gift which was "in their hand" we have
translated previously where it occurred in the chapter
(v. 12 and v. 15) merely as "along" or "along with
them," for the idea certainly was not that the money
was to be carried all the way "in their hand" (*beyedh-
khem*). But here (v. 26) the expression could be
translated literally. The pregnant construction "to
the house" (*habbayethah*) means "bringing it into the
house." Again the dream of chapter 37 is manifestly
fulfilled as "they bowed down before him to the
ground," the customary gesture of oriental respect.
Joseph, no doubt, made his inquiries as casual as

possible. First he inquires after their own "well-being" — Hebrew: "peace," *shalôm*. So as not to make the inquiry concerning the father appear too pointed he adds, "the old man of whom ye told me." Deep attachment dictated the solicitude of the question, "is he well; is he yet alive?" The sons reply with the courteous idiom of their day, designating their father, as they do themselves, as Joseph's "servant"; and they acknowledge the courtesy of the inquiry by "doing obeisance" (*yiqqedhû* from *qadhad*) and by "bowing down" (*yishtachawû*) — a pair of words often appearing together.

29. The next step comes naturally. Next to his father, Benjamin is the object of Joseph's concern. The greater length at which the meeting with Benjamin is dwelt upon shows the importance of this meeting to Joseph; for Benjamin is in a stronger sense "his brother," for he is "the son of his mother." All this must have run strongly through Joseph's feelings at the sight of his brother, who was perhaps a year old when Joseph last saw him and now was a young man of twenty-two years. Joseph dare not admit that he really knows him, and so he inquires as a stranger might. Throughout the interview thus far Joseph has very correctly played the part of the high-standing Egyptian lord: he has not troubled to acknowledge their gift; now he does not wait for an answer to his question. But his deeper feelings at this point break into utterance in the brief but touching: "God be gracious to thee, my son." "Son" is quite permissible because of the prominent difference in age. Besides, it is a part of Joseph's disguise. *Yechonkha,* imperfect optative from *chanan,* the "o" having receded into the first syllable before the suffix. Till now Joseph's self-control has been admirable. We do not at all wonder that he now "hurriedly (*yema(h)her* — translated as an adverb, being auxiliary to 'sought') sought a

place to weep." *Nikhmerû* literally means "to grow warm," here "were stirred." The final *shammah* apparently gets its "*ah* locative" by attraction to the *ah* of *hachchadhrah* (K. S. 330 h). The interruption dare not be long if Joseph is to play his role successfully. He washes his face, indicating that he must have wept rather freely, returns, keeps himself under control, and bids the meal be served — Hebrew: "set on bread." The *dagesh* in *'aleph* of *yabhî'û* (v. 26) marks the *'aleph* as not having lost its natural Hebrew character of a smooth breathing and as not having become like double "y" between two vowels as is the case in the Aramaic.

32-34. **And they served him alone and them alone, and the Egyptians eating with him alone; for the Egyptians cannot eat a meal together with Hebrews; for that would be an abomination to the Egyptians. And they were seated before him according to age, the eldest first, the youngest last; and the men looked at one another in astonishment. And he provided portions for them from his own table, and Benjamin's portion was five times as great as the portion of all the rest of them. So they feasted and drank freely with him.**

The exclusiveness of the Egyptians over against foreigners is well known, especially the exclusiveness of the priests. It would hardly have done for Joseph to incur Egyptian displeasure by flagrant disregard of custom. So everything proceeds in approved fashion. He, who belongs to the priestly cast, is served alone. So are his brothers. So are his Egyptian guests. All caste distinctions are thus faithfully upheld. Egyptians regarded eating together with foreigners as *tô'ebhah*, "an abomination" — (Meek good: "abhorrent"). Here Joseph again introduces a touch of mystery which, as Keil says, "necessarily impressed them with the idea that this great man had been supernaturally enlightened as to their family affairs." How could they think otherwise? They had never revealed a thing about the matter to anyone in Egypt, and here they sit, accurately arranged according to age. They cannot but "look at one another in astonishment" — Hebrew: "they were astonished, a man toward his fellow" — pregnant construction of *'el*. The phrase *lephanay* can hardly mean "according to his judgment," as K. C. strangely translates. They actually sat before Joseph — "before him" — so that he could in a measure feast his eyes upon them, but perhaps primarily for the purpose of keeping their unusual Egyptian patron distinctly before their eyes.

34. Now Joseph does something that provides a further test of the brethren. He purposely shows preference for Benjamin. Had the same feeling prevailed over against Benjamin that had once animated them over against Joseph, such preference would have stirred resentment that could hardly have been kept under cover. But they meet the test successfully. Even when the more generous use of wine has removed the restraint from their tongues, the men still ring true. The distinction conferred on Benjamin was "portions" of honor from Joseph's table, five "portions" to the one received by every other brother. *Mas'ah* is a noun derived from the root *nasa'*, "to lift up," by prefixing an "m." Such gifts, not required to be eaten but to be regarded as honorary distinctions, have their parallels in antiquity, as Dillmann shows, quoting Knobel. Spartan kings always received a double portion; Cretan archons a quadruple portion. However, among the Egyptians five was a number enjoying a special distinction. *Shakhar*, the last verb, sometimes means to become drunk, but apparently the milder meaning prevails here: they "drank freely."

The chapter is assigned by critics to J with the possible exception of about v. 12-15, or 16 and 23 b. But the arbitrary distinctions made offer no new problem here and have been answered by us above.

HOMILETICAL SUGGESTIONS

There is hardly any danger that this chapter will ever fall into neglect in the Church, for all children hear the substance of it and readily remember it. As a whole or in its various parts the chapter is so intimately bound up with the unravelling of the knot of the plot of the Joseph story that there is very little about it that suggests itself for use as a sermon text. Every part is so clear in itself that, should any man take a portion of the chapter as a text, he should have no difficulty about the treatment of it.

CHAPTER XLIV

8. The Test Successfully Met by Joseph's Brethren
(Chapter 44)

The approach that Luther makes to this chapter is worth noting. He asks why it should have pleased the Holy Ghost to write down things seemingly so trivial; for the individual steps in the development of this sacred drama are, indeed, recorded very minutely. He answers that this was done in order that men might learn to perform faithfully the duty assigned them. Joseph displays a fine attitude toward his duty and his calling when he performs all parts of it in a conscientious way. Such works done in the way of one's calling are right and pleasing to God.

Aside from that, Joseph's brethren have not yet been tested to the fullest extent nor led to the point where they have an opportunity to retrace their steps and to make good their shameful treatment of Joseph. To this point Joseph guides them, being himself directed by God's Holy Spirit to display a wisdom and an unselfishness which call forth our highest admiration.

1-3. **And he gave commandment to the man who was over his household, saying: Fill the sacks of the men with as much food as they will be able to carry away, and place each man's money in the mouth of his sack. And place my cup, the silver cup, in the mouth of the sack of the youngest as well as the money for his grain. And he did according to the orders that Joseph gave. Morning came and the men were dismissed with their asses.**

Joseph's steward co-operated perfectly with his master in a very discreet way. But behind this discretion and the very practical wisdom of Joseph one involuntarily feels the guiding hand of the good Lord, who gave success to a plan that might have miscarried in a number of ways.

The steward's orders were to give the men all the grain their sacks would hold. This generosity would be noticed, and the elation of the brethren would be increased thereby. Again the money was to be laid in the mouth of the sack — *késeph* — "silver," again for "money," as in the preceding chapters. The purpose of this was to be what it had been in the first instance. This mysterious money preyed on the mind of the brethren and roused a sense of the presence of a higher hand in all these proceedings. Besides, as it roused a sense of involuntary guilt on the part of the brethren, we believe that Delitzsch is right when he claims that "the brethren forfeited the right to give up Benjamin because all had in their bags something incriminating." Yet we doubt whether that was felt or realized at the time, because not a word is said in the further course of the narrative about this second money in the bags. This money simply faded into the background because of the prominence of the fateful cup. This *gabhi'a'* was apparently a cup of special design, for it is mentioned in connection with the sevenbranched candlestick as being upon each branch. According to the root the term means something "convex" or "swelling." No doubt, a typically Egyptian cup is meant. This cup is to be placed in the mouth of the sack of the youngest, in order to create the impression that he had filched it, and so, of course, the brothers would be put to the test as to whether they were ready to abandon him to his fate. These orders from Joseph are carried out. A certain abruptness characterizes the style at this point, first, by the use

of the asyndeton: "morning came" or "became light"
(*'ôr*) ; then, by the use of successive perfects, also in
v. 4 (K. S. 119).

**4-9. They on their part went forth from the
city. They had not yet gone far when Joseph said
to the one who was over his house: Up, follow
after the men, and when thou hast overtaken them,
thou shalt say to them: Why have ye requited evil
for good? Is not this that out of which my master
drinks? in fact, he practices divination thereby. Ye
have done evil in so doing. And he overtook them
and spoke these very words? And they said to him:
Why does my lord say such things? Far be it from
thy servants to do anything like this. Look, silver
that we found in the mouth of our sacks we returned
to thee from the land of Canaan. How then could
we steal from thy lord's house, silver or gold? He
of thy servants with whom it might be found, both
he shall die, and we on our part shall be slaves to
my lord.**

It is not difficult to imagine with what cheerful
hearts and almost exultant behavior these men took
their departure ("go forth" with direct object in
the sense of "*leave* the city"). They had been treated
like royalty. The man whom they had dreaded to
encounter had proved a genial host. Their grain sacks
were well filled. Eagerly they recounted every detail
of their experience. In the meantime Joseph barely
allows them time to get beyond the city when he
instructs his steward to make haste lest the men by
discovering the cup themselves and returning it thwart
his purpose. The perfect tenses still continue the
impression of abrupt haste in the narrative. Much
depends on the very words used, therefore Joseph lays
the very statements to be made upon his steward's
lips. First comes the general accusation calculated to
arouse a measure of apprehension: "why have ye

requited evil for good?" an arresting question while the memory of the favors received was still remarkably fresh.

5. The vague "this" spoken as though all of the men must know that he referred to the stolen cup is a clever approach and very realistic. The steward makes it appear that this was in a very special sense Joseph's cup ("to drink" is construed with *be*, "in," because the lips touch the cup in drinking). Some translators, like the Greek Septuagint and the Vulgate, certainly missed the fine point of the steward's clever approach on the indefinite "this" without an antecedent, when they felt it necessary to prefix the explanatory remark: "Why have ye stolen the silver cup?" However, the steward's next remark causes us a measure of perplexity when he says: "in fact, he practices divination thereby." Practicing divination is a heathen custom. The type referred to here is cup-divination, called κυλικομαντεία by the ancients. As far as the practice as such is concerned, it is said to have been used in several forms. Some poured clear water into a bowl or a cup and then strewed into the water small pieces or particles of gold and of silver or even of precious stones. Some poured oil into the water. Still others observed the manner in which light rays broke on the surface. Usually the resulting designs to be observed in the water, whether from the particles thrown into it or from the oil, were construed after certain rules in order to draw conclusions as to the future. Surely, if Joseph had imitated these customs, he would have been guilty of heathenish and sinful practices. Or does he merely feign that he uses them? Such feigning would have been a form of deception both here and in v. 15. There still remains the possibility, as Vilmar points out, that it may actually have pleased God to use some such means in order to convey higher revelation to Joseph. In fact, we know too

little about the whole matter to pass judgment upon
it in one way or in another. The last charge to be
spoken is, "Ye have done evil in so doing," (literally:
"ye have done ill what ye did").

6. The steward does his part of the work successfully. He delievers his message correctly. A
strong protestation of innocence is the reaction on the
part of the brethren. Conscious of their innocence,
their reply bears all the earmarks of sincerity: strong
assertion of innocence coupled with a respectful attitude. They cite a very good illustration of a typical
attitude on their part. There was some "silver" involved here recently in a certain case ("silver" =
"money" — no article, a thing overlooked by the familiar versions; the absence of the article generalizes the
statement more). They had found this in their bags;
and though they had been in "the land of Canaan" and
so beyond the range of observation, they had brought
the silver back from a sense of obligation. Surely,
such men could not desire to take from the house of
the steward's lord "silver or gold." That is really a
forceful argument. The consciousness of their entire
innocence leads them to make an extravagant offer:
Should this cup be found in the possession of any,
that one shall die, and they as a body are ready to
return as slaves. The imperfect *nighnobh* here (v. 8)
acquires an optative or potential meaning: "how *could*
we steal?" (K. S. 187). The relative clause of v. 9
practically has a conditional meaning: "if it be found
with any of thy servants" (K. S. 390 e).

10-13. **And he said: Even though now this
is to be settled according to your words, yet only
he with whom it is found shall be my servant, whereas ye shall be innocent. So they made haste, every
man of them, and set their sacks on the ground,
and they opened every man his sack. And he made
the search — with the eldest he began, with the**

youngest he finished — and the cup was found in Benjamin's sack. And they rent their garments, and each man reloaded his ass, and they returned to the city.

The usual translations of v. 10 (A. V. and Luther) make the verse contain a contradiction: for first the steward says: "let it be according to your words," then he sets up terms radically different from those proposed by the brethren. Apparently, the difficulty can be settled as K. C. proposes by taking *gam*, "even," in a concessive sense: "Even though now this is to be settled according to your words" — the thought being implied: in a general way. Then the apodosis reads: "Yet only he with whom it is found shall be my servant, whereas ye will be innocent." The steward speaks thus, well knowing what the outcome of the search will be.

11. The brothers make haste to have the unpleasant interruption disposed of as soon as possible. The sacks are set on the ground ready for inspection. They are opened for the steward. The words, "with the eldest he began, with the youngest he finished," are best treated as parenthetical. We can hardly imagine the astonishment when they, practically sure of vindication, see the cup emerge from Benjamin's sack.

13. We are struck by the reaction of the brothers of Benjamin. They do not inquire of Benjamin; they do not remonstrate with him; they do not seem to think of the possibility of a piece of deception being practiced on them; they do not seem to think Benjamin guilty. They merely rend their garments, reload their asses, and return to the city. The mysteriousness of what happened in just singling out Benjamin seems to impress them all so strongly with the thought that a higher hand is at work, that they actually overlook a few obvious possibilities and reckon only in

terms of how their duty demands that they act in
reference to Benjamin and in reference to their father.
Dods lets his imagination run riot when he actually
conjures up the possibility that Benjamin may have
made boastful remarks beforehand of the things he
was going to do to show that he was not the child
they seemed to think he was; and so the brethren
at this point may actually have thought Benjamin
guilty of having done the bold thing of actually
taking Joseph's cup in order to make good his proud
boast.

14-17. **And Judah and his brethren came to
Joseph's house and he was still there, and they fell
down before him on the ground; and Joseph said
to them: What is this deed which ye have done?
Did ye not know that a man such as I am, is indeed
able to use divination? And Judah said: What
shall we say to my lord; what can we speak; how
can we justify ourselves? God has found the guilt
of thy servants. Behold, we are servants to my
master, both we and he with whom the cup was
found. But he said: Far be it from me to do
this. The man with whom the cup was found, he
shall be my servant. But as far as ye are concerned,
go up in peace to your father.**

Judah is mentioned separately, apparently because he at this point definitely took the whole situation in hand. The busy food administrator of Egypt
in this instance made all things else wait till he had
reached the conclusion of the unusual trial that was
pending: "he was still there." Again the brethren
prostrate themselves. For this was the necessary
token of courtesy for all who would approach a person of such a standing as Joseph had. Joseph first
heaps reproach on the brethren, because, surely, in
the light of yesterday's favor shown to them they

were apparently rank ingrates. Then he increases the
sense of higher powers at work in the case by referring to gifts of prognostication which were admittedly
his. He may actually, as our remarks on v. 5 indicate,
have been known in the past to have received revelation from on high. Perhaps he refers to the example
known throughout Egypt, how it was he that foretold
the event indicated by Pharaoh's dream. The abso-
solute infinitive makes the expression strong: "I
am *indeed* able to use divination" (*nach(ch)esh
yenach(ch)esh*).

16. The strong feeling of helplessness is reflected
in Judah's triple question: "What shall we say; what
can we speak; how can we justify ourselves?" — potential imperfects; in the last instance *mah* = "how."
Some here speak of the brethren as being aware of the
fact that an adverse fate had caught up with them. We
believe such a statement to be out of place. Joseph's
brethren knew better than to believe in a blind fate.
Their better instruction in the paternal home had
taught them concerning the true God. Into His hands
they now believed themselves to have fallen: "God
has found the guilt of thy servants." They do not
actually confess their wrong against Joseph here, but
that is what they all thought of at these words of
Judah. They felt that divine retribution had caught
up with them. Judah's next statement is the utterance
of a faithful heart. The idea of Benjamin's remaining
alone in Egypt simply could not enter the mind of
one of them. If one stays, they all must stay. A
good feeling of the solidarity of their group was here
recreated in all of them. But Joseph tries them to
the uttermost to give the deepest feelings of the heart
an opportunity to display themselves. He protests
strongly against the idea of keeping back all of them.
He even makes release seem delightful by practically

guaranteeing them all safe conduct: "go up in peace."
But Joseph's mention of their father made them all
the more keenly aware of their obligation to him.

18-24. **And Judah came up to him and said:
Please, lord, let thy servant speak a word in my
lord's hearing, and do not become angered at thy
servant. For thou art just as Pharaoh is. My lord
asked his servant, saying: Have you still a father
or a brother? And we said to my lord: Yes we
have a father, an old man, and a son of his old
age, a youth; and his brother is dead; and he alone
is left of his mother's children, and his father dearly
loves him. And thou didst say to thy servants:
Bring him down to me that I may set eyes on him.
And we said to my lord: The lad cannot leave his
father; his father would die if he should leave him.
And thou didst say to thy servants: If your
youngest brother does not come down along with
you, you cannot appear in my presence. And it
came to pass, as we went up to thy servant, my
father, we told him the words of my lord.**

This is one of the manliest, most straightforward
speeches ever delivered by any man. For depth of
feeling and sincerity of purpose it stands unexcelled.
What makes it most remarkable, however, is the fact
that it comes from the lips of one who once upon
a time was so calloused that he cared nothing about
the grief he had caused his father. The speech is well
ordered, being a historical presentation of the facts
of the case: how Joseph had learned of their brother
and had demanded his presence as a condition of
their appearing again before his face; how their
father had been apprised of the demand and had
grieved over letting the youngest depart; what the
effect of the non-appearance of Benjamin on the father
would be; and finally it contains a moving plea that
Judah might be permitted to stay in Egypt in his

brother's stead. It presents no particular exegetical difficulties. But a few things call for explanation. First of all, it is difficult to determine whether as Juhah stepped up to Joseph the others remained prostrate on the ground. It seems more likely to us that when he arose they also arose. Then, there is an honest compliment in the words, "for thou art just as Pharaoh is." It means: you have as great power as Pharaoh and must be respected as he is. It supplies the reason why Judah speaks so respectfully; K. C. makes the clause concessive, but without good reason.

In v. 20 "he alone is left of his mother's children" runs literally: "and he is left, he alone to his mother." Apparently the *le* before *'immô* is the *le* used as a substitute for the construct relationship (K. S. 280 c). In v. 22 the co-ordinated clause, "and he shall leave his father, then he would die," plainly necessitates rendering the first clause conditional, much as K. C. protests; cf. K. S. 369 s. Therefore we render, "his father would die, *if* he should leave him," patterning after Meek's good suggestion.

25-34. And our father said: Purchase a little food for us again. And we said: We cannot go down, unless our youngest brother be with us. Then we could go down; for we cannot see the face of the man, if our youngest brother be not with us. And thy servant, my father, said to us: Ye know that my wife bore me two sons, and the one went forth from my presence; all I could say was: surely he hath been rent by a wild beast, and I have not seen him to this day. If ye shall take this one too from me, and evil should befall him, ye should bring down my gray hairs with trouble to Sheol. And now, should I come to thy servant, my father, and the lad be not with me, seeing that his and his father's soul are closely knit together, it will happen that when he sees the lad is not there, he will

die; and thy servants shall bring down the gray hairs of their father with sorrow to Sheol. For thy servant went bond for the lad with my father, saying: If I do not bring him back to thee, I shall be guilty before my father forever. And now let thy servant stay in place of the lad as servant to my lord. And let the lad go up with his brethren. For how could I go up to my father and the lad be not with me? Oh that I might not be obliged to see the evil that would come upon my father!

Here, as in the previous portion of Judah's speech, we notice that the whole account must have been condensed quite a bit. The fact mentioned in v. 22 has not been recorded heretofore. Yet none of these facts is out of harmony with the original version. Now v. 27 and 28 appear as words of Jacob which were not previously reported as belonging in this connection.

In v. 28 "and I said, Surely, he is torn in pieces" (A. V.) is intended as a summary of the whole experience after he "went forth" from his father's presence. We sought to reproduce this purpose by rendering: "All I could say was, Surely, he hath been rent." Verse 30 presents a good statement of the case where two are bound together by a close love, "his and his father's soul are closely knit together" (*qeshûrah*). In v. 34 appears that particular use of *pen*, usually "lest," which introduces negative wishes, "Oh that not." A son that can say: "Oh that I might not be obliged to see the evil that would come upon my father," is a son who really cares for his father and is much concerned not to cause him grief. Judah was a transformed man. That is clearly displayed by his words. No doubt, the entire attitude of all the rest showed just as clearly that Judah was speaking the inmost thoughts of their heart. There could be no more doubt as to whether the brethren were minded toward their father and his most dearly beloved son as they once were. They were all transformed men.

HOMILETICAL SUGGESTIONS

We feel that our remarks concerning the use of the material of the preceding chapter as a text for a sermon apply also to this chapter.

CHAPTER XLV

9. Joseph Revealed to His Brethren; Summons the Family to Egypt (45:1-28)

The test planned and carried through by Joseph had now gone far enough and had proved entirely successful. The deepest feelings of the heart of these men had been laid bare. They were heartily sorry for what they had done to Joseph. In a similar situation they had not thought of dealing heartlessly with their father again. They had refused to take advantage of Benjamin when a very easy way of escape from evil had offered itself for them by abandoning him. They felt that divine justice was slowly but surely catching up with them for their betrayal of Joseph. One of them in particular, Judah, had given proof of heroic self-sacrifice to spare the father. There was no need of probing further. God had so effectually blessed Joseph's course with these brethren of his that manifestly the crowning touch could now be given to it all by Joseph's revelation of his own identity.

1-4. **But Joseph could no longer control himself before all those who stood round about him; so he called out: Have everyone go out from my presence. And so there was no one standing about when Joseph made himself known to his brethren. Joseph raised his voice so loudly in weeping, that the Egyptians heard it, and even the house of Pharaoh heard it. And Joseph said to his brethren: I am Joseph. Is my father still alive? But his brethren were not able to answer him, for they were terrified at the sight of him. But Joseph said to his**

brethren: Come nearer to me, and they came nearer. And he said: I am Joseph, your brother, whom ye sold into Egypt.

The whole scene as it now follows is a family matter. Our deeper emotions are not to be displayed before the general public. What is sacred to a family group may only be an object of curiosity or of amusement to those outside the group. Very wisely and properly Joseph bids all others leave the room. Then with only the twelve sons of the one father present in the one room comes the revelation. Joseph's overwrought emotions find relief in giving vent to loud weeping, the weeping of joy. It is specifically remarked that they who just had been dismissed, "the Egyptians," (Hebrew: "Egypt") heard him weep. They naturally carried the report to Pharaoh's house. So he heard of it. The simple statement, "I am Joseph," must have come like a thunderclap out of a clear sky on these unsuspecting men. It was spoken, besides, without the assistance of an interpreter and in their own native tongue. The question immediately following could be construed as incongruous and unnecessary. For their previous words had just referred to the father repeatedly as still living. However, upon second thought we discern that everything follows in natural sequence. Before he had asked as a stranger; now he asks as a brother, expecting such an account as one brother might give to another. Besides, as has been repeatedly pointed out, Joseph softens the harshness of the startling announcement, "I am Joseph," by an eager, friendly inquiry about the father. He wants to draw their thoughts away from the alarming disclosure he has just made. We can well understand the reaction of the brothers. Here they were completely in their brother's power, whom they knew for the most part as a harsh and rather cruel man. If the sense of

guilt was strong before, now it was overwhelming
and entirely alarming. "They were terrified" (*nibh-
halû* — "trembling" "dismayed") at the sight of him.
Perhaps, too, they now recognized a resemblance to
their brother's facial traits, mannerisms, bearing and
expressions characteristic of him. In horror, wonder
and dismay they naturally started back.

4. But Joseph's entire attitude was one of sincere friendliness. He invited them to "come nearer."
Perhaps more or less automatically they came nearer,
feeling that the man must be obeyed. Apprehension
still marked every countenance. Fear would not relax
its hold on them. Joseph had to win their confidence.
His next step serves to establish his identity fully,
if that were still necessary, when he mentions that
he is the one whom they sold. Lange very correctly
sees in this statement on Joseph's part a delicate
attempt to make their difficult confession for them,
so that for the present this very painful experience
does not need to come to the forefront any more.

5-8. **And now be not grieved, neither be angry
with yourselves that ye have sold me here; for it
was for the saving of life that God sent me on before you. For it is now two years that the famine
has been in the land, and there are yet five years
that there will be neither plowing nor reaping. But
God sent me on before you in order to set up for
you a remnant on earth and in order to keep alive
for you a great number of such who escape. And
now it was not ye that sent me here but God, and
He has appointed me a father to Pharaoh and lord
over all his household and ruler over all the land
of Egypt.**

A double reaction was liable to appear on the
part of Joseph's brethren. They that had contrived
the sale of their brother were liable to "grieve" unduly over the wrong they had done, and so might

embitter their own lives as well as those of the rest.
But they who were relatively innocent might be
"angry" (*'al yich(ch)ar* = "let it not burn" [in your
eyes], i. e., do not let anger rise within you as you
view this case). The summary statement of the
deeper purpose involved is, "it was for the saving
of life that God sent me on before you." *Michyah* =
"life," or "saving of life" — *Leben, Lebensunterhalt*
(K. W.). It should be noted that Joseph very appropriately ascribes these higher divine plans to
'Elohim, for He it is who as the mighty Ruler of
the world providentially controls the affairs of His
children. Here another reason becomes apparent
why these matters were not divulged before the ears
of the Egyptians. Egyptians would hardly have ap-
preciated the peculiar destiny of Israel. Joseph reminds his brethren that five more years like the last
two must be reckoned with. When he says, "there
will be neither plowing nor reaping," the statement
is meant relatively and not absolutely. Here and there
in the land a few may have attempted the one or the
other, but with little success.

7. The difficulties of this verse are largely removed if it be remembered that the "remnant"
(*she'erîth*) is Joseph himself. He was "set up" (*sîm*,
"put" or "place") as something left over, a remnant,
in order that the others might cluster around him.
In the second place, the *le* before *pelêtah* indicates
the direct object (K. S. 289 b). And lastly, *pelêtah*,
literally, "escape," here signifies "the number of such
who escape." The verse, therefore, means that Joseph
is the nucleus appointed by God, that the men of
Israel might rally around him, and so there will be
kept alive a great number of such who escape.

8. Now Joseph's explanation grows more pointed.
It was not really they who sent him here but God.
This is a strong way of asserting the fact of God's

overruling providence, stated so strongly for the comfort of his brothers. Here Joseph shows himself particularly wise in ministering to the souls of his brethren. If their sorrow does not learn to reckon with God, His mercy and His mighty providence, it will remain a mere earthly sorrow, which serves no particular purpose. To see God's purpose and judge from His point of view, that throws clear light on everything. Joseph has no overwrought notions about himself, but He clearly sees that his exalted position is arranged for Israel's advantage. His relation to Pharaoh is that of paternal advisor or "father" (*'abh*). His relation to the royal household is that of supreme controller or "lord," *'adhôn*. His relation to Egypt is that of "ruler over all the land." There is no boastful ring in what Joseph here asserts. Strangely, the monuments have titles for men as exalted as Joseph, titles which sound almost the same as *'abh* and *'adhôn* but have a meaning which is quite different. Joseph may intentionally have used these titles as a play on terms. In this verse we have *Ha-e'lohîm*, "the personal God," designated as the one who placed Joseph in the position he occupied. It hardly seems permissible to translate *beqérebh ha'árets*, v. 6, "in the midst of the world," as Strack suggests; such a thought is not motivated in this connection, even though in 46:16 and in Exod. 8:18 such a translation might prove admissible.

9-13. **Go up quickly to my father and say to him: Thus saith thy son Joseph: God hath appointed me lord of all Egypt; come down to me; delay not. And thou shalt dwell in the land of Goshen and thou shalt be near to me, thou, thy sons and thy grandchildren, and thy flocks and thy herds and all that belongs to thee. And I shall provide for thee there, for there are yet five years of famine, lest thou come to poverty, thou and thy sons and**

**all that belongs to thee. For, look, your eyes as
well as the eyes of my full brother Benjamin see
that it is my own mouth that is speaking to you.
And ye shall tell my father of all my renown in
Egypt and of all that ye have seen, and bring my
father down here quickly.**

A further means of setting his brothers' minds
at rest is for Joseph to disclose in detail his plans
for the future. He has just said that he has been
brought to Egypt providentially. What, then, does
he purpose to do? The resourceful Joseph, quick at
formulating effective plans, has everything arranged
for and tells his brothers exactly what is to be done.
They are to lose no time: "Go up quickly" (Hebrew:
"make haste and go up"). They are to inform their
father of Joseph's position of authority and that his
message is: "Come down to me; delay not." Joseph's
adequate plans have even selected the very place
where all are to settle — "the land of Goshen." This
land lies in northeastern Egypt. Here Jacob shall
be near Joseph, an added inducement for coming
down. It is believed that in these days the Egyptian
court was held in Zoan or Tanis, perhaps twenty
or twenty-five miles directly north of Goshen. Joseph's
plan further stipulates that a complete transmigration take place, involving the head of the family, his
children and grandchildren, flocks and herds and all
that belongs to him. He himself, Joseph, agrees to
provide for all these while they are there during
the five years of famine that still remain. Otherwise the family would "come to poverty" (*tiw-
waresh* = "be dispossessed," i. e., because of debt).
That this entire plan has been unfolded with the purpose of also setting the brothers' minds at ease,
appears from the next statement (v. 12): "Your
eyes . . . see that it is my own mouth that is
speaking to you." Joseph means: there can no

longer be any doubt as to my identity and my purpose;
the clearest proof that I am really your brother is
the fact that without an interpreter I with my own
mouth am talking with you in your native tongue;
Benjamin, whom the father will most readily believe,
sees these same tokens and will corroborate what
you say. *'Achî,* "my brother," must here mean "my
full brother."

Lastly Joseph enjoins upon his brethren to tell
their father of all his "renown" (*kabhôdh,* "glory,"
"honor," etc.) in Egypt. The purpose of this information is not to be self-glorification on Joseph's
part, for this is mentioned last and briefly, and certainly not in a vainglorious fashion. The purpose of
telling of Joseph's renown must then simply be to
convince the father that Joseph possesses sufficient
power to carry through all that he has agreed to do
for his family. Conclusion: "Bring my father down
here quickly," (*mahar* — Piel — again translated as
an adverb, though it is the chief verb in Hebrew;
cf. v. 9). In v. 12 the participle *hammedabber* is not
subject, as G. K. claims (126 k), but predicate (K.
S. 409 a). Strack, as others, concludes without warrant that, since v. 13 is practically the same in substance as v. 9, the former must be from J. Critical
intent on detecting parallel sources lets these critics
overlook such plain facts as that our own words often
offer repetitions. Here, however, both statements are
necessary to a well-rounded out statement for the
father: first he must be informed of Joseph's position
and plan (v. 9). Then, after the details of Joseph's
plan of providing for the family have been stated,
it is proper again to remind the father that Joseph's
position will enable him to achieve this plan.

**14, 15. And he fell upon his brother Benja-
min's neck and wept, and Benjamin wept on his**

neck. And he kissed all the brethren and wept over them. Afterwards his brethren talked with him.

The identification is complete; the first restraint has worn away; the revelation of Joseph's plans has quieted misgivings; now a more brotherly greeting is in place. But it still behooves Joseph to take the initiative. This he does, greeting Benjamin, his full brother, first and giving free vent to his emotions, though not so loudly as at first. The expression in reference to Benjamin seems to imply a measure of greater affection displayed in his case — they "wept on one another's neck" implies clinging to one another. The rest were "kissed" and "wept over" — all a truly oriental display of emotion. Then, finally, the barriers are down, and the brethren feel free to talk with him.

16-20. The report was heard at Pharaoh's court, Joseph's brethren have come, and it pleased Pharaoh well and his servants. And Pharaoh spoke with Joseph: Tell thy brethren: This is the thing to do: load your beasts; up, and go to the land of Canaan, and take your father and your households and come to me, and I will give you the good things of the land of Egypt and ye shall eat the fat of the land. And as for thee, thou art under orders — this do: Take wagons for yourself from the land of Egypt for your little ones and for your wives and bring your father and come. Do not bother about your utensils, for the good things of all the land of Egypt are to be yours.

So stirring an experience cannot remain hid. Its effect upon Pharaoh's court is particularly noteworthy. First of all, "the report" (*qôl* — not "sound" for v. 2 spoke of that) came through to "Pharaoh's court" (here *bêth par'oh,* i. e., "house of Pharaoh"), accu-

sative of place. Since Joseph was so universally
esteemed, all things connected with his fortunes were
a matter of interest to all. In this instance Pharaoh
might well be pleased, for a kind of stigma had been
attached to Joseph's origin; for he had been accounted
a slave. Now proof is offered that Joseph comes of
an honorable family of free nomads, who were generally held in high regard in those days. Joseph's
universal popularity is attested to by the fact that
Pharaoh's command coincides with Joseph's plan,
which he had just made known to his brethren — a
providential coincidence: They are now to load their
beasts, return to Canaan, get their father and their
households (Hebrew: "houses"), and come to Egypt.
He promises to give "the good things of the land
of Egypt." The word *tûbh* means "the good." Here
it hardly means "the best," for why should foreigners
get the best? Nor does it mean the "best part of
the land." as many since Rashi have contended. For
in v. 20 and in v. 23 where the expression recurs it
cannot refer to Goshen. So it means the good things
of the land, generally speaking, as Keil claims, and
so is a far broader expression than "the fat of the
land," which follows and expressly emphasizes the
food for the present time of famine.

19. It has been correctly observed (Lange) that
whereas the king allows Joseph much liberty in the
matter of disposing of the affairs of the realm, he
lays strict orders upon him in the matters concerning
his own welfare and says: "as for thee, thou art
under orders"(*tsuwwethah*, Pual). In fact, he shows
himself to be a man also accustomed to issuing
orders; for his commands are curt: "this do" — "take
wagons," etc. A strictly Egyptian touch is introduced
at this point, for "wagons" were found only in Egypt
in those days, though it is said that the *'aghalôth*
were originally introduced from Canaan and the

Semitic name was retained. They were two- or
fourwheeled carts without seats; they were not the
"chariots" heard of elsewhere (e. g., Exodus 14:6)
called *rékhebh*, or *merkabhah*. They merely served to
transport those who could neither walk nor ride.
Pharaoh's orders further bid the family: "Do not
bother about your utensils" — a peculiar Hebrew
idiom: "As for your eyes, do not pity your utensils"
— *keli*, vessels or tools of any sort. The matter was
urgent. Utensils would have encumbered or delayed
them, and so Joseph would have been caused added
anxiety. Pharaoh purposes to deal very liberally with
Joseph's family out of gratitude for the great deliverance Joseph wrought for Egypt. "The good things
of all the land of Egypt" will be at their disposal to
recompense them for what must be left behind.

21-25. **And the sons of Israel acted accordingly. Joseph gave them wagons, as Pharaoh had
ordered. He also gave them food for the journey.
To each separately he gave extra garments and to
Benjamin he gave three hundred skekels of silver
and five extra garments. And to his father he
accordingly sent ten asses laden with the good things
of Egypt, and ten she-asses laden with grain and
bread and provisions for his father for the journey.
And he sent his brethren and they went; and he
said to them: Do not grow angry on the way. And
they went up from Egypt and they came to the land
of Canaan to Jacob, their father.**

The writer begins with one of those summary
statements so common in Hebrew narrative, "and
the sons of Israel acted accordingly." The details
of what they did follows. Joseph gives them wagons
and food for the journey. Incidentally Joseph gives
further tokens of his goodwill: each man of them
separately receives "extra garments" — perhaps two
of them. The Hebrew calls them "changes of gar-

ments" — *chaliphoth semaloth* — the second noun being assimilated to the plural of the first. The thing
meant, of course, is a garment for special occasions.
Meek translates "festal garments," patterning after
Luther's *Feierkleider*. Benjamin, who stands nearest
to him, is given "three hundred shekels of silver" —
"shekels" being understood according to a common
Hebrew construction (G. K. 134 n; K. S. 314 h) — and
five "extra garments." As a gift of courtesy and a
token of esteem he sends his father "ten asses laden
with the good things of Egypt" — the good things
corresponding perhaps to the gift Jacob had sent.
Besides, Joseph sends what is of greater value under
the circumstances, "ten she-asses laden with grain
and bread and provisions for the journey."

24. But Joseph knows human nature. The
brethren scarcely dare to do a thing; they are so over-
awed by his authority and capacity for management.
Joseph sends them on their way. But he sees what
must necessarily develop on the way: "they are liable
to grow angry (not 'grow excited' — that is too
trivial) on the way." They will attempt to allocate
the share of guilt of each participant in the nefarious
sale. Each one will try to exculpate himself and
make the guilty ones appear more guilty. So fruitless anger and ill-will could result. Apparently they
gave heed to his admonition, for the journey is reported as uneventful: "they went up and came to the
land of Canaan to Jacob, their father."

26-28. **And they told him: Joseph is still living, and that he was ruler over all the land of Egypt.
But his heart grew numb, for he did not believe
them. But they spoke to him all the words of
Joseph which he had spoken to them, and he saw
the wagons which Joseph had sent to bring him.
Then the spirit of Jacob, their father, revived. And**

Israel said: Enough! Joseph my son is still alive; I will go down and see him before I die.

The substance of all their message is, of course, "Joseph is still living." This they tell first as they encounter their father. Next the very remarkable circumstance clamors for utterance that he is "ruler over all the land of Egypt." With the *kî* the report passes from direct to indirect discourse. But the two reports together seem so far beyond the pale of the possible that they serve to stupify the father: "his heart grew numb," (*pûgh*, "to grow cold"). The brothers can well understand the father's difficulty. They keep right on, as men who know first hand what they are reporting, and their reports all agree. They keep telling what Joseph had told them to arrange. Stupefaction gave way to understanding, and when Jacob finally saw the wagons, that distinctively Egyptian thing, sent besides by Joseph to transport the aged father to Egypt, then conviction grew on him and "his spirit revived." The old energy began to assert itself. The customary gloom of resignation vanished. Old "Jacob" again became "Israel," as the significant change of name indicates, an aggressive combatant in the battle of life, ready to overcome obstacles in the power of his God. He needs no more argument or proof — "enough!" he says, "Joseph my son is still alive." We should not venture to measure the deep joy reflected in this word. Jacob has now just this one ambition before he dies: to go down to Egypt and to see Joseph. The soberness of old age is not deeply impressed with the glories of Joseph's position in Egypt.

Here criticism has an objection to raise which may at least be noted. Gunkel (see K. C.) finds that the author ought at this point to have made mention of the brothers' repentance, supposing that they would naturally have made a full confession at this point. Procksch seconds him in this, claiming that our ethical feeling would demand that the brothers admit their wrong. Such subjective criticism has little value. In fact, do not these men see that the record as it stands is the more true to life? Joseph forgave them. The father learned from the account of his sons how Joseph had come to Egypt. The wound in the conscience of the brothers is too deep to call for much probing. This sore point is touched no more. Joseph knows of the sincerity of their repentance; so does their father. Least said, soonest mended, applies to such sorry cases when there is true repentance.

All of which reminds us that the whole narrative from the literary point of view displays the finest skill. It is a narrative pearl. The skillful portrayal of the psychological reaction of the different characters reveals the touch of a master hand.

But a few more things must be mentioned. As the fulfillment shows, there is a deeper typical import behind the things narrated. As the nation, which is designated as God's son (Exod. 4:22), here goes down to Egypt during the time of suffering as to a haven of refuge and is recalled thereafter, so God did for His only-begotten Son and called Him again after the danger had passed (cf. Matt. 2:15 and Hos. 11:1). So, as Vilmar points out, shall it be in the time of the last persecution, when a place of refuge shall be provided for the church according to Rev. 12:6.

Criticism, in its source analysis, is pretty much at sea despite its display of ingenuity. Skinner definitely asserts "the preponderance of E." Procksch assigns the major part to J and gives a rather generous portion to P besides. All this work is speculation that draws the thoughts of men from the truth revealed to uncertain externals.

HOMILETICAL SUGGESTIONS

The chapter is a unit as far as serving as a text is concerned. It centers on the theme of God's marvelous provisions for the maintenance of His Church. For, strictly speaking, the children of Israel, few as they are in number, constitute the Old Testament Church in its then state of development. Certainly one should guard against losing the broader viewpoints of a chapter such as this. Merely to think in terms of domestic scenes or along the line of personal ethics loses sight of the bigger issues.

CHAPTER XLVI

10. The Temporary Emigration of Israel to Egypt
(46:1-34)

A rather momentous step for this small nation to transfer its abode to another land! That it is momentous is indicated by the fact that the patriarch does not venture to take it until he has full divine sanction. Yet from the very outset it is borne in mind that God does not intend it to be a permanent settlement. All the promises since Abraham concerning the ultimate possession of Canaan by the Israelites still stand. God's people do not move blindly at such important junctures of their history.

The tendency that we have observed repeatedly before this, to summarize at critical turning points, (6:9, 10; 10:1-32; 11:27-32) displays itself here again. The heads of clans are mentioned, practically the same persons as those who went down to Egypt with Jacob. Such summaries serve to place very definitely before one's eyes just what the situation was at a given period.

At this point it may be desirable to examine the deeper providential motives that lay behind this momentous step of the migration to Egypt. The one manifest purpose that lay prominently on the surface was, of course, to preserve the nation, small as it was, during the time of famine. Deeper reflection reveals the following additional points that were apparently also involved in the divine plan.

First of all, a distinct and separate consciousness of being a nation by itself was begotten and nourished by being isolated in Egypt. For the Egyptian pride, which led that nation to disdain all foreigners, is well

(1104)

known. Israelites were, therefore, isolated geographically and nationally as long as they were in Egypt. Intermarriage with Israelites was out of the question. Consequently, there was no danger of Israel's amalgamating with the Egyptians as there had been of amalgamating with the Canaanites; cf. Judah's and Simeon's (v. 10) Canaanitish wives. In such an amalgamation Israel, the smaller group, would naturally have been absorbed. In Egypt such a misfortune was precluded. At the same time Israel was guarded against falling into the idolatry of its neighbors as a nation. For the strict isolation of the nation as long as it was in Egypt naturally extended also to matters of religion. Safeguarded thus against idolatry, Israel was at the same time outside of the reach of Canaanite immorality and its contaminations, a very real danger as chapter 38 shows. Yet during all this time of isolation from the culture of Canaan, which was of the first order, Israel was, nevertheless, in contact with another type of eminent culture, namely the Egyptian, and so was not in danger of cultural retrogression. For good culture could prove to be a very valuable asset also for the people of God during all the years of its development. At the same time faith and hope were nurtured by having the land of promise in prospect on the basis of clear promises of the God of their fathers. The persecutions in Egypt, however, served to make this hope of the possession of the promised land more fervent. (The above summary in general is based upon Hengstenberg's *Geschichte des Reiches Gottes,* with certain modifications; especially do we concede the high cultural level of Canaanite civilization of patriarchal days, as it is established by the researches of archaeology).

1-4. And Israel set out and all who belonged to him, and he came to Beersheba and sacrificed to

the God of his father Isaac. And God said to Israel in a night vision: Jacob, Jacob! And he said: Here am I. And He said: I am the true God (El), the God (Elohim) of thy father. Do not be afraid to go down to Egypt, for a great nation will I make thee there. I myself will go down with thee to Egypt, and I myself will most certainly bring thee up again; and Joseph shall close thy eyes (in death).

Jacob is very appropriately called "Israel" as he starts out; for, strictly speaking, it is not a personal but a national venture. Criticism does not see this simple fact, for according to its critical canons vv. 1-5 belong to E, but E always says "Jacob." Consequently the unscientific expedient is resorted to of attributing the presence of "Israel" in v. 1 to some Redactor, R. By such critical devices almost anything can be proved. So, then, the nation, small as it is, sets out, as is further indicated by the words, "and all who belonged to him." It seems that the point of departure was Hebron (37:14). The road to Egypt from Hebron runs directly over Beersheba. Here Jacob "sacrificed (Hebrew: 'sacrificed sacrifices') to the God of his father Isaac." This expression cannot mean that this God was a god different from other gods Jacob had worshipped; but it does strongly remind of the fact that at Beersheba Isaac had offered sacrifices to God 26:25; in fact (28:13), by this name God had designated Himself over against Jacob. The expression reminds of all the promises given to Isaac. The primary purpose of the sacrifice was to have it embody the petition for guidance and for protection on this journey. Other purposes will have entered in secondarily, such as gratitude for the impending deliverance; praise for the promises given to the nation; renewed consecration to the divine purpose respecting the nation. But raising the

question, Why were the sacrifices made here and
not in Hebron? we are inclined to view the case as
follows: Providential guidance had seemed so clear
when Joseph's message came to Hebron that Jacob
got under way for Egypt at once. At the southern
extremity of the land of promise the momentous character of such a step came home to him with greater
clearness. God had not yet spoken directly. Abraham's going to that land had led to his fall into sin
(12:10 ff). Isaac had been forbidden to go to Egypt
(26:2). The prophetic word, 15:13-16, must have
been in Jacob's thoughts. Yet the decisive step was
not to be taken without clear divine sanction.

2. The desired answer comes "in a night vision."
Hebrew: plural: "visions" *marôth* "of the night" —
the plural being indicative of the various steps of a
process (K. S. 261 c) or of the magnitude and the
glory of the experience. This was the last of the
patriarchal visions. It is given not to the individual
as such but to the one who is the father of the
nation, to "Israel." He is addressed by his old, personal name "Jacob," perhaps to remind him of what
he once was, or to indicate that as long as he doubts
and hesitates he is the old Jacob rather than the
new Israel. Criticism renders a hasty judgment when
it pronounces: this is "a sentence, which no original
writer would have penned." The repetition of the
name "Jacob" indicates a strength of divine interest
in the nation's welfare.

3. First God identifies Himself, recalling his
earlier promises by His manner of doing it. He
designates Himself first as *Ha'el,* i. e., "the true God,"
'el itself meaning "Strong One." With the article
it means: the one who especially deserves the name.
Very appropriately He is "the Strong One" here, because His ability to help and to protect is being considered. Then the more general title "God of thy

father," *'elohey 'abhî'kha,* reminds Jacob that God will deal as faithfully with him as He did with Isaac. Then the paramount issue is definitely decided: "Do not be afraid to go to Egypt." Jacob's fear must have been primarily a fear of acting contrary to the divine will, less a fear of the dangers otherwise to be encountered there. What Jacob and the nation need to know besides for their guidance during the time of their stay there is that in Egypt they will be made "a great nation." So that is revealed next. When K. C. declares the translation, "I am the true God, the God of thy father," to be wrong, he does this not on grammatical grounds but on dogmatic He simply does not believe that true monotheism prevailed at so early a date, whereas the true people of God never had any other faith than the monotheistic faith. *Redhah,* usually *rédheth,* is infinitive construct of *yaradh* (G. K. 69 m).

4.   The promise becomes more intimate and gracious. With emphasis God says that He Himself ("I" *'anokhî* — emphatic by position) will be the one that will go along down to Egypt, as well as the one that will bring Jacob back. By metonomy Jacob, the individual, refers to his descendants as a group. "I will bring thee up again" naturally refers to the return of the whole nation and not to the relatively trivial return of Israel's bones for burial. The emphasis of the divine statement shows that the biggest issues are involved. The absolute infinitive following the verb — Kal after Hifil (G. K. 113 w) — makes the promise as positive as possible. One purely personal touch is added when Jacob is assured that Joseph shall close his eyes — Hebrew: "he shall lay his hand upon thy eyes." Many nations of antiquity speak of this special last duty to the dead (cf. Dillmann).

5-7. **And Jacob set out from Beersheba, and the children of Israel transported Jacob, their**

father, and their little ones and their wives in the
wagons which Pharaoh had sent to transport him.
And they took their cattle and their possessions
which they had acquired in the land of Canaan and
they came to Egypt, Jacob and all his descendants
with him — his sons and his sons' sons with him,
his daughters and his sons' daughters, and all his
descendants — he brought them with him to Egypt.

Till now the interest has centered more on the
vision which God sent to confirm Jacob's purpose, less
on the transmigration as such, because that was still
in a sense problematical. After the vision Jacob
burns all his bridges behind him, and now the attention centers on the big train that travels to Egypt.
A unique feature in that train was found to be the
"wagons" Pharaoh had sent up. That is why they
are first mentioned here, although they had already
served to transport Jacob, the little ones, and the
wives from Hebron. Criticism sees in the appearance
of the wagons first in v. 5 a crude joining together
of the sources. Pharaoh's rather generous demand
to leave their "utensils" (A. V. "stuff") behind and
to be supplied by the rich Egyptian resources can hardly have involved leaving "the cattle" behind. Perhaps
the heards had already been much reduced during the
time of famine, and they were further reduced by the
rigors of the journey to Egypt. However, a true sense
of frugality induced Jacob's sons to take along all
"their possessions." Perhaps sound common sense
taught them to evaluate boastful royal munificence
somewhat lightly. More to the point is the consideration that as godly men Jacob's sons regarded their
possessions as good gifts of God, which they did not
dare to abandon rashly. With unusual fulness of expression, calculated to draw a clearer picture before
our eyes of this train that went down to Egypt, we
are told that "all his descendants" went with him,

and that these included "his sons and his sons' sons,
his daughters and his sons' daughters, and (here =
'namely') all his descendants." And we are again
reminded that in the last analysis this was an act for
which the old patriarch himself was responsible: "he
brought them with him to Egypt." *Miqnehem* is not
a plural noun, for the *y* represents *h* of *miqneh* (G. K.
93 ss).

**8-15. And these are the names of the children
of Israel that came down to Egypt — Jacob and his
sons: Reuben, Jacob's first-born. And the sons of
Reuben: Hanoch and Pallu and Hezron and Carmi.
And the sons of Simeon: Jemuel and Jamin and
Ohad and Jachin and Zohar and Shaul, the son of
the Canaanitish woman. And the sons of Levi:
Gershon, Kohath and Merari. And the sons of
Judah: Er and Onan and Shelah and Perez and
Zerah — now Er and Onan died in the land of
Canaan — and the sons of Perez: Hezron and
Hamul. And the sons of Issachar: Tola and Puvah
and Job and Shimron. And the sons of Zebulon:
Sered and Elon and Jahleel. These are the des-
cendants of Leah whom she bare unto Jacob in
Paddan-aram — and Dinah, her daughter. The
total number of his sons and his daughters was
thirty-three.**

The mental picture becomes a bit clearer if we
use the following grouping:

Leah's Sons

Reuben	Simeon	Levi	Judah		Issachar	Zebulon
Hanoch	Jemuel	Gershon	Er		Tola	Sered
Pallu	Ohad	Kohath	Onan		Puvah	Elon
Hezron	Jachin	Merari	Shelah		Job	Jahleel
Carmi	Zohar		Perez	{Hezron {Hamul	Shimron	
	Shaul		Zerah			

A count of names reveals: Reuben 6, Simeon 7,
Levi 4, Judah 8, Issachar 5, Zebulon 4 = 33. Consequently Dinah, though mentioned, is not counted. For
verse 15 also lists a total of 33.

Now at least two paralled lists are available —
disregarding the partial list of Exod. 6:14 ff. — namely Num. 26 and I Chron. 4-6. A comparison with
these indicates that certain of the names found above
were in circulation also in another form, usually pretty
much like the ones above, sometimes radically different
as to form but similar in meaning. For, as the margin
of A. R. V. briefly indicates, "Jemuel" v. 10 in both
Num. and I Chron. appears as "Nemuel." "Jachin"
has the parallel form in Chron. of "Jarib." "Zohar"
appears as "Zerah." "Gershon" (v. 11) has the
parallel "Gershom" (I Chron.). "Puvah" (v. 13) and
"Job" have parallels "Puah" and "Jashub" (I Chron.).
These variants need disturb no one. The similarity
of forms is usually apparent at a glance. From many
instances of the Scriptures we conclude that in every
period of Israel's history men had several names which
were legitimately theirs.

A few additional facts should be noticed. *Beney*
Jisra'el (v. 8) cannot be translated "sons of Israel,"
for all that follows indicates that the broader term
"descendants" or "children of Israel" is meant. Of
Simeon it is specifically asserted that Shaul, his son,
was begotten of a "Canaanitish woman." Since this
is mentioned in this manner, it would appear that it
was rather the exceptional thing for Jacob's sons to
have taken Canaanitish wives. They must, therefore,
have followed the patriarchal example of procuring
their wives from Mesopotamia or at least from such
racial groups that had kept themselves from the contamination of Canaanite corruption. Another strange
thing is to be observed in the case of Er and Onan,
Judah's sons, who died in the land of Canaan (chapter
38). Yet they are listed among those, who are the
heads of the clans (*mishpachoth*) of Israel. Some
adjustment must have been made, as a result of which
clans nevertheless bore their names. For we can hard-

ly accept the surmise of Procksch that "dead names
appear in our list, names of men who had never
actually existed" — a claim which would rob our list
of its historical validity. The concluding statement,
that here is the total of "his sons and his *daughters*"
from Leah is a bit unusual from our point of view,
for Dinah, though mentioned, is not counted — as we
showed above. The remark may, therefore, include
the daughters-in-law in so far as they are thought
of as the mothers of Jacob's grandsons, and may be
thought of as living in their sons.

**16-18. And the sons of Gad: Ziphion, and
Haggi, Shuni and Ezbon, Eri and Arodi and Areli.
And the sons of Asher: Imnah and Ishvah and
Ishvi and Beriah; and Serah was their sister. And
the sons of Beriah: Heber and Malchiel. These
are children of Zilpah, whom Laban gave to Leah,
his daughter; and these she bare unto Jacob, six-
teen persons.**

Rearranged, the names present the following
picture:

Zilpah's Sons

Gad	*Asher*
Ziphion	Imnah
Haggi	Ishvah
Shuni	Ishvi
Ezbon	Beriah {Heber / Malchiel}
Eri	
Arodi	Serah—(sister)
Areli	

This makes a total of 16 names. However, in
this instance the name of the sister Serah is counted
along with that of the brothers and not passed by like
that of Dinah. A few variant forms occur here too.
"Ziphion" is listed in Numbers as "Zephon." "Ezbon"
becomes "Ozni," and "Arodi" appears as "Arod."

**19-22. The sons of Rachel, Jacob's wife:
Joseph and Benjamin. And there were born unto**

Joseph in the land of Egypt (sons), whom Asenath,
the daughter of Potiphera, priest of On, bore to
him, Manasseh and Ephraim.   And the children
of Benjamin: Bela and Becher and Ashbel, Gera
and Naaman, Ehi and Rosh, Muppim and Huppim
and Ard.   These are the sons of Rachel, who were
born to Jacob, all together fourteen persons.

The picture is the following:

	Rachel's Sons
Joseph	*Benjamin*
Manasseh	Bela
Ephraim	Becher
	Ashbel
	Gera
	Naaman
	Ehi
	Rosh
	Muppim
	Huppim
	Ard

A few of these have different forms of names
which were also in circulation. "Eli" (v. 21) appears
as "Ahiram" in Numbers, "Muppim" as "Shephu-
pham," but in I Chron. as "Shuppim." "Huppim"
appears as "Hupham" in Numbers only. Already
above (v. 16) "Arodi" was a clan or race name. Here
appear two more, namely as plurals "Muppim" and
"Huppim."   This confirms what we must allude to
again: The individuals as such are not so much under
consideration; rather the clans derived from them.

In the case of Benjamin a new factor comes up
for consideration.   Till now Benjamin has been regarded as comparatively young.   A sober computation could hardly rate him higher than twenty-three
years old.   Ten sons at that age is virtually an impossibility.   The Septuagint translation, following, it
would seem, a reliable tradition, has given us a state-

ment of the case which may be more literally correct. It regroups Benjamin's descendants. It gives him three sons: Bela, Becher and Ashbel. To Bela it gives six sons: Gera, Naaman, Ehi, Rosh, Muppim and Huppim. But to Gera it ascribes one son: Ard. We shall draw upon this fact in a moment in making our final conclusions as to the object of this entire list.

One sees the difficulty of the critical approach to v. 19 (Dillmann). Had the writer followed strictly the pattern previously used in the chapter, he would have said: "The sons of Joseph: Manasseh and Ephraim." Instead we find: "The sons of Rachel, Jacob's wife." The critic does not deem the Biblical writer capable of so much originality and ascribes the words to a reviser. What wooden fellows some of these ancient Biblical writers would have been had they not even been able to depart from a form they had begun to use! Critical verdicts on such points are so purely subjective and unscientific as to be worthless. Apparently Moses varied his style at this point to remind us that Rachel actually counts as Jacob's wife.

23-25. And the sons of Dan: Hushim. And the sons of Naphtali: Jahzeel, and Guni, and Jezer, and Shillem. These are the sons of Bilhah, whom Laban gave unto Rachel, his daughter, and these she bore unto Jacob; all persons were seven.

According to our previous arrangement:

Bilhah's Sons

Dan	*Naphtali*
Hushim	Jahzeel
	Guni
	Jezer
	Shillem

Variant forms are: for "Hushim" "Shuham"; for "Jahzeel" "Jahziel"; for "Shillem" "Shallum."

It must be very apparent that the opening verse
in this catalogue of names (v. 8) uses the statement
in a very loose sense when it says: "these are the
names of the children of Israel that came down to
Egypt." It means: shortly after the children of Israel
had come to Egypt there were to be found those seventy fathers from whom were derived the seventy clans
that were the prevailing clans throughout Israel's
early history. Some seem to treat the author as
though he had sought to deceive his readers by exag-
gerating or by misrepresenting. Others charge him
with being confused a bit himself. Yet even upon the
first reading of the list of names one is struck
with the fact that Benjamin cannot have had ten
sons, and so it becomes clear in what sense this list
is meant.

Now a word as to the different totals. In v. 26
the count is sixty-six; in v. 27 we have seventy. Acts
7:14 creates an added problem by offering the total
seventy-five. A few difficulties of a minor character
appear insoluble. The major facts are clear enough.
The four lists we presented above give totals as follows: Leah's sons = 33; Zilpah's = 16; Rachel's =
14; Bilhah's = 7. Now 33 + 16 + 14 + 7 = 70. Here
the difficulty is that Jacob is not counted in. Yet,
perhaps, he may be counted in on the first group of
thirty-three. For if the two who died in Canaan —
Er and Onan — be dropped and Dinah recounted along
as is Serah, the sister, in the second group and
Jacob's name be added, the requisite thirty-three is
arrived at. This seems to be the simplest solution.
Then the sixty-six of v. 26 would quite naturally omit
Jacob and Joseph and his two sons, for the latter
already were in Egypt. For there the statement is
meant literally: "all the souls that came with Jacob
into Egypt."

But how about the New Testament statement Acts 7:14: "Jacob . . . and all his kindred, three-score and fifteen souls"? It must be that Luke in writing the Book of Acts followed the Septuagint translation, which gives five grandsons of Joseph. For Manasseh's son Machir and his son Gilead are there listed as well as two sons of Ephraim, Soutalaam and Taam, and also one son of Soutalaam, namely Edem. This Septuagint list may also be strictly historical. These five descendants of Joseph may actually have become heads of clans in later years. These clans may not have endured as long as some others or may have been counted in with the two Josephite clans: Ephraim and Manasseh. So, then, from one point of view there were seventy clans, according to another count seventy-five — all depending on a man's point of view.

But Moses emphasized that seventy clans were in existence in their clan fathers at this early date, for the number "seventy" has symbolical significance. Being composed of "seven" times "ten" — seven is the number which marks a *divine covenant work*; ten is the number of *completeness* — this number then signifies that at this point God had done a *complete divine work* upon Israel and had made a substantial people, which was able to weather the storms which were only too soon to break upon their head. The Greek translators had less of the Jewish viewpoint. For them the round number seventy-five was more significant than the symbolical number seventy. Seven also is the covenant number: this involves that God's covenant was to hold in the land of Egypt.

26, 27. **The total number of persons belonging to Jacob that came to Egypt, his direct descendants, apart from the wives of Jacob's sons, all these persons numbered sixty-six. And the sons of Joseph, which were born to him in Egypt, were two persons.**

All the persons of the house of Jacob that came to Egypt were seventy.

The main issue of these verses regarding the numbers involved was settled above. The *le* before *ya'aqobh* is the dative of the possessor; it does not mean "with." *Yotse'ey yerekhô*, "going out of his loins," is well covered by Meek's rendering: "his direct descendants." In v. 26 *habba'áh* is the participle with the article agreeing with *néphesh*. In v. 27 *habbá'ah* is a verb form with the article, in which case the article serves as a relative pronoun.

28-30. And he sent Judah on before him to Joseph to point out before him (the way) to Goshen. And they came to the land of Goshen. And Joseph hitched up his chariot and came up to meet Israel, his father, to Goshen. And he appeared unto him and fell upon his neck and wept long upon his neck. And Israel said to Joseph: Now I can die after I have seen thy face and that thou still art alive.

Goshen may have been available for settlement. But that does not mean that the children of Israel might have settled anywhere in that land. No doubt, Joseph knew best where Israel should settle. So Israel send Judah, the energetic and competent son, who now had the father's confidence in fullest measure, to inquire of Joseph what his plans were and then to come back and to guide Israel's family to the most suitable part of Goshen. Though the pronouns are not all expressed, as we might express them, there can be no doubt about it that this is the simple meaning of the verse. Critics like to make things hard for themselves in an effort to discredit the present text and they say: "The Hebrew here gives no tolerable sense."

29. As soon as it is certain that Israel has arrived, Joseph rides by chariot — "his chariot" im-

plying some splendid state chariot — and comes up
to Goshen to meet his father; the verb used here is
very unusual, as we have tried to show by our translation, "he (Joseph) appeared unto him," *wayyera'* —
a verb usually used for a divine appearance. This
indicates that it was an experience like unto having
the Lord appear, or better, an appearing in which
at least the hand of the Lord was manifest. Joseph
falls upon his father's neck and weeps there a long
time. Overcharged emotion long pent up seeks a
natural outlet. Not a word is spoken. There is no
need of words. Words cannot utter the deep feelings
of this hour.

30. Finally the father voices his reaction. We
do not feel that he desires death and actually says:
"Now let me die," as A. V. translated, but *'amûthah*
is rather potential: "Now I can die," implying: whenever my hour comes, I can die at ease, which is practically Luther's rendering: *Ich will nun gerne ster-
ben.* Father and son must have loved one another very
dearly and been deeply attached to one another.

31-34. **And Joseph said to his brethren and to
his father's house: I shall go up and tell Pharaoh
and I shall say to him: My brethren and my father's
house, who were in the land of Canaan, have come
down to me. And the men are shepherds, for they
are men who have dealt in livestock; and they have
brought with them their flocks and their herds and
all that they possess. And it shall be if Pharaoh
summons you and shall say: What is your business?
Then ye shall say: Thy servants have been dealing
in livestock from our youth up to this day, both we
and our fathers, in order that ye may dwell in the
land of Goshen. For every shepherd of flocks is an
abomination to the Egyptians.**

Joseph said these words "to his brethren and to
his father's house" or household. Naturally, his

"brethren" are a part of "his father's house." But such combinations are.rather common in Hebrew and are always to be construed in the sense of: "to his brethren" in particular, and generally speaking also "to his father's household." In these verses the issue is not, and cannot be, to convey information to Pharaoh chiefly concerning the arrival of Israel in Egypt. Pharaoh had anticipated that and practically arranged for it. Naturally, courtesy demanded that he be informed of the arrival. But Joseph has wisely chosen Goshen as the prospective dwelling place of his kindred, and now he desires to secure Pharaoh's free and hearty approval. To that intent he conveys the information that had not come to Pharaoh heretofore, namely, that these men are all shepherds. Joseph informs his brethren in advance that he purposes to do this. For Joseph is dealing with a somewhat delicate situation, the key to which is given in the second half of v. 34 in an explanatory remark of the author of the book to the effect that "every shepherd of flocks is an abomination to the Egyptians." The brethren must have known this fact, for they were now coming down to Egypt for the third time; in fact, they may have heard of it in Canaan, which was a country bordering on Egypt. Now this situation required delicate handling from two points of view. Joseph dare not offend his brethren by making them feel that he, perhaps, had adopted the Egyptian attitude merely to please the Egyptians and was treating his brethren as social inferiors. So perfect frankness in the whole matter and securing for them a position of comparative isolation geographically was the happiest solution of the problem. On the other hand, the situation was delicate in reference to Pharaoh. For as king he was bound by Egyptian customs and prejudice. He would, however, not want to offend Joseph or his brethren. To have the matter disposed of practically

ir advance by the geographical isolation of Israel,
which practically required only his stamp of approval
— all this was a very wise adjustment on Joseph's
part. So he personally first informs Pharaoh (v. 32)
that they are shepherds; that they have always dealt
in livestock; that they have brought their flocks and
herds with them. He also coaches his brethren as
to what they are to say, should Pharaoh put the question: "What is your business?" i. e., *ma'aseh,*
originally "deed" or "work." They are to speak
frankly and unashamed as men who feel that no
stigma is attached to their calling, but at the same
time very deferentially ("thy servants"), and are to
make it plain that they have always followed this
occupation. The *hayû* is interesting: they "have been"
— implying: should it please Pharaoh to decree otherwise, they would desist from this work. Joseph's dis-
crete handling of the whole situation is usually not
evaluated as highly as it deserves. He discerns quite
clearly that the easiest course for Pharaoh will be to
confirm the whole arrangement and let them stay in
Egypt. For Pharaoh's original suggestions had left
this question as to exactly where they should settle
open; cf. 45:16-20. It was Joseph who made the selection of Goshen, a fertile country, known as such from
antiquity and well adapted to the keeping of cattle.
Whitelaw summarizes well the advantages of this land
for Israel: (1) "It was suitable for their flocks and
herds; (2) it would secure their isolation from the
Egyptians; (3) it was contiguous to Canaan, and
would be easier vacated when the time arrived for
their return." In v. 34 *tô'abhath,* though construct
before a definite noun, does not acquire definiteness,
"*the* abomination," as the general rule requires. Exceptions are allowable (K. S. 304 a) when the sense
demands it: here plainly other abominations of the

Egyptians must be allowed for. Therefore: "an abomination."

The statement, "every shepherd of flocks is an abomination to the Egyptians," has provoked much discussion. This explanation is applicable not only to foreign shepherds but, as Keil has shown, to natives as well, who are represented on monuments in a way calculated to express the fact that they were of a low and despised caste, for they "are constantly depicted as lanky, withered, distorted, emaciated, and sometimes almost ghostly figures." Herodotus confirms this in words that appear to be applicable to all shepherds (Keil). The Hyksos domination will have served to establish this natural aversion. Quite naturally such a feeling will have been displayed still more strongly toward foreigners.

References made to the Israelites in this connection, as though they came down to Egypt as a strictly nomad group, are quite misleading. In reality they were only half-nomadic in their habits. Isaac already had sowed and reaped (26:12). Jacob continued in a settled life. Goshen, having abundant pasturage, would discourage nomadic wanderings and make them unnecessary. Being a fertile land, it would encourage agriculture. So Israel came in as a semi-nomadic group and became a predominantly agricultural group in very short order.

Only a few critical problems can be treated by way of samples. K. C. feels that he must concede that the words, "for they are men who have dealt in livestock" (v. 32), are a gloss, for they seem to say the same thing as the preceding words, "the men are shepherds." As our explanation indicates, the verse marks a threefold progression of thought: 1) they *are* shepherds; 2) they have always *been* shepherds; 3) they have brought their flocks along. Consequently : the best thing would be to let them settle in Goshen. Gunkel holds that Joseph coached his brothers to tell a lie: for they were not strictly shepherds. They, however, who are half-nomads and half-agriculturalists may with perfect honesty refer to their experience as shepherds as Joseph's brethren did; they are only describing their experience along one particular line. There was no attempt at deception.

The critical source analysis presents the usual problems, weaknesses and lack of agreement among the critics.

HOMILETICAL SUGGESTIONS

The first seven verses of the chapter furnish a good basis for a sermon on the theme "Thy will be done." A godly man's concern about having certainty in the matter of a momentous decision in life, even where the decision seems to involve only his advantage—such concern, we say, should teach men to let God's will be paramount in all decisions, great or small.

CHAPTER XLVII

11. Establishment of Israel in Goshen and Egyptian Famine Measures (47:1-26)

This chapter ties up so closely with the subject of the preceding one as to require no further introduction.

However, we may consider briefly at this point the question of chronology — in what dynasty or under which of the Pharaohs did this famine take place? We believe that most writers on the subject are guilty of misdating this event as a result of their distrust of the Biblical chronology. The usual assumption, made quite apart from strictly chronological issues, is that Joseph must have had contact with the Hyksos kings, whose rule is commonly dated from 1680-1580 B. C. This assumption builds on the somewhat plausible contention that the Hyksos rulers, themselves shepherd kings, will have been friendly disposed toward Israel and his family — also shepherd folk. Yet the assumption is gaining ground that "Hyksos" meant "Ruler of Countries."* Besides, we still maintain that the chronology of the Bible points to a date for the Exodus in the fifteenth century — about 1449 B. C. We also believe that Exod. 12:40 is a correct statement — "the time that the children of Israel dwelt in Egypt was 430 years." This should lead exegetes to look for the famine in the days of Joseph about the year 1880 B. C. If now available historical data of Egyptian history reveal nothing concerning Joseph or the famine or the agrarian policy developed by Joseph, such silence by no means discredits the

---

*George A. Barton. *Archaeology and the Bible* (1937) p. 18.

Mosaic record. It means nothing more than that the available records concerning things Egyptian are incomplete.

1-4. Then Joseph went in and told Pharaoh and said: My father and my brethren, together with their flocks and herds and all that they possess, have come from the land of Canaan; and, see, they are in the land of Goshen. Now he had taken five men from the total number of his brethren, and he presented them unto Pharaoh. And Pharaoh said to his brethren: What is your business? And they said to Pharaoh: Shepherds of flocks thy servants are — both we and our fathers. They said moreover unto Pharaoh: To sojourn in the land have we come; for there is no pasture for the flocks which thy servants have — for the famine is heavy in the land of Canaan. May thy servants, pray, settle in the land of Goshen.

Joseph knew the exact situation in reference to all things Egyptian and had coached his brethren how to meet this particular occasion. Yet much would depend on his own approach to Pharaoh. Pharaoh's attitude had been very generous (45:17 ff). But royalty has been known to speak generously and afterward to forget what it had promised. Besides, though Joseph was overlord over the whole land, he would have laid himself open to criticism had he provided for his own family in so liberal a manner as Pharaoh had suggested. It was the part of wisdom to have Pharaoh confirm publicly what he had originally suggested, and so to let it appear that the settlement of Israel was Pharaoh's work. Consequently, the account does not conflict with the representation of the full power conferred upon Joseph according to the rest of this record. Neither is there anything "naive" about the view that these simple shepherds appeared before the very presence of the great Egyptian king,

as Israelites did in the days of David and Solomon.
These men were brothers of the grand vizier Joseph.
Another diplomatic move on Joseph's part was to
settle his brethren in Goshen first and then to tell
Pharaoh about it. To settle them and their flocks and
herds and all their possessions in Goshen is the
simplest way of getting the Pharaoh's confirmation.

2. We can hardly suppose that Joseph would
first have reported to Pharaoh that Israel was
settled in Goshen, then would have gone out and
selected five men, to take them out of the land of
Goshen, and then would have presented them at court.
No doubt the selection was made in advance, and the
five were presented at once. Therefore *laqach*
ranks as a pluperfect (K. S. 117)). *Miqtseh* (from
min and *qatseh*) here means from "the whole" (B D
B), i. e., "from the total number of his brethren."
We are not able to determine whether they were the
eldest or the youngest or a mixed group. No doubt,
Joseph's wisdom taught him to discern which men
were most presentable at court.

3. Joseph had also rightly discerned what question the Pharaoh would put on this occasion. The
Egyptian monarch may well have put other questions.
One that was bound to arise was: "What is your
business?" The full truth is the safest course, un-
diplomatic as it might appear to be. The brethren
do as Joseph had instructed them: they say with unmistakable plainness — *ro'eh* first for emphasis —
"shepherds of flocks thy servants are." *Ro'eh* ("shepherds") stands first in the singular, as the verb often
does, though the subject following is plural, "thy
servants" (K. S. 348 m). To correct the text to *ro'ey*
(plural construct) is unnecessary. With a true pride
in an honorable and ancient calling they are ready,
for that matter, to inform the Pharaoh that both they
and their "fathers" have long followed this calling.

4. The brethren also explain very satisfactorily how they conceive of the dwelling in the land (46:34). They say, again with emphasis, "to sojourn in the land have we come." It certainly will make Pharaoh still better disposed toward them if they say truthfully that they intend only to "sojourn," i. e., to settle for the time being. They added by way of explanation what Joseph had not told them to say, but what was eminently proper: "for the famine is heavy in the land of Canaan." In other words: they have left their native land only as a matter of utter necessity. To this explanation they then attach the modest request to be allowed to settle in Goshen — the imperfect *yeshebhû* is optative — "may they settle."

5, 6. **And Pharaoh said to Joseph: Thy father and thy brethren have come to thee. The land of Egypt is at your disposal; settle thy father and thy brethren in the best part of the land; let them settle in the land of Goshen. And if thou knowest of competent men among them, appoint them to have charge of the stock which belong to me.**

Pharaoh's first statement by way of response summarizes the situation, much as we might say: "So I see your father and your brothers have arrived." This is a gracious royal acknowledgment of the fact, and it is not to be regarded as an idle or unlikely statement. From this acknowledgment the Pharaoh proceeds to reiterate what he had promised in advance (45:18), only here, if anything, he makes his proposition more generous, as though, as far as he is concerned, they might settle wheresoever they pleased. The statement in the original has it: "The land of Egypt is before thy face." That must here mean, "lies open before you" or "is at your disposal" (Meek). He then proceeds to confirm the arrangements toward which Joseph's initial steps pointed, namely, he

gave command that Joseph should "cause them to
dwell" (*hôshebh*), i. e., "settle" them "in the best part
of the land" — a noun *metabh* used to express a superlative (K. S. 309 f). By a kind of self-correction or
by way of making his statement more specific Pharaoh
adds, "let them settle in the land of Goshen" — just
what Joseph had wanted him to grant. Then, by way
of a further indication of royal goodwill, he suggests
that any "competent men" (*'anshey cháyil*, i. e., "men
of might or capacity") from among their number be
appointed "to have charge (i. e., be *sarey miqneh* —
'chief of the cattle') of the stock" of Pharaoh.

These two verses fit so excellently into the picture
and make such excellent sense and such good sequence
of thought that we must confess to be greatly surprised at certain claims advanced by the critics at this
point. The critics had expected something different
or liked particularly a different sequence of clauses
as found in the Septuagint (5 a, 6 b, 5 b, 6 a) and
so they claim that "the overlapping of J and P at
this point can be proved and corrected from G," i. e.
the Greek translation. We venture to assert: no-
body can prove anything of the sort; there is no overlapping; criticism is making unwarranted assertions
by claims which a straightforward interpretation of
the text proves entirely untenable.

**7-10. And Joseph brought in Jacob, his father,
and set him before Pharaoh; and Jacob blessed
Pharaoh. And Pharaoh said to Jacob: How many
are the days of the years of thy life? And Jacob
said to Pharaoh: The days of the years of my pilgrimage are a hundred and thirty years; few and
evil have been the days of the years of my life and
they have not reached the days of the years of
the lives of my forefathers in the days of their
pilgrimage. And Jacob blessed Pharaoh and went
forth from Pharaoh's presence.**

A fine token of filial respect is given by Joseph when he next presents his father at court. His father always was his best friend, and Joseph, knowing the true worth of character of true saints of God, felt that in character and personality Jacob was more than Pharaoh's equal. The simple old shepherd contrasts very favorably with the Egyptian monarch. In fact, the very report of the incident seeks to convey the impression that Jacob actually stood forth as the greater figure according to a true analysis, for "Jacob blessed Pharaoh." "But without any dispute the less is blessed of the better" (Heb. 7:7). Some render *waybhárekh,* "and he blessed," very poorly as "greeted" or "paid his respects." The truth of the matter is that these old men of God greeted by blessing, as B D B correctly renders, "greet with an invocation of blessing, (stronger than *shalôm*)." Conscious that he, a true child of God, has more to offer by his blessing than any earthly monarch can offer him, Jacob here blesses as by an act and a display of true faith. For we should hardly venture to go as for as Luther does in this connection and to suppose that Joseph had converted Pharaoh and the Egyptians to the true and living God. Nor does Ps. 105:20-22 allow for so extreme a position. At most Joseph "taught" the "elders wisdom." Nothing is said of their having accepted it.

8. We know not what matters besides may have been discussed by Pharaoh and Jacob. We are loath to believe that no more was said than what we here read. But the answer of Jacob in particular has been handed down to us as a memorable one. The Hebrew idiom, "How many are the days of the years of thy life?" for our simpler question: "How old are you?" lays emphasis on the individual days that go to make up the total of our life.

9. Jacob was then 130 years old. He describes
his life as a "pilgrimage" (*meghûrim*, potential plural,
indicating the many and the varied episodes involved). The noun is derived from *ghûr*, "to sojourn"
or "dwell as a stranger." The outer circumstances
involved are these: in Canaan Jacob had had a fixed
possession or property as little as Isaac or Abraham;
in Mesopotamia he had dwelled as a stranger twenty
years; since his return to Canaan he had dwelled
mostly around Hebron but always as a sojourner
"having no abiding city." Without a doubt, such an
unsettled outward state of life would have served to
such a man of God as Jacob was as an excellent
type of the spiritual truth that all of a man's life is
but a pilgrimage to the eternal home where we no
longer stay for the time being as strangers. Therefore Heb. 11:13-16 is entirely justified in laying
emphasis upon this deeper spiritual meaning and in
describing Jacob also as having his hope fixed upon
the "heavenly country." Yet Jacob's statement of the
case covers the outer and the inner meaning. To
translate *meghûrim*, therefore, as "my life as an
immigrant" is far too shallow and superficial. The
rest of Jacob's statement regards his life as practically finished, and so he looks back upon it as a unit
by way of retrospect. This is but a natural thing
for old people to do. They often think that their
life is practically ended and then go on to live ten
or fifteen years more. In this retrospect Jacob contrasts his life with that of his forefathers — especially Isaac and Abraham, but also the post-diluvians
since Noah — and finds that his life's days have been
"few and evil." For *rayim*, "evil," we might use
"wretched" or "unhappy." Surely, it cannot be
denied that not one of his ancestors had so many
hardships and disappointments to encounter as he,

who was compelled to flee from home, was treated wretchedly and deceived by his father-in-law in a strange land, encountered the hostility of Esau, was grieved by the rape of his daughter Dinah and by the murder perpetrated by his sons, Simeon and Levi, was deeply pained by Reuben's incest, and grieved almost to the point of death by the loss of Joseph and Benjamin, as well as by the death of Rachel. The man can well foretell that his years will not come up to those of Abraham, who became 175 years old, or of Isaac, who reached 180. But that the same spirit animated them as well as him appears from this that he calls their life too a "pilgrimage."

10. Again upon leaving Jacob, the man of God, bestows a blessing upon the king, a blessing by way of a farewell greeting. On the use of the word to "bless" (*berekh*) we may yet add that the secondary meaning which borders on "greet" so little impresses K. W. as not even to be mentioned.

11, 12. **And Joseph settled his father and his brethren, giving them a possession in the land of Egypt, in the best part of the land, in the land of Rameses, as Pharaoh had commanded. And Joseph provided his father and his brethren, and all his father's household with bread according to the number of the children.**

Since Pharaoh concurred, Joseph made the settlement of his father and brethren permanent. There must have been unoccupied land in Goshen at the time. This is given them as a "possession" (*'achuzzah*) ; therefore they had a more permanent foothold in Egypt than they had had thus far in Canaan. Joseph, knowing the aversion of the Egyptians to foreigners, confirmed this grant so as to make later difficulties less likely for the days when the popularity which he and his family enjoyed should have begun to wane. So well did this guardian, whom God raised up for His people, provide for them in their extremity. Besides, (v. 12) the "bread" (by metonomy for "food") needed was provided "according to the number of the children," Hebrew: "according to the mouth of the little ones" — an unusual phrase whose meaning seems plain enough: he who had many children received just so much more food. The children are mentioned, for they will be the chief concern of parents in days of want. The verb "provide" is followed by a double accusative (G.K. 117 cc; K. S. 327 r).

The expression "land of Rameses" (Hebrew — *Ra'mses*) is used by Moses proleptically to describe more accurately for his contemporaries the region which they in their day knew as Rameses. For the store cities Pithom and Raamses (Exod. 1:11), which the children of Israel built, seem to have stood on this site. The other claim, usually made in this connection, that Rameses must have derived its name from Rameses II, their supposed builder, is unsound; for according to Biblical chronology the Exodus took place about 1449 B. C., whereas Rameses II first ruled beginning about 1300 B. C. A city may be named after a king; but so may a king be named after a city, or both king and city after some other person or other object bearing a familiar name. This Rameses is usually located by geographers about midway between Lake Timsah and the Nile. For further location of the land of Goshen we add some facts to which Keil has drawn attention. It must have bordered on the east on Arabia Petraea because the Septuagint translators' term is Γεσὲμ 'Αραβίας. On the west it must have reached to the Nile, because "the Israelites had an abundance of fish" (Num. 11:5). Then, it "must have skirted the Tanitic arm of the Nile, for the fields of Zoan, i. e. Tanis, are said to have been the scene of the mighty acts of God in Egypt" (Ps. 78:12, 43).

13-17.   But bread there was none in all the rest of the land, for the famine was extremely severe and the land of Egypt as well as the land of Canaan was exhausted because of the famine.   And Joseph took in all the money that was found in the land of Egypt and in the land of Canaan for the grain which they were buying, and Joseph brought the money into Pharaoh's house.   When the money was used up from the land of Egypt and from the land of Canaan, all the Egyptians came to Joseph and said: Give us food; why should we die before thy very eyes; for the money is all spent.   And Joseph said: Give your livestock, and I will supply you for your livestock if your money is all spent.   So they brought their livestock to Joseph, and Joseph gave them food for their horses, for their livestock in sheep, their livestock in cattle and for their asses; and he supplied them with food for all their livestock that year.

By contrast with the unusual provisions made for Israel and his children "the rest of the land" has no bread or food.   The Hebrew says, "bread there was none in all the land," meaning: "in all the rest of the land," for we have just been told that the Israelites in Goshen had their wants provided for. The severity of the famine involved "Egypt as well as the land of Canaan."   This reference to Canaan may merely have been due to the fact that the two lands primarily affected by this famine actually were Egypt and Canaan.   Since it later develops (v. 15) that the money from Canaan flowed also into Egypt's coffers, it is quite likely that during this period Canaan was under Egypt's dominion, as happened so often both before and after this time.   With this obvious explanation at hand, it seems very strange that critics

cannot account for the reference to Canaan and
describe it as "quite uncalled for" (*ein unberechtigter
Seitenblick*, K. C.). Several terms make us feel how
very severe the famine was; it is said that these
lands "were exhausted." Naturally the money is used
up first — *késeph* is regularly used: "silver" for
"money," because of the metal that served as a
medium of exchange. Joseph "took in" (*laqat* — Piel
— "collect") all this available money both from Egypt
and from Canaan, and brought it "into Pharaoh's
house" or palace, into the royal treasuries.

15. When their money was used up, the
Egyptians come to Joseph, to whom they feel they
can appeal with confidence, for he has proved himself the nation's savior thus far. Apparently no
Egyptian in those days mistrusted Joseph's motives
or misconstrued them. Though he had their money,
they seemed to recognize that the course he was pur-
suing was the wisest. The emergency of those days
called for emergency measures. Nothing so unnerves
a nation and breaks down its morale so much and
so rapidly as complete support by relief long continued. Unfortunately, some otherwise sober commentators sharply censure Joseph's famine measures,
as though they proceeded from sinister motives and
were aimed directly at the enslavement of the nation.
Yet, apparently, afterward Joseph restored their cattle
and livestock and provided the Egyptians with seed
grain and merely charged what was not an exorbitant
tax for a fertile land. The Scriptures neither commend nor censure Joseph's measures, but these
measures are quite readily defended. The objections
made are largely the inventions of theorists who
cannot realize what stern measures extreme emergencies may call for. There is something pathetic-
ally helpless about the plea of the Egyptians: they
want food; they have no money; they do not appear

ready to make further sacrifices. But Joseph has a workable plan.

16. Joseph has the bold plan of having them pay with their "livestock" (*miqneh*). It really was a relief for the people in famine days to have the care of their cattle taken off their hands. The resources of the goverment apparently could carry the cattle through famine days better than individuals could have done. Horses, sheep, cattle, asses are sacrificed. The fact that the people brought them all shows their dire need. Silence on the question whether they protested is no proof that protests were not forthcoming. But protests of individuals are in themselves no gauge of the folly or the wisdom of a course in which they are involved. To expect patient and entirely acquiescent acceptance of Joseph's measures on the part of all is to expect the impossible. The price paid was deemed sufficient to maintain the purchasers for a year. Yet the nation had not lost its self-respect: they were paying for what they got.

One difficulty created by the critics on this section must be alluded to. Some hold since Wellhausen that since the scene is laid neither in Ephraim nor in Judah, therefore neither E nor J can be the source. Nothing points to J. Consequently some entirely foreign source is involved, they claim. Note how the weaknesses of the critical theory demand hypothesis after hypothesis to bolster it up.

18, 19. **When that year was ended, they came to him in the next year and said to him: We will not hide from my lord that if the money and the livestock owned is all spent, for my lord's disposal there is nothing left before my lord except our body and our land. Why should we die before thy very eyes, both we and our land? Buy us and our land for bread, then we on our part and our land shall belong the Pharaoh; then give us seed that**

we may live and not die, and that the land may not be desolate.

The Hebrew says "second year" (*hashshanah hashshenîth*) but it means the year after the cattle had been purchased and not the second year of the famine. So we translate "next year" to avoid confusion. The people approach Joseph, for he on his part had to make his hoard of grain stretch as far as possible, and so naturally he would not approach them but would wait till their need drove them to him. They on their part cannot forget the loss of their money and their cattle; so they mention it in their plea, although Joseph well knows that both are gone. Consequently, all they have left is their body and their land. We must translate *kî 'im* as we did above "that if," for it does not mean "how that" (A. V.). Perhaps for: "we will not hide" (*nekhachchedh*) we should translate the verb as a potential, "we could not hide" (K. C.). *"My lord"* for *"our* lord," a natural irregularity, because it is a stereotyped expression.

19. The people speak of their land as dying by a kind of zeugma, for the land deteriorates if it be not worked, and here their plea is for seed. Now this may bring us in point of time to the last year of the famine where they may justly reckon with the idea of again working their lands; or this may mean that a bit of sowing was attempted annually in a few portions where this might yield slight returns. But, in any case, the plan to sell themselves and their land for bread emanated from the people; it was not a scheme of Joseph's to enslave them, as some seem to imply. Besides, this plan shows that the people are learning a lesson from Joseph's approach to the problem. Outright donations have no place in his relief measures. So they compute very correctly that the next step is to sell themselves

and their lands. The price paid is not too high, for
the thing at stake is their very life ("that we may
live and not die"). *Namûth* — "should we die" — the
potential imperfect (K. S. 187). *Léchem,* "bread,"
has the article to express the idea: the bread needed
under these circumstances (K. S. 298 b).

20-22. **So Joseph bought all the land of Egypt
for Pharaoh, for the Egyptians sold every man his
field, because the famine was very severe on them.
So the land came into Pharaoh's possession. And
as for the people, he removed them to the cities from
one end of Egypt to the other. Only the land of the
priests he did not buy, for there was an allowance
of food for the priests by Pharaoh's command, and
they lived off the allowance which Pharaoh gave to
them. Therefore they did not sell their land.**

Pharaoh was the one whose power and influence
were greatly enhanced by Joseph's acquisition of
land, another one of the wise and considerate features
of Joseph's plan, whereby both king and people were
led to trust him the more. The added statement,
"the Egyptians sold every man his field," shows how
entirely universal was the situation that prevailed.
Moses is recording a thing of special historic interest
for those times, for it is the explanation of a peculiar
situation which actually prevailed in Egypt. Therefore Moses says very distinctly: "So the land came
into Pharaoh's possession."

21. Now another famine measure — how about
the people after Pharaoh had them on his hands?
Joseph simplifies the matter of food administration by
"removing them to the cities from one end of Egypt
to the other." Food could be distributed far more
readily to groups collected in and about the cities.
Again the completeness of Joseph's plans is indicated:
they cover the situation "from one end of Egypt to
the other" — half-measures had no place in Joseph's

administration. Changes in the text to make it conform with the Septuagint are not indicated by any
worth-while consideration. The Hebrew text makes
such good sense; the Septuagint text flounders help-
lessly: "he enslaved them into being slaves" could
hardly be called an improvement. Procksch produces
a rare gem of critical results when he modifies the
text to the point where it reads: "He made the
people pass in review before him by cities from one
end of Egypt to the other." What an idea to stage
parades, all the population of the cities, the famishing multitudes! That would have been about the last
thing Joseph would have done.

22. One exception was made when the land
passed into Pharaoh's hands — the land of the priests
was not bought. This was a concession either to the
respect they enjoyed or to their strong influence in
the nation, or to both. Instead, a *choq*, "a portion"
or "an allowance of food," (B D B) was designated
for their use "by Pharaoh's command," *me'eth par'oh*,
literally = "from Pharaoh."

23-26. **And Joseph said to the people: See,
I have bought you and your land for Pharaoh; lo,
here is seed for you that ye may sow your land. It
shall be at the time of your harvest then ye shall
give a fifth part to Pharaoh, and four parts shall
be your own for seed for your fields and for your
food, and for those who are in your households, and
for food for your little ones. And they said: Thou
hast saved our lives; may we find favor in my lord's
sight and we will be Pharaoh's servants. And
Joseph made it an ordinance concerning the land
of Egypt unto this day for Pharaoh in the matter of
the fifth part. Only the land of the priests belonged
to them alone; it did not become Pharaoh's.**

Joseph's words on the day that these new land
regulations went into effect are here reported. They

embody the regulations that were to prevail as laws
covering taxes. Joseph tells the people plainly that
what he has done profits him nothing; the land was
bought together with the people for Pharaoh. Indeed, that involves the setting up of a kind of feudal
relationship, a thing apparently unavoidable under
the circumstances. In return Joseph at once gives
them the seed they were bargaining for. He also
defines for them very clearly what their obligations
will be in the future. "At the time of harvest" (*bat-
tebhû'oth* = "in the harvest" — *be* being temporal
rather than partitive) they are to make five parts,
give one to Pharaoh and keep the remaining four.
Twenty per cent is a high tax rate but quite moderate
for the Orient where one third and one half have
been demanded (cf. I Macc. 10:30 — Luther v. 29).
Our tax-ridden age ought not find reason for objection here. These four parts remaining were thought
sufficient by Joseph for "seed," and "food," both for
their entire "households" as well as particularly for
their "little ones," who here, as in v. 12 (*taph*),
are a matter of special concern. *La'asher* expresses
a genitive relationship: "for (or of) those who are
in your households," for *le* often serves to express
the genitive (K. S. 281 b).

25. The Egyptians understand Joseph's motive
and appreciate what he actually did for them. They
admit: "Thou hast saved our lives" (Hifil from
chayah). All they desire is that Joseph's goodwill
may continue to rest upon them — "may we find
favor in my lord's (for: *our* lord's) sight." Though
they recognize that they will have lost their liberty,
yet so long as Joseph is kindly minded, they know
their lot will not be an unpleasant one: "we will be
Pharaoh's servants." So the whole thing is published
as an ordinance which prevailed till the Mosaic age
— "unto this day" — *lephar'oh la(ch)chómesh,* lit-

erally, "in reference to Pharaoh in reference to the
fifth" — two datives of reference. Only the land of the
priests was exempt.

12. Jacob's Preparations for His End
(47:28-49:32)

a)   Provisions for His Burial (47:28-31)

28-31. **And Jacob lived in the land of Egypt
seventeen years. And the days of Jacob, that is
the years of his life, were one hundred and forty-
seven years. And the days of Israel came near to
the point of death; and he called for his son Joseph
and said to him: If now I have found favor in
thy sight, place thy hand under my thigh, that thou
wilt show kindness and faithfulness toward me:
do not, I pray thee, bury me in Egypt; but I would
lie with my fathers, and do thou take me away from
Egypt and do thou bury me in their grave. And
he answered: I for my part will do according to
thy word. And he said: Give me thy oath. And
he gave him his oath. Then Israel bowed down in
prayer upon the head of the bed.**

There is little more of theocratic interest to be
reported in the life of Jacob than his last words. So
we are informed that though he thought death was
near at the time when he stood before Pharaoh, yet
he lived a total of seventeen years more near his
beloved son in the land of Egypt, bringing his total
age (i. e. "the days of Jacob" or, as the appositional
statement has it: "the years of his life") up to 147
years. When it became apparent that the end was
inevitable, Jacob felt the necessity of seeing Joseph
for one last time. He has a special request to make
of Joseph. He prefaces it with a respectful statement
used in addressing a person of some consequence. By
these words Jacob expresses his respect for one who

occupies an eminent and responsible position. "Honor to whom honor is due." The words are: "If now I have found favor in thy sight." The gesture used in connection with the oath administered is to "place the hand under the thigh," which gesture we showed in connection with 24:2 to refer to the descendants, in particular to the most prominent descendant hoped for, namely the Christ. The oath, therefore, means: "I adjure thee by the Christ in whom is embodied our dearest hope." Executing the oath is both "kindness and faithfulness." Jacob makes his entreaty very solemn by all these means, for the thing he asks for is a token of a fine faith in God's promises. The eagerness of the petition finds further expression in the *na,'* "I pray." Upon first hearing the petition one is inclined to regard it as relatively trivial. Why should it be a matter of such moment to ask for burial in Canaan not in Egypt? It is not merely a matter of sentiment when he says besides: "I would lie with my fathers." With men of strong faith, such as the patriarchs had, such petitions would have a deep and worthy motivation. Heb. 11:21 gives the right direction to all investigation, telling us that this was done "by faith." Jacob believed God's promises in reference to Israel, the land of Canaan, and the blessing of all the nations of the world through the Savior to come. His deepest hopes were tied up with these promises of the Word of God. Jacob wanted even his burial to give testimony to this faith. But the only suitable land the patriarchs owned was the cave at Machpelah where Abraham and Isaac lay buried. Therefore he requests that he be laid to rest there. This may all agree very well with the statement of 50:5 that he had dug the grave for himself, for the cave still required that each new grave be separately dug within its confines.

30. "To sleep with one's fathers" does not refer to being buried but to falling asleep. Therefore this verse cannot be translated: "But when I sleep with my fathers, thou shalt carry me out of Egypt." (A. R. V.). It must be rendered: "But I would lie with my fathers, and do thou take me away from Egypt" (converted perfects!). Joseph promises: "I for my part will do according to thy words." The emphasis on the initial *'anokhî*, "I," means, Joseph will do what lies in his power. That an oath was intended by the gesture used (v. 29) is made unmistakably clear by Jacob's next demand: "Give me your oath," (Hebrew: "swear to me"). Joseph readily grants this favor. Jacob is so well pleased with the assurance, for the whole matter was one of greatest importance to his faith, that he proceeds at once to worship. *Yishtachû* does mean "bow down in reverence," and it might mean a gesture of respect to Joseph, which, however, in this case is hardly seemly. Meek translates, "he settled back on the head of his bed" — unnatural; a weary old man would settle down on the entire bed. The whole setting indicates that an important need of faith had been met. That would most naturally suggest that Jacob "bowed down in prayer," thanking God that He had granted him this deep satisfaction. The added phrase, "upon the head of the bed," conveys the sense that the headend (*ro'sh*), being a bit elevated, would offer a natural point upon which more comfortably to bow his head in prayer.

A point occasioning some confusion in this connection is the fact that the words "head of the bed" are rendered "top of his staff" (Heb. 11:21), this translation being based upon the Greek version which says: ἐπὶ τὸ ἄϰϱον τῆς ϱάβδου. The Masoretic Hebrew text has *mittah*, "bed." The Greek translators pointed the text *matteh,* "staff." This is manifestly a wrong translation, but the author of the letter to the Hebrews used the Greek version because no vital point was involved.

One naturally raises the question in connection with this chapter, whether the agrarian reforms ascribed to Joseph can be traced in other available records of a secular character. Keil takes the sanest view of the whole subject. He points out that Diodorus Siculus (I, 37) reports that all land in Egypt belonged either to the priests, to the king, or to the warriors. Strabo (21—60 A. D.) tells that farmers and traders held taxable lands, but that the peasants were not landowners. Again Herodotus, the old Greek traveler, (425 B. C.), on the one hand tells how Sesostris had once divided the land among all Egyptians, giving every man a square piece, and had derived his revenue from an annual tax on them (2, 109). But later he reports (2, 168) that the warriors had received, every man of them, twelve sections of land exempt from taxation. These various accounts point to the fact that a situation such as Joseph created must have prevailed in Egypt, except that Joseph knows of no tax-free lands for warriors. But at a later date, when the original arrangement had already undergone extensive modification, except as far as the priests were concerned, the memory of how it all had originated was already lost, and so some attributed it to "the half-mythical king" Sesostris. In the last analysis this, then, is the situation: Egyptian sources do not happen to reveal these agrarian measures that the Biblical records have preserved; modification of Joseph's policies in the course of years is to be expected; what later Egyptian sources describe suggests policies of earlier days like those inaugurated by Joseph.

HOMILETICAL SUGGESTIONS

We feel that the only portion of this chapter suitable as a text for a sermon is the section v. 1-12. It seems to us that the part v. 13-26 is too definitely involved in a specifically Egyptian situation which cannot be duplicated anywhere at any time. Regarding the last paragraph, v. 27-31, we feel that it corresponds too closely with situations in Abraham's life to afford anything new. But for v. 1-12 we have always felt that the focal point lay in v. 10, and we regard the whole as an excellent portrayal of the supreme worth of the character of God's saints: God's saints are kings, kings by a higher right than the kings of this earth can claim. This, of course, involves nothing derogatory to civil authorities.

CHAPTER XLVIII

12. **Jacob's Provisions for His End** (Continued)

b. **The Blessing of Joseph's Sons** (48:1-22)

Death was not as near as Jacob (47:27-31) had supposed, yet he made the needed preparations for it in due season. Now a second event transpires as death is seen to have drawn much nearer: Jacob blesses Joseph's sons. It would seem that at most several months elapsed between these two events. For the first occasion Jacob summoned Joseph to him; in this case a report came to Joseph in an incidental way.

1, 2. **And it came to pass after these things that the report came to Joseph: Behold, thy father is sick. So he took his two sons along with him, Manasseh and Ephraim. When it was told to Jacob: Behold, thy son Joseph is coming to thee, Israel made himself strong and sat upon his bed.**

It is of no moment for us to know how much time elapsed between the previous event and the one about to be related, therefore the writer uses the very general phrase "after these things." "The report came to Joseph" — for this expression the Hebrew has the impersonal "one said" (*wayyó'mer*). Apparently, then, Jacob did not summon Joseph and his two sons. Yet the event about to be related seems altogether too important to regard it as a mere chance occurrence: Jacob just happened to see Joseph's two sons and conceived the idea on the spur of the moment to adopt and to bless them. Such an approach leaves vital issues to be the outgrowth of whims and impulses. More acceptable by far is the approach which suggests that

(1144)

some plan like the one here carried out by Jacob had
been discussed between the father and the son on a previous occasion. The carrying out of it may not have
been feasible at the time. When Joseph hears of his
father's weakened state, he promptly gets under way
though he has not been sent for, bringing his two
sons. Jacob is not greatly surprised when told of
Joseph's coming. He had evidently expected it. Here
we read "thy father is sick." Apparently Jacob had
felt only the general debility of old age in the situation
described at the close of the last chapter. Now actual
sickness has come besides.

2. Again a double impersonal construction, "one
told Jacob and said." We combine the two clauses
in the translation and make them a subordinate clause.
Very likely the verb form *ba'* is a participle, because
participles are used regularly after *hinneh,* "behold."
Such participles usually convey a future or a present
(progressive) sense; therefore: not "has come" but
"is coming." How considerately proper names are
employed in the Scriptures. "Jacob," the father,
received the message, but in his capacity as "Israel,"
the theocratic and divinely appointed head of the
race, he "made himself strong," i. e., summoned up
his reserve energy, and "sat upon his bed." An
important work was to be done and he wanted to
do it well.

3, 4. **And Jacob said to Joseph: God Almighty
appeared unto me in Luz in the land of Canaan
and he blessed me, and He said to me: Behold,
I am about to make thee fruitful, and I shall multiply thee and make of thee a company of tribes;
and I shall give this land to thee and to thy seed
after thee as an everlasting possession.**

The adoption and the blessing of Joseph's sons
is Jacob's manifest purpose. The adoption is to be
spoken of in v. 5. These two verses (v. 3, 4) must

be a natural preparation for the adoption. Jacob
recalls how God had appeared to him in Luz, the
later Bethel, in the land of Canaan — this appearance is the one of 35:6-13 rather than the one of
28:10-19, although in Jacob's thoughts the two may
have blended into one, since the substance of the
divine revelation was both times practically the same.
The blessing imparted had centered around great
posterity and permanent possession of the land. Again
hinneh, "behold," with a participle *maphrekha,* "am
blessing thee," points to the future. The familiar
fulness of expressions is used to indicate strongly that
there shall be a remarkable multiplication of offspring: "be fruitful," "multiply," "make thee a company of tribes." "Tribes" is better than "people"
here for *'ammîm,* because in reality Jacob did not
develop into separate "peoples" in the course of time
as did Abraham; cf. K. W. *sub verbo.* Many people
as descendants need a land to occupy. Consequently,
multiplication of offspring and the land occupied
are items of the blessing which are frequently joined
together. The idea of an "everlasting possession"
is familiar since 17:8. However, in the nature of
the case that promise is conditioned by the separate
existence of Abraham's or Jacob's offspring. When
these descendants are scattered abroad, they no
longer have need of the land and no guarantee or
title to it.

The transition from these two verses to v. 5 now
is this: since Jacob is to multiply greatly in numbers,
he is justified in adopting such devices as are in
themselves right and calculated to further this multiplication. Such a device he is about to employ.

5-7. **And now thy two sons that were born
unto thee in the land of Egypt before my coming
to thee to Egypt, they shall belong to me: Ephraim
and Manasseh shall belong to me as Reuben and**

Simeon do. And thy descendants whom thou shalt beget after them shall belong to thee. After the name of one of their brethren shall they be designated in their inheritance. **But as for me, when I was coming from Paddan then Rachel died to my great grief in the land of Canaan during the journey when we were still a stretch removed from Ephrathah; and I buried her there on the Ephrathah road — also called Bethlehem.**

Jacob formally adopts Jospeph's sons, who may now have been at least eighteen to twenty years old (cf. 47:28 and 41:50). His words are, "they shall belong to me." To indicate that they are not to be reckoned as loose appendages but as full-fledged sons Jacob places Ephraim and Manasseh on a par with his two eldest sons, Reuben and Simeon, mentioning the latter merely as examples. This does not imply that Ephraim and Manasseh replace Reuben and Simeon, for the latter cannot cease to be sons. Yet in one sense, as we shall see in a moment, Joseph's sons acquire the pre-eminence that the two first-born should normally have held by right of primogeniture. Jacob is conferring a favor, and yet as head of the theocratic family he also has full authority to make an adjustment such as this. He knows that Joseph will concur wholeheartedly in this arrangement. The preposition *'adh* introduces the infinitive clause, here used in a temporal sense; besides *'adh* is used in the "exclusive" sense in this case (K. S. 401 w).

6. In constructing genealogical tables, however, any future sons of Joseph's are to be counted as Joseph's own. In the matter of inheritance, however, a special provision has to be made. Apparently Jacob is thinking of ordinary inheritances as well, but primarily of the inheritance of the promised land, which he knew would be distributed according

to tribes. Such sons, counting as Joseph's, would receive an inheritance under the name of the one or the other of these adopted sons. For that reason we translated, "after the name *of one* of their brethren," though the words "of one" are not needed in the Hebrew. We have no knowledge of any further sons born to Joseph, and so this apparently remained an idle provision. *Hóládhta* is to be construed as a kind of future perfect, best rendered as a future in the translation: whom "thou shalt beget" (K. S. 129).

7. Reading superficially, we might suppose that Jacob's thoughts went wandering at this point after the manner of old men, who are not as keen of mind as they once were; and so he seems to run off into a bit of reminiscing, which comes to an abrupt close with this verse. However, as Luther already goes to some pains to prove in his commentary, Jacob's words show a logical progression. Here Jacob motivates his choice of Joseph's sons a bit more fully. Not only are they adopted because of God's promise to make Jacob fruitful, but also because Rachel, his beloved wife, of whom he had anticipated further issue, had died prematurely at Ephrathah — Bethlehem — at the time of the return of the family from Paddan (usually called Paddan-Aram). The sentence structure betrays heightened emotion on Jacob's part as he recalls the bitter scene — the pronoun *'ani* stands first, "as for me." Jacob recalls how grievous the experience was and what a burden it laid upon him (*'ali* = "upon me," i. e., "to my bitter grief," K. C., *zu meinem Leidwesen*). Now Jacob had naturally destined Rachel to be his only wife. Her sons should have been the first-born. By this arrangement of the adoption of her son's sons, Ephraim and Manasseh receive this position as is indicated by I Chron. 5:1, 2. From another point of view this

is very proper, inasmuch as the portion of the first-
born always was a double one, and here, then, Joseph
in his two sons actually receives that double portion.
From another point of view this was extremely proper,
because Joseph certainly had been the benefactor
of the entire family in a most eminent way. Such
services called for recognition. The place of honor
was his by merit.

All these deeper points of view seem hidden to
those who are critically minded. Usually it is
assumed that in the source from which this is taken
(P) this statement led up to something which has
now "been displaced in the redaction." This something K. C. thinks was the request to be buried by
Rachel's side. But since that would have harmonized
but poorly with 47:30 it is left out; in fact, Jacob is
made to say something entirely without a point.

**8-10. And Israel saw Joseph's sons, and he
said: Who are these? And Joseph said to his
father: They are my sons, whom God gave to me
here. And he said: Bring them to me that I may
bless them. Now Israel's eyesight was poor because of old age; he could not see well. So he
brought them near to him, and he kissed and
embraced them.**

Joseph now understands sufficiently well why his
father is minded to bless Ephraim and Manasseh.
Everything is ready — Jacob may proceed to bless.
The successive steps follow as one might have surmised. The grandfather feels that the two dim shapes
that he sees are the sons in question. To verify the
impression he asks: "Who are these?" We may add
that he may have seen Joseph but rarely and Joseph's
sons still more rarely and may not have expected that
they would have grown to such full manly stature.
How often we are surprised at young people's stature
if we do not happen to have seen them for a time!

Joseph responds, confirming his father's surmise, as
much as to say: Yes; "they are my sons whom God
gave me here." So Jacob naturally requests:
"Bring them to me that I may bless them." Blessing one's descendants was by this time a kind of
established tradition among the patriarchs. It was
the regular custom. The parenthetical remark that
follows explains why Jacob had asked: "Who are
these?" Jacob was not actually blind; his "eyesight
was poor." That must be the meaning of the Hebrew
idiom: "his eyes were heavy" (*kabhedhû*). That
does not mean that he was blind. Consequently the
Hebrew "he could not see" is meant in the sense "he
could not see well." Viewed thus, all items in the
narrative yield a natural harmony. There is no room
for the critical position that E says (v. 8) Jacob
saw; whereas J says (v. 10) he could not see. Because
of the unlikeliness of such a contradiction within two
almost contiguous verses, ordinary common sense has
always reconciled them without effort. Joseph com-
plies with his father's request and "brought them near
to him." Then the venerable patriarch "kissed and
embraced them" in a manner that made these young
men understand the better what their grandfather
had meant to their father. The imperative *qachem*
(v. 9) is followed by a converted imperfect *wa'abha-
rakhem* — a rather common sequence (K. S. 364 n)
The clause (v. 10) *lo' yakhûl*, etc., is asyndetic, expressing result; the imperfect is a *yaqtul concomitans*
(K. S. 152).

11-14. **And Israel said to Joseph: To see thy
face — I had never expected it; and now God allows
me to see even thy descendants. And Joseph
brought them away from beside his knees and fell
down before him to the ground. And Joseph took
both of them, Ephraim in his right hand at Israel's
left hand, and Manasseh in his left hand at Israel's**

right hand, and so he brought them to him. And
Israel put forth his right hand and laid it upon
Ephraim's head — and he was the younger — and
his left hand upon Manasseh's head, and so crossed
his hands; for Manasseh was the elder.

Who can blame Jacob for lapsing into reminiscences? All the more not since they are remembrances
of God's mercy. The order of the sentence gives the
true shade of meaning: "to see thy face" stands
first. He had never hoped to catch even a passing
glimpse of Joseph's face, and he is permitted by God's
providence to be in his son's company and even to
behold grandsons. The infinitive *re'oh* is unusual
for a construct, yet it is found 50:20 and 31:28 (G.
K. 75 n).

12. Joseph naturally wishes to thank his father
for the favor granted him. In true oriental courtesy
"he fell down before him to the ground," bowing his
face to the ground. But in order to be able to do
this he first "brought them away from beside his
knees," for there they stood in the way between him
and his father. They had not been "between his
knees," A. R. V., that would have required a different preposition. They had not been sitting on his
knees, as some imagine. What a picture! Two youths
of twenty sitting on their grandfather's knees! When
brought to the old man who was sitting upon his
bed, they naturally stood at either side of his knees
while he embraced them. The preposition involved
is *me'im* = "from at," which is best rendered "beside" in this case. No need of rare conjectures about
some occult adoption rite. A reference to 30:3 is
out of place, for nothing indicates that he took them
on or between his knees.

13. What now follows is quite simple. Joseph
reckons in terms of the rights and the advantages
of the first-born. So he takes his two sons and guides

them to his father in such a way as to bring the eldest to the father's right hand; the youngest to his left. But here again nature gives no advantages in the kingdom of God; it must be entirely in terms of free grace. Isaac was preferred before the elder Ishmael; Jacob before Esau; now Ephraim to Manasseh. The Spirit of prophecy, who enlightened Jacob to speak his blessing, guided him in this case to let the right hand rest upon the younger. By the way, here we have the first specific mention of the laying on of hands as a rite of benediction. The verb *sikkel*, used here only, may mean "crossed," as the Greek version already construed it. K. C. imports rather a heavy meaning into the verb from the parallel Arabic root meaning "to be dark," when he translates this verb alone as: "with secret purpose he laid on" his hands. The verb might come from the root which means "to deal wisely or prudently," and then the Piel meaning might be "to do (it) purposely," or "guiding his hand wittingly" (A. V. and Luther). But this seems rather an unwarranted jump in thought from "prudently" to "purposely." (The article in *hatstsa'îr* — "the younger" — marks the comparative, K. S. 308 a).

15, 16. **And he blessed Joseph and said:**

**The God before whom my fathers walked —
Abraham and Isaac,
The God who shepherds me from of old to this
day,
The Angel that redeems me from all evil —
may He bless the lads;
And may my name be named upon them and
the name of my fathers, Abraham and
Isaac;
And may they multiply exceedingly in the
midst of the land.**

This arrangement shows that Jacob's blessing is
really poetical in form according to the Hebrew law
of poetic parallelism. Quite properly it is said that
"he blessed Joseph," for in blessing the sons he
blessed and purposed to bless the father. The Greek
Septuagint, as usual, removes the difficulty by a
textual change and says "them" for "Joseph." The
noun *'Elohîm* with the article means "the true God."
The blessing begins rather majestically with a threefold address to God, which we may well regard as
designed by the Spirit of inspiration, whether Jacob
at the time fully realized this import or not. For
Jacob here spoke as a prophet, and not always was
the fullest meaning of the prophetic word entirely
apparent to the mouthpiece God employed (though
by this we in no wise imply mechanical inspiration).
The first reference is to the Father; the last is to the
Son, the Redeemer; the second does not specifically
refer to the Holy Spirit, though in a sense He may be
said to shepherd God's children.

When Jacob describes the true God as the one
before whom his "father walked," he suggests the
necessity of knowing the true God according to the
true tradition that the fathers, Abraham and Isaac,
possessed concerning Him. He knows God as one
whom his fathers knew intimately and whose religion was a vital, living issue with them. This word
testifies to a type of godly life that was deeply
sincere. In thinking of the fathers he recalls how
the preceding generations had already stood under
God's gracious blessing.

Then he describes God as *ro'eh,* "the one shepherding," the participle expressing continuity: God
still shepherds. Himself a shepherd, Jacob well understood what a measure of tender care the figure involved. In this case Jacob could well testify that
this care had extended "from of old to this day." This

is the first of those frequent references to the Divine
Shepherd (Ps. 23:1; 80:1; Isa. 40:11; John 10:11;
Heb. 13:20; I Pet. 2:25, etc.).   The A. V. blurs this
thought by rendering "fed."   Without a doubt, the
third reference is also to God, for it is in strict
parallelism with the preceding two and ascribes a
truly divine work to the Angel, namely the work
of redeeming from all evil.   Consequently this is
a reference to the divine Angel of the Lord or Angel
of Yahweh, whom we already met with 22:11, and
who was there already discovered to be more than
a created angel.   See the remarks on that passage.   Cf.
also 16:11.   For the Son is God's messenger or Angel,
sent to deliver man.   Here again the participle is
used, *go'el*, "the Redeeming One," i. e., one who still
redeems or continually redeems.   After an experience
of a lifetime marked by many a deliverance Jacob well
knew how often He had been delivered.

In this case there is no need of specifying wherein
the blessing upon "the lads" (*ne'arîm* = "young men")
is to consist.   "May He bless the lads" covers the
case, for it involves that He is to continue to manifest
the same care, first suffering them to walk before
Him; secondly, shepherding them uninterruptedly;
thirdly, redeeming them also from all evil.   Yet the
three mentioned are one, as the singular verb "may
He bless" (*yebharekh*) indicates.   In the statement
"may my name be named upon them" the term "name"
(*shem*) signifies "character"; i. e., may my and my
father's character find expression in them, or: may
they express the true patriarchal character and be
conscious of what deeper responsibilities are involved.
The blessing concludes with a thought that was vital
in those days of small beginnings: "may they multiply exceedingly (Hebrew: *larobh* = "to a multitude")
in the midst of the land" — *beqérebh ha'árets* in-

volves holding secure possession of the land and not only holding the fringes of it.

In this blessing not only did the Spirit of God speak through the venerable old patriarch, but he himself on his part gave proof of a strong and cheerful faith. Such words were an effective benediction and much more than a pious wish.

17-19. And Joseph noticed that his father was placing his right hand upon Ephraim's head, and it displeased him, and so he took hold of his father's hand to remove it from Ephraim's head to Manasseh's head; and Joseph said to his father: Not so, my father; for this one is the first-born; put thy right hand upon his head. But his father refused, saying: I know, my son; I know. He too shall become a people, and he too shall be great. However, his younger brother shall be greater than he, and his descendants shall be a multitude of people.

Everything is apparently recorded just as it happened. The two men are placed before Jacob; he places his hands crossed upon their heads and at once pronounces his blessing. Joseph observes the irregularity but cannot act at once, for he is also giving heed to what his father says. Furthermore, so solemn a word dare not be lightly interrupted. But as soon as the father has spoken the benediction, Joseph aims to correct what he thinks is a strange oversight. In fact "it displeased him" — *yera'* (imperfect from *ra'a'*) literally: "it was evil in his sight." Having less discernment than his father, he had reckoned the right of the first-born as naturally belonging to the eldest. He even "took hold of his father's hand to remove it from Ephraim's head to Manasseh's." But Jacob has been induced by the Holy Spirit, the Spirit of prophecy, to do this unusual thing and recognizes that his action is the result of superior, divinely wrought insight. So he refuses very positively and tells Joseph that he himself was aware of the actual situation. Then he proceeds to tell definitely just what difference is involved. Manasseh too shall he "a people and he too shall be great." But Ephraim shall outstrip him, so that "his descendants shall be a multitude of people." This last expression *melo' haggoyîm* — "the fulness of peoples" with the article means: he shall constitute a real multitude of people (*die wahre Voelkerfuelle,* K. C., potential article, K. S. 296 b). Strange to say, in the first census of Moses' time the tribe "Ephraim had 40,500 men, while that of Manasseh could only reckon 32,200; in the second, the numbers received a temporary alteration, Ephraim counting only 32,500, and Manasseh 52,700" (Whitelaw) ; cf. Num. 1:33-35 with 26:28-37. Moses gives proof of his faith in prophecy by recording a word which in his day was not yet being fulfilled.

20-22. **And he blessed them on that day saying: In thee shall Israel bless, saying: May God make thee as Ephraim and as Manasseh. So he put Ephraim before Manasseh. Then Israel said to Joseph: Behold, I shall die, but God will be with you, and will bring you back unto the land of your fathers. And I myself do give to thee one portion of ground above thy brethren, which I took from the hand of the Amorites with my sword and with my bow.**

Joseph had interrupted the blessing as soon as he had dared, but Jacob had not said all that was on his mind. After gently repelling Joseph's suggestion, he continues to state that these two tribes shall be so greatly blessed that they shall in the course of time become proverbial for blessing and shall provide the formula to be used, i. e., "In thee (= by referring to the one or the other of you) shall Israel bless" or "invoke a blessing" (Meek), saying: "May God make thee as Ephraim and as Manasseh." *'Elohîm* occurs here rather than *Yahweh* because the Creator's power in multiplying descendants is being reflected on. But one noteworthy point was that Jacob still continued to "put Ephraim before Manasseh." Such is the certainty of men of God when they speak prophetically. In *yesimekha* the future is optative. The Jews are said to use this formula of blessing to this day.

21. But Jacob has a word for Joseph in particular. He knows death is at hand. He states the fact with the calm courage of faith. But he leaves the assurance with Joseph that Egypt is not the land of their destiny. God in His power (*'Elohîm*) will bring back Israel's children "to the land of their fathers." They should not allow this prospect to become submerged. Jacob foresaw very clearly on the basis of words spoken to the fathers (cf. chap. 15) what the next important developments in God's people would be. God's children do not walk on toward a dark and uncertain future.

22. Jacob has a last bequest for his favorite son Joseph. He gives it as something to which he, Jacob, has a particular right — "I myself do give" (*'ani*, emphatic). It is a special "portion," a *shékhem*, that is a "shoulder" or "ridge" — just "one above thy brethren" (*'a(ch)chadh min* — construct, before a preposition, G. K. 130 g). He asserts that he took this "from the hand of the Amorites with sword and bow." This is a reference to an event not recorded elsewhere in the Scriptures but referred to John 4:5, and so, apparently, the parcel of ground in question was clearly identified for many a century. This cannot be a reference to chapter 34, for in that deed Jacob had no hand and sharply rebuked

his sons for it. Therefore the word *shékhem,* "portion," does not contain a subtle allusion to the town Shechem and the event there recorded. Practically all commentators see such an allusion because of the accidental correspondence of words, but they create great difficulties for themselves by such an assumption. The patriarchs did more things than Genesis records. But some will protest, as does Delitzsch, that such an act of conquest is contrary to the attitude of the patriarchs, who did nothing to further their own interests but waited patiently till God gave what He had promised to give. Yet here is a situation that would cover the case: Jacob may on some occasion have been wrongfully attacked and resolutely defended himself — for the patriarchs could on occasion bear arms, as Abraham did Gen. 14 — and as a result in driving off the Amorites he may have acquired right and title to a "portion" or "ridge" of ground. The other explanation resorted to by not a few is to make the perfect *nathatti* a prophetic perfect, "I shall give," and to refer it to the time of conquest under Joshua when the Ephraimites did take Shechem and the surrounding territory from the Canaanites. But the Hebrew construction opposes itself first of all with the emphatic "*I do give*": what *Ephraim* has to conquer is not emphatically *Jacob's* gift. Lastly, note: *nathátti* is a *perfectum praesens,* "herewith I give" (G. K. 106 i).

The critical approach to the subject matter of this chapter is what one would be inclined to expect. Since the chapter purports to set forth a prophecy, and criticism does not believe very much in prophecy, we are assured that this must be a prophecy after the event, *vaticinium post eventum,* and therefore a later account which is cast into the form of a prophecy, as though Biblical writers were not above the use of such morally doubtful devices, and as though the message of the passage were just as valuable whether it be a true, straightforward prophecy or a pious fraud. Along the same line is the critical assumption that the "threefold invocation" (v. 15, 16) "has some resemblance to a feature of Babylonian liturgies." Such an accidental "resemblance" may exist, but it takes much more than that to warrant the assumption that therefore the thought of the patriarch must be derived from some Babylonian source.

HOMILETICAL SUGGESTIONS

We feel that v. 8-20 may be used to demonstrate the potency of the prayers and the blessings of God's saints. This approach involves, of course, that blessings are prayers, and that prayer is heard. One could use the section v. 1-20 for the same purpose.

CHAPTER XLIX

14. Conclusion of Jacob's History (Continued)

c. The Blessing of His Own Sons (49:1-27)

Jacob concludes his life in a manner worthy of the patriarchs, among whom he stands as one fully deserving this honor. Other saints of God are presented in the Scriptures as having spoken a blessing before their end. In this class are Isaac (chap. 27), Moses (Deut. 33), Joshua (Josh. 24), Samuel (I Sam. 12). What is more natural than that a saint of God departing this life should desire to lay a blessing upon the head of those whom he leaves behind!

Upon closer study this blessing of Jacob stands revealed as a piece of rare beauty. Lange has summarized the elements of poetic excellence as "rhythmical movement, a beautiful parallelism of members, a profusion of figures, a play upon the names of the sons, other instances of paronomasia, unusual modes of expression, a truly exalted spirit, as well as a heartfelt warmth." It seems but natural to us that a man of Jacob's energy of mind and character should have cast his thoughts into a mold of fine poetic beauty in order to make his utterances the more clear-cut and also the more easily remembered. They who have a mean conception of the patriarchs as being prosy and trivial characters, standing on a low level of faith and godliness, are inclined to take offense at so noble a production and to pronounce apodictically that Jacob could not have been its author. But before we reckon with the weaknesses of the critical position, we shall set forth a few other features of this blessing that contribute to a correct understanding of it.

The sequence of the names is readily understood. The six children of Leah are mentioned first, though it is not clear why Zebulon, the sixth, should be mentioned before Issachar, the fifth. Then come the four sons of the handmaids, though the two sons of Zilpah, Asher and Gad, are inserted between the two sons of Bilhah, Dan and Naphtali. Lastly come Rachel's children, Joseph and Benjamin. Another observation is in order on this matter of grouping. Among the first six Judah definitely stands out by receiving a much more substantial blessing than the rest. His is the pre-eminence in point of leadership. Among the last six Joseph excels by virtue of his blessing, although his is the pre-eminence in the matter of possession. Joseph is blessed by including Ephraim and Manasseh in one. The distinction between these two sons of his was taken care of in the preceding chapter.

Some question whether this poem should be designated as a blessing; they emphasize v. 1, "that I may tell you that which shall befall you in the latter days." They would prefer to label it prediction or perhaps prophecy. Yet v. 28, rightly construed, labels the words spoken by the patriarch a "blessing." So if the Scriptural estimate is at all normative — and for us it is absolute — we have here both blessing and prediction, or a prophetic blessing. This claim is by no means impaired by the fact that four of the sons must hear words spoken that involve a censure, in fact, in the case of the first three sons a severe word of censure. Issachar (v. 15) gets a milder rebuke. The entire problem, however, is viewed in the wrong light if it is claimed that certain sons were cursed. Reuben is censured (v. 4). Simeon's and Levi's *anger* is cursed (v. 7) not they themselves. And rightly considered, these criticism are blessings in disguise, for they point out to the tribes involved the sin that the tribe as a whole is most exposed to and against which it should be particularly on its guard: Reuben against moral instability and licentiousness; Simeon and Levi against hotheaded violence; Issachar against indolence. Yet, for all that, not one of the tribes is removed from the concord of blessings laid upon the rest, for the blessings laid upon some redound to the welfare of all the rest. The blessed land is denied to none. The benefits of the covenant of the Lord in which all stood are cancelled for none. The dying father recognized that what some needed was not further gifts but restraint in the use of what they already possessed.

From the human point of view another matter must be stressed. The father had long observed his sons and knew them perhaps better than they knew themselves. In a pithy final word he gives to each man the counsel that he needed most. Upon this natural foundation the Spirit of God builds up and helps Jacob to foretell in a number of instances how the tribal development tends in the future. So with a fine mixture of councel and encouragement the father speaks a word that the sons from the very outset value as a divinely inspired oracle. A godly man's oracles are very potent prayers made according to God's heart and answered by Him.

We can, therefore, hardly agree with those who stress the improbability of a decrepit old man's being able to utter thoughts so clear-cut and virile. We know of two possibilities: first, man's intellect may grow feeble and decay before his end; secondly, men have been known to retain full possession of their faculties, in fact, to have their powers of mind and heart at the keenest point of development just prior to their end. Jacob happens to belong to the second class.

Some have found fault with the fact that no judgment is pronounced on religious conditions in the course of these last words of Jacob — *kein Urteil ueber die religioesen Verhaeltnisse* — Dillmann. Such a criticism is rather wide of the mark. That is not what Jacob set out to offer. He says (v. 1) that he proposes to tell his sons what would befall them in the latter days. From another point of view this is also a blessing (v. 28). A man can hardly be criticized for not having said what he did not aim to say.

The critical position in regard to these words of Jacob is well known. With almost united mind and voice the critics hold that these are not words of Jacob, at least not in their present form. Instead, the words are relegated to the time of the Judges, perhaps the latter portion of that age. It is claimed that the whole chapter indubitably reflects this later age, and that it received its present shape and form perhaps no later than the days of David and Solomon. A few notable exceptions are still to be found: Hengstenberg, Keil, Delitzsch, Whitelaw, Koenig (with reservations), Strack still have the courage to hold that the words are Jacob's.

However, it must be remembered that certain presuppositions condition the critical attitude. In the first place, actual prophecy or prediction as such is regarded as virtually impossible. In the second place, the patriarchs are without good grounds regarded incapable of so significant an utterance. Thirdly, some men are obsessed with the idea of denying outstanding productions like this poem to outstanding characters and of ascribing them to insignificant, obscure and usually unknown authors — a strange course of procedure. Then we should yet note a fatal weakness of the critical contention: Levi is spoken of in terms of an inferior position, which actually was his in the earlier days and which constituted a disadvantage and in a sense a reproof of the tribe. But this situation underwent a radical change in Moses' day, when Levi rallied to the cause of the Lord (Exod. 32:25-28), redeemed itself from disgrace, and advanced to a position of honorable and blessed dispersion among the tribes of Israel. Jacob's words (v. 5-7) reflect the earlier situation and would not be the statement of the case for the Age of the Judges. When, then, some critics (Land mentioned by Skinner) "distinguish six stages in the growth of the song," that must be regarded as the type of proof that covers up deficiency of sound logic by bold assertions, none of which are susceptable of proof.

Keii has very properly reminded us that the thing that actually appears in the song of blessings is "not the prediction of particular historical events" but rather a "purely ideal portraiture of the peculiarities of the different tribes." This is a point that must be borne in mind continually. Critics make of these generalized statements specific allusions to particular events or situations and so gain ground for their type of interpretation, which sees the Age of the Judges reflected again and again.

One last point of view is not to be lost sight of — this blessing was one of the things Israel needed to guide its course through the dark days to be encountered during the stay in Egypt. A blessing like this was a spiritual necessity. By the use of it men of Israel could look forward to the blessed time when the tribes would be safely established in the Promised Land, every tribe in its own inheritance. Without words like this and 15:12-14 Israel would have been a nation sailing upon an uncharted sea.

This chapter was a necessity for Israel's faith during the days of the bondage in Egypt.

We mention perhaps the strangest of exegetical curiosities, the interpretation of Jeremias (*Das Alte Testament im Lichte des alten Orients*) which makes of the twelve sons of Jacob in this blessing the twelve signs of the Zodiac. To arrive at this result he reconstrues a number of these signs, deliberately changes portions of the Hebrew text, and discovers allusions so subtle and remote that only a very few — Nork and Zimmern Lepsius, e. g. — have ventured to follow him. But even if his construction should be correct, to what purpose would the chapter have been written? Men such as Jeremias would say: these are Israel's astral myths. We cannot substitute such vague reconstructions for the sound purposeful meaning that a sober exegesis knows to be the true sense of the Scriptures.

Several types of figures are found in this chapter, especially comparisons or metaphors. Judah is a lion; Issachar, an ass; Dan, a serpent; Naphtali, a hind; Benjamin, a wolf. Yet not one of these comparisons of itself involves anything derogatory. Least of all have they any reference to a totemistic state of religion through which the tribes are said to have passed earlier in their history.

There are many more minor problems relative to this blessing, but we have touched upon all that are essential to a correct understanding of it and have shown the fallacy of at least the major misconstructions that are put upon it.

1. **And Jacob summoned his sons and said: Assemble yourselves and I will tell you what shall befall you in the end of the days.**

For "summoned" the Hebrew says, "he called unto" them. This is meant in the sense of dispatching messengers to gather them together. There is a definite consciousness on the old father's part that he like other old men of God is being granted special insight in reference to his sons' lives, the knowledge of which can be a substantial blessing to them. Jacob never saw more clearly and never spoke more truly. We have here more than *pia desideria,* "pious wishes." The solemn formal announcement on the father's part also indicates that he is clearly aware of the fact that he is about to pronounce substantial blessings. Besides, these words are to be common property heard and known by all. Each brother is to profit by what the other hears and receives. "Befall" *yikra'* for *yikrah* — a common exchange of the verbs of these two classes (G. K. 75 rr).

Much depends on the right evaluation of the expression "in the end of the days." So we have translated quite literally *be'acharîth hayyamîm.* Koenig says very generally *in der Folgezeit,* "in coming days." Luther was content with the general phrase *in kuenftigen Zeiten,* "in future days." A. V. uses too strong an expression, "in the last days," laying itself open to the criticism that much of what Jacob foretells does not lie at the end of time. Literally, of course, *'acharîth* is "the latter part" (B D B). Some make the expression refer merely to the future, but that is made impossible by the literal meaning, "the latter part." Others construe in a fanciful way, contending that it runs up to the end in so far as an individual may see in the direction of that end, some seeing much farther than others. Most interpreters are ready to concede that the Messianic age is involved in some passages where this expression occurs and that it, therefore, in those passages bears a Messianic connotation. K. W. will allow this to be the case from Isa. 2:2 onward. That is the attitude of the majority of expositors. But, as we hope to demonstrate, the Messianic future is very definitely in this chapter. Consequently, from the very first instance of its use as well as in all others the phrase points to the future, including the Messianic future. But it points not to this only but to any preceding part of the future as well, as long as this future is covered by God's promises and is a part of the divine developments culminating in the days of the Messianic age. This meaning holds good also for Num. 24:14; Deut. 4:30; 31:29, as well as for the later prophetic passages. Consequently Keil says correctly, on the one hand: This phrase "in prophetic language denotes not the future generally but the last future, the Messianic age of consummation"; and adds, on the other hand: "It embraces 'the whole history of completion which underlies the present period of growth.'" Now as far as Jacob himself was concerned, the first instance of fullfillment naturally was the occupation of Canaan by the tribes descended from his sons. As far as Israel as a nation was concerned, that was the first thing to be realized. We need not wonder greatly that his blessing speaks very largely in terms dealing with this first fulfillment. To see this first word realized would serve as a pledge for the realization of all things that God might yet be pleased to reveal and to do. Perspective, as far as time is concerned, was not in evidence in prophetic words. Revelation presents all the elements of the future in its prediction without troubling to reveal the time intervals that may come between the events foretold. This explains how Jacob can see in one picture the occupation of Canaan and the Messiah's kingdom but hardly anything that lies in between. Dillmann makes an unwarranted statement in reference to this phrase: he claims that it was customary in the age of the prophets; therefore it must have been added by some narrator living in that age. Proof for such a claim is not adduced and cannot be.

We must also take issue with the question whether it is Jacob who pronounces this blessing or not. For us the question is permanently settled by the statement, perfectly clear in itself — "Jacob . . . said." The statements of v. 6, 7 b and 10 are supposed to demonstrate that it was not Jacob who spoke, for these verses seem to move in terms of the later tribes. Quite so. But it is Jacob thinking in terms of the tribes descended from him — not at all an unnatural thing, seeing he knew he was to develop into a number of tribes. But the critics claim that some writer of the Age of the Judges sought to recall the tribes that were fast disintegrating and losing their spiritual heritage, and to make his appeal more effective the writer assumed the name of the venerable Jacob — this literary assumption does not strike us as particularly effective. It is far from convincing. We fail to see how a message cast into such a form could exert any particularly salutary influence.

2. **Come together and hearken, ye sons of Jacob,**
   And hearken unto Israel, your father.

At this point the poem proper begins, as is indicated by the parallelism of structure. In substance v. 1 is repeated, in so far as the sons are bidden to gather round their father. The added feature of the verse is the double summons to "hearken." Good sons would in any case be ready to do that. The father's double exhortation grows out of the knowledge that his words will be doubly precious, since they voice his own best counsel as well as wisdom imparted by God's Holy Spirit. For no man ever yet by the cleverness of his own ingenuity fore-

told future developments in the kingdom of God.
That Jacob is thus speaking in a double capacity is
further indicated by the two names he uses, "Jacob,"
the name of the man naturally clever and ambitious,
and Israel, the name of the new man who had submitted to God's leadings, had prevailed in prayer, and
had been content to go as God led when native human
ingenuity had failed.

> 3, 4. **Reuben, thou art my first-born,**
> **My strength and the beginning of my might,**
> **The pre-eminence of dignity and the pre-**
> **eminence of power,**
> **Seething as water does — thou shalt not enjoy**
> **pre-eminence,**
> **For thou hast gone up upon thy father's bed,**
> **Then didst thou defile — my couch did he**
> **mount.**

The father cannot forget that Reuben is his "first-
born," nor all the fine hopes that attached themselves to him. The father multiplies himself and
grows strong through his children. Therefore the
first-born may well be regarded as a pledge of what
the others yet to come may achieve together with
him. He may, therefore, well be designated "my
strength (*kochî*) and the beginning of my might"
(*'ônî*). This latter expression, "beginning of might,"
is on several other occasions used in the Scriptures
in reference to the first-born: Deut. 21:17 b; Ps.
78:51; 105:36. For, surely, with all purity we may
make the assertion that manly strength best displays
itself in procreation. More dignity still may be
ascribed to the first-born, for truly in a sense it
was divine providence that ordained that a certain
one be the first-born among the children of a man.
Universal customs and the law itself to an extent
at least recognize this distinction. Among the chosen
people such a dignity is not lost. If anything, it is

like all good things enhanced in value by being found
in the kingdom. Jacob expresses this thought by
designating Reuben as "the pre-eminence of dignity
and the pre-eminence of power." *Yéther,* here rendered "pre-eminence" could have been rendered
equally well as "superiority, excellency" (B D B).
Se'eth is the construct infinitive from *nasa',* which
means "to lift up," "to bear." From the great variety
of meanings possible from this root "dignity" seems
best suited to the context. Luther, following the
Vulgate, arrived at a similar meaning, using the idea
of *nasa'* in so far as it is also used for offering up
sacrifices; so Luther renders *der Oberste im Opfer,*
"the leader in sacrifice." Yet the A. V.'s rendering has more to commend it. In any case, Reuben's
dignity and honor due to his being the first-born are
strongly set forth in this verse. The rendering "excessively proud and excessively fierce" is grammatically possible but conflicts with whatever else we know
about Reuben. The criticism and the reproof are confined to the next verse.

4. There was within Reuben's character a certain unbridled element, a boiling-up, a "seething,"
which was in itself "wantonness" (B D B). For
páchaz involves both these ideas, being derived from
a root which implies "to be reckless" but used in the
Scriptures in the sense of "being lascivious." Seething lust, "unbridled license," was within the man.
This root fault incapacitated him for the position of
leadership which would normally have been his. So
the father pronounces the sentence, "thou shalt not
enjoy pre-eminence" (*tôthar* — Hifil imperfect from
yathar). For, apparently, all of the family knew
what Reuben's unbridled license had led him to
do. If any did not, here the father makes specific
mention of the crime of incest reported 35:22. At
that time Jacob did not score Reuben's sin, if we are

justified to argue thus from the silence of the Bible.
There can be no doubt as to what his attitude was
toward this foul piece of licentiousness. Here he
leaves a public condemnation on record and condemns
the deed in no uncertain terms at a time which serves
to make his condemnation all the more impressive.
This was a rebuke that none who heard it could ever
forget. Jacob speaks very plainly, "for thou hast
gone up upon thy father's bed." He says nothing by
way of accusing Bilhah. Of the two she may have
been the less guilty party of the crime. "Then,"
speaking in more general terms, Jacob adds, "thou
didst defile" (*chillálta*). Nothing is gained by refer-
ing to sexual irregularities by terms that specifically
describe them. It is enough to note "he defiled," that
is, himself, the partner to his misdeed, his father's
name, the family's reputation. Then Jacob turns
away from his son as from a stranger in sad reflection and speaks in the third person about him (K.
S. 344 m), "my couch did he mount" — a statement
accompanied, as it were, by a sad shaking of the
head as over an unbelievable thing. *Mishkebhey*,
"bed," seems to be a dual (K. S. 260 h).

This solemn rebuke was the best thing that
could have befallen Reuben, and it will, no doubt, have
produced a salutary reaction. One more outbreak
of his licentious lack of restraint appears in his descendants when Korah's rebellion flares up in the
wilderness (Num. 16). Aside from that, Reuben
never furnished a prominent leader for Israel. According to Joshua 20:10ff. the Reubenites at least acted
inadvisedly if not wickedly. In the days of the Judges
Reuben failed in an emergency when put to the test
(Judg. 5:15). The tribe settled east of the Jordan,
demanding its share of the inheritance of Israel a
bit prematurely (Num. 32). In the course of Israel's
further development Reuben grows more and more

unimportant. So the father's word became a reality
— "thou shalt not enjoy pre-eminence." With deep
insight the father detected the major flaw of this son's
makeup and read his character aright.

> **5-7. Simeon and Levi are brothers,**
> **Their tools are implements of violence.**
> **May my soul not enter into their council,**
> **And may my glory not join in their assembly.**
> **For in their anger they slew men,**
> **In their self-will they hocked cattle.**
> **Cursed be their anger, for it is fierce,**
> **And their wrath, for it is cruel!**
> **I will parcel them out in Jacob.**
> **And scatter them in Israel.**

It is rather obvious that Simeon and Levi are
brothers after the flesh, for Leah was their mother.
Here "brothers" implies that they are besides of
one mind and disposition. The unfortunate episode
in which they figured found them in complete agreement: one was as much to blame as the other. The
rebuke administered has reference to the vengeance
these two brothers took on the Shechemites because
a prince of that city had violated the honor of their
sister Dinah. At that time already (34:30) Jacob
had condemned their deed strongly. Apparently, the
native perversity of the two was yet unbroken.
While the minds of the twelve sons were still shocked
over the plain speech used in reference to Reuben,
all of them, but especially the two addressed, hear
a salutary reproof that is equally strong. Perhaps
nothing more helpful could have been spoken for these
two; and so again we have a blessing, though in disguise. The word *mekherôth*, used only here, presents
difficulties. From days of old grammarians have
sensed the root *khûr* in this noun and have been
struck by the similarity of the Greek μάχαιρα, "short
sword." Very likely this resemblance is purely acci-

dental. *Khûr* means "to dig"; a *mekherah* would be
a digging tool, i. e., a "mattock" (K. W., *Karste*).
On that memorable occasion Simeon and Levi, perhaps lacking swords and also to avoid suspicion, may
have come down upon Shechem with heavy mattocks
in their hands and used them as "implements of
violence." Jacob first expresses his disapproval of
the deed and the method employed to achieve the deed
when he says: "may my soul not enter into their
council." His inmost being, his "soul" (*néphesh*),
abhors such crafty schemes. Not only would he
not be partner to their deeds; he would not even have
it said that he in any wise shared in such nefarious
gatherings where the plot was hatched out. For
emphasis' sake he repeats the thought in a parallel
statement: "May my glory (i. e. again: my soul —
see Ps. 7:6; 16:9; 30:13; for the soul is the most
glorious part of man) not join in their assembly."
Some render the imperfect of the verbs involved as
potentials and gain a still more acceptable form of
statement: My soul would not enter (*tabho'*) into
their council and my glory would not join (*techadh*
— from *yachadh*) in their assembly. "My soul"
and "my glory" are, of course, Hebrew substitutes for
"I" (K. S. 7 and 325 o), being reserved for more
elevated strains of diction. Thus far the deed stands
condemned as highhanded "violence," the planning of
it as done in an iniquitous assembly, which all
righteous men should abhor. Now the source of the
deed or its deeper motive is scrutinized. The brothers
had flattered and, no doubt, at first prided themselves
upon what they had done, as though it had been a
deed born out of righteous indignation. But good
motives do not produce murder. So Jacob, reading
their hearts better than they themselves did, instructs
them that they did it "in their anger" (*'aph*) and
"self-will" (*ratsôn*). For "men" the Hebrew has the

singular *'ish,* "man," as the language often does
in the case of nouns whose plural form would be
the normal thing (K. S. 256 b); so also "cattle"
singular *(shôr).* "Hocked" means "hamstringed"
(Meek), i. e., cut the leg tendons. "Digged down
a wall" (A. V.) is not correct. It is true that
34:27-29 told of the *capture* of the cattle. In v. 6,
however, we have supplementary information: what
these two men did not lead away as plunder they
destroyed in the fierceness of their anger. In our
day we should say that these two brothers were
actuated by a nationalistic, carnal pride. They particularly resented that their sister, born of the superior
stock of Jacob as they felt, had been treated dis-
respectfully. They did not regret so much that a
daughter of the race of promise had been dealt with
dishonorably.

7. Jacob wishes to remove all questions as to
the estimate that was to be put upon a deed growing out of such carnal pride in the Israelite race.
He pronounces a curse upon such "anger," for it
was not holy but "fierce." It was "wrath," *'ebhrah,*
that is "overflow," "arrogance," or "outburst," something that had gotten beyond control and was also
"cruel." Apparently, Jacob spared no man's feelings.
It seems as though Simeon and Levi needed a bit
of disillusioning, and their father did not lack the
courage necessary to administer it. Lastly, a restraint is laid upon both: they are to be "parcelled
out" and "scattered" in Israel. Jacob ascribes this
act to himself, for in his authority as head of the
race he determines that this shall happen. Apparently, this was also a word of prophecy: Jacob spoke
what was God's will. Consequently this result was
providentially brought to pass. There was a wisdom and a propriety about this punishment. They
who had banded together to their own hurt were to

be dispersed for their own good. Apparently, after they were scattered, their native bent for hatching out evil plots died out.

The fulflllment of this word is instructive. Simeon increased rapidly at first. The first census not long after the Exodus (Num. 1) revealed the count of 59,300. The second census shortly before the Occupation of Canaan (Num. 26) showed that the tribe had shrunk to the number of 22,200. The tribe received its portion of the Promised Land "in the midst of the inheritance of the children of Judah" (Josh. 19:1). Its fortunes are identified with those of Judah (Judg. 1:3). Already in his blessing (Deut. 33) Moses had passed it by. Its extinction apparently involved being absorbed by other tribes, especially by Judah. Such as did survive to a later date (I Chron. 4:38-43) sought out for themselves regions outside of Canaan and dwelt there. All this, especially the absorption by the other tribes, may have been for the good of this tribe. Had it stood alone as a strong tribe, it might have perpetuated the father's sinful ways.

In the case of Levi the situation is different. The Levites were, indeed, dispersed throughout the whole land in the cities mentioned Josh. 21:1-40. But in their dispersion these ministers of the sanctuary served as teachers of Israel and so really became a wholesome leaven, whose influence was felt for good by all. Of course, the turn for the better in the case of the Levites came with Exod. 32:26ff., as noted above. Here it is most evident how an apparent setback may yet be a blessing (v. 28) if those upon whom it is laid accept it as a wholesome bit of discipline. No writer of the days of the Judges could have written these words.

Thus far the father's last words have not been of a kind to cause joy or to raise hope. Rebuke and

correction have been their theme. But, surely, there
must be something in the future of these sons of his
to give rise to words of a more hopeful and more
cheerful character. The next son comes under this
second classification.

8, 9.   **Judah, thee, yes thee will thy brethren
praise:**
**Thy hand shall be on the nape of the neck of
thine enemies;**
The sons of thy father shall bow down to thee,
A whelp of a lion is Judah;
**Thou hast mounted up, my son, after eating
the prey.**
**He crouches, then lies down, as would a lion,
or a lioness.**
Who would dare to rouse him?

One at once feels the glad animation that takes
possession of the father as he comes to his fourth
son. It is as though he had sought one upon whom
to bestow the blessing of the first-born and now had
found him. For Judah and Joseph share in this
honor, as I Chron. 5:1, 2 show, Joseph having received the double portion, Judah carrying on the
line from which came "the prince." The emphatic
pronoun (G. K. 135 e) *'attah* follows the name
"Judah," emphasizing particularly the object of the
verb "praise." As in 29:32 we have a play upon
the name Judah, Hebrew *yehûdha,* for *yôdhûkha* involves the same root — Hifil of *yadhah.* As Hengstenberg has shown, this verb especially figures in
cases where Yahweh is praised for His faithful goodness. So here: thy brethren shall praise the Lord
for what He shall bring to pass through thee. However, the reason for the brothers' praise is immediately stated: in the history of this tribe it shall
be particularly evident that God achieves victories

through him. His hand is on the *'o'reph,* i. e., "the
nape of the neck," for the enemies are represented
as in flight before him. He leaps upon them and
throws them to the ground. When his capacity for
overthrowing foes will have become apparent, then
"the sons of his father shall bow down" before him,
yishtachawû, i. e. "do reverence" as before one who
deserves reverence. The most significant instance
appears in II Sam. 5:1-3, where all the tribes of
Israel are compelled to admit Judah's superiority in
David. "Sons of thy father" includes more than "sons
of thy mother" — namely half-brothers as well as
brothers, here all the tribes of Israel.

9. A fuller description of this outstanding trait
of heroic courage in Judah now follows by the use
of the figure of the lion. First he is labelled a *gûr
'aryeh,* i. e. "whelp of a lion," which here certainly
does not mean a young cub but a young lion in the
freshness of his just matured strength. He is pictured at the point where he has captured and eaten
his prey; literally "from the prey thou art gone up,"
mittéreph, the *min* being temporal like "after eating the prey" (K. S. 401 e). Thereafter he
"mounted," i. e. went up to the mountain fastnesses
(Song 4:8). When he comes to his den, "he crouches"
with that peculiar grace characteristic of the strong
beast; then he "lies down" in that bold security
equally characteristic of the bold lion (*'aryeh*) or,
for that matter, of the still bolder and fiercer "lioness"
who has cubs to guard. After such a bold beast
has thus lain down, "who would dare to rouse him?"
All this furnishes a bold, clear picture of Judah's lion-
like courage and strength. By these words a foundation is laid for great achievements yet to follow.
Verses 8 and 9 create a sense of expectation, for they
ascribe to Judah acknowledged pre-eminence, courage
and strength.

10. **The scepter shall not depart from Judah,**
Nor the ruler's staff from between his feet
Until Shiloh come.
And to him (shall be) obedience of peoples.

"The sceptre" (*shébhet*) symbolizes rule and dominion or capacity for rule. The qualities mentioned in v. 8 and 9 result in this, that rule over the tribes of Israel will sooner or later be conceded to Judah. The statement is to be set forth with emphasis, for a parallel clause that follows presents the same idea, substituting "ruler's staff" (*mechoqeq*) for "sceptre." This term can mean "prescriber of laws" or "commander," as Deut. 33:21; Judg. 5:14; Isa. 33:22 indicate. Consequently, "law-giver" (A. V.) as such is not wrong. But the ensuing phrase causes difficulty, for "from between his feet" can only with difficulty be understood of descent. However, the meaning "ruler's staff" is also appropriate in Num. 21:18; Ps. 60:7 (A. V.); 108:8. This translation agrees so very well with the following phrase, because the long ruler's staff would be placed between the feet as the ruler sat on his throne and would then either rest against his shoulder or be held in the hand. Commentators here usually refer to monumental carvings of old Persian kings. A very good illustration, more readily accessible to the average reader, is that of King Tutankhamen found in Barton's, *Archaeology and the Bible* (1937), Figure 304. The verb "depart" (*yasûr*) does not quite represent our point of view in the matter, for it is an active, where we should have used a passive (K. S. 97). For the idea is that no one shall remove Judah's sceptre, or Judah's dominion will not be taken away from him until a certain climax is achieved, which is here stated in double form: first "until Shiloh come"; secondly, this climax will be overtopped by a second — "and to him shall be the obedience of peoples."

First we must determine what "Shiloh" means.
It is a noun form which, as K. W. concedes and Keil
and Hengstenberg have long contended, may well
be derived from the root *shalah*, which means "to
rest." *Shiloh*, therefore, can mean "rest" (*Ruhe*, K.
W.), or "man of rest" or "giver of rest" by metonomy. Such a meaning could very readily have suggested itself to those familiar with Hebrew. In this
passage, then, the general meaning might be found:
Judah shall continue to hold rule until rest come.
But then the concluding statement comes limping after
rather lamely, almost without thought connection,
"and to him (i. e. Judah) shall be the obedience of
peoples." Into this rather pale picture one could
implant the Messianic thought, letting the words be
a description of the Messianic age. However, this
interpretation proceeds on the assumption that nothing in Messianic prophecy even intimated that a
personal Messiah would ultimately come, a thought
involved, by the way, already in Gen. 3:15, though
not yet clearly expressed. However, another approach
is possible — that which regards *Shiloh* as a proper
name of a person and construes the sense of the
whole verse thus: Judah's capacity for rule and
sovereignty shall not be lost; in fact, it shall come
to a climax in a ruler so competent that he shall be
able to achieve perfect rest, and who shall because
of his achievement in this field of endeavor be called
"Rest" or "Restgiver" — *Shiloh*; and when the "peoples" become aware of these superior achievements
of his, they shall willingly tender "to him obedience."

Against this interpretation it may, of course, be
urged that it does not appear in the church in this
form prior to the last century. But we may well
press the counterclaim that from the earliest interpretation onward the passage was always understood
as Messianic, an interpretation which has the fullest

support in the New Testament, where, most apparently, St. John is alluding to our passage when he speaks of Christ as "the lion that is of the tribe of Judah" (Rev. 5:5) ; and this interpretation appears already in the Targum in the very plain form — "until Messiah come." No version prior to the A. V. offered the word "Shiloh," for they all sought to give the *interpretation* of the name, and, it must be confessed, they had not approached the problem from the right etymological angle, but yet all from the days of the Septuagint onward felt very strongly the Messianic implications.

Now, before we subject the other interpretations that have been suggested to a closer analysis, let us examine more closely the second half of the climax to which the statement rises, that is to say, the words, "and to Him shall be obedience of peoples." The "and to Him" (*welô*) definitely points back to Shiloh who was just named, and it stands first in the sentence by way of emphasis, as if to say: He shall be so great that men will readily yield him obedience. In fact, not only men but "peoples" (*'ammîm*). Very likely here the article is merely omitted because the statement is poetic — a common thing in Hebrew — and the familiar versions are correct when they say "the people" (A. V.) or "the peoples" (Luther and A. R. V.). In other words, the nations of the world shall willingly submit, for *yiqqehath* refers to inner submission cheerfully tendered. This, then, is an attractive description of the conquests of the Gospel, and so the critical objection falls to the ground which charges that the term *Shiloh*, if construed as above, is "at most a negative word, denoting mere tranquillity." For in the first place, we are justified in construing the word personally as "Rest-bringer," and secondly, that this one is not merely passive appears from the conquests that he makes among "the peoples" the world over.

From all that has been said it would appear clearly that we are not following the interpretation which makes "until" the limit to which Judah's dominion endures; in other words, we are not construing *'adh kî* in the exclusive but in the inclusive sense, even as it is found in 26:13; 28:15; Ps. 112:8; Ps. 110:1. For if this dominion were to endure only up to a certain point, the word as such would constitute a threat rather than a blessing. A rather common interpretation was the one that said that this verse means Judah must first lose her position of eminence and sovereignty; then the Messiah would appear. Yet is not the sovereignty of Judah brought to its highest point and in reality never lost when the Messiah appears?

Aside from this interpretation the one most commonly held by constructive expositors, who feel they must hold fast to a Messianic element, is the one which makes *Shîloh* mean "rest," *Ruhe* or *Beruhigung*, i. e. pacification. Aside from the objection we raised above, we also find the whole statement of the climax which is supposedly involved rather pale and ineffective.

Then there is the rather specious claim which asserts that in every other instance where *Shîloh* occurs it is a proper name, namely that of the city mentioned in Joshua 18:1 and thereafter till the time of Eli (I Sam. 1:3), and referred to in the psalms and in prophetic writings, the modern *Seilûn* lying about 9½ miles NNE of Bethel. That claim is very inaccurate, for the form spelled *shîloh* — long "î" and final "h" — occurs only here. The name of the town has three different spellings, as accurate dictionaries indicate — *shilô, shîlô* and *shiloh*. Langensheidt's *Pocket Dictionary* is inaccurate in listing our

word and the name of the city under one head. Buhl,
B D B, and K. W. list both words separately. It
will help the case of the opposition but little to point
to a variant reading *shîlô* which about forty manuscripts offer. The majority of good manuscripts
have the form with final "h." And then, if the
sense of this interpretation is weighed — "until he
(Judah) come to Shiloh" — the difficulties grow still
greater. Grammatically such an interpretation is possible. But it is extremely difficult to make it appear
as if Judah's leadership continued till he came to
Shiloh (Judg. 18:1) together with the other tribes.
For though this coming to Shiloh marked an epoch in
the history of the tribes, it was in no sense epochal
for Judah. In fact, Judah had not yet come into its
own at that time, in fact, it did not do so for three centuries to come. All that had appeared thus far of
Judah's capacity for greater things was that the tribe
was appointed to lead the march through the wilderness (Num. 10:14). Then in the Land of Promise
Judah's inheritance was allotted first, Josh. 15:1;
and then shortly thereafter Judah began the work
of completing the conquest of Canaan (Judg. 1:1ff).
Yet, to tell the truth, up to this point actual rule
over the other tribes ("sceptre" = rule) had not yet
been conceded to Judah. *Shiloh,* the town, never
was of particular moment in *Judah's* history. Procksch
claims very correctly: "It cannot be demonstrated
that Shiloh, the Ephraimite capital, ever was of any
importance for the history of Judah. Besides, none
of the versions ever thought of the city Shiloh."

The Septuagint translation is instructive; it runs
thus: ἕως ἂν ἔλθῃ τὰ ἀποκείμενα αὐτῷ = "until the things
laid up in store come into his possession." Behind
this lies a Hebrew *shello,* i. e. *shel* for *'asher* =
"which" and *lô* = "to him." So apparently the
Greek translators had a defective reading — short "i"

and final "h" missing. They seem to have thought
of Ezek. 21:32 (English, v. 27) which reads, "until
he come whose right it is." In any case, they thought
of one to whom particular rights and prerogatives
appertained.

The Vulgate translates at this point *qui mitten-
dus est* = "who must be sent." Consequently, this
presupposes the altering of the final consonant *he* to
cheth, namely *shalúach*. But the Hebrew text nowhere suggests that vowel change. Other modern
attempts at textual alterations are equally unwarranted, like *mosheloh* = "his ruler."

Lastly, there is an old Jewish interpretation that
has no firm ground on which to stand. It is based
on the root *shiljah* which is taken to mean "son" —
therefore *shîloh* = "his son." Helpful as that might
be, it is in reality quite impossible, for *shiljah*
does not mean "son" but "afterbirth." Or *shîl* =
shalil which in *New Hebrew* means "embryo." Calvin
and Luther favored this. But there is a world of difference between "son" and "afterbirth."

One last objection to the Messianic import of the
last clause has not yet been met. K. W. especially
contends that *'ammîm*, "peoples" here means "tribes."
The facts are these: tribes may sometimes in a looser
sense be spoken of as peoples, but nothing here indicates that only the submission of the other Israelitish
tribes is under consideration. A word should be taken
in its primary basic sense unless the connection in
which it appears definitely indicates another legitimate
meaning.

11, 12. He tethers his ass to the vine
And his ass's colt to the choice vine.
He washes his garments in wine
And his robes in the blood of grapes.
His eyes are dark from wine,
And his teeth white from milk.

A difficulty will be encountered if one insists on referring these two verses to the Messiah. But two possibilities must be conceded: either the author of these words, having reached a high point in the reference to the Messiah, may continue on that thought level, or he may drop down again to the level of Judah and conclude in describing what blessings Judah will encounter. If these verses are to be explained in reference to Shiloh, a rather fantastic and fanciful meaning is extracted from them. If they are referred to Judah, they do nothing more than to describe the exuberant fertility that is to prevail in his land, the unexpressed condition being that the uninterrupted enjoyment of these blessings would depend upon Judah's fidelity to his God. "He tethers (*'oserî* — participle with old genitive case ending — K. S. 272 a; G. K. 90 l) his ass to the vine." The participle used indicates that Judah habitually does this. His reason for so doing is because vines grow in such profusion in the land — as they still do in the vicinity of Hebron in Judah — that a man will have no hesitation about tethering the ass to them. What if one vine be damaged? The loss is not felt because there is no end of vines. For that matter, a man would not even show hesitation about binding the more restless "ass's colt to the choice vine" (*sereqah*). Even these abound. If, then, the noblest and finest plants thrive so profusely, the more ordinary plants without a doubt shall also. Certainly, the verb "wash" in the next comparison is not to be taken literally. It merely describes graphically a picturesque episode from the time of treading out the grapes after the grape harvest. So full will the press be that they that tread out the grapes will stain their garments so profusely that they will come out of the press looking like men who have washed their garments in wine. Since these grapes were for the most part

dark and the resultant wine dark, in the parallel
expression the wine is called "the blood of grapes."
The remaining two lines are entirely in the same
spirit and involve absolutely no censure. In a land
where wine is drunk regularly there is practically no
drinking to excess. Yet the abundance of nourish-
ing food and drink imparts a healthy color to the
inhabitants of the land: the eyes have a ruddy darkness from the wine — "his eyes are dark from wine."
There is no thought here of the bloodshot eye of the
drunkard. "His teeth, i. e., the teeth of the typical
inhabitant of Judah's land, are white from milk" —
a shrewd observation agreeing with the dentist's
recommendation in our day. *Lebushô*, "his garments," and *sûthô*, "his robes," are collective singulars
(K. S. 254 c). *Chakhlîlî*, "dark," is a genitive: (He
is) "dark of eyes from wine" — *min* causal; on the
genitive see K. S. 272 a.

13. Zebulon shall dwell toward the seashore,
Yea, he shall be toward the shore where ships
come,
And his flank shall be toward Sidon.

In the Spirit Jacob foresees that Zebulon's
heritage in Canaan shall lie up toward the north
where he can have contact with those that go down
to the sea in ships. Yet it is not definitely stated
that he is to dwell *at* or *on* the seashore but "toward"
it — *lechôph yammîm*. For though Zebulon's territory touched the Sea of Galilee on the east and swept
westward over a big portion of the Plain of Esdraelon,
it yet went only two-thirds of the way to the Mediterranean coastline, having Asher between it and the
sea. Yet the people of Zebulon were to have contact
with those whose ships touched the shore, as the
further statements indicate — "he shall be toward
the shore (*lechôph* again) where ships come," literally,

"toward the shore of ships," and the second statement: "and his flank shall be toward Sidon." Zebulon faces south; its flank is to be toward the old commercial city Sidon, prominent long before Tyre. The products of this commerce shall be transmitted through Zebulon to the rest of the tribes. The opening words constitute a play upon Zebulon's name, which means "dwelling." Consequently, Zebulon "shall dwell" (*yishkon*) emphasizes his being definitely located in that area. No particular achievement or blessing of Zebulon's is mentioned but merely an attendant circumstance that shall be in evidence after his settlement in the land. The prophetic vision of this fact, however, held up before this tribe a definite prospect of what God held in store for it. This fact explains why the sentence structure is cast as it is, the phrase "toward the seashore" standing first for emphasis. In fact, the Hebrew reads "toward the shore of the seas" (plural), the article being omitted in a poetic piece (K. S. 292 a). It is also very true that the Spirit of prophecy did not give Jacob the ability to foresee the entire history of this tribe; but what Jacob saw that he proclaimed. This, of course, is the case in reference practically to most of the tribes. The whole future does not need to be unrolled before them.

14. **Issachar was a strong-boned ass,**
Couching between the sheepfolds.
He saw that rest is good,
And that the land is pleasant.
So he stooped over with his shoulder to take
on a burden
And became a toiling labor band.

Jacob speaks of the past; he describes a trait that he has observed in Issachar's character. But the father means these words in the sense that what Issachar the individual did is a trait that the entire

tribe will develop. So the word becomes a prophecy.
Construing the whole word as spoken in the past tense
agrees best with the sequence "and he saw" (*wayyar'*). Now the chief feature observable about
Issachar is that he had a generous amount of sturdy
physical strength, expressed figuratively: he is "a
strong-boned ass" — Hebrew "an ass of bones" —
the noun for the adjective. The participle "couching between the sheepfolds" describes the tribe as
such rather than the ass. Either sheepfolds abound
in his territory, and the members of the tribe are
thought of as settled in a country where sheepfolds
abound; or else the tribe is thought of as a unit
being situated between tribes where sheepfolds
abound. Both thoughts, for that matter, may even
blend into one. Most dictionaries and most commentaries regard the word *mishpeth\u00e1yim* as of somewhat doubtful meaning. The meaning "sheepfolds"
is reasonably sure however; see K. W.

15. But though the tribe has the advantage of
sturdy physical strength, it is spiritually and perhaps mentally lethargic and utterly unambitious.
Seeing the prospect of "rest" and a good "land"
and "pleasant," this tribe would rather surrender
other advantages and become a group who would
"stoop over with the shoulder to take on a burden,"
working for others in work that required only the
contented exertion of brute strength. Yea, they were
ready to become a "toiling labor band" for others
as long as a fair measure of ordinary creature comforts could be enjoyed. Such an unprogressive, unambitious attitude has nothing noble about it. To
make the understanding of this word comparatively
easier for all who first heard it there may have been
a specific instance available remembered by all, where
Issachar had done just this. Jacob's word to this
son is a rebuke mildly but clearly administered.

Issachar is thereby warned against aiming too low, against burying his talent in a napkin. Skinner's translation is too strong for *lemas 'obhedh,* "a toiling labor-*gang.*" So also Meek's: "a gang-slave." In this case, too, a play on words is involved. The name Issachar is related to the root *sakkîr,* "a day laborer," and so Jacob interprets the *omen* of the *nomen.*

16, 17. **Dan shall administer justice for his people**
As any other of the tribes of Israel.
May Dan be a serpent in the way,
A horned serpent in the path,
One that bites the horse's heel
So that his rider falls off backward.

Again a play upon words: *Dan,* the name, and *dîn,* the verb "to judge" or "to administer justice." For the word usually translated "judge" signifies to hold an administrative office or, practically, "to rule." We are at a loss to know why Jacob should emphasize this fact in the case of Dan, that he will always be able to provide the needed rulers to "administer justice for his people," that is, within his own tribe, as the following statement suggests. For "as any other of the tribes of Israel" will hardly mean that they all in their turn supplied judges. For that was not the case. *Ke'a(ch)chadh,* "as one," must be taken in the sense of "as any other" (K. S. 73).

17. Now the word takes on the form of a wish, *yehî,* "may he be." The wish expressed is Jacob's own. The godly patriarch in blessing his son would hardly desire an evil and ungodly thing. Consequently the comparison involved is complimentary, a thing to be desired. Naturally, then, this thought cannot involve that all who have dealings with Dan may find him treacherous. But rather that all who wickedly oppose him may find him as deadly an opponent

as "a serpent," (*nachash*) or more specifically "a
horned serpent," (*shephiphon*) might be. For of
the latter it is said that it is of a pale yellowish dust
color and so blends successfully with the dust of the
road in which it coils itself. Then wayfarer or horse-
man — here the mounted enemy is thought of, since
horses particularly shy at the deadly thing — treading near it find their "heel" bitten in a lightning-
like flash. In fright the horse rears and throws its
rider. So may Dan successfully overthrow all who
wrongfully antagonize him. This may be considered
as prophetically covering also the case of the Danite
Samson, for who would have supposed that such
dangerous powers lurked in that muscular young
hero. Yet, though we claim this, we do not regard
the word as a specific prophecy concerning Samson.
It describes a tribal trait, which was also displayed
in the case of the Danites who struck like a serpent
in capturing the inhabitants of Dan-Laish (Judg. 18).
It may be that Jacob put a veiled warning into the
comparison of the serpent, implying that Dan had
a tendency towards treachery and should guard against
it. That other fanciful notion that some fathers held
we may well regard as fantastic when they claimed
that from the tribe of Dan Anti-Christ would ultimately come forth, and based this largely upon the
fact that in Rev. 7 the tribe of Dan is passed by,
and concluded also without warrant that some of the
persons who conspired to bring about Christ's death
were of this tribe. The singular *sûs*, "horse," represents the plural — K. S. 256 b.

18. For thy salvation do I wait, O Yahweh.

This plainly interrupts the thought sequence, but
with good reason. Repeatedly Jacob has spoken of
self-help on the part of the tribes: of Judah the lion,
of Issachar the strong-boned ass, of Dan the deadly

serpent. Yet Jacob would not be misunderstood.
Not from that source does he expect true salvation.
Even when men help themselves, only then are they
truly delivered if God helps them. On the latter help
Jacob has grounded his personal salvation and every
deliverance, hard though it was for him to learn
that submission and trust. On that help he would
have his sons ground their every hope. The perfect
qiwwithî expresses the thought: in many instances
of the past have I waited or trusted and I do trust
still. Therefore it is best translated as a present
(K. S. 125). Meek renders very nicely: "For succor
from thee, O Lord, I wait." Is it not trivial to regard
such a significant word as merely a short prayer for
strength on the part of the fast weakening old man,
that he might be enabled to finish blessing the other
sons? More correct is the claim that Jacob's prayer
also includes the Messianic hope: "salvation" = full
salvation.

19-21. **As for Gad, troops troop against him
But he presses upon their heel.
As for Asher, his food is rich,
And he provides royal delicacies.
Naphtali is a liberated deer,
He also is wont to use clever speech.**

The word concerning Gad amounts to this:
though he be pressed hard, he in turn presses hard
upon those that assail him. The word play is intensified, because "Gad" and "troop" and "press" build
upon almost one and the same root. So the Hebrew
has: *Gadh gedhudh yeghudhenû.* We tried to catch
at least a part of this by rendering, "a troop shall
troop against him," but we were obliged to alter the
verb to "press" in the next line in order to make
sense. Jacob, therefore, foresees that Gad will be
especially exposed to the raids of marauding bands.

Gad was exposed to the bands of roving marauders
from the desert — Midianites and Ammonites and
Arabians. But though that was the case, Gad was
not slow about defending himself and striking back.
Of the courage of those of Gad we read in David's
time I Chron. 12:8 and before, 5:18. The idea of
pressing upon their heel involves that he comes in
close pursuit, following hot upon the enemy. We
have taken the initial letter of v. 20 and attached
it as the final letter to v. 19 and read *'aqebham,*
"their heel," and so, besides making good sense, we
are rid of an uncomfortable and practically sense-
less "m" at the beginning of v. 20. The Greek translators, the Samaritan Pentateuch and the Latin version did the same. The word on the whole is encouragement for a son who in his day will need it, because he will be particularly exposed to attack.

20. "Asher" — the lucky or fortunate one, as
his name indicates — has a portion which conforms
to his name. Situated along the seacost north of
Carmel, he has one of the most fruitful areas in the
land — "his food is rich," or "fat," *shemenah. Lach-
mô,* "his bread," signifies "his food" — *pars pro toto*
— synecdoche. From the abundance of rich things
that are produced he is able to provide what would
grace any king's table, "royal delicacies." Here it
matters little whether one thinks in terms of Israel's
kings or of those who were in Phoenicia or of none
in particular. Delicacies worthy of a king are meant.
Moses in his blessing (Deut. 33:24) states the case
thus: "let him dip his foot in oil," i. e., a profusion
of rich olive oil shall overflow so that men at times
will tread upon the rich overflow. All this by no
means contains an allusion, as is foolishly claimed,
to the oil pipeline that now has its western terminus
at the Bay of Haifa in Asher's territory.

21. "A liberated deer" or "a hind let loose" (A. V.) is a deer hemmed in by no restraint. By comparison with II Sam. 22:34, where the fleet strength of warriors' feet is pictured by the same figure, we may conclude that the fleet strength of the average man of Naphtali is the point involved. Such men were Barak and the ten thousand of Naphtali and Zebulon that came with him for the deliverance of Israel. The same judge illustrates "the clever speech" here referred to. For *'imrey shápher* are "words of beauty" like the song of Deborah and Barak (Judg. 5). These may not be the most notable of achievements but they will be the distinguishing marks of this tribe. The critics try many reconstructions of this verse as though it were quite unsatisfactory, but their best is not an improvement. We regard the last participle *nothen* as expressing the habitual: "he is wont to use" or "give."

22-24. **Joseph is a shoot of a fruitful branch,**
A shoot of a fruitful branch by the side of a
    fountain,
Whose branches have already climbed up on
    the wall.
    The archers have sorely grieved him, shot
        at him and persecuted him,
    But his bow stayed firm,
And the arms of his hands remained supple.
As a result of the work of the Strong One of
    Jacob
From there where the Shepherd, the Stone of
    Israel, is.

As the blessing upon Judah is richer and better than that of the tribes grouped around him in this chapter, so that of Joseph stands out in the same fashion, and its phrases and pictures are rich and rare. Some of the comparisons involved require a measure of thought before they are grasped, but the

case is far from being as hopeless as some claim. It
is not true that "the section is full of obscurities and
the text frequently quite untranslatable." This impression of obscurity is fostered by presenting the
most difficult of several possible translations. The unnecessary textual alterations resorted to as pure conjectures result in an amazingly different rendering.
Note how Meek translates:

22. **Joseph is a young bull,**
     A young bull at a spring,
     A wild ass at Shur,

23. **Shooting at him in enmity,**
     The archers fiercely assailed him.

24. **But their bow was broken by the Eternal,**
     And their arms and hands trembled
     At the might of the Mighty One of Jacob,
     At the name of the Shepherd, the Rock of
     Israel.

The impression created upon the uninformed by
such a translation is that the Hebrew text must be
in a deplorable state — a thing which is by no means
the case. Besides, such unwarranted alterations
undermine very effectually the confidence in God's
Word. We hope to show both that the text makes
sense and that the sense is good. First of all Joseph
is described as "a shoot of a fruitful branch,"
literally, "son of a fruitbearer" (B D B), with the
common use of *ben,* "son," for anything derived
from another thing; this means, of course, that since
it is derived from a fruitful branch, it is itself fruitful. Consequently, the translation, "Joseph is a fruitful bough" (A. V.), covers the case very acceptably.
Porath is the feminine of the participle of *parah,*
"to bear fruit" (G.K. 80 g). As a choice phrase the
expression "shoot of a fruitful branch" is repeated
with the addition of the descriptive phrase "by the

side of a fountain." The Hebrew says *"over* a fountain" using *'al,* because the sturdy vine does stand
higher than the fountain. Even so far we have a
situation that gives a guarantee of fruit. The "shoot"
was derived from good stock; its water supply is
ample. So the picture does not delay to depict the
meagre beginning. At once it gives the shoot in the
advanced stage of growth where it has "already
climbed up on the wall" — so the perfect *tsa'adhah*
is meant: it has been growing and now is quite spread
out over the wall. The supporting wall, of course, furnishes a good hold for the vine and protection from
inclement weather. Such a healthy, thriving, full-
grown, well-supported, fruit-bearing vine well por-
trays the fruitful sturdy tribe of Joseph or Ephraim
and Manasseh. Perhaps a play on words is here
intended. For the root *parah* appears in *Ephraim* —
the fruitful one. The distributive singular verb
tsa'adhah after a plural subject merely concentrates
more on the individual shoot that spreads out (cf. G.
K. 145 k).

23. The figure of this verse draws our attention
to a situation radically different from the former. The
successful tribe is antagonized because of its success.
His enemies are thought of under the figure of
"archers," called in Hebrew "masters of the bow," *ba'a-
ley chitstsim* (a peculiar double plural, "masters of
bows"; K. S. 267 b). These archers "have grieved
him sorely" — from the root *marar: yemararuhû =*
"to make life bitter for one." Besides, they have
"shot at him" — *robbû* from *rabhabh.* They have
lastly "persecuted him," *yishtemuhû,* i. e. "proved
themselves adversaries." Apparently, the brunt of
hostile opposition to Israel will have to be borne by
Joseph, next to Judah. The three verbs indicate that
he will have plenty of it. However (*waw* adversative
in *wattéshebh*) "his bow stayed firm" (v. 24). He,

too, has a bow for defensive purposes when attacked.
He uses it, and his hands do not weaken as they draw
the tough bow again and again; it stayed "firm" ═
"as a strong one," *be'eythan.* The arms behind the
bow are described thus, "the arms of his hands remained supple." Arms and hands are seen in quick
movements, snatching the arrow from the quiver,
placing it in position on the bowstring, bending the
bow, steadying it for aim, letting it fly. Every movement is eloquent with suppleness. And yet, in harmony with v. 18, even this purely physical asset is
not to be ascribed to man's native powers. Tracing
it back to its true Source, Jacob says that it comes
"as a result of the work of (literally: 'from the
hands of') the Strong One of Jacob." By this time
Jacob well knows God as strong and as the Source
of all strength, and he knows that God will engage
in behalf of his loved ones. By a second parallel
statement Jacob traces back the strength Joseph will
display as coming "from there where (Hebrew:
'from where') the Shepherd, the Stone of Israel, is."
A protecting "Shepherd" is a thought Jacob and his
shepherding sons could well appreciate. "The Stone
of Israel" (*'ébhen yisrael*) is not meant any differently
than is the other common phrase: "the Rock" of
Israel. This pictures Yahweh's sturdy strength and
unwavering helpfulness.

One would hardly venture to claim that the verses
about Joseph considered thus far are lacking in clear,
forceful meaning. Any tribe might well have desired
such a rich blessing.

25, 26. **From the God of thy father — and may**
He help thee —
And with the help of the Almighty — and may
He bless thee —
With blessings of the heavens above,

> With blessings of the deep that coucheth be-
> neath,
> With blessings of breasts and womb.
> The blessings of thy father have prevailed
> Above the blessings of my progenitors,
> Even unto the border of the everlasting hills;
> May they be upon the head of Joseph,
> Upon the crown of the head of the choice one
> among his brethren.

The blessings now become superlatively rich. It is hard to say whether Judah or Joseph gets the greater blessing. Jacob it still tracing all gifts and blessings back to their true Source, particularly the deliverance of Joseph. It will be offered from the God (*'el,* "the Strong One") of Jacob's father. Eagerly Jacob inserts the prayer for his beloved son, "and may He help thee." The next statement, also spoken in an exalted strain of thought, begins with *we'eth,* "and with,' here used in the sense of "and with the help of" as it appears in 4:1. Having told of Joseph's fortunate lot and having now again inserted a brief prayer that God might bless Joseph, the father goes on to heap blessing upon blessing upon his son. If any son was worthy of such wonderful blessings, it surely was Joseph. The following blessings are specialized: first "blessings of the heavens above" — those would be such blessings as the heavens hold within their grasp — rain, sunshine and pleasant breezes. Then follow "blessings of the deep," i. e. *tehom,* the deep source of the subterranean waters, which is pictured as a being "that coucheth (or croucheth) beneath" the earth. This involves the waters stored in the earth that are so essential to all vegetable growth as well as the sources of the much needed streams and of the fountains. Thirdly follow "blessings of breasts and womb" which means abundant offspring of man and of beast and the

capacity of caring successfully for them in their early
days. If it still seem strange that Jacob in pronouncing blessings offers none of a character that may be
termed spiritual blessings, we must again recall to
mind that Jacob set out v. 1 to foretell "what shall
befall." So even the blessings are largely predictions.
Then, if no spiritual blessings are foretold in the case
of the offspring of this favorite son, it seems to us
that this was because the Spirit of truth Himself
could foresee none of particular moment. This very
silence must have constituted a warning and a lesson
to Joseph's descendants. Spiritually they never ex-
celled. It was among the tribe of Ephraim that one of
its sons, Jeroboam, instituted the calf worship, whereby he "made Israel to sin."

26. It is difficult at first to determine the exact
import of the expression "the blessings of thy father."
Is the genitive "of thy father" objective or subjective?
If it were subjective, i. e., "the blessing that thy father
bestows," then Jacob's word would convey the thought:
I can bless more potently than my own forefathers.
That would be presumption on Jacob's part. There is
left the objective genitive, i. e. "the blessings that thy
father received." Then the following statement involves: God has blessed me more abundantly than
my fathers — a word spoken, indeed, in all humility
in the sense of, "Lord, I am not worthy." Abraham
had one son of promise; Isaac had two children; Jacob
had twelve sons destined to be heads of tribes. When
Jacob came down to Egypt with his family according
to 46:27, his descendants numbered seventy. What
wonderful provisions for the preservation of this
group God had made! Truly: "the blessings of thy
father have prevailed above the blessings of my
progenitors" (that is *horay*, participle of *harah*,
plural with the first person suffix). Only here the
word appears as meaning "parents" or "progenitors."

But though this is unusual, there is no need to change
to the text which would substitute "mountains" (*hara-
rey*) for "progenitors." Another line added to this
statement says that these blessings enjoyed by Jacob
extended "even unto the border (*ta'avah* is admitted
to have this sense, even by B D B) of the everlasting
hills." The land seems to be thought of as encircled
by mountains. The blessings are thought of as growing in rich profusion up to the very borderland of
the mountains, thus filling the whole land. With these
rich blessings he himself received filling his thoughts,
Jacob pronounces the wish over the head of Joseph:
may they be also upon his head "and upon the crown
of the head of the choice one among his brethren."
Nazîr is the word from which "Nazirite" comes. Now
that word may mean "one consecrated, devoted," but
since that again according to the root means "a
separated one," we could also find the meaning in
it "the one standing apart" or here practically "the
choice one" or "the prince" (A. R. V. m.). Without
a doubt, Joseph was the most eminent one among his
brethren, eminent in character and in godliness. If
any one of the twelve deserved pre-eminence, it was
Joseph. Jacob practically claims as much in these
words. The *'al* of the first line is practically equivalent to a comparative, for the line may be translated:
"The blessings of thy father have been stronger than
the blessings of my progenitors" (K. S. 308 d).

27. Benjamin is a ravening wolf,
In the morning he devours prey,
In the evening he divides spoil.

This is the last word, spoken in reference to the
second son of Rachel. There is no criticism involved
in the use of this comparison; it is complimentary.
The rapacity of the wolf is not under consideration.
Yet even as v. 17 contained a veiled warning, so

we may also regard this word as suggesting to Benjamin as a tribe that he take heed unto himself lest the undesirable qualities of a wolf develop in him. The original says, "Benjamin, a wolf, rends prey." We prefer to translate as Luther does: *Benjamin ist ein reissender Wolf.* To describe him as successful in his depradations Jacob speaks of him as always having prey; in the morning he devours it; in the evening, with a change of figure, he is the warrior dividing the spoil. This expression, touching upon the two limits ("morning" and "evening"), is one of many similar expressions designed to cover the entire intervening area. Here, therefore, this means, he is *always* successful in despoiling his foes. At the same time, when he must encounter his foes, he is a fierce opponent like a wolf. Representative men of this type were Ehud "the Benjamite" (Judg. 3:15) and Saul (I Sam. 9:1) and Jonathan. The whole tribe displayed this attitude, though not in a holy cause, in Judg. 20.

d) **Jacob's Last Charge and His Death** (49:28-33)

28. **All these constitute the twelve tribes of Israel, and this is what their father spoke to them; and he blessed them, individually he blessed them with what was in conformity with each man's blessing.**

Quite naturally the author now summarizes his results. He reminds that the twelve tribes have just been blessed — twelve being the covenant number, and this, therefore, being an event that has bearing upon the covenant existing between Israel and God. The numeral strangely after a definite noun lacks the definite article (K. S. 334 u). To emphasize that Jacob actually spoke all these remarkable words the author then reiterates (cf. v. 1), "this is what their

father spoke to them." Of course, this statement
is either a truth or a lie. We accept it as truth. It
had, however, not been said previously that this was
a blessing. So after we have the words before us
the author reminds us of what is really quite self-
evident, that these individual words were in reality
blessings, strictly adapted to each man's case and
needs, as Jacob foresaw that God would bestow them.
This is the meaning of the words, "individually he
blessed them with what was in conformity with each
man's blessing."

Skinner calls the construction *'ish 'asher* "impossible," for he seemingly overlooks what K. C.
points out by his translation that *'asher* is the cognate
or factative object and to be translated "with which."
Besides, criticism insists that at this point (v. 28) P
again begins (v. 28-33); and so J, who spoke v. 1-
27, is regarded quite incapable of any summary statement or formal remark such as this is — a rather unfounded limitation laid on J. Capable writers like these
are capable of quite a number of different types of style.
To deny to them this capacity, which all good writers
have, makes of the Biblical writers a peculiar set of
literary dummies of very limited ability. Very queer
is the claim of Koenig that the blessing now spoken
of in this verse has nothing to do with the preceding
verses of the chapter. Rather, it is claimed, having
spoken these words (v. 1-27), he then proceeded to
add a blessing, but the blessing as such is not recorded.
How can a man fail to see that in all its parts almost
v. 1-27 are blessings?

29-32. **And he laid a charge upon them and
said: I for my part am now being gathered unto
my people. Bury me together with my fathers in
the cave which is in the field of Ephron, the Hittite,
namely in the cave which is in the field of Machpelah which is over against Mamre in the land of**

Canaan, which field Abraham bought from Ephron,
the Hittite, for a burial place of his own possession.
There they buried Abraham and Sarah, his wife;
there they buried Isaac and Rebekah, his wife;
and there I buried Leah — the property consisting
of the field and the cave which is in it, bought of
the sons of Heth.

Joseph had already been placed under oath to
see to it that Jacob be buried in Canaan. Now all
the sons have the same charge laid upon them. Jacob
very clearly realizes that he is dying: "I for my
part" — *'ani* for emphasis, namely I, as formerly my
fathers — "am now being gathered unto my people."
Ne'esaph as Nifal participle describes an act or experience which is beginning at the time the speaker
utters the word and continues into the future (K. S.
237 d). Jacob regards "his people" as still existing
though dead, and so he gives testimony of his faith
in the life to come. It is an act of faith on Jacob's
part that he desires burial in Canaan in the grave
acquired by Abraham. Abraham's provision for his
and for Sarah's burial (chapter 23) was a testimony
of faith for the generations that were to come after
him. That "being gathered unto his people" is one
thing, and that "being buried with his fathers" is
another, appears from the fact that the two are mentioned separately. His sons may well have heard of
this family sepulchre. He repeats in detail where it
is, to whom it formerly belonged, that it is a cave,
what other name the field bears, that it lies over
against Mamre in the land of Canaan, and that Abraham had bought it of Ephron for this very purpose,
that he might at least have "a burial place of his
own possession" in the land where he was not
privileged to own any other property or fields. The
expression *'ahuzzath qébher*, "a possession of a grave,"
means "a burial place of his own possession." Luther

renders it well *Erbbegraebnis,* "a hereditary burial
plot."

31. *Shammah,* "thither," is often weakened
down to a mere "there," though it involves a kind
of pregnant construction: they took him to that place
and buried him there. We already know that Abraham (chapter 35) and Sarah lay buried there (chapter
23). Now we are informed of what we would have
surmised, that Isaac and Rebekah lay there also.
There Jacob himself had buried Leah. Jacob now
repeats how much the property actually involved, for
he wants his sons to perpetuate a correct tradition
concerning it. It is "the property consisting of the
field and the cave which is in it." All these directions
are not the garrulous reminiscences of an old man
but specific directions which are of importance for
the future. All three patriarchs wanted their children to have clear testimony that they had believed
God's promises also in reference to the land that
was ultimately to be theirs. These clear directions
help to carry this testimony down to successive generations, clear-cut and correct.

33. **And Jacob finished giving his charge to
his sons and drew up his feet into his bed and expired and was gathered unto his people.**

Jacob's very last act on earth was an act of faith.
When the charge is finished, he draws up his feet into
his bed. Apparently, he had summoned up his last
strength and had sat up in bed to bless his own sons,
even as he had done to bless Joseph's sons (48:2).
Practically immediately thereafter he "expired,"
whether the process of dying was instantaneous or
whether it occupied several hours. Apparently, death
was almost instantaneous. Such remarkable instances
occur from time to time where men remain in full
possession of their faculties to the end and are also
entirely certain that their end is just at hand. On

the expression "was gathered unto his people" see v. 29. It means here as there to go to the company of those who live in the life to come in a happier existence. For a full discussion of this phrase read our remarks on 25:8.

HOMILETICAL SUGGESTIONS

It strikes us that at least two parts of Jacob's Blessing have possibilities as texts: the blessing of Judah and the blessing of Joseph. The blessing of Judah should center definitely around the Messianic thought. It offers a good text for preaching Christ in so far as He displays the characteristics of "the Lion of the tribe of Judah." Note how the Restgiver idea ties up with this. Only one who is capable of achieving such conquests as are His can also establish and provide true rest. The blessing of Joseph displays "how richly God can bless His own."

CHAPTER L

13. Jacob's Burial (50:1-13)

The story of Jacob's burial is told in a rather detailed fashion, more so than is any other burial except Sarah's in the book of Genesis (chapter 23), because it gives a fine example of faith on the part of the patriarchs. Jacob desired burial in the land of promise, thereby testifying to his faith in the promise. His sons did not treat the father's request as an unimportant whim but executed it with fine conscientiousness. Besides, the entire material of the chapter is an excellent preparation for the book of Exodus. The sons of Israel had come down into Egypt at the behest of divine providence. They purposed to stay no longer than that same providence ordained. Jacob's burial testifies that their thoughts and their hopes lay in Canaan. Joseph's dying injunction points in the same direction.

1-3. **And Joseph fell upon his father's face and wept over him and kissed him. And Joseph gave charge to servants of his, who were physicians, to embalm his father. So the physicians embalmed Israel, being occupied in the task a full forty days; for so many are the days used in embalming. And the Egyptians made mourning for him seventy days.**

No doubt the other sons were also present at their father's death, not only Joseph. The closing verses of the last chapter indicate this. They, too, grieved greatly to lose their father; but Joseph's grief is especially mentioned, because he had all his days stood closer to his father than the other sons. Consequently

his pain was greater. We must remember, too, that
the very close relationship existing between Joseph
and his father has stood in the forefront of the narrative especially since Jacob's coming to Egypt. For
that matter, there was also the promise of 46:4
that Joseph would be at hand to close his father's
eyes in death. The fulfillment of that promise deserved to be recorded. First of all "Joseph fell upon
his father's face," *'al peney 'abhiw,* a phrase reminding us of 23:3, where Abraham is said to have arisen
after Sarah's death from *'al peney* Sarah. Natural
grief usually finds an outlet in tears; so "he wept
over him." A last token of the close affection that
existed between the two was the parting kiss bestowed upon the dead lips. Enough is reported to
indicate the depth and the sincerity of Joseph's grief.
But the manly grief of God's saints has a certain
restraint, for even in the Old Testament there was
the sure hope of life eternal.

2. It might have been misunderstood if we had
translated literally, "he gave a charge to his servants,
the physicians," as though all his servants were physicians. So we have rendered: "to servants of his who
were physicians." No doubt, the eminence of Joseph's
position called for a very great retinue. Even a
special group of physicians was detailed to watch
over his health. These seem to have been particularly
adapted to such a task as embalming the dead, perhaps
even more so than the professional embalmers. The
process of embalming, described already in some
detail by Herodotus, involved the removal of the brain
through the nose by a hooked instrument as well
as the removal of the entrails through an incision
in the side made with a sharp stone knife. The
entrails were placed in a jar. The cranial cavity
was filled with spices, likewise the abdominal cavity;
but it as well as the entire body were thoroughly

treated with saltpeter for seven days. Afterward the whole body was washed with a palm wine. Then it was daubed with pitch or gums, swathed in many folds of white cloth and laid away in its mummy case. Jacob and Joseph are the only two Israelites of whom the Scriptures tell that they were "embalmed," *chanat*, a verb having close Arabic and Ethiopic parallels and meaning first to "ripen" then to "embalm." In the case of these two Israelites this distinctly Egyptian type of preparation for burial was resorted to in order to make it feasible to transport the mummified remains to Canaan.

3. By way of explanation for later generations Moses relates how much time the entire process entailed. First he tells of their "being occupied with the task a full forty days." The Hebrew idiom is a bit different. It says: "And they made full for him forty days, for thus they fulfill the days of embalming." But the entire mourning extended over a period of "seventy days," including, of course, the forty days during which the embalming took place. Other writers of antiquity assign a period of seventy-two days to the entire process, though that may have been a custom prevalent in another place. The two statements can for all practical purposes be said to agree. But if "Egyptians" (Hebrew: *mitsráyim* = "Egypt") mourn, that is an indication in what high esteem he was held, both as a prince in his own right as well as the father of Joseph. Luther remarks that there is no burial recorded in the Scriptures quite as honorable as this or with such wealth of detail. The imperfect *yimle'û* expresses the thing that is customary (G. K. 107 g).

4-6. **When the days of weeping for him were passed, Joseph spoke to the household of Pharaoh and said: If now I have found favor in your eyes, speak, pray, in the hearing of Pharaoh and say:**

**My father exacted an oath of me, saying: Behold,
I am to die; in my grave which I digged for myself in the land of Canaan, there bury me. And
let me go up, pray, and let me bury my father;
thereafter I shall return. And Pharaoh said: Go
up and bury thy father as thou art bound by oath
to do.**

Joseph asks the "household" (literally — "house,"
báyith) to present his request to Pharaoh. The
reason for this roundabout mode of procedure is not
the fact that Joseph was not presentable at court as
a mourner, unwashed and unshaven. For we note
that he preferred his request to Pharaoh's household
"when the days of weeping for him (Jacob) were
passed." It would have been a simple matter to wash
and to shave and then to go to Pharaoh. Perhaps,
then, some defilement according to the Egyptian conception of death and of mourners may have stood
in the way. But more suggestive is the explanation
which says that this was a wise tactical move on
Joseph's part to allay suspicion as to Joseph's perhaps trying to leave Egypt now that his father was
dead. In any case, they who had sponsored such a
request at court could hardly be the authors of some
suspicion concerning Joseph's purpose. If this explanation be correct, Joseph would have given just one
more proof of unusual wisdom in dealing with men.
Less to the point is the explanation which works on
the supposition that Joseph must have been in disfavor at court just at this time. We also reject the
opinion which says that Joseph was careful not to
prefer any request in matters pertaining to himself.
For he should hardly have hesitated to ask a favor
that pertained more to his father than to himself.
"If now I have found favor" is an expression of fine
courtesy commonly met with in Genesis and not the
property of the author of some one source (like J).

5. The preference of the Hebrew for direct quotation appears in this verse — a quotation within a quotation within a quotation. A strong point to win his request for him is that the dying man had "exacted an oath" of him (Hebrew: "he caused me to swear"). Nor was this oath a rash one, for the man Jacob had made preparations for burial during his lifetime, for he had digged his grave in the land of Canaan. It is unwarranted to claim about v. 5 that "on any view, the contradiction to 47:30 remains." What if it was the burying place of the fathers? If they did acquire it, did they dig out of its sides as many separate tombs as the next generations needed? Most probably each man during his lifetime made provisions for himself and his family. So Abraham bought the cave and digged his grave and Sarah's. Isaac digged his and Rebekah's. Jacob digged his and Leah's. So the statements of Scripture are in perfect harmony. It is a reprehensible thing continually to speak of contradictions in Sacred Writ, where a bit of patience could soon have discerned the underlying harmony. *Karîthî* means "digged" and not "bought." The request is to be presented last, "Let me go up, pray, and let me bury my father." Hardly anybody could deny so proper a request. To set all minds at ease about his purpose Joseph adds the promise, "thereafter I shall return." All the three imperfects used here have the "*ah* hortative" added (*jaqtul elevatum*), a common form with the first person imperfect. The words of the oath are here not introduced by the customary '*im* or *îm lo*' but by *le'mor*, "saying" (K. S. 391 f).

6. Pharaoh graciously gives his royal permission. "Go up" ('*alah*) here as in v. 5 is naturally used because the mountains of Palestine lie higher than the land of Egypt. On the whole question of Joseph's asking permission to go and bury his father

there is one more consideration that carries weight.
So important a man as Joseph, ranking second only
to the reigning Pharaoh, had to guard himself lest
he create the impression that he no longer needed
to consult his king. All important steps that could
be construed as undue self-assertion had to be covered
by a very clear, royal pronouncement. Joseph knew
his place also in this respect.

7-10. **So Joseph went up to bury his father;
and there went up with him all the servants of
Pharaoh, the elders of his household, and all the
elders of the land of Egypt; also Joseph's entire
household and his brethren and his father's household. Only their little children and their flocks and
their cattle did they leave behind in the land of
Goshen. There also went up with him both chariots
as well as horsemen. Their company was a very
considerable one. And they came to Goren Atad
which is across the Jordan, and there they lamented
with great and very heavy lamentation; and he made
a seven-day mourning for his father.**

One would hardly have expected so numerous a
funeral cortege. Several classes felt it incumbent
upon them to grace the occasion. The monuments
indicate that the Egyptians dearly loved imposing
and elaborate funeral processions. Joseph's position
in itself was so influential that these persons who
attended were in duty and in courtesy bound to do
so. They comprised the following classes: "All the
servants of Pharaoh" (*'abhadhim* here cannot mean
"slaves"; all chief courtiers must be meant); "the
elders of his household" — a staff of officers who were
Pharaoh's personal attendants; "all the elders of the
land of Egypt" — all who held positions of any consequence as leaders. Besides there was "Joseph's own
household" — a considerable number apparently —
also "his brethren" and lastly "his father's house-

hold." One can only venture to suppose how many
hundreds made up this entire retinue. The only ones
of Israel left behind were those that were unable to
bear the rigors of such a trip — "their little children," "flocks and herds." Since Goshen was practically their own, they could with safety leave these behind in that land.

9. Such a caravan required food and protection.
So there went along with it "chariots and horsemen."
Somehow the noun *rékhebh* is usually a collective
singular, whereas *parashim* (with long "a" in the
antepenult) is not governed by such usage. Perhaps
"wagons" for *rékhebh* would be the better rendering.
Then "wagons" would have carried the provisions,
and the "horsemen" would have constituted the mili-
tary protection. With good reason the narrator summarizes, "their company (*machaneh* — originally
"camp," then also "army" or "company") was a very
considerable one." The correlative of v. 9 a is the
more uncommon *gam . . . gam* for "both . . .
and," K. S. 376 b).

10. The place where this funeral train came to
a standstill was "Goren Atad." Now *góren* is a
"threshing floor," and *'atadh* signifies "bramble or
buckthorn." Yet the latter may also have come to
be the name of a person. In case it is not, then the
"bramble" will have to be regarded as the type of
hedge that perhaps enclosed the threshing floor. For
the threshing floors were level spaces preferably on
hilltops and situated outside of villages, and naturally
were not roofed over. This one is located as "across
the Jordan." Because of v. 13, which asserts that
Jacob's sons carried their father "into the land of
Canaan," we are practically compelled to place Goren
Atad on the east bank of the Jordan. For the expression *be'ébher hayyarden*, "across the Jordan," may
signify either side depending on the speaker's stand-

point. Here, however, it cannot be urged that the
writer must have resided or written in Canaan, because the writer, Moses, may just as well have written this in the land of Egypt, or, what is equally
valid, his mental point of view may have been Egypt,
the startingpoint of the caravan. Then the course
taken by this long funeral train would have been more
to the south than the usual route along the Mediterranean, then past the land of Philistaea, then over toward Hebron. Yet this would not have necessitated
a route as far south as that taken later by the Israelites
of the Exodus. The reason for this more southerly
course may have been the antagonism of certain
nations or groups along the northern route. Then,
of course, the route will have curved around the
southern end of the Dead Sea up to a place like the
Plains of Moab (Num. 22:1). A few writers from
Jerome to this day contend that "across the Jordan"
must mean the west side, assuming that Moses wrote
Genesis while Israel was encamped in the plains of
Moab, or else supporting what seems the wrong location of Goren Atad. The Egyptian custom of those
days apparently required an additional seven days'
lamentation near or at the point of burial. Oriental
custom required to make such a lamentation quite
demonstrative — "very heavy." Apparently, Joseph
himself made the arrangements required. The Israelites are never known to have indulged their grief
so profusely. For Moses they mourned but thirty
days (Deut. 34:8) ; also for Aaron (Num. 20:29).

11-14. **And the Canaanites, the inhabitants of
the land, beheld the mourning in Goren Atad and
they said: Heavy mourning ('e'bhel) is this for the
Egyptians. Therefore they called its name meadow
('abhel) of the Egyptians, which is across the Jordan. And his sons did for him even as he had
ordered them. And his sons bore him to the land**

**of Canaan and buried him in the cave of the field
of Macpelah, which field Abraham bought for a
burial place of his own possession from Ephron,
the Hittite, over against Mamre. Then Joseph returned to Egypt, he and his brethren and all who
had gone up with him to bury his father, after the
burial of his father.**

So unusual was the display of mourning on the
part of an assembly largely Egyptian, perhaps by this
time entirely Egyptian as to appearance, that the
natives who witnessed it, called "the inhabitants
(*yoshebh* — singular collective) of the land" and
"the Canaanites," the general name for all who dwelt
in those parts, remarked about it, calling it a "heavy
mourning." *'Ebhel* signifies "mourning"; *mispedh*
signifies "lamentation," the public and usually vocal
display of the inner mourning, assuming rather extravagant forms in oriental countries, at least if
judged by our standards. Therefore the thing that
the Canaanites noticed was that the inner grief really
appeared to be heavy. As a result of this observation they gave a name to the meadow on which this
Egyptian assembly encamped for at least a week,
calling it "the meadow of the Egyptians." This name
involved a slight play on words that we cannot reproduce but which made this new name suggestive.
"Mourning" is *'ébhel;* "meadow" is *'abhel.* Naturally
the latter term suggested the former. This explanation follows the pointing of the Hebrew text which
appears to us to follow a very reliable tradition. Because even though the two words have the same consonants in the unprinted original text, it is yet far
more likely that a place will be called a "meadow"
rather than a mourning, even though some render-
ings obliterate this distinction. The Septuagint renders *'abhel* as πένθος = *'ébhel;* Luther says *der
Aegypter Klage.*

12. After this notable display was ended, Jacob's sons become the chief actors in the scene. They take in hand very properly the more intimate part of the burial service, the actual laying of the patriarch in his last resting place . Whether the Egyptians stayed behind or followed along as persons of secondary importance is of so little moment to the writer that he says nothing about them. The part of the sons must be mentioned because their father had laid a strict charge upon them and the author wishes to describe them as dutiful sons. They personally "bore him to the land of Canaan and buried him in the cave of the field of Macpelah." Then follows a description of the field and an account of the manner of its purchase agreeing almost verbatim with the charge given by the dying Jacob (49:29, 30). That, then, is another way of stating the fact that his behest was carried out to the very letter. Critics cannot believe Moses capable of using such flexibility of style, involving a formal repetition, so they assign these two verses (12, 13) to P, who is supposed to have written all things that savor of formal statement. Then to bolster up their contention more firmly they claim that these two verses also fail to agree with the rest of the account, for the preceding verses, it is claimed, make the Egyptians the chief actors, whereas these two put Jacob's sons in the forefront, as if both could not be true and in perfect harmony with one another. J is said to have written the rest of v. 1-14.

14. To leave no doubt in any man's mind whether Joseph actually returned to Egypt as he had promised (v. 5) the writer informs us of his own return as well as of that of his brethren and of that of all the rest who "had gone" (*ha'olîm* — participle referring to past time as 43:18) up with him. As the group was a unit in its going up, so it apparently

continued as a unit in its return, a still further testimony to the honored memory of Jacob; for out of courtesy to Joseph and to Jacob's memory they did not scatter on the homeward way.

15-17.   When the brethren of Joseph realized that their father was dead they said: What if Joseph should turn against us and should actually pay back all the evil which we did him —!   So they sent a message unto Joseph saying: Thy father gave a commandment before his death, saying: Thus shall ye say to Joseph: Pray, do forgive the crime of thy brethren and their sin, for they have done thee wrong.   And now do forgive the crime of the servants of the God of thy father.   And Joseph wept at the message that they sent to him.

The Hebrew says "they *saw*" that their father was dead.   This here means they *"realized"* it and began to see that the restraining influence that the father may have exercised upon Joseph was now at an end. They all seem to feel about the same, except perhaps Benjamin, who naturally was excluded; for they express but one sentiment — apprehension: "What if (*lû* introducing a conditional clause, more vivid) Joseph should turn against us (*shatam* — "antagonize") and should actually pay back (verb with an absolute infinitive) all the evil which we did him" —. The apodosis is not stated — aposiopesis.   This silence makes their apprehension appear all the more vivid: there was no end of possibilities that their excited imagination conjured up before them.   So they "sent a message" — *tsiwwah* means this in the Piel — to Joseph, perhaps through the person who would meet with the favor of both parties — Benjamin.

17.   The best aid to the understanding of the entire situation is to use the approach set forth with greatest emphasis by Luther, who pictures graphically

what a bitter thing sin is — easy to commit, but after
it has come to light it rears its ugly head, and its
prick keeps rankling, "so that no forgiveness and
comfort are strong enough to alleviate the bite and
to remove the prick." Consequently, their feeling of
guilt is their primary trouble; it tends to make
them suspect Joseph. We should hardly do them
justice to suppose that the message which they claim
to have from their father is merely a fictitious one.
It seems fair and right to regard these brethren of
Joseph as men of good and seasoned character, who
speak the truth as godly men should. They all seem
worthy of their rank as patriarchs. Consequently we
must probe more deeply into Jacob's motive and purpose in commanding his sons to proceed after this
fashion. For Jacob had actually given a commandment (*tsiwwah*) before his death. It seems unreasonable to suppose that Jacob questioned the sincerity of
Joseph's forgiveness of the sin of his brothers. So
very likely this step was taken for the sake of the
ten brothers, who had hitherto really made no open
confession and full disavowal of their treachery over
against Joseph. The episode 42:21, 22 cannot be interpreted to amount to a true confession. Yet heavy
sins require to be confessed, especially over against
the person whom they wronged. Otherwise they leave
behind the seed of further misunderstanding. Besides, confession eases the conscience of those who
are troubled over their wrong. So Jacob commands
them to take this step, partly to put their own mind
at ease, when they hear Joseph's assurance of the
fullest pardon; and partly to remove any possible
remnant of misunderstanding that might yet remain. Jacob as well as those sons use a strong term
for their wrong — *pésha'* = "rebellion," of course,
against God. Here it seems very proper to render
it "crime" (Meek). Very naturally "Joseph wept at

the message that they sent to him" — literally, "at
their speaking to him"; but above we noted that they
spoke through a messenger. There is a measure of
mistrust revealed by the brethren. But it was un-
grounded. Joseph's forgiveness had been without
condition or proviso. To have sincere motives questioned is painful.

**18-21. Then came the brethren themselves
and fell down before him and said: Here we are
ready to be thy slaves. And Joseph said to them:
Do not be afraid; for am I in God's place? Ye on
your part did devise evil against me. God devised
it for good, in order that he might do as has this
day actually happened, namely keep alive a great
multitude. And now do not be afraid. I myself
will provide for you and for your little ones. So he
consoled them and spoke comforting words.**

Their sorrow is so genuine and their repentance
so genuine that these brethren come on the heels of
their messenger and offer themselves to Joseph as
his slaves. Their words run thus, "Behold us to
thee for slaves." That must mean, "Here we are
ready to be thy slaves." Joseph seems to understand
by this time why his father had ordered his brethren
to take this step and reassures them very effectually.
His way of doing it is to point primarily to a rare
token of divine providence which was immediately
before their eyes: God had used their evil deed
and turned it for good. All that so openly declares
that God has the case in hand that Joseph may well
ask, What could I do to interfere with God's plans
even if I desired to do so? This is the meaning of
the question, "Am I in God's place?" Delitzsch has
very correctly pointed out that the same thought
is found in 30:2, where it means: have I the *power*
to interfere in God's doings? Here, however, its meaning is: have I the *right* to do so? Joseph explains

this by saying that the proof of God's control of the
situation lies in the fact that where they on their
part did devise evil against him, God devised it for
good — a remarkable example of God's concurrence,
overriding the evil consequence of the wicked deed
to bring about results remarkably blessed. For on
God's part it was all planned in order "to keep alive
a great multitude" — a result which is clearly in
evidence. For the expression "as of this day" means
as it "has this day actually happened" (cf. K. S.
402 u). It surely is one of the most astounding examples of God's control of all things to see a group
like Israel's descendants and household preserved
in famine as an indirect result of the treachery of
men who thought only in terms of bloody vengeance.

A second time Joseph reassures his brethren,
"do not be afraid," and promises to use his best
endeavors in providing for them and their little ones.
This does not imply that the famine was still in
progress. But it does suggest that as strangers in
Egypt, Jacob's sons could well use an influential person like Joseph to guard their interests and represent
fairplay. To this Joseph adds words calculated to
comfort and reasure them, and he "spoke comforting
words," for which the expressive Hebrew says: "he
spoke to their hearts."

22, 23. **And Joseph dwelt in Egypt, he and his
father's household and he lived a hundred and
ten years. And he saw in reference to Ephraim
children of the third generation. Also the children
of Machir, the son of Manasseh, were born upon
Joseph's knees.**

Joseph's story is briefly concluded. So important
a character cannot be dismissed without some report
as to how his life ended. He "dwelt" — we would
prefer to say "lived" — in Egypt all his days. All
involved understood from chapter 15 that the time

involved in their stay in Egypt was not yet concluded. So did also the rest of his father's household continue to reside there. The age to which
Joseph attained shows still more clearly how the
span of human life was slowly shortening — Isaac 180,
Jacob 147, Joseph 110. During these years Joseph
enjoyed the blessing of seeing three generations after
him develop and expand in normal growth. For
the expression "children of the third generation"
(*beney shilleshim*) means grandchildren, for in the
expression "third generation" the original father, here
Joseph, is counted along. K. W. rightly contends
that Exod. 20:5 and Deut. 5:9 settle the case; for
if there *shilleshim* meant great-grandchildren, then
these two passages would strangely have omitted the
grandchildren. In Manasseh's line the same development occurred during Joseph's lifetime, with the exception that it appeared only in the line of Machir.
The expression "were born upon Joseph's knees" is
without a sufficient number of parallels to allow us
to decide exactly what it means. 48:12 does not belong here. The only other occurrence of the expression is 30:3. There are two possibilities. Either these
words describe some rite of adoption, a meaning suitable in 30:3 but not in our passage. Or else they
are a concise way of expressing the double thought that
Joseph lived till they were born and he on his part
was able to take them upon his knees. This appeals
to us as the more reasonable.

24-26. **And Joseph said to his brethren: I am
about to die, but God will most assuredly visit you
and bring you up from this land to the land which
he promised by oath to Abraham, to Isaac, and to
Jacob. And Joseph imposed an oath upon the children of Israel saying: When God does finally visit
you, then ye shall bring up my bones from here.
And Joseph died at the age of one hundred and**

ten years, and they embalmed him and put him in
a mummy case in Egypt.

When Joseph felt his end approach, he spoke these
last words and made this last provision. The participle *meth* describes an act which takes its beginning in the present and runs on into the future (K.
S. 237 d). The pronoun "I" (*'anokhî*) is emphatic
by the contrast involved: "*I* die, but *God* will visit."
The statement implies that during Joseph's lifetime
Israel's sons derived much comfort from the fact
that Joseph sponsored their best interests. Now he,
indeed, must die. Joseph emphasizes that they will
have a Greater than himself to provide for them.
In giving assurance of positive divine deliverance
Joseph is not uttering a prediction which came to
him by divine revelation. He is merely perpetuating
a truth revealed already in Abraham's time (15:16),
a truth of which Israel will stand in need more and
more as the stay in Egypt grows protracted. "Assuredly visit" is expressed by the strong construction
of a verb reinforced by an absolute infinitive. God's
promise to the patriarchs justly looms up as of fundamental importance from these times onward especially. So much for the momentous word of encouragement from the lips of the dying Joseph.

25. In addition he has a solemn word of request
to make, to which he binds the Israelites by oath,
namely that they are ultimately to bring his bones
up to the land of promise, that is to say at the time
when they are themselves brought up by God, an
act here again rightly described as a "visiting"
(*paqodh*), a term descriptive of every act of divine
intervention in the lives of men. Joseph does not
expect his brethren to execute this commission at once.
The circumstances are so different at his death from
what they were when Jacob died. Then an immediate granting of the request was feasible because of

Joseph's influential position. After Joseph's death there was no man of Israel influential enough to make the needed arrangements. It would be misconstruing Joseph's purpose to regard the oath imposed as little more than an act designed for the gratification of a cherished hope. By laying it upon his people he gave eloquent testimony to his faith in God's promises, and by leaving his body in their midst he gave them a continual reminder of that gracious promise.

26. The initial step in the keeping of that promise is recorded. When Joseph dies — the age being repeated in the more solemn style of narrative, as is common in epic poetry also — they embalm him and put him into an 'arôn, a word whose primary significance is "box," used also of the ark of the covenant. Here the term might mean: "coffin," but the type of box or coffin used for mummies is the familiar painted wooden "mummy case."

With this close, which eloquently calls for the continuation provided by Exodus, Genesis comes to a conclusion, which betrays that it, like the others of the five books of Moses, from the very outset constituted a finished literary product designed to be complete in itself but also to be an integral part of a greater work.

HOMILETICAL SUGGESTIONS

May one not use v. 1-14 as a text suggesting what the Christian or Biblical concept of burial is? The display connected with Jacob's burial, the pomp and the ceremony, emanated from the heathen Egyptians. For believers true grief, honest lamentation, proper entombment all have a place. Even in the death of a saint of God his faith may be commemorated. Or he himself may make provision that in some natural way or other he may testify as to his faith. Then v. 15-21 furnish an illustration of what is involved in displaying a forgiving spirit. Or in an effort to touch upon both sides of the question one might treat the general theme "True Reconciliation."